# THE TEACHING OF THE
# CATHOLIC CHURCH

# The
# TEACHING
## of the
# CATHOLIC CHURCH

*A Summary of*
*Catholic Doctrine*
*arranged and edited by*
Canon GEORGE D. SMITH, D.D., Ph.D.

## *Volume I*

AROUCA
PRESS

NIHIL OBSTAT: EDVARDVS CAN. MAHONEY, S.T.D.
CENSOR DEPVTATVS

IMPRIMATVR: E. MORROGH BERNARD
VICARIVS GENERALIS

WESTMONASTERII: DIE X IVNII MCMXLVII

Volume 1 originally published by
The MacMillan Company in 1949
Reprinted by Arouca Press 2021

ISBN: 978-1-989905-72-2 (pbk)
ISBN: 978-1-989905-73-9 (hardcover)

Arouca Press
PO Box 55003
Bridgeport PO
Waterloo, ON N2J 3G0
Canada
www.aroucapress.com

Send inquiries to info@aroucapress.com

# EDITOR'S PREFACE

The majority of the essays here presented as a composite work were published originally as separate volumes in the *Treasury of the Faith* series, now for some time out of print. It is felt that re-edited in two volumes they not only fulfil better the intention with which they were designed but also lend themselves more easily to be used as a work of reference. They appear now almost exactly as they were first printed, with such abridgements only as have appeared necessary where the same ground is covered by more than one writer. Even so, a certain number of repetitions, almost inevitable when the closely knit fabric of Catholic doctrine is woven successively by different hands, have been suffered to remain if the fuller treatment thus afforded has seemed useful and illuminating. Still less has it been considered necessary or even expedient to eliminate permissible differences of view from this combined presentation of the teaching of the Church ; such divergencies of theological opinion within the unity of the faith are a mark of the true liberty of the children of God.

Of the original contributors some have died since the *Treasury of the Faith* series was first published. Those still living have since received various degrees of ecclesiastical preferment, three of them—the present Archbishop of Liverpool, the Bishop of Lancaster, and the Bishop of Lamus—having been raised to the episcopate. It has nevertheless been thought fitting to describe them here by the titles that they held at the time of writing. To all of them I take this opportunity, the first hitherto afforded, of recording my sincere thanks. No editor could have been blessed with more willing and friendly collaborators.

G. D. S.

*St. Edmund's College,*
   *Old Hall,* 1947.

# CONTRIBUTORS

Rev. J. P. ARENDZEN, D.D., Ph.D., M.A.
Rev. JOHN M. T. BARTON, D.D., L.S.S.
Very Rev. Mgr. Canon C. CRONIN, D.D.
Rev. M. C. D'ARCY, S.J.
Rev. RICHARD DOWNEY, D.D., Ph.D.
Rev. T. E. FLYNN, Ph.D., M.A.
Most Rev. Archbishop GOODIER, S.J.
Dom AELRED GRAHAM, O.S.B., S.T.L.
Rev. H. HARRINGTON, M.A.
Dom Justin McCANN, O.S.B., M.A.
Dom J. B. McLAUGHLIN, O.S.B.
Rev. E. J. MAHONEY, D.D.
Rev. C. C. MARTINDALE, S.J.
Rev. B. V. MILLER, D.D., Ph.D.
Rev. J. P. MURPHY, D.D., Ph.D.
Right Rev. Mgr. Canon E. MYERS, M.A.
Rev. A. L. REYS.
Rev. G. D. SMITH, D.D., Ph.D.
Rev. E. TOWERS, D.D., Ph.D.
Rev. O. R. VASSALL-PHILLIPS, C.SS.R.
Abbot ANSCAR VONIER, O.S.B.

# ANALYTICAL LIST OF CONTENTS

## I—FAITH AND REVEALED TRUTH

By the Rev. GEORGE D. SMITH, D.D., Ph.D.

## II—AN OUTLINE OF CATHOLIC TEACHING

By the Rev. GEORGE D. SMITH, D.D., Ph.D.

## III—THE ONE GOD
### By the Rev. A. L. REYS

## IV—THE BLESSED TRINITY
### By the Rev. RICHARD DOWNEY, D.D., Ph.D.

## V—THE HOLY GHOST

By the Rev. J. M. T. Barton, D.D., L.S.S.

## VI—GOD THE CREATOR

By the Rev. B. V. Miller, D.D., Ph.D.

## VII—DIVINE PROVIDENCE

By the Rev. RICHARD DOWNEY, D.D., Ph.D.

## VIII—THE ANGELS

By Abbot ANSCAR VONIER, O.S.B.

## IX—MAN AND HIS DESTINY

By the Rev. C. C. MARTINDALE, S.J.

## X—THE FALL OF MAN AND ORIGINAL SIN

By the Rev. B. V. MILLER, D.D., Ph.D.

## XIV—CHRIST, PRIEST AND REDEEMER

### By the Rev. M. C. D'ARCY, S.J.

## XV—MARY, MOTHER OF GOD

### By the Rev. O. R. VASSALL-PHILLIPS, C.SS.R.

## XVI—SANCTIFYING GRACE

### By the Rev. E. TOWERS, D.D., Ph.D.

## XVII—ACTUAL GRACE

By the Rev. E. TOWERS, D.D., Ph.D.

## XVIII—THE SUPERNATURAL VIRTUES

By the Rev. T. E. FLYNN, Ph.D., M.A.

# I

## FAITH AND REVEALED TRUTH

### §I: INTRODUCTORY

" I so run, not as at an uncertainty ; I so fight, not as one beating the air." [1] The Catholic, strong in faith, might well describe his attitude towards life in these confident words of St Paul. He is in no doubt as to his destiny, nor as to the manner in which he must achieve it. God, his attributes, his providential designs in man's regard, man's own duties to his Creator and to his fellow men—all this, and much more, he knows with a certainty that is supreme. These religious truths are the basis of his life ; his appreciation of them determines the whole course of his existence ; and if concerning them he had the slightest real doubt, his outlook would be radically changed. He is certain that there is a God, his Creator and Lord, whose loving friendship he must at all costs retain ; did he doubt it, his obedience to what he conceives as divine commands would falter. He is certain that there awaits him a life after death in which, if he has been faithful, he will enjoy God's eternal embrace ; did he doubt it, his life on earth would be deprived of all meaning and purpose.

If, therefore, a man is to lead a religious life—and a religious life is synonymous with a good one—he must have firm and sound convictions concerning God and his duties in God's regard. He must have convictions, otherwise his life will be purposeless ; they must be firm, else he will be inconsistent in practice as his theory is vacillating ; they must be sound, for upon them depends the success or the failure of his life. The Catholic has certainty on these vital matters because God has revealed them to him. His hope rests upon the firm foundation of God's word. " Faith is the substance of things to be hoped for."

But to judge the value of revealed truth merely by its use in action would be to estimate it incompletely. Revelation extends the field of our knowledge, and this itself is a perfection of the mind, the noblest faculty of man. By revelation we receive something of the inner radiance of God's glory ; by faith we learn divine truths of which humanly we should never have dreamed. By faith we are given a foretaste of the wonders which will be fully disclosed only when we see God, no longer " through a glass in a dark manner," but face to face. In the meantime the radiance is too bright for our finite minds. We adore, but we cannot see. " Faith is the evidence of things that appear not."

[1] 1 Cor. ix 26.

To display the riches contained in revelation is the object of the subsequent essays.   In this, the first, we must study the meaning of revelation itself, and the act of faith by which we accept it.

## §II: RELIGION AND HUMAN REASON

*Validity of human reason*

THE Catholic theologian sets out with the supposition—which as a philosopher he is prepared to vindicate—that the human mind is able to know truth.   If anyone, therefore, in that unhappy state of mind which despairs of attaining certain knowledge upon any subject whatever, should hope to find in this essay a philosophical proof of the validity of mental processes, then he is doomed to disappointment. The sceptic, before he can approach the study of theology, or in fact of any science at all, must first find his remedy in a sound and true epistemology.   Nor is it within the province of the theologian as such —although again as a philosopher he may be well equipped—to justify the first principles of analytical reasoning, to prove that the conclusions which issue from the application of those principles are valid, even though they may lead the mind into a realm of reality of which no actual experience is given, and thus cannot be verified by experiment.   The demonstration of these and kindred truths belongs to a branch of knowledge which is antecedent to the science of theology.

*Anti-intellectualism*

I venture to hope, however, that those who read this series of essays have remained unaffected by the wave of scepticism and agnosticism which has swept over Europe during the last two or three centuries.   It is an interesting phenomenon of religious history that the heresy of Luther, taking its rise in a proud rebellion against the teaching authority of the Catholic Church, issued in a pessimistic theology which, exaggerating the effects of original sin, presented human nature as intrinsically corrupt.   The human will, bereft of freedom, was radically incapable of pursuing the good, the human reason was powerless to know the truth.   As man's broken will must submit passively to the grace of God, so must his mind now, darkened by sin, allow itself to be led by an occult and irresistible force, a blind and unreasoning faith.   The agnosticism of Kant and his disciples, which, denying the validity of metaphysical argument, takes refuge, in order to justify religious belief, either in the dictates of the practical reason or in an unreasoning religious sense, is an essentially Protestant philosophy ; and of this tendency to rely upon a blind instinct in religious matters the modern forms of exaggerated—and therefore false—mysticism, the systems of religious pragmatism and sentimentalism, so common outside the Church, are the more or less direct descendants.

From all such attempts to disparage the powers of the human reason the Catholic Church has remained ever aloof.   Some of her children, it is true, have not been immune from the anti-intellectualist atmosphere of their time ; but they have been solemnly warned and, when occasion demanded, condemned by the ever-watchful guardian of Divine Truth. Thus the Traditionalists of the nineteenth century, convinced by the German agnostics that the foundations of religious belief and practice, such as the existence of God, the freedom of the will, the immortality of the soul, could no longer be justified by an appeal to reason, had recourse to the inheritance of truth which the human race has received by tradition from antiquity, and ultimately from God. The suggestion was well-intentioned and, like most errors, contained a considerable measure of truth. The Traditionalists rendered valuable service by emphasising the great part played by human authority in the acquisition of knowledge ; it is true, moreover, that we receive much of our religious knowledge from divine revelation. But these faint-hearted apologists, by denying to human reason the power to prove the existence of a God who reveals, rendered all faith in him unreasonable. To save the ship they cast away the compass ; and the Church was not slow to reject this ill-judged compromise with scepticism.

More recently certain restless spirits within the Church, anxious *Modernism* to reconcile Catholic doctrine with the so-called exigencies of " Modern Thought," formed the school known as Modernism. Rejecting with Kant all rational demonstration of religious tenets, and borrowing from his disciple Schleiermacher " the religious sense " as a criterion of truth, the Modernists found the source and the explanation of all religion in a subconscious " need of the divine." Thus the revelation which the Traditionalists (rightly) sought from God the Modernists (wrongly) thought to find within the nature of man himself. From this the way lies open to pantheism, to the rejection of all dogmas, and indeed of all objective religious truth. It would be beyond the scope of this short essay even to enumerate the manifold errors which Modernism involves ; it was rightly stigmatised by Pope Pius X as " a compendium of all heresies." [1]

The teaching of the Catholic Church on this all-important subject *Attitude of* is stated clearly by the Vatican Council : " Holy Mother Church *the Church* holds and teaches that God, the beginning and end of all things, may be certainly known by the natural light of human reason by means of created things." [2] The terms of the oath against Modernism render impossible any misunderstanding of this definition. By " created things " are meant, not merely human testimony, not merely a subconscious religious sense, but the " visible works of creation " ; and lest there should be any doubt as to the manner in which our knowledge of God is acquired, the formula tells us that it is by applying the principle of causality to the data of experience : " God . . . can be known as a cause through his effects."

[1] I write of Modernism in the past tense, because for Catholics it is a thing of the past. Nevertheless the tendency is still strong outside the Catholic Church. [2] *Const. de fide cath.*, chapter ii.

The Church, in thus vindicating the power of human reason to know God, is but reaffirming what St Paul had said in his Epistle to the Romans : " The invisible things of him, from the creation of the world, are clearly seen, being understood by the things that are made." [1]   But the power of the human mind is not limited to the mere knowledge of the existence of God.   Man is able unaided to know much concerning the nature of God ; he can know many of his own duties in regard to his Creator, duties of worship, love and thanksgiving ; he can learn naturally much concerning his own nature and destiny, his duties to himself and to his fellow men. There is, in short, a whole body of religious truth—the truths of the natural order—which man is able to acquire with certainty by the normal use of his natural powers.

*Necessity of revelation*   But while the Church is solicitous to vindicate the just rights of the human reason, while she has no sympathy with those who unduly disparage it, she strenuously resists the claim of Rationalism that it is " the sole judge of the true and the false . . . that it is a law to itself and sufficient by its natural powers to procure the good of men and peoples." [2]   She asserts the essential soundness of the human mind and its radical capacity for learning all natural truth ; but she is mindful that man is in a fallen state, that disordered passion and the manifold distractions of material things hamper and retard him in his pursuit of religious knowledge.   What I have called truths of the natural order can be known and demonstrated by the proper application of the principles of reasoning ; but such a process requires a special type of mind, it needs leisure, concentration, an environment conducive to thought.   Experience shows that not all men have the ability to follow reasoning, be it of the most elementary kind ; some men have a practical rather than a speculative bent. Many who have the ability have not the leisure for these studies. The practical difficulties become more evident when one considers that the rational proofs of such truths as the spirituality of the human soul, the freedom of the will, if they are to stand the test of modern objections, require as a preliminary a long and arduous study of metaphysics and psychology.   Add to this that religious knowledge is of paramount importance for man's daily life, necessary especially in youth, when the character is in process of formation, necessary precisely at the time when, through mental immaturity and lack of concentration, he is least likely to be able to acquire it.

Thus if we view mankind as a whole, if we consider the difficulties with which men are beset, it is clear that, left to their own resources, very few would gain adequate knowledge even of the truths of natural religion.   Nor does human authority offer an adequate solution of the difficulty.   History shows that the great thinkers of antiquity— not to speak of more recent or contemporary philosophers—have been unable to impose their doctrine beyond a certain school.   The

---

[1] Rom. i 20 ; *cf*. Wisd. xiii 1-9.            [2] Syllabus of Pius IX, n. 3.

clamour of diverse views, the difficulty of the subject-matter, the lack of authority in the teacher to impose belief upon those who cannot understand his reasoning—all this rendered, and still renders, merely human teaching authority powerless to supply the need of mankind for religious instruction. On this subject above all man needs an omniscient and infallible Teacher.

Hence, even though the field of religious doctrine were confined to " natural " truth, man's need of divine aid is apparent. But it should be carefully noted that this need arises, not, as the Traditionalists contended, from the radical impotence of the human mind as such, but from other circumstances of human life which render it practically impossible for all men to discover these truths for themselves with any sufficient degree of accuracy and certainty. Briefly, just as in the practical order grace is morally necessary in order that each man may observe all the precepts of the natural law, so is revelation necessary so that all men may reach a sufficient knowledge of the truths of natural religion.[1] The exaggerated claim of Rationalism is thus seen to be unreasonable.

But here again, in a most important particular, the Church opposes the Rationalist. According to the latter, not only can the human mind unaided know all natural truth, but natural truth is all that there is to know. The Church, on the contrary, teaches that there is an order of reality above that of nature, an order of reality which is beyond the reach of the human mind : the supernatural order.

And that such an order exists does not seem *a priori* unlikely. God, as St Paul tells us, has left traces of himself in his handiwork, and man is able from the consideration of created perfections to learn much concerning his Creator. Even the little that we naturally know of God would lead us to conjecture that there is much more of which we know nothing ; that there are divine perfections of which no clear trace appears in the works of creation ; that besides the natural truths of religion there may be hidden truths concerning God and things divine, " mysteries "—*i.e.*, truths which must remain God's secret unless and until he vouchsafes to make them known.

The supernatural order, therefore, by its very character is outside the scope of our natural knowledge and comprehension. We can know nothing of it unless God wills to reveal it. The impotence of human reason in respect of supernatural truths is physical and absolute. Natural truth is within the reach of the human mind. The reasons which show an adequate and universal knowledge of this order to be morally impossible without revelation are concerned not with the powers of the human mind itself, but with such concomitant circumstances as lack of ability, or time, or concentration. But no course of study, however long, however arduous, could bring the human—or indeed the angelic—mind to the discovery

[1] *Cf.* Essay xvii : *Actual Grace*, pp. 589 ff.

of a supernatural truth. This calls for a special intervention of God, for the inauguration of a divine intercourse with man whereby he communicates knowledge otherwise unattainable ; in other words a supernatural revelation.

Man's need of revelation is therefore twofold. He needs it for ease and security even in the sphere of natural research ; he needs it absolutely if he is to know God's secrets. The first need God might have supplied by help of the natural order, by an enlightenment or an inspiration which would have been included in God's natural Providence in man's regard. God, however, has willed to destine man for a supernatural end, and every help that he grants is bestowed with that end in view. Man's twofold need is met by one divine revelation which is supernatural in character, and in its content partly supernatural and partly natural. By one and the same revelation he supplies a remedy to man's natural weakness, and discloses truths which no finite mind could ever have learned.

### §III : SUPERNATURAL REVELATION

*Meaning of revelation*  IT is important for a proper understanding of our subject to have a clear idea of what is meant by divine revelation. The word " revelation " is used in many senses. In common parlance it often means the disclosure of a fact hitherto unknown : " What you say is a revelation to me " ; and in theology the word sometimes has this meaning. Or, again, it is said that God has " revealed " himself in the works of creation ; and in this sense the Psalmist sings that " the heavens tell forth the glory of God." Moreover, God may manifest some truth to man by an interior enlightenment of his mind in such a way that the favoured soul is unaware of the origin of his knowledge ; he simply begins to know what he did not know before. Of such a kind was the infused knowledge granted to many of the saints. Such a mysterious illumination also may be called a revelation. The Modernists used the word in a special sense. By revelation they meant the manifestation of a religious truth made in consciousness by the religious sense ; for them it was nothing else than a personal religious experience.

But when the Church uses the word " revelation " in connection with faith, it has the definite meaning of a *divine testimony*. Revelation is the act whereby God speaks to man, making a statement to the truth of which he testifies. " God who at sundry times and in divers manners spoke in times past by the prophets, last of all in these days hath spoken to us by his Son." [1] Hence the Vatican Council describes faith as a " virtue whereby . . . we believe that the things which he has revealed are true . . . because of the authority of God himself who reveals them, and who can neither be deceived nor deceive." [2] The oath against Modernism, to exclude

---

[1] Heb. i 1.                    [2] Chapter iii.

the perverted sense given to the word in that theory, uses even clearer terms. Faith is there defined as " a true intellectual assent given to a truth received *by hearing* from without, whereby . . . we believe to be true the things that have been said, testified and revealed by a personal God, our Creator and Lord."

Revelation, then, is not an interior emotional experience ; it is a statement of truth made to man in a definite place, at a definite time, by a personal God who is outside and distinct from the recipient. Moreover it is essential to the concept of revelation as understood by the Church that the statement in question be authenticated : the statement is received by the believer as made by God, and accepted because it is made by God. Infused knowledge, therefore, unless it is infused with clear notification of its divine origin, is not the revelation which faith presupposes. Furthermore, this revelation is distinct from the manifestation of his perfections which God has given to us in creation. It is true to say that God " speaks " to us in the works of nature, inasmuch as those works " reveal " his presence and activity ; it is true, but it is metaphorical. Revelation properly understood implies a personal intercourse between God and man, wherein God truly speaks—*i.e.*, makes an assertion, which man accepts on God's personal authority.

Hence revelation is supernatural—supernatural not only because *Supernatural* it contains supernatural truths, but also because the very act whereby *character of* God reveals is beyond the ordinary course of nature. In the ordinary *revelation* course of nature God teaches us through created things, through the voice of conscience, through our own conscious needs and desires. By supernatural revelation God teaches us himself. " All thy children shall be taught of God." [1]

I have said that God's revelation contains supernatural truths. *Mysteries* The essence of revelation does not demand that what is revealed should be hitherto unknown or otherwise unknowable. Much of what God has revealed man may already have discovered by the natural light of reason ; in which case the authority of divine teaching but confirms the conclusions of the human mind. But even if the truth revealed is a mystery properly so called—that is, a truth which the human reason itself is incapable of discovering or of comprehending when it has ascertained it—yet it contains an element which is not new : the terms in which the revelation is made are familiar. It is not true to say that the mysteries of our faith are unintelligible. The unintelligible, the meaningless, precisely because it is meaningless, can have no relation to the human mind. Thus an unknown language is unintelligible, because it conveys no meaning ; it corresponds to no idea in consciousness. A mystery is incomprehensible, if you will, but it is not meaningless ; it conveys a very definite meaning. The proposition that Jesus Christ is both God and man, that he is one person who has two natures, the human and the divine,

[1] Isa. liv 13.

is incomprehensible indeed; but it is not without meaning. It is full of meaning, so full that man with his finite mind will never exhaust it.

If divine revelation is supernatural in character, if it is beyond the ordinary course of nature, it follows that man can have no natural title or claim to it. It is a grace, an entirely gratuitous gift of God. Hence, although, as we saw in the previous section, the conditions of human existence indicate the need of some help from God for a universal and sufficient knowledge of religious truth, yet we cannot argue from this to the existence of a *supernatural* revelation. Apologists rightly point out how wonderfully revealed truth harmonises with the intimate needs and desires of mankind. But it is too little to say: " This is exactly what we needed." It is far in excess of what we had any right to expect. In this as in all else God has been more than just, he has been generously bountiful to his creatures.

*Manner of revelation*    And how has this supernatural revelation been made? Its history may be given in the inspired words of Holy Writ: " God who at sundry times and in divers manners spoke in times past to the fathers by the prophets, last of all in these days hath spoken to us by his Son." [1]  " And Jesus spoke to his Apostles, saying: Going therefore, teach ye all nations ; . . . teaching them to observe all things whatsoever I have commanded you ; and behold I am with you all days, even to the consummation of the world." [2]

Undoubtedly, had God so willed, he might have communicated his testimony directly to each member of the human race as soon as he was capable of receiving it. The contention of Protestantism is (or was) that he does so. There is no need to insist here on the inconveniences of such a method, had it been adopted ; it would have led to hallucinations of every sort. Sad experience has shown how easily men may be led to think that they are inspired. But apart from any other reason, an individualistic revelation seems antecedently improbable because it would not be in keeping with what we know of God's providential dealings with mankind. God deals with man according to his nature ; and man is naturally social. This being so, we should have expected God to make his revelation to men as a body ; and such in fact was the case.

" God spoke to the fathers [*i.e.*, to the ancestors of the Jews whom St Paul was addressing] by the prophets." Whether by visions, or by an interior illumination of the mind, or by the ministry of angels, God entrusted his message to certain chosen men, who in their turn were to deliver it to God's chosen people. Of that chosen people would be born Christ, the Word Incarnate, who was to complete the divine message and found on earth a universal kingdom in which God's word would be carried to the ends of the earth until the end of time.

[1] Heb. i 1.                    [2] Matt. xxviii 18-20.

But God's message must be authenticated, his messenger must *Authentica-* present his credentials. In vain will the seer claim divine authority *tion of divine* if he cannot vindicate his mission. Hence that all men might know *message* that the words of the prophet were the words of God, he marked their teaching with unmistakable signs of its divine origin. " They will not believe me," protested Moses,[1] " nor hear my voice, but they will say : The Lord hath not appeared to thee . . . And the Lord said : Cast thy rod down upon the ground. He cast it down, and it was turned into a serpent . . . that they may believe, saith he, that the Lord God . . . hath appeared to thee." Leaving to its proper place [2] the discussion of miracles and prophecies as motives of credibility, we must remark here on the consistent appeal made by God's messengers to these irrefragable evidences of their divine authority. Suffice it to quote the words of the greatest of all the prophets, the Son of God himself : " Go and relate what you have heard and seen. The blind see, the lame walk, the dead rise again, the poor have the gospel preached to them." [3] In answer to the Jews who ask him to say plainly if he is indeed the Christ, he says : " I speak to you, and you believe not ; the works that I do in the name of my Father, they give testimony of me." [4] Finally, we read of the Apostles of Christ who " going forth preached everywhere ; the Lord working withal, and confirming the word with signs that followed." [5]

The revelation which God made to his chosen people was a *Revelation* gradual one. Speaking to them " at sundry times," he suited his *gradual* message to the degree of culture and the condition of his hearers. The promise that God would send a Redeemer was made at the very beginning, and that hope, fostered by repeated revelations through the Patriarchs and Prophets, was the heart and centre of the Jewish religion. Belief in the one true God was safeguarded by constant divine warnings against the idolatry of the surrounding nations and by detailed instructions for the manner of divine worship. The precepts of the natural law were fully expounded in the Commandments and enforced by legal sanctions. Gradually in the books of the Old Testament beliefs concerning the future life, at first fragmentary and crude, become more and more detailed and definite. Of the great mysteries of Christianity, the Incarnation and the Trinity, we find little more than mere traces—traces, however, which become clearer and clearer as the fulness of time approaches. It was a period of preparation and expectation, during which truths were successively revealed according as they served to prepare men's hearts to receive him who was to come. But this progressive unfolding of God's providential plan was not to be indefinitely prolonged. At last Christ came, and with him the completion of God's message of mercy.

[1] Exod. iv 1.      [2] P. 13.      [3] Matt. xi 4-5.
[4] John x 24 ; cf. ibid., 37-38 ; xi 41-42.      [5] Mark xvi 20.

*Definitive revelation in Christ*

The Son of God became man and, living in the midst of men, showed by his fulfilment of the Messianic prophecies that he was indeed the divine messenger whom all generations had expected ; and of his divine mission he gave still further proof—if further was needed—by the wonders that he worked. The prophets of old had conveyed God's word to the chosen people alone ; Christ's message was for the whole world. Their revelation was but partial, to be supplemented by those who should come after ; his was definitive and complete. They were the creatural mouthpieces of God ; he, while truly man, was God himself.

To the Jews first he preached his gospel, to the nation which throughout its history had been so signally favoured by God ; and by these he was rejected. But from the beginning of his ministry he laid the foundations of his Church, collecting a chosen band of disciples who were to be witnesses of his gospel, not merely in Palestine, but throughout the whole world ; they were his twelve Apostles. These with infinite care and patience he trained for their important mission ; to these he revealed " the mysteries of the kingdom of God " so far as they were then able to bear them, promising that when he should leave them he would send the Holy Ghost, who would teach them all truth. To these, under the primacy of Peter, he gave special powers : a teaching authority such that to hear them was to hear Christ himself, that they might preach in its integrity the doctrine that they had received from his lips ; powers of jurisdiction over all believers, that they might govern Christ's spiritual kingdom on earth.

*Committed to the Catholic Church*

In this way the Catholic Church was instituted, the visible, infallible society in which and through which the revelation of Christ was to be preserved and propagated. The Church, the mystical body of Christ, was to perpetuate his work, to bear witness to the truth until the consummation of the world. As the doctrine of Christ was the doctrine of the Father who sent him, so the teaching of the Church is the teaching of Christ who instituted her. Just as Christ had proved his divine mission, so the Church bears in the sight of all men the manifest marks of her divine origin. " The Church herself," says the Vatican Council,[1] " by reason of her wonderful extension, eminent holiness and inexhaustible fruitfulness in all good things, her Catholic unity and invincible stability, is . . . an irrefutable witness to her own divine mission."

## §IV: PRELIMINARIES TO FAITH

*Faith man's assent to revelation*

HAVING studied the need, the nature and the manner of divine revelation, we now possess the elements necessary to understand the act whereby that revelation is accepted, the act of faith ; and if in the pages which precede points of doctrine have been touched upon

[1] *Loc. cit.*, chapter iii.

which are treated more fully elsewhere in this essay, it has been in order to provide data for the solution of the problem before us.

In fact, the nature of the act of faith has already been implied in what has been said about revelation. Revelation is a divine testimony. But if God has spoken, if he has testified to the truth of a statement, then it is man's bounden duty to accept it by an act of belief, by an act of faith. For our present purpose, then, it will be sufficient to describe the act of faith as that act whereby, on the authority of God, we give mental assent to a truth which he has revealed. All that is involved in such an act will form the subject of the succeeding section, but here it should be noted that the motive of assent is not the intrinsic evidence of the statement itself, but the authority of God who makes it ; in other words, I believe simply because God has said it. Already it becomes clear that the act of faith cannot be made without certain preliminaries. A motive, before it can give rise to an act, must first be perceived by the mind ; the authority of God, then, must be known before I can make an act of faith. I must know that there is a God, and that he has the authority—i.e., the knowledge and the veracity—which is to command my assent. Moreover, by the act of faith, I give my assent not merely to a vague generalisation—" whatever it may be that God has revealed "—but to a definite truth, or body of truth, which I know to have been revealed. A further preliminary, therefore, is to know " the fact of revelation "—i.e., that God has revealed this or that truth to which I am required to give my assent.

We begin to see, then, that the act of faith is no " step in the *Evidence of* dark." Faith is not an unreasonable credulity ; still less is it a blind *credibility—* instinct to believe whatever one is told. Man is a rational being, *faith* and God does not call upon him to do anything ill-befitting his nature. It is reasonable, prudent, to believe what one is told by a trustworthy witness. It is imprudent, and even foolish, to believe a statement purporting to be made by one whose existence is unknown, or at the best doubtful, or of whose knowledge and veracity, even if he exists, one has little or no guarantee. St Thomas Aquinas has been accused of being a Rationalist, but indeed he only vindicates the just rights of a reasonable being when he says : " Man would not believe (revealed truth) unless he *saw* that he must believe it." [1] Hence, before a man can reasonably and prudently believe a statement, that statement must be credible to him ; he must have " evidence of credibility." That evidence of credibility he obtains from the knowledge of those preliminary truths which we have enumerated, called for the sake of convenience the " preambles of faith."

How are we to know these preambles ? Should we not, some *Fideism* have suggested, rely for this knowledge on the authority of God himself, so that not only the act of faith but also its foundations should rest upon the firm ground of God's infallible truth ? Even

---

[1] *Summa Theologica* II-II, Q. 1, art. 4 ad 2.

granting for the sake of argument, say the Fideists, that the existence of God and the fact of revelation can be discovered by the unaided human mind, yet even the Catholic Church is forced to admit that without revelation man finds it practically impossible to learn natural truths with certainty. Is our faith, then, to rest upon so insecure a foundation ? It needs little reflection to see that such a process involves a vicious circle, and, far from strengthening the foundations of faith, removes them altogether. How can I reasonably rely upon the authority of God when he reveals to me his existence, his omniscience, his veracity, the fact that he has revealed this or that truth, unless I am antecedently and independently of that same authority convinced that the revealing and truthful God exists ? Others have had recourse either to a blind instinct, or to an act of will, to bring about adherence to these preliminary truths.

All such systems betray that distrust of the human reason to which we referred in our second section. The Church, we repeat, has no sympathy with those who disparage the powers of the human mind ; nor is there any antagonism between reason and faith. In the words of a famous preacher, " they are two sisters who dwell together in the same home. The hospitable doors of our soul are opened to receive these two daughters of God. Faith dwells on high, reason a little lower. But faith will never kill her sister ; she will not betray the hospitality accorded her to reign alone in the palace of them both." [1]   " The use of reason," says the Church in condemning Traditionalism, " precedes faith and must lead us to it." [2]

The human mind, then, must discover for itself the truths which are the basis of faith, and these must be known with certainty. It is not enough to conjecture with some degree of probability that there is a veracious God who has made a revelation. While doubt concerning the preambles of faith remains the act of faith cannot be reasonable. No man believes reasonably unless he sees that he must believe.

*Motives of credibility*   But how are all men to acquire this certainty ? In the first place it is to be remarked that the existence of God, at least, can be certainly known by the light of human reason. In fact, so clear are the indications of this truth that the Gentiles were upbraided by St Paul as inexcusable for failing to recognise it. Moreover, the arguments which prove the existence of God show also that he is all perfection, and therefore omniscient and incapable of deceiving. As to the third preamble, the fact of revelation, we have seen that God accompanied his message with clear signs of its divine origin, particularly by miracles and prophecies, and that, moreover, the Catholic Church, founded by Christ for the specific purpose of teaching men what God has revealed, bears upon her unmistakable marks of her divine institution.

[1] Monsabré : *Introduction*, Conf. II.
[2] Denzinger, *Enchiridion*, 1626.

To set in full relief the arguments which show the divine origin *Miracles and* of the Christian religion—to expound, in other words, the " motives *prophecy* of credibility "—is the function of the apologist, and therefore lies outside our scope. These motives are many and varied ; among them are some which alone are fully convincing, others which convince only by their accumulated force ; some will appeal to all minds, others will appeal only to a few. It is just, therefore, to that extent, that the apologist should accommodate his procedure to the mentality of those whom he seeks to persuade. But of the absolute efficacy of at least one motive of credibility no Catholic may doubt, since it has been made the subject of an infallible definition in the Vatican Council, namely, miracles worked in confirmation of a divine mission. " Anathema to him who says . . . that by miracles the divine origin of the Christian religion is not rightly proved." [1] In the corresponding chapter the Council goes further ; it declares that miracles and prophecies [2] " are most certain signs of divine revelation, and suitable to the intelligence of all." They are suited to the intelligence of the learned as to that of the ignorant, to that of the scientist as to that of the layman, to the modern mind, too often supposed to be infallible, no less than to the mind of the ancients, too often presumed to be lacking in common sense.

That a miracle, granted the existence of God, is possible is shown elsewhere.[3] If a true miracle, which is the work of God alone, is performed by a man *as a sign that his teaching is divine*, it argues an extraordinary intervention of divine power to vindicate his claim, and, since the true God cannot confirm falsehood, the argument is peremptory. His statement is thus rendered credible on the divine authority. It may not, however, be superfluous to add that the miracle as such does nothing more. It is not an intrinsic proof of the statement made ; it is a completely adequate motive of credibility.

The human mind, then, is able to learn with certainty the ex- *Certitude in* istence of God ; is able, by the proper investigation of the facts, to *preambles of* conclude that Christ is the bearer of a divine message, that he *faith* founded an infallible Church for the purpose of propagating that message ; and finally, by the process indicated in apologetics, to conclude that the Catholic Church is that divinely appointed teacher of revelation. These things, I say, can be known and proved, and by those who have the requisite leisure, opportunity and ability, are actually known and proved with all the scientific certainty of which the subject is patient. The preambles of faith, therefore, rest upon the solid ground of human reason.

[1] *De fide*, can. 4.
[2] I make no distinction here between miracles and prophecies, since the value of each, *mutatis mutandis*, is equal in showing the divine mission of the wonder-worker or the prophet. In fact, a prophecy is simply a miracle of the intellectual order.
[3] Essay vii, *Divine Providence*, pp. 226 ff.

*Relative
certitude*

But while the human mind *can* satisfy itself by rational demonstration of the existence of God, and by historical investigation of the " fact of revelation," it remains true that for a great proportion of the human race such a process of scientific demonstration is a practical impossibility.    A secure conviction that a good God exists is obtainable by all men, and by the large majority is actually obtained.    But how many are able, besides justifying that conviction to themselves, to construct a scientific proof of the existence of God which satisfies all the demands of human reason, with all the apparatus of objection and answer which is needed by the modern apologist ?    Most men believe in the existence of God because they have satisfied themselves, by reasons which for them are sufficient, that God really does exist.    Again, the divine origin of the Christian religion, the divine character of the Catholic Church, being attested by so many motives of credibility, is known by all Catholics, can be recognised by non-Catholics.    But relatively few Catholics have either the leisure or the ability to investigate the historical documents, to sift for themselves the evidence required for a scientific historical demonstration : relatively few non-Catholics would have the opportunity of thus verifying the claims of the Catholic Church.    Moreover, the difficulty in the way of such scientific certitude is infinitely increased when we consider the condition of the uneducated and the young.    Can these make no act of faith until they have completed a course of philosophy, until they have satisfied their minds by answering every objection that can be made against the existence of God, proved the divinity of the Christian religion by a rigid demonstration, and thus arrived at perfect evidence concerning the preambles of faith ?

Such perfect scientific evidence is unnecessary.    The reason why one must, before believing a statement, be convinced of the existence and trustworthiness of the witness who makes it, is that otherwise the assent given would be unreasonable, imprudent.    Thus it is imprudent to believe a statement supposed to have been made even by a most knowledgeable and trustworthy person, if there is reasonable doubt as to his having made it.

I say, advisedly, if there is reasonable doubt, because there are doubts which are unreasonable, imprudent.    Nowadays, at any rate, whatever may have been the case years ago, it is unreasonable to doubt the safety of travelling by rail.    It is unreasonable to doubt a proposition which you have clearly demonstrated simply because an objection is made to it which, by reason of your lack of ability or technical knowledge, you are unable to solve.    Briefly, without going into the vexed question of certitude and its various kinds, we may remark that there is a state of mind which a reasonable man demands before he will engage upon any serious undertaking.    Call it moral certitude if you will ;  I prefer to call it a prudent conviction.    Complete scientific evidence in many cases, either for circumstantial or personal reasons, he cannot have.    He asks those who are competent to know, in whose judgement he has full confidence, and with the conviction thus obtained he sets out upon his task. Absolutely speaking, he may have been deceived ; but in the circumstances he acted prudently ; it would have been imprudent, unreasonable to doubt.

And here follows a consequence of vital importance for the solution of our question. What is prudent in some circumstances is imprudent in others ; what is prudent for one person is not prudent for another. This state of mind, which I have called " prudent conviction," is not absolute but relative.[1] So, for example, it is prudent for the unlearned to believe implicitly the teaching of those who " ought to know." A child acts prudently on the advice, however misguided, of his mother. School-children believe what their teachers, however incompetent, teach them ; and to act upon such information is prudent and reasonable—for children. In fact, they would be imprudent to act otherwise.

And now let us apply these principles to the question before us. In order to make a reasonable act of faith the prospective believer must achieve a prudent conviction concerning the preambles of faith : a conviction—*i.e.*, he must be convinced of the existence of God and the fact of revelation : a *prudent* conviction—*i.e.*, there must be no reasonable doubt. Such a state of mind, then, is compatible with unreasonable doubts such as we have exemplified above. Thus a child who learns from his teacher, or from his catechism, that there is a God who has revealed certain truths through his Church, of which the parish priest is an official representative, has a prudent conviction regarding the preambles sufficient for a reasonable act of divine faith. Again, motives of credibility which would not convince the scientist, to the unlearned may carry a conviction upon which he could prudently rely. Hence, a scientific demonstration of the preambles, so far from being a necessary preliminary to a reasonable act of faith, is in most cases impossible ; in those cases, therefore, it would be *unreasonable* to demand it.

Nevertheless, in all cases the legitimate demands of reason are met. Reason demands that no man believe a thing unless he *see* it to be credible. Even in the case of the child, even in the case of the unlearned, whatever be the objective reliability of his grounds for admitting the existence of God or the fact of revelation, the conclusion to which he is led—namely, the judgement of credibility —is perfectly evident. He concludes that it is evidently reasonable to believe on the authority of God a truth, or a group of truths, which he is prudently convinced that God has revealed. But it should be carefully noted, even now, that the motives which have led to the

[1] Obviously this view has nothing in common with the theory of " relative truth," according to which a proposition objectively true to one is false to another. I am speaking here not of objective truth but of a subjective state of mind.

"judgement of credibility" are not the motive of faith. The act of faith remains yet to be made, and its motive is quite distinct ; it is the authority of God who reveals.

*Other factors in the approach to faith—The function of the will*   When the inquirer has reached the stage at which he regards revealed truth as "credible," when, further, he has realised his obligation to believe, he is on the threshold of faith. But before we consider the act of faith itself, we have still to take into account other important factors in the approach to it. In what has been said hitherto we have considered only the intellectual activity of man ; and we have purposely confined our attention to this aspect of the question in order to stress the essentially reasonable character of submission to divine revelation. But man is not a mental machine. When he thinks of a subject he does so because he wills to think of it. As we shall see later, the will plays a prominent and essential part in the act of faith itself. But also in the preparation for faith good-will is absolutely necessary. Moreover, man has various emotions and desires which to a greater or less extent are under his control ; these too must be taken into account. It is not simply the human mind that prepares itself for faith ; it is the whole man, a vital unity, with all the complex interaction of his mental, volitional, and emotional powers.

The first thing necessary in the approach to faith is attention to the subject of religion ; the inquirer must first make up his mind to think about God and his duties in God's regard. And here, besides the effort of will, the emotional factor may well enter to attract or to repel. Some have begun their inquiry simply out of affection for a Catholic friend whose good opinion they valued ; others have desisted when they saw that such inquiry would lead to self-denial. Some have been first attracted to the Catholic Church by the beauty of her ceremonial ; others have been repelled by the squalor of an ill-kept church. Thus the most insignificant circumstance may exert its effect, inclining a man this way or that ; but finally it is the will that directs the mind to God.

It is not only in the initial impulse, however, but throughout the preliminary stages too, that these factors exert their influence. Distractions must be firmly set aside that the mind may devote its attention to a serious and difficult subject ; prejudices must be overcome so that the full force of the motives of credibility may be appreciated ; the temptation to dally with sophistical objections when they are seen to be groundless must be suppressed ; unworthy considerations of self-interest, pride and human respect must be excluded lest they interfere with the earnest inquiry after truth. In short, there are innumerable ways in which desires and feelings may help or hinder man in his preparation for faith. The will cannot make a thing to be true which is false ; the will cannot give force to an invalid argument. But it can and must prevent extraneous considerations from obscuring the issue, and exclude from the mind anything that may distract a serene and unbiassed attention to the arguments proposed. In the study of a purely speculative subject there is little danger of such interference ; one is not liable to unreasonable prejudices in the solution of an algebraic problem. But religion is vitally connected with man's moral duties, and for that very reason a purely unprejudiced and rational study of it is particularly difficult. If a man is to devote himself to it wholeheartedly and with unruffled mind, he needs above all things good-will.

There remains the last, and yet really the first and most import- *Grace* ant factor. With the intellect of a Plato, with the iron self-control of a Stoic, with all the good-will of which man is capable, he can do nothing to prepare himself for faith without the help of God's grace. "No man cometh to me unless the Father draw him." Man's destiny is a supernatural one, entirely beyond his natural powers to achieve. His acts, to be salutary—that is, to be conducive to his eternal salvation—must be supernatural, must have a quality, a modality, which raises them above their natural power and value, making them proportionate to a supernatural end.[1] It is by the act of faith that man first sets himself in the path of salvation, and, as will be seen, that act must be supernatural. But even before this vital step is taken man must be guided by God's grace. God's supernatural providence, which wills all men to be saved and to come to the knowledge of the truth, watches over all men, guiding them gently, but surely, to himself. The child who learns his religion from his mother, whose mind is gradually opened to the wonders of God's revelation, is acting under the impulse of God's grace. The unbeliever who becomes conscious of a desire to know God, who earnestly and perseveringly, in spite of obstacles, seeks after the truth, is being led, enlightened and inspired by supernatural grace. The eloquence of St Paul would not have converted a Lydia had the grace of God not opened her heart to hear his words. The Apostle may plant the seed and tend it carefully, but it will not grow unless God give the increase.[2]

In all these preliminaries, therefore, man must do his part. He must endeavour, with good-will, to see that God's truth is credible ; it is his duty and his right as a rational being. But he must not rely upon himself. "Our sufficiency is from God."[3] His very good-will must derive from him who "worketh in us both to will and to accomplish."[4] The urge of passion, a deep-seated prejudice, a whole complex of circumstances for which he may be but partly or even in no degree responsible, may blind him to the truth. For such a one the grace of enlightenment is at hand, if he will but accept it. His prayer must be that of the blind man : "Lord, that I may see." The answer and the result will be the same : "And immediately he saw, and followed him."[5]

---

[1] See Essay xvii, *Actual Grace*, pp. 595 ff.  [3] *Cf.* Acts xvi 14 ; 1 Cor. iii 4-6.
[2] 2 Cor. iii 5.  [4] Phil. ii 13.  [5] *Cf.* Matt. xx 30-34.

## §V: THE ACT OF FAITH

*Definition of faith*   IN the previous section we accompanied the believer in his progress towards the act of faith until the stage at which, having acquired a firm conviction concerning the preambles of faith, he forms an evident "judgement of credibility": "This truth, which I am convinced has been revealed by God, is to be believed on God's authority." Passing to a judgement of the practical order, he says: "I must believe it." Then, and not till then, he proceeds to give his assent to the revealed truth: "I believe this truth because God has revealed it." This assent is the act of divine faith which we must now study.

The subject is of such vital importance that our definition of the act of faith must be taken from the infallible pronouncement of the Vatican Council. The Council directly defines the virtue of faith, but in doing so it necessarily defines the act: "Faith . . . is a supernatural virtue whereby, inspired and assisted by the grace of God, we believe that the things which he has revealed are true ; not because the intrinsic truth of the things is plainly perceived by the natural light of reason, but because of the authority of God himself who reveals them, and who can neither be deceived nor deceive."

*Motive, the authority of God*   Faith, then, is an act whereby we believe something to be true. It is an assent to truth, and therefore an act of the intellect : for truth is the object of the intellect.[1] There is, however, this important difference between the assent of faith and the assent of immediate knowledge. The assent in the latter case is caused by the perception of the intrinsic truth of the statement ; so that when it is made I say : "I see ; of course, that must be so " ; and, when once the truth is seen, nothing further is required to gain my assent. In the case of faith, I see indeed—otherwise there could be no assent—but I do not see within the truth itself. I understand the terms of the revealed proposition, but neither the analysis of those terms nor my own experience assures me that they should be connected. The ground, or the "motive," of my assent to the proposition is extrinsic to it, and that motive is the authority of God, who tells me that it is true. In both cases there is evidence : in the former the evidence is intrinsic, in the latter it is extrinsic. The believer sees the truth, says St Thomas, "as credible ; . . . for he would not believe unless he saw that he must believe." [2]

*The will in the act of faith—a free act*   I have said that when once the inward truth of a proposition is seen, nothing further is required to evoke the assent of the mind ; it is drawn of necessity to adhere to its connatural object. But without that internal evidence the mind, of itself, is powerless to

---

[1] *Cf.* the oath against Modernism : " Faith . . . is a true act of the intellect."

[2] *S. Theol.*, II-II, Q. 1, art. 4 ad 2.

assent. " Faith," says St Paul, " is the evidence of things that appear not." [1] Revealed truth is not seen in itself ; it is seen as credible, as clothed, so to speak, in the garment of divine authority. Invested with such authority, it becomes indeed a fit object for intellectual acceptance ; but the intellect alone, eager to " read within " (*intus-legere*) the truth, makes no spontaneous move to accept it. It is here that the intervention of the will becomes necessary. It has been seen in the previous section that the will has an important function in the preliminaries to faith. To arrive at the judgement of credibility the believer must focus his attention upon the motives of credibility and set aside all that might distract from their unbiassed consideration. All this needs a firm and constant effort of will. But in these preliminary stages the will has no direct causative influence upon the assent of the mind.[2] The intervention of the will in the act of faith itself is of a different and more direct character. The act of faith, though, as we have seen, it is elicited by the mind, is *caused* by an act of will. By faith, says the Vatican Council, " man yields a *voluntary* obedience to God himself." The mind sees the revealed truth as credible, and the will bends the mind to accept it.

Now it is important at once to preclude a possible misunderstanding of the function of the will in the act of faith. The will cannot make the mind believe anything it chooses ; it is not that " the wish is father to the thought." Before the mind can accept a statement, even at the behest of the will, the statement must be " credible " ; it must be attested by a trustworthy witness ; and, moreover, it must not be nonsense. Nonsense is meaningless and can have no relation to the mind. Briefly, a revealed statement *can* be accepted by the mind provided that it fulfils the conditions necessary to render it credible—*i.e.*, fit for intellectual acceptance. It is seen to be not unfit for acceptance because it has an intelligible meaning ; it is seen to be positively fit for acceptance because it is attested by an infallible witness. In fact, since the witness in this case is God himself, who has a right to our homage and obedience, the fitness is presented as a positive duty.

The will therefore now deliberately intervenes and commands the *Motive of* assent of the mind to revealed truth ; and the motive of the act is *faith* the authority of God who attests that truth. This motive, it *further* should be remarked, is one which appeals to both mind and will, but *explained* under different aspects. To the mind it appeals as endowing the statement with credibility ; to the will it appeals as a divine perfection to be worshipped : his love in revealing to be repaid by a loving acceptance on our part, his wisdom and his veracity to be

---

[1] Heb. xi. 1.

[2] This, of course, is true only of those preambles of which rational demonstration is given. If the preambles are accepted—as they often are—on human testimony, then the function of the will is the same as in every act of faith, whether human or divine.

adored by an unquestioning homage.[1] "Since man," says the Council which is our infallible guide in this matter, "is utterly dependent upon God as upon his Creator and Lord, and since created reason is absolutely subject to uncreated Truth, we are bound, by faith in his revelation, to yield him the full homage of our intellect and will." [2] Hence, although the act of faith is an intellectual act, yet it is also an act of homage which is in the power of the will to withhold. By faith "man yields *free* obedience to God." To explain the freedom and other properties of faith, it is necessary to examine a little more closely the precise nature of its motive, the authority of God.[3]

It might seem at first sight that if a man is firmly convinced that a statement has been made by one who is certainly telling the truth, then he cannot possibly withhold his assent to it ; nor is it apparent that such assent would be an act of homage to his informant. If a man accused of murder admits a fact which is damaging to his case, the jury—granted that they find no other reason for his admission—cannot but believe his testimony. And apart from all discussion as to the freedom of such an assent, by no conceivable standard could such belief be termed a homage to the veracity of the witness. The jury accept his statement because they know that in the circumstances it must be true. Of a like nature is the credence that we may give to an historian whom, however otherwise unreliable, we have proved by the application of tests to be here and now telling the truth. Critical students of history rely upon human testimony, but their acceptance of it implies no personal compliment to the narrator of the event. They believe that this happened because, and in so far as, they know that he is saying what is true. Is not the case the same with the act of divine faith ? I know that God has revealed the Trinity. I know that God is Truth itself. Surely the logical conclusion is inevitable : the Trinity is true.

---

[1] The act of faith, therefore, involves an act of *trust*, of confidence in God's authority. But this trust is not the act of faith itself ; it is anterior to it because it belongs to the motive of my assent. As a consequence of my faith in what God has revealed I may then make a further act of confidence in God that he pardons my sins ; this is an act of hope. The Protestant error concerning the "faith that justifies" consists in confusing hope with the faith which it presupposes. But see Essay xvi : *Sanctifying Grace*, p. 550.

[2] Chapter iii.

[3] Here a preliminary remark may not be out of place. As in many matters of theology, where it is a question of explanations, so in this matter theologians differ. The explanation of the act of faith involves the science of psychology wnich, although, or perhaps because, it deals with ourselves, is full of difficulties and mysteries. It is fair, therefore, to warn the reader that while all Catholics are agreed—as they must be—that the motive of faith is the authority of God, not all are agreed as to the manner in which this should be explained. The view here put forward appears to the writer a reasonable one, and is held by many theologians of repute.

Here is no free acceptance of God's word, no free homage to his Person. I am forced by the laws of evidence.

But there is a radical difference between the assent of divine faith and the assent given under the circumstances above described. The jury believe the witness, the historian believes his informant, because and in so far as they know him to be relating what is in conformity with reality. The motive of their assent is the evidence that they have of the truth of the statement; and such assent is probably not a free act; it is certainly no personal compliment to the witness. The believer accepts a revealed truth not precisely *because he knows* that God has revealed it and *knows* that God is infallible. This knowledge is the necessary condition, but it is not the motive, of his faith. He believes because *God*, who is infallible, has said it. The difference is perhaps subtle, but it is important. The motive of the act of divine faith is not *my knowledge* of that authority as accrediting revealed truth, however certain, however evident that knowledge may be, but the divine authority itself. My knowledge is finite, my knowledge is fallible. God's authority is infinite; God can neither deceive nor be deceived. If, when I believe, I rely upon my knowledge, I rely upon what is human; if I rely upon God's authority I rely upon what is divine. In the act of divine faith the believer abstracts from the arguments which have led him to the judgement of credibility. They were a necessary preliminary; they were, if you will, the tinder that lit the torch. But the torch burns now by its own brilliance; the light of God's authority illumines revealed truth with its infinite radiance; and this is the motive of faith : I believe because God has said it. Reason has led me to faith. Reason has told me that God's revealed word is credible, and in accordance with her advice I freely and unreservedly submit myself to the guidance of his Truth.

An instructive incident in the life of our Lord illustrates the nature of divine faith. The Pharisees, as is well known, were constantly rebuked by our Lord for their unbelief. They had seen, as others had seen, evident signs that Christ spoke the words of God ; and yet they stubbornly refused to believe him. One day after they had made one of their frequent attempts to discredit him,[1] he took a little child and said : " Amen I say to you, whosoever shall not receive the kingdom of heaven as a little child, shall not enter it." [2] The act of divine faith has more in common with the trusting belief of a child in his mother than with the assent of the critical historian. For the child it is enough to know that his mother has said it, and he believes on that authority. His assent is a prudent one, for he has motives of credibility which for him are sufficient ; everything leads him reasonably to suppose that his mother knows everything and would not deceive him. But when he believes, he believes

[1] Matt. xix 3.  [2] Mark x 15.

simply and solely because his *mother* has said it. He does not advert
to the reasons which have led him to regard his mother as trustworthy. His belief is an unaffected and trusting homage of love to
his mother. So also in the Act of Faith which every Catholic child
recites : " O my God, I believe . . . because thou hast said it, and
thy word is true." To the motives of credibility the child does not
advert ; he has probably forgotten them. But the motives of credibility are not the motives of his faith. He relies not upon them, but
upon the authority of God itself. What is true of the child is true
of the Christian adult ; and this the experience of each will confirm.
When he makes an act of faith, he thinks not of the proofs of the
existence of God, not of the miracles which Christ worked, but of
the authority of God, who can neither deceive nor be deceived.

This is why faith is a " theological " virtue, this is why faith is an
act of free obedience to God ; this, finally, is the reason of its
sovereign certitude.

*The certitude
of faith*    The certitude of faith is supreme because the believer's assurance
rests upon a ground more secure than all human science, upon the
infallible authority of God. " If we receive the testimony of man,"
says St John,[1] " the testimony of God is greater " ; infinitely, unspeakably greater, since God is very Truth. But, as in regard to
the freedom of the act of faith so also in regard to its certitude, a
difficulty often arises from a misconception of the precise motive of
faith. It is sometimes urged that since no chain is stronger than
its weakest link, therefore the assent of faith can enjoy no greater
certitude than the assent given to any of the preambles of faith which
are its foundation. Metaphors are misleading here. Even the
word " foundation " may lend itself to misunderstanding. The
preambles of faith are the foundation of faith in the sense that they
are a necessary prerequisite. But they are not its foundation in
the sense of supplying the security of the edifice. The metaphor
of the chain is no less fallacious. There is no continuous " chain"
of reasoning that leads from the first argument which proves the
existence of God to the truth, for example, that in one God there
are three Persons. If the act of faith were the logical conclusion of
such a chain, then evidently that conclusion could have no greater
weight than is warranted by the series of arguments that lead
to it. But the act of faith is not an inference from preceding
arguments.

The series of truths which we have called the preambles of faith
leads logically to the judgement of credibility, but no further. I
aver, in view of my previous reasoning, that it is reasonable, prudent,
in fact obligatory, to believe that, *e.g.*, there are three Persons in
one God. I then proceed, impelled not by my previous reasoning,
but by God's authority, to believe it. I believe it, not precisely
because and in so far as I know that God has revealed it, but

[1] I John v 9-10.

because God has revealed it. Hence the firmness of my assent is measured not by the cogency of any one, or indeed of the sum, of the reasons which led me to judge the truth as credible, but by the infinite weight of the divine authority which is the motive of my faith.

But although the certitude of faith is supreme, supreme as is the divine authority upon which it is based, yet the mind of the believer is not completely satisfied. Under the influence of the will it holds firmly to the truth ; but within the truth it does not see ; and nothing save vision can satisfy the mind. Faith is an evidence—*i.e.*, a firm conviction—but it is a conviction " of things that appear not." As long, then, as intrinsic evidence is denied, the mental assent is not spontaneous and requires the concurrence of the will. Hence it is misleading to compare the state of mind of the believer with the complete repose of the mind in a truth clearly demonstrated, or with the evidence of the senses. In the latter case there can be little or no temptation to doubt. The believer, on the other hand, precisely because he does not see within the truth, may be subject to many such temptations. But temptations are not doubts, and the believer is able by an effort of will to dispel them, to concentrate his attention upon the infallible motive of his faith, and thus to achieve a state of security from error as superior to that of human knowledge as the Truth of God infinitely transcends the fallible reason of man.

The whole process of the act of faith, such as we have described *The super-* it, does not seem, absolutely speaking, to exceed man's natural *natural* powers. If we consider those powers in the abstract, there seems to *character of* be no reason why, granted that God has made a revelation, man *faith* should not be able for himself to investigate the preambles of faith, naturally to recognise his obligation to accept it, and finally to believe on God's authority the truths that he has revealed. But even if we grant this to be physically possible, we have seen that the difficulties which occur even in the preliminary stages are such as to render it extremely unlikely of achievement, without the help of God's grace. When, moreover, we consider that the act of faith, being the initial step in man's progress towards his supernatural end, must itself be supernatural, the need for grace becomes quite imperative.

We must now, therefore, give our attention to those words of the *Grace* Vatican definition which we have hitherto neglected. " This faith," says the Council, " which is the beginning of man's salvation, is a *supernatural* virtue, whereby, *inspired and assisted by God's grace*, we believe," etc. And later in the same chapter, quoting the Council of Orange (529) the Council asserts the absolute impossibility of a salutary faith " without the illumination and inspiration of the Holy Spirit, who gives to all men sweetness in accepting and believing the truth."

Grace is necessary for the act of faith, in the first place, to make it supernatural ; to give it that quality which makes it conducive to a supernatural end, in other words, to make it salutary. If that supernatural character is needed—as we have seen that it is—even in the preliminary steps to faith, still more is it needed in the very act by which man submits to God's authority. " By grace," says St Paul,[1] " you are saved through faith, and that not of yourselves, for it is the gift of God." For faith man must strive to his utmost ; he must use all human endeavour to learn the truth and to submit to it. But all his striving, all his endeavour, would be utterly useless without the grace of God. He might even—we have surmised that it is not impossible—make an act of faith unaided ; but that act would not serve for his salvation unless it were made under the inspiration and assistance of God's grace. It must be *inspired* by grace. God does not wait until man conceives the desire to believe ; he puts that desire supernaturally in his heart. It must be *assisted* by God's grace. In the very act of submission to God's truth, the mind is enlightened, the will is strengthened by God, who works in us " to will and to accomplish."

The grace of God is essential ; but to none is it ever lacking. If even during man's progress towards faith God enlightens the mind and strengthens the will, anticipating every act with his grace, still more abundantly, when the act of faith itself is to be made, will God give his supernatural help. It is not the lack of grace that man should dread, but rather his own power to resist it.

But grace does more than make the act of faith supernatural ; it renders it easy and delightful. The Holy Spirit gives " sweetness in believing." Grace enlightens the mind, setting in vivid relief the desirability of paying intellectual homage to God, giving to it a supernatural insight into the meaning even of mysteries, and into the treasures of grace and glory which will be the reward of our faith. Grace helps the will to adhere firmly to God's word, putting aside all considerations of self-interest, all distractions of worldly things, to cleave to God, the inexhaustible source of every good.[2]

*Faith God's gift— Perseverance in faith*   In the fullest sense of the term, therefore, faith is God's gift. Hence it is for man to treasure and preserve it. Until we see God face to face the mind will be restive, and temptations to doubt will be frequent. The will must be prompt to reject them, and in this task man has always the abundant help of God's grace. He who has once committed himself to the keeping of God's Truth need not fear that he will be deserted in time of temptation. But he must do his part. He must take all those measures which are humanly possible to guard his treasure against attack. The mind of man is fickle ; error seduces by its very novelty, sophistical reasoning by its display of ingenuity. The Church, therefore, while she en-

---

[1] Ephes. ii 8.
[2] The effects which, in those who have the supernatural virtue of faith, proceed from that virtue are produced in others by actual grace. *Cf.* Essay xviii : *The Supernatural Virtues*, p. 643.

courages her more learned children to study, in order to refute, the written works of those who attack the faith, wisely forbids the dissemination, and above all the indiscriminate reading, of such books. She knows well that many who have the intelligence to understand an objection have not the ability to find, or even to understand, its answer ; that not all the faithful have the leisure or the power to meet reason with reason and learning with learning, and to rebut the objections so lightly made.

Those of the faithful who are troubled with such difficulties will do well to meditate upon these infallible words of the Vatican Council : " Although faith is above reason, there can never be any real discrepancy between faith and reason ; since the same God who reveals mysteries and infuses faith has bestowed the light of reason on the human mind, and God cannot deny himself, nor can truth ever contradict truth. The false appearance of such contradiction is mainly due, either to the dogmas of faith not having been understood and expounded according to the mind of the Church, or to the inventions of opinion having been taken for the verdicts of reason." [1]

A further duty regarding perseverance in faith arises from what was said in the previous section. It was there established that in order that the act of faith may be reasonably made it is sufficient to have a conviction concerning the preambles which, relatively to the circumstances of the individual, is prudent. But what is the duty of the child, for instance, when he grows to manhood and discovers— as he may—that the motives upon which he relied for his judgement of credibility no longer satisfy him ? Is he to give up his faith until he has once more gone over the preliminary ground and satisfied himself concerning the preambles ?

The answer of the Church as far as Catholics are concerned is peremptory : a Catholic can never have a just reason for abandoning the faith that he has once embraced. And the first reason of this is that the Catholic has constantly before him an absolutely, and not merely a relatively, sufficient motive of credibility—namely the Church herself, divinely instituted, and assuring her children " that the faith which they profess rests on the most secure foundation." [2] The second reason is that faith is not only a supernatural gift of God, but is accompanied by the graces necessary to preserve it. God's providence will not allow the faithful to lack the helps which they need to protect their faith. The ever-watchful Father, to whom his children daily pray, " Lead us not into temptation," will never allow them to be in such circumstances that the loss of their faith would be inculpable. Whatever be the greater or lesser degree of blame that may attach in individual cases, whatever be the mysterious means that God may use to protect his faithful ones, it is certain that " God does not abandon us until we first abandon him." [3]

[1] Chapter iv.     [2] Vatican Council, *loc. cit.*, chap. iii.
[3] St Augustine, *De natura et gratia*, c. 26.

It is clear, then, that in this matter the Catholic has serious duties. Not only must he avoid temptations against the faith, not only must he pray for an increase of faith, but he is bound to take care that his mental development in secular branches of study shall be accompanied by equal development in the knowledge of his religion. If he feels difficulties regarding fundamentals it is his duty to inquire of those who are able to solve them ; and here he needs a humility of mind which recognises that what he does not know is well known to many others. There can be little doubt that many defections from the Church are due to a culpable lack of knowledge—culpable because the ordinary means of information upon this important matter, whether they be Catholic books, sermons, or instructions, have been culpably neglected.

But it is otherwise for those who belong to non-Catholic religious bodies. None of these possesses, or indeed claims exclusively to possess, those characteristic marks of divine institution which so clearly distinguish the Catholic Church. Although members of such bodies may indeed assent by divine faith to some truths which are revealed by God, yet that very grace of faith, which strengthens Catholics in their adherence to the Church which Christ has instituted as the pillar and the ground of truth, will lead others to correct their errors and to submit to the infallible teacher of God's word. The essential difference in this matter between the position of Catholics and that of others is that whereas other religious bodies do not claim to be divinely instituted as the only infallible teacher of divine revelation, Catholics by their very faith profess that the Church is their divinely appointed guide. As Tertullian said to the unbelievers of his day, " We need no curious searchings, when we have Jesus Christ ; we need no further inquiry, when we have the gospel. When we believe, we need to believe nothing more. For this we believe at the very beginning, that there is nothing more to believe." [1]

*Necessity for salvation*    A word in conclusion on the necessity of the act of faith. That in all adults a supernatural act of divine faith is necessary as an indispensable means of salvation is the doctrine of the Catholic Church, and may be readily inferred from all that has been said concerning faith and supernatural revelation. The primary truth of that revelation is that man is called to a supernatural destiny which consists in the vision of God face to face. Of this destiny man could know nothing without revelation, and knowing nothing could never strive for it. Hence, in all who are able to act rationally and to think for themselves the first and indispensable step towards salvation is their recognition, by an act of divine faith, of God as their supernatural end. " Without faith," says St Paul, " it is impossible to please God." [2]    That act of faith, it is clear, must embrace at least implicitly every truth that God has revealed, for the motive of faith,

[1] *De praescr.*, c. 8.    [2] Heb. xi 6.

the authority of God, applies equally to them all. As to the minimum that must be known, and therefore believed explicitly, so that even its inculpable ignorance would exclude from the hope of salvation, it is commonly held that the two truths mentioned by St Paul [1] are sufficient : " He that cometh to God must believe that he is, and is a rewarder of them that seek him." But however few, however many be the truths believed, they must be accepted by an act of faith strictly so called. It is not enough, therefore, to hold, simply because one thinks it reasonable to hold, that there is a God who will reward those who seek him. It is necessary for salvation to hold this *because God has revealed it*, whatever be the means by which God's word has been made known. And the reason is that the reward which is in store for man is a reward which he could never have expected without God's revelation.

But apart from exceptional cases, it is normally necessary to know and to believe explicitly far more than the two truths mentioned, for Christ has instituted his Church to teach all that God has revealed. And this brings us to the subject of the next section.

§VI: THE CHURCH AND THE OBJECT OF FAITH

A NECESSARY condition for the act of faith, as we have seen, is that *The Church* the believer should know what God has revealed ; the object of *the appointed teacher of* faith must be presented to him as credible on the divine authority. *revealed* But it is evident that, so far as the act of divine faith as such is con- *truth* cerned, it matters little by what means it is thus presented. The study of Jewish and Christian literature simply as historical documents may convince a person that certain doctrines are revealed by God ; in that case he is bound to believe such doctrines on the authority of God's word. There are undoubtedly many outside the Catholic Church who, inculpably rejecting or not knowing her claim to be the infallible guardian of divine truth, yet believe some Christian doctrines by a supernatural act of divine faith. They have their motives of credibility, they have the assistance of God's grace ; they have, in short, all that is necessary for the act of divine faith which we have described.[2]

But—and the antithesis is to be noted—these are exceptional cases. They presuppose inculpable ignorance of the Catholic Church, the divinely appointed means for the teaching of revealed truth. Although by God's admirable mercy many outside the Church are enabled providentially to believe some small part of that divine doctrine, yet these must be content, as it were, with crumbs from the table of that rich repast which is spread for those who dwell within. " That we may be able to satisfy the obligation of embracing the true faith and of constantly persevering therein, God has instituted the Church through his only-begotten Son, and

[1] *Loc. cit.*            [2] See Essay xvii : *Actual Grace*, pp. 605 ff.

has bestowed on it manifest marks of that institution, that it may be recognised by all men as the guardian and teacher of the revealed word." [1]   This, then, is the way of approach to God's truth which Christ himself has ordained : a visible Church with a living teaching authority, infallible because the Holy Ghost is with her, preserving her from error. [2]

*Revelation complete in Christ*

The revelation made to the Apostles, by Christ and by the Holy Spirit whom he sent to teach them *all truth*, was final, definitive. To that body of revealed truth nothing has been, or ever will be, added.   The duty of the Apostles and their successors was clear : to guard jealously the precious thing committed to their care and to transmit it whole and entire to posterity.   "Therefore, brethren," says St Paul, "stand fast, and hold the traditions which you have learned, whether by word or by our epistle." [3]   "Hold the form of sound words which thou hast heard of me in faith and in the love which is in Christ Jesus . . . The things which thou hast heard of me by many witnesses, the same commend to faithful men who shall be fit to teach others also." [4]   Hence this important consequence : when the Church teaches that a truth—*e.g.*, the doctrine of original sin—is revealed by God, she does not mean that God has just now revealed it to her ; but, in virtue of her office as the infallible custodian and interpreter of God's word, she declares that this truth is contained, and always has been contained, in the deposit of revelation committed to her care.   In other words, when the Church teaches a revealed truth she draws upon the " sources " of revelation.

*Sources of revelation*

What are these sources ?   It would be true, in a sense, to say that there is but one source of revelation—namely, divine Tradition —understanding thereby the body of revealed truth handed down from the Apostles ; and it is in this sense that St Paul uses the word when he urges Timothy to " hold the traditions which you have learned, whether by word or by our epistle."   Nevertheless, since a great and important part of that tradition was committed to writing and is contained in the inspired books of Holy Scripture, it is the custom of the Church to distinguish two sources of revelation, Tradition and Scripture, the former name being reserved for that body of revealed truth which was not committed to writing under the inspiration of the Holy Ghost, but has been handed down through the living teaching authority of the Catholic Church.   We must deal briefly with each.

*Tradition and its organs*

And first, that oral tradition is a source of revelation distinct from Scripture there is little need to demonstrate.   The manner in which Christ instituted his Church is a sufficient indication of this. He instituted a visible society to the rulers of which he gave power to teach infallibly ; in other words, he founded a living teaching

---

[1] Vatican Council, *loc. cit.*, chap. iii.
[2] *Cf.* Essay xx : *The Church on Earth*, pp. 711 ff.
[3] 2 Thess. ii 14.          [4] 2 Tim. i 13 ; ii. 2.

authority. He may indeed have given his Apostles instructions to write some account of his life on earth, and of the chief points of his teaching ; but the Gospels themselves do not tell us so. At any rate not all of them did, or if they did their writings have not come down to us. But he told them explicitly to *preach* the gospel to every creature ; and the accounts that we have of the early apostolic ministry—and the Pauline texts above quoted—show that it was by oral instruction that the revealed word of God was chiefly propagated. St Paul, in fact, presupposes as a necessary prerequisite for faith the *hearing* of the word and the *preaching* of the gospel.[1]

The Tradition which is a source of revelation is divine Tradition ; and this differs from human tradition not only because it is of divine origin, but also in that, unlike its human counterpart, it is divinely guaranteed against corruption and alteration. Daily experience offers examples of statements which, made to one person and by him related to another who, in his turn, relying partly on a faulty memory and largely on a vivid imagination, relates them with embellishments to a friend, are brought back to the original speaker mutilated, mangled, and unrecognisable. Divine Tradition is authoritative and infallible ; infallible because authoritative—that is, transmitted through the teaching authority of the Church, under the assistance of the Holy Ghost.

Circumstances may demand that the Church should exercise her teaching office in a solemn manner, either by an infallible pronouncement of the Head of the Church, by the definitions of an Oecumenical Council, or by the authoritative proposition of some creed or formula of belief ; all such statements of doctrine form a part of divine Tradition. Ordinarily, however, the Church teaches the faithful through their more immediate legitimate pastors, and their universal consensus on a point of doctrine—expressed either in official pronouncements, in catechisms issued by episcopal authority, or through other channels—is an organ of divine Tradition. Similarly the universal practice of the Church, if it essentially implies a dogmatic truth, is a source of divine revelation. Thus St Augustine rightly pointed to the universal practice of the Church of baptising children as an indication that the doctrine of original sin is divinely revealed. Moreover, many of the theologians of the early centuries of the Church, conspicuous for their sanctity and learning, are called " Fathers." The consensus of these, similarly, considered as witnesses to the general belief of the Church, is an indication that the truth which they unanimously hold to be divinely revealed is in fact a part of the deposit of faith. The same is true of the consensus of later theologians. For although neither Fathers nor theologians *as such* represent the teaching authority of the Church, yet they are witnesses to the universal belief of the faithful which is the result of that teaching. Hence, finally, the belief of the faithful themselves,

[1] *Cf.* Rom. x 14-17.

expressed unanimously, is a further indication that a truth is contained in the deposit of faith.   For the faithful, considered as a body,
believe infallibly what they have been infallibly taught.

*Holy*
*Scripture*
The other source of revelation is Sacred Scripture.   The books
of the Old and New Testaments are held by the Church as sacred,
not merely because they contain revealed doctrine, not merely because they are free from error, but because they are the work of God
himself.   God is their author.   This is not the place in which to
deal with the important subject of inspiration ;   it is treated fully
elsewhere in this work.[1]   Suffice it to note here that inspiration is
a supernatural work of God.   Hence we can know nothing of it
except from revelation.   No natural perfection of a book—*e.g.*, the
fact that it contains true and holy doctrines, that its perusal gives
rise to pious thoughts—can show it to have been written under the
supernatural influence of the Holy Spirit.   We can know that God
is the author of a book only through the testimony either of God
himself, or of the writer whom he has used as his instrument, provided
that he was conscious of being divinely inspired.   In the latter case,
unless the sacred writer is able to present divine credentials for his
assertion, the testimony is but human and fallible.   Whether,
therefore, in regard to inspiration in general—that there do in fact
exist divinely inspired books, or in regard to the canonicity of the
sacred books—that this or that book is divinely inspired, our sure
and infallible knowledge can come only from divine revelation.
Now we have seen that the complete divine revelation is transmitted
to us from Christ through the Apostles in the divine Tradition of
the Church.   Hence the only certain guide as to the inspiration and
canonicity of all the books of Sacred Scripture is the authoritative
pronouncement of the Church.   " I should not believe the gospel,"
says St Augustine, " unless I were impelled thereto by the authority
of the Catholic Church." [2]

Moreover, since the Church is the divinely appointed custodian
of revelation, it is evidently her office to preserve not merely the
letter of the Scriptures, but also their meaning.   The Church,

[1] Essay v :   *The Holy Ghost*, pp. 166-179.
[2] *Contra ep. fundament.*, c. 5.   With regard to some books of Scripture
that revelation may be found in Scripture itself, where we find the testimony
of Christ and his Apostles to the inspiration of many of the books of the Old
Testament.   Moreover, it may still be not unnecessary—although it has been
done so often before—to point out that the Catholic is not guilty of a vicious
circle in arguing " from the Bible to the Church and from the Church to the
Bible."   The Catholic apologist does indeed argue (partly, not entirely)
from data found in the Bible to the divine institution of the Catholic Church ;
but at this stage he does not use the Bible as inspired, but simply as a trustworthy historical document. The logical sequence, therefore, is not simply
" from the Bible to the Church and from the Church to the Bible," but
rather from a *trustworthy* Bible to a divinely instituted Church.   Then
follows an act of faith (made on the authority of God and under the direction
of his Church) in the *inspiration* of the Bible.

therefore, is the authentic and infallible interpreter of Scripture. Nevertheless, this intimate connection between Tradition and Scripture does not imply that the inspired writings are not a source of revelation distinct from the oral Tradition which transmits them to us. The Church, infallibly assisted by the Holy Ghost, tells us what God has revealed. In the Scriptures it is God himself who gives us his revelation. But so deep is the reverence in which the Church holds the inspired word of God that she guards it most jealously, encouraging scholars, indeed, in their endeavours more profoundly to penetrate its meaning, but keeping upon them a salutary check, lest human ingenuity should corrupt the wisdom that is divine.

These, then, are the two sources of divine revelation : Tradition preserved by the living and infallible teaching authority of the Church, and Scripture, the inspired word of God : sources of truth which the Church preserves pure and undefiled, and from which she derives that divine revelation which she proposes for belief in all ages.

What the Church, therefore, teaches as divinely revealed, that *Dogmas* most certainly is revealed by God and must be believed on the divine authority. These truths, revealed by God—*i.e.*, contained in Tradition or in Scripture, or in both, and taught by the Church either in her solemn definitions or in her ordinary teaching—are called by the technical name of *dogmas*.

A little reflection will serve to show that the act of faith by which *Divine and* a Catholic believes the dogmas of the Church does not differ essen- *Catholic* tially from the act of divine faith. The motive of faith is always the *faith* authority of God who reveals. Yet such an act of faith has an additional perfection, in that, besides accepting the authority of God, it includes also submission to the Catholic Church as the infallible and authentic interpreter of revelation. This act of faith is therefore called by the special name of " divine and catholic " faith. It is divine because its motive is the divine authority ; it is catholic because the truth is accepted as divinely revealed on the authority of the infallible Catholic Church.

But the infallible authority of the Church is by no means con- *"Secondary* fined to the teaching of " dogmas." The Church is not only the *truths"* teacher of revealed truth, she is also its guardian ; and in the office of protecting God's truth against error she needs to pronounce infallibly upon many matters which, although they are not formally revealed by God, are nevertheless intimately connected with revelation. It cannot be too strongly emphasised that Catholics are bound under pain of grave sin to believe the truths thus infallibly taught by the Church. They are not dogmas, indeed, because in themselves they have not been revealed by God. Hence the motive of the assent which we give to them is not the divine authority. We believe them on the authority of the Catholic Church, inasmuch as she is exercising her office of guardian of revealed truth, an office committed to her by God himself. Evidently, therefore, refusal to believe them would be a serious sin against the virtue of faith.[1]

*Further explanation*

Having thus duly stressed the strict duty of Catholics in this matter, we may now proceed, without fear of being misunderstood, to explain more fully the important distinction between what for purposes of convenience I will call these " secondary truths," and " dogmas " in the proper sense of the word. The distinction is important for at least three reasons, for upon it depends the understanding (1) of what is meant by " heresy," (2) of what is meant by the " immutability " of Catholic dogma, and (3) of the restrictions placed upon theological discussion. The third point will be dealt with in the last section ; of the first it is sufficient to say that " heresy " is the wilful denial of a dogma ; [2] with the second we must deal here more fully.

A dogma, then, as opposed to a secondary truth, is a truth contained " in the word of God, written or handed down, and which the Church, either by a solemn judgement or by her ordinary and universal teaching, proposes for belief as having divinely been revealed." [3] That the sources of revelation are two has already been sufficiently emphasised. Two points, however, in this definition need to be explained, since the neglect of either may lead to the exaggeration or to the undue limitation of the field of dogma.

In the first place the truth must be *contained* in either of the sources of revelation. That is to say, it must have been revealed by God either expressly or in equivalent words—*i.e.*, as the theologians say, " formally." Hence from the field of dogma properly so called are to be excluded those truths which are only connected—however intimately—with revelation. Thus a truth which is deduced by human reasoning from revealed truth—a theological conclusion— even though it may be infallibly taught by the Church and therefore binding on our assent, is not a dogma. Thus varying practical or devotional applications of revealed truths are not dogmas ; the infallible decisions of the Church on points of historical fact, such as the oecumenicity of certain Councils, though they are closely connected with revealed truth, are not, properly speaking, dogmas. Nor does the use of certain philosophical terms in the proposition of revealed truths consecrate as a dogma any tenet proper to that philosophical system.

On the other hand, a truth, to be a dogma, need not be contained expressly in the sources of revelation. It is sufficient that it be revealed at least in equivalent words. Thus if two statements are revealed which together involve a third, then that third is revealed equivalently. If, for example, it is expressly revealed that man has free-will, and that Christ has a true human nature, then it is equiva-

---

[1] *Cf.* Essay xviii : *The Supernatural Virtues*, p. 645. Since the motive of this assent is the authority of the Church, such faith is called " ecclesiastical."
[2] *Ibid.*, p. 644.          [3] Vatican Council, *loc. cit.*, chap. iii.

lently revealed that Christ has free-will.  In this and many similar instances the third proposition is not deduced by human reasoning, but gathered directly from the meaning of what God has revealed.

In the second place, it is to be observed that to be a dogma a revealed truth need not be solemnly defined by the Church.  It is sufficient, as the Church herself has repeatedly declared, that it be proposed as being divinely revealed in her ordinary official teaching.  But this at least is necessary.  Hence, regularly, a private revelation —*i.e.*, a revelation made by God for the benefit of one individual or group of individuals—binds only those to whom and for whom it is made.  It is not intended for all the faithful, it is not accompanied by any divine guarantee that it will be transmitted to others without adulteration, nor is it, as such, contained in the deposit of faith committed to the Church.  The approbation granted by the Church to these revelations means nothing more than " permission, given after due examination, to publish them for the edification and utility of the faithful." [1]  Moreover, by such approbation the Church does not—at any rate infallibly—guarantee even their authenticity. [2]  Truths so revealed form no part of the dogmatic teaching of the Church.

Having thus, so far as space allows, cleared the ground of misconceptions, we may now answer the questions : What is the meaning of the immutability of Catholic dogma ?  Does it in any way develop ? *Immutability and development of Catholic dogma*

The answer to the first question is contained in what has already been said.  The revelation of Christ is definitive.  He, with the Holy Spirit whom he sent, has revealed to his Apostles all truth.  But a dogma, as we have seen, is a truth which is contained in that revelation.  Therefore dogma, in the sense that it proposes for belief no truth which was not thus revealed to the Apostles and by them handed down to the Church, is immutable.

But undoubtedly a certain development is to be admitted.  The subject is most complex and demands a far fuller treatment than can possibly be accorded it in the present essay ; we must be content with the merest outline.  In the first place clearly any " development " must be excluded from dogma which would result in the adulteration of the original meaning of God's revealed word.  This would be incompatible with the immutability already established.  Thus the view that dogmas, being mere symbols to represent the evolution of the universal religious consciousness, may in course of time come to mean the opposite of what they meant before ;  the view that dogmas develop in the sense that they are re-stated—and this often means contradicted—to suit the practical or scientific needs of the age ;  these and similar views must be definitely rejected as incompatible with the essential immutability of divine revelation.

[1] Benedict XIV : *De Beatif.*, etc., lib. 2, c. 32.
[2] Pius X : Encyclical *Pascendi*.

How, then, does dogma develop ?   Albertus Magnus [1] succinctly describes this development as " the progress of the faithful in the faith, rather than of the faith within the faithful."   In other words, the whole of revealed truth is contained in the sources of revelation, but in the course of ages it has undergone, and still undergoes, a process of " unfolding," whereby the faithful, under the infallible guidance of the Church assisted by the Holy Ghost, arrive at a fuller understanding of the truths which God has revealed.   Of this " unfolding " process, however, the cause is not the understanding of the faithful, but the infallible teaching authority of the Catholic Church.

It is inevitable, in the nature of things, that a body of truth committed to human understanding should undergo a process of development.   The truth is apprehended by the mind now under one aspect, now under another ; every new point of view is a development.   A universal truth contains implicitly its application to many individual cases ; every such application is a development.   The human mind relates one statement to another by a logical sequence, and thus is enabled more fully to understand them both ; the fuller understanding of truth is a development.   Such development occurs in every science.   But there is this important difference in regard to revealed truth, that whereas in human science progress is made from the totally unknown to the known, often from error to truth and *vice versa*, in the development of dogma there are no such vicissitudes, because the only cause of development in Catholic dogma is the infallible teaching of the Church.

Theologians may study revealed truth, may find new modes of expression, may discover or set into clearer relief new implications thereof ; the denial of a truth by heretics may orientate discussion towards aspects of the truth hitherto but little studied ; old formulas may be found to be not false, but no longer adequate, in consequence of misunderstanding or misconstruction, for the controversial needs of the day ; the devotion of the faithful may lead to a greater emphasis being laid upon certain aspects of the truth.   But when all is said and done, it is the Church, assisted by the Holy Ghost, that unfolds the truth, since, until she has embodied in her official teaching the results of theological study or of devotional impulse, there is no development in Catholic dogma.

*An illustration*   To illustrate this development of revealed truth " in one and the same doctrine, one and the same judgement," [2] many examples might be taken from history.   One characteristic instance must suffice. The dogma of the Immaculate Conception of our Blessed Lady was solemnly defined by Pope Pius IX in the year 1854.   It was defined, not as a conclusion drawn from revealed doctrine, but as being con-

[1] Quoted by Franzelin : *De Divina Traditione* . . . p. 260.
[2] Vatican Council, *loc. cit.*, chap. iv, quoting Vincent of Lerins : *Common.*, n. 28.

tained in the revealed word of God. And, in fact, if we examine the sources of Revelation (Scripture and Tradition) we find that this is so. In the Scriptures, as interpreted by Tradition, this truth is implicitly contained in the statement that Mary is " full " of grace, that between her and Satan there is complete enmity, such that she could never have been under Satan's power. During the first three centuries we find in Tradition the constant teaching—as a doctrine divinely revealed—that Mary is the new Eve, that she plays a part in the Redemption analogous to that which Eve had played in the Fall—i.e., that she is ever on the side of the Redeemer against sin. Hence the Fathers teach that she is all-pure, so much so that St Augustine, in spite of his insistence against the Pelagians upon the natural sinfulness of mankind, yet refuses to mention the name of Mary in connection with sin. With the impetus given to devotion to our Lady by the Council of Ephesus we find lyrical outbursts, especially among the Eastern Fathers, extolling the purity of our Lady, and—from the seventh century onwards—not infrequent mention of the feast of her Conception. Differences of opinion among the theologians of the Middle Ages as to the precise essence of original sin prevented many of them from explicitly exempting our Lady from this hereditary taint ; but with the clearer understanding of that doctrine came the explicit statement and universal belief that not for one moment of her existence was our Lady stained with original sin.

The history of this dogma is very instructive as showing how a particular truth, implicitly contained from the very beginning in a more general one, may, under the successive influence of theological study, devotional impulse, and even theological disagreement, come to be explicitly understood, universally believed, and, in the end, solemnly defined by the Church.

But the dogmas of the Church, though they are the most important part of her doctrine, form but a part of her infallible teaching. Besides dogmas strictly so called, our heritage includes a wealth of doctrine derived from revealed truth, the fruit, in great measure, of the loving meditation of our forefathers in the faith and of the devoted study of theologians.

## §VII: THEOLOGY

THEOLOGY may be briefly described as the science of revealed truth. *Definition* Presupposing revelation and faith, it applies the scientific method to the study of revealed truth. The theologian not only accepts the truths which God has revealed, but he links them together in their logical sequence, showing the connection of one with another, their mutual harmony and their analogy with the conclusions of human reason. Nor does he deal only with revelation as such ; by applying to revealed truth the principles of human reasoning he deduces conclusions, and these in their turn he links up with other conclusions and with other revealed truths, thus forming a complete and harmonious system.

*Sources and Method*    The chief sources used by theology are, clearly, the sources of Revelation : Scripture and Tradition. The theologian shows how the various dogmas of the Church are contained therein, traces their development from implicit to explicit belief, the different aspects under which they have been studied at different periods of the Church's history, and deals with the heresies and the controversies that have arisen in regard to each. But he does not confine his study of Tradition to the truths which have always been believed as revealed by God. He investigates the conclusions which in the past have been drawn from revealed truth, testing the consensus of Fathers and theologians concerning them as a criterion of their accuracy, and as indicating the common belief of the faithful on matters closely connected with revelation.

Like other sciences, theology has its subsidiary sources. Chief among these is philosophy, by means of which the theologian is able not only to demonstrate the preambles of faith, not only to show that the data of revelation are in perfect harmony with the conclusions of human reason, but also to gain a most " fruitful understanding even of mysteries." These must, of course, remain veiled in a certain obscurity as long as we walk " by faith " ; yet by the aid of philosophy the theologian vindicates their reasonable character, defends them against the accusation of absurdity, and is able to learn much of their meaning. As we have already seen,[1] the terms in which mysteries are revealed are familiar to us. Philosophy enables the theologian to define more accurately the meaning of those terms, and in this way to acquire a better understanding of the mystery itself.

But philosophy, though useful in theology, is subsidiary, and must take a subordinate place. There comes a stage in the study of mysteries where the philosopher must bow his head and be content, and even rejoice, to walk by faith alone. Moreover, he must submit to learn from revelation the limits of his own science. If a philosophical tenet is found to be in contradiction with a revealed truth, then the philosopher must retrace his steps to see where he has wrongly reasoned. To this extent the theologian must always argue *a priori*. If a truth is certainly revealed by God—and that, through the infallible teaching of the Church, he can always ascertain—then any human conclusion or hypothesis, whether it be philosophical, historical, or scientific, which contradicts it, is most certainly erroneous. The theologian, on the other hand, must beware lest in such matters he himself introduce confusion by expounding the word of God otherwise than the Church understands it.[2]

[1] P. 7.    [2] *Cf.* above, p. 25.

Similarly other sciences, especially history and the natural sciences, are used as subsidiary in theology. These are valuable as supplying knowledge concerning the created universe, and particularly concerning the nature of man, the most noble of God's visible creatures. But they too must be used under conditions and safe-guards analogous to those already described. It has been said before, but it is worth while repeating, that between the natural revelation which God has made of his perfections in the universe and the supernatural revelation which he has given us through his Church, there can be no real contradiction. In God's providence the one is complementary to the other.

One important observation must be made before we conclude. Theologians are fallible and therefore they differ. In the essays of the series of which this is the first, there will be set forth not only the dogmas of the Church, not only quite certain theological conclusions which, since they are taught by the infallible Church, must be accepted by " ecclesiastical " faith,[1] not only more remote conclusions which, by reason of the common consent of theologians, it would be " rash " to deny, but also other statements, intended to explain, to amplify, or philosophically to justify some doctrine of the Church, statements which have not the same infallible certainty. On these matters, in which the integrity or the security of revealed truth is not in question, theologians enjoy freedom of discussion. Upon such controversies, since the sincere object of the participants is the fuller understanding of revealed truth, the Church looks with no unfavourable eye, solicitous ever to promote charity among the disputants with that single-minded desire for truth, and loving appreciation of the word of God, which are the heart and soul of theology.

G. D. SMITH.

[1] See above, p. 32, n. 1.

# II

# AN OUTLINE OF CATHOLIC TEACHING

## INTRODUCTORY NOTE

CATHOLIC doctrine is not a series of disjointed statements. It is an organic body of religious truth, in which one dogma cannot rightly be understood save in its relation to the others, a part cannot be denied without rejecting the whole. Hence the utility—perhaps even the necessity—in a work of this character, of a brief outline of the whole of Catholic teaching.

The space at the disposal of the writer does not allow of lengthy explanations ; these are to be sought in other essays. It may well be, therefore, that some of the truths here stated will appear difficult, some of the terms used require elucidation. But it has seemed opportune, even at the risk of some obscurity in matters of detail, to deal in its broad outlines with the whole doctrine of the Church, so that the truths of our faith may appear in their proper perspective, each in its connection with each of the others, as an integral part of an harmonious whole.

## §I: THE DIVINE TRINITY

*The three divine Persons*

WHEN we were baptised three august names were pronounced over us—the Father, the Son, and the Holy Ghost—and in the name of these three we were made children of God. At the beginning and the end of every day, before and after meals, whenever we enter or leave a church, whenever we make the sign of the Cross, these same three names are on our lips. When, finally, we breathe our last, it is in the name of the Father, and of the Son, and of the Holy Ghost that the Church will speed us on our journey to eternal life.

Who are these three Persons with whom the whole Christian life is so intimately and essentially connected ? They are the one God whom we worship. Who is the Father ? He is God, who from eternity begets the Son. And the Son ? He is God, eternally begotten of the Father. And the Holy Ghost ? He is God, the Spirit from eternity breathed by Father and Son. They are really three, really distinct ; distinct, because the begetter is not the begotten, the breather is not the Spirit breathed ; distinct by their reciprocal relations, and yet in nature, in Godhead ineffably one. One in nature, not as you and I are one, united by the bond of our common human species, under which we are classified together as individuals. Your human nature is not mine, nor is mine yours, and therefore we are not one man, but two. Father, Son, and Holy

38

Ghost are not three Gods, but one God, because the divine nature which the Holy Ghost eternally receives from Father and Son, which Son eternally receives from Father, is numerically one and the same. One Person is not greater than another, one is not before another; all three are equal and co-eternal. Seek no perfection in the Father which is not equally in the Son, no perfection in these which is not in their Holy Spirit; their perfection is their Godhead, which is identical in each. They are distinct really, but merely, by their reciprocal relations. Think of no time in which Father was without his Son, or Father and Son without their Holy Spirit. Father, Son, and Spirit are the one God, without beginning or end, changeless, eternal.

And of this Godhead, one in three Persons, what can we say? *The Godhead and divine attributes* "We shall say much, and yet shall want words: but the sum of our words is: He is all." [1] By what name shall we call him? He has told us his name. He is Being. "I am who am." [2] He is all perfection, limitless, infinite. Read upon the face of the universe which he has made, and there you may see some reflection of the Maker. The sun that rises and sets, the trees that with the change of the seasons pass from death to life, and from life to death, the animals that are born to die, man himself, "who cometh forth like a flower and is destroyed, and fleeth as a shadow and never continueth in the same state," [3] all speak the same language, all say that they are made, that they have received their being from another, that they were not, and now are, that they owe their being to him who is not made, but makes all that is, who receives being from none, whose essence is to be, who is the necessary Being, God.

Whatever is good and beautiful in the work of his hands, that you may say of him, provided you do not limit or disfigure his perfection. He is not material; for a body has parts, a body changes and tends to dissolution. God is supremely one and simple; he is a Spirit. In him is no transition from one state of being to another, no lack of anything, no capacity unfulfilled; he is changeless. But, for God, to be without movement is not to be quiescent, inactive. To act is his very being; he is essentially active. But his acts do not succeed one another; he has no beginning and no end. What he is and does, he is and does outside of time; for him there is no "before" and "after," but one all-embracing "now." The creatures and their activities which succeed each other in time to him are ever present. God is eternal. And where is God? He is everywhere. To all things that are, God is present, because he is the cause of their being. And yet the universe cannot contain him; his power, infinite as all his perfections, extends immeasurably beyond the limits of the things that he has made. "If heaven," cries Solomon,[4] "and the heaven of heavens cannot contain thee, how much less this house which I have built!"

---

[1] Ecclus. xliii 29.  [2] Exod. iii 14.  [3] Job xiv 2.  [4] 3 Kings viii 27.

The fount of life is himself most perfectly and infinitely living. But the life of God is not, like ours, dependent on external objects. We cannot live without some material upon which to nourish our vital activity. The divine life is infinitely self-contained, supremely immanent. His life is the life of Spirit, of mind and will. God is subsistent, essential mind, and the object of his contemplation is himself. He is immediately and immutably conscious of the infinite perfection of his being. There is nothing that gives him knowledge, for his being is the all-sufficient reason of his mental activity, the adequate object of his thought. Of the creatures that he has made he has most perfect and intimate knowledge, but he knows them in knowing himself, the First Cause of all being. Nothing is hidden from his all-seeing eye, which with one eternal glance comprehends in the Source of all being everything that in any way is, has been, can or will be. The thoughts and intentions of man, so jealously hidden from others, lie open before God, who knows what is in man; the future holds no mysteries for him to whom all things are present; not a leaf falls, not a seed shoots, not an atom changes, but with the knowledge of him who is the Cause of all.

To know the good is to love it. God is subsistent Will, and the necessary, all-sufficient object of that will is himself. In God, to will, to love is not to desire, for he lacks nothing that is good. In him is only joy and delight; he is infinitely happy in the contemplation of his goodness. As his mind needs nothing to give him knowledge, so his will needs no other being upon which to lavish his infinite love; he alone is truly and totally self-sufficient. Creatures have their being, creatures have their goodness and their beauty; but they have it from him who is Being, who is Goodness, who is Beauty. It is not because they are that God knows them, not because they are good that God loves them. God knows them, and his knowledge creates them; he loves them, and his love, freely bestowed, gives them some faint reflection of his infinite goodness.

These truths concerning the nature of God are mysterious indeed, and the human mind would be other than it is could it fully understand them, could it ever fathom the depths of the Infinite Being. But, mysterious though they are, man recognises that God must be so, and rejoices in the knowledge which human language is but ill-fitted to express. But of the Trinity of Persons, of that mystery of the life of God, belief in which may be said to be the touchstone of Christianity, man could have known nothing, had God not willed in his mercy to reveal his secret. Where all is simple and indivisible, we should have thought that there is place for nothing but unity. Yet there—wonder of wonders—is a Trinity of Persons. The divine life of mind and will is fruitful, productive, and the one eternal God is not one Person, but three. We cannot understand this mystery; but yet, enlightened by faith in God's revelation, we strive to find in our own life of mind and will some analogy by which we may illustrate the adorable life of the Trinity.

God the Son is called the Word; he is "the image of the invisible God,"[1] "the brightness of his glory and the figure of his substance."[2] Is he not, then, the eternal subsistent thought, the Word conceived by the Father, wherein he perfectly expresses himself, the object of his eternal contemplation? And the Holy Spirit, is he not the subsistent breath of divine love, proceeding eternally from the Father and his Word? We lisp like children when we speak of things divine. But we are destined one day to know the answer. We are called to share in that divine life, in that intercommunication of knowledge and love, which is the life of the Blessed Trinity. Until God's face is openly revealed, we adore by faith in his word.

## §II: GOD AND CREATURES

INFINITELY happy in the contemplation of himself, in the mutual knowledge and love of the three divine Persons, God has no need of anything apart from himself. Nothing, therefore, could constrain him to create, to produce other beings. That act of divine love, whereby he eternally decrees that creatures shall begin to exist, is perfectly and supremely free. By an exercise of his almighty power God willed, commanded, and creatures began to be. There was nothing out of which he might make them—not from his own substance, which is simple and indivisible—and apart from him there was nothing. "He spoke and they were made, he commanded, and they were created."[3] He cannot increase his perfection, for it is infinite; then he will manifest it. There shall be beings distinct from him, and yet in some manner resembling him, for they will each show forth something of the infinite perfection of their Maker.

*Creation, its freedom and purpose*

That infinite perfection we have tried to contemplate and to describe; but our minds are as impotent to grasp as our language is inadequate to express it—it is as if we tried to gaze upon the noonday sun. Yet look at the western sky when the sun has dipped below the horizon, and see how each tiny cloud portrays a different tint, how the sun's white brilliance is reflected now in a gorgeous variety of colour; it is the glory of the setting sun. The divine perfections, as mirrored, participated in by creatures, are the external glory of God. He has freely willed that the supreme perfection which in him is one, simple and undivided, should be reflected in myriads of beings, each having its own goodness and beauty, each manifesting in some degree the goodness and the beauty of its Maker, each dependent entirely upon that Maker for all that it has and is.

The result of that eternal decree is the universe, the finite mirror of God's limitless beauty, the visible pledge of his infinite

*Angels*

[1] Col. i 15.     [2] Heb. i 3.     [3] Ps. xxxii. 9.

love.  Supreme in the hierarchy of created being are the angels, pure spirits, separated indeed by an abyss from the infinite simplicity of God, to whom they pay homage as their Creator, yet most perfect among creatures because they are pure intelligences, most like to the great Spirit who is the cause of all.  Over these death has no power, matter has no hold.  Untrammelled by bodily limitations, their intellect needs no laborious reasoning to arrive at the truth, but reaches it by simple, immanent acts, receiving its knowledge by a mysterious radiance from the eternal Sun of Truth.  Their will-activity is proportionately perfect, free and unconstrained, but decisive and irrevocable, with none of the groping hesitancy of our human deliberations.  Their name describes their office ; they are God's messengers, the ministers of his power, the bearers of his commands.  Their life and their joy is to sing in spiritual canticles the praises of their God.[1]

*Various orders of being*

Lowest in the scale of being are inorganic material substances ; and yet in these what wonderful variety and harmony are discovered by the scientist, what immense, uncharted spaces have been revealed by the astronomer !  Such is the awful majesty, the splendour, the beauty of the heavens, so clear is the voice with which they " tell forth the glory of God " that many have been led to see there, not the works of his hands, but the Maker himself.  " With whose beauty, if they being delighted, took them to be gods : let them know how much the Lord of them is more beautiful than they.  For the first author of beauty made all those things." [2]

More perfect in their order than these are the innumerable forms of plant-life with which land and sea have been adorned by the unstinting generosity of the Creator.  They are living beings ; a higher force has entered into matter and formed it into the living cell.  Here in its least perfect form is animate existence.  The plant assimilates the inorganic matter around it and grows unconsciously, but vitally, to its own perfection, transmitting its life to others of the same species.

Higher still in the scale are the animals, which in addition to the functions of plant-life possess an even more perfect activity.  By sensation they perceive their object, and, desiring it, move spontaneously in search of it, in this manner knowingly seeking and securing what they need for their growth and propagation.

*Man—his nature*

Finally, at the very centre of the universe, all the perfections of created being meet in the " microcosm," " the little universe," man himself, in whom a body, immeasurably superior in beauty and proportions to that of the other animals, is animated by a principle whose essence and activity are unbounded by the limits of matter ; man is endowed with a spiritual, immortal soul.  In this noble being the perfections of the spiritual and of the material spheres, of the visible and of the invisible worlds, are wonderfully combined.  With

[1] Isa. vi 1.          [2] Wisd. xiii 3.

inanimate material substances he has in common a body ; with plants he shares vegetative life, whereby he absorbs nourishment from without for his development and begets others like himself to propagate his species ; like other animals, he has the faculties of sense and instinct—but what raises him far above all these is his spiritual soul, whereby he is like the angels.

And yet man is a unity. It is by virtue of the one spiritual principle that he lives and moves, feels and sees, knows and wills. He has not three souls, but one—a spiritual soul, whereby he exercises all his functions, both those which he has in common with other creatures and those which are proper to himself. Like the animals he receives sense-impressions, but with his immaterial intellect he elaborates them, purifies them, disengages them from their material conditions, forms spiritual and universal ideas, and is able by these to rise above matter and to live in the world of the spirit. His feet are upon the earth, but his head soars to the heavens. Dependent in all his vital operations upon material things, he is yet able to lift himself beyond them. He alone of visible creatures has the conception of moral good, of his duty to his Maker ; he alone is able to know God, to rise from the contemplation of visible things to the knowledge—imperfect indeed, but how precious !— of the invisible Creator of all.

Side by side with intelligence he has the faculty of free will. Man is not drawn of necessity to embrace any of the finite goods that he apprehends. They are arraigned before the judgement-seat of his intelligence, they are weighed in the balance. Desiring the good, he chooses between the various means that present themselves as conducive to it, and in this choice consists his freedom. He is material, but not wholly so ; then he will satisfy his material needs, but only in so far as they assist in his spiritual development. He is spiritual, but not wholly so ; then, while attending primarily to his spiritual development, he will not neglect the needs of the body. By his free will man is master in his own house and, for good or for ill, freely directs his own activities.

" Thou hast made him a little less than the angels, thou hast crowned him with glory and honour, and hast set him above the works of thy hands." [1] The whole material creation is subject to man. The new splendours, the immense spaces, the overwhelming vastness of the material universe that are being daily revealed to us by science—these may indeed make us exclaim with the Psalmist : " What is man that thou art mindful of him ? " [2] We may wonder the more at the prodigal generosity of the Creator who has made all these things for man, but none may take from him the glory and the honour with which God has crowned him. It is not for man to abdicate his throne. The vastest planet is as nothing compared to the mind of man that studies its evolutions ; the whole of the material

[1] Ps. viii 6-7.      [2] Ps. viii 5.

universe is less in God's sight than the tiniest child endowed with intelligence, upon whom the light of the Lord's countenance is signed.[1]

Man is lord of the visible universe ; but he is also its priest. For no other reason have all things been subjected to man than that he in turn may offer them to God. God has created all things for himself, since he who is the First Cause, the First Mover, himself unmoved, can have no other motive. If man, the " pontifex," the bridge-builder between matter and spirit, has been crowned with glory, that glory is not his own, but God's ; it is to God, then, that he must offer it. " Thou art worthy, O Lord our God, to receive glory and honour and power ; because thou hast created all things, and for thy will they were and have been created." [2]

*God the end of all creatures*   The object, then, that creatures are to achieve is the external glory of God ; and it is in achieving this object that they achieve their own perfection. All creatures are destined to " serve God " ; not that they can give anything to God, from whom they have their very being and all that they possess ; but they are to serve God by showing forth in their own finite perfections something of the infinite goodness and beauty of their Maker. In this see how the sublime self-love of God is supremely disinterested. Receiving nothing he gives all ; creating all things for his own glory he thereby perfects all creatures. Creatures themselves, in fulfilling the purpose of their existence, which is to manifest the goodness of God, thereby perfect themselves ; for the more perfect they are, the more do they redound to the glory of him who made them.

God, therefore, is not only the beginning, he is the end of all creatures. " I am Alpha and Omega, the beginning and the end, saith the Lord God." [3]  From God all creatures come, to him all creatures tend. He is the sovereign Good, the first source of all good ; in whom, then, if not in the Author of their being, can creatures seek their ultimate perfection ? It is this fundamental truth that we express whenever we speak of the " universe " : it is " towards one " that all created things, diverse though they are in their nature, varied in their activities, must ever tend, towards him from whom, in whom, and to whom are all things [4] that are made.

*Divine conservation and co-operation*   That same eternal activity that creates them, that preserves them in being, that co-operates with their every movement, also directs them providentially to their end. The material elements that act and react according to their nature, the heavenly bodies that move unswervingly on their appointed course, the tiny seed that swells in the soil and reaches out roots to absorb nourishment for its growth, the animal that with sure instinct finds the food that it needs, that mates with its similar to propagate its species, that tends and cares for its young—all these are obeying, each according to its respective nature, the law of him who made all things for himself. A creature

[1] *Cf.* Ps. iv 7.    [2] Apoc. iv 11.    [3] Apoc. i 8.    [4] *Cf.* Rom. xi 36.

may suffer loss, but it is for the perfection of a higher ; a part may seem to fail, but it is for the good of the whole. In the decree of God's Providence there is no chance. All is according to plan ; all is directed to good.

Men and angels too, free agents though they are, are none the *Providence* less subject to the all-wise Providence of God. That infinite Wisdom, which " reacheth from end to end mightily and ordereth all things sweetly," [1] respects the noble gifts that he has given to intelligent creatures, and the law of nature, which others fulfil unconsciously and of necessity, becomes in them the moral law, recognised by the mind and freely obeyed by the will. Man knows that he can do wrong, but he knows also that he ought to do right. He sees in his duty the obligation, not merely of acting in accordance with the proper aspirations of his nature, but of submission to the will of his Creator. He knows that he can, if he will, act as though created joys were the ultimate object of his existence, but he knows too that by inordinate indulgence in such pleasures he disobeys the law of him who is his supreme Good, his last End. He can choose between the creature and the Creator ; but, whatever his decision, he remains subject to God's law. If with full deliberation he rebels, then he rejects the Sovereign Good, he renounces his own perfection and his happiness which can be found only in the God whom he has spurned. He can rebel, but yet he cannot frustrate the plan of God's Providence ; for in that eternal decree it is ordained that Justice will punish all who refuse to submit to his merciful and beneficent law.

In God, therefore, consists man's final perfection. Earthly joys, however noble, however spiritual, cannot content the longings of his immortal soul for a good which is all-inclusive, limitless, and indefectible. God alone can satisfy man's infinite desires ; in him alone who is self-existent Truth, the measure of all truth, can his mind have complete repose ; in him alone, the Sovereign Good, the standard and cause of all good, can his will find peace and full delight.

And how will he attain his end ? What destiny awaits him beyond the darkness of the grave ? Were we left to rely for our answer solely upon human reasoning, if in order to learn the truth we had as evidence only man's nature as we know it and God's generosity as we can conjecture it, then we might have said that, when death had put an end to the time of probation, when man's body had crumbled in the dust, then the soul, spiritual and immortal, would live on to be delighted with the contemplation of still more perfect creatures, of beings in whom the beauty of their Maker would be more clearly resplendent and, by an indefinite progress through unending life, would continue more and more perfectly—yet never completely— to know and love God in the mirror of his creatures ; that the body, too, faithful companion of the soul on her earthly pilgrimage, essential

---

[1] Wisd. viii 1.

part of man's composite nature, might perhaps be raised by God from corruption to share this unending bliss. . . .

All such conjectures, reasonable though they are, fall far short of the truth. God has dealt more generously with his creatures than the mind of man could ever have conceived.

## §III: THE RAISING OF CREATURES TO GOD

*Beatific Vision, man's supernatural end*

WHILE we admire the almighty Power of God which gives being to everything that is, while in the universe, this pageant of beauty, this harmonious blending of every conceivable perfection, we adore his infinite Wisdom, still there is one divine attribute which outshines all others in the works of his hands ; it is his infinite Love, his insatiable delight in giving. And yet we have scarcely begun to tell the story of his benefits.

God, in creating, has communicated many and marvellous perfections to his creatures ; but the greatest of these is yet infinitely distant from him who is essential goodness. He has created beings who resemble him, for the artist cannot but reproduce something of himself in his work. He has communicated to them a likeness of himself, but he has not communicated himself. Man especially, it is true, is made in the image and likeness of God, for in him are intellect and will whereby he presents some reflection of the spiritual life of God. God lives by knowing and loving himself ; man too can know and love God. But what a difference ! Man's nature is such that by his natural powers he can never know God immediately and directly ; he can know him only in the mirror of his creatures, in the imperfect—necessarily imperfect because created and finite—image of the divine perfections which is the universe that he has made. Intimate though this knowledge might become in that state of natural beatitude at which our reason has conjectured, it must ever remain imperfect, immeasurably inferior to that knowledge whereby God sees himself face to face.

Our knowledge, which is nothing else than a spiritual representation within ourselves of the objects that surround us, must be conditioned by our nature. That nature is compounded of body and spirit, and hence our knowledge of the spiritual world, though true and objective, is necessarily imperfect and inadequate. At the very best our concept of God must be a limited idea, by which we represent singly and separately the infinite perfections which in God are one and undivided. Every finite concept, therefore, whether in men or in angels, must be of an infinitely lower order than God, and for that reason infinitely incapable of representing God as he is in himself. To know God directly and immediately, to contemplate in all its radiant beauty the Divine Essence, to see all loveliness in its first fount and origin—this is the life of God himself, this is the eternal life of Father, Son, and Holy Ghost, the life of the Blessed Trinity ;

and from that life the creature, because he is a creature, is naturally for ever excluded.

Yet it is this divine life that God decreed to communicate to intellectual creatures. The limitations of the creature set no limit to the Creator's delight in giving. The vision of God, which is the essence of the divine activity, is beyond the natural power of any finite being; yet it is to this "supernatural" end that God has destined us. Creatures are to be made "partakers of the divine nature," [1] sharers in his life; we are to be made "like to him; because we shall see him as he is " [2]—no longer groping after the light of God in the dim twilight of created beauty, no longer seeing him "through a glass in a dark manner," but "face to face," [3] bathed for ever in the light of eternal Truth.

This, then, is the ultimate perfection of man, in this will all his *Divine* faculties receive perfect satisfaction : " I shall be satisfied when thy *adoption* glory shall appear." [4]   God the Son, eternally begotten of the Father, image of the invisible God, will be the firstborn of many brethren, for creatures will be made conformable to his image.[5] He indeed is the Son of God by nature, true God of true God, while men will be but adopted sons, by God's free will given the right to a heritage which naturally could never be theirs, remaining for ever distinct from God and immeasurably distant from his infinite perfection ; but yet they are to be admitted within the sanctuary of the Trinity, within the divine Holy of holies, to partake of the divine vision. They are to be adopted by the Father as brethren of his Son in the love, the charity, the sanctity of the Holy Spirit. It is no longer a likeness of himself that he communicates to creatures ; it is his very Self.

But it were a poor generosity on the part of God to destine us to an end which we are quite incapable of attaining, did he not also raise our nature to a proportionate state of perfection. Our nature, while remaining essentially the same, must yet be transfigured, supernaturalised by gifts which will adapt it for so high and glorious a destiny. Nor is it enough that in the moment of attainment God should elevate our nature ; he willed that by our own acts we should merit our reward, that our works should have a real relation and proportion to our supernatural end. Already in this life we must be " sons of God." Let us see the loving Father at work.

To Adam, the first man, from whom the whole human race was *Elevation of* to be descended, God gave, in addition to his natural powers, all *our first* those supernatural and preternatural endowments which were to fit *parents : sanctifying* him for his noble destiny. To his soul was given " sanctifying *grace* grace," a real spiritual quality that raised his nature, transforming it after the likeness of God, giving to it a real participation in the nature of God, enabling him to perform supernatural acts meritorious of his supernatural reward, making him an adopted son of God. He was

[1] 2 Pet. i 4.       [2] 1 John iii 2.       [3] 1 Cor. xiii 12.
[4] Ps. xvi 15.              [5] Rom. viii 29.

thereby given a new life, not substituted for, but superimposed upon his natural life. His natural faculties were reinforced, etherealised, so to speak, by the infused virtues, by reason of which his acts took on a new and infinitely higher value, for they were supernatural ; they were, if we may say so, the recognised currency with which man might purchase his supernatural end.

An even more wonderful effect of this grace : the three divine Persons, Father, Son, and Holy Ghost, came to dwell within the soul of man, consecrating it as a temple with a special and sanctifying presence. It is of this mysterious presence that Christ says : " If any man love me . . . my Father will love him and we will come to him and make our abode with him." [1]  By grace God dwells in the soul as friend, guest, and lover ; already by grace is begun that intimate union between God and the creature which will be consummated in the glory of heaven.

Enlightened by faith to know his supernatural destiny, strengthened by hope to have confidence in God's aid to attain it, his will adhering by charity to God the sovereign Good, every power of his being elevated and ennobled by the infused moral virtues, man was now no longer merely a servant but a son of God, partaking already of the divine life, capable by his acts of meriting the fulness of his inheritance, when it should please God to call him to his final reward.

*Preternatural gifts*   But there is more.   The nobler faculties of man have been richly endowed ; but what of the body, what of his senses ?  Will not the demands of his lower self distract him from the thought of his high destiny ?   His soul is spiritual, but his immediate needs are material ; is there not a danger that in satisfying these he may forget those of the spirit ?   His very spiritual faculties are conditioned by sense ; may it not be that his senses take an inordinate part in his life ?  We are but too familiar with these difficulties, and St Paul in a well-known passage [2] has given a description of them which will be famous for all time.   But in the first father of the human race such difficulties, natural though they are to man, had no place.   It is natural to man, composed of matter and spirit, that his body should tend to dissolution ;  God gave him the privilege of bodily immortality.   It is natural to man that he should be subject to pain and sickness ;  Adam was by God's gift preternaturally immune from them.   It is natural to man that there should be conflict between the desires of the flesh and those of the spirit ; there was no such conflict in Adam, endowed with the gift of " integrity " whereby the surge of passion was quelled.   The whole of his nature was thus in perfect equilibrium ;  his sentient faculties in complete subservience to his mind and will, and these subjected by grace to God.

From the body of Adam God formed Eve the first woman, whom he similarly endowed, to be a worthy helpmeet to the father of mankind.   It was then that God instituted and blessed the sacred bond

[1] John xiv 23.         [2] Rom. vii 14-25.

of matrimony, whereby the human race should be propagated. From this pair should be descended a blessed progeny ; all men would receive as their birthright the same gratuitous endowments that adorned their first parents—a birthright due, not to the nature of man, but to the lavish generosity of the Creator who, not content with leaving man in his natural state, had willed to raise him to a destiny nothing short of divine. Their life on earth would be a happy one, the future unclouded by the shadow of death, their daily labour a joy and a delight, their leisure spent in sweet and intimate converse with God, until they should be rapt immortal to his eternal embrace.

## §IV: THE FALL OF CREATURES FROM GOD

IT might well have seemed that our first parents, in a state of perfection such as has been described, could not have failed to achieve their end, that God in his generosity had given all that was necessary for the fulfilment of his beneficent plan. And, indeed, on God's part nothing was lacking to assure the happy issue. But among the natural prerogatives of man there is one which, while it is his greatest dignity, was also the source of his downfall ; man has free will. The whole of his being, in that state of " original justice," was in complete subjection to his will—within himself there could be no rebellion ; but his will, adhering indeed to God by grace and charity, had yet lost nothing of its freedom and defectibility. The service that Adam was to render to his Maker was in his power to give or to withhold. Through the wiles of Satan and by the suggestion of his consort he withheld it.

The angels had been raised by God to a destiny identical with *Fall of the* that of mankind ; they too, after a period of probation, were to enjoy *angels* the vision of God. Called upon to recognise the supremacy of their Creator, many of them, led by Lucifer, rebelled. For them there could be no repentance ; such is the perfection of the angelic nature that their decision between good and evil, though free and unconstrained, is final and irrevocable. Cast out for ever from God's sight and condemned to a just and eternal punishment, the rebel angels would spend their existence in endeavouring to drag mankind with them in their fall. To others God would entrust the task of protecting men against their crafty machinations. The great drama was about to begin.

The head of the fallen angels approaches the head of the human *Temptation* race—not directly, but through the woman Eve. " Ye shall be as *and fall of* gods." Such is the bait with which he tempts her. And Eve first, *Adam and Eve* and then her consort, deceived by the glamour of an impossible independence, rebel against the supreme authority of their Creator— they sin. This was the first in that long series of revolts which has continued through the ages, whereby to God, his last End and supreme Good, man prefers the finite, created good which is himself, whereby the creature sets himself in the place of the Creator. In this consists the awful malice of sin, that the sinner, weighing up in his mind the comparative merits of the creature and of the Creator, decides in favour of himself. Sin, in the words of St Augustine,[1] is " the love of self to the contempt of God."

*Effects of sin in them*  With one act of disobedience, prompted by pride, our first parents wrecked that edifice of supernatural beauty and harmony which the loving hand of their Father had built. Charity departed from their souls, for how could they love God above all things when they loved themselves in his despite ? With charity were lost grace and the noble array of infused moral virtues ; lost, in fact, were all the supernatural gifts with which they had been endowed to reach their destiny ; they had ceased to be the sons of God. The Trinity withdrew its holy presence from that desecrated temple, from the souls in which they were dishonoured guests.

And now, with the rebellion of the spirit against God, there began at once in man the insubordination of flesh to spirit. The preternatural gifts given to our first parents in order that without difficulty and distraction they might devote the whole of their energies to the loving service of God—these gifts were now withdrawn, for they had ceased to serve their purpose. They began to feel the weaknesses inherent in human nature. Those inordinate desires that come to us unbidden, those tendencies that seem to carry us away before we can advert to their presence, those base cravings that draw us to evil and hardly suffer control, the importunate stings of concupiscence that give no peace till we assent to them—of all this they tasted the first bitter experience after their sin. Unruly passion, held hitherto in check by the gift of integrity, reared itself unrestrained ; the mind, hitherto clear and serene, became clouded with uncertainty and error ; the daily toil that had been man's pleasure now became a painful task ; the natural forces that make for the dissolution of the human body were now allowed full sway, and man's life became the path to the tomb towards which he wends his way, reminded daily of his mortality by the stimulus of pain and disease. All these are natural defects, but man had not been intended to experience them ; the purely gratuitous endowments which had obviated them had been lost through man's sin ; they are natural, and yet also the penalty of rebellion.

But lamentable and painful as were these natural infirmities, they were as nothing compared with the loss of supernatural grace. In this was the great tragedy, in this essentially consisted the state of sin. With the loss of grace man was in a state of enmity with God. Destined for an end far in excess of his natural powers, he remained deprived of all supernatural gifts, totally incapable of attaining the object of his existence. His nature remained in its essentials intact, but, compared to that former state, what a ruin ! Seek as he might

[1] *De civ. Dei*, xiv, 28.

to serve God in future with his natural powers, his acts could have
no proportion to the exalted destiny of the sons of God; repent as
he might with bitter tears to atone for his offence against God, no
act of his could make reparation for that insult to God's infinite
majesty. Man was now a purposeless thing, like a rudderless, dis-
masted ship at the mercy of wind and waves, bound for a port which
she has no conceivable hope of reaching.

The first sin of Adam, tragic in its consequences for him, is *Transmission*
tremendous in its effects upon us; for his sin is our sin too. All men *of original sin*
who are naturally born receive their nature from Adam, the fountain-
head of the human race; and together with that nature they inherit
his sin. We cannot inherit his wilfulness, we cannot inherit his
responsibility, but we inherit the state of sin which he induced by
his sinful act.

God had designed that the natural means which he had instituted for the propagation of the human race should fill the earth
with men who, from the first moment of their existence, would be
endowed with grace and integrity; they were to be born men, yet immortal sons of God. The supernatural and preternatural gifts which
we have described were to be attached to man's nature as a specific
human property, so that to be a man would involve—by God's
bounty—being also the adopted son of God. Of all these precious
gifts Adam, by his sin, despoiled his nature, and in that state of
privation he transmitted it to us. We have lost nothing of the
essentials of our nature; we have lost gratuitous privileges. But
the lack of grace means a state of sin, a state of enmity with God.
For man, destined to a supernatural end, constituted from the beginning in the state of " original justice," to be without that supernatural rectitude which should be his normal condition, is to be in
the state of " original sin."

If all men must die, it is because Adam, by his sin, forfeited for
himself and for us the gift of bodily immortality; if man is condemned
to a painful and laborious existence, if in his search after truth he is
hampered by error and discouraged by ignorance, if his will is in
conflict with inordinate desires, if, with St Paul,[1] he sees another
law in his members fighting against the law of his mind, if " concupiscence," child and father of sin,[2] is the lot of all men in their
daily lives—all this is due to that first sin which brought death and
sorrow to mankind. " Unhappy man that I am," cries St Paul,
" who shall deliver me from the body of this death ? "

The answer comes as a joyous echo : " The grace of God, by
Jesus Christ our Lord."

---

[1] Rom. vii 23-25.     [2] *Cf. ibid.* and Jas. i 14-15.

## §V: PLAN AND PREPARATION OF REDEMPTION

IF the limitations of the creature could set no bounds to the generosity of God, neither could the malice of the sinner baulk the designs of his mercy. Man had sinned, he had stripped himself of the precious garment of grace with which the loving hand of God had clad him ; he was an outcast on the face of the earth, shut out from the intimacy to which God had willed to admit him, the enemy of God who had loaded him with benefits. The glory of God's love has appeared in his lavish gifts ; we have seen his wisdom and his power in the works of his hands. Surely the moment had come in which he would manifest the perfection of his justice by casting man out for ever from his sight ?

*The Redeemer promised*  His justice, indeed, will appear, but infinite mercy will attend it. The condemnation of man is accompanied by the promise of salvation ; the sentence of death is mitigated with the promise of life. As the man and the woman stood trembling before God's offended majesty, they heard that there would come another man and another woman who should undo the work of the triumphant demon ; a woman and her seed should crush the serpent's head. Sin, far from thwarting God's beneficent design, will be the occasion of a still greater manifestation of his goodness. Out of the darkness of sin shines forth the bright figure of the Redeemer.

*Meaning and necessity of redemption*  The sin of Adam was disastrous, whether we consider man in himself, or in his relation to God. In man himself it meant the loss of all that made possible the attainment of the supernatural end to which he was destined. That loss, as far as man was concerned, was irreparable ; he could do nothing by his own act to merit its restitution, for the very quality which could make his acts meritorious was the gift of supernatural grace which he had lost. What was his condition in the sight of God ? He had offended God ; he had withheld from him the honour that was his due ; he had preferred the creature to the Creator. The insult, the offence was in a manner infinite, infinite as the majesty of God against whom it was committed. He had offered an insult for which he was powerless to make adequate satisfaction ; for if the gravity of an offence is to be measured by the dignity of the person offended, the value of the honour paid in compensation is proportionate to the worthiness of the offerer. Man could commit an " infinite " offence ; he could not make infinite atonement. Nothing could make condign satisfaction for sin save an infinite act of adoration, and that no creature could offer.

To repair this twofold ruin : to restore to man the gifts that he had lost, to make condign satisfaction to God for the offence committed against him ; this is the work of " Redemption."

But might not God have waived his right to satisfaction, and have condoned man's offence ? Might he not have accepted the poor satisfaction that man himself could contrive to offer by his tears and lamentations ? Might he not have reinstated man immediately in his supernatural dignity, treating him as if he had never sinned ? To our puny human minds there seems to be nothing in such suggestions incompatible with the perfections of God. But to no human mind could it ever have occurred to conceive the plan by which Redemption was actually to be accomplished ; it was such as only an infinite wisdom could devise. In this plan, infinite justice is satisfied, infinite mercy is displayed, God's power, his wisdom and his love find most perfect and marvellous expression. Let us glance at it now.

Divine justice demanded adequate satisfaction such as no finite *Plan of* being could make ; none but God can give infinite honour to God. *redemption* Then God himself, the second Person of the most Holy Trinity, will become man in order to give it. Man, he will offer prayer, adoration and sacrifice to God, and because he is also God his offering will be of infinite value. By his sacrifice he will appease divine justice, he will merit for man the grace that he has lost. He, the Son of God, will be the second Adam. Through the first came death, through the second will come life. All mankind born of Adam are born to sin by virtue of their solidarity with him ; all who are reborn in Christ, by reason of their mystical union with him, will be reborn to grace. From the Son of God made man, as from a fruitful vine into its branches, will flow into all men united with him the grace that makes them once more the sons of God and heirs of eternal life. Man had cast away his birthright as son of God ; God the Father will not spare his own Son that his adopted sons may be restored to their inheritance. God will become man in order that man may be restored to his share in the nature of God. Can we be surprised that the Church, celebrating this wonder of God's mercy and goodness, this mystery in which " mercy and truth have met each other ; justice and peace have kissed," [1] does not hesitate to cry : " O *felix culpa !* " " O happy sin that gave us so noble a Redeemer ! "

No sooner is the promise made than the salutary work of Redemption is begun. He, the Redeemer, will not come until the time appointed for his advent, but already the Sun of Justice has appeared above the horizon, already he is present in the expectation of men, and through faith in the Saviour to come they are sanctified by his grace. First to profit by the fruits of the Redemption were our parents, who by their sin had rendered it necessary. But to them now, as to all men henceforth, grace was given as a personal gift, and not as a legacy which they might transmit to their children. It is no longer by carnal generation from the first Adam, but by spiritual regeneration in Christ, that men will be made the sons of God.

The promise made to Adam and Eve, handed on by them to *Preparation* their children, is treasured through the ages, and with the dispersion *of redemption*

---

[1] Ps. lxxxiv 11.

of men over the face of the earth the Redeemer becomes " the expectation of nations." [1]   The fall of our first parents was followed by a gradual moral and physical degradation of the human race ; sin took its toll of the spiritual and bodily health of mankind, and the hope that had shone so brightly in the earliest times became neglected and obscured.   But nowhere, even among those nations in which error and vice especially prevailed, was that primitive revelation entirely lost.   In the chosen people, the race of whom the Redeemer himself was to be born, the hope of a coming Saviour remained ever green ; in them, in spite of their inconstancy and repeated delinquencies, God kept alive the faith in him who was to bring salvation to mankind.   Their heroes are types of the coming Redeemer ; their religious hymns are filled with inspired references to the Messias ; their religious rites, their sacrifices, are types to foreshadow his great sacrifice which should redeem the world.

Why was his coming delayed ?   God was awaiting the fulness of time, until men had learned by long and bitter experience how weak their nature is, until the pride that had given birth to Adam's sin should be humbled in the dust, so that men might cry out for a Saviour ; the world must be prepared to receive the Son of God made man.

As time goes on, the expectation becomes more and more clearly defined.   The Holy Ghost, speaking through inspired writers and prophets, announces that the Redeemer will be of the seed of Abraham, of Isaac and Jacob ; he will be the son of David.   With Isaias and Jeremias the prophecies become still more detailed regarding the origin and the life of the Redeemer to come.   Every woman of Israel had cherished the hope that she might be his mother. Isaias announces the providential decree that he will be born of a virgin :   " Behold a virgin shall conceive and bear a son, and his name shall be called Emmanuel (God with us)." [2]   " A child is born to us, a son is given to us, and the government is upon his shoulder ; and his name shall be called Wonderful, Counsellor, God the Mighty, the Father of the world to come, the Prince of Peace . . . he shall sit upon the throne of David and upon his kingdom, to establish it and strengthen it with judgement and with justice, from henceforth and for ever." [3]

*The Immaculate Mother of the Redeemer*   And now, when the fulness of time was come, the grace of the Redeemer, whose merits are ever present in the sight of God, that grace, which had sanctified the souls of all men of good will since the fall of Adam, was poured out in the greatest abundance upon her whom God had eternally chosen as the Mother of the Redeemer. The woman whose seed was to crush the serpent's head, the woman between whom and Satan there was to be complete enmity, the second Eve, who by her co-operation with her Son the second Adam was to repair the ruin brought about by our first parents—this was

[1] Gen. xlix 10.          [2] Isa. vii 14.          [3] Isa. ix 6-7.

Mary. She alone [1] of all the children of Adam was preserved immune, through the merits of her Son, from the stain of original sin. She, who with her Son was to overcome Satan, should not for one moment be subject to his dominion. Mary was to be the Mother of the Redeemer ; it was fitting that she should be most perfectly redeemed. She was to be the Mother of God ; it was right that she should ever have been a child of God. She was to be the Mother of the spotless Lamb ; it was just that she should be spotless, untouched with the slightest stain of original or of actual sin. The first Eve had been formed pure and holy from a pure and sinless Adam ; the second Adam should take his immaculate flesh from an ever-immaculate Mother.

The world was ready for his coming, the pure womb that was to *The* bear him was prepared. The great and awful event awaited by men *Annunciation* since the moment of that first promise may be worthily recorded only in the inspired word of God : " Behold " (says the Angel Gabriel to Mary), " thou shalt conceive in thy womb and shalt bring forth a son ; and thou shalt call his name Jesus. He shall be great, and shall be called the Son of the Most High. . . . The Holy Ghost shall come upon thee and the power of the Most High shall overshadow thee : and therefore also the Holy which shall be born of thee shall be called the Son of God." [2]

Centuries before, a malignant angel had come to a woman upon an errand of death, and the woman's disobedience to God's command which had ensued was the beginning of the sin of the world. The Archangel Gabriel came to Mary with the message of eternal life, and the ready obedience of the second Eve gave us him who is the fount of all grace. Mary, who had designed to know no man, had been troubled at the announcement of the angel that she should conceive and bear a son. Her fear was groundless ; the Holy Ghost was to be her Spouse, and Mary, still clad in the white veil of virginity, was yet to wear the crown of motherhood. " And Mary said : Behold the handmaid of the Lord ; be it done to me according to thy word." The obedient submission of Mary gave to the world the divine Redeemer. In that moment " the World was made flesh and dwelt amongst us."

## § VI : THE REDEEMER

BY creating, God communicates an image of himself. By raising creatures to the supernatural order he gives himself, his own infinite beauty and perfection, to be the object of their supernatural knowledge and love, that they may see and love him as he is ; he makes the creature a partaker in his own intimate life.

[1] Christ, since his body was miraculously formed in the womb of his Virgin Mother, is not a child of Adam in the sense in which we are, and was therefore not subject to the law of sin.

[2] Luke i 31-32, 35.

To create was an act of disinterested love ; to raise creatures to the condition of adopted sons was infinite liberality, beyond anything that man could have conceived, beyond any legitimate yearning of his nature. Made in God's image and likeness, man had been crowned with glory ; made a son of God, he had received a greater glory still. And yet God's love—it seems incredible—had a more wonderful gift in store. Not content with the intimate embrace of man's knowledge and love, he has deigned to become personally one with him, so that there is one divine Person who is both God and man. The Incarnation is the culmination of man's glory, the supreme act of God's love. " We speak the wisdom of God in a mystery," says St Paul,[1] " a wisdom which is hidden, which God ordained before the world unto our glory." More than this—we have the authority of God's own word—he could not give. " He that spared not even his own Son, but delivered him up for us all, how hath he not also with him given us all things ? "[2]

*The hypostatic union*

" The Word was made flesh." The second Person of the most Blessed Trinity, God the Son, became man. Has God, then, ceased to be God ? Impossible ; for the changeless cannot change. Eternally and immutably God, he began at a moment of time to be man also. Becoming man, he lost nothing of his Divinity. Nor yet did he become richer by assuming humanity. Just as by creation nothing was added to God's infinite perfection, so God incarnate is not more perfect by reason of his manhood. When God creates it is the creature that is perfected. When God assumed a complete and real human nature, a body formed by the power of the Holy Ghost in the most pure womb of the Virgin Mary, a soul created and infused into it by the same divine power, he conferred an unspeakable dignity upon that humanity, because it began to exist, not as a human person, but as the human nature of God the Son ; but God himself remains unchanged.

The Person of Jesus Christ, then, is one : the second Person of the Blessed Trinity. In him subsist two natures, really distinct : the Divinity, uncreated, eternal, almighty ; and a human nature, created, temporal, mortal, passible. Of Christ we may say with equal truth that he is God and that he is man, that he is eternal and that he died, that he is our Creator and that he redeemed us with his blood. He who is eternally begotten of the Father is the same Person who was born at Bethlehem of the Virgin Mary. The Son of Mary is God ; Mary is the Mother of God.

Jesus Christ is God, and we adore him. We adore the second Person of the Blessed Trinity, and from our worship we exclude nothing of what is personally united to him. We adore his humanity, not because it is human, nor yet because it is perfect, but because it is his ; we adore his sacred body and soul because they are the body and soul of the Word made flesh. We adore his Sacred Heart

[1] 1 Cor. ii 7.                [2] Rom. viii 32.

because it is the human heart of God incarnate, because with every beat it speaks of the infinite love of God for mankind. We adore Christ because he is God, and adoring we revere all that belongs to his Person.

If the Word is man without prejudice to his Divinity, the man Jesus Christ is also God without detriment to his true humanity. The two natures, ineffably united in the one divine Person, remain distinct and physically unaltered by each other. That sacred body, formed from the virgin flesh of his blessed Mother, is a true human body similar to ours. The tiny fingers that clutched at Mary's hand were alive with the sense of touch ; ears, eyes, and the rest functioned as our organs function. In him, as in us, shines the light of intelligence, and he acquired knowledge by the same means as we. He willed, even as we do, and his will is free. Human feelings, human affections and sentiments of joy and sorrow, human desires, all the natural yearnings of man were in him, for all these are good and pertain to the perfection of our nature.

His humanity, then, in all essential respects is the replica of our own. But words fail when we attempt to describe its perfection. *Christ full of grace and truth* " We saw his glory," says St John, " the glory as it were of the only-begotten of the Father, full of grace and truth." [1] Full of truth because that human intelligence is the mind of God made man. The man Jesus Christ is humanly conscious from the first moment of his human life that he is God, and from that first moment with his human mind he contemplates the Godhead face to face. Not for one instant, even while his soul was sorrowful unto death, even during the awful desolation of Calvary, was the glorious light of God's countenance withdrawn from his human understanding. During the whole of his life on earth he enjoyed the beatific Vision, and in that Vision all his pain and sorrow—and these were greater than man can tell—appeared to him no longer as an evil, but as God's justice to be appeased, his infinite love to be manifested, his glory to be consummated by the salvation of human souls. In all his agony his soul rejoiced.

He is full of truth because he is the Word of God, Truth itself, who is come to bring truth to mankind ; he is " the true light that enlighteneth every man that cometh into this world." [2] He speaks what he knows, he testifies what he has seen ; [3] his doctrine is the doctrine of the Father who has sent him. [4] He alone has seen the Father, for he is in his bosom ; he alone has revealed him to mankind. [5] He is full of truth because as man he is the Judge to whom all judgement has been committed by the Father ; [6] he reads the heart, he knows what is in man, [7] and will judge every man according to his works.

Jesus Christ, full of truth, is also full of grace. We, by grace,

[1] John i 14.  [2] John i 9.  [3] John iii 11.  [4] John viii 26-28.
[5] John i 18.  [6] John v 22.  [7] John ii 25.

are the adopted sons of God. He is not the adopted son, for he is the Son eternally begotten of the Father ; the grace that is abundantly in him is his birthright as God's own Son. It is from him that all men receive grace ; and the fount of grace is itself overflowing.[1] If St Augustine,[2] speaking of the holiness of Mary, refused to have the word " sin " even mentioned in her regard, how much more is a like silence imposed when we revere the sanctity of the God-man ! The human mind that contemplated the beauty of the Godhead could find no good in the creature save what was ordained to God's glory ; his human will, while supremely free, is yet infallibly and completely subject by grace and charity to the will of God, so that the two wills in him, the human and the divine, may, in a sense, be said to be one. The Holy One of God experienced, as we have said, all the affections, all the yearnings of man's nature, but he was never swayed by these ; he was subject to them only in so far as his perfect will allowed.

*His virtues*    He, indeed, is the Model of manhood, in whom every virtue after which we so laboriously strive is found in the highest degree of supernatural perfection. Let us pause in our summary description to admire the all-wise and loving Providence of the Father who, having destined men to be his adopted sons after the likeness of his own divine Son, in the charity and communication of the Holy Spirit, has willed to send that Son in human flesh, that in him, our brother— doubly our brother now, because a man like ourselves—we might see and copy in our lives what God desires that his human sons should be.

*His sufferings*    Dearer, perhaps, to our hearts, because they are our own familiar experience, are the human limitations of the Saviour ; for as the truth of his Divinity is no bar to the reality of his manhood, so the perfections of that manhood do not exclude human infirmities. Some of these, natural to man, yet also the penalty of sin, are so closely allied to sin itself that they could find no place in him who is full of grace and truth. Thus disordered desire, or " concupiscence " could not be in him, for his will held full sway over all his natural feelings, over every movement of his being ; in him flesh was completely subject to spirit. Christ is " full of truth " ; no error, no ignorance clouded the human mind of the Light of the world.

But to all the other penalties of the sin of our first parents he willed to be subject. He who came " to take away the sin of the world " assumed them to make use of them for our sake. They are the consequence of sin ; it is by their means that sin will be destroyed. Manual toil is consecrated, for he worked with his hands at the carpenter's bench. The poor are blessed, for poverty was his lot who possessed all the riches of the Godhead. He suffered hunger and thirst, and had no place to lay his head. He suffered mental anguish beyond what we are able to appreciate, because we cannot fully understand the perfection of his mind and will, a perfection which must have increased his every suffering. What must the

---

[1] John i 16.      [2] *De natura et gratia*, c. 4.

sight of sin have been to the Holy One of God! Nor was his suffering mitigated, as is ours so mercifully, by the limitations of his knowledge; the sorrows of the past—and still worse, those to come —were ever present to his mind. Of the bodily pain which he suffered during his Passion we need not speak—it is so often the subject of our meditation; suffice it to say that the exquisite sensibility of that soul must have added a refinement to every torture. Last of all, he willed to suffer death. He who was without sin, the immaculate Lamb of God, willed to suffer the penalty of sin for our sake; in the vivid words of St Paul: " Him that knew no sin, for us he hath made sin, that we might be made the justice of God in him." [1]

The deep significance of the human limitations of Jesus cannot be better described than in the inspired words of the Epistle to the Hebrews : " Because the children are partakers of flesh and blood, he also himself in like manner hath been partaker of the same, that through death he might destroy him who had the empire of death —that is to say, the devil. . . . Wherefore it behoved him in all things to be made like unto his brethren, that he might become a merciful and faithful high priest before God, that he might be a propitiation for the sins of the people. For in that wherein he himself hath suffered and been tempted, he is able to succour them also that are tempted." [2]

One other aspect of the humanity of Christ we must yet consider *His power* before we can understand the function and the work of the divine Redeemer; it is his miraculous power. The human nature of Christ is the instrument—joined with the Godhead in unity of Person—whereby God gives grace to man and works those miracles which are at once the sign of his divine mission and the necessary means for the accomplishment of the Redemption. God, it is clear, is the sole source of the divine life; he alone can be the first and principal cause of grace. He alone, too, can neutralise by an exercise of almighty power the forces of nature of which he is the Author; miracles can have only God for their principal cause. Yet this power resides in the human nature of the Word Incarnate; it is there, communicated from the Godhead, and used by Christ at will. It is the man Christ who forgives sins by the power of the Divinity which is personally one with him. That same divine power, working through his human nature, healed the sick, gave sight to the blind, commanded the winds and the sea so that they obeyed him. By the same power our divine Saviour, as he hung bleeding upon the Cross, brought at length to the utmost limit of human endurance, his body reduced to that state of feebleness in which the soul could no longer naturally animate it, was yet able, had he so willed, to retain his life. Freely he laid it down, as freely as after three days he took it up again.[3]

These acts of our Saviour are human, and yet they are divine. *Theandric actions*

[1] 2 Cor. v 21.    [2] Heb. ii 14-18.    [3] John x 18.

They are human because they proceed from a human nature ; they are divine by reason of the power that pervades them. Indeed, not only those actions of Christ which are the vehicles of God's miraculous power, but every act of the Word Incarnate is in a sense theandric, human and divine : human by reason of his human nature, divine by reason of the Person in whom that humanity subsists. They are the human actions of the second Person of the Blessed Trinity ; human and yet of infinite dignity, infinite as the dignity of God who performs them.

Christ, therefore, is truly and perfectly God, truly and perfectly man. He is man without losing anything of his Divinity, God without prejudice to his humanity. While the manhood assumed by God the Son is as perfect as manhood can be, yet Christ did not disdain to be subject to the weaknesses of our nature. Finally, side by side with the natural and supernatural perfections of his manhood, in which he presents himself as our Model, we discern others—his extraordinary knowledge and his miraculous power—which are bound up with the peculiar condition of one who is both God and man, and with his functions of Teacher and Redeemer of mankind.

*Mediator*     From this necessarily brief description of the adorable Person of our Redeemer, it will be seen that no name more aptly describes him than that of " Mediator." " One is the mediator of God and men, the man Christ Jesus." [1]  By reason of his twofold nature the God-man is the natural Mediator between God and man, uniting as he does the Divinity and humanity in his own Person. He is the corner-stone who has made both one. With this thought in mind let us study the work of the Redeemer.

## § VII : THE WORK OF THE REDEEMER

As the Person of the Word Incarnate may be best described by saying that he is the natural Mediator between God and man, so also it is under the general office of Mediator that his functions in man's regard may most conveniently be grouped.

I

*Christ as*     The primitive revelation of divine truth which had been made to
*Teacher*     man through our first parents had been obscured by sin and error and in great part lost. God had, indeed, brought man once more to some knowledge of himself by a gradual manifestation to the chosen people. But the fulness of revelation came with Christ. " God, who at sundry times and in divers manners spoke in times past to the fathers by the prophets, last of all in these days hath spoken to us by his Son." [2]  " He is the light that enlighteneth every man that cometh into this world." [3]  Christ is Prophet and Teacher.

[1] I Tim. ii 5.          [2] Heb. i 1-2.          [3] John i 9.

It is no mere human prophet who teaches us ; it is the Word himself, the personal Image of the Father, who comes to bring divine revelation. And what is the doctrine that he came to teach ? He came to reveal that Trinity of Persons whose divine life we are destined to share. " No man hath seen God at any time ; the only-begotten Son who is in the bosom of the Father, he hath declared him." [1] He revealed the Father, not only as his own Father by nature, but as the Father of us his adopted sons. He revealed his Holy Spirit, not only as the Spirit proceeding from Father and Son, but as the Spirit by whom, if we possess him, we are made the adopted sons of the Father,[2] made conformable to the likeness of the Son,[3] filled with the supernatural love of God, which by that Spirit is poured forth in our hearts ; [4] as the Spirit in whom we are reborn to the divine life of grace.[5]

The three divine Persons working—nay, dwelling—in the souls of men and raising them to a participation in their divine life—this is the compendium of Christianity. The whole teaching of which I am endeavouring in this essay to give some account is nothing else than the story of how man once received, then rejected, and finally, through the Incarnation of the Son of God, received once more those great and precious gifts by which he is made partaker of the divine nature.[6] To recognise this truth, that we by grace are made the adoptive sons of the Father, this is " eternal life." The Word of God, who alone has the words of eternal life,[7] has said it : " This is eternal life, to know thee the only true God, and Jesus Christ whom thou hast sent." [8]

But it is not merely a speculative doctrine that Christ teaches us. He is not only the Truth, he is also the Way and the Life. If he teaches us that we have been raised to the dignity of sons of God, it is in order that we may live worthily of so high a vocation. Raised by grace to this noble destiny, man must achieve his salvation by his own works. The love of God that Christ demands of us is a practical love, a love which is shown by our observance of his commandments. He came not to destroy the moral code which had been given under the Old Testament, but to fulfil it, that is, to perfect it, to render it more detailed and more exacting. The standard of perfection at which Christ asks his disciples to aim is nothing short of divine : " Be ye perfect as your heavenly Father is perfect." [9] And lest we should despair, lest we should think that such perfection could not be found in man, he shows us, by the example of his own life, what the life of a son of God should be. He is the model of every virtue, and he points to himself as the example which all Christians are to follow.

When we consider the authority with which he spoke, the un-

---

[1] John i 18.    [2] Rom. viii 15 ; Gal. iv 6.    [3] Rom. viii 29.
[4] Rom. v 5.    [5] John iii 5.    [6] 2 Pet. i 4.
[7] John vi 69.    [8] John xvii 3.    [9] Matt. v 48.

wavering certainty—so far removed from the hesitancy of human teachers—which characterised his utterance, the simple yet sublime language in which he solves those problems which had ever exercised the human mind—deep problems concerning the origin, the nature, and the destiny of man—when we see that his doctrine is signed and sealed with the divine approbation through the working of miracles, when, finally, we contemplate the grandeur and the harmony of that doctrine itself, then we can well understand how the Samaritans could say, "We ourselves have heard him and know that this is indeed the Saviour of the world," [1] and the exclamation of those who had witnessed his wonderful works : "A great Prophet is risen up amongst us, and God has visited his people." [2]

## 2

*Christ as Redeemer*      But it is in the work of Redemption strictly so called that the office of the Mediator is especially apparent. The doctrine that Christ taught, even the example of his life, might conceivably have been given to mankind by purely human agency. God might have used a man specially inspired, as were the prophets of old, as the bearer of his revelation. But the divine plan of Redemption, such as we have briefly described it above, could be fulfilled by no other than the God-man.

We have seen that Redemption involves two elements : that of satisfaction, whereby adequate atonement should be made for man's offence ; and that of merit, whereby grace, which man had lost by sin, should be restored to him. Now such satisfaction, such merit, is completely beyond the power of a mere man. The atonement offered by a creature could have no proportion with the magnitude of an offence against God's infinite majesty. And how could man merit grace, when the very grace which he lacked was necessary that his acts might be meritorious ? Only the God-man could offer infinite satisfaction ; only the God-man, who, as the only-begotten of the Father, is full of grace by right of his divine Sonship, could gain merit sufficient, and more than sufficient, for the whole human race.

Only the God-man could redeem us. But it is clear from what we have said of the adorable Person of our Redeemer that his merest act would have sufficed. Every human act of Christ during his life on earth was the act of a created, finite nature, and as such, could be, and was, an act of homage to God the Creator of all. But each of those acts was also, as we have seen, the act of God ; for the Person of Christ is one, the second Person of the most Holy Trinity. It is God who is born of the Virgin Mary, God who is subject to his human parents at Nazareth, who preaches divine truth in human words, is rejected, suffers, and dies upon the Cross. Each of these

[1] John iv 42.          [2] Luke vii 16.

acts, therefore, is human and yet, because it is the act of a divine Person, is of infinite, divine value. A sigh, a tear of the divine Child would have been sufficient to redeem the world. But the infinite Love of God—we have seen it again and again—is not content with what is merely sufficient. His infinite Wisdom had devised a nobler plan. His infinite Mercy had provided for man's every need.

There are many ways in which we can show our love for our fellow-men, but there is one proof, the greatest of all, which even the most sceptical cannot gainsay ; it is to die for another. Christ, who came to show by his human acts how great is the love of God for men, chose to give this supreme proof—to lay down his life for his friends. He gave his life " a redemption for many." [1]

Suffering and death, but for sin, would never have afflicted mankind. These evils, the punishment of sin, were to play a central part in the all-wise plan of Redemption. Our Redeemer would use the very penalty of sin as the means by which to destroy it. Pain and sorrow would be sublimated by the pain and sorrow of Christ, and would become the means of man's perfection for all who unite them with his.

The need of man was for an all-sufficient sacrifice. Man needs to express by this external act his homage to God, his will to atone for sin, his thanksgiving for divine benefits, his petition for divine assistance. But how could sinful man offer a sacrifice that would be acceptable in the sight of God ? What victim could he offer that would be worthy of God's infinite majesty ? Christ would offer an infinite sacrifice by his Passion and Death on the Cross.

For these reasons, then—and for others which Christian piety has discerned—Christ, who might have redeemed us with a prayer, willed to redeem us by his Passion and Death. Calvary is the throne of the King of Love, the school of Pain and Sorrow, the scene of the great Sacrifice. Freely laying down his life, our High Priest offered the all-sufficient sacrifice, and the Victim is none other than himself. Greater homage God himself could not demand, more worthy thanksgiving God could not receive, fuller atonement for sin, more prevailing petition could not be offered than the infinite Sacrifice of Calvary. By that Sacrifice our Redeemer blotted out the handwriting of the decree that was written against us,[2] and merited once more for us all the grace that Adam had lost. By his death on Calvary he accomplished the Redemption ; by his death he consummated the supreme act of his Eternal Priesthood.

### 3

Christ, our Teacher, our Priest and Redeemer, is also our King. *Christ as* He is King by reason of his eternal Divinity ; but he is King also as *King* man. Assuming a human nature, the Word Incarnate received from

---

[1] Matt. xx 28.                    [2] Col. ii 14.

the Godhead the royal dignity as the rightful attribute of his humanity. The angels are commanded to adore him, the winds and the sea obey him, every creature does him homage, because he is the Word Incarnate.

But he is King of men by a special title, for we are his subjects by right of conquest. Under the domination of Satan, reduced to the servitude of sin from that fatal moment in which Adam sinned, involving us all in his ruin, we have been freed by Christ from captivity, and we are now justly subject to his salutary rule. " As King," says St Augustine, " he fought for us, as Priest he offered himself for us. . . . He is our King, he is our Priest, in him let us rejoice." [1]

The Kingship of Christ, spiritual in character, is exercised " by truth, by justice, and above all, by charity." [2] By truth he subjects the minds of all men to himself, for all must believe by faith in his word. By justice he will punish in the world to come all those who have refused in this life to submit to his dominion. By charity, by love, by his grace, he draws all hearts to himself, bringing them " mightily and sweetly " [3] to union with God.

Upon Christ, therefore, Mediator, Prophet, Priest, and King, all things converge. To him all creatures, and in a special way all men, are subject, and he, uniting in his own Person humanity—which is itself a compendium of all created perfection—with the Divinity, as King and Priest offers all creatures to his Father. " All things," says St Paul, " are put under him . . . and when all things shall be subdued unto him, then the Son also himself shall be subject unto him that put all things under him, that God may be all in all." [4]

### 4

*Head of his Mystical Body*
There remains, finally, to be considered what is in many respects the most important of all the functions of Christ the Mediator. It consists in this, that he is the Head of his Mystical Body.

Christ has made full satisfaction for the sins of mankind ; he has merited abundant grace for us all. But that atonement, that merit, that grace, is not ours—it is his. The atonement of Christ can become our atonement, his merits our merits, his grace our grace, only in so far as we become in some manner one with him. This principle of solidarity we have seen verified in the case of original sin. We did not commit original sin ; yet because we receive our nature from Adam, in that sense being one with him, we inherit a sinful nature. It is in virtue of a similar solidarity with Christ, the second Adam, that mankind partakes of the fruits of the Redemption.

As Adam was in a sense the whole human race, being the fountain-head of our human nature, so Christ is mystically, but really, one

---

[1] Comment. on Ps. cxlix.
[2] Pope Leo XIII, Encycl. *Annum Sacrum.*
[3] Wisd. viii 1.      [4] 1 Cor. xv 28.

with all who partake of his grace. " As in Adam all die, so also in Christ all shall be made alive." [1] " As by the offence of one man, unto all men to condemnation, so also by the justice of one, unto all men to justification of life." [2]

Christ having died for our sins, rose again for our justification.[3] Death has no longer any power over him ; [4] he is the living, glorious Christ. It is the living, glorious Christ of whose " fulness we have all received " ; [5] he is the Head, from whom the divine life of grace flows into all the members of his mystical body.

But of that mystical body we must treat apart in a special section.

## § VIII : THE MYSTICAL BODY OF CHRIST

### I

It is not uncommon to give the name of " body " to a number of persons who are banded together under an authority for a particular purpose ; and if, when we speak of Christians as a " body," we had in mind nothing more than the ordinary meaning of the term— namely, that of a properly organised society—then it would be scarcely necessary to insist especially upon the propriety of such an expression, since it may be applied with equal justice to any group, under whatever authority and for whatever purpose it may be formed. *Meaning of the expression*

But when Christians are called " the body of Christ," the term is used in a special sense, to indicate a unity far more intimate, far more real than that which it commonly designates. The bond that unites the members of any human society can never be other than external. Each member lives his own life, and the only sense in which he can be said to be one with his fellow-members is that, in common with them, he desires the same end and is subject to the same authority. The bond which unites the members of the mystical body of Christ is an internal, a vital bond ; the members of Christ are one with Christ—and with each other—in the sense that each lives the same supernatural life of grace which he receives from the Head of the body, the living Christ. As in the body of man it is from the head, from the nerve-centres, that his vital activity is set in motion, so in the mystical body of Christ it is from the Head that every member receives that grace by which he lives the divine life.

This mystical union of the redeemed, of which St Paul so often speaks under the symbol of a body, is taught by Christ himself under a slightly different figure. He is the vine and we are the branches : " he that abideth in me and I in him, the same beareth much fruit ; for without me you can do nothing." [6] The essential meaning is the same ; the member that is cut off from the rest of the body is dead, inactive ; the branch that is cut off from the stem of the

---

[1] 1 Cor. xv 22.  [2] Rom. v 18.  [3] Rom. iv 25.
[4] Rom. vi 9.  [5] John i 16.  [6] John xv 5.

vine can bear no fruit because it can no longer receive the sap that gives it life. It is in this sense that St Paul speaks of the faithful as being " grafted in Christ " as branches in an olive-tree.[1]

The necessity of a real union with Christ, if we are to partake of his grace, becomes apparent also if we consider those passages of the teaching of Christ and his Apostles in which our reception of grace is described as " regeneration," as a new birth. It is by reason of our birth " in Adam " that we inherit original sin ; it is by re-birth, regeneration in Christ, that we are to receive grace. And just as natural descent from Adam, or, if we may say so, " incorporation into Adam," is the indispensable condition of our receiving human nature with its dread heritage of sin, so incorporation into Christ is the necessary means whereby we may be re-born and made partakers of the divine nature.

2

*Life of the mystical body*

It will be convenient here, before we proceed to study further the nature of Christ's mystical body, to examine more closely the life which animates it. Briefly, the life which we receive in virtue of our incorporation into Christ is none other than a participation in the life of God, which, in its inceptive state during our earthly pilgrimage, is sanctifying grace ; in its perfect and consummated state, is the glory of the Beatific Vision.

*Sanctifying grace and virtues*

We have had occasion already, in describing the original state of our first parents, to explain that sanctifying (or habitual) grace is a spiritual quality ennobling the soul, elevating man's nature to a new order of being, making him the adoptive son of God and heir to eternal life. It has been said also that this grace is accompanied by other supernatural habits—the infused virtues—which perfect and elevate the natural faculties of man, enabling him to perform super-natural acts of virtue, proportionate to the reward which he is to merit. By the virtue of faith he is enabled to give a supernatural assent to the truths of God's revelation, by hope to place full con-fidence in the divine assistance, and by charity to love God as his sovereign good, to whom, as his supreme end, his whole life is to be directed. In addition to these " theological " virtues, the soul is endowed with infused moral virtues and other gifts perfecting it in the supernatural order.

Here I should like to insist upon two very important points. The first is that these gifts, although they perfect and bring about a real change in man's nature and faculties, do not destroy or replace them. It is an axiom, which should never be lost sight of, that " grace does not destroy nature, but perfects it." Man must co-operate by his own acts in the work of his salvation. Raised by these gifts to the supernatural order, he remains in all the essentials

[1] Rom. xi 23.

of his nature unchanged.  He lives a supernatural, a divine life ; but he lives that life with his natural powers elevated by grace and the supernatural virtues.  The act of faith, the act of love is supernatural, and meritorious of a supernatural reward ; but that act of faith, that act of love is impossible without the act of intellect or of will which is, so to speak, its substratum.  It would be a pernicious error to suppose that God's supernatural operation in the soul supersedes man's natural activities.  Those natural powers, although of themselves they have no proportion with man's supernatural end, are nevertheless in themselves good, and, in spite of original sin, intrinsically unimpaired, and their exercise is necessary for salvation even as, on the other hand, is the assistance of God's grace.

The second point to which I would draw special attention is that, *Actual grace* since man's end is a supernatural one, the whole work of man's salvation must begin and end with the grace of God.  If he had been left in his purely natural state, it is clear that, given his natural faculties, given God's providential co-operation—without which no creature can exist or act—man would have been able by the use of those powers, without any further special aid from God, to achieve his salvation.  But since his end is one which surpasses his natural powers, therefore his motion towards that end must have its first impulse from the supernatural grace of God.  Hence the first thought, the first aspiration of the will towards God in the supernatural order, must be the effect of grace.

In addition, therefore, to the permanent gifts already described, man needs to receive from God a supernatural illumination of the mind, a supernatural inspiration of the will, in order that he may freely turn to God, the source of his sanctification.  This transient enlightenment and inspiration is called actual grace.  But here, too, is verified the same principle of co-operation.  Invited by God to become his adoptive son, man can refuse to answer the call ; urged to repentance, he can oppose to grace the resistance of his will.

Man's salvation, then, is in his own hands, and yet it is completely *Predestina-* in the hands of God.  Eternally God has prepared the gifts of grace *tion* that will call all men to himself, that will assist them in times of stress and temptation ; for all he has prepared the grace and the virtues by which they may merit their supernatural reward.  Some will answer the call, others will reject it.  Those who have answered, by God's grace, truly merit their reward ; but they owe it to God, who has called them that they might hear.  Not only the call, but also man's answer to the call, is God's gift ; man has nothing that he has not received from God's bounty ; his very merits are the gift of God.  And what of those who reject the call ?  Their failure is their own, in that, when they might, had they so willed, have corresponded with grace, they refused to do their part.  In this free consent of the just to God's grace, in this wilful rejection of God's call on the part of the impious, lies the mystery of Predestination.  While leaving to its proper place a full treatment of this subject, let me say only this : man's malice is but too apparent ; of God's abundant mercy we have had ample proof. The mystery, therefore, may bewilder, but it cannot appal us.

*Sin*

The life of grace—in this not unlike the natural life of man— becomes intensified by the activity of him who lives it. By good works done in the state of grace the members of the mystical body of Christ increase that grace within themselves, becoming more and more closely united with God by charity, partaking more and more fully of the divine life. But if this be the effect of good works, what will be the effect of mortal sin ? By that dread act the son of God rebels against his Father ; he sets his heart upon a creature in the place of God. By sin he loses the virtue of charity, and with charity are lost grace and the other supernatural virtues which depend upon charity for their being. There remain only—unless the unhappy sinner has rejected his belief in God's word or his trust in God's mercy—the supernatural habits of faith and hope, two slender strands which still hold him to the body of Christ, of which, however, now he is but a withered member. Although still able by his natural powers to do some good works, yet he cannot by these merit eternal life, for he has lost sanctifying grace, which gave his works their supernatural value.

*Forgiveness of sin*

This being the effect of mortal sin, it is clear that the forgiveness of sins, or justification, involves a real change in the soul. When God forgives sin he does more than merely overlook man's past offences ; he gives him life once more. Moving him by actual grace to repentance of his sin, he enriches his soul again with sanctifying grace and the virtues, reinstating him in his dignity as the son of God, generously restoring to him every gift that he had lost.

*Soul of the mystical body*

The life of the body of Christ is sanctifying grace together with the supernatural gifts which accompany it ; the head of the body is Christ, from whom that life is communicated to all its members. But a living body has a soul, and the soul of the mystical body is none other than the Holy Ghost. It is through the Holy Spirit that the charity of God is poured out in our hearts ; it is because we possess the Spirit of his Son that we are able to call God our Father ; it is through the work of the Holy Spirit dwelling in us that we are made in the likeness of the Son. Dwelling in the souls of each of the just, the Holy Ghost pervades with his life-giving presence the whole of the mystical body. He is the Spirit of life,[1] and the Church proclaims her belief in this truth daily as she recites the Creed : " I believe . . . in the Holy Ghost, the Lord and giver of life."

---

[1] Rom. viii 2.

3

St Paul, in speaking of the mystical body of Christ, which is the *Merit* Church, uses a very significant expression. He says that it is " the fulness " of Christ.[1] The mystical Christ, then, is the complement, the prolongation of the physical Christ, of the Word Incarnate. To the physical Christ nothing can be added, but the mystical Christ is in a state of growth, of gradual development. It is to grow until it has reached " the measure of the age of the fulness of Christ." [2] And, just as the physical body grows by its own life and activity, so the mystical body of Christ will develop through the works of its members performed under the vital influence of Christ the Head.

The merits, the satisfaction of Christ are superabundant, and to them nothing is wanting. And yet something is lacking to the accomplishment of the Redemption. There is lacking the appropriation by each member of the human race of the merits which Christ has gained for all. Incorporated into Christ, living his life, as he lives the life of the Father, we make those merits our own. They are his merits and they are ours—ours because we are one with him from whom we receive our supernatural life. Our works are meritorious and have satisfactory value, but that merit, that satisfaction adds nothing to the merits and atonement of Christ; for the life of the member is not distinct from the life of the head. In this sense, then, we " fill up those things that are wanting of the sufferings of Christ," [3] that by becoming members of his body we make his life our own, and by our good works multiply our merits and intensify in ourselves the life of grace.

But it is not only ourselves that we perfect by our good works. *The* Precisely because we are not isolated units but members of a body, *communion* our actions have their repercussion upon the other members of that *of saints* body. Each member of the body of Christ takes his part in circulating the divine life among the other members. We are able to help one another by our prayers and merits. In this manner we can assist one another on earth; the saints in heaven—and particularly the blessed Mother of God—can assist us; and both the saints and we are able to help the souls in purgatory. Not only are we members of Christ, but, in the words of St Paul, we are " members one of another." [4] This inter-communication of prayers and merits is known as " the communion of.saints," and it is upon this doctrine that rests the Catholic practice of praying to the angels and saints, and of interceding for the souls of the faithful dead.

After these general considerations concerning the mystical body of Christ it remains now to study the Church more particularly in her various stages.

[1] Eph. i 22-23.   [2] Eph. iv 13.
[3] Col. i 24.   [4] Rom. xii 5.

## §IX: THE CHURCH ON EARTH

*Visibility of the Church*

SINCE the Church on earth is the " fulness of Christ," the prolongation on earth of the Word Incarnate, we should expect to find verified in her that combination of the human and the divine, the visible and the invisible, which is the proper note of the Incarnation. It is peculiar to the mixed nature of man that he perceives the things of the intellect through the medium of the senses, the things of the spirit through things material, the invisible things of God through the things that are made. Hence God in his loving wisdom sent his Son in human flesh, that through him we might be brought to the knowledge and love of the invisible God. This incarnational or sacramental dispensation he has willed to continue to the end of time, and it is in the Church of Christ that it is embodied.

As it is of the essence of man to be body and soul, as in Christ the visible human nature and the invisible Divinity were personally and indissolubly united, so in the Church of Christ there is the human and the divine, the visible and the invisible. It is of the essence of the Church that her members live by the invisible, divine life of grace. It is equally essential to her that her members are visibly united by external bonds, subject to the same visible authority. The same conclusion—that the Church is essentially visible and invisible—follows from the general considerations that we have made concerning the mystical body of Christ. We are not isolated in the work of our salvation ; our redemption is social and organic in character. If we human beings are united with Christ and with each other in receiving the fruits of the redemption, then we form a visible society ; for it is natural to men to be grouped together by visible means, to be governed by a visible authority. God deals with men according to their nature ; and a society among men is naturally visible and external.

*Hierarchical constitution*

What we might have been led to expect is actually the case. Christ willed that his mystical body on earth should be a visible society, governed by a visible head, its members united by visible links of communion. He, the invisible Head, would be represented on earth by a visible head, Peter—and his successors—whom he himself appointed. Subject to the head, but divinely appointed too, and endowed with real authority over the members of his body, are the Apostles—and their successors, the hierarchy of bishops, pastors of the flock of Christ. As he had been sent by the Father, so he sent these to continue the work of salvation—nay, to continue on earth his very self, for to hear them is to hear him, to despise them is to despise him. Hence the inevitable—and vital—consequence : to be a member of that living organism which we have described, to belong to the mystical body of Christ, is nothing else than to be a member of the visible Church on earth which Christ has founded. As it is impossible for the branch to live which is not united to the stem, so outside the body of Christ, outside the Church which he has founded, there can be no salvation.[1]

That the Church of Christ is One none can doubt who has under- *One, holy,* stood the organic nature of the body of Christ. It is as essential to *Catholic,* the Church to be one as it is essential to her to be the body of Christ. *apostolic* But since she is visible, that unity is not only a unity of life—which is invisible—but a visible unity consisting in subjection to the same visible authority, in a common faith in the teaching of that visible Church, in a common worship, manifested in the use of the same external rites instituted by Christ.

The Church, because she is the body of Christ, is holy ; holy because she lives by the divine life which she receives from her Head ; holy because union with Christ and with God is the essence of her being ; holy because apart from her there is no holiness.

Because all who are members of Christ's body are the children of God, because all are one in Christ, so that " there is neither Jew nor Greek, there is neither bond nor free," [2] therefore the Church is Catholic or Universal, with the mission to teach all nations, to preach the Gospel to every creature.

" Built upon the foundation of the Apostles," [3] fulfilling the mission entrusted to the Apostles, her members recognising as their head the Pope, the successor of St Peter, Prince of the Apostles, the Church is Apostolic.

The Church which, by reason of the twofold element in her— the human and the divine, the visible and the invisible—continues the person of the God-man, continues also the work of the Redeemer. The Church fulfils the functions of Christ as Teacher, Priest, Head, and King.

I

The revelation brought to man by Jesus Christ is definitive. *Teaching* " Last of all he hath spoken to us by his Son." [4] To the truths *Authority of* taught by Christ nothing new is to be added. It is the office of the *the Church* Church, therefore, in fulfilling Christ's function as teacher, not to make new revelations, but to guard from error the deposit of faith, and authentically, authoritatively to proclaim and interpret the Gospel of Jesus Christ. " Going therefore, teach ye all nations . . . teaching them to observe all things whatsoever I have commanded you ;

---

[1] To some that Church has not been made known, to others she has been made known, but inculpably they have not recognised her for what she is. In their case we may be sure that God will take account of their good faith, of their sincere desire to please God, and will make it so that they receive grace from the life-giving Head. He will take the will for the deed, and those who are in inculpable error will be united " by desire," though not in fact, to the visible Church of Christ.

[2] Gal. iii 26-28.    [3] Eph. ii 20.    [4] Heb. i 2.

and behold I am with you all days, even to the consummation of the world." [1]

The teaching authority of a visible society resides, not in its individual members, but in its visible head. The subject of that authority, therefore, is first the visible head of the Church, the Pope, and secondly the hierarchy of bishops under that head and considered as forming one with him. The teaching of the Church is to be accepted by her members, not as a matter for discussion, but as the word of God himself ; for through that living voice it is Christ himself who speaks. To the insistent questionings of man : Whence do I come ; what is my nature ; whither do I go ? the Church returns unhesitating and infallible answer. Of the law of God, concerning which man is so often in doubt, the Church is the authentic interpreter, the unequivocal teacher. It is as necessary that she should be infallible in her teaching as it is impossible that Christ himself, the Word of God, should err ; for the Church is none other than Christ the Prophet, living and teaching in his mystical body.

## 2

*Priesthood in the Church*    The sacrifice of Calvary, by which Christ our Priest consummated the work of the Redemption, is all-sufficient, and no further sacrifice can be needed. Is the religion of Christ then—alone of all religions—to have no external rite, whereby its adherents may daily express to God their worship and their thanksgiving ? Are the members of Christ to be content with the mere memory of a sacrifice that was offered long ago ? The loving Wisdom of God has provided also for this need. No other sacrifice can be pleasing in God's sight when our High Priest has offered himself, the immaculate Victim. Then that same Sacrifice will be continued to the end of time. The Church, the mystical body of Christ, continues the function of his eternal Priesthood.

The night before he suffered, our Redeemer, as he sat at table with his Apostles, took bread and broke it, saying : " This is my Body " ; and then, taking wine, he said : " This is my Blood. . . . Do this in commemoration of me." By virtue of the words of Christ, the bread, though to all appearances still bread, was not bread but his Sacred Body ; the wine, though to the senses it appeared to be wine, was his most Precious Blood. In this manner Christ instituted the Sacrifice of the New Law, the Eucharistic Sacrifice, in which the true Body and Blood of Christ, under the appearances of bread and wine, are offered to God for the remission of sins. It is more than a mere commemoration of the sacrifice of Calvary ; it is that sacrifice itself. The Victim is none other than Christ, really, though sacramentally, present. The Priest is Christ, though he

[1] Matt. xxviii 19-20.

offers now in his mystical body, through the ministry of his priests, who from him have the power to work the eucharistic miracle. The Sacrifice of the Mass differs from that of Calvary solely in the manner of offering.

Daily, therefore, ascend to God the infinite honour and thanksgiving that are due to him ; daily to each of the members of the mystical body, who with Christ and in Christ offer the Eucharistic Sacrifice, are applied the fruits of the Redemption, the inexhaustible merits and atonement of Christ our Saviour. As the sacrifice of Calvary was the supreme act of the life of Christ on earth, so the Mass is the supreme act of worship in the Church. In the Eucharist, where our Redeemer is really present under the sacramental veils, the whole life of Christians must ever be centred.

In the sacrifice of Calvary is the whole efficacy of the Redemption. Hence it is around the Eucharistic Sacrifice that we must group all those external rites which Christ has instituted as the means of our sanctification.

## 3

Fulfilling on earth the function of Christ the Teacher and of *The sacra-* Christ the Priest, the Church fulfils also his function of life-giving *ments* Head by the administration of the Sacraments. God might, had he so willed, have distributed invisibly the grace which Christ had merited for mankind ; he might have decreed to bestow the fruits of the Redemption directly and immediately in answer to man's prayer. But it was in keeping with the nature of man, with the incarnational dispensation of which we have spoken, that the invisible grace of God in the soul should be signified—and produced—by visible, external rites. These external rites, seven in number, instituted by Christ to signify and to produce grace, are the Sacraments. God the Son, as we have seen, used his humanity, personally united with him, as the instrument of grace. The Sacraments are the instruments which Christ himself, through human ministry, uses to communicate the divine life to the members of his mystical body.

Most noble among them all is the Sacrament of the Eucharist, which contains Christ himself, the author of grace. Really present as the Victim of the Eucharistic Sacrifice, he invites all men to partake of the Victim. To eat the Body of Christ, to drink his Blood under the sacramental species—this is the principal means of our incorporation into Christ. " He that eateth me, the same also shall live by me." [1] We are solemnly warned that unless we partake of this Sacrament, we shall not have life in us. [2] As all grace flows from Christ the Head, as it is by the sacrifice of Calvary that we are redeemed, so does the efficacy of all the Sacraments depend

[1] John vi 58.          [2] John vi 54.

upon their essential relation to the Eucharist, in which is Christ the source of all sanctification. " From this sacrament as from a fountain is derived the goodness and the perfection of all the other sacraments." [1]

But before we can eat of the food of life we must be born, before we can be nourished with the food of the strong we must be strengthened. Washed in the waters of *Baptism* we are cleansed from original sin and, dying to the old Adam, are re-born to the new, incorporated already into the mystical body of Christ by the rite of regeneration, which destines us to eat of the living bread. Anointed with the oil of *Confirmation* we are strengthened in faith, that we may be valiant witnesses to the truth of Christ's teaching, and be prepared to suffer and, if necessary, even to die in its defence. But such is human weakness that even though we have been nourished with the heavenly food of the *Eucharist*, we may yet fall away and offend God grievously. For this calamity Christ has provided a remedy in the Sacrament of *Penance*. He has given to his priests the power to forgive sin. Humble and contrite confession, with the will on our part to make satisfaction, together with the sacramental absolution of the priest—these are the elements of the sacrament by which Christ restores the life that we have lost. The contract of *Matrimony*, blessed already by God in the very beginning, is now raised by Christ to the dignity of a sacrament, giving grace to those who are to be parents of more members of Christ's body. So holy is this union that it is compared by St Paul to the union between Christ and his Church. When death is imminent, and our powers are weakened by disease, the grace of God is at hand in the Sacrament of *Extreme Unction*, to destroy the remnants of sin that are still in us, to strengthen us against the final efforts of Satan, and to prepare us for our final journey to God. More evidently connected with the Eucharist and with the Priesthood of Christ is the Sacrament of *Holy Order*, by which Christ has provided for the continuation in some chosen men of the power of his Priesthood. At their word the bread and the wine become the Body and Blood of Christ ; by their power the bonds of sin are loosed or retained in the members of his mystical body. To the bishops the priesthood is given in its fulness, that, subject to the successor of St Peter, they may rule the flock of Christ and, by communicating to others the powers of the priesthood, provide unfailing succession of ministers in the Church of God.

These are the means by which Christ, the invisible Head, communicates his life to his visible members. Man is sanctified by the means most adapted to his nature. A material thing, a visible rite, is used by Christ to produce in man a spiritual, invisible effect, and the visible Church lives by the invisible life of God.

[1] Cat. Council of Trent, Part II, ch. iv, n. 48.

### 4

The Church, then, is the Kingdom of Christ on earth. Here *The kingdom* Christ reigns visibly as King over the minds of men ; to subject *of Christ on earth* one's mind to the Church by faith is to acknowledge the reign of Christ, King of Truth. Here, too, the King of Love rules the hearts of men by the grace which, by visible means and through his human ministers, he communicates to all the members of his body. The Pope, the head of the Church, exercising his boundless spiritual jurisdiction over all the faithful, is the earthly representative of Christ the King.

To the King of Truth and of Love many have not submitted, perhaps will never submit. But over these also Christ must reign, for no man can withdraw himself from his universal dominion. Those who resist the attractions of his grace will not escape the punishment of his justice, when the day comes in which he will offer all things to his Father.

It is time now to consider the Kingdom of Christ in its consummation.

### §X: CONSUMMATION

RESTORED by the grace of Christ to the condition of sons of God, we *Death* remain none the less subject to those ills which are the penalty of original sin. The sting of concupiscence reminds us that, sons of God though we be, we are still the children of Adam. Pain and suffering are our daily lot in this life, though we are destined to a joy of which no man can tell. And before that joy can be ours all must suffer the penalty of death.

But while our Redeemer has not freed us from these evils, yet he has transformed them. The rebellion of the senses has no terrors for the Christian who is strong in the grace of Christ ; for in overcoming temptation by the help of God, which is never lacking, he wins a more glorious crown. Suffering and death, since Christ has suffered and died, have taken on a new meaning. Uniting his suffering and his death with the Passion and Death of Christ, the Christian appropriates the atonement of the Saviour and becomes more and more formed to his likeness ; like St Paul he glories in his tribulations for Christ's body, which is the Church.

At length, then, the body, worn out with age or disease, is unable *Particular* any longer to co-operate with the soul in its vital functions ; and the *judgement* immortal soul departs from it, leaving it to crumble in the dust. The time of trial, the time during which, by struggling with temptation and corresponding with God's grace, we may store up merit of eternal life, finishes with death. At the moment of dissolution man has already made his final and irrevocable decision ; after death there is no repentance. He has chosen as his sovereign good either God or the creature. If the former, then he is in the state of grace, and he has merited his eternal reward. If the latter, then he is in the state of sin, supernaturally dead, and he can have no part in the inheritance of the sons of God. In that moment the disembodied soul is judged ; its eternal doom is pronounced.

*Hell*   Upon the unhappy fate of the lost soul there is little need to dwell. The heart falters at the thought of the immortal soul, made for God and unable to find contentment save in him, doomed to live for all eternity and to yearn for God with a gnawing hunger that can never be appeased. Then at length the emptiness of creatures becomes apparent, when the soul, cut off from God for ever, turns for solace to them and to itself, only to be cast back, still unsatisfied, upon the God whose countenance is eternally withdrawn. In the creatures where man had expected to find satisfaction he will find only his torment, and especially the torment of an ever-consuming, yet never-destroying fire. Hitherto we have contemplated the infinite love and mercy of God. Of his justice, let it suffice to say that it is infinite too ; and we adore it in that dread sentence : " Depart from me, you cursed, into everlasting fire." [1]

*Purgatory*   We turn willingly to consider the lot of those who die in peace with God. Among these will be some who in God's sight are entirely guiltless, or, if they offended him, have completely atoned. There is nothing to delay their eternal reward. Others there will be who, by reason of venial sins, or of atonement due to mortal sins whose guilt has been forgiven, have yet to make full satisfaction to God's justice. These souls must undergo after death a period of suffering in purgatory, until the last remnants of sin have been removed which keep them from their Father's loving embrace.

*Heaven*   Of the reward of the blessed one would be happy to write. But if St Paul, who was rapt to the third heaven, tells us that " eye hath not seen nor ear heard what God hath prepared for them that love him," [2] then it were folly for the writer to attempt to describe it. We must be content with what little God has revealed. In heaven the life of grace blossoms into the life of glory. Each soul, in proportion to its merits, receives a new supernatural gift—the light of glory—adapting and strengthening it for the vision of God. And then at last they look upon God's face. It is no longer a feeble image of God that the human mind conceives ; it is God who immediately and directly shows himself to the soul. " We shall see him as he is." Faith has given way to vision, darkness to the brilliance of the midday sun ; and the mind is not dazzled, but illuminated, by the brightness. The life of God in the Trinity of Persons is no longer a mystery, for in that life the blessed have, and now fully enjoy, their share. The sons of God have entered into their inheritance.

The human mind, in its search after truth, has now reached its goal, for it sees all truth in Truth itself. Man's will has ceased to

[1] Matt. xxv 41.    [2] I Cor. ii 9 ; *cf.* Isa. lxiv 4.

desire the good, for he is in complete and eternal possession of the Supreme Good, apart from whom nothing can be desired. For him now, as for God eternally, to will is not to desire, but to love, and in that love to find his eternal delight. Faith and hope are no more ; there remains only charity, the greatest of all. As God infinitely surpasses the creature, so does the joy of heaven infinitely surpass the most exquisite joy of earth. The happiness of the blessed is none other than the happiness of God ; for, in what else is God happy but in the eternal contemplation of his infinite Self ?

This visible world will have an end. The moment appointed by *Resurrection* God will come in which the earth and the heavens will be destroyed, *of the body* and all men who are then living will pass through the gates of death to immortality. The heavens and the earth will be renewed, and then the Saviour will make all men sharers in his triumph over death. The bodies of all who have died, from Adam to the last child who is born, will rise again from the dust to partake of the eternal lot of the soul. The body that has been the soul's partner in sin will rise again to share in its everlasting torment. The body that has worked with the soul for sanctification will rise to share in its glory. The glorious body, perfectly subject to the soul in all its actions, will now no longer suffer pain ; completely subject to the commands of the spirit, it will annihilate space by the agility of its movements ; and if, even on earth, the happiness of the soul can transform even the most homely human countenance, then the glorious body will shine with light and be resplendent with a supernatural beauty, as it reflects the perfect bliss of the soul.

Then the Son of Man will come " with much power and majesty."[1] *Last Judge-* The triumphant Redeemer will come at last to judge all mankind. *ment* The doom that has been pronounced upon each at the moment of death will then be publicly proclaimed, and, in the gathering of all mankind before the judgement-seat of Christ, the love, the mercy, and the justice of God will receive solemn vindication. Then all who have wilfully rejected the grace of the Redeemer will be cut off for ever from his body, and Christ will present the " glorious Church, not having spot or wrinkle, or any such thing . . . holy and without blemish,"[2] to his Eternal Father.

\*　　\*　　\*　　\*　　\*　　\*　　\*

I began this account with the names of the Father, the Son, and *Conclusion* the Holy Ghost, the Three who are ineffably One.

Man's life is a search after unity. His mind is not content until he has reduced to an harmonious unity the multiple phenomena of experience. That unity he will find, but only in God, the first Cause of all. Men have dreamed of unity among themselves. They have lamented the discord of wills which sets man against man,

---

[1] Matt. xxiv 30.　　　　　[2] Eph. v 27.

family against family, nation against nation. The unity which will combine all men into one great family is also to be accomplished ; but only in God. Sin is the origin of discord ; the bond of perfection is charity. The unity which mankind is destined to achieve is none other than that which unites the three Persons of the Godhead— the unity of one divine life in which all men share under Christ the Head of his body. That this unity may be consummated is the last prayer of Christ to his Eternal Father :[1]

" All my things are thine, and thine are mine ; and I am glorified in them. And now I am not in the world, and I come to thee. Holy Father, keep them in my name whom thou hast given me ; that they may be one as we also are. . . . And not for them only do I pray, but for them also who through their word shall believe in me. That they all may be one, as thou Father in me and I in thee ; that they also may be one in us. . . . And the glory which thou hast given me, I have given to them, that they may be one as we also are one ; I in them and thou in me, that they may be made perfect in one."

G. D. SMITH.

[1] John xvii 10-26.

# III

## THE ONE GOD

### §I: GOD THE ONE SUBSISTENT BEING

THE supreme fact naturally known to man is that the ultimate reality *Subsistent* is a self-subsistent Being. We realise that there is some reality which *being* is altogether uncaused, which exists of itself, having and requiring no antecedent whatsoever. The ultimate being has not *become* itself, or received existence as an event, it simply *is*, and never has been otherwise. It is in every respect independent of all else, because it embodies in itself all the fulness of which being is capable. That is to say, its existence is not an activity distinct from the ultimate being, but such being intrinsically involves its existence in its very nature. Its " nature " and " existence " are one single eternal fact. In all other things we are able to distinguish their particular natures from the fact of their existence, but in the original being there can be no such composition of distinct principles, for all " composition " implies some power still more ultimate which provides the explanation of the compounding. The question of causal origin cannot possibly arise when once the meaning of ultimate subsistence, is understood. This supreme Being, eternally self-sufficient, whose nature is *to be*, we call God.[1]

In contrast to this undifferentiated oneness essential to ultimate *Essence and* being, the universe and the minds of men are composite, for in them *existence* essence and existence are not one, but are two distinct (though inseparable) principles forming a composite unity as distinct from a simple unity. The distinction between " essence " and " existence " in the universe (whether considered in part or whole) is no invention of the human mind, but, like all other real distinctions, is objective in things themselves. Observation makes us aware that things not only have existence, but over and above existence they have each also a distinct fabric of a given kind which we call their nature or essence. Existence tells us *that* a thing is, while knowledge of its essence tells us *what* a thing is.

To know *that* a thing exists is very different from knowing *what* particular nature it consists in. Consequently we always think of things and persons as *possessing* existence rather than as constituting it. Their existence is in no sense included in the definition of their essences : it is therefore a principle or activity distinguishable from

---

[1] *Cf.* the declaration of Jehovah to Moses : " I am Who am. . . . Thus shalt thou say to the children of Israel : He who is hath sent me to you " (Ex. iii 14).

their qualitative nature as such. Conversely, the nature of things is not included in or postulated by the definition or meaning of existence. So clear is the distinction between the essences of things and the fact that they exist, that, even if we wished, we could not avoid making it. Indeed we cannot combine the different meanings of " essence " and " existence " in a single idea, inasmuch as our concepts are derived from composite being. This shows that we cannot *positively* conceive " subsistent being." Our very ability positively to conceive the universe is a sign to us of its non-subsistent character. Thus all material and spiritual reality present in the universe of direct experience, being composite, is dependent for its composition of essence and existence upon a more ultimate being ; it is a product whose existence is conferred upon it by a superior cause. Such natural objects are, of course, not to be considered as having been first constituted as essences and then subsequently receiving their act of existence : that is an obvious impossibility, for though distinct, essence and existence in things are inseparable. The creation of the natures and the giving of their existence is simultaneous.

*The contrast between God and creatures* There is thus a great contrast between God and his creatures. He alone is self-subsistent. Deity is Being *par excellence*, and as such cannot be multiplied. Even the word " being " cannot be used in one and the same meaning of the ultimate being and dependent beings. Creatures do not constitute an addition to " being " in the sense that being is predicated of God. But just as mind and matter can co-exist because they are different orders of being, so matter and finite minds can on a lower plane co-exist with God.

The meaning of subsistent being, common to the three persons of the Blessed Trinity, is perfectly comprehended by the subsistent mind itself, but our finite minds, even when aided by the revelation of our Lord Jesus Christ, can form but inadequate conceptions of it. " No one knoweth who the Son is, but the Father : and who the Father is, but the Son and to whom the Son will reveal him." [1] In this stage of our experience we do not see God directly, but in his works. The creation and the redemption indirectly represent to us the being, truth and goodness which is the life of Deity. In the incarnate Logos, the way, the truth and the life, is the meaning of God most clearly reflected : " For God, who commanded the light to shine out of darkness, hath shined in our hearts, to give the light of the knowledge of the glory of God, in the face of Jesus Christ." [2]

*Our natural knowledge of God* The universe, life, and thought likewise in their own order give us knowledge of their one primal Cause. " The invisible things of him from the creation of the world are clearly seen, being understood by the things that are made. His eternal power also and divinity." [3] Jehovah is thus never an " unknown God." " It is he who giveth to all life, breath, and all things : and hath made of one, all mankind, to dwell upon the whole face of the earth, determining appointed

[1] Luke x 22.  [2] 2 Cor. iv 6.  [3] Rom. i 20.

times and the limits of their habitation. That they should seek God, if haply they may feel after him or find him, although he be not far from every one of us. For in him we live, and we move, and we are."[1] Inasmuch as God has so ordained that during its probation mankind should know him indirectly, our reflecting minds find in every realm of nature clear indications of his supreme activity and presence. Yet the finitude of our minds cannot adequately represent Deity in any of its absolute perfections. Thus wrote St Paul: " O the depth of the riches of the wisdom and of the knowledge of God ! How incomprehensible are his judgements, and how unsearchable his ways ! For who hath known the mind of the Lord ? Or who hath been his counsellor ? Or who hath first given to him, and recompense shall be made him ? For of him, and by him, and in him, are all things : to him be glory for ever." [2]  The nature of Divinity is not corporal or attainable by the five senses. " God is a Spirit and they who adore him must adore him in spirit and in truth." He is more perfectly spiritual than the mind of men or of angels. " God, who made the world and all things that are in it, he being Lord of heaven and earth, dwelleth not in temples made with hands. Nor is he served by the hands of men, as though he needed anything." [3]

" We see now through a glass in an obscure manner." [4]    *Analogy*

The terms we use of God are verily full of meaning, but none of our concepts can be referred to Deity without an accompanying proviso that their limitations have no counterpart in God himself.[5] Our ideas themselves are partial, and in analogically referring them to God we mentally negate these partialities and attribute to him only their perfect meaning. Our concepts are superlatively verified only in the infinite perfection of subsistent holiness which we call God. We think truly of all reality in terms of our own nature. When therefore we consider orders of being which are higher or lower than our own we properly employ the principle of analogy. Thus we can think of purely inorganic matter and the purely spiritual life of the angels only by analogy with our human nature which is neither pure matter nor pure spirit, but a compound of both matter and spirit.[6] Such analogical application of our concepts is more remote according as the mode of being concerned is different from our own, and Deity is supremely different therefrom. Yet inasmuch

---

[1] Acts xvii 25-27.    [2] Rom. xi 33-36.
[3] Acts xvii 24, 25.    [4] 1 Cor. xiii 12.
[5] The validity of the principles of human knowledge is affirmed by all minds, for those principles are based ultimately upon experience and self-evidence. That mankind possesses true natural knowledge cannot be logically denied. A denial implies that we have positive knowledge of the meaning and conditions of truth. But to affirm that there is such a quality as validity is incompatible with a contrary attitude of doubt.
[6] It is likewise owing to the analogical character of our knowledge of the consciousness of animals that the facts of animal psychology are so difficult to ascertain.

as our minds, in common with the natural objects of our experience, are made according to the exemplar of the Divine Mind, the knowledge gained from God's material and spiritual creations brings us valid, though partial, understanding of their primary Cause.

Christianity teaches us that subsistent being is self-complete living spiritual activity, wherein the one being of God self-manifestly appertains to itself in three distinct relations. The qualitative superiority and triune independence of Deity in no way detracts from the reality of creatures, nor does it render them illusory. On the contrary, their chief value and dignity results from the very fact that the Absolute Being has determined that they should participate in being, and simultaneously achieve his purpose and their own. They are not, indeed, emanations from God's unique nature, but being made in his likeness they are what they are because God is what he is, and are freely willed in the pure subsistent act whereby God is God.

## § II : THE NECESSITY AND FREEDOM OF GOD

*Intrinsic absolute necessity*

IN general usage the term necessity bears a relative sense. One thing is said to be necessary to another, or circumstances are regarded as necessitating a given result. God's necessity, however, is of an entirely different order and is unique. It is not relative or due to anything extrinsic to himself, but absolute. Deity in itself is necessary irrespective of everything else. It is indeed owing to the contingency of the universe that we first realise that God is necessary, but that does not imply that the Divine necessity itself arises from his creation or conservation of the worlds. Necessity is, on the contrary, an excellence intrinsic to ultimate being.

Deity cannot but exist ; it must be, and must for ever be. Divine necessity concerns not merely the principle of existence, but the whole reality of subsistent being. The rational nature of Deity, being numerically one with its actual existence, has an identical necessity therewith.

There is thus one unique inevitability wherein God's superlative nature both necessarily is, and is Deity. Negatively stated, this means that the final ontological impossibility is that the Blessed Trinity should not be, or should not be what it is.

*The contingency of the finite*

The universe of matter and mind does not possess intrinsic necessity, and is therefore said to be contingent. Apart from the duality of essence and existence already referred to, the contingence of the whole universe upon the Divine will and power is revealed by the relative dependence of its parts. It is a system of interdependent components, inorganic, organic and rational. This organisation of multiple parts is obvious whether we consider the individual atom, or single elements, or the cosmos as a whole. Composition of all kinds, however, implies a prior agent as the reason and cause of the compounding. Constitutive elements do not involve each other in their very essence and meaning, otherwise they would not be distinct but identical. They cannot therefore be themselves the ultimate cause of their union.[1] The composite union which they form shows that they are not ultimately reducible to each other, and thus their unification as a system is dependent upon some power superior to themselves. It is not guidance or rearrangement that is implied, but total production as a cosmos. They are mutually incomplete and dependent upon each other as secondary causes, and also dependent upon a primary cause which, in the act of giving being to the whole, produces the parts in intimate relation.[2]

The relative completeness of the system of nature does not obscure the fact that unless it had been originally constituted as a composite whole it could not have existed at all. Nor does the resultant unity of operation itself explain the original composition, and no addition of dependent elements can constitute necessary being. The fact that the universe changes from state to state also shows that it is not an absolutely necessary being. A thing that changes its states is never wholly all it can be. Were any state necessary that state would be unalterably permanent, and if no state is permanently necessary such being cannot be necessary at all. *The sufficient explanation of all being*

Beings that are essentially subordinate, existing for a compound unity or system, cannot therefore be necessary in themselves, nor can they render more than a relative explanation of their existence. The very queries that arise in our minds as to origins and purpose are evidence of this contingency, for such ideas represent impressions received from the world's inadequacy.

By all paths of thought we are thus led inevitably from contingent minds and objects to Necessary Being as the explanation of all reality and existence. Therein the sufficient reason of being is perfectly embodied and comprehended. A necessary being has in and of itself the reason of its existence, whereas contingent beings have not. God, being one and self-manifest, is thus self-explanatory: the subsistent Reason, wherein ultimate being and ultimate meaning are identical. Deity and Deity alone has intrinsically the ability and right to exist, for the reason of its existence is identified with its very nature.

The necessity of God, unlike certain relative forms of necessity, has nothing in common with determinism. Absolute necessity in subsistent spiritual life means absolute freedom and independence. To identify determination with necessity would render freedom *Divine necessity is not determinism*

---

[1] Pampsychism and theories of *anima mundi* posit a duality of matter and mind and therefore are not ultimate explanations.

[2] The contingency of the universe relates to the dependence of its being and is distinct from the question whether the universe had a temporal beginning. Even if the universe had always existed its dependence upon a prior constituting cause would be no less obvious.

impossible. Things that are determined are extrinsically under compulsion to something other than themselves or to something within themselves which is distinct from their will. God's necessity is not compulsion, and thus it includes the perfection of freedom. He is remote from the influence of beings on a lower plane, and within his own being there is no distinction of nature and will. Therefore in God freedom, which is independent personal judgement, is so identified with the life of God that it partakes of his very necessity ; he is necessarily free. God is not composed of necessity and freedom as distinct principles. Thus freedom is involved in the necessary love whereby God appreciates his own infinitely perfect being. Divine freedom is not restricted to creation or contingent upon his will to create. It is not a temporary expedient. He does not acquire it or confer it upon himself, or produce it by his essence or his will ; it is eternally identified with both. He does not will himself by a mere resultant or static acquiescence in the inevitability of his own being. That would imply that God's volition was determined by his nature. On the contrary, his volition is free ; it is as much involved in the very life of Deity as is subsistence. God's will is never determined. Its freedom, therefore, is not an isolated activity exclusively applied to creation and providence, but is intrinsic to, and indistinguishable from, the infinite life of God.

Necessity in a given nature is according to the type of that nature. Material natures are determined, while spiritual natures have freedom. Thus, inasmuch as the Blessed Trinity is super-spiritual, its necessity is not the necessity of compulsion but the necessity of spirituality—that is, of mind and purpose. God's necessity, then, is one with subsistent freedom. Eternal freedom is integral to the very meaning of Deity.

*Necessity and freedom unified*  God's necessity implies that he cannot will to be other than he is, or act otherwise than according to his nature. His nature and powers are one ; there can be nothing contingent in necessary Being. He is both necessary and free. These two attributes are complementary as known to us analogically ; in Deity they are one single Divine fact. First Cause cannot be regarded as a principle of blind fatalism or unconscious fortuity. It must be the creative Exemplar of personal liberty and merit in angels and men. The adage that " what is to be, will be," is true therefore only if it is recognised that destiny includes liberty in God, as well as in the constitution of human beings. The partial necessity and freedom which finite beings possess in regard to each other derives its meaning from the perfect necessity and freedom of the Divine nature. Things are what they are because the Blessed Trinity is inevitably what it is, for it communicates being according to its own meaning and value.

*The origin of right and sanction*  The merit of our Lord's sacrifice, the authority of the Church's doctrine and penitential system, as well as all lesser rights, duties and privileges, derive from the necessary presence of God. In that same triune life natural laws of mechanics, physics, biology, thought, ethics and society have their ultimate origin and sanction.[1] Moral obligation, or the ethical " ought," may be taken as an example of God's necessary intelligence and will impressing itself within the very fabric of beings he has formed. The nature of man being self-conscious and rational is able, by experience of the self and the bearing of its actions, to become acquainted with the meaning and ineradicable laws of its own constitution. Man's rational life and ethical goodness are consequently due to his compliance with and fulfilment of these natural tendencies. Such human action is therefore nothing less than direct obedience to the First Cause as to a personal lawgiver, whose purpose for human life is revealed in that synthesis of mental and physical inclinations which is distinctive of the human compound.

## § III : DIVINE PERFECTION

PERFECTION is the completeness of goodness and truth. Truth and goodness are ontological and ethical. All things have ontological truth and goodness, in that they are knowable and useful. They achieve a certain end of their own and contribute to the needs of other things and minds. In rational and responsible beings there are also ethical truth and goodness, which place them still higher in the hierarchy of reality.

The universe regarded as a united whole, comprising matter, *The relative* energy, life, thought and will, has a certain completeness in virtue *perfection of* of which it so admirably fulfils its purpose. The whole, however, *finite being* is in no respect greater than the sum of its parts, but is merely coincident with them. It possesses no quality such as a " world soul " over and above the totality of the active and passive powers of its constitutive elements. Each quality is therein restricted to distinct material elements or to modes of life and consciousness. Moreover, these partial qualities set limits to each other by the very fact of their mutual interaction. And not only do elements, such as iron and gold, spatially exclude each other, but, in general, the possession of one quality renders its possessor incapable of qualities of another kind. Thus " the heavens show forth the glory of God " but are lacking in any consciousness of it, so that their own glory is incomplete, while man, though able to appreciate their grandeur, lacks in physical life the relative permanence of the suns.

Chemical affinity renders the elements incapable of freedom ; the inertia of inorganic matter excludes life ; instinct in man is modified by reason ; and human intelligence is extrinsically conditioned by the five senses.

---

[1] Thus that $2 + 2 = 4$ has only a relative necessity. It results from the fact that God has put us in relation with a number of things from which our minds can derive the notions of unity, difference, plurality and addibility.

Ontological and ethical qualities and powers within the universe are thus obviously partial and conditioned. No quality exists therein in absolute perfection. Hence the durability of the rocks or the synthetic power of the human mind cannot be regarded as respectively the perfection of strength or of knowledge.

Qualities and powers are found restricted in the order of nature solely on account of the limitations of the things and persons in which they are present. Further it is clear that such perfections, qualities, or powers are not precisely identical with the things and persons which possess them, but are departmental activities thereof. Activities are not their *substance*, but, as we say, the attributes, faculties, properties or accidents of those things—*e.g.*, gold is not precisely its atomic weight, and an animal is distinct from its instinct to imitate its parents ; similarly in regard to all other substances. Man likewise has many activities distinct from each other as well as from his substance, which manifests itself by means of each in turn— namely, by sense perception, reasoning, will, movement, and so forth. Throughout nature there is an irreducible duality of mass and kinetic energy, whether of the atom or of the solar systems.

This fact, that activities or qualities are not identical with the substances of things, means that substances and their properties are compounded into a unity which is traceable to that same supreme constituting Cause to which the composition of their essence and existence is referred.

*Unqualified completeness* But qualities and powers as such are not in their essential meaning limited to those partial and incomplete forms in which they are found in nature. On the contrary, there is only one mode that can be thought of as the *necessary* mode of any quality, attribute or power, and that is a superlative mode which completely realises *the whole meaning* of that quality or power. If power and quality and goodness are ultimate they must be identified with ultimate reality, and as such be perfectly complete in the degree of their realisation.

The ultimate being must therefore be superior to all composition. In subsistent being nature and activity are necessarily identical. Thus the ultimate subsistent reality possesses in one non-composite triune activity, immanent to its essence, all the qualities and powers, ontological and ethical, which in the universe are apportioned partially to many diverse types of being.

In that divine mode all attributes are realised in absolute completeness or perfection, for God cannot restrict his own nature to any lesser degree, and nothing else is capable of causing any restriction therein. God is therefore uniquely complete in one all-embracing perfection which we call " Deity."

*Our analogical concepts of God* Such absolute perfection surpasses our comprehension ; we can only think of it analogically. It is true that our concepts and ideals surpass to a certain extent all " comparative " degrees of being, unity, truth and goodness embodied in nature. Nevertheless our ideas fall immeasurably short of that unique "superlativeness" which we know must characterise ultimate being.

Such analogical knowledge of Deity arises mainly from two facts —viz. : (1) that the universe is contingent, or in other words that it has a Cause more perfect than itself capable of producing the composite system ; and (2) that the Subsistent Cause is not composite but identical in essence and activity. From these two considerations it follows that God acts or works according to his very essence, and therefore his creations represent his nature far more definitely than the works of man can embody human qualities. All causes bear some resemblance to their effects, but whereas a creature's causality is but an extrinsic modification of things that exist independently of itself, God's productions, inasmuch as they derive their entire being immediately from the Divine essence, are more truly representative of their Cause.

Our knowledge of the immediate products of God's essence is therefore a knowledge of the essence itself, though indirect. According to the capacity of finite things the Creator endows them with qualities analogous to his own. The exemplar or pattern of all finite qualities is the one all-comprehensive Quality of Deity itself. By knowing things he causes them, and they in their turn evoke in our minds the meaning and value they are thus made to represent. God's omnipotent apprehension of contingent beings in himself is itself the act which originates them. Thus in knowing them we are sharing his self-manifestation.

There is no other adequate explanation of the ultimate origin of truth. To know the partial qualities and values represented by creatures is thus proportionately to know the attributes of their perfect Cause.

Our most direct and intimate knowledge of God's work is that revealed in our own personality, for of that we have both exterior perception and interior consciousness. Human personality therefore most fully embodies for us the meaning and character of the Blessed Trinity. The meaning and purpose of any product is manifested by the dominant tendencies and laws of action and reaction which characterise it. We have seen that the reason and law of God are impressed within man's nature. Rational and ethical right and duty, thus dominant, reveal the spiritual purpose of God in the conscious purpose of man.

Natural experience as well as Christian teaching clearly indicate that knowledge and goodness (and not merely the prosperity or enjoyment which may accompany them) are the objects for which the human race and the conditions of its life were instituted.

The whole creation is subordinated to the attainment by men of personal wisdom and devotion, with happiness accompanying. Thus revealed in the tendencies given to the universe, of which man is the centre, the Blessed Trinity is manifested as Goodness and Truth in unlimited perfection.

*The best*
*possible world*

NOTE.—God has created the best possible world, but that world is not this present earth but the supernatural Kingdom of God. This present imperfect earthly state has its place, however, as a condition without which the most perfect world could not be realised. A " heaven " whose free inhabitants were retained irrespective of their own will would be inferior to earth and hell. There would be a still more excellent world conceivable. Personal merit is more perfect than passive sinlessness.

The best possible world, then, is that wherein the Blessed Trinity is supernaturally known by those who by grace and personal determination have merited that dignity, and whose confirmation in goodness is but a divine perfection coinciding with the creature's own deliberate character. The best possible world thus involves this present preliminary world (itself adequate as a sphere of probation) in order that man may, by avoiding possible wrong, freely attain the right with that merit of faith, hope, and personal devotion which restricted and obscure conditions of life alone make practicable. Angelic probation and the intermediate state of purgation are likewise conditions preparatory to the most perfect world which is the participation by rational beings in the life of perfect God.

## §IV: DIVINE INFINITY

*The finitude*
*of the*
*universe*

ALL things and persons of which we have direct experience are finite ; they are, indeed, subject to many limitations. The universe is a system of composite interdependent factors modifying and restricting each other as a natural condition of their co-existence. Each person and thing is limited in being, meaning, value, and in its complement of active and passive powers. It is, in fact, largely by means of their limitations that ordinary things can affect our senses or otherwise become known to our consciousness. Moreover, matter is essentially finite ; the divisible quantity which characterises its extended surfaces is the chief source from which we derive the idea of limitation. The material universe is thus not infinite even in volume, and the measurability of its surfaces or limits is itself the basis of physical science.

The limits of the universe are as clearly revealed by those of its surfaces which are adjacent to us, as would be the case were we able to see the outline of the furthermost stars. The surfaces accessible to us are typical of all material volume, and thus, however numerous and distant the stars may be, their fabric still has limited bounds.

Our realisation of the finitude of the material universe is not due to the fact that our minds are limited. On the contrary, it is solely because the universe is finite that our finite senses are able to observe it at all. Only an infinite mind can directly know the infinite and in so doing be conscious of its own infinity. That which is infinite has, by definition, no limits, and thus no parts, for parts are limits. An infinite reality, then, cannot be known by observation of parts ; it is directly knowable either in its entirety or not at all. The material universe has really distinct parts. Our five senses, as differentiated parts of the universe of matter, are characteristically restricted. Our minds also are limited, though their limits are of a non-material character. Ignorance, error, forgetfulness, the serial character of our reasoning processes, as well as our dependence upon external evidence, make us conscious of our mental limitations. The human will is subject to a corresponding finitude.

Limitation is likewise shown in both matter and mind by the fact of their development. All changes from one state to another involve either the loss or the gain of some ingredient or factor : loss implies present limitation ; gain reveals limitation in the past ; moreover, what is once finite can never become infinite. No addition of finite increments can accumulate to form infinity.

Infinity cannot be acquired ; if it is not possessed eternally it *Mathematical* can never be possessed. That which is infinite in any respect is *"infinity"* necessarily infinite in all respects, for infinite being cannot be limited to this or that quality, but by definition includes all in all. It follows that whatever is finite in any respect is by that fact alone known to be finite in every respect.

In order to take infinity seriously it is necessary to distinguish the true and real infinite from the so-called " infinity " of logic and mathematics. Mathematical infinity (applicable to the infinitely small as well as to the infinitely great) is sometimes qualified as " the potential infinite," but it is more accurately termed " the indefinite " or " the indeterminate," for it does not exclude limitation as such, but merely implies that any given particular limit is not to be identified with the abstract ideal or imaginary continuum of space or of time. No one can ever positively imagine or conceive an infinite or eternal series of stages or subdivisions in the mathematical sense ; the most we do is to commence an enumeration, and then represent the remainder by a symbol. Moreover, a developing infinity or an infinite series of parts is a contradiction in terms, for infinity has no parts or limits.

We can, indeed, mentally prescind from all imagery of place, time and division, and set our minds to contemplate exclusively the idea of quantity or extension as an abstraction, but any actual line or surface in the real world cannot be without definite limits. The " indefinite " is thus but a mental generalisation applicable at once to every possible degree of quantity and thus incapable of being realised in any one given real being.

In contrast to the " indefinite," the *real* infinite cannot be a mere *The real* abstraction in our minds, but must be an existing being having one *infinite* unique and unalterable meaning. Real infinity is being without any possibility of limits. The term " in-finity " is not positive but negative, and the idea we have of such a being is correspondingly negative. But the character of the negation must not be overlooked. It is the negation of a negation, for limitation is the *negation* of further being, and the idea of " limitless being," though negative in form, thus represents positive super-eminent being.

Our finite minds cannot form a positive concept of the real infinite, though our negative idea has a luminous meaning. From our awareness of the multifarious limitations of the universe of experience arises the abstract idea of " the finite," as a general concept applicable to every type of restriction and limitation. This idea of the finite cannot, however, be conceived in isolation, but only as accompanied by an idea of its opposite, the infinite. The meaning of either of these depends precisely upon their being thought of together in a relation of contrast. We can, of course, think about the nature and powers of things that are finite, without adverting at once to the fact of their finiteness, but when once we recognise that they are finite, then we do but set up a mental contrast between them and the non-finite or infinite. Such complementariness in meaning shows that as ideas they are not conceived successively, but simultaneously. Together they are a compound idea which occurs to us as an expression of our realisation that our rational ideals and capacities find no adequate and exhaustive object either in themselves or in the world around.

*Unique spiritual greatness*

The mind's capacity for meaning and value is realised to be exhausted or exhaustible by nothing that is limited, and therefore only by the unlimited. Thus by experience of the finite our minds inevitably become aware of the fact that visible or limited entities cannot be the total object of which human reason is consciously capable. No degree of the finite realises the fulness of meaning of which the human understanding is capable. Though indeed we have no positive idea of, or adequate desire for, the infinite, we are clearly aware of the insufficiency of everything *other than* the infinite.

The verdict of our whole nature is that the finite is not the All of meaning or being. The partial cannot be the whole. We do not directly see the intrinsic possibility of the infinite, but we do directly see the impossibility that limited beings should constitute the whole of existence or exhaust the meaning of reality. This brings us clear knowledge that the meaning of being implies the real existence of the Infinite. It is precisely because we realise that things and persons are limited that we are unable to suppose that being as such must be restricted solely to them. They cannot embody the whole possibility of being, or comprise a sufficient reason even of their own finite existence. The inadequacy of the finite thus indicates that complete or perfect reality and meaning exist in the Infinite alone, constituting the sufficient reason of the infinite itself as well as of the finite.

Infinite being is therefore superior to the limitations of material volume and of discursive reason. *Infinity is spiritual greatness* of a unique and superlative order. Our mental imagery and our relative concepts of spatial extension are therefore incapable of representing it.

*Divine omni-presence*

God's Omnipresence or spiritual immensity is thus entirely different from the mode of " presence " whereby finite objects " occupy " a defined place and sustain a relative position in regard to each other. The Infinite is " present " according to its subsistent mode of being. All that is related to the infinite is related to the whole of infinity, for no partial relation is possible in regard to that which is indivisible. To be restricted to any spatial position is itself a limitation. The human mind, though finite, is in some respects superior to material or spatial restrictions, and Infinite Spirit transcends them all. It is by uniting the idea of spiritual life with the negation of all limitations that we can attain the most adequate mental " analogue " of the positive infinity of supreme being. The phrase " infinite matter " would be self-contradictory, for matter is essentially finite. Subsistent Mind can alone be consistently thought of as Infinity, as the philosophies of East and West abundantly illustrate.

## §V: DIVINE UNITY

" THE Holy Catholic Apostolic Roman Church believes and confesses that there is one true and living God, Creator and Lord of heaven and earth, almighty, eternal, immense, incomprehensible, infinite in intelligence, in will, and in all perfection, who, as being one, sole, absolutely simple and immutable spiritual substance, is to be declared as really and essentially distinct from the world, of supreme beatitude in and from himself, and ineffably exalted above all things beside himself which exist or are conceivable."

" This one, only, true God, of his own goodness and almighty power, not for the increase of his own beatitude, nor to acquire, but to manifest his perfection . . . created out of nothing . . . both the spiritual and corporal creature, namely the angelic and the mundane, and then the human creature as partaking, in a sense, of both, consisting of spirit and body." [1]

Unity is differently realised in diverse orders of being. In the *Types of unity* realm of inorganic matter there is a merely structural and functional unity within the elements. Higher than this is the unity involved in chemical compounds. Vegetation presents above this again a unity of life. The animal represents a still more complex unity of organic life, involving also sense-consciousness. Man is a synthesis of matter, life, sensibility, rational mind and will, while the human soul, considered in itself, is the highest type of unity of which we have immediate knowledge.

The unity of the soul and its operations is more complete than that attainable in any material compound or organism. Its ideas interfuse without spatial separateness, and its volition is intrinsically involved in the activity of the intelligence, so that ideas and motives coalesce. Unlike sense impressions, ideas are not localised, but modify the whole fabric of the mind, so that the mind is greater than the mere sum of its ideas. Unlike sense imagery, ideas, being immaterial, each contribute to a general unity of meaning which

[1] Vatican Constitution *De Fide,* 1.

reveals itself in principles of thought and reasoning applicable to all reality. Single states of consciousness do not, indeed, manifest this essential simplicity of the mind's spiritual life, but any series of states bears witness thereto. The soul, or mind, is not, however, a perfect unity. It is composite in that its existence and other powers, such as reasoning and volition, are constitutionally distinct, though inseparable, from its essence ; moreover, its states of consciousness are variable.

The unconditioned perfection of unity is thus not possible in anything which is composite, partial, or mutable. It is exclusively proper to the infinite. Perfect unity means simplicity. In contrast to changing composition, it is a single fact involving in one reality a spiritual fabric, existence, meaning, value, activity. Triune God who is One Spirit is the sole complete reality, having in himself supereminently all the perfections of being, whether known to us or not.

We learn aspects of the meaning of God from the vast universe involving us which are not at first so obviously recognisable in the otherwise more wondrous realms of the human personality. The Divine omnipotent energy, supremacy, immensity, eternity, grandeur, have a peculiarly impressive embodiment in external nature, while man's personal and social life supplies the analogues of the Divine unity, intelligence, meaning, freedom, right, and purpose. Moreover, our own composite nature, inasmuch as it embodies vegetal and animal life in conjunction with rational powers, helps us to think of the still higher unification of all perfections in the supreme unity of God.

*Simplicity of all qualities in one Being* The nature of God is spiritual, for the unlimited source of reality cannot be subject to the specific limitations and passivity of composite matter. But it is equally clear that rationality in God is not subject to the limitations conditioning finite spirits. The incomparably complete spirituality of God is neutral both as to the characteristic restrictions of finite mind as well as of finite matter. God is a Spirit of such transcendence that his essence unifies all those qualities which finite matter and mind inadequately represent in all their respective modes of duration, energy, life, emotion, understanding, and will.

Attributes in Deity are not supplementary but are all present in a single transcendent subsistent act. Our minds, being finite, cannot combine our various negative and analogical ideas of God into one concept or state of consciousness. Consideration of those concepts, however, shows that each implicitly involves all the others in intimate relation. Subsistence and infinity are complementary, perfection and intelligence ally themselves to infinite unity, power, will, immutability, and eternity. Each is an aspect to our minds of spiritual greatness.

The import of Divine unity is thus distantly realised by the partial synthesis formed by different thoughts regarding him. In the attempt distantly to understand what unity is in God we think first of the possibility of a perfect form of each quality separately, and then of the possibility of one sole transcendent perfection, still greater than each, which in its limitless fulness includes them all more wondrously, without differentiation or dependence. " Simplicity " in God, however, is not acquired by synthesis, but is a necessary oneness eternally original.

In virtue of this absolute perfection of his unity God is unique. *One only God* Deity is numerically singular in its subsistent infinity. It does not include a plurality of divinities. It is not a genus but a single being. The composite system of the universe, including human life, implies a unity of authorship which the providential alchemy rendering evil contributory to good serves to emphasise. All creation has a single cause and tendency. There is only one First Cause, for God is One. Deity excludes all composition of different elements or beings, yet it is the very nature of absolute unity to be triune.

Reason naturally tends to explain the complex in terms of the simple, and to resolve differences of the many in a higher unity. There is thus a general belief in the unity of truth and reality in ultimate being. With equal naturalness the mind concludes that the ultimate unity must be a transcendent spiritual nature capable of self-manifestation, a sufficient reason evident to itself, unifying all perfections of matter, life, and society. All possibilities of being must therein be perfectly subsistent, for we cannot assume that the ultimate is limited to those perfections which are discoverable by unaided reason. On the contrary, by reason we know that God is knowable to himself in a manner that surpasses our negative and analogical knowledge of him.

His revelation then helps us to understand that ultimate being is not a mere abstract oneness or mathematical unity without distinctive quality and meaning.

From that revelation we learn that the absolute perfection of unity *Trinity in* consists in the sublimity of triune self-realisation. The co-equal *unity* persons are three relations in which the one indivisible Divine Subsistence possesses, knows and values itself. Trinity in Unity involves no distinction which differentiates the Divine Nature from itself, but, on the contrary, alone involves all that is required in order that it should *be itself perfectly* in consummate appreciation. It is the " necessary " unity of being, unifying the absolute and the relative in unlimited meaning. The One and the Many are thus ultimate in virtue of the relative mutual coinherence of the adorable Trinity in that self-sufficient Unity which is the One Godhead.

## §VI: DIVINE OMNIPOTENCE

POWER is the intrinsic energy of being realised in activity. The *The dynamic* Blessed Trinity, infinite in the immanence of its life, is the perfect *aspect of* self-realisation of Power. In one omnipotent and eternal experience *divine life*

all powers of being, both absolute and relative, are completely actualised without the possibility of increase or diminution.   Omnipotence
suffuses all the Divine attributes, and is identical with the Godhood
of God.   It represents for us the dynamic aspect of the triune life of
the divine essence, wherein the fecundity of the one subsistent nature
expresses, manifests, and comprehends its own meaning and value,
and all things within that fulness.

*The divine*
*processions*
Omnipotence involves every possible mode of origination and
production, and is thus more than the power of causation whereby
things other than itself are brought into existence.   The eternal
origination or procession of the Son and the Holy Ghost is omnipotent life ; but it is not causal activity, inasmuch as the persons are
identical with the one divine nature.   They are not additions to its
life, they are its life.   The three persons are self-expressions and
self-realisations of life, knowledge, love, and sanctity which constitute
the very being of Deity.   Thus subsistence is power, knowledge is
power, will and eternity are power, all infinitely one.   Omnipotence
is distinctive of Deity, and creation is but a revelation of it in the
order of finite being.

Hence our idea of supreme power is but a distant analogy of that
almightiness which characterises the ultimate being.  Power in
creatures passes from a state of potential capability to the actual
performance of an act.   But Omnipotence is the subsistent energy
of eternal being, and is not transient but immanent and permanent
in its infinite actuality.

*Creation*
Creation is to us but an aspect of an eternal activity.   The
statement of Genesis that God " rested " on the seventh day is
metaphorical of the eternal contentment of God in the knowledge of
all things in himself.   In regard to the universe his activity has neither
beginning nor end, and involves no change.   Creation is not a local
transference of power from God to the creature, nor is the creature
a terminus of his power.   The motive of that power is not the creature
itself but God's knowledge of his own being.   Apart from God's
power the creature has no existence, and therefore cannot be regarded as an object antecedent to his production of it.   Nor can the
creature ever become an " object " reacting upon God in the sense
in which objects react upon us.   Likewise the continuance of the
creative act in the conservation of and concurrence with creatures
involves no new or different activity in Omnipotence.

*Creation and*
*omnipotence*
The contingency of the universe reveals the fact that it was
created by Omnipotence.   The dependence of finite beings upon
God is not accidental or partial but total, involving their entire
reality.   Thus contingent mind and matter are essentially and qualita-
tively different from subsistent Being.   They cannot therefore be
regarded as natural emanations from the Divine Nature or as par-
ticipating in its distinctive life.   This complete distinctness of God
and finite being implies that the universe was produced in no way

other than *creation* in the full meaning of that term. For it is clear that creation is the only mode of causation whereby a cause can produce other being entirely distinct from itself.

It is evident, too, that creation is within the competence of Omnipotence alone. The universe, which is the product of the Creator, is indeed finite, but no power less than infinite could have produced it. Finite being cannot create ; its activities presuppose already existing material upon which to operate. Not being subsistent, finite being cannot even maintain itself in being, and does not control its own existence. It follows, therefore, that finite being cannot create other finite being, as that would be equivalent to causing being equal to itself. The origination of being therefore requires a productive energy which is positively infinite. Subsistent being alone can create the finite, and the gift of grace which perfects nature and forgives sins by creative regeneration is likewise possible to Deity alone.

Thus all modes of created being, whether natural or supernatural, normal or miraculous, are finite evidences of that power, wisdom, and mercy which is triune Omnipotence.

## § VII : DIVINE IMMUTABILITY

To be mutable is proper to composite beings within an interdependent *Mutability* system. The elements and orders of being in the universe exist for *implies* each other, and the capacity to change is a condition of their inter- *dependence* action. No chemical element or living species has any reason or capacity for existence except as part of a reciprocal system culminating in rational being. Material things do not possess independent spontaneous activity, motion, or life. In order that they may be active it is necessary that they should be influenced by other things. As truly as colour depends upon light, so truly do all properties of matter involve interaction. Animal dependence upon the vegetable kingdom is still more obvious. Also our own mental as well as bodily dependence upon other things is with us an abiding consciousness.

Finite activity, life, and development thus demand interaction of diverse entities. Movement can only take place when one thing is influenced by another either directly or indirectly. Without interaction there can be no change. To receive impressions from other things is of the very meaning of change or development. Mutual influence and interaction, moreover, necessitate heterogeneity. Things must be of different kinds in order to produce that modifying influence upon one another which is requisite for development, life, movement, or change of any kind.[1] The energy of chemical elements

[1] Evolution from perfectly homogeneous matter is thus impossible, for undifferentiated matter could not act causally upon itself and change its homogeneity into heterogeneity.

is only potential if considered apart from that interaction with other elements which is necessary for complete activity.

There are three types of change, namely, qualitative change, as in intensification or waning of attention; quantitative change, as in the growth or withering of a tree; and local change, which concerns movement from place to place. To bring about any kind of change some type of mutual influence between diverse things is requisite. Given the necessary stimulus a thing changes, but never can it modify itself in the absence of such extrinsic influences. This indicates that change is not identical with the thing that undergoes it.

The motion of the universe is thus an endowment distinct from matter as such, though intimately allied therewith. Matter is indifferent to rest or motion, hence it can be in either of these states. Of itself matter does not possess motion; if it did it could not be indifferent to movement.

*What is moved is moved by another*   Nothing can of itself change or move in any respect. Whatever is in motion is moved thereto by something other than itself. And inasmuch as each element in the universe needs itself to be influenced in order that it may in turn exert influence, the beginning of motion cannot be traced to any element *within* the universe. The whole system, as a system, must therefore have been originally endowed with motion, otherwise those relative movements within it with which we are familiar could never have originated. There must have been a first arrangement or ordering of the system as a system which was neither the effect of material energy nor essential to matter as such. That is to say, the motion of the whole finite series or group of elements which constitute the universe must have been produced simultaneously with their fabric, otherwise the system could not have existed at all. As a system they depend upon motion. But the motion itself requires the actual presence of the system. The system cannot be antecedent to the motion on which it depends, and so cannot be the cause of the motion. System and motion must exist simultaneously or not at all. *The universe, therefore, was produced in a state of movement* by a cause superior both to matter and to motion.

To summarise the foregoing considerations, the conclusion is clear that the universe is the product of a cause capable of producing instantaneously : (*a*) the group of heterogeneous elements having each its own potentialities, (*b*) their mutual complementariness, and (*c*) their actual motion throughout the system. Only thus actually in motion can the universe have originated.

*The first cause unchanging*   It follows, therefore, that the activity whereby the system of nature is produced is of a higher order than the activity of movement or change. The originating Cause of being cannot have the same limited type of activity as it gives to its products. Their changeful mode of activity depends upon influence from without, but there is nothing which can change or move the First Cause, for no being other than that Cause exists on the plane of subsistent being. Nor could that Cause move or change itself, for no being, whether finite or infinite, alone can cause limitation, change, or movement in itself. It follows that the activity of this Cause is not any form of change or movement. The causal activity superior to all change must therefore be ever present in, and identical with, the very nature of the First Cause. The causation of the universe must thus represent a permanent and changeless natural activity of God as distinct from a transient or departmental change of state. The first change in matter, as well as all subsequent changes, is therefore caused by a being which itself is changeless. Movement ultimately owes its origin to a Prime Mover, himself unmoved, whom we call God.

Mutability is not an absolute perfection. On the contrary, the possibility of loss or gain denotes the absence of perfection. Change is the transitory stage of beings while they are actualising or ceasing to actualise their capacities in conjunction with influences from their environment. Changeability spells incompleteness and dependence. Being as such does not necessarily involve change; indeed, change can only occur in composite being, which is limited and dependent.[1]

By definition, therefore, change cannot be absolute and can have no place in ultimate being. Infinity admits of no variation. God the Primary Being is thus unique in his superiority to change. He has the perfection of which change implies the lack. In the activity of Deity " there is no change, nor shadow of vicissitude." [2] The triune life involves no subsequent realisation of capacities previously undeveloped or passive. It has always been fully actualised. Its internal manifestations share the changelessness of the essence in which they eternally originate. Deity is pure omnipotent Act excluding instability and deflection. Subsistent goodness is necessarily constant and independent, for it is the fulness of being.

The activity whereby God creates the worlds involves no altera-  *The change-*
tion in God's life, which has always included it. Creative and *lessness of*
miraculous power involves no new state or procedure within his *pure act*
timeless fulness. Whatever God is in any respect, he is changelessly.[3]
The meaning of Eternity, which is studied in the next section, shows that God as Subsistent Creator has never been other than he is.

---

[1] Modern scientific philosophy has discarded Darwinism in favour of a theory of a God evolving with the universe in which he works creatively. But to require development in God is sheer anthropomorphism.

[2] James i 17.

[3] In our own finite experience freedom is normally associated with a change of state, but change is not of the essence even of our freedom. It is not the fact of change which renders an act free. The freedom of an act is due solely to the spiritual nature which posits the act. Thus God's freedom in creating represents the eternally changeless state of his will.

His free creative act is itself necessarily eternal, though its finite product is naturally subject to time and change.[1]

Immutability in the life of God is thus the antithesis of inertness, and is in contrast to the relative incompetence of beings that are subject to successive variation. Changelessness implies intensity of value in the Infinite as, on the highest plane, unifying the qualities of the static and the dynamic. Human beings normally attain their social values gradually through changing experience. But qualities which are occasional in men are permanent in God. Triune Deity involves these perfections in one all-comprehensive experience which is always identical with its being. God does not need to change in order to act. God *is* Act. Divine knowledge is not an acquisition ; God *is* truth. The implications of all being are in him self-known and eternally realised. In that sublimest Companionship the Blessed Trinity does not need to learn to love. Love is in no way subsequent to being ; it is integral to the very life of Deity. God *is* love.

*Compassion without passibility*
Hence all theories suggesting that " passibility " is needful to God in order that he may be sympathetic to human beings, fall far short of that loving kindness and emotional compassion which is intrinsic to God's own triune experience. Every quality which such theories desiderate has been in God always, without his needing *per impossible* to submit to the imperfection involved in change.[2] Is not the exquisite delicacy of " the lilies of the field " an exemplification of unutterable tenderness as well as of inscrutable greatness ? Thus not only all that creatures can acquire by changing, but literally *all that being can be*, in value, understanding, emotion, and active sympathy, the God who answers prayer is unchangeably in very essence.

## § VIII : DIVINE ETERNITY

*Time*
THE duration of a being is its continuance in existence. When duration consists in a series of different states succeeding each other it is called temporal, and can be measured by our standards of time. Duration which is not composed of a series of successive states, but is one invariable state ever-present without end or beginning, is called

---

[1] God's constant providence in our world and in the unseen is included in his one creative activity. To will a series of changes is not to change the will. Thus answers to prayer, miracles, the intermediate state of disembodied souls, the Limbo (or Borderland) of those who die innocent of actual sin but unbaptised, equally with the preparation of heaven itself, are not revisions or after-thoughts in the Divine plan of the ages, but form an integral part of one supreme interrelated purpose, the inner significance of which can never be adequately realised in our present state of probation.

[2] Self-limitation is impossible to God in regard to any of his attributes, for all attributes are identical with his subsistent essence and are thus necessarily eternal.

eternal, and the idea of time cannot apply to it. Time depends upon the comparability of one stage or state with another, and, therefore, where there is no change of state there cannot be comparative duration or time.

Our own consciousness of time is thus due to the recognition of successive changes in ourselves and in the world around, and by conventional means we measure the periods occupied by the different states. Each state is " limited " by the state which precedes it and the state which follows it, and the knowledge of these limits enables us to measure any given state, and record it in terms of minutes or other time-standards. Changing states are so numerous in ourselves and our environment that the idea of time becomes from early years an element in our habitual consciousness. Nevertheless time is applicable only to things that change. We have seen, however, that change itself is not essential to being as such, and, indeed, changing activity can take place only in beings that are incomplete and dependent. In order to exist, live, and act, they need the co-operation of other things. They are always becoming what they were not before, and are never wholly all that they can be. They thus possess their actuality only by successive degrees or increments. This is true of individual things and persons and of the universe as a whole. They are never completely the whole reality of their being. Change may involve loss or gain departmentally, but in any case change spells limitation, and the serial process of their duration involves everlasting incompleteness.

The more complete a being is, the less it changes. A perfectly *Timeless* complete being would not change or need to change at all. It would *duration* possess its whole being permanently, and not in a variable series of successive stages. It would be capable of embracing its whole reality in one permanent experience. It would be always wholly itself, and for ever identical with itself in every respect. It would realise all its possibilities and meaning at once. There would be no past or present or future in our relative sense, but all would be an abiding " now," or transcendent " present." It would not merely (as we can partially) include the " past " by representative memory, and the " future " by anticipation based on past and present knowledge. In perfect being " past and future " would be actually present and fully possessed without differentiation of periods. Perfect duration would involve an unrestricted consciousness of the fulness of being. Time would not apply to it : it would be eternal life.

But such must be the character of Deity. Subsistent, the blessed *Eternal lif* Trinity is its own fulness. Necessary, it knows no dependence. Perfect, it is complete in itself and has need of nothing. Infinite, it has no limits intrinsic or extrinsic. Immutable, it is unvarying. One, it possesses itself in undifferentiated identity. There is nothing that God will be that he is not yet, or has not always been. In him nothing awaits future development, no state needs to be acquired.

The " now " or " present " of our finite consciousness may be regarded as an instant or a moment or a day or a longer period, but it is never a state complete in itself. Consciousness changes incessantly owing to our limitations. But the " now " of superlative consciousness is not restricted to a passing state. It comprehends all being in one act and vision, its " present " is not a moment but the whole of eternity. God has, so to speak, always been present in our future as he has been in our past. Time is but the gradual and partial experience by creatures of the eternity of God.

*Eternal knowledge and will*

Perfect Knowledge does not need to look back in memory, nor does Perfect Will need to look forward in anticipation.[1]   All is known and willed together in the power of one subsistence. Man's soul is naturally immortal, and by its vast range of thought and imagination can, in measure, embody all things and represent a synthesis of universal history. Man is a microcosm. But God is the Macrocosm in whom the universe of nature and of history has its original exemplar, its possibility and actuality. It is known in his eternal life as a temporal manifestation. We by direct knowledge know only finite things in their passing finitude, and thus inevitably our knowledge involves the idea of time. But finite things are not the whole of reality. The Infinite is, to itself, far more consciously real than anything can be to finite minds.

The Divine mind and will cannot regard Deity under the aspect of time. And it is in that timeless nature that the Infinite knows the finite. The finite is known and willed by God according to his own mode of consciousness, which, unlike ours, is transcendent and eternal. God, in knowing the imitability of his nature, knows his creatures. In willing his own perfection he purposes theirs, and has never lacked the full realisation of his creative power and purposive providence. In what we call the distant future his activity will be no greater and no less than it has ever been. Thus sang the Psalmist : " In the beginning, O Lord, thou foundedst the earth : and the heavens are the work of thy hands. They shall perish, but thou remainest : and all of them shall grow old like a garment : and as a vesture thou shalt change them, and they shall be changed. But thou art always the self-same, and thy years shall not fail." [2]   " The mercy of the Lord is from eternity and unto eternity upon them that fear him." [3]

*Complete self-realisation*

Eternally complete self-realisation is possible to God only, who is the infinite and omnipotent mind. Eternity is not cumulative or acquirable by countless ages of existence : it is a single infinite fact without process or temporal qualities. Hence the universe can never become eternal ; it is characteristically changeful and therefore

---

[1] Terms such as " fore-knowledge," " pre-destination," " pro-vidence," " pre-vision," and " pur-pose," reflect the limitation of our minds in conceiving analogously their Divine equivalents.
[2] Ps. ci 26-28.                    [3] Ps. cii 17.

temporal. Even could we suppose that it never had a beginning it would be in no sense eternal, since it can never include its future at any given stage. We learn from revelation that the world had, in fact, a first stage or beginning. Furthermore, eternity is nothing other than infinity under the aspect of duration. Thus only that which is infinite is eternal, and what is eternal must be infinite in every respect. Infinity is possessed in its entirety or not at all. The universe not being infinite, but finite, is thus known to be limited in duration. Thus temporal, it is incapable of eternity in the past and in the future. In no respect does it transcend the category of time, though the age of the suns has not yet been finally calculated by man.

The universe, at each moment, is, however, related by dependence *Relation of* to the whole of eternity. God's creative act being eternal has no stages *the universe* corresponding to the events of time. The eternal is one and in-*to eternity* divisible. Whatever, therefore, is ever related to eternity is related to the whole of eternity. But to coexist with the whole of eternity is not to coexist *always* with eternity. Hence, though in the eternal comprehension of God things neither begin nor end, their own changeful and temporal character remains.

## §IX: DIVINE INTELLIGENCE

THE highest type of being in the universe of our experience is the *Human* human personality. Man recognises his own supremacy in the *personality* natural order because he knows his own nature to be spiritual as well as material, whereas all things lower than himself are non-spiritual. Thus we speak of human beings as persons, while refer-ring to other beings as things or individuals. Personality is attributed only to those higher individuals who are rational or spiritual. The human personality is not indeed purely spiritual; it is a unique compound of matter and mind. According to the Scholastic ex-planation the vital principle of the human body is not entirely im-mersed in matter, since it is spiritual. The normal condition of the soul is to be united to the body, and thus a disembodied soul is meanwhile an incomplete human personality.

The human spirit has thus a twofold operation. Its inferior *Spirituality* function is the energising of the bodily organism, while its higher *and meaning* activity is man's reason. Animals are capable of an instinctive response to environment, and have a lower type of memory in the form of spatial imagery of past material scenes and actions. Man in addition to this is spiritually aware of meaning, value, and purpose in nature and existence. He is capable of a rational appreciation of the higher significance of all being in terms of his own. He classifies phenomena and events according to non-material and abstract principles of order, and conceives the universal aspects of reality and truth. Such abstract ideas cannot be seen with the eyes, or other-wise be the object of the senses. They are not material objects outside the mind but immaterial or spiritual states on a plane beyond the range of nervous impressions.

The human mind therefore possesses, within the foil of its own fabric, what is known as " meaning." In virtue of this meaning man understands his experiences along with the laws and relativity of natural objects.

*Mind*

From such non-material states of rational meaning and voluntary appreciation of values we thus gain our idea of spirituality. Meaning and value, as such, are not in material things, but are rational relations within our consciousness. Only as experienced in mind can meaning and value be present. Therefore, it is the mind itself which supplies the subject within which they can exist. The qualities of matter are knowable to us because we are able to form in our minds the ideas which material things embody on a lower plane. Meaning does not come ready made from without to the mind. It cannot exist outside the mind, and inheres only within it. That is to say, the mind is that type of reality the experienced modifications or activities of which take the form of meaning and appreciation. The terms " Spirit " and " Spirituality " thus designate meaning-fabric in contrast to material and sense-fabric, and it is this spiritual character of life which distinguishes human persons from sub-human types of individuality.

*The highest form of activity*

We see, then, that personal self-realisation in immanent spiritual life is the highest form of activity of which we have experience. It is superior because of that immanence whereby, though complex in its powers, its life is relatively independent and complete, and can contain within itself its own term and process.

In the ascending scale of being, each higher form embodies the activities of the lower forms with the synthetic addition of its own higher characteristics. Thus plants possess, over and above the atomic energy common to all types of matter, an immanent individual life, assimilate nutriment, grow and propagate their kind, and have a degree of sensitivity. Animals further possess, in a superior order, all these vegetative functions while adding thereto their distinctive qualities of high sensibility, imagination, memory, appetition, emotional language, and progressive movement. Man, in a still higher mode, embodies in his physical life vegetal and animal powers, but in such a manner as to subserve a higher than animal individuality and purpose, finding expression in a language which is rational and ideal. Revelation teaches us that the life of an angel is more intensely immanent even than that of the human mind.

The higher, therefore, the mode of life, the more activity it embraces, and thus is the more immanent and independent. The supreme life is that which is perfectly immanent, complete, and independent. Hence the ultimate subsistent life of triune Deity, which is necessarily self-sufficient and independent, includes immanently all activities of being in a super-spiritual mode.

God is necessarily spiritual because he is superior to dimensive *Pure imma-*
parts, and yet embodies the fulness of meaning and value of all-being. *nent activity*
He includes within himself, in the highest possible form, all the
activities which angels, men, animals, plants, and inorganic elements
possess in various lower grades of being. The spiritual substances of angels and men can partially embody all reality in their
knowledge and volition, in virtue of modifications of their own
meaning-fabric. But the ultimate being who is cause of all by the
power of his life is not thus conditioned. God does not derive
knowledge and purpose from objects as external to himself, but from
within his own nature. Deity is subsistent meaning and value,
omnipotent intelligence and will. In God the perfection of the
real and of the ideal are one actuality. His self-knowledge is infinite,
all-involving consciousness. He eternally possesses the completest
knowledge of creatures in recognising that his own perfections are
creatively representable in finite modes. The actual existence of
finite being can provide no new object or knowledge for the Being
who alone is in every respect their ultimate explanation.

Truth is eternal because it is identical with eternal Deity. Finite *Eternal*
minds participate in truth in the same manner in which they par- *truth*
ticipate in being. God is necessary truth, envisaging finite beings
within an infinite unity of conscious meaning, in which alone lies
their original possibility.[1]

God's knowledge, therefore, is for ever complete and changeless.
Being eternal he knows, in unalterable vision, as actually existent, all
the beings of the universe according to their proper and individual
natures, together with every series of changes in matter and living
things, as well as all acts of freewill in angels and men. We ourselves
cannot even predict our own free acts, because the whole meaning
of our natures never appears in our finite consciousness at any one
time. But the whole reality of all free spirits is completely obvious
to God in his creative act. The acts of a man are not creative of new
being, but utilise powers which are the immediate product of the
divine life itself; they are thus fully comprehended in God their
primary Cause. In this perfect and changeless meaning of God
things are not observed as past or future, or viewed as from afar.
All states of being, all events, conditions, intentions, rights, duties,
merits, demerits, joys, sorrows, hopes and fears, are "present" in
an eternal and comprehensive awareness.

The intelligence of the supreme Being is revealed: (a) in the *Proofs of*
composite and relative order within the universe, (b) in the gift of *the divine*
*intelligence*
intelligence to men, (c) in the very meaning of truth.

(a) We have seen that compositeness cannot be ultimate. The *The order of*
universe implies a prior constituting cause to which it owes this *the universe*

[1] We cannot regard our minds as one with the Divine Mind, since we
are incapable of a direct and positive consciousness of the infinite. The
finitude of our minds is further shown by our relative ignorance.

composition of finite elements. We have seen, too, that neither the universe nor its activities are necessary in themselves. Inasmuch, therefore, as the reason why things are compounded is not involved in the components themselves (for mind, and not matter, is the principle of order), the ordering and compounding involved in the constitution of the universe is due to a Cause which has some intelligent reason for producing such a system. And as such reason can be present only in an intelligent being, it is clear that the cosmic order of interdependent elements is due ultimately to a Cause which is intelligent.

The order of the universe is not a mere remodelling or redistribution of pre-existing material. It is the creative constitution of the whole system in a state of relative activity. Hence it does not consist in the giving of " guidance " to material otherwise chaotic. Even independently of the relative movements discoverable in the material universe itself, there is evidence of God's intelligent ordering in the very fact that external objects are knowable to man's mind. Absolute chaos is therefore inconceivable, for any knowledge of things, in whatever state they may be, is itself order, and not chaos. Indeed, the knowability of things external to the mind is the supreme example of order. Each aspect of cosmic order implies sovereign intelligence in the universal Architect.

*Human intelligence*

(b) We have seen in the section on Perfection that qualities are unlimited in their source. Where, therefore, they are only partially possessed, they do not originate, but are the gift of a higher cause in which they exist completely in identification with being. This is true of the properties of both matter and of mind. Each is a manifestation in different grades of the attributes of their common cause. Thus just as material energy symbolises Divine power, so man's possession of finite intelligence is a sign of perfect intelligence in God its original Cause.[1]

*The meaning of truth*

(c) Truth is an aspect of being. It is that aspect under which being is knowable or intelligible to mind. Over and above the question of universal order or relativity, there is the question of the ultimate reason or intelligibility of being as such. To be intelligible at all, being must be related to a mind. Thus the meaning of truth implies a knowing mind as well as a knowable object. We are able analogically to see the purpose of God in the purpose of men, but that does not give us direct knowledge of the ultimate purpose or meaning of being in itself. Being is thus only partially intelligible to finite minds. Ultimate meaning is beyond our comprehension.

---

[1] Theology declares that mind cannot have developed by any *natural* process from matter or from semi-material " neutral stuff." Self-conscious meaning, which is the essence of mind, is an entirely different type of reality from all modes of material energy or organic imagery. Therefore, to change matter into mind would only be possible by God's *supernatural* power, for it would be equivalent to transubstantiation.

Partial truth does not include the ultimate reason of being, whether finite or infinite, as it is subsequent to, and dependent upon, the previous actual existence of the universe. Yet the fact that being is known by us to be partially intelligible implies that being is perfectly intelligible to some mind which is greater than our own. Perfect intelligibility, or the ultimate explanation or reason of being, must be identical in act with the being in whose mind that explanation is present, for a mere explanation *in* a mind is not, as such, an explanation of that mind. Hence in subsistent Deity intelligibility and being are one reality. In other words, if relative truth is valid, its validity depends upon absolute truth, and what is absolute excludes all dependence, even the dependence of subject upon object.

The meaning of Truth and intelligibility thus reveal the presence of a being whose nature is to be perfectly intelligible in itself ; that is to say, a being of which spirituality is the very essence. God, therefore, being subsistent, is self-existent Reason and Meaning. Perfect and infinite in every respect, he is not limited to the lesser qualities of being, but involves all in a transcendent life of spiritual meaning and eternal value.

### §X: DIVINE VOLITION

VOLITION is spiritual will whereby value is appreciated and loved. *Value and* It is devotion to being under the aspect of goodness, the counterpart *spiritual will* of the same consciousness wherein the meaning of being is understood. Volition and intelligence are the complementary activities distinctive of personality and self-realisation.

Thus the principles of explanation already employed in the *Perfect will* section on Intelligence are applicable generally to the immanence, *in God* completeness, and independence of spiritual volition. Likewise those facts of nature which reveal intelligence in the Divine Cause imply also the presence of his perfect will : (*a*) in the institution of the orderly system of nature whereby the components mutually contribute to the common purpose of all ; (*b*) in the gift to finite man of a nature inherently tending to goodness ; and (*c*) in the fact that partial values are real only as implications of absolute Value in the ultimate being upon which all depend, just as partial truth depends upon absolute truth for its final validity.

From such considerations we know that supreme volition is enshrined within the very life of the three Persons who are one Spirit, so that Deity is its own purpose of subsistent value, its own personal appreciation in supreme mutual love.

In human volition there are two forms, namely, desire and delight. *Divine voli-* Desire is the imperfect or unfulfilled state of will, wherein is sought *tion supreme* that which is beneficial and advantageous. Delight is the superior *delight* state of will realised and fulfilled in the actual possession or attainment of its object. Divine Volition, however, involves no imperfection, and is therefore supreme delight, the significance of which we can only contemplate by analogy. Lacking nothing and possessing all, the triune perfection knows no desire. Divine volition is perfect because will and object are one in the fullest realisation of subsistent life. The intrinsic might of triune sanctity embraces within itself an infinite appreciation of perfect being. God loves all being by being All, not by composition but by very excellence of reality, truth, and value.

*Divine sanctity*

In this identification of will with perfect being consists God's merit and goodness, both relative and absolute. God *is* sanctity in virtue of his immanent love of the most sacred perfection of his own nature as manifested in the triune life and in its benevolence to creatures. " He that is mighty hath done great things to me, and holy is his name." [1] In itself the Divine will thus possesses its infinitely adequate object, for love and being are identified.

*Divine self-love*

The complaisance of power whereby God loves himself supremely is according to the very meaning of ultimate and subsistent being. There can be no error or disproportion in God's eternal activity. Therefore, in Deity, self-love is necessarily infinite. It is impossible that it should be otherwise. God's will is naturally identified with the perfection of his being. There is no selfishness in the Blessed Trinity, for selfishness is an inordinate self-aggrandisement which despises others and unjustly withholds from them their rights and esteem. Self-seeking in men or angels is doubly false in that it imputes undue importance to oneself whilst undervaluing God and one's neighbour. But proportionate self-love in all is both necessary and praiseworthy, and the absence of self-esteem would be incongruous and unnatural. God's gift of being to creatures is liberality, the opposite of selfishness, and shows that his self-love embraces all things. The reason of love is the goodness involved in rational beings, as well as, secondarily, their value to ourselves, and the Divine Exemplar of being is honoured in all respect shown to finite perfections. True love for the lesser good can therefore only exist as involved in devotion to the highest Good.

*God's love of creatures*

The partial revelation of the mystery of the Blessed Trinity helps us to appreciate the meaning of eternal love. God's love is necessary and changeless, yet voluntary and free. It is the exemplary originating source of all affection, fervour, enthusiasm, and worship in his creatures. In the mutual self-realisation of the three Persons is embraced the Divine love of creatures : as expressed in the words of the natural Son of God : " I in them, and thou (Father) in me : that they may be made perfect in one ; and the world may know that thou hast sent me, and hast loved them as thou also hast loved me." [2]

*The problem of evil*

In Deity there is the highest recognition of human and angelic worth. It may be that this will not be evident to the whole universe

---

[1] Our Lady's words in the *Magnificat* (Luke i 49).
[2] John xvii 23.

until the era of judgement, but meanwhile, with that faith which is appropriate to our state, there can be no real doubt of the Divine concern for creatural benefit. Suffering, calamity, bereavement in peace and war : these are the obscurities attending the overture of immortality. " The sufferings of this present life are not worthy to be compared with the glory to come." [1] Exemption from pain is not the ideal of happiness or the emblem of success. Pain and death are natural to sensitive human and animal nature, and the body can only be rendered immune from them by a preternatural gift which no man can claim as a right. Death and its attendant distresses are an appropriate tribute to the eternal sanctity in view of the sin of the race. In that mystery of sacrifice lies the means of redemption, and the more innocent the sufferer the greater benefaction he brings to mankind. " Bear ye one another's burdens, and so fulfil the law of Christ." [2] Thus can be paid the debt of temporal punishment for corporate transgression.

The " problem " of evil is the problem of angelic and human selfishness, and the " origin " of evil is nothing else than the origin of pride. God constitutes free creatures in being and co-operates with their actions. Guilt lies in just that deliberate relation of acts to motives in which the distinct activity of men and angels consists. Evil is a relation of disproportion within the creature's volition, for which he alone is responsible.[3]

Pain, death, and other physical calamities are called " evil " only by analogy. In themselves they are appropriate in the circumstances, and God is their primary author. God is said to cause physical evil in the sense that he creates things which are good in themselves, and yet incidentally capable of causing harm to others. " Good things and evil, life and death, poverty and riches, are from God. Wisdom and discipline, and knowledge of the law are with God. Love and the ways of good things are with him." [4] Hereby the sacred writer precludes the error of those who suppose two primitive principles, good and evil.

The will of God is a will to holiness, not to the mere prosperity *God's will* of man. That saving will is shown by the gift of sufficient grace *and the free* to all, along with the gift of freedom. God's will is absolute, using *acts of* no means, but directly willing all events in the one infinitude of *creatures* power which is essential holiness.[5] Nothing can resist that will. Man's being and destiny are willed as one in God's timeless volition,

---

[1] Rom. viii 18.  [2] Gal. vi 2.
[3] Our difficulty in understanding God's co-operation with his creatures' activities is due to our inability to form a positive conception of action which is creative.
[4] Ecclus. xi 14-15.
[5] Terms such as " overruling," " tolerating," " overlooking," and " anger," and equivalent phrases, are but metaphors, contrasting with opposing wickedness the divine activity of which we have only analogical knowledge.

and what we call predestination and reprobation are but aspects to our minds of that total productivity of creation in regard to responsible creatures. God created man's being as possessed of certain powers and the ability to act freely. God's concurrence with man's deliberate acts does not diminish their freedom but maintains it. Man's purpose is the fulfilment of the Divine purpose in the manifestation of Divine power and sanctity. "We can do nothing against the truth, but for the truth," [1] and all human acts inevitably fulfil that purpose. Thus "in the name of Jesus every knee should bow, of those that are in heaven, on earth, and under the earth : and every tongue should confess that the Lord Jesus Christ is in the glory of God the Father." [2]

*The reason of creation*    Creation thus expresses God's delight in the sanctity of his own Deity, as including his imitability on creatural planes. God who is Being in the highest degree is himself the sole principle and reason of all lesser modes of being. Composite natures have not of themselves the reason of their being ; their very possibility arises from the fact that they are known and purposed by God in imitation of his own perfection. Their type of being is such that they could not exist unless they were created. They are by nature dependent ; that expresses both their frailty and their charm.

Being subsistent and infinitely perfect, God has no need of creatures, nor can they add to his beatitude or involve change in his activity. Whatever is related to his eternal life is related to the indivisible whole of that eternity. To be Creator is God's eternal state, though finite creatures are naturally of limited duration, and are thus conditioned by time. Eternally Creator, he knows and wills all always. The production of creatures is not a subsequent fulfilment of an antecedent "desire," but has place in the eternal realisation of his omnipotent life.

By creating the universe God therefore acquired no additional glory, but manifested it to rational beings who, in Christ the universal King, are the central feature of that creation. To finite minds that manifestation is known in time, while to God himself it is known and possessed in his eternity. God is his own purpose. His own excellence, self-manifested and made known to creatures, is the complete object of his infinite volition. His glory is no other than his own intrinsic perfection, and this is the motive of his works.

God's ultimate reason in creating the finite is thus identical with his very being. He is the Alpha and the Omega. The purposive or "Final Cause" of creatures is therefore God himself.

In considering the ultimate reason why God created the world we must distinguish the two very different meanings of the word creation. The term "creation" is used to denote : (1) the Divine activity as creative, and (2) the finite universe as the product of creation. The

---

[1] 2 Cor. xiii 8.        [2] Phil. ii 10-11.

reason of the omnipotent act itself is one with God's essential delight in his perfection and power as possessing that exemplary excellence whereby all else must depend creatively upon himself. The sufficient reason of the creative act as such is thus totally immanent to the Divine Cause. But the finite universe, considered in itself as the product of omnipotence, contributes nothing to the Divine reason or motive in creating. Finite things cannot contain within themselves the ultimate reason of their nature or existence. They are not purposed for their own sakes, but because they represent the glorious nature of their triune Maker.

It follows that Deity is under no obligation to create finite entities, and is perfectly free in conceiving their possibility no less than in giving them actual existence. Even the human will cannot be compelled to act by a finite object, still less the Divine.

Creation, then, has its complete and eternal reason in the Divine Perfection which is the Glory of God, and the manifestation of God in the universe is evidence of the freedom of Divine love. During the present preparatory stage of our existence that glory of God is seen but indistinctly. The fuller manifestation of the glory of the Blessed Trinity and the meaning of creation is attainable only in that experience which makes heaven what it is, namely, the supernatural intuitive vision of the perfection of Deity.

## §XI: ADORATION

To give honour where honour is due is a dictate of our very nature. Where there is excellence of being or goodness or knowledge or power, there reverence is accorded inevitably.

Because of his ineffable value and our complete dependence upon him, God merits our deepest adoration. Humanity has ever borne testimony to the Supreme Ruler. Magic and sceptical anti-intellectualism may always be present as outgrowths upon human religion, but mankind *is* what it has been, and thus the race can never lose its sense of responsibility to its God. Religion is connatural to us. It is not only a mode of consciousness. It is a physical state of man's dependent being. It is, further, the response of man's complete personality to the ultimate facts as known to us. The knowledge of God is humanity's greatest boast, and a lowly worship, both private and public, is consequently man's pre-eminent vocation. This natural tendency to worship God is itself a proof that such is the will of him who conceived our being, and constituted it so that it should recognise him as its Alpha and Omega, its efficient, exemplary, and final Cause.

The propriety of interior and exterior worship is still further enforced by the revelation of Christ, which at once clarifies our natural knowledge and brings further insight as to the status of man in the Divine purpose. " God is a spirit, and they that adore him must adore him in spirit and in truth."[1] Our Lord, who spoke these words, himself embodies the supreme example of that spiritual worship. The filial spirit of harmony with the divine will, recognition of God in all creation, gratitude, prayer, praise, adoration, especially the adoration of sacrifice, pervaded our Lord's every intention in joy and sorrow. The subjective element of personal preference and advantage was entirely subject to the objective element in his devotion to the Blessed Trinity. The sublime transcendence of God, which added so much grandeur to the Divine condescension, was the central theme of his life and teaching. So it must ever be.

It is inappropriate to regard God primarily under the aspect of his beneficence to his creatures. Gratitude for existence and for every privilege there must indeed be, but that element must be subordinate to the still higher recognition of all that Deity is in itself. Things are what they are because God is what he is, and this order must ever be observed. Even self-regarding prayer has its proper motive in adoration of God as subsistent reason, value, and sanctity. Praise to the holiest contains no element of flattery, but its absence would be an unnatural affectation.

God must be recognised, we cannot avoid it. It is vain to strive after an artificial indifference in a matter that is so intimate to our whole being. Vain likewise, and idolatrous, would be any attempt to deflect our admiration from its true object by imputing to humanity or to nature and its tendencies the attributes which are proper to Deity alone. Human worship of God is no such Narcissism, or worship of ourselves as reflected in our own conceptions. We contemplate God as objectively as we do the material world of which our ideas are similarly analogical.

We are fully conscious that the reality of the Blessed Trinity is inexpressibly more wondrous than our ideas are capable of representing. Whereas we need to restrict the meaning of our concepts when applying them to finite persons and things, the whole range of our ideas finds exhaustive applicability in regard to Deity, the subsistent fulness of all that man admires and enjoys in finite nature.

A. L. REYS.

[1] John iv 24.

# IV

# THE BLESSED TRINITY

## §I: THE DOGMA OF THE TRINITY

By the Blessed Trinity we mean the mystery of one God in three *General* persons, the Father, the Son, and the Holy Ghost, each subsisting *notions* distinct in the same identical divine nature.

It will be well if, at the outset of our study of this fundamental dogma of the Christian religion, we acquire precise and clear-cut ideas as to the exact significance of such terms as nature and person, since they must needs occur frequently in any treatise on the Trinity.

They are words which we employ commonly enough in ordinary conversation, and in writing in a loose literary way, without adverting to their more precise philosophical and theological connotations. Both words are of ancient lineage and have played no mean part in the history of dogma. For centuries they were the watchwords, the touchstones of orthodoxy, during the great controversies which distracted the early Church as to the divinity and humanity of Christ. In the welter of theological argument, ambiguities were gradually removed, and in course of time the meaning of these two words gradually crystallised into definite technical form.

The word nature, derived from the Latin *natum*,[1] means literally *Nature* that which is born, or that which is produced. We use the term nature, in its widest sense, to indicate everything that has been produced, the totality of finite things, the whole created universe which in its various parts furnishes the objects of what are called the natural sciences. These objects, the earth, the sea, the animals, the stars, differ very considerably : each, we say, has its own nature. And so by an easy transition from its etymological significance, we arrive at the philosophical meaning of the term nature as that which makes a thing what it is ; in other words, the essence, or quiddity of the thing.

" Nature, properly so called," says Aristotle, " is the essence of beings, which have in themselves and by themselves the principle of their movement." [2] The nature of any being, then, is simply its essence considered from the dynamic standpoint, that is, precisely as the principle of its peculiar activities. It is the nature of a fish to swim, of a bird to fly, of a reptile to crawl ; and it is by observing their characteristic operations, their native activities, that we are able to classify things according to their natures.

---

[1] *Nasci*, to be born.  　　　　[2] *Met.*, lib. v, c. 4.

*Person*

The word person is derived from the Latin *persona,* which originally meant the mask worn by ancient Greek and Roman actors on the stage. These tragic and comic masks were so constructed as to magnify the voice which sounded through (*per sonare*) the spacious cavity in front of the actor's mouth. That through which the voice sounded, the mask, was naturally called *persona.*

The term was then transferred from the mask to the actor who wore it as he portrayed some god or other mighty potentate. Next, it came to be applied to any assumed character of distinction, and finally to any human being as a name of dignity. For, it will be noted, person is primarily a name of honour, indicating rank and importance ; and consequently, in philosophical usage, it came to be applied exclusively to the highest grade of the things which exist in nature, namely, substances endowed with rationality. Accordingly, in the fifth century, Boethius defined *persona* as " *rationalis naturæ individua substantia,*" *i.e.,* " an individual substance of a rational nature." St Thomas Aquinas, Leibnitz, Kant, and others have made valuable contributions to the study of personality, but the classical definition of Boethius remains substantially unchanged and unchallenged.

Hence the requisite qualifications for personality are :

1. In the first place, *subsistence* or substantiality ; a person is first and foremost a substance, that is, something which exists in itself, something which subsists, as for instance an apple, and not something which merely inheres in something else, like the colour of the apple.

2. In the second place, the substance must be *distinct,* that is, it must have complete individuality, so that it is not in any sense part of, or common to, something else. Consequently neither the human body nor the human soul, separately, is a person.

3. And, finally, this distinct substance must be of a *rational nature.* We cannot, therefore, predicate personality of dogs or horses, however clever they may be, and still less can we predicate it of lower forms of life, or of inanimate objects. By a person, then, we mean a distinct substance endowed with the faculty of reason.

*A mystery*

We speak of the *mystery* of the Blessed Trinity, because clearly we are stating a truth which is above or beyond reason, when we say that in the same divine nature there are three distinct persons. As far as our experience goes, wherever we have a plurality of persons, we have also a plurality of individual natures. Apart from revelation we should never even have conceived the possibility of such a thing as absolute identity of nature in three distinct persons.

The Council of the Vatican has declared that the deposit of revealed truth contains some mysteries which can neither be understood nor demonstrated by reason, and in the whole ambit of divine revelation there is nothing more profound than the doctrine of the Trinity. Here, then, if anywhere, we have a truth above reason. It is beyond the wit of mortal man to fathom it, to sound its depths and

shoals, for " no one knoweth the Son but the Father : neither doth
anyone know the Father but the Son, and he to whom it shall please
the Son to reveal him." [1] Nevertheless, with St Athanasius, St
Augustine, and St Thomas Aquinas, we contend that the doctrine
of the Trinity is not against reason, and, furthermore, that we can
establish to the full the rationality of the obedience of the faith which
accepts this great mystery.

To say that unaided human reason could never have excogitated
the doctrine of the Trinity is not to say that the doctrine is incomprehensible or evidently repugnant to reason. The fact being made
known to us by revelation that there are three persons in one God,
reason, as we shall see, is well able to dispose of the objections which
reason can bring. Truth is not at war with itself, and consequently
reason and revelation play perfectly harmonious parts in the service
of Eternal Truth.

From the very beginning the doctrine of the Trinity was in the *The Catholic*
forefront of Christian teaching. It is enshrined in the final com- *doctrine*
mission of our Blessed Saviour to his Apostles : " going therefore
teach all nations . . . baptising them in the name of the Father and
of the Son and of the Holy Ghost " [2] ; and, as we shall see, it is
taught explicitly in many passages of the New Testament. In fact
the germ of the Apostles' Creed would seem to be the statement of
the doctrine of the Trinity set forth by St Irenaeus in the second
century in the following formula : " I believe in one God the Father
Almighty, who made the heaven, the earth and the sea, and all things
contained therein ; and in Jesus Christ the Son of God, who became
incarnate for our salvation ; and in the Holy Ghost, who through the
prophets preached the dispositions of God." [3]

Now the preaching of this new doctrine, affecting as it did the
vital concept of God, not unnaturally led to considerable confusion
of thought amongst some of the early converts to Christianity, who
brought with them into the Church preconceived notions with regard
to the Deity.

No less than three distinct influences are discernible, distorting *Errors*
the doctrine of the Trinity, each in a different way. First of all,
there was the Jewish influence, stressing monotheism as opposed to
the polytheism of the pagans ; then there were the Platonists with
their ingrained tendency to multiply divinities ; and, finally, rationalism was represented by the Gnostics whose general preoccupation
was to harmonise the Christian religion with current philosophical
speculation.

1. The Jewish influence made itself felt in the heresy of the
Sabellians who, through over-emphasising the unity of the Godhead
against the Platonists, ended by making the three divine persons mere

---

[1] Matt. xi 27.　　[2] Matt. xxviii 19.　　[3] *Adversus haereses*, I, x, 1.

modes or manifestations of the divinity. They seem to have taken the word person in its original sense of mask or character, and to have conceived the Trinity as an outward manifestation of the threefold character of God as creator, as redeemer, and as sanctifier. Obviously, here, there is merely a trinity of concepts and not of persons.

2. Many of the Platonists went to the other extreme, and multiplied not only the divine persons, but also the divine nature itself, so as to afford a real basis for the charge of polytheism levelled at them by the Sabellians.

3. The Gnostic influence favoured Arianism and other forms of Subordinationism, which made the second and third persons of the Trinity subordinate, or inferior, to the Father, and consequently in reality made the Son and the Holy Ghost emanations, as it were, outside the divine nature altogether, and therefore in essence creatures.

All these different forms of error were condemned in the celebrated dogmatic letter which Pope Dionysius (A.D. 259-269) addressed to Denis, Bishop of Alexandria. In this epistle are formulated the principles which later governed the decisions of the Council of Nicaea (A.D. 325) in defining the divinity of the Son, and the Council of Constantinople (A.D. 381) in defining the divinity of the Holy Ghost.

*The Athanasian Creed*  The whole doctrine of the Trinity is summarised in the Athanasian Creed. This creed, though not the work of St Athanasius, is admittedly not of later date than the first half of the fifth century, since it contains no echoes whatsoever either of the Council of Ephesus (A.D. 431) or of the Council of Chalcedon (A.D. 451). It solemnly proclaims : " Now the Catholic Faith is this : that we worship one God in Trinity, and Trinity in unity." Then follows a detailed exposition of the precise meaning and theological implications of this fundamental formula, embodying the majestic declaration : " the Father is God, the Son is God, and the Holy Ghost is God ; and yet there are not three Gods, but one God." The symbol ends in the uncompromising spirit of the great Athanasius whose name it bears : " This is the Catholic Faith, which, except a man believe faithfully and steadfastly, he cannot be saved."

§ II: THE TRINITY IN SCRIPTURE

I

*In the Old Testament*  IT was the peculiar glory of the Jews, as God's own chosen people, to have preserved upon the earth, amidst the welter of surrounding polytheism, the worship of the one true God. As a nation, the Jews never wavered in their belief that there was but one God, Jehovah ; and consequently the idea of a trinity of divine persons would be alien to their natural mental outlook.

The mystery of the Blessed Trinity was not formally revealed in the Old Testament, but in accordance with what St Bonaventure calls " the general law of preparation," this distinctively Christian doctrine is foreshadowed on many pages of the Old Testament. For it appears to be God's way not to allow the fulness of revealed truth to break upon the world suddenly. There is a long period of adaptation, as it were, during which the way is prepared gradually for the final revelation. Thus, the Fathers declare the Paschal Lamb to be the type, the symbol, the figure of the Divine Victim by whose blood we have been redeemed. They see in the initiation rite of circumcision an adumbration of the sacrament of baptism, and in the manna a foreshadowing of the true bread of life in the Holy Eucharist. In the same way there are assuredly indications in the Old Testament of the stupendous revelation which was to come in the New Testament as to the inner fecundity of the Divine Life itself.

Thus St Augustine detects the implication of a plurality of divine persons in such utterances on the part of God as " Let us make man to our image and likeness," [1] " Behold Adam is become as one of us," [2] " Let us go down, and there confound their tongue "[3]; wherein other commentators see only the plural of majesty. The triple *Sanctus* of Isaias, " Holy, holy, holy, the Lord God of hosts," [4] and the triple blessing recorded in Numbers,[5] have also been pointed out as heralding the sublime mystery of the Trinity in Unity.

Again, the theophanies, or manifestations of God in the Old Testament, in which an angel of the Lord appeared to one or other of the patriarchs, were interpreted by all the Fathers prior to St Augustine as manifestations of the second person of the Trinity in the form of an angel. St Augustine takes exception to this view on the ground that God is incorporeal and therefore invisible to the human eye, but nevertheless he holds that the angel represents God. The most notable of these apparitions is that which was vouchsafed to Abraham in the valley of Mambre : " And when he had lifted up his eyes, there appeared to him three men standing near him : and as soon as he saw them he ran to meet them from the door of his tent, and adored down to the ground." [6] St Augustine, St Ambrose, St Hilary, and the Fathers generally, interpret this incident as a veiled manifestation of the mystery of the Trinity ; and this patristic exegesis receives corroboration from the Roman Breviary which, in the response to the second reading from the Scripture occurring for Quinquagesima Sunday, setting forth the above-cited passage of Genesis, says of Abraham : " he saw three and adored one."

From the time of Daniel onwards there are clearer references to the second and third persons of the Trinity in the not infrequent personifications of the Word, Wisdom, or the Spirit. Thus we read, " By the word of the Lord the heavens were established ; and all the power of them by the spirit of his mouth." [7] And again, " I have not spoken in secret from the beginning : from the time

[1] Gen. i 26.     [2] Gen. iii 22.     [3] Gen. xi 7.     [4] vi 3.
[5] vi 24-26.     [6] Gen. xviii 2.     [7] Psalm xxxii 6.

before it was done, I was there, and now the Lord God hath sent me, and his spirit." [1]  In the sapiential books, Wisdom is constantly hypostatised and speaks as a Divine Person ; as, for instance, in Ecclesiasticus : " I came out of the mouth of the Most High, the firstborn before all creatures." [2]

Naturally the second person of the Trinity has a peculiar prominence in the Old Testament owing to the number of prophetic passages which predicate divine attributes of the coming Messias. Thus, " The Lord hath said to me : Thou art my son, this day have I begotten thee " [3] ; " and I will make him my firstborn, high above the kings of the earth . . . and his throne as the days of heaven." [4] In fact many of these passages in the Old Testament are explicitly applied to Christ in the New Testament.[5]

However, the doctrine of the Blessed Trinity is certainly not revealed in the Old Testament, which at best, in accordance with the general plan of the divine economy, merely foreshadows " the revelation of the mystery which was kept secret from eternity, which now is made manifest by the Scriptures, according to the precept of the eternal God, for the obedience of faith, known among all nations." [6]

### 2

*In the New Testament*  Whereas at best the doctrine of the Blessed Trinity is only dimly foreshadowed in the Old Testament, in the New Testament it shines forth with unmistakable clearness, lighting up many difficult passages with regard to the Incarnation, the redemptive work of Christ, the mission of the Holy Spirit, the operations of grace, and the infinite perfection of God.

Lest we lose ourselves in the maze of material at our disposal, it will be well, perhaps, if we set forth, first of all, the chief texts which treat of all three persons of the Trinity taken together, and then consider briefly the more important texts concerning the different persons of the Trinity taken separately.

#### A. THE DIVINE PERSONS CONSIDERED COLLECTIVELY

#### (i) *In the Gospels*

We shall consider, first of all, passages from the Gospels, and then from the Epistles.  In the gospels all three divine persons are mentioned in an emphatic way on four momentous occasions.

*At the Annunciation*  At the Annunciation the angel Gabriel declared unto Mary, " The Holy Ghost shall come upon thee, and the power of the Most

---

[1] Isaias xlviii 16.  [2] xxiv 5.  [3] Psalm ii 7.  [4] Psalm lxxxviii 28-30.
[5] Compare, for instance, Ps. ii 7 with Heb. i 5 ; Isaias vii 14, with Matt. i 23 ; Isaias xl 3-11 with Mark i 3 ; Zacharias xii 10 with John xix 37.
[6] Rom. xvi 25, 26.

High shall overshadow thee, and therefore also the Holy which shall be born of thee shall be called the Son of God." [1] Here, clearly, we have an unmistakable distinction of subsisting individuals. That the "Most High" refers to God the Father is obvious from a comparison with verse 32, where we read of the Son, "He shall be great, and shall be called the Son of the Most High." Now the Father is necessarily distinct from his own Son, and from the Holy Ghost, who is carrying out the work of the Most High. So, too, the Son and the Holy Ghost are really distinct from each other, since, as will be shown, the latter proceeds from the former.

Furthermore, each of the three persons, the Father, the Son, and the Holy Ghost, subsists in a rational nature, namely, the divine nature itself. That this divine nature is common to all three persons is seen from a cursory consideration of the text. The divinity of the Father, "the Most High," is beyond question : as to the second person of the Trinity, the term "Son of God" is here used in its strictly literal sense to express true, real, sonship in such a way that the Son is of the same divine nature as the Father : the divinity of the Holy Ghost is revealed both in the miraculous work which he performs, and in the fact that he is described as "the power of the Most High," in the same manner that Christ is said to be "the Son of the Most High."

In this text, then, we have set before us both the reality of the distinction between the three subsisting individuals, the Father, the Son, and the Holy Ghost, and also their real community in the divine nature. In other words, we see that there are three divine persons.

Again we have a striking manifestation of the Trinity of divine persons at the baptism of Christ in the Jordan by John the Baptist, *At the baptism of Christ* as recorded in St Matthew's Gospel, where it is written : "And Jesus being baptised, forthwith came out of the water : and lo, the heavens were opened to him : and he saw the Spirit of God descending as a dove, and coming upon him. And behold a voice from heaven, saying : This is my beloved Son, in whom I am well pleased." [2] We have here an external manifestation of the three persons as distinct. The Father speaks from the heavens, the Son rises up out of the water, and the Holy Spirit appears in the form of a dove. Here at least, it would seem, that all possibility of "confounding the persons" is precluded.

In this solemn incident at the beginning of our Blessed Saviour's public ministry we have more than a mere hint or inkling as to the community of the divine nature in all three persons. We cannot reasonably doubt that the "Spirit of God" is consubstantial with the Father, "the glory equal, the majesty co-eternal." As to the divinity of the Son who, it has been objected, in this incident occupies a subordinate rôle, especially in that he has been baptised by John,

[1] Luke i 35.  [2] iii 16, 17.

it has been pointed out by many Scripture commentators that the full force of the words spoken from heaven is somewhat weakened in our English translations, which ignore the significance of the definite article before the word Son, in the Greek original. What the voice proclaimed was : " This is *the* Son *par excellence*, mine, the beloved, in whom I am well pleased " ; in other words, we have here a proclamation of the divinity of the Son, of his consubstantiality with the Father.

*After the Last Supper* When our Blessed Saviour was taking leave of his disciples after the Last Supper, he said to them : " I will ask the Father, and he shall give you another Paraclete, that he may abide with you for ever, the Spirit of truth whom the world cannot receive. . . ." [1] In this passage the real distinction of persons is evident. No person asks himself for anything, nor does a person ever send himself on a mission. The language used by Christ on this august occasion is at once unintelligible and unjustifiable unless the three divine persons are really distinct. Our Blessed Saviour asks for *another* Paraclete. The word paraclete means literally " one who is called in beside " to assist in some way. It has been variously translated as counsellor, consoler, comforter, advocate, guide, friend ; but the word is so rich in meaning that it would need a sentence at least to plumb its depths. Christ himself gives us the key to its expansive meaning when he speaks of *another* Paraclete. He himself had been a Paraclete to the disciples. He is about to leave them. He asks the Father to send someone to take his place, to discharge his divine office, to be another Paraclete. If the divinity of Christ is once admitted, it is impossible to deny the divinity of the Spirit of Truth who was to be another Paraclete.

*In the divine commission* Both the distinction of persons and the unity of the divine nature are emphasised in the well-known passage of St Matthew's Gospel in which Christ's final commission to his Apostles is recorded : " Going, therefore, teach ye all nations ; baptising them in the name of the Father, and of the Son, and of the Holy Ghost." [2]

The three distinct names, Father, Son, and Holy Ghost, in accordance with common usage, indicate three distinct persons, that is, three subsisting beings of a rational nature each complete in its own individuality in such a way as to preclude the possibility of any identification or confusion of one with another. The distinction of persons is stressed in the Greek by the presence of the definite article before each name, *the* Father, *the* Son, *the* Holy Ghost ; it would be contrary to Greek usage thus to repeat the definite article before mere attributes of one and the same subject.

The divinity of each of the three persons is equally clear. For he in whose name baptism unto the remission of sins is administered must needs be God, and this baptism is to be administered in the name of the Father, and of the Son, and of the Holy Ghost. The

[1] John xiv 16.  [2] Matt. xxviii 19.

Vulgate reading *in nomine*, which we translate " in the name of," indicates the one by whose power or authority the sacrament is administered ; whilst a literal rendering of the Greek words would be " unto the name of," indicating rather, as Franzelin has pointed out, the one to whose honour and worship the recipient of the sacrament is consecrated.   In either case divinity is clearly implied, divinity undivided, and possessed equally by all three persons.   This interpretation is confirmed by a comparison of the text before us with 1 Cor. i 13 where St Paul indignantly asks the Corinthians, "were you baptised in the name of Paul ? "   Here both the Latin and the Greek expressions for " in the name of " are the same as in St Matthew's text, and St Paul's meaning is abundantly clear, namely, " Is Paul the author of your baptism ? "   It is as though he said to them, " Why extol me, or Peter, or Apollo, or any mere mortal as the source of grace ? "   In other words, " Is Paul *God?* "

### (ii) *In the Epistles*

As in the Gospels, so in the Epistles, there are four classical passages having reference to the persons of the Trinity considered collectively.

The most famous of these is the Johannine Comma [1] : " And there are three who give testimony in heaven, the Father, the Word, and the Holy Ghost.   And these three are one."   That this passage *The heavenly witnesses text* sets forth the true Catholic doctrine, and that it is in perfect harmony with the teaching of St John's Gospel, there can be no doubt.

Nevertheless this statement as to the " Heavenly Witnesses " has been the subject of considerable controversy.   The text itself comprises two verses of the First Epistle of St John.[2]   The undisputed text reads :  " For there are three who give testimony."   Then follow the disputed words :  " in heaven, the Father, the Word, and the Holy Ghost : and these three are one.   And there are three that give testimony on earth."   And then, again, we have the undisputed text :  " the Spirit and the water and the blood : and these three are one."   It will be observed that the undisputed words make sense in themselves if the disputed be omitted.   Westcott and Hort, in their important edition of the New Testament text, state in the note on this passage that " there is no evidence for the inserted words in Greek, or in any language but Latin, before the fourteenth century " ; and also that " the words first occur at earliest in the latter part of the fifth century," that is, in Latin.   This summary may be said to express the general view of the evidence, though there are not wanting scholars who trace the passage into earlier times, even to Tertullian at the end of the second century A.D.   In any case it is evident that the textual case against the " Comma " is a strong one ; no Greek manuscript of any consequence, for example, contains it.

[1] 1 John v 7.    [2] 1 John v 7-8.

Something of a sensation was therefore caused when a decree of the Holy Office appeared under date of January 13th, 1897, replying in the negative to the question "whether it can safely be denied, or at least be called in question," that the disputed text is "authentic." An official explanation, however, was then given ·privately, and has lately been published officially in the *Enchiridion Biblicum* issued under the authority of the Biblical Commission [1] to the effect that this was not intended "to prevent Catholic writers from investigating the matter more fully, and after weighing the arguments on both sides . . . from inclining to the view unfavourable to the genuineness of the passage, provided they profess themselves ready to stand by the judgement of the Church. . . ." Thus we may conclude that the evidence is strong against the passage, but that the Holy See reserves to itself the ultimate decision in a matter which obviously falls within its competence.[2]

*The teaching of St Paul*

St Paul's own teaching with regard to the Blessed Trinity is unequivocal, notwithstanding the rationalist contention that he makes of Christ only a celestial man, a being removed by many degrees from divinity. Writing to the Corinthians, St Paul says: "Wherefore I give you to understand that no man, speaking by the Spirit of God, saith Anathema to Jesus. And no man can say the Lord Jesus, but by the Holy Ghost. Now there are diversities of graces, but the same Spirit; and there are diversities of ministries, but the same Lord; and there are diversities of operations, but the same God, who worketh all in all." [3] In the first sentence we have a clear statement of the equality of the Lord Jesus and the Holy Ghost, and then follows what has been described as at least an insinuation of the doctrine of the Trinity in Godhead, since diversities of graces are ascribed to the same Spirit (the Holy Ghost); diversities of ministries to the same Lord (Christ Jesus); and diversities of operations to the same God who worketh all in all (the Father). All these operations are divine, but by appropriation they are attributed to the different persons of the Trinity according to that peculiar fittingness which led the writers of Holy Writ, in treating of divine operations, to assign external works of power to the Father, external acts of love to the Son, and external works of sanctification to the Holy Spirit. In this particular text, it will be noticed, the three persons are mentioned in reverse order, and this, according to some commentators, with a view to emphasising their absolute equality.

*The Trinitarian invocation*

No one can fail to see the implications of St Paul's direct invocation of the three persons of the Trinity in the final verse of his Second Epistle to the Corinthians: "the grace of our Lord Jesus

[1] Rome, 1927 : pp. 46-47.
[2] The Council of Trent declared the traditional Vulgate "authentic" (Session iv) in a context which shows the meaning of "authentic" to be primarily "official". It is not declared authentic in the purely *critical* sense.  [3] 1 Cor. xii 3-6.

Christ, and the charity of God, and the communication of the Holy
Ghost be with you all.  Amen."

In precisely the same manner does St Peter pen the first words *The*
of his First Epistle : " Peter, an apostle of Jesus Christ, to the *apostolic salutation*
strangers dispersed . . . according to the foreknowledge of God
the Father, unto the sanctification of the Spirit, unto obedience and
sprinkling of the blood of Jesus Christ. . . ."

In the Epistles, then, as in the Gospels, the Holy and Undivided
Trinity is shown forth both in the bewildering multiplicity of operations outside the divine essence and in the ineffable intercommunion
of the divine persons in that inner life which is from eternity unto
eternity.

### B. THE DIVINE PERSONS CONSIDERED SEPARATELY

We are now in a position to consider the divine persons separately,
that is, in their individual and distinctive relationships towards each
other.  The fact of the distinct relationships and of the common
nature of the three persons is abundantly clear from the manner
in which each of the three is spoken of in Holy Writ.  It would
be tedious and superfluous to give an exhaustive list of all the
texts in the New Testament which treat of the divine personality
of one or other of the three persons.  We shall therefore content
ourselves with making mention only of the more celebrated texts
with regard to each of the persons.

Whereas ancient heresies assailed the divine personality of *God the*
the second and third persons of the Blessed Trinity, Modernists have *Father*
in addition attempted to make of God the Father a kind of limited
deity, still in process of evolution, ever blindly striving and groping
to find himself in the universe as in the medium of his self-expression.
Needless to say, such a view finds no warrant in Holy Scripture.  In
the Old Testament, Jehovah is portrayed as the omnipotent sole
creator who rules and governs the world according to his will ;
whilst in the New Testament, he is the first person of the Trinity,
the principle from which all else proceeds, even the Son and the
Holy Spirit from all eternity.  Thus he is set before us not merely
as the Father of all creatures in the metaphorical sense, but as the
Father of our Lord and Saviour, Jesus Christ, in the strictly literal
sense : " Blessed be the God and Father of our Lord Jesus Christ " [1] ;
" the God and Father of our Lord Jesus Christ, who is blessed for
ever " [2] ; " Blessed be the God and Father of our Lord Jesus Christ,
who hath blessed us with spiritual blessings." [3]  That the Father is
also the principle of origin for the procession of the Holy Spirit is
clearly stated by St John : " When the Paraclete cometh, whom I
will send you from the Father, who proceedeth from the Father, he
shall give testimony of me." [4]  How precisely the second and third
persons proceed from the Father we shall consider presently.

[1] 2 Cor. i 3.        [2] 2 Cor. xi 31.        [3] Eph. i 3.        [4] John xv 26.

*God the Son*    The teaching of revelation with regard to the second person of the Blessed Trinity centres in the doctrine of his real and perfect sonship. If he is the real Son of God, then he must be consubstantial with the Father, that is, of the same divine nature as the Father, or, as the Creed has it, " true God of true God." There will be community, in fact identity, of nature. On the other hand, if the sonship is real, so too must be the distinction of personality. Now, that the sonship is real is stated in the New Testament in the most unequivocal manner : " God so loved the world, as to give his only-begotten Son " [1]; " the only-begotten Son who is in the bosom of the Father, he hath declared him." [2] This real sonship of Christ is even contrasted by St John with adoptive sonship, for Christ is " only-begotten," whereas " as many as received him, he gave them power to be made the sons of God." [3]

St Paul, too, stresses the fact that the filiation of Christ is of a different and higher order than that of the adoptive sonship even of the angels. He says that God " in these days hath spoken to us by his Son, whom he hath appointed heir of all things, by whom also he made the world," and who is " the figure of his substance." St Paul then goes on to say that this Son, being made higher than the angels, hath inherited a more excellent name than they, " for to which of the angels hath he said at any time, Thou art my Son, to-day have I begotten thee ? And again, I will be to him a Father, and he shall be to me a Son ? And again, when he bringeth in the first begotten into the world, he saith : And let all the angels of God adore him." [4]

The scriptural language used of Christ is unintelligible unless he is the Son of God in the most literal sense of sonship. It is clear, then, that the second person of the Trinity proceeds from the Father by generation ; by some real process of generation which is from all eternity.

*God the*    That the Holy Spirit is not a mere attribute of God, or some form
*Holy Ghost*  of impersonal divine energy emanating from the Father and the Son, is obvious from the fact that, as we have already seen, baptism is administered in the name of, that is, by the power of, the Holy Ghost, just as much as by the power of the Father and the Son. We have seen that the Holy Spirit is a distinct rational substance, in other words, a distinct person. He is a divine person, since the spiritual regeneration which he bestows in baptism is assuredly a divine gift. Moreover, the special functions attributed to the Holy Spirit in the Scriptures proclaim his Godhead : " The Holy Ghost said to them, Separate me Saul and Barnabas for the work whereunto I have taken them " [5]; " Receive ye the Holy Ghost : whose sins you shall forgive, they are forgiven them " ; [6] " Take heed to yourselves, and to all the flock, over which the Holy Ghost hath placed

---

[1] John iii 16.          [2] John i 18.          [3] John i 12.
[4] Heb. i 1-6.          [5] Acts xiii 2.          [6] John xx 22.

you bishops, to rule the Church of God." [1]   The Holy Spirit, then, is a divine person "who proceedeth from the Father" [2] and from the Son who sends him.

Now just as the name Son indicates a necessary likeness in nature to the Father, so, too, the term " Spirit of God " implies a necessary likeness to the essence of God.   This point is stressed by St Paul in the classical text in which he argues from an analogy with the human cognitive process.   He says :   " For what man knoweth the things of a man, but the spirit of a man that is in him ?   So the things also that are of God no man knoweth, but the Spirit of God." [3] St Paul has just been speaking of certain hidden mysteries, and in answer to the unspoken query as to how he knows these things, he answers that he knows them by the revelation of the Holy Spirit. He then proceeds to explain that just as no one can know a man's secret thoughts except his own spirit or self, so no one can fathom the deep things of God but the Spirit of God, that is, the Holy Ghost, co-essential with God, and possessing the same identical nature.

Now though the Holy Spirit proceeds similar, in fact identical, in nature with the Father, as does the Son, nevertheless the Holy Spirit must proceed by a process different from that by which the Son proceeds.   The second person of the Blessed Trinity is called the *Only*-begotten.   Clearly, then, the Holy Spirit proceeds by a process other than that of generation.

We are now in a position to enquire into the character of the divine processions, and into the fundamental constituents of the distinctive personality of the Father who proceeds from none, of the Son who proceeds from the Father, and of the Holy Spirit who proceeds from both.   But we will do well to approach this sublime study in the spirit of the true humility of learning as voiced by the Psalmist : " Lord, my heart is not exalted, nor are my eyes lofty." [4]

### §III: THE FECUNDITY OF THE DIVINE LIFE

ARISTOTLE reached the highest point of pagan theological speculation *The* when he defined God as " Thought of Thought."   In Aristotle's *Aristotelian* philosophy there is an ever-ascending scale of being ranging from *conception* of God pure passivity to pure activity.   God must necessarily be the supreme activity in which there is no alloy of passivity of any kind whatsoever. Now the highest activity of which we are aware is intellectual activity, the spiritual activity of thought.   God, then, in the Aristotelian theodicy, is pure, unadulterated thought which, on account of its very perfection, can think only of the infinitely perfect, namely, itself. To think of anything lower than itself, according to Aristotle, would be derogatory to the infinite perfection of the pure activity of thought. Hence God is defined as the " Thought of Thought," the Infinite

---

[1] Acts xx 28.      [2] John xv 26.      [3] I Cor. ii 11.      [4] Ps. cxxx 1.

Intelligence wrapt in eternal self-contemplation.  But the God of this philosophy is at best but a pale abstraction subsisting in awe-inspiring isolation.

*The Jewish conception*  On the contrary, when we come to consider the God of the Jews, there is warmth, there is light and shade, there is colour, for this is a personal God who governs the universe by his providence.  He is the God of Abraham, Isaac and Jacob, and the God too of the mortal enemies of the Jews, the Philistines.  He is the omnipotent God of heaven and earth who " made the little and the great, and hath equally care of all." [1]  Above all, the God who is revealed in the Old Testament is a *living* God, a God endowed with the fulness of life, a God whose very essence it is to live, a God who describes himself in the stupendous words, " I am who am." [2]  " He who is," is his distinctive title, for he is the unique being who exists necessarily, whose very existence is his essential characteristic ; but not the remote impersonal colourless existence of the God of Greek philosophy.  Far from it : he is personally nigh to each one of us.  " Let all fear the God of Daniel," says Holy Writ, " for he is the living God." [3]  He is the source, the fount, the teeming principle of all life, sustaining and governing the whole of creation at every moment, the God to whom we must render an account of the life that he has given to us.

*Contrast with Mohammed-anism*  Islam's conception of God is well known, and represents a kind of *via media* between the Greek and the Jewish notions :  " There is no God but God ; and Mohammed is his prophet."  So, too, Christ Jesus was his prophet, and indeed many another, since the *Qur'an* proclaims, " there is no nation but has had its warner."  Nevertheless, the greatest of the prophets and apostles, such as Moses, Christ, and Mohammed, are mere mortals, and the same gates of spiritual advancement that were open to them are open to all mankind.  They are " warners," admonishers, voices calling men always to the contemplation of the sublime unity of the Godhead.  In no sense are these prophets intermediaries between God and his creatures : there are no intermediaries.  However proficient in sanctity these " warners " may be, at best they are but guides.  They do not even reflect the light of divinity, for just as the sun in the heavens is the sole source of light to this planet, so God in his isolation is the sole source of light to the spiritual world. . . . This is indeed a beautiful and arresting piece of imagery, but it must be confessed that the concept of deity which it sets forth is so dazzling that we are intellectually blinded by it.  It is like looking at the sun with the naked eye : we are so dazed by its brilliance that we learn nothing about it.

The plain fact is that Mohammedanism, equally with paganism, though in a different way, failed to realise the true nature of God,

---

[1] Wisdom vi 8.          [2] Exod. iii 14.          [3] Dan. vi 26.

failed to understand that he is the God of life and love, of that life which is supremely active, and of that love which is infinitely diffusive. He is not a god who dwells like a lone star apart, but the God whose pulsating life and illimitable love find expression in the gracious condescension of his self-revelation. It is to one's intimate friends that one reveals the secrets of one's inner life, and consequently it is in the New Testament, with the coming of the Eternal Son of God in the flesh for the love of man, that the veil is drawn aside from the majesty and mystery of the divine life, so that we may catch some glimpse of it as it is in itself, and not merely as it was known hitherto in its outward and visible manifestations.

From revelation it is obvious that the divine life in itself is not solitary either in the Aristotelian or the Mohammedan sense. As we have seen, we are given many inklings of this basic truth in the Old Testament, especially in those passages wherein Wisdom is personified and speaks in accents which are unmistakably divine, as, for instance, in the following : " The Lord possessed me in the beginning of his ways, before he made anything from the beginning. I was set up from eternity, and of old before the earth was made. The depths were not as yet, and I was already conceived. . . ." [1]

But it is from the New Testament that we learn definitely of the *The divine* origins or processions, as they are called, which are intrinsic to the *processions* divine nature, and which give rise to the distinction of persons in God. Thus our Blessed Saviour says of himself, " For from God I proceeded and came." [2] According to the Fathers, the words " and came " refer to the outward manifestation of the eternal Son of God in the flesh at his coming in the Incarnation ; whilst the expression " from God I proceeded " is taken to be a statement of his eternal origin from the Father. This interpretation is confirmed by St Paul's direct application to Christ of the words of the Psalmist, " Thou art my son, to-day have I begotten thee." The use of " to-day," indicating the immediate present, in conjunction with the past tense " begotten," must be regarded as a forcible way of expressing the eternal " now," the generation which always was, is, and ever shall be.

Furthermore, there is clear indication of another origin or procession, equally from all eternity and terminating, as does the first procession, within the divine essence itself. It is Christ himself who tells us of the Paraclete " whom I will send you from the Father, the Spirit of truth, who proceedeth from the Father." [3] The Holy Spirit is sent by the Son, and therefore proceeds from the Son equally as from the Father.

There are, then, two distinct processions or origins in the divine essence which, as we see, is represented in Scripture as being

[1] Prov. viii 22.     [2] John viii 42.     [3] John xv 26.

manifestly fruitful in itself. The key to the nature of the divine fertility is to be sought in the fundamental concept of God as the supreme spirit who alone exists of himself, and is infinite in all perfections. " God is a spirit," [1] and therefore his intrinsic activities must be entirely spiritual, and the divine processions or origins must be of a purely spiritual character.

Now the essential activities of a spiritual agent are thought, by which he understands the true, and volition, by which he loves the good. Therefore of God, who is the supreme spirit, we must predicate thought and volition in their fullest perfection. This much was recognised by Aristotle, though without the guiding light of revelation he was unable to penetrate deeper into the mystery of the hidden things of God.

Since it has been made known to us by revelation that there are, intrinsic to the divine nature itself, two different processions or origins, it is clear that one of these processions will be according to the activity of the divine intelligence, and the other according to the activity of the divine will. This is implied in the names which the Scripture applies to the second and third persons of the Trinity. The second person is called the Logos, that is, the word or the concept, something begotten by an intellectual process ; whereas the third person is called the Holy Spirit. Here the term " spirit," derived from the Latin *spirare*, to breathe, is used by analogy with the manner in which we draw a deep breath or sigh as expressive of the attraction of the will to some loved object.

## §IV: THE PROCESSION OF THE SON FROM THE FATHER

*The Logos*    IN the prologue to the Fourth Gospel St John says : " In the beginning was the Word, and the Word was with God, and the Word was God." The term " the Word," " the Logos," was in common use amongst the philosophers of St John's day. As far back as 500 B.C. it was employed by Heraclitus to express that which gives rationality or order to the universe. With Plato, the Logos became an intermediary between God and the material world ; with Aristotle, the energy in touch with finite things. The Stoics seem to have endowed the Logos with intelligence and consciousness, whilst the Jew, Philo, who was a contemporary of St John, even personifies it in much the same way that the Hebrews personified Wisdom in the Old Testament. [2]

It would seem, then, that St John, of set purpose, made use of a word which was well known in the schools of his day. Ephesus was the hub of the learned world, and there scholars were wont to meet together to exchange ideas, to speculate and philosophise. We

[1] John iv 24.        [2] Wisdom xviii 15 ; x 1, 2.

can hardly doubt that a favourite theme of their discussions must have been the precise nature of the mysterious intermediary between God and man which every system of philosophy seemed to regard as a first postulate. St John says to them in effect : You argue mightily amongst yourselves, Platonists, Stoics, and disciples of the Jew Philo, as to the true character of the Logos. Behold the veil is drawn aside, and you are permitted to look into a region where pure reason cannot penetrate. It is revealed unto you that the Logos is indeed the eternal Son of God made man.

St John proclaims an entirely new *doctrine* of the Logos. For, *The new* in the first place, the Logos of current speculation was at best a *doctrine of* vague abstraction ; even the Logos of Philo " floats indistinctly *the Logos* midway between personal and impersonal entity." [1] But for the author of the Fourth Gospel, the Logos was made flesh and dwelt amongst us, in the person of Christ Jesus. In the second place, the idea of the Logos becoming incarnate was utterly beyond the conception of any contemporary thinker, since they all regarded matter as essentially impure, and bound up with evil. That the Supreme Being should really assume a human nature and become man, man made of a woman, as St Paul has it, was beyond their most exalted vision. And finally, neither Greek, nor Roman, nor Jew regarded the Logos as of the same identical nature with the omnipotent God whose supreme will the Logos merely executed ; whereas for St John, the Logos is consubstantial with the Father (x 30), so that by the Logos all things were made, and without him was made nothing that was made (i 3).

This will become clearer if we consider the teaching of St John himself.

Twice in the Prologue to the Fourth Gospel, the Logos is called *The " only-* the " only-begotten " of the Father. Thus, in verse 14, we read : *begotten "* " And the Word was made flesh, and dwelt among us (and we saw his glory, the glory, as it were, of the only-begotten of the Father) full of grace and truth." St John is here testifying that he himself had witnessed Christ's divine attributes shining through his sacred humanity. For St John had seen " the glory, as it were [ὡς], of the only-begotten of the Father." The Greek particle ὡς does not mean " as if," but " such as belongs to." As St Chrysostom has pointed out, it does not express similitude, but identity, as is true of our own use of the particle " like " in such expressions as " he acted like a man." St Chrysostom therefore renders the passage : " We have seen his glory, such glory as it was *becoming and right* that the only-begotten and true Son of God should have."

Again, in verse 18, St John says : " No man hath seen God at any time : the only-begotten Son who is in the bosom of the Father, he hath declared him." Instead of " the only-begotten Son," the

[1] Zeller : *Die Philosophie der Griechen*, Vol. III, p. 378, 3rd edn.

reading " God only-begotten " is found in many ancient manuscripts, so that this second reading is regarded as equally probable by the late Cardinal MacRory.[1] It is an explicit statement of Christ's divine sonship, and even if this reading be not adopted, it can hardly be ignored as a valuable commentary on the text.

In any case St John's meaning is clear. His point is that he could not have acquired the doctrine which he has set forth in the Prologue from any source other than the divine source itself. But Christ could declare it because he was " in the bosom of the Father," that is, in the secret counsel of the Father. St Thomas Aquinas, commenting on this passage, writes : " In that bosom, therefore, that is, in the most hidden recess of the paternal nature and essence which transcends all created power, is the only-begotten Son, who is therefore consubstantial with the Father."

Père Lagrange shows that the term " only-begotten," as used in the Prologue, is a much stronger expression than that used by St Paul in Romans viii 9, where Christ is called " the first-born amongst many brethren." The Prologue states that the Logos, as God, is the only-begotten of the Father, whilst St Paul states that the Logos, as man, is the natural Son of God, and first-born among all others, who are only his adopted sons. Everything considered, it is impossible to doubt that the term " only-begotten Son " implies real, as opposed to every form of metaphorical, sonship.

*The " Son of God "*  The expression " Son of God " has various meanings in sacred Scripture, but there are certain passages of the New Testament in which the term obviously refers to the real eternal generation of the second person of the Trinity. Before indicating these passages it will be helpful to glance at the use of the term in the Old Testament and by Christ's contemporaries.

*In the Old Testament*  In the Old Testament it is used (1) to indicate any kind of special relationship to God. Thus it is predicated of angels,[2] and even of magistrates.[3] However, this vague use of the term is comparatively rare. (2) It is commonly applied (a) to the people of Israel, as for instance in such texts as " Be ye children of the Lord your God," [4] and " Israel is my son, my first-born " [5] ; and (b) it is commonly applied especially to the king of Israel : thus we have, " I will be to him [David, the king] a father, and he shall be to me a son," [6] and " Thou art my son, this day [that is, the day of the coronation or anointing] have I begotten thee." [7]  (3) By an easy transition it came to be applied in a special manner to the Messias, the anointed one *par excellence*. This obviously would be the sense in which the term would be used of Christ by his contemporaries apart from divine revelation.

*In the New Testament*  With regard to the New Testament usage, it is pretty generally admitted, even by rationalist critics, that in the Epistles the term

[1] *The Gospel of St John*, p. 33.   [2] Gen. vi 2 ; Job i 6.   [3] Ps. lxxxi 6.
[4] Deut. xiv 1.   [5] Exod. iv 22.   [6] 2 Kings vii 14.   [7] Ps. ii 7.

" Son of God " applied to Christ is meant to express his divinity ; that it is in fact a statement of his real generation from the Father. Again, there can be no doubt as to its precise meaning when the expression is used by Our Lord himself. He teaches men to call God " our Father," but he himself always speaks of " my Father."

The twofold nature of Christ and his divine origin are well brought out in Matthew xxii 41-45 [1]: " And the Pharisees being gathered together, Jesus asked them saying : What think you of Christ ? whose son is he ? They say to him : David's. He saith to them : How then doth David in spirit call him Lord, saying : *The Lord said to my Lord, Sit on my right hand, until I make thy enemies thy footstool ?* If David then call him Lord, how is he his son ? " The problem is, how can David be the father of one whom he sees at the right hand of God ? The answer is that David, though he is the father of Christ according to the flesh, cannot be his only father. He who sits at the right hand of God the Father, sharing divine authority, must indeed be the consubstantial Son of God. [2]

Even reason may throw some light on the mysterious generation of the Son by the Father. Already, the very name Logos, the word or concept, gives us an insight into it. For there is a remarkable analogy between the way in which the mental word or idea of some external object is conceived in our minds and the ordinary biological process of generation. For instance, I look at some object outside myself, say an oak tree. Thereupon there is formed in my imagination a visual image or phantasm of that oak tree. The active intellect now proceeds to strip that image of its pictorial or sensory elements until there is left only the nude impression of the oak tree, and this purified image then penetrates of its own accord into the womb of the passive understanding, where it is assimilated and brought forth as the concept or logos of the oak tree. *Theological study of the divine generation*

In this rough and ready account of the Aristotelian-Thomistic theory of intellection, it will be noticed that the external object, the oak tree, plays the part of the father ; the purified image, the part of the fruitful seed ; and the passive understanding, the part of the matrix or womb. Moreover, the concept resembles both its parents, for the concept of the oak tree is indeed like the oak tree, but each individual concept of the oak tree is modified somewhat, and moulded, by the particular understanding in which it is formed.

When we speak of the generation of a concept in the human mind, obviously we are using the term generation in an analogous sense. The formation of an idea of an extra-mental object is not, literally and strictly speaking, generation at all. Nevertheless, as we have seen, the process may very well be likened to the process of

----

[1] *Cf.* Mark xii 35-37.  [2] See also Matt. xvi 16 ; Mark i 11 ; Luke i 35.

generation. But the procession of the Logos within the divine essence *is* generation in the strict sense.

Generation in the wide sense, says St Thomas Aquinas, is nothing but change from non-existence to existence. Thus, for instance, we speak of generating hope, or love, or fear in the human soul. It is to be noticed that whatever is produced in this fashion is produced, not out of nothing as in creation, but out of previously existing material. But generation in the strict sense belongs properly to living things, and is defined by St Thomas as *origo alicuius viventis a principio vivente coniuncto* ; [1] that is, "the origin of a living being from a conjoined living principle."

St Thomas, however, immediately adds, "not everything which proceeds from a conjoined living principle is called begotten ; for, strictly speaking, only what proceeds in the specific likeness of the parent is really generated, as a man proceeds from a man, and a horse from a horse." [2]

There seem, then, to be three requisite conditions for real generation.

1. It must be a vital operation resulting in the communication of life.

2. The generating principle must be actually conjoined with that which is begotten, so that the offspring is of the very substance of the parent.

3. The offspring must be of the same species as the parent precisely in consequence of the manner of his origin. Hence, though Eve was formed from the living substance of Adam, in the same species as Adam, she was not Adam's daughter, because her specific identity with Adam was not due to her origination from Adam, but to the extraordinary process of God's moulding her to the pattern of human nature.

Now St Thomas contends that the procession of the Logos in the divine essence satisfies these three conditions.

1. In the first place the Logos proceeds "by way of intelligible action, which is a vital operation." [3] The eternal Father contemplating the divine essence gives origin to the Logos. Now with us the logos, or the concept which is formed in the mind, is certainly not a living thing. It is an accident, a modification or quality which is distinct from the mind itself.

But the Logos which is begotten by the Father is not something accidental to the divine essence, since this is incapable of modification or qualification of any kind. Whatever proceeds within the divine essence must be identical with it, and consequently the Logos does not proceed as an accident, but as something substantial, as the divine essence itself in fact, under a special relationship by reason of its eternal origination. The Logos, then, is not merely living, but the inexhaustible source of all life.

[1] *S. Theol.*, I, Q. xxvii, art. 2          [2] *Ibid.*          [3] *Ibid.*

2.  In the second place, whilst it is obvious that the logos or concept which we mortals form is not of our own substance, is not, so
to speak, bone of our bone and flesh of our flesh, but merely a sort
of mental accessory, it is clear nevertheless from what has been said
that the Logos which proceeds from the Father *is* of his very substance, *is* of the same divine essence in every respect, differing from
the father only by his proper relationship of filiation as opposed to
that of paternity.

3.  Finally, it follows that the Logos proceeds not merely with
the same specific nature, but with numerically the same nature as
the Father, and this precisely because of his mode of origin.   We have
seen that every concept bears the likeness of the intellect that conceives
it.   The concept in the human mind, it is true, bears but an intentional resemblance to the object with which it corresponds ; that
is to say, the resemblance is entirely in the intentional order, in that
sphere of thought wherein the human mind assimilates to itself the
things to which it has in-tended or stretched forth.   In this case the
resemblance is not even specific.

But it is far otherwise with the divine Logos.   That which
proceeds in the divine intelligence, or essence, namely, the Logos,
is similar to the principle from which it proceeds, not merely in
an intentional way, nor even specifically as in natural generation,
but in the most perfect possible way, namely, by substantial
identity.

Hence in the procession of the Son from the Father we have real
generation stripped of all its imperfections ; for we have the origin
of a living being from a conjoined living principle, in such a way that
this living being proceeds with the selfsame nature as its progenitor.
But this origination is eternal, without change, without causation,
without dependence, without time, without succession, without
multiplication of the divine nature, from everlasting unto everlasting.

## § V:  THE PROCESSION OF THE HOLY SPIRIT FROM
## THE FATHER AND THE SON

It is evident from the New Testament that besides the procession *The second*
of the Logos there is another procession within the divine essence, *procession*
namely, the procession of the Holy Spirit.   For the incarnate Logos
says :  " But when the Paraclete cometh, whom I will send you
from the Father, the Spirit of truth, who proceedeth from the Father,
he shall give testimony of me." [1]   Here we are told that he proceeds from the Father, that he is sent from the Father by the Son ;
in other words, that the Holy Spirit proceeds both from the Father
and the Son.

[1] John xv 26.

*From the Father and the Son*

That he proceeds equally from the Son as from the Father is clear from a number of texts from which we may select the following words of Our Lord uttered at the Last Supper : " He [the Holy Spirit] shall glorify me ; because he shall receive of mine, and shall show it to you. All things whatsoever the Father hath are mine." [1] Since the Holy Spirit is a divine person, he is infinite in perfection, and therefore cannot receive anything except in his eternal origin. To receive from the Son, then, is to proceed eternally from the Son. But our Blessed Saviour adds immediately, " all things whatsoever the Father hath, are mine," to show that the things that were essentially his were communicated to him with his essential existence in his eternal generation from the Father. In this passage Christ tells his disciples that in the future the Holy Spirit, who is to come, will reveal divine knowledge, which has been communicated to him in his procession from both the Father and the Son. For this divine knowledge, like all divine attributes, is possessed equally by all three divine persons, since, as the Athanasian Creed has it, " the whole three persons are co-eternal to one another, and co-equal."

With the second divine procession we need deal only briefly here, as it will be described fully in Essay V.

*Not generation*

We have seen that the Son proceeds from the Father by a strict process of generation because the Logos proceeds according to the operation of the divine intellect. Is it conceivable that the second procession in the divine essence is also according to the operation of the divine intellect ? A little reflection makes it obvious that it is not conceivable. For if the Holy Spirit also proceeded as the divine concept, as the Logos, he also would be the Son, and this would contradict the Scriptures which tell us that the second Person is the " *only-begotten* of the Father."

Now there are only two conceivable activities of a purely spiritual being, namely, the activities of the spiritual faculties of intellect and will. If, then, the Holy Spirit does not proceed according to the operation of the divine intellect, he must proceed according to the operation of the divine will. Such is the reasoning of St Thomas Aquinas, following St Augustine. Just as in the intellectual process there is begotten within us a concept which is the image of the object understood ; so, too, in an act of love, there arises within us an inclination towards the loved one which may be rightly regarded as the spiritual force of the loved one motivating within us. Naturally poets have a good deal to say about this attraction, or inclination, or urge ; they honour it with many fine names indicative of its nature from " the breath of life " to " the sigh suppressed, corroding in the cavern of the heart." [2]

[1] John xvi 14, 15.  [2] Byron.

Now the procession of the Holy Spirit is considered to be a pro- *"Spiration'*
cession of love, that is to say, the third person of the Blessed Trinity
proceeds from the Father and the Son according to the operation of
the divine will.   To know the supreme good in such a way as to
comprehend it, is necessarily to love the supreme good.   Consequently the Father from all eternity contemplating the Son, and
the Son from all eternity contemplating the Father, necessitate an
eternal act of mutual love, a divine spiration, common to both the
Father and the Son.   This spiration issues within the divine essence
itself in what we can describe only as the divine breath personified,
the Holy Spirit of God, subsisting in the divine essence, but distinct
from both the Father and the Son by reason of his eternal origin
from them.

Just as in the intellective act, the logos or concept which we form
is an accident, whereas the divine Logos is the subsisting divine
essence itself ;   so, too, in the volitional act, though the spiritus or
breath with us be merely an accident, in God it is the divine essence
itself, with the special relation which is proper to that which proceeds
according to the immanent act of divine love.   But, whilst the Logos
is consubstantial with the Father precisely because of the manner of
his eternal origin, namely, by generation ;   the Holy Spirit is consubstantial with the Father and the Son, not by reason of the process
of his origin, but for the simple reason that whatever proceeds in
the divine essence itself must be in substance identical with that
undivided and indivisible essence.

We have seen, then, that the second person of the Trinity is
properly called the Son, since he proceeds from the Father by a
process of real generation.   But the third person proceeds by a
totally different process, and moreover by a process which, from the
psychological standpoint, is little understood even in the analogical
form in which we experience it.   It is so elusive that it seems to
defy introspective analysis, and consequently we have no proper
name for that attraction or urge, or impulse, which is, as it were,
the internal issue of the volitional process.   That being so, it is not
surprising that we have no proper name for the third person of the
Trinity, as we have for the second ;   but in view of the fact that the
Holy Ghost proceeds according to the operation of the divine will
as distinguished from the divine intelligence, he is called in Scripture
by such names as " Spirit," " Gift," or " Pledge " of love.   These
names clearly express the characteristic outpouring of love, which
manifests itself in gifts and pledges, but above all in the supreme
gift or pledge to the loved one of the lover's whole self.

We may sum up what we have said with regard to the eternal
origin of the third person of the Trinity in the words of the Athanasian
Creed :   " The Holy Ghost is from the Father and the Son, not made,
nor created, nor begotten, but proceeding."

## §VI: THE DIVINE RELATIONS

THE study of the divine relations is a matter of supreme importance, for the Council of Florence, in the *Decretum pro Jacobitis*, after declaring that in the three persons there is one substance, one essence, one nature, one divinity, one immensity, and one eternity, formulates the general principle, that everything is one, except where relative opposition intervenes.[1] It follows therefore that the distinction between the persons is due to their relations to each other.

The whole doctrine of relation has been worked out elaborately by Scholastic theologians and used by them to elucidate, as far as may be, the sublime mystery of the Trinity. But here it must be admitted frankly that we are largely in the region of philosophical speculation. The Church has made no formal pronouncement in this matter, but it is instructive for us to see how her devoted theologians have attempted to harmonise the content of revelation with the findings of reason.

*Relations real and mental*

By relation we mean the habitude of one thing to another, or, as Annandale's Dictionary has it, " the condition of being such or such in respect to something else." For, says St Thomas, " the true idea of relation is not taken from its respect to that in which it is, but from its respect to something external."[2] Thus, as I sit at my desk, I have a definite positional relation to the paper on which I am writing ; a totally different kind of relation to the words in which I express my thoughts ; and a third kind of relation to the dog who lies at my feet. Meantime there are also my varying relations to my spiritual subjects, my fellow-citizens and my readers.

Now it is obvious that some relations are purely mental since they have no foundation except in the mind which links up the related objects. It is in this way that the lily is related to purity, and the red light to danger. Nevertheless there are real relations whereby certain objects are linked up, not merely mentally, but in point of actual fact in the order of extra-mental reality. Thus the perfection of a wall consists in the real positional relation of each brick to every other one ; the perfection of a squad at drill lies precisely in the relative attitudes of the members of the squad.

Three conditions are seen to be required for real relationship : (a) the related objects must be real, and not merely figments of the mind ; (b) they must be really distinct from each other ; and (c) the relation of one to the other must be founded on a solid fact outside the mind which apprehends the relationship. Hence the relations of paternity and filiation existing between any human father and his son are real, because the father and son are real persons, really distinct from each other, and the relationship is founded on the physical act of generation.

[1] *Omniaque sunt unum, ubi non obviat relationis oppositio.* Denzinger, 703.
[2] *S. Theol.*, I, Q. xxviii, art. 2 c.

Now we have seen that in God from all eternity there are two *Four real* real processions or origins, since both the Son and the Holy Spirit *relations in* proceed as real persons. Each real origin gives rise to two real *God* relations. Thus the first procession gives rise to paternity and filiation, and the second procession to spiration and procession. These relations satisfy the requirements of a real relation, for (*a*) the Father, the Son, and the Holy Ghost are real ; (*b*) the persons related are distinct from each other ; and (*c*) the first pair of relations are founded on the eternal act of divine generation, whilst the second pair are founded on the eternal act of divine spiration, both real vital processes.

But, whilst there are four real relations, there are not four divine *But three* persons. We have already defined a person as an individual sub- *persons* stance of a rational nature, and we have said that the requisite conditions for personality are substantiality, individuality, and rationality.[1] Now, all four divine relations are substantial, since they subsist by reason of their identity with the divine essence ; all four again are rational, since the divine essence is the divine intelligence ; but all four are not individual. We have shown that for personality the rational substance must be individual in such a way that it is not in any sense part of, or common to, anything else.

Clearly in the Blessed Trinity the relation of paternity is peculiar and proper to the Father ; the relation of filiation is peculiar and proper to the Son ; and the relation of procession from the Father and the Son is peculiar and proper to the Holy Ghost. Each of these three relations is individual in the strictest possible sense, for between them there is opposition. But not so the relation of active spiration. This relation is not individual, but common to both the Father and the Son, and consequently it cannot possibly constitute a distinct person. Hence, since there are three, and only three, distinct subsisting relations in the divine essence, there are three, and only three, divine persons.

In the Preface to holy Mass appointed for Trinity Sunday and *Definition of* the Sundays throughout the year, the Church solemnly prays *ut* . . . *a divine* *in personis proprietas* . . . *adoretur ;* "that in the persons that" *person* which is proper or individual should be adored." That which is proper or individual to each of the divine persons is his distinct relation to the others. It follows, therefore, that the distinct subsisting relations in the Trinity are to be adored. But adoration can be given only to the divine persons themselves, whence we arrive at the definition of a divine person as a distinct subsisting relation.

This is confirmed by analysing the generic definition of person and applying it to the Trinity. The distinctive characteristics of personality are rationality, substantiality, and individuality. What precisely is it in the Trinity which satisfies these requirements ? It is clearly not the divine essence itself as such, for it is common to all

[1] See p. 112.

three persons, as witness the Church in her Trinity Preface when she prays aloud, *et in essentia unitas . . . adoretur ;* "that in the essence unity may be adored." Neither is it simply a subsisting relation, that is, a divine relation subsisting of itself, for, as we have seen, there are four such relations, one of which, active spiration, being common to both the Father and the Son, is lacking in the essential note of individuality. Only those relations which are mutually opposed to each other by reason of their origin are completely individual, or, as the Scholastic theologians have it, incommunicable. Thus paternity is by its very connotation opposed to filiation, and filiation to paternity ; and since the Holy Ghost proceeds by a common spiration from both the Father and the Son, this relation of procession by an act of the mutual love of the Father and Son is necessarily opposed equally to paternity and filiation. We see then that, in the Trinity, that which is at once rational, substantial, and individual, is an incommunicable subsisting relation ; incommunicable, because by reason of its very origin it is diametrically opposed to other individual subsisting relations.

*Subsisting relations*
Apart from revelation we could hardly conceive such a sublime notion as that of a subsisting relation ; but reason alone is able to demonstrate that the concept does not involve any self-evident intrinsic repugnance. We have seen that the essential note of relation is its respect, regard, or habitude to something else. If the relation is a real one, it derives its reality from the substance in which it inheres ; thus, paternity is a real relation in a real man who has begotten a real child. The notion of reality, then, is quite distinct from that of relation. However, a real relation in the Trinity cannot be something inhering in the divine essence, something modifying or qualifying the divine essence, for in that case the divine essence would be subject to composition. A real divine relation must subsist of itself, must be in fact the divine essence itself in its eternal intrinsic origins. Reason can find no repugnance in that a real relation derives its reality, not from inherence in a subject, as it does with us, but in a higher way, from the divine subsistence in its immanent fecundity.

With regard to the mysteries of faith, it is the function of reason to show that these truths which are above reason are not against reason. Herein lies the "reasonable service" of speculative theology. To penetrate into the hidden recesses of the wisdom of God is beyond man's capacity and reach, for, as the Book of Wisdom has it, "hardly do we guess aright at things that are upon the earth : and with labour do we find the things that are before us. But the things that are in heaven, who shall search out ? " [1] And of all the things in heaven none is higher, more remote from, and inaccessible to, human reason than this august mystery of the Trinity, before which,

[1] Wisdom ix 16.

as the great Athanasius assures us, the very Seraphim veil their faces and fall prostrate in adoration.[1]

Etymologically, the word appropriation means "to make some- *Appropriation* thing one's own," and from that it came to mean "to make something personal which before was common," and hence, in the theological treatise on the Trinity, it signifies "the ascription of the common names, attributes, and operations to particular divine persons."

We have already seen that in the Trinity everything is common to the three divine persons with the exception of the properties which are radicated in the relative opposition between the persons. Thus, filiation is proper to the second person, and cannot be predicated of either the Father or the Holy Ghost. But there are many attributes which, because they refer to the unity of the divine substance, can be predicated indiscriminately of all three persons. For instance, we may say equally of the Father, or the Son, or the Holy Spirit, that he is God, that he is eternal, omnipotent, infinitely holy, the searcher of hearts. However, it is the constant usage of Holy Writ to ascribe certain of these common attributes to particular divine persons, and it will be found on examination that neither in Scripture nor tradition is the ascription or appropriation merely arbitrary.

It is true that appropriation is a mental operation on our part by which we attribute in a special manner to one person what really belongs to all three, and it is obvious that the appropriation does not make whatever is appropriated belong more to the person to whom it is ascribed than to the other persons. Nevertheless appropriation must have some foundation other than, and independent of, our minds.

As a matter of fact there are many different grounds of appro- *Grounds of* priation which may be classified under three headings, according as *appropriation* we consider (*a*) the divine essence or substance in itself, (*b*) the divine essence in its outward activities, or (*c*) the divine essence in relation to its external effects.

(*a*) As an example of the first kind of appropriation we have the well-known attribution of St Hilary[2]: *Infinitas in Aeterno, Species in Imagine, Usus in Munere*, which we may render, "the Infinitely Eternal, the Image and Likeness, the Supreme Enjoyment." Infinity and eternity are ascribed to the Father so as to stress the fact that, though he is the principle from which all else proceeds, he himself proceeds from none. None is thought of as before him. The Son is called the image and the likeness because he proceeds by real generation from the Father in such a way that there is between

---

[1] *Ep. ad Serap.*, n. 17.    [2] *L. 2 De Trinitate*, n. 1.

him and the Father the likeness of numerical identity of nature. And, finally, the Holy Spirit is portrayed in a peculiar expression, which I have rendered Supreme Enjoyment, since St Hilary's meaning is that the Holy Spirit is in the active unitive possession of the supremely lovable, and this because the Holy Spirit proceeds as the uncreated Love of the infinitely good.

(b) In the second method of appropriation, the divine essence is regarded from the standpoint of its extrinsic activities, partly with a view to distinguishing the divine persons from one another, and partly with a view to distinguishing them from creatures who bear the same names. Thus, power and its products are attributed to the Father, wisdom and its offshoots to the Son, goodness and its fruits to the Holy Spirit. This attribution is partly based on the divine origins, and partly also, as St Thomas points out,[1] on the removal of the imperfections which are found in creatures. A human father on account of his age is apt to be infirm, so works of power are ascribed to God the Father ; a human son on account of his youth is inexperienced, so wisdom and its manifestations are attributed to God the Son ; the word *spiritus*, breath or wind, indicates something which through its impetuosity is apt to be destructive, and so by contrast goodness in all its beneficent activities is appropriated to the Spirit of God.

(c) The third kind of appropriation is made from the standpoint of the divine essence in relation to its external effects. The classical instance of it occurs in St Paul's Epistle to the Romans (xi, 36), where he writes, " Quoniam *ex* ipso, et *per* ipsum, et *in* ipso sunt omnia " ; " For *of* him, and *by* him, and *in* him, are all things." Here the particle *ex*, *of*, indicates the efficient cause, and is therefore appropriate to the Father who is the principle from which all else proceeds ; the particle *per*, *through* or *by*, indicates the plan, or the idea, or the concept, according to which the agent works, and this kind of causation is naturally ascribed to the Son ; the particle *in*, which the Authorised Version translates as *to*, denotes the ultimate or final end, to or towards which all creation moves : the Supreme Good which draws all things and brings all things to itself, the end for which they are made. For, as we have seen, it is peculiarly fitting that goodness should be appropriated to the Holy Spirit.

It will be understood readily that, as Billot has remarked,[2] all the different methods of appropriation are ultimately reducible to one, and to one which is radicated in the divine origins themselves. For whatever is appropriated to the Father will be found to imply in some way that he is the fount, the source, the principle which proceeds from none, but from which all else derives ; whatever is appropriated to the Son will have necessarily some reference to the intellectual operation according to which he proceeds from the

---

[1] In I, D. 34, q. 2.　　　　[2] *De Trinitate*, thesis XXXIV.

Father; and finally, whatever is appropriated to the Holy Spirit will be traceable to the action of the divine will according to which he proceeds from both the Father and the Son, consubstantial with them, but distinct in personality.

## §VII: THE TEMPORAL MISSION OF THE DIVINE PERSONS

BY the term *mission*, in its primary significance, we understand the sending of an agent, delegate, or messenger, and the inspired writers do not hesitate to predicate such a mission of the second and third persons of the Blessed Trinity. Thus, Our Lord says, " He that sent me, is with me," [1] and again, " If I go not, the Paraclete will not come to you ; but if I go, I will send him to you." [2] *The notion of divine mission*

Now it is clear that the external mission of the divine persons cannot involve the imperfections which are necessarily bound up with the mission of any human person. With us, the person who sends is of higher authority than the person sent. But, because of the perfect equality of the divine persons, there can be no question of the subordination of one person to the other. We have seen that all three persons have everything in common except what arises from the opposition of relationship of origin. Therefore the external missions of the divine persons must be radicated in their processions ; they must be, as it were, continuations of their eternal origins.

All theologians are agreed that for a divine mission in the technical sense it is required

1. that there shall be a going forth or a procession of the person who is sent from the person who sends ; ·
2. that the person sent shall acquire a new relationship to creatures ;
3. and acquire this new relationship precisely by reason of his procession from the sender.

There can obviously be no change in the divine persons themselves, and therefore whatever change results from a divine mission must be in the creature, in whom the divine person begins to be in a new, *i.e.* in a supernatural way.

It is equally clear that only those persons are sent who proceed, and that they are sent only by those from whom they proceed. Hence the Father is sent by none ; the Son is sent by the Father ; and the Holy Ghost is sent by the Father and the Son.

These missions may be of two kinds : visible or invisible, according as the divine messenger comes to creatures in a visible or invisible manner. Thus in the Incarnation of the Son of God we have a visible mission in its greatest possible perfection, whilst visible missions of the Holy Ghost in the form of a dove and of parted tongues of fire are recorded in the New Testament. An *Visible and invisible missions*

---

[1] John viii 29.          [2] John xvi 7.

invisible mission is one which takes place without any external signs, as whenever sanctifying grace is infused into the soul, according to the divine ordinance.

*The visible missions*    Of the invisible missions we shall not speak here, since these will be described fully in the following essay. Among visible missions the most important is the coming of the second person of the Trinity in the flesh in the mystery of the Incarnation. The second person of the Trinity became man to redeem us from our sins and to lead us to the beatific vision. The visible mission of God the Son was the preliminary to his invisible mission to our souls, as he tells us in the prayer to his Heavenly Father, in which he sets forth the object of his mission : " that the love wherewith thou hast loved me may be in them, and I in them." [1]

In the Old Testament there were no visible missions, because, as St John points out, a visible mission is a manifestation of grace which is already conferred. For, says St John : " as yet the Spirit was not given, because Jesus was not glorified." It must be borne in mind that though the just of the Old Testament were participators of grace within their souls, externally and legally they belonged to the order of servitude and not to that of adopted sonship. [2] In order that it might be manifest that it is through Christ, true God and true man, that all men shall acquire the power to become sons of God, it was fitting that no legal or formal dispensation of grace should precede his coming, but that the second person of the Trinity made man for us should himself inaugurate the external economy of grace. In the old dispensation God operated through the visible forms of angels, who were his messengers, the harbingers of his favours ; in the new dispensation he manifests in outward form the actual gift of sanctification which he has already bestowed upon the soul.

Other visible missions of the Holy Spirit, to the early Christians, to the Apostles, and to Christ, are recorded in the New Testament. Of the visible mission of the Holy Spirit to our Blessed Saviour in the days when he walked the earth John the Baptist testifies : " I saw the Spirit coming down, as a dove from heaven, and he remained upon him." [3] This mission had indeed been prophetically foretold by Isaias in the Old Testament, when he said : " And the Spirit of the Lord shall rest upon him : the spirit of wisdom and of understanding, the spirit of counsel and fortitude, the spirit of knowledge and godliness. And he shall be filled with the spirit of the fear of the Lord." [4]

In the New Testament the Holy Spirit appeared under several emblems or sensible signs : at Our Lord's baptism, as we have just said, in the form of a dove, bringing the message of reconciliation, symbolising the advent of salvation to the human race, just as the

---

[1] John xvii 26.       [2] Gal. iii-iv ; Heb. ix-x.
[3] John i 32.       [4] Isaias xi 2-3.

dove of old was used to indicate that the ancient world was saved from inundation ; again the Holy Spirit is manifested as a gentle breathing signifying the spirit of God ; and yet again under the forms of parted tongues of fire, showing forth the manifold operations of the Holy Spirit.

It is to be noted that a visible mission always implies an invisible one, though not vice versa. Moreover, in the visible missions, with the sole exception of the Incarnation, the part played by the external element is merely symbolical. Both kinds of missions, the visible and the invisible, are found in their highest perfection in the Incarnation of the eternal Son of God. Herein the Word assumed our human nature in such a way that it became his. His body was not merely a sign or symbol of the divine ; it was God's own body. For the human nature which the Son assumed was united hypostatically with the divine nature which he already possessed, in the one person, the historical Jesus ; and since he is in himself uncreated grace, in his visible mission all invisible missions find their bounteous source.

We have seen that the Trinity is a mystery in the strict sense of *Conclusion* the term, that is to say, a truth which unaided human reason could never have discovered for itself, and which human reason cannot fathom even after the existence of the Trinity has been revealed to us. We are told distinctly in Holy Writ : " no one knoweth the Son but the Father : neither doth anyone know the Father but the Son, and he to whom it shall please the Son to reveal him." [1] The " no one " obviously means " no one outside the Trinity," for the Holy Ghost is no more excluded from the knowledge of the Father in this passage than the Son is excluded in the following text, in which St Paul explains how he came to a knowledge of the hidden things of God : " But to us God hath revealed them by his Spirit. For the Spirit searcheth all things, yea, the deep things of God. For what man knoweth the things of a man, but the spirit of a man that is in him ? So the things also that are of God no man knoweth, but the Spirit of God." [2] Clearly perfect knowledge of God as he is in himself is an essential attribute of the three divine persons and pertains to them alone.

But by the Redemption we have been made partakers of the divine nature, and raised to the dignity of adopted sons of God. Our adopted sonship is a derivative, a consequence, a corollary of the natural sonship of the second person of the Blessed Trinity. He is the first-born, we are his brethren. For the natural sonship of Christ is the ideal of our relationship to the Father, an ideal to which, through the grace of Christ, it is possible for us to make some distant approach in this life. This indeed we do, in the supernatural order, by way of that consuming charity which is a reflection, an after-glow,

[1] Matt. xi 27.                [2] 1 Cor. ii 10-11.

as it were, of that divine love of the Father for the Son, and of the Son for the Father, of which the Holy Spirit is the Pledge and the Seal. " The Spirit himself giveth testimony to our spirit, that we are the sons of God." [1]

It is to us, then, as sons of God, to us who have been elevated by grace to the supernatural plane, to us who have been made co-heirs with Christ, to us, his intimate friends, that the sublime mystery of the inner life of God has been revealed. There is opened up to us a vision of the incalculable richness of the divine life in its eternal fecundity. We catch a glimpse of the true meaning of communion with God by contemplating the divine sociability by which each person of the Trinity penetrates and pervades each other and possesses the essence of each other person as his own.

Here is the ideal unity unattainable outside the beatific society of the undivided Trinity, but nevertheless the essential exemplar of our fellowship in the Church of Christ and of our ultimate union with God. At the beginning of his first Epistle St John tells us that as an Apostle he is proclaiming the sublime mystery of the coming in the flesh of the second person of the Trinity precisely " that you also may have fellowship with us, and our fellowship may be with the Father, and with his Son, Jesus Christ." [2]

We are called to fellowship with God himself. Truly no other people hath its God so nigh. In thankfulness for the revelation made known to us we are moved to say with reverential awe, " This is our God, and there shall be no other accounted of in comparison of him." [3]

RICHARD DOWNEY.

[1] Rom. viii 16.     [2] 1 John i 1-3.     [3] Baruch iii 36.

# V

# THE HOLY GHOST

## § I: INTRODUCTORY

" AND (we believe) in the Holy Ghost, the Lord, the Life-giver, who proceeds from the Father *and the Son ;* who with Father and Son is together adored and together glorified ; who spoke through the prophets."

With the exception of the words in italics, which were added later, this is the form in which the doctrine concerning the Holy Ghost is set forth in the Nicene-Constantinopolitan Creed, a formulary commonly attributed to the First Council of Constantinople of 381.[1] The words were an answer to the heresies of the time ; they have been constantly reaffirmed by the Church as the official summary of her doctrine, in particular by the profession of faith of the Council of Trent.[2] It will be shown in the course of the present essay that all the Church's teaching on the Holy Spirit may conveniently be grouped under the various clauses of the Creed.

Under the clause affirming the equal adoration due to the three divine persons, we shall treat of the divinity and consubstantiality of the Holy Ghost. Under the clause regarding his procession from Father and Son, we shall deal with the sources of that doctrine. The words " The Lord, the Life-giver " will serve as a text for some account of the Holy Spirit's work in the Incarnation, in the Church, and in the individual soul. Finally, the phrase commemorating the prophetic office of the Spirit will give an occasion for a short treatment of the inspiration of Holy Scripture.

It has been regretted at times that no explicit mention was made by the great Creeds of the Holy Ghost's office as Paraclete and of his visible mission on the day of Pentecost. But it may be urged in reply that this office is summarised in the one phrase, " The Lord the Life-giver," and that, in Cardinal Manning's words, " it is not by accident or by mere order of enumeration, that in the baptismal creed we say, ' I believe in the Holy Ghost, the Holy Catholic Church.' These two articles are united, because the Holy Spirit is united with the Mystical Body." [3]

---

[1] Denzinger's *Enchiridion*, n. 86. The Creed may well be earlier by some years than the Council of 381, and must be if it is that quoted by St Epiphanius in 374.

[2] Denzinger, n. 994.

[3] *The Temporal Mission of the Holy Ghost*, p. 35.

143

## § II: THE DIVINITY OF THE HOLY GHOST

### I

*The Old Testament* THE central dogma of the Christian faith, that of the Blessed Trinity, is one that was only foreshadowed under the old dispensation. It is not to be denied that, in the light of the New Testament revelation, many traces of the doctrine may be observed in the pages of the Old Testament. Furthermore, it is the opinion of some Catholic writers that certain of the Fathers who died before Christ's coming may have received a special enlightenment regarding the trinity of persons in the Godhead. But it is commonly maintained that the generality of mankind under the Old Law could find only scanty and indecisive warrant for such a belief in the pages of the sacred text.

This is especially true as regards the Holy Ghost. Though the term " Spirit (of God) " occurs no less than ninety-four times in the protocanonical books alone [1] it is far from clear that the readers or writers of those books were aware of any distinction of persons in God. A few representative passages will give some clue to the nature of the evidence.

In the first place, it is the Spirit of God (in Hebrew, Rûªh 'elôhîm) who is regarded as inspiring the holy prophets. Thus one reads of the seventy elders [2] that " When the Spirit had rested upon them, they prophesied." Later, at the close of the period of the judges, Saul, the first Israelite king, is assured by Samuel that " the Spirit of the Lord shall come upon thee and thou shalt prophesy with them." [3] For Osee [4] a prophet is above all " the man of the Spirit," while Micheas contrasts the reality of his mission with the ravings of the false prophets in the phrase, " As for me, I am filled with strength, thanks to the Spirit of God." [5]

It is a further office of the Spirit to move the prophet to utter words of exhortation and warning and to set his seal upon a divine mission. It is said of Balaam [6] that " The Spirit of the Lord came upon him " and inspired him to prophesy good things regarding Israel. David declares in his last words [7] that " The Spirit of the Lord hath spoken by me and his word by my tongue." The Prophet Isaias is even more explicit : " And now the Lord God hath sent me and his Spirit " (*i.e.* he and his Spirit have sent me).[8] And again, in the words cited by Our Divine Lord in the synagogue at Nazareth [9] : " The Spirit of the Lord is upon me, because the Lord hath anointed me . . ." [10]

But the action of the Spirit is not restricted to prophecy. There

---

[1] See the Oxford *Hebrew Lexicon*, pp. 925b-926a.
[2] Numbers xi 25.   [3] 1 Kings x 6-10.   [4] Osee ix 7.
[5] Micheas iii 8.   The Douay Version differs slightly.
[6] Numbers xxiv 2.   [7] 2 Kings xxiii 2.   [8] Isaias xlviii 16.
[9] Luke iv 18-19.   [10] Isaias lxi 1.

is frequent mention of his influence upon kings and rulers and judges in ancient Israel. He it is who moves them to deeds of warlike valour and virtuous judgement. Thus we read of the judge Othoniel [1] that " the Spirit of the Lord was in him and he judged Israel," and of Jephte [2] that, on the eve of his departure for his campaign against the Ammonites, " the Spirit of the Lord came upon " him. Gedeon and Samson, Saul and David are likewise mentioned as receiving in abundant measure the Spirit of fortitude and wisdom.[3] It is the Spirit who will rest in a special and most intimate manner upon the Messianic King, who is to receive a sevenfold influence of his might.[4] And in another passage of Isaias [5] it is said of the suffering Servant of the Lord that " I have given my Spirit upon him : he shall bring forth judgement to the Gentiles." This endowment with gifts is twice found in Exodus.[6] In the former passage God says of Beseleel that he has " filled him with the Spirit of God, with wisdom and understanding and knowledge of all manner of work."

Again, the Spirit is regarded as the source of life and energy. At creation's dawn " the Spirit of God moved (better, hovered) over the waters." [7] And Job says in reference to the beginning of his life, " the Spirit of God made me and the breath of the Almighty gave me life." [8]

Finally, an even more intimate doctrine of the Spirit is found in such passages as Isaias lxiii 10 : " They provoked to wrath and afflicted the Spirit of his holiness," [9] and in Aggeus : [10] " My Spirit shall be in the midst of you. Fear not." Perhaps the most explicit of all Old Testament references occurs in Wisdom, [11] " And who shall know thy thought, except thou give wisdom and send thy Holy Spirit from above," where the Spirit seems practically to be identified with divine wisdom.

Turning to the books outside the Old Testament Canon, one finds little definite teaching on the Holy Ghost. He is called " the Spirit of understanding and sanctification," [12] and it is said of Isaias that " his lips spake with the Holy Ghost until he was sawn in twain." [13] But, in general, the doctrine is not especially prominent.

From these and other passages in the pre-Christian literature, it might appear that the doctrine of the Spirit as a distinct person was revealed with some degree of clearness in Old Testament times. A careful examination, however, will go far to negative this impression and to confirm the dictum of a well-known theologian that, in spite

---

[1] Judges iii 10.      [2] Judges xi 29.
[3] Judges vi 34 ; xiii 25 ; xiv 6, 19 ; xv 14 ; 1 Kings xi 6 ; xvi 13-14.
[4] Isaias xi 2.    [5] xlii 1.    [6] xxxi 3 ; xxxv 31.     [7] Gen. i 2.
[8] Job xxxiii 4. See also Isaias xxxi 3 ; Ezechiel i 12 ; x 17.
[9] Cp. Ephes. iv 30.      [10] Cp. Ephes. ii 6.
[11] ix 17. See also i 4-7.      [12] Testament of Levi, xviii 7.
[13] Martyrdom of Isaias, v 14. See also 1 Enoch lxvii 10 ; Psalms of Solomon xvii 42 ; Targum of Onkelos to Gen. xlv 27 ; Jerusalem Targum to Gen. xli 38.

of the frequent allusions to the " Spirit of God " and the " Holy Spirit," which would be readily understood by Christian readers of the third person of the Trinity, " no passage, so far as I know, is brought forward, which, considered in itself [that is, apart from the full revelation of Christ] could not suitably be explained as the personification of a divine attribute or a divine operation." [1] With this temperately expressed opinion the present writer is in hearty agreement.

2

*The New Testament*

To pass from the obscure teaching of the Old Testament on the Holy Ghost to the clear and abundant testimony of the Gospels and apostolic writings is to enter another world. Whole volumes have been written that are solely occupied with a discussion of the New Testament teaching and here one can only offer a selection of some of the more important texts and passages.

In approaching these texts it is to be noted that three scriptural uses of the word " Spirit " must be carefully distinguished. First, the term is used to signify the divine essence as wholly immaterial. It was in this sense that Our Lord said to the Samaritan woman, " God is a spirit and those who worship him must worship in spirit and truth." [2] Secondly, there is the use of the word so common in the Old Testament, as noted above, in which the term might be understood of a divine attribute or operation. [3] Thirdly, there is the frequent and unmistakable use of the term in the New Testament for a distinct person in the Godhead, who is called in a peculiar sense the Spirit, the Holy Spirit, and the Spirit of Father and Son. It is our claim that the New Testament witnesses to a Person, who is divine and is distinct from the Father and the Son.

The fact that the Holy Ghost is a person appears, in the first place, from the titles given to him by Our Lord in his last discourse to the disciples. [4] Our Lord calls him " the Spirit," and though the Greek word for " spirit " ($\pi\nu\epsilon\hat{\upsilon}\mu\alpha$) is of the neuter gender, the pronoun used in referring to it is in the masculine gender. [5] Again, he calls him by another name, the " Paraclete," which more probably means an advocate or pleader, a friend of an accused person called to testify to his character or to enlist sympathy in his favour. This term is used four times in regard of the Holy Spirit in St John's Gospel, [6] but occurs in his first Epistle as a title of Our Lord, who is our " Advocate with the Father, Jesus Christ the just." [7] The title, therefore, is evidently a personal one.

---

[1] Van Noort, *De Deo Trino*, p. 133.      [2] John iv 24.
[3] Cp. Gen. i 2 ; Psalm l 13, etc.
[4] John xiv 15-18, 26 ; xv 26 ; xvi 7-15.
[5] ἐκεῖνος.  See especially xvi 14.
[6] John xiv 16, 26 ; xv 26 ; xvi 7.      [7] 1 John ii 1.

The same fact may be seen from a comparison between the Holy Ghost and other persons. Besides the one just mentioned, we find in the gospels a comparison between blasphemy against the Son of Man and blasphemy against the Holy Ghost, which brings out even more clearly the personality of the Spirit.[1] And again the formula of baptism contained in the risen Christ's commission to his Apostles [2] associates the Holy Ghost with the other two persons of the Trinity in a manner that shows clearly that he too is a person.[3]

Thirdly, it is made clear from the attributes of the Holy Ghost, which testify to his personal character. He speaks, teaches, and testifies. "When he, the Spirit of truth, is come, he will teach you all truth." [4] He chooses and constitutes ministers in the Church. "Take heed to yourselves and to the whole flock, wherein the Holy Ghost has placed you (as) bishops to rule the Church of God." [5] The Holy Ghost said to them : "Separate me Saul and Barnabas for the work whereunto I have taken them." [6] He issues decrees to the Church through his Apostles. "It hath seemed good to the Holy Ghost and to us." [7]

Moreover, the Holy Ghost is a person distinct from the Father and the Son. Apart from the evidence of the baptismal formula in St Matthew, we may gather from St John's Gospel that the Holy Ghost proceeds from the Father, is sent by the Father, is demanded by the Son from the Father. Further, he receives of the Son, is sent by the Son, gives testimony of him, and takes his place. "I will ask the Father and he shall give you another Paraclete." [8] "The Paraclete, the Holy Ghost, whom the Father will send in my name." [9] "But when the Paraclete cometh, whom I will send you from the Father, the Spirit of truth who proceedeth from the Father, he shall give testimony of me." [10] "He shall glorify me, because he shall receive of mine." [11] "If I go not, the Paraclete will not come to you ; but if I go, I will send him to you." [12]

That the Holy Ghost is a divine person may be seen from the frequency with which he is identified with God. So to lie to the Holy Ghost is to lie to God,[13] and to offend him is to offend God. Again, to be the temple of the Spirit is the same as to be the temple of God. "Know you not that you are the temple of God, and that the Spirit of God dwelleth in you ? " [14]

It may also be proved from the divine operations that are attributed to him. He fully knows the secrets of the divine counsels. "For the Spirit searcheth all things, yea, the deep things of God. . . . So the things also that are of God no man knoweth but the Spirit of God." [15] To him are appropriated the inspiration of the prophets [16]

---

[1] Matt. xii 32 ; Luke xii 10.    [2] Matt. xxviii 19.
[3] See Essay iv, *The Blessed Trinity*, pp. 118-119.
[4] John xvi 13.    [5] Acts xx 28.    [6] Acts xiii 2.    [7] Acts xv 28.
[8] John xiv 16.    [9] John xiv 26.    [10] John xv 26.    [11] John xvi 14.
[12] John xvi 7.    [13] Acts v 3-4.    [14] 1 Cor. iii 16.
[15] 1 Cor. ii 10-11.    [16] 2 Peter i 21.

and the foretelling of the future.[1] He is the giver of various gifts and graces, and, on this count, one finds a striking reference to all three persons of the Blessed Trinity in St Paul.[2]

" Now there are varieties of gifts but the same Spirit,
And there are varieties of ministrations but the same Lord.
And there are varieties of workings but the same God, who worketh all things in all . . .
But all these things are the work of one and the same Spirit, who apportioneth severally to each as he will."

To him is also attributed the conception of Christ in the womb of the Blessed Virgin. The verbal parallelism in St Luke's narrative is to be noted.[3] The angel says to Mary :
" The Holy Ghost shall come upon thee,
And the power of the Most High shall overshadow thee."

Here " the power of the Most High " is clearly a synonym for the Holy Ghost.

Again, it is his function to sanctify and regenerate fallen men. " Unless a man be born again of water and of the Holy Ghost, he cannot enter into the kingdom of God." [4] " The charity of God is poured forth in our hearts by the Holy Ghost who is given to us." [5] Finally, it is his office to be at once the earnest and the agent of the resurrection. " He that raised up Jesus Christ from the dead, shall quicken also your mortal bodies, because of his Spirit that dwelleth in you." [6]

One may summarise the teaching of this section in the last words of a martyr, St Polycarp, Bishop of Smyrna, who suffered for his faith in the year 155. After he had been bound to the stake, he lifted his eyes to heaven and prayed, saying, " Lord God Almighty, Father of thy only and blessed Son, Jesus Christ, I bless thee that thou hast counted me worthy of this day and hour, that I may have a part in the number of thy martyrs, in the Cup of thy Christ, unto resurrection to life eternal of both soul and body in the incorruptibility of the Holy Spirit. . . . I glorify thee through the eternal and heavenly High Priest, Jesus Christ, thy only Son, through whom be glory to thee, together with him and the Holy Ghost now and for ever." [7]

§III: THE PROCESSION OF THE HOLY GHOST FROM THE
FATHER AND THE SON

*The Divine processions*  So far it has been established that revelation makes known to us a divine Person, the Holy Ghost, who is distinct from the Father and the Son. It remains for us to show that the intrinsic reason of this

[1] Acts xx 23.
[2] 1 Cor. xii 4-6, 11. Here I follow the Westminster Version.
[3] Luke i 35.   [4] John iii 5.   [5] Romans v 5.   [6] Romans viii 11.
[7] *Martyrdom of Polycarp*, xiv 1-3.

distinction is to be found in the doctrine of the divine origins or processions of the Son from the Father, and of the Holy Ghost from Father and Son.

It has been stated elsewhere [1] that there are in the divine nature two processions or origins of one divine person from another or from others ; that they are from all eternity and terminate in the divine essence itself ; that they imply no imperfection or posteriority of time or nature in the two persons who proceed ; that they correspond to the two activities of a purely spiritual nature, since the one is according to the operation of the divine intellect and the other according to the operation of the divine will. Further, it has been stated that the Father alone does not proceed, but is the principle of all processions, and that the Son proceeds from the Father alone by a special mode of procession known as generation. This, then, is the first procession, that of the divine Word, who is the perfect " reflection of his (the Father's) glory and the expression of his substance." [2]

With the second procession, that of the Holy Ghost, we must *The second* here deal more fully. It is of divine faith that there is in God a *procession* procession of the Spirit, which is distinct from that of the Word. The chief scriptural authority for this procession is to be found in Christ's discourse in the supper-room, to which reference has already been made. [3] There is mention of the Father from whom the Son proceeds ; of the Son who asks the Father to send, and who himself sends, another Paraclete distinct from himself ; of a Paraclete Spirit, who is expressly said to proceed from the Father. It will be shown later that he proceeds also from the Son.

It is furthermore of faith that the second divine procession is not generation, and that he who proceeds is not the begotten or the Son, but the Spirit. In Holy Scripture the third person is called the Holy Ghost, the Paraclete, the Spirit of truth, but he is never called the Son. In fact, in various passages of Holy Scripture it is made clear that the Second Person is the *only* Son, the only-begotten of the Father. [4] The Creeds also may be invoked as witnesses to this tradition ; of these the Athanasian is the most explicit in its wording : " The Holy Ghost is from Father and Son, not made nor created *nor begotten* but proceeding." [5]

The patristic evidence bears valuable witness to the truth in that the Fathers, while confessing their ignorance as to the precise *reason* why the Holy Ghost does not proceed by generation, are most certain as regards the *fact*. [6]

---

[1] Essay iv, *The Blessed Trinity*, pp. 123-133.
[2] Hebrews i 3, according to the Greek.     [3] John xiv-xvi.
[4] John i 14, 18. The word, ἀγαπητός, in Matt. iii 17 ; xvii 5, etc., ordinarily translated " beloved," should more properly be rendered " only," for it means : " *that wherewith one must be content* . . . hence of only children." See the new *Liddell and Scott*, s.v.
[5] Denzinger, n. 39.     [6] St Gregory of Nazianzos, *De Spiritu Sancto*, 8.

Various insufficient explanations have been put forward by St Augustine and other Fathers and schoolmen. It has been said, for example, that the Holy Spirit does not proceed by way of generation because he proceeds from two divine persons and the Son only from one. But this, in fact, would only prove that the Holy Ghost is not the Son who proceeds from the Father alone, and would not exclude his being *another* Son proceeding from the first and second persons. Again Richard of St Victor, St Bonaventure and others have sought the distinction in this that the Son receives a nature communicable to another, whereas the Holy Ghost does not receive such a nature. But it might be answered that filiation does not call for the reception of a communicable nature, but for the reception of a nature similar to that of the principle from which the son proceeds. These and other explanations fail in that they assign no adequate reason for distinguishing between the manner of the processions of the Son and of the Spirit.

The best explanation may be found in St Thomas.[1] To understand it we must realise that the first procession is according to the divine intellect and the second is according to the divine will. For generation properly so called it is necessary that the begotten should be similar in nature to the principle from which he proceeds *precisely by reason of the mode of his procession.* Now this condition is verified in the procession by way of intellect, and not in the procession by way of will. The Word, by the very fact that he proceeds according to the operation of the divine intellect, is the express likeness of the principle from which he proceeds, since the intellect is essentially an assimilative faculty. But it is not due to the very nature of his procession that the Spirit is like to the principle from which he proceeds, for he proceeds by way of will. " The intellect," says St Thomas, " is actualised by the object understood residing according to its own likeness in the intellect . . . the will is actualised not by any likeness of the object willed within it, but by its having a certain inclination towards the thing willed." [2] In other words, the will is not an assimilative faculty, but tends by an impulse towards the thing loved. That this impulse or inclination in God is the divine essence itself is not due to the very character of Love, but to the fact that nothing can proceed in God which is distinct from the divine essence. Hence, says St Basil [3] : " We do not speak of the Holy Spirit as unbegotten, for we recognise one unbegotten and one principle of things, the Father of Our Lord Jesus Christ ; nor (do we speak of the Holy Ghost) as begotten, for we have been taught by the tradition of the Faith that there is one only-begotten ; but, having been taught that the Spirit of truth proceeds from the Father, we confess him to be from God in uncreated wise."

[1] *S. Theol.*, I, Q. xxvii, art. 2-4 ; *Contra Gentiles*, IV, cc. 11, 19.
[2] *S. Theol.*, I, Q. xxvii, art. 4.          [3] *Ep.* cxxv.

The first and most common name of the Person who proceeds according to the divine will is the Spirit. " The name ' Spirit ' in things corporeal seems to signify impulse and motion ; for we call the breath and the wind by the term spirit. Now it is a property of love to move and impel the will of the lover towards the object loved. Further, holiness is attributed to whatever is ordered to God. Therefore, because the divine person proceeds by way of the love whereby God is loved, that person is most properly named the Holy Spirit." [1] It may be added that the term more commonly used in English, " the Holy Ghost," is simply a derived form of the Anglo-Saxon gāst, which means soul or spirit. There is no name that formally designates the mode of origin of the Holy Spirit. Theologians have contented themselves with calling it " procession," or, later, " spiration."

A second personal name of the Holy Ghost is that of Love. Love in respect of God can be taken in a twofold sense. It can be used essentially in so far as it implies an act of the divine will or a relation to the thing loved, and, in this sense, it is common to the three divine persons, as when St John says that " God is love (or charity)." [2] But it can also be used in a personal sense for the love that proceeds from Father and Son and is the resultant of their loving, and, so taken, it is a proper name of the Holy Ghost. In this sense, the " Veni Creator Spiritus " speaks of " the living fountain, fire and Love."

There is a third personal name of the Spirit, and it is that of Gift. The Holy Ghost proceeds as the mutual love of the Father and the Son, and it is of the nature of love to be a gift, to be, in fact, the first of all gifts from which all others flow. Hence, in the hymn just quoted, the Holy Ghost is called " Altissimi donum Dei "—" the gift of God most high."

It is, furthermore, of divine faith that the Third Person of the *The Holy* Blessed Trinity " proceeds eternally from the Father and the Son . . . *Ghost* as from one principle . . . and by one spiration." [3] These are the *proceeds from the* words of the Second Council of Lyons, the fourteenth General *Father and* Council, held in 1274. They have been constantly repeated and *the Son* reinforced in later Councils of the Church and in professions of faith. This dogma is denied, as regards the Son, by the Orthodox Eastern Church, which claims that the Holy Spirit proceeds from the Father only, on the ground that this alone is explicitly stated in Holy Scripture.[4] To the uninstructed this point might seem to be one of minor importance. In reality it is essential not only for a true profession of the Catholic Faith, but for the establishing of any consistent theology of the Blessed Trinity.

We will begin with the Scriptural data, premising the remark that

[1] *S. Theol.*, I, Q. xxxvi, art. 1.  [2] 1 John iv 16.
[3] Denzinger, n. 460.  [4] John xv 26.

we do not claim to find in Holy Scripture any perfectly explicit statement of the Holy Spirit's procession from the Son, but that the force of various equivalent statements is unmistakable. Holy Scripture declares that the Holy Ghost is the Spirit of the Father. " The Spirit of your Father that speaketh in you." [1] But it also speaks of him as the Spirit of the Son. " God hath sent the Spirit of his Son into your hearts." [2] " The supply of the Spirit of Jesus Christ." [3] The natural meaning of " the Spirit of the Son " is that which is spirated, or breathed by the Son. In other words, it is equivalent to that which proceeds by spiration from the Son. Furthermore, it is admitted by the Orthodox themselves that the Holy Ghost is called the Spirit of the Father for no other reason than because he proceeds from the Father. Hence, one may conclude that the Spirit of the Son is so called because he proceeds from the Son.

Again, in certain passages the Holy Spirit is said to hear the Son and to receive from him. This would have no real signification, unless he proceeded from the Son. Our Lord in his last discourse to the disciples [4] says of the Holy Ghost : " When he, the Spirit of truth, is come, he will teach you all truth " (better, " He will guide you into all the truth "). " For he shall not speak of himself ; but what things soever he shall hear, he shall speak. . . . He shall glorify me, because he shall receive of mine and shall show it to you." Here, then, there is question of the communication of divine knowledge by the Son to the Holy Spirit. Evidently, this cannot imply any ignorance on the part of the Holy Ghost, or any need of illumination from the Son. It can only mean that, as there is no real distinction between the divine knowledge and the divine nature,[5] the Holy Ghost receives wisdom by receiving the divine nature from the Son. In other words, the Son communicates to the Holy Spirit the divine nature, which he has himself received from the Father. Passages of similar implication are to be found regarding the Son's reception of the divine nature from the Father. " The things I have heard of him, these same I speak in the world." [6] " As the Father hath taught me, these things I speak." [7] " My doctrine is not mine, but his that sent me." [8] This interpretation of John xvi 13 ff. receives additional support from a text that immediately follows it. " All things whatsoever the Father hath are mine." [9] In the light of these texts and of the general teaching on the divine relations,[10] we may argue as follows : All things whatsoever the Father has, the Son has with the exception of paternity. But active spiration, or the act of breathing the Holy Ghost is not paternity. Therefore, as the Father has active spiration, the Son also has it.

[1] Matt. x 20.    [2] Gal. iv 6.    [3] Phil. i 9.    [4] John xvi 13-14.
[5] See Essay iii, The One God, pp. 86, 92.
[6] John viii 26.    [7] John viii 28.    [8] John vii 16.    [9] John xvi 15.
[10] See Essay iv, The Blessed Trinity, pp. 134-136.

The same truth may be gathered from the texts relating to the mission of the Holy Spirit by the Son. Our Lord said : " And I will ask the Father and he shall give you another Paraclete that he may abide with you for ever." [1] And again, more explicitly : " When the Paraclete cometh, whom I will send you from the Father." [2] And again : " If I go, I will send him (*i.e.* the Paraclete) to you." [3] It is clear from such passages that there is a mission of the Holy Ghost and that the principle of this mission is the Son. Now it will be seen later that a divine person can only be sent by the person from whom he proceeds. But, if the Holy Ghost is sent by the Son, it is clear that he proceeds from the Son. A divine mission necessarily presupposes an eternal procession. *Missio sequitur et manifestat processionem.* A mission follows upon a procession and makes it manifest.

We conclude, then, that the temporal mission of the Holy Spirit points clearly to his eternal procession from both Father and Son. St Augustine, commenting on John xx 22, writes : " Why do we not believe that the Holy Ghost proceeds also from the Son since he is the Spirit of the Son also ? For if he did not proceed from him, he (Our Lord) when he manifested himself to his disciples after the resurrection would not have breathed upon them, saying : Receive the Holy Ghost. For what else did that breathing signify than that the Holy Spirit proceeds also from him ? " [4]

A word may be said regarding an important text to which reference has already been made. It is Our Lord's phrase regarding " the Spirit of truth, who proceedeth from the Father." [5] It will be noticed that this text in no way states that the procession is from the Father only. Furthermore, it follows immediately upon the words : " Whom I will send you from the Father," a mission, which, as we have seen, clearly postulates an eternal procession from the Son.

The teaching of the Fathers may here be summarised, though a careful individual study of their writings is essential for the formation of an independent judgement. [6] We may leave on one side the testimony of the Latin Fathers, which on the Orthodox theologians' own admission is entirely favourable to the Catholic doctrine. We may also with good reason refrain from any attempt to find very clear testimonies to the doctrine in the Fathers of the three centuries before the Council of Nicaea in 325. Having established these limitations, we can go on to say that the Greek Fathers teach with moral unanimity the procession of the Holy Ghost from the Son.

Sometimes the doctrine is taught equivalently and implicitly, as when Origen (185-254) says that : " The Son communicates to the

---

[1] John xiv 16.  [2] John xv 26.  [3] John xvi 7.
[4] In Joan. Evang., tract. 99, cap. 16.  [5] John xv 26.
[6] There is an admirably full account of the question in the *Dictionnaire de théologie catholique*, t. v, coll. 773-807.

person of the Holy Spirit not only being, but also wisdom, intelligence and justice." [1] Or again, in the words of St Basil (ca. 330-379) : " As the Son is in regard of the Father, so is the Spirit in respect of the Son. . . . No dissection or division can be in any way conceived whereby the Son should be understood without the Father, or the Spirit separated from the Son." [2]

At times, however, the doctrine is taught distinctly and expressly. St Epiphanius (ca. 315-403) speaks of " the Spirit of the Father and the Spirit of the Son, intermediate between the Father and the Son and from the Father and the Son." [3] Or, as St Ephraem the Syrian (ca. 306-373) writes : " The Father is the Begetter ; the Son the Begotten from his bosom ; the Holy Spirit proceeding from the Father and the Son " [4]—Or, again, in the words of Didymus of Alexandria (ca. 313-398), " Our Lord teaches that the being of the Spirit is derived not from the Spirit himself, but from the Father and the Son ; he goes forth from the Son, proceeding from the Truth ; he has no substance but that which is given to him by the Son." [5]

We must note particularly the phrase that often occurs in the Greek Fathers, and is not unknown in the Latin writers : " The Holy Spirit proceeds from the Father *through* the Son." St Athanasius says that : " As the Word before the Incarnation dispensed the Spirit as his own, so now that he is made man he sanctifies all with the Spirit. . . . Through whom and from whom could the Spirit be given, but *through* the Son, whose Spirit he is ? " [6] St Basil states that " the native goodness and the natural hallowing and the royal dignity reach the Spirit *from* the Father *through* the Only-Begotten." [7] This formula is recognised by the Council of Florence as perfectly orthodox.[8] It merely lays stress upon the fact that breathing or active spiration is in the Father as in its principle and in the Son as it is communicated to him by the Father.

*An argument from reason*  In the light of Scripture and Tradition, theologians have found an argument from reason that may fairly be described as unassailable. It is stated by St Thomas as follows [9] : " It must be said that the Holy Ghost is from the Son. For if he were not from him, he could in no wise be personally distinguished from him." In other words, the Holy Spirit is really distinct from the Son ; but in the divine nature there can be no real distinction between the persons except by reason of the origin or procession of one from the other. " For it cannot be said that the divine persons are distinguished from each

---

[1] *In Joann.* ii 6.  [2] *De Spiritu Sancto*, c. 17, n. 43.
[3] *Ancoratus*, 8.
[4] *Hymnus de defunctis et Trinitate ;* Ed. Lamy, 3, 242.
[5] *De Spiritu Sancto*, 34-37.  [6] *Or. c. Arianos*, I, 48, 40.
[7] *De Spiritu Sancto*, c. 18, n. 47.
[8] Denzinger, n. 691.  [9] *S. Theol.*, I, Q. xxxvi, art. 2.

other by anything absolute ; for it would follow that there would not
be one essence of the three persons." Therefore they are distinguished only by relations.  Nor can the divine persons be distinguished by relations that are merely dissimilar, for in the Father
there are two dissimilar relations, Paternity and active spiration,
" but these are not opposite relations, and therefore they do not
make two persons but belong only to the one person of the Father."
In like manner, filiation and active spiration in the Son, since they
are merely dissimilar relations, do not constitute two persons.  Hence
the reason for the distinction must be found in relations that are
opposed to one another.  " Now there cannot be in God any relations opposed to each other except relations of origin.  And
opposed relations of origin are those of a principle to that which
proceeds therefrom.  Therefore we must conclude that it is necessary
to say either that the Son is from the Holy Ghost, which no one says ;
or that the Holy Ghost is from the Son, as we confess."

The Orthodox position is based on the affirmation that the Father
is the source of all things, and that to admit the procession of the
Holy Ghost from the Son would be to admit two sources in God.
Catholic theologians have replied by allowing that the Father is the
ultimate principle of the divine processions, who alone does not
proceed, while disallowing expressions that might seem to imply any
inferiority in the other two persons.  They also insist that, although
there is a relation of generation between Father and Son, there is no
opposed relation between them in so far as they are the common
source of the Holy Ghost's procession.  At the Councils of Lyons
II (1274) and Florence (1438-45), the Pope and the Latins were
willing to make certain concessions in terminology—to admit that
the Father is the " cause " (understood in the sense of principle) of
the other two persons and to allow the complete orthodoxy of the
formula " from the Father, through the Son."  Unfortunately for
any hope of permanent reconciliation, our opponents are not strong
in either logic or metaphysic, they have tried to convert a point of
abstruse theology into a popular war-cry, and the end of their opposition is not yet.[1]

One of the principal Orthodox grievances is that the Latins have *The*
tampered with the historic Creeds by inserting the clause known as *Filioque*
the *Filioque*, that is, the words " and from the Son."  It is true that
the considerable additions made to the Nicene Creed by the Council
of Constantinople in 381 did not include these words, and that the
article originally read :  " The Holy Ghost . . . who proceeds from
the Father."  Later, however, the words " and from the Son " were
added, first in Spain, as the evidence of several Spanish councils of
the 5th, 6th, and 7th centuries shows, and then in France and
Germany.  In 809 the Synod of Aachen (Aix-la-Chapelle) petitioned

[1] See in particular Dr. Adrian Fortescue's *The Orthodox Eastern Church*,
pp. 372-384.

Pope Leo III to introduce the formula at Rome. He refused to make any change in the official creeds, though the doctrine itself of the procession from both Father and Son was universally believed in the West. Finally, Pope Benedict VIII (1012-1024) allowed the introduction of the *Filioque* at Rome. It had long been in use throughout the Roman Patriarchate.

The legitimacy of such an addition in the first place, on the authority of a local council, may well be questioned. But there can be no doubt concerning its lawfulness since its approval by the supreme magisterium of the Church. Nor have the Orthodox any reason for saying that such an addition contravenes the decree of the Council of Ephesus forbidding anyone to " compose another faith than that one which was defined by the holy Fathers who were gathered together with the Holy Ghost at Nicaea." [1] The Council's intention was to anathematise any contradictory formula. It had nothing to say against legitimate additions to the Creeds or against clearer statements of the unchanging Faith.

A few lines will suffice for the remaining words of the Second Council of Lyons—that the Holy Ghost proceeds from Father and Son *as from one principle and by one spiration*. The clause has already been equivalently stated. All things are common to Father and Son with the exception of paternity and filiation, and the only distinction between them is one of origin. It follows, then, that active spiration is numerically the same in the Father and the Son. So, in the words of St Augustine [2] : " The Catholic Church holds and preaches that God the Holy Spirit is not the Spirit of the Father only, or of the Son only, but of the Father and the Son. . . . He is their common life (communitas). It was therefore their will to give us communion with one another and with themselves through that which is common to them both ; to gather us together in one by this Gift which both have in common, namely, by the Holy Ghost, who is God and the Gift of God."

We must now pass from the inner life of the Blessed Trinity to consider the Holy Ghost in his temporal mission and in the gifts he gives to men.

## §IV: THE TEMPORAL MISSION OF THE HOLY GHOST

*The divine
missions*

" By the Temporal Mission of the Holy Ghost, Catholic theologians understand the sending, advent, and office of the Holy Ghost through the Incarnate Son and after the day of Pentecost. . . . The Eternal Procession of the Holy Ghost completes the mystery of the Trinity *ad intra ;* the Temporal Mission . . . completes the revelation of the Trinity *ad extra.*" [3]

[1] Denzinger, n. 125.          [2] Sermon 71, 12, 18.
[3] Cardinal Manning, *The Temporal Mission of the Holy Ghost*, p. 14 and pp. 22-23.

Our Lord himself tells us that " He that sent me, is with me," [1] and that " If I go not, the Paraclete will not come to you, but, if I go, I will send him to you." [2]  These sendings, or missions, may be defined as the processions of one divine person from another as implying a new mode of existence in creatures.  They involve no change in the divine persons themselves, nor, since the divine persons are everywhere present, can they be understood of any change of place or local motion.  But they demand a new manner of existing in a rational creature, and this new operation must take place in the creature in whom the divine person is received after a new manner.  It is to be noted that all divine operations in creatures are common to all three persons of the Trinity, but, as regards these operations, the Son and the Holy Ghost are sent, whereas the Father is not sent, but sends.  The Son is sent by the Father, and the Holy Ghost by the Father and the Son.

These missions are either visible or invisible ; in the former, the divine person manifests himself visibly ; in the latter, his manifestation is invisible.  The invisible mission is effected by the gifts of grace without any exterior manifestation, but the visible missions are brought about with some external effect perceptible to the senses, as, for example, in the Incarnation of the Word or in the descent of the Holy Ghost on the day of Pentecost.  The former is the only example of a substantial visible mission, for the Word by becoming hypostatically united to a human nature appeared visibly in that nature.  Four visible missions of the Holy Ghost are commonly enumerated ; and they were all not substantial but representative since, although the Holy Ghost was specially revealed in them, he was not united personally and hypostatically with creatures.  The first visible mission took place at Our Lord's baptism and was under the appearance of a dove [3] ; the second was at the Transfiguration and took the form of a luminous cloud [4] ; the third took place after the Resurrection, when Christ conferred the Holy Spirit upon his Apostles under the form of breath [5] ; lastly, the fourth occurred on Pentecost in the form of tongues of fire.[6]

We have now to consider the invisible mission of the Holy Ghost and the varied ways in which " He, who is the divine goodness and the mutual love of the Father and the Son, completes and perfects by his strong yet gentle power the secret work of man's eternal salvation." [7]  Following Pope Leo's Encyclical, we shall consider three of the principal manifestations of the Holy Spirit's temporal mission under the headings, the Holy Ghost and the Incarnation, the Holy Ghost and the Church, and the Holy Ghost in the souls of the just.

[1] John viii 29.    [2] John xvi 7.    [3] Matt. iii 12.
[4] Matt. xvii 5.    [5] John xx 22.    [6] Acts ii 3.
[7] Pope Leo XIII : Enc. *Divinum illud*, p. 426.  The pages referred to are those in *The Great Encyclical Letters of Leo XIII*, an American edition published by Benziger.

The Holy Ghost and the written word of God will be the subject of our final section.

*The Holy Ghost and the Incarnation* "Among the external operations of God, the highest of all is the mystery of the Incarnation of the Word. . . . Now this work, though it belongs to the whole Trinity, is appropriated especially to the Holy Ghost, so that the gospels thus speak of the Blessed Virgin : *She was found with child, of the Holy Ghost,* and *That which is conceived in her, is of the Holy Ghost.*[1] And this is rightly ascribed to him, who is the Love of the Father and the Son, since this great *mystery of godliness* [2] proceeds from the infinite love of God towards man, as St John tells us : *God so loved the world, as to give his only begotten Son.*" [3]

It is of faith that one divine person can assume to himself a human nature without this union being shared by the other divine persons. In fact, only the Word assumed human nature. But the act of raising that nature to union with the Godhead is common to all three persons, since it is an operation of the Trinity in relation to creatures. As St Thomas has it : "The three persons effected the union of a human nature to the one Person of the Son." [4] But this act, for the reasons given by Pope Leo, is most fittingly attributed to the Holy Ghost.

Moreover, the dignity of personal union with the Word to which a human nature was elevated was bestowed by reason of no merits of ours. It is therefore essentially a grace and, as such, proper to the operation of the Holy Spirit. Other graces remain in the accidental order ; even the gift of the Holy Ghost to the just, though in itself substantial, does not effect a substantial union, as we shall remark later, but the personal union of Christ's human nature with the Word *is* a substantial union. Hence the grace of union is accounted the greatest of all graces ; and this grace, by which in the judgement of most theologians the humanity of Christ was formally sanctified, is rightly attributed to him who is regarded as peculiarly the source of sanctification.

To the Holy Ghost we also attribute the fulness of sanctifying grace with which Christ's soul was endowed, and which is called in Holy Scripture his *anointing.*[5] In the synagogue at Nazareth Our Divine Lord applied to himself those words of Isaias the prophet : "The Spirit of the Lord is upon me, wherefore he hath anointed me," [6] and this anointing of the Spirit was bestowed not only in the grace of union, but in all the other graces and gifts that adorned the soul of Christ, so that in him resided the absolute fulness of divine grace in the most perfect manner possible. Isaias had foretold that these gifts of the Spirit would be bestowed upon the offspring of

---

[1] Matt. i 18, 20.  [2] 1 Tim. iii 16.
[3] John iii 16 ; *Divinum illud*, p. 427.
[4] *S. Theol.*, III, Q. iii, art. 4. See Essay xi, *Jesus Christ, God and Man*, p. 383.
[5] Acts x 38.  [6] Luke iv 18 ; Isaias lxi 1.

Jesse [1] and, at Christ's baptism, the descent of the Spirit and the Father's voice glorified the divine Son. "Therefore by the conspicuous apparition of the Holy Ghost and by his invisible power in his soul, the twofold mission of the Spirit is foreshadowed, namely, the mission which is evidently manifest in his Church and that which is effected by his secret descent into the souls of the just." [2]

We must now consider the Holy Ghost's office in founding the Church and in her guidance and administration throughout the Christian centuries. Pope Leo says that "the Church which, already conceived, came forth from the very side of the Second Adam, when he was, as it were, sleeping upon the cross, first showed herself in a marvellous manner before the eyes of men on the great day of Pentecost." [3] It was the fulfilment of Our Lord's promise to send "another Paraclete," who should be the "promise of the Father." [4] It was the last of the visible missions of the Spirit. And Our Lord by this gift to his disciples intended "to complete and, as it were, to seal the deposit of doctrine committed to them under his inspiration."[5]

*The Holy Ghost and the Church*

The conception of this deposit and the sources of revelation in which it is contained are more fully dealt with elsewhere.[6] But, at the risk of some repetition, one must insist upon the fundamental truth that one of the effects of the Holy Ghost's mission to the Church is to ensure the safe custody of an unchanging revelation. The Church teaches us that after the death of the Apostles no new economy or new revelation was to be expected, and, further, that there never has been nor will be any objective increase in revealed truth. Holy Scripture assures us that the present economy is final; it is the "fulness of time"[7]; that Christianity stands, as it were, midway between the types and figures of the Old Testament and the final consummation of God's kingdom in heaven; that, in opposition to the levitical ministry that passed away and needed renewal, Jesus, "for that he continueth for ever, hath an everlasting priesthood." [8] It was to be the office of the Apostles' successors to "keep that which is committed to their trust," to "hold the form of sound words" which they had heard, to avoid all that was "contrary to the doctrine" which they had learned, to "contend earnestly for the faith once delivered to the saints." [9] And Tradition teaches the same lesson—that from the earliest times Catholics sought to follow in all things the apostolic teaching and regarded novelty in doctrine as an unmistakable sign of heresy.

This is not to deny that there could be, and indeed has been at times in the Church's history, a somewhat more explicit or more

---

[1] Isaias xi 1 ff.    [2] *Divinum illud*, p. 428.    [3] *Ibid.*
[4] John xiv 16; Luke xxiv 49.    [5] *Divinum illud*, l. c.
[6] Essay i, *Faith and Revealed Truth*, pp. 28 ff.
[7] Gal. iv 4; Eph. i 10.    [8] Heb. vii 24.
[9] 1 Tim. vi 20; 2 Tim. i 13-14; Rom. xvi 17; Jude 3, etc.

distinct or more technical presentation of certain dogmas.[1] It remains true that, in the words of the Vatican Council, " the doctrine of faith which God has revealed has not been proposed, like a philosophical invention, to be perfected by human intelligence, but has been delivered as a divine deposit to the Spouse of Christ to be faithfully kept and infallibly declared." [2]

The deposit must be " faithfully kept "; there have been occasions when it has had to be " infallibly declared." The Holy Ghost is twice called by Our Lord " the Spirit of truth," [3] and it is to him that the Church looks for that gift of infallibility, that divine assistance that safeguards her supreme authority in its doctrinal definitions and in its ordinary teaching of the faithful. This assistance should not, as is evident from what has been said, be regarded as a means of communicating new truths to the Church, nor is it a positive influence inspiring the Popes and members of General Councils to utter definitions and declarations of Catholic doctrine. It is rather in the nature of a negative influence that restrains the episcopate and its Head from teaching or proclaiming anything contrary to the revealed deposit. But, though it may be called negative in its essential character, it is not negative in its effect— the preservation of the ecclesiastical magisterium within the limits of the truth. Such assistance does not necessarily preserve the Church from error except in regard of revealed truth and truths intimately connected with revelation, nor does it dispense the authorities of the Church from exercising ordinary prudence and diligence in preparing matter for a definition. This, then, is the special divine assistance promised by means of the Holy Spirit's mission to the Church. " You shall receive the power of the Holy Ghost coming upon you, and you shall be witnesses unto me in Jerusalem, and in all Judea and Samaria, and even to the uttermost part of the earth." [4]

But the Holy Spirit comes to the Church not only as the Spirit of Truth, but as the Spirit of Holiness. He is the principle of regeneration in baptism,[5] and of the forgiveness of sins [6] and of all supernatural life. St Paul exhorts us not to " grieve the Holy Spirit of God, whereby you are sealed unto the day of redemption," [7] and by whom we are united together in one body. " For in one Spirit were we all baptised into one body," [8] and that body is the Body of Christ, a visible and a mystical Body.

Finally, the Holy Ghost is the principle of unity in the Church, of her organisation, and of all the gifts conferred upon her members. " There are diversities of graces, but the same Spirit. . . . But all these things one and the same Spirit worketh, dividing to every one

[1] See Essay i, *Faith and Revealed Truth*, pp. 33 ff.
[2] Sess. 3, cap. 4, Denzinger, n. 1800.
[3] John xv 26 ; xvi 13.      [4] Acts i 8.      [5] John iii 5.
[6] John xx 22.      [7] Ephesians iv 30.      [8] 1 Cor. xii 13.

according as he will." [1]   He is the source and the secret of that
" unity of the Spirit in the bond of peace.   One body and one Spirit ;
as you are called in one hope of your calling.   One Lord, one faith,
one baptism.   One God and Father of all." [2]   And what is true of
the body as a whole is true also of its organs.   " Take heed to yourselves and to the whole flock," said St Paul to the priests of Ephesus,
" wherein the Holy Ghost hath placed you (as) bishops to rule the
Church of God." [3]   " Let it suffice to state that, as Christ is the
Head of the Church, so is the Holy Ghost her soul," says Pope Leo.[4]
And he quotes St Augustine's words :  " What the soul is in our
body, that is the Holy Ghost in Christ's body, the Church." [5]

The Holy Ghost is also called the heart of the Church, for, as
St Thomas says [6] :  " The heart has a certain occult influence, and
therefore the Holy Ghost is compared to a heart, which invisibly
gives life to and unites the Church."

It is to be noted that the Church as a society is not merely the
sum of the individual members, and he who is the Church's soul, in
addition to his indwelling in the souls of the individual members,
dwells in the Church as a society, an organism, a body, and acts
principally through the gifts bestowed upon the society—priesthood,
ecclesiastical magisterium, and sacred authority.

" This being so,  no further and fuller ' manifestation and revelation of the divine Spirit ' may be imagined or expected ;  for that
which now takes place in the Church is the most perfect possible,
and will last until that day when the Church herself, having passed
through her militant stage, shall be taken up into the joy of the saints
triumphant in heaven." [7]

It is not possible within the compass of this short essay to say *The Holy*
very much regarding the work of the Holy Spirit in the individual *Ghost in the*
soul.  A large part of the subject is treated in other essays, notably *just*
*souls of the*
in Essays XVI and XVII on *Sanctifying Grace* and *Actual Grace*, and
in those, ten in all, that deal with the Sacraments of the Church.  But
something more than a word must be said here concerning one of
the principal effects of sanctifying grace in the soul, namely, the
inhabitation of the divine Persons in the souls of the just.  But, as
this is a special divine presence, it is necessary first to have some
conception of God's ordinary presence in the things he has created
out of nothing.

Holy Scripture accustoms us to the truth that God is everywhere
really and substantially present.  " Do not I fill heaven and earth,
saith the Lord " by his prophet Jeremias,[8] and the fact of that divine
presence in all creation is one of the child's first lessons in the things

---

[1] 1 Cor. xii 4, 11.          [2] Ephesians iv 3-6.          [3] Acts xx 28.
[4] *Divinum illud*, p. 430.    [5] Serm. 267, 4.
[6] *S. Theol.*, III, Q. viii, art. 1 ad 3.
[7] *Divinum illud*, p. 430.    [8] xxiii 24.

of God. The mode of that indwelling is less generally explained. Theologians commonly say that the formal reason for this divine presence is not the divine substance itself, but the divine operation. God is a spirit, and a spiritual substance, unlike a bodily substance, is not in a place by its extension, but by its operation therein. Hence God is present in things by his operation. So the reason assigned by Holy Scripture for this presence is that " in him we live and move and are," [1] or, in other words, that God is present in his creatures as a cause is present to its effect, namely, by the application of his power. An enlargement upon this conception is given in St Thomas's dictum that God is present and exists in all things, " by his power, inasmuch as all things are subject to his power ; by his presence, inasmuch as all things are naked and open to his eyes ; by his essence, inasmuch as he is present to all as the cause of their being." [2]

This is the ordinary presence of God in the order of nature, but there are other more intimate modes of his presence in the supernatural order. We have already spoken, in treating of the Incarnation, of the most special of all these modes—the substantial union between a divine person and a human nature that gave to the world Jesus, Our Lord, true God and true man. Now we come to the special manner of God's presence in the just, whereby the divine Persons reside by grace in the just soul as in a temple in a most intimate and special manner.

The fact of this inhabitation is a dogma of the Faith, which is most explicitly stated in Holy Scripture and Tradition. As regards the Holy Ghost, we have already considered the texts regarding his mission and gift to men. The words in St John were addressed in the first place to the Apostles, but many other passages prove that the divine gift was not restricted to them but was bestowed on all the adopted sons of God. " You have received the spirit of adoption of sons," writes St Paul to the Romans.[3] " . . . For the Spirit himself giveth testimony to our spirit that we are the sons of God." And he writes to the Galatians : [4] " Because you are sons, God hath sent the Spirit of his Son into your hearts. . . ." And it is not only a divine gift, but a permanent divine presence. " Know you not that you are the temple of God, and that the Spirit of God dwelleth in you ? " [5] " Your members are the temple of the Holy Ghost, who is in you, whom you have from God." [6]

This presence of the Holy Ghost is also the presence of the other divine persons. Our Lord himself says : " He that eateth my flesh, and drinketh my blood, *abideth* in *me*, and I *in him*." [7] And again he says, " If any one love me, he will keep my word, and my Father will love him, and *we* will come to him and will make our abode with him." [8] The chief condition is love of Jesus ; as a reward he

[1] Acts xvii 28.
[2] *S. Theol.*, I, Q. viii, art. 3.
[3] viii 15-16.
[4] Gal. iv 6-7.
[5] I Cor. iii 16.
[6] I Cor. vi 19.
[7] John vi 57.
[8] John xiv 23.

and the Father will dwell supernaturally and permanently with the lover.

Hence it is clear that, as a result of sanctifying grace, the human soul becomes the temple of God, who inhabits it in a special manner not merely by His created gifts, but by the real presence of the divine Persons. This is especially evident from the Epistle to the Romans,[1] where the Holy Ghost and his gift of charity are sharply distinguished. " The charity of God is poured forth in our hearts by the Holy Ghost, who is given to us."

So fundamental a truth was commented upon even by the Apostolic Fathers. Thus St Ignatius of Antioch writes to the Ephesians [2] : " You are then all travelling companions, bearers of God, bearers of his temple, bearers of Christ, bearers of sacred things, having no other vesture than the precepts of Jesus Christ." And this divine indwelling is distinguished from God's created gifts as St Cyril of Alexandria tells us : " We are made *partakers of the divine nature* [3] and are said to be born of God ; we are therefore called gods, being raised not by grace alone to supernatural glory, but having already God dwelling in us and abiding in us." [4]

This permanent inhabitation of the divine Persons in the souls of the just necessarily calls for some change on the part of the creature, and for the setting up of a new real relation in him whereby he is intimately joined with God. But, as St Thomas says, " No other effect (*i.e.* no other change) can be the reason for the divine persons existing in a rational creature in a new manner *except sanctifying grace.*" [5] Evidently there can be no change on the part of God, who is immutable ; hence some new divine effect is required that operates in the just and not in others. And Sacred Scripture, the Fathers and the theologians agree in finding no other effect of this kind except sanctifying grace. So it is that our union with God is effected by means of the supernatural, created accident of sanctifying grace. Hence by the reception of sanctifying grace the just truly become the temples of the divine Persons, who truly and really inhabit their souls. This is confirmed by the consideration that the divine Persons do not inhabit the souls of those who are not in a state of grace, for, in the words of St Athanasius, " He who has fallen is no longer in God, since the holy Paraclete Spirit, who is in God, has receded from him." [6] It is, of course, true that God can *move* the sinner by his actual graces, but he does not thereby inhabit him, since actual graces are of their nature transient.

But we must further determine the manner of this divine inhabitation. By its very definition as a special presence and as an effect of sanctifying grace, it evidently cannot be reduced to God's

[1] v 5.　　　　　[2] ix 2.　　　[3] 2 Peter i 4.
[4] *In Joannem comm.*, i 9.
[5] *S. Theol.*, I, Q. xliii, art. 3.
[6] *Or. contra. Arianos*, III, 24.

ordinary manner of existence in his creatures by his power, his presence, and his essence. Nor can we accept the view of certain theologians that the Holy Spirit is only present in the just in so far as he preserves in them the supernatural gifts of grace and the infused virtues. This would call, indeed, for some supernatural presence, but not for a divine inhabitation, since God preserves the habits of faith and hope in sinners, but does not thereby inhabit them. Inhabitation implies a permanent reception as a guest and a friend, a reception not merely of a friend's gifts, but of the friend himself. Any theory that minimises this fact may be ultimately reduced to what St Thomas calls " the error of those who say that the Holy Ghost is not given but only his gifts." [1]

For the true explanation of this divine presence we turn to St Thomas. After mentioning God's common manner of existence in creatures, he continues : " There is one special mode, belonging to the rational nature, wherein God is said to be present *as the object known is in the knower and the beloved in the lover.* And since the rational creature by its own operation of knowledge and love attains to God himself, according to this special manner, God is said not only to exist in the rational creature, but also to dwell therein as in his own temple." [2] The keynote to this teaching is to be found in the words in italics. First, " God is said to be present *as the object known is in the knower.*" This may be explained in the following way. Among the infused virtues and gifts that accompany sanctifying grace the gift of wisdom, since it arises out of charity, has a pre-eminent place. It is the gift of such knowledge as gives true delight and peace to the soul. But knowledge, if it is to be truly delightful, calls for a certain real presence of the thing known, by reason of which the knower really enjoys the object of his knowledge. Hence the gift of wisdom calls for such a real presence of God in the soul as is possible in this life. But, in the present life, a real union with the intelligence is not possible ; we should then already enjoy the beatific vision. It is, however, possible to have this union with the essence of the soul and with the faculty of enjoyment, which is the will. Therefore the gift of wisdom requires the real presence of God in the essence of the soul and in the will. And this is effected by sanctifying grace according to St Thomas's dictum, " To have the power of enjoying a divine Person can only be according to sanctifying grace." [3]

Secondly, St Thomas says that God is present " *as the beloved in the lover.*" Sanctifying grace, by the intermediacy of charity, constitutes perfect friendship between God and the soul. But

---

[1] *S. Theol.*, I, Q. xliii, art. 3, arg. 1.
[2] *Ibid.*, I, Q. xliii, art. 3.
[3] *Ibid.*, l.c. For this argument and the following the writer is much indebted to his old master, the late Père Edouard Hugon, O.P., S.T.M. See his *Tractatus de Gratia*, pp. 175 ff.

friendship, as a condition, calls not only for unselfish and mutual love, but also for a certain communication of good things, establishing some measure of equality between friends. This communication of good things is effected by sanctifying grace, for, since grace is a participation of the divine nature, it is something common to God and ourselves, namely, that supernatural life which is given to us by God and is most truly ours. And so God gives us something of his, namely, a participation of his divine life, and we are permitted to give something of our own to God, in so far as we promote his extrinsic glory by good works done in a state of grace. Furthermore, friendship to be perfect calls not only for an affective union of the lover with his beloved, but also, so far as is possible, for a real and effective union, so that the beloved is not only extrinsically present to the lover, but exists within the lover as a most intimate object of his knowledge and love. And so this supreme intimacy and friendship between God and man calls for a special and intimate presence of God in the soul.

Hence the whole argument turns upon the nature of charity, which is intimate friendship with God. Our *knowledge*, indeed, is in this life imperfect and obscure and does not effect a real union of God, by way of object, with our intellect. But our charity, since it is specifically the same as the charity of our heavenly fatherland, demands and effects a real union of the divine persons with the will of one in a state of divine grace. Hence, by way of sanctifying grace, in which charity is rooted, the divine Persons are really and substantially present in our souls.

Is this divine presence common to the three divine Persons or does it pertain in any exclusive manner to the Holy Spirit ? The question is already answered by the fundamental principle that all external operations of the Trinity are common to the three divine Persons, though, as we have seen in the case of the Incarnation, a formal substantial union could exist between the Word and a created nature without this union being shared by the other divine Persons. A special union with the Holy Ghost would involve a hypostatic union with every soul in a state of grace, and Catholic teaching recognises no hypostatic union other than that of the Incarnate Word. But it may freely be allowed that this divine indwelling, as a work of divine love and the effect of the divine friendship, manifests in a special manner the personal character of the Holy Ghost, who is subsistent Love, the infinite Love of the supreme Good. So this inhabitation is fittingly appropriated to the Holy Spirit, and it is in this sense that we must understand those texts of Scripture and Tradition which state that the Father and the Son dwell in us through the Holy Ghost.

The effects of this marvellous indwelling are not far to seek. Since we have a share in " that wonderful union, which is properly called ' indwelling,' differing only in degree or state from that with which God beatifies the saints in heaven," [1] we enjoy most intimate converse with the divine Persons. We have dwelling within us one who is our Advocate in the sorrows and misfortunes of the present life, and who makes known to our souls the deep things of God.[2] We have within us the source of all the virtues, gifts, and fruits bestowed by the Holy Ghost upon men, and even our mortal bodies, since they are the temples of the Blessed Trinity, are in a special manner made holy, and sacred, and worthy of the general resurrection.

What are our duties towards our divine guests? We must avoid anything that may occasion the withdrawal of this special inhabitation in our souls or that may hinder the fulness of the divine activity within us. We may also consider some words of Père Hugon reminding us that, "Since friends are accustomed to converse with each other and to pay each other visits, we ought very often to visit the Blessed Trinity, as we visit Jesus in the Blessed Sacrament. A double visit should be paid by us frequently in the course of the day: a visit to the Blessed Sacrament, though this is not always possible, and a visit to the Most Holy Trinity, which is always and at all times possible and passing sweet indeed!" [3]

§ V : THE HOLY GHOST AND THE WRITTEN WORD OF GOD

*The prophets of the Old Testament* WE have already seen that it was one of the functions of the Spirit in Old Testament times to inspire "the holy prophets, who are from the beginning." [4] The subject of Hebrew prophecy is an intricate one, not to be lightly attempted in less than a treatise. For our purpose it suffices to say that throughout the Old Testament literature we find frequent mention of prophets. A prophet by definition is "one who is moved to speak by God, one who delivers his messages or reveals his will." [5] The word is also used in the sense of one who predicts future events, but, according to the authority just quoted, this is "an idea merely incidental, not essential." Granting that the foretelling of the future, sometimes of the far distant future, was frequently a part of the prophetic office, we may still hold that the principal office of these great figures that arose from time to time in Israel's history, particularly at times of national infidelity or disaster, was, like St John the Baptist's, to "turn the hearts of the fathers unto the children, and the incredulous to the wisdom of the just, to prepare unto the Lord a perfect people." [6] From Samuel to Malachias, that is from the eleventh to the fifth century before Christ, we can trace an uninterrupted succession of these divinely sent and divinely inspired messengers, whose office it was "to assert Eternal Providence and justify the

[1] *Divinum illud*, p. 433.
[2] 1 Cor. ii 10.
[3] *Tractatus de Gratia*, p. 182.
[4] Luke i 70.
[5] See Liddell and Scott's *Greek Lexicon*, 8th ed.
[6] Luke i 17.

ways of God to men." As regards their call and mission we are frequently reminded that these were supernatural. They presupposed an enlightenment of the mind (though, as we shall see, not necessarily the communication of new ideas), a special mission and an impulse given to the will to communicate to others the message received.

Now, among these prophets, some of them were moved to set down in writing the truths they had emphasised in their preaching, and so we find among the Old Testament books some seventeen which contain the summarised teaching and preaching of the so-called writing prophets. Many of the other prophets never wrote at all, or, if they wrote, their writings have perished. With these non-writing prophets we are not here immediately concerned, though we believe that their supernatural illumination and mission should be attributed to the Holy Spirit of God. Our concern is with the prophets and other holy men of old in both Old and New Testament times, who were moved by God not only to preach but to set down in writing the divine library of the Scriptures " in apt words and with infallible truth." [1]

The divine impulse given to the sacred writers is known to us as " inspiration," though it is to be noted that the great St Thomas, in his *Summa Theologica*, has no treatise on inspiration as such, but deals with the whole matter under the heading of Prophecy, to which it most rightly belongs. [2] We must now inquire how far the Scriptures affirm their own inspiration and how far this truth is grounded in Tradition, before we pass on to the nature of that divine gift.

The fact of the divine character of the holy Scriptures is laid *The existence* down with the greatest clearness by the Vatican Council of 1870. *of divine in-* " These books (*i.e.* those of the Tridentine Canon) of the Old and *spiration* New Testament are to be received as sacred and canonical . . . because, having been written by the inspiration of the Holy Spirit, they have God for their author, and have been delivered as such to the Church herself." [3] And among the canons on Revelation there is one that anathematises anyone who should deny the sacred and canonical character of these books, or " that they have been divinely inspired." [4] We shall have occasion to go deeper into the sense of this definition, but meanwhile we can note two points in passing: first, that the Church's approbation follows and does not constitute inspiration; that is, the Church receives them because they are divinely inspired; they are not inspired simply because she receives them; secondly, that, although we have not, as yet, given any complete definition or description of inspiration, it is clearly stated that there is a divine influx of some sort whereby God influences

---

[1] Leo XIII, *Providentissimus Deus*, p. 297.
[2] *S. Theol.*, IIa-IIae, QQ. 171-174.
[3] Denzinger, n. 1787.     [4] Denzinger, n. 1809.

the sacred writers and by reason of which the books are said to have God for their author.

Among those who deny or limit this divine influence are, first of all, the Rationalists. Since they question the existence of God and deny the fact of revelation, it is hardly surprising that they also deny inspiration, which supposes a God who inspires and a revelation having, as one of its sources, the sacred books of Scripture. Then there are the liberal Protestants, who frequently use the word, but in a quite uncatholic sense. For them inspiration is a kind of religious exaltation of the same order as poetic inspiration, or else it is nothing more than the natural genius of a great writer, calling for no special divine intervention. Thirdly, we have the Modernists, whose denial of inspiration in any Catholic sense is based upon the two chief dogmas of the Modernist programme—denial of the supernatural and denial of absolute truth. One of the leading Modernists has said,[1] " God is the author of the Bible, as he is the architect of St Peter's, Rome, or of Notre-Dame de Paris," that is, by his general concursus, and in no special and supernatural manner.

*The witness of Scripture*    The Scriptures themselves bear witness to their own divine character. First, we find numerous passages in both Testaments in which certain books or parts of books are said to possess a divine authority. In the Pentateuch God moves Moses to write. " And the Lord said to Moses : Write this for a memorial in a book." [2] " And the Lord said to Moses : Write thee these words by which I have made a covenant both with thee and with Israel." [3] In the New Testament, reference is made to David, who, according to Our Lord, " saith by the Holy Ghost : *The Lord said to my Lord*, etc." [4] And the words of God to Moses are taken by Our Lord as said to the Jews of A.D. 30, who could only have received them in writing. " Have you not read that which was spoken by God, saying to you : I am the God of Abraham, and the God of Isaac, and the God of Jacob ? " [5] Therefore these words were written under the divine influence, or, in other words, were divinely inspired.

In many other passages it is stated, either implicitly or explicitly, that the Scriptures *as a whole* are inspired. In the Old Testament there is no explicit statement, but a large part of the Scriptures is said equivalently to be inspired, in that it is attributed to the prophets, who themselves affirm the divine character of their mission and preaching. Our Lord himself frequently refers to the Old Testament Scriptures as a firm and infallible proof of his divine mission, and as having final authority. " Ye search the scriptures : for

---

[1] A. Loisy, *Simples réflexions sur le Décret du Saint Office " Lamentabili,"* pp. 42 ff.
[2] Exodus xvii 14.            [3] Exodus xxxiv 27.
[4] Mark xii 36.              [5] Matt. xxii 31-32.

you think in them to have life everlasting. And the same are they that give testimony of me." [1] "How then shall the scriptures be fulfilled?" [2] "The Scripture cannot be broken." [3] In particular one has the formula that occurs some 150 times in the New Testament, "The Scripture saith" or "It is written," which attributes to the Scriptures an authority that belongs to God alone. The appeal is made to the Old Testament Scriptures as a whole, as is proved by Our Lord's reference [4] to "the Law of Moses and the prophets and the psalms" concerning him, a phrase which includes the three divisions of the Jewish books, the Law, the Prophets, and the Writings.

The most explicit proof is furnished by St Paul's second Epistle to Timothy. [5] The Apostle exhorts Timothy, who was the son of a Gentile father and a Jewish mother, to remain firm in his faith, and puts forward two motives, the apostolic authority of his teacher [6] and the authority of the inspired Scriptures, which Timothy has known from his infancy, and which " can instruct thee to salvation, by the faith which is in Christ Jesus." He continues: " Every scripture is inspired of God and is also profitable to teach, to reprove, to correct, to instruct in justice." [7] It is clear from this verse that the word " scripture " is the equivalent of the " sacred scriptures " used in the preceding verse. It includes at least the books of the Old Testament and may well be extended to include such books of the New Testament as had already been written. " Every scripture " is better than the Douay Version's " All scripture," since it emphasises the inspiration of each single part of Scripture, in addition to being a better translation of the Greek. The most important word, "inspired" ($\theta\epsilon\acute{o}\pi\nu\epsilon\nu\sigma\tau os$), means literally, " breathed by God," and so, divinely inspired. It is not found elsewhere in the New Testament or in the Septuagint. Its sense may be illustrated by a verse in II Peter [8] though the immediate reference there seems to be to spoken prophecy. " Prophecy came not by the will of man at any time: but the holy men of God spoke, inspired (literally, moved) by the Holy Ghost." Hence we may conclude that all Scripture and every part of it is inspired by the Holy Ghost.

The value of these proofs from Scripture must be correctly understood. It is true that they have real force of proof; that they are in sufficiently clear terms ; and that they enjoy indisputable authority, since many of them come directly from the lips of Our Lord and his Apostles. But the witness of the Scriptures remains imperfect and incomplete. If we look for a criterion or standard for determining the inspiration of any particular book of the Old or New Testament, we shall find that there are many insufficient ones and only one that is fully satisfactory.

[1] John v 39.  [2] Matt. xxvi 54.  [3] John x 35.
[4] Luke xxiv 44.  [5] iii 14-16.  [6] iii 14.
[7] This version slightly differs from the Douay.  [8] i 21.

The Catholic teaching is that this criterion is not to be found in any intrinsic excellence of the books themselves nor in the testimony of the authors of these books, nor in the interior illumination of the reader by the Holy Spirit. No human testimony, and not even the apostolic character of the writer will suffice, for the gift of the apostolate was conferred for the preaching of the Gospel, and here there is question of written works. The only testimony that abstracts from subjectivism and is truly infallible, universal (*i.e.* having application to all the inspired books) and at the disposal of all is that of God, which is made known to us through the teaching authority of the Catholic Church. Apart from the insufficiency of all other criteria, it should be clear that the fact of inspiration is a dogma of the Faith and that a dogma of the Faith is not to be believed upon merely human testimony. Therefore the fact of inspiration is to be believed upon the authority of God alone. The appeal of the Fathers and Doctors of the Church is made to Scripture not as an inanimate book at the mercy of everybody's private judgement, but to the Scriptures as interpreted by the voice of Tradition, which is that of the Church, "to whom (alone) it pertains to judge concerning the true sense and interpretation of Holy Scripture." [1]

*The witness of tradition*    We cannot here go fully into the history of the doctrine of inspiration, but we may attempt some general summary, which can be divided into two periods—the first three centuries and the period from the fourth century onwards. As regards the first three centuries we have, as is well known, relatively few Christian documents, and of these fewer still make any reference to the authority, and the reason for the authority of Holy Scripture. However, we find allusions to the biblical writers as the organs, or the instruments, or the ministers of God, and especially of the Holy Spirit, who is represented by St Justin (martyred A.D. 163-7) [2] as playing on their minds as a musician plays on a lyre. The books themselves are the "oracles of the Holy Spirit," "the divine utterances." A striking phrase is that of St Clement of Rome (who wrote about A.D. 96),[3] "Ye have searched the scriptures, which are true, which were given through the Holy Ghost." Careful distinction was made between the genuine books and those judged to be apocryphal, and it was the aim even of the earlier Fathers and writers to discover the exact sense of Scripture, because there, they were persuaded, was to be found truth pure and undefiled.

From the fourth century onwards there is abundant witness to the regard in which Scripture was held and the teaching of local councils, Popes, Doctors, Fathers, and theologians shows that the general inspiration of the biblical books was firmly held, taught,

---

[1] *Council of Trent*, Sess. iv ; Denzinger, n. 786.
[2] *Cohortatio ad Græcos*, c. 8.
[3] First Epistle to the Corinthians, 45.

and believed. But the more exact theological inquiry into the nature of inspiration was yet to come, and this must be the next subject of investigation.

In the decree already quoted in part, the Vatican Council says : *The nature of* " These (books) the Church holds to be sacred and canonical, *not divine* because, having been carefully composed by mere human industry, *inspiration* they were afterwards approved by her authority, *nor* merely because they contain revelation without any admixture of error, *but because, having been written by the inspiration of the Holy Ghost, they have God for their author,* and have been delivered as such to the Church herself." [1]

Before stating the true doctrine the Council deals with two of the errors concerning the nature of inspiration that flourished for a time even among some Catholic writers. The first error confused inspiration with the subsequent approbation of the Church, holding that a book written by human industry alone could be reckoned as inspired Scripture if the Holy Spirit subsequently testified by the judgement of the Church that it contained no error. It may be answered that, apart from the Church's condemnation, this theory, which was not proposed before the sixteenth century, does not explain the view of inspiration current for centuries, and that such approbation by the Church cannot change the manner in which the book was written. It could give it a certain extrinsic authority, but it could not make a purely human work the direct work of God. Again, the second error must be avoided. Inspiration is not to be identified with revelation, which is a divinely made manifestation of truths previously unknown or less clearly understood. Inspiration, on the other hand, is an influence of the Holy Spirit moving men to write down certain things, which may or may not be specially revealed for the purpose. Finally, the Council implicitly condemns the error of confusing inspiration with the assistance given to the authorities of the Church in their teaching office. The one is a positive motion to write, whereas the other is a negative preservation from error in doctrinal definitions or teaching.

The true doctrine of inspiration is set out at some length in Pope *The doctrine* Leo XIII's great encyclical *Providentissimus Deus.* After quoting *of Leo XIII* the words of the Vatican Council, the Pope goes on to say that " because the Holy Ghost employed men as his instruments," we cannot therefore allow that error exists in the sacred works, on the plea that it might be attributed to the human authors and not to God. " For, by supernatural power, he so moved and impelled them to write, he was so present to them, that the things which he ordered, and those only, they first rightly understood, then willed faithfully to write down, and finally expressed in apt words and with infallible truth. Otherwise it could not be said that he was the

[1] Denzinger, n. 1787.

Author of the entire Scripture." [1] The explanation of this passage will furnish us with a satisfactory concept of inspiration.

*The notion of instrument*  First, the Pope adopts the scholastic terminology and speaks of the human author as the instrument. The distinction between the principal efficient cause or agent and the instrumental efficient cause is well known. The principal cause is one that acts by its own virtue or power ; the instrumental cause acts not by its own power, but in so far as it is moved by the principal cause. The simplest example, perhaps, is that of the woodman and his axe. In felling a tree the woodman is the principal efficient cause and the axe the instrumental cause. It is clear that the axe itself is incapable of attaining the effect and needs the guidance and directing skill of its owner for the achievement of the purpose for which it is used. One must, however, distinguish a double virtue in the instrument, one proper to itself and the other communicated to it by the principal agent. Thus the axe has one action that pertains to its very nature, namely, the power of cutting, and another action, communicated to it by the principal agent, that is, the power of giving grace or beauty or, at least, a regular shape to the thing cut. Now two things are required in regard of the instrument : first, that it should concur in the production of an effect which is more excellent than any it could attain by its own power alone ; secondly, that it should receive from the principal cause a transitory virtue, or motion, or guidance to raise it above its connatural powers, and to apply it to the production of the effect. The exact nature of this transitory influence is disputed. Thomists generally demand a physical entity, essentially transitory in character, which begins and ceases with the act to which it contributes. In other words, the instrument is rendered active by physical premotion, whereby the instrument is physically elevated above its natural efficacy by the transitory influence that it receives. In St Thomas's words : " The influence of the mover precedes the motion of the thing moved by a priority of nature and causality." [2]  It is to be observed that this influence does not change the nature of the instrument, though it adds a new efficacy to its connatural operation. Moreover, this communicated power is only exercised through the power that is proper to the instrument, for " it is by cutting that an axe makes a bed." [3]

The instrument, then, has its own proper action and also the influence communicated by the principal cause. If the former were lacking it would be not an instrument, but a mere occasion for the operation of some cause wholly extrinsic to it—in no sense a medium between the principal cause and the effect. If the latter

[1] *Providentissimus*, p. 297. (References are to the pages of the work mentioned p. 157, n. 7.)
[2] *Summa contra Gentiles*, III, 150.
[3] *S. Theol.*, III, Q. lxii, art. 1 ad 2.

were wanting, that is, if there were no principal cause, there would be no question of instrumental causality.

Before applying this teaching to the inspiration of Scripture, we must realise that, though the full development of the scholastic explanation is not earlier than St Thomas's time, the doctrine of God as the author of Scripture and man as God's instrument is found in the sources of revelation.

St Thomas himself applies his general teaching on instrumental causality when he says: " The principal author of Holy Scripture is the Holy Spirit . . . man was the instrumental author." [1] Admitting the fact of inspiration, one must say that Holy Scripture has two authors, for it was written by men and, none the less, is the Word of God. In other words, God is the author of Holy Scripture by means of the human author, and this subordination of the sacred writer to the influence of the Holy Spirit is best explained by the doctrine of the principal and the instrumental efficient causes.

For greater clearness we may make the above-mentioned application by considering the nature of inspiration in God, in man, and in the resulting sacred work.

A. *In God.* ("*For by supernatural power, he so moved and impelled them to write. . . .*") Inspiration is an extraordinary grace given to the recipient not for his own sanctification but for the benefit of the Church, and infallibly efficacious. First, it is a *grace*, for it is a supernatural motion from God, given to bring about a truly supernatural effect, and wholly distinct from God's ordinary concursus. It is an *extraordinary grace* given only to a few in the course of human history and given by way of a transitory movement, and not as a permanent habit. It is a grace given not for the benefit of the individual but for that of the Society. Finally, there is an *infallible connection* between this grace and the effect intended by God, so that the sacred writer infallibly though freely was moved to carry out all that was involved in the production of a book. *[margin: Inspiration considered in God]*

B. *In man.* ("*The things which he ordered and those only they first rightly understood, then willed faithfully to write down, and finally expressed in apt words and with infallible truth.*") By these words the Pope makes reference to the intellect of the sacred writer, to his will and to the executive powers required for the carrying out of the work. Leaving on one side any preparatory labours, it may readily be seen that this sentence affirms the reality of the divine motion throughout the whole process from the first conception of the ideas to the actual production of the book. *[margin: Inspiration considered in man]*

We have said that it is of the nature of a principal cause to move the instrument to act. " The instrumental cause acts through the motion by which it is moved by the principal agent." [2] It

---

[1] *Quodlibet.*, VII, art. 14 ad 5.
[2] *S. Theol.*, III, Q. lxii, art. 1.

follows that any of the opinions mentioned above that make inspiration consist in subsequent approbation by the Church or in merely negative divine assistance, falls short of the true conception of the divine causality.

We have said, again, that it is the nature of the instrument to have a twofold virtue, the one proper to it, the other communicated ; and that the latter does not destroy the former but uses it. It is to be held, then, that the human instrument acting under divine inspiration acted in a human manner, that is, intelligently and freely. This excludes any direct suggestion or dictation of words, which would imply that the Holy Spirit was not only the principal author, but the sole author of an inspired book. On the contrary, it is certain that in choosing men for his instruments, he allowed them the free use of their natural powers and of their ability or relative lack of ability, as the case might be, and the resulting works show clearly that the authors preserved their own literary styles and modes of expression. Further, we are told by the author of the second book of Machabees that his abridgment of the five books of Jason of Cyrene was "no easy task, yea, rather a business full of watching and sweat," [1] and by St Luke that he had "diligently attained to all things," that is, that he had made an accurate study of his materials, before he began to write. [2] This does not agree with any theory of mechanical dictation, and from this it follows that various sayings of the Fathers, which compare the sacred writers to the "pens" or the "secretaries" of the Holy Spirit must be rightly understood. They were pens and secretaries in so far as they wrote nothing of Scripture except under the divine influence, but they were also free and intelligent human beings, not mere mechanical agents.

*Divine action on the intellect* Now, as regards the divine action upon the intellect (" *They, first, rightly understood* "), we must distinguish between the reception of new ideas and the judgement passed on ideas already in the mind of the thinker or writer. The former is essential to the concept of revelation, which is the reception of new truths, but, in all true prophecy, there is another element, namely, a divinely assisted judgement passed upon the truths received, whether these were received by revelation or in some natural manner. In the book of Genesis we are told that God made known to the Pharaoh in dreams what he was about to do. [3] But the divinely assisted judgement on the interpretation of the dream was given to Joseph, and he was a prophet, whereas the Pharaoh was not. So in biblical inspiration the essential notion is that of a supernatural judgement passed upon the truths that God wishes to have handed down in writing to his people. Many, or even all, of these truths may have been arrived at by ordinary human means. Inspiration, as regards the intellect,

[1] ii 27.    [2] Luke i 3.    [3] Gen. xli.

is a divine light that elevates and assists the mind of the sacred writer to judge with absolute certainty and truth that certain things are to be set down in writing. This practical judgement regarding the things to be written is undoubtedly the principal action of the intellect under divine inspiration. But it would seem, though this is disputed, that the mental processes preceding this judgement, namely, the theoretical judgement regarding the truth of the propositions and even the conception of the ideas, were divinely influenced, though this divine influence was in the nature of an illumination and not necessarily of a revelation of new ideas.

A question arises : How far were the inspired authors conscious of their own inspiration ? In default of more evidence it is difficult to be positive. St Thomas [1] distinguishes the " spirit of prophecy " from the " prophetic impulse " (*instinctus propheticus*) and calls the latter : " A certain most secret impulse, which human minds experience without their knowledge." But the majority of theologians are inclined to admit at least some general knowledge of the divine motion on the part of the sacred writer, though it seems clear that the writers did not always appreciate the full depth and full importance of what they were writing.

We come to the divine action upon the human will of the inspired *Divine action* author. (" *Then willed faithfully to write down.*") There is *on the will* question here of a divine motion, truly efficacious but not destructive of freedom, that moved the writer to set down in writing the things he had conceived under the divine impulse. This action on the will was not confined to a preliminary impulse, but " was present " to the author " in a special and uninterrupted manner " [2] up to the time of the completion of his work. It partly preceded the conception of the matters to be written and partly followed upon this conception, in so far as there was first the general proposal to write, then the thinking out of the concepts to be expressed, and finally the will to set them down " *in apt words and with infallible truth.*" In these last words we see expressed the final stage of the work and the divine impulse given to the executive powers through the intermediacy of the will.

C. *In the Sacred Work.* Reverting once more to the teaching *Inspiration* on instrumental causality we can now answer the question : Who is *considered in* the author of a book of Holy Scripture ? And the answer is : God *the sacred* and man. God is the author of the whole book, and man is also *work* the author of the whole. There is no question of attributing part to one and part to the other. The whole is to be attributed to each, but to God as the principal cause and to man as the instrumental cause.

We may sum up this teaching on the nature of inspiration in the light of Zanecchia's now classic definition. Inspiration is :

---

[1] *S. Theol.*, IIa-IIae, Q. 171, art. 5.
[2] Encyclical *Spiritus Paraclitus* of Pope Benedict XV.

"A divine, physical, and supernatural influx, elevating and moving the faculties of men that the things which God willed might be committed to writing for the good and utility of the Church, and in the manner which he willed."

In treating of inspiration as it is in God, we saw that it was a physical influx upon the faculties of the writer and that it was in the supernatural order. Its action, as the definition says, is to elevate and move the faculties—the intellect, the will and the executive powers that contribute to the complete effect. The end or purpose is to bestow a library of divinely-written books upon the Church of Christ. Finally the object of inspiration is *the things which God willed . . . in the manner which he willed*. As God is the principal author, Holy Scripture must contain all that God wished to hand down to man in this manner and nothing more.

So we have first, the truth that is of faith—that God is the author of Holy Scripture ; secondly, the fact that is clear from Tradition —that the books of Scripture were visibly produced by human writers in subordination to God ; finally, the explanation of this duality of authorship by means of St Thomas's doctrine of instrumental causality. For, as he says, " It is clear that the same effect is ascribed to a natural cause and to God, not as though part were effected by God and part by the natural agent ; but the whole effect proceeds from each, yet in different ways : just as the whole of the one same effect is ascribed to the instrument and again the whole is ascribed to the principal agent." [1]

*The extent of divine inspiration* It is clear from the decrees cited above that all the books of the Old and New Testaments are divinely inspired. But a further point has to be noted, namely, that, according to Catholic teaching, inspiration extends not only to all the sacred books, but to all the authentic contents of these books. This is sufficiently implied in St Paul's words : " Every Scripture is inspired of God," where no distinction is made between one part of Scripture and any other. All were written under divine inspiration. The Councils of Trent and of the Vatican declare that the sacred books in their entirety and with all their parts are to be received as sacred and canonical, since they were written under divine inspiration. [2] Pope Leo XIII is quite explicit on the point : " It is absolutely wrong and forbidden, *either* to narrow inspiration to certain parts only of Holy Scripture, *or* to admit that the sacred writer has erred." [3] This is the teaching of the Fathers and Doctors of the Church, to whom any distinction between inspired and non-inspired Scripture was entirely unknown. Pope Benedict XV said of St Jerome what could be said of all the Fathers : " He affirms that which is common to all the sacred writers : that they in writing followed the Spirit of God, so that God

[1] *Summa contra Gentiles*, III, 70.  [2] Denzinger, nn. 784, 1787.
[3] *Providentissimus Deus*, p. 296.

is to be considered the principal cause of the whole sense and of all the judgements of Scripture." [1] In fact, one may say that this doctrine follows from the nature of inspiration, which postulates divine guidance for the entire composition of the whole work written by the inspired writer.

A further question, which, unlike the preceding, is freely dis- *Verbal* cussed among Catholics, is whether inspiration extends to the very *inspiration* words used. And here one must distinguish. If by "verbal inspiration" is meant mechanical dictation, we have already rejected any such conception as being irreconcilable with the writer's freedom, with the varieties of style and expression found in the different books, and with the testimony of the writers themselves. But, if by verbal inspiration we mean that the divine action of elevating and moving the writer's faculties ought to extend to the effect, namely, to the composition of the book, then we may say that this view seems to be more reasonable and more consistent than any other. It is more in harmony with the Vatican Council's words that the books " having been written by the inspiration of the Holy Ghost, have God for their author," and with Pope Leo XIII's expression : " The Holy Ghost employed men as his instruments *to write.*" It is also more in accordance with the doctrine of instrumental causality—that the whole of the effect is to be attributed both to the principal and to the instrumental causes. Again, ideas and the words in which they are expressed are so closely connected in the human mind that it is hard to see how God could have influenced the concepts without extending his divine action to the words. This, then, is the view, which, to distinguish it from any dictation theory, has been called that of " plenary " inspiration. As has been said, it remains a theory and has not been imposed upon the Church by her authorities.

From the fact of divine inspiration it follows, as a necessary *The effect of* consequence, that the sacred books are free from all error. We *divine in-* have already quoted Pope Leo's words that " It is absolutely wrong *spiration* and forbidden . . . to admit that the sacred writer has erred." And a little later he writes : " It follows that those who maintain that an error is possible in any genuine passage of the sacred writings, either pervert the Catholic notion of inspiration or make God the author of such error." [2] It is clear from these words that absolute inerrancy belongs only to the original manuscripts of the sacred books, and that errors due to copyists or translators may have crept into the texts and versions of Scripture in the course of centuries. We are reminded of this latter fact by Pope Leo, but he adds that its existence in a particular instance " is not to be too easily admitted, but only in those passages where the proof is clear." [3]

[1] Enc. *Spiritus Paraclitus.*      [2] *Providentissimus Deus,* p. 297.
[3] *Op. cit.,* p. 296.

*Infallible truth of Scripture*

The Catholic teaching is that the principal effect of divine inspiration is the infallible truth of all things contained in Holy Scripture. For any full discussion of such a statement with applications to the various difficulties brought forward against it, the reader must be referred to manuals of Scriptural introduction and to commentaries on the separate books. But here one may well note that not all things contained in Holy Scripture have precisely the same degree of truth. The words that are recorded as spoken by God himself, or by angels, or by inspired men are inspired in themselves and intrinsically and in consequence are divine words. Again, the writer's own words are inspired and divine in so far as he spoke in God's name or made known truths that exceeded his natural powers and could only be known by divine revelation, such as prophecies, mysteries of faith, and so forth. But there is a third class consisting of those utterances recorded in Scripture that are only inspired by reason of their consignation, that is, by reason of their occurrence in a sacred book, but are not thereby made intrinsically divine and infallible. Such are the words uttered by non-inspired men, and these do not obtain a greater authority by being recorded in Holy Scripture, and can be true or false, unless they are approved by God or by the inspired author. So " the vain reasonings of the wicked," as our Douay Version calls them, in the book of Wisdom [1] receive no divine approval by being recorded in Holy Writ. It is often necessary to consider carefully the writer's method of presentation, and so, in the book of Job, one may see that many false statements are put forward during the dialogues for the sake of making the truth more apparent. Finally, if the sacred writer sets forth his own opinions or feelings or doubts, these are inspired by reason of consignation only and are not intrinsically divine and infallibly true.

One may end this brief statement of a most vital question with two quotations, one from the greatest of the Latin Fathers, the other from a papal document. Both are peculiarly applicable to the interpretation of Holy Scripture.

St Augustine, writing to St Jerome, distinguishes his attitude towards Holy Scripture from his attitude towards secular literature. As regards the first, he says : " I confess to your Charity that I have learned to yield this respect and honour only to the canonical books of Scripture : of these alone do I most firmly believe that the authors were completely free from error. And if in these writings I am perplexed by anything which appears to me opposed to truth, I do not hesitate to suppose *either* that the manuscript is faulty, *or* that the translator has not caught the meaning of what was said, *or* that I myself have failed to understand it." (Letter 82, 3 to Jerome.)

[1] ii 1 ff.

Again, we find Pope Pius IX in his encyclical *Qui pluribus*,[1] emphasising the truth that: " Although faith is above reason, there can never be found any real dissension or real disagreement between them, since they both have their origin from the same source of unchanging and eternal truth, God." In other words, between the certain sense of Holy Scripture and the certain conclusions of natural reason or natural science, there can be no real opposition, for " all these things one and the same Spirit worketh." [2]

JOHN M. T. BARTON.

[1] November 9, 1846. Denzinger, n. 1635.    [2] 1 Cor. xii 11.

# VI

# GOD THE CREATOR

## § I : INTRODUCTORY

How man himself, the world in which he lives, and the greater world of the heavens came into being are questions that men have asked themselves from at least the earliest times of recorded human thought. And vast numbers of men have failed and still fail to find a satisfactory answer. The human reason, indeed, is capable, by its own natural powers, of finding the right solution to the riddle ; but, in fact, the difficulties are so great, the obstacles put by men themselves in the way of straight thinking are so many, the influences leading their minds astray are so powerful, that it is very rare for civilised man, left to his own devices, to discover the true answer, and rarer still for him consistently to hold to it. Men in the more primitive state, with their simpler and more direct and natural outlook, and without the distractions and impediments arising from a complex civilisation, seem, on the whole, to have a truer view of the question, and to be less troubled by the doubts, uncertainties, and speculative fancies that afflict the mind of civilised man. In the course of our exposition we shall have occasion briefly to speak of some of the theories to which men have had recourse ; at present it is enough to note the simple fact that many different opinions have been and are held.

It is easy to see and needs no proof that this question of the origin of the world and, more particularly, of man himself is of the highest importance, is, indeed, one of the few fundamental questions as to which the holding of right or of wrong views means having a true or a false outlook upon the whole of life. A right view is the necessary foundation of a true philosophy of life, of a true individual and social ethic, of a true religion ; whereas by a false view philosophy, ethic, and religion are of necessity falsified, confused, and misdirected. The question, then, being so weighty, and its inherent and incidental difficulties so many and so grave, it has pleased God, in his mercy, not to leave men without divine help and direction in the matter. He has come to man's aid ; by clear and repeated revelation he has made it easy for him to discover the certain truth, and by his grace he enables him, without much difficulty, to hold to it firmly and consistently. This truth is summed up in the opening words of the Apostles' Creed : " I believe in God the Father, Creator of heaven and earth." The revelation of this truth is, however, far older than Christianity. The Jews from the earliest times held the same belief. It is taught constantly and explicitly throughout the Old Testament. This doctrine is, therefore, one of those which, as regards their main lines, have undergone no development since the first days of the Church's existence. At the same time, however, all its implications have not been fully and clearly perceived from the beginning, nor have all its particular applications been always rightly understood. In these respects there have been development and growth of clarity which it will be our business to note as we proceed. But first of all certain fundamental things must be made clear, and certain points elucidated as being necessary to a proper understanding of the whole dogma.

## §II: IDEA AND MEANING OF CREATION

THE verb "to create" does not necessarily mean to make something *The meanin·* from nothing; this is true, also, of the equivalents of the English *of creation* word in Latin, Greek, and Hebrew. But the word in all these languages does contain the idea of a productive action that, in one way or another, is more than ordinarily powerful. Thus we speak rightly of the creations of a genius in music and sculpture, or we talk of the Sovereign creating new peers of the realm. Consequently the word is properly applied in a special and distinctive way to that action, requiring the exercise of infinite power, by which God—to use the ordinary but not wholly satisfactory phrase— makes something out of nothing, or—to speak more precisely— makes something to be where there was absolutely nothing. This is the strict theological meaning of the word; this is the sense in which we shall use it throughout this essay, unless we make it clear that it is to be taken less strictly.

We see at once that this act differs wholly from any of which we have experience. Nothing at all like it is known to us. All the productive actions within the range of our experience need a subject to work upon, and merely effect some change in a thing already existing. The sculptor who produces a statue does not make a new thing, he but changes the form or shape of an old thing, the stone or marble upon which he works; the musician playing on his instrument produces vibrations in the existing air; the chemist makes new substances by combining or dividing existing ones; even thoughts or ideas, which may at first seem to be really new creations, are not so. In the first place, they have no independent existence apart from the thinker, being nothing but passing modifications of his mind; and secondly, in order to produce them he must have pre-existing material, objects of thought, to work upon. Without these human thought is impossible. All these productive actions, and all others possible to men, are therefore reducible to some sort of change effected in some subject that was already in existence before the action began. But creation is not like any of these. Creation is not a transformation of one thing into another, nor is it an emanation or outflow of something from the creator's own being, nor any kind of action about or upon some pre-existing subject or material. Creation means just this : that besides God, and apart from God, there was nothing, no being of any sort whatsoever ; God willed, commanded, and behold, at his command and by the sole power of his will, things, substances, beings, sprang into existence. Where nothing had been, now there is something ; something that is neither God, nor a part of God, nor an emanation from his substance ; something having its own being and its own special nature, and yet dependent upon God for all it has and all it is.

*Not self-contradictory*   How this creative action proceeds we know not ; its mode is beyond our understanding. We can have no experience of it. It is beyond the ken of physical science, which, dealing only with the phenomena of human experience, and with their flow and succession under the impact of finite forces, cannot reach to the very first beginning of things when infinite power acted. Yet in the idea itself there is nothing contradictory, nothing offensive to human reason. On the contrary, not only has God clearly revealed that such was the origin of all things, but human reason itself can prove and does prove that so it must have been, while no theory can satisfy, as does this truth, all the imperious exigencies of human thought.

I said just now that the common description of creation as "the making of something out of nothing" is not wholly satisfactory. This is so because, in common speech, the words "out of" in the expression "to make out of" refer to the subject or the material from which someone, by working upon it, produces something else, as when we say that a carpenter makes a table out of wood. But it is clearly impossible even for God to work upon nothing, or to use nothing as the material or stuff from which to produce something. The idea is self-contradictory. This may seem a small, even a trivial matter, but the point must be made and even pressed, because at least from the third century, right down to our own times, opponents of creation have used this definition as a peg on which to hang the charge that the concept of creation is self-contradictory, since, as they have triumphantly pointed out, it is quite impossible for anything to come out of nothing. Creation, then, would be more accurately defined as the production of something in its totality, or, again, as the action that, without working upon any already existing subject or material, produces something wholly new.

It will help to complete and to make clearer our notion of this fundamental concept if we glance at two or three more of those aspects of creation which put it into a class by itself. In the first place we need hardly say that no created being can itself create. Creatures are, of necessity, limited in nature and capacity, whereas to create needs the exercise of unlimited, that is, of infinite power.

A creature can act only if he has some other created being to act upon ; put him, even the highest and noblest of creatures, up against sheer nothingness, and, having nothing to take hold of, his utmost power is powerless. Creation is so far removed beyond the possibility of created power that we might almost say that God himself, in order to create, must bring into action the full force of his infinite might.

Secondly, we may remark that creation cannot be a gradual process ; there can be no measurement in time, no succession of movements or states in the creation of anything. Between simple not-being and being there can be no middle state of half-being, for this would already be something. Nothingness cannot grow and gradually change into something. And consequently, since it is growth, change, succession, movement that require time and there is none of these in the creative process, creation is, in the strictest sense, instantaneous, or even more exactly, timeless.

From this it follows directly that the fact of creation is one of those truths that are altogether beyond the reach of investigation, of proof or disproof by physical science. This can deal only with the measurement of time processes, with the succession of phenomena in time, with the relation of state to state of things subject to movement and so to time, with the mutual activities of things acting in time ; to go beyond this into the region of timeless production, of production without movement, growth or succession, belongs primarily to the philosopher and metaphysician, while the theologian, using the data of revelation, may be said to act as a court of higher appeal.

We make no attempt to disguise the fact that the notion of creation is hard to understand ; rather, we fully acknowledge that in its inward reality, as in its mode of realisation, it is beyond our power adequately to grasp ; it is truly a mystery. It is as much beyond our power to understand the idea, as it would be to perform the act of creation. But no apology is needed on that score, no valid objection can be based on the difficulty involved. Ease of comprehension is not necessarily a sign-post to truth, especially when we are dealing with the higher and the bigger things. In looking for a way to account for what we see and experience in the world, in searching for the first cause and the final reason of things, we are bound, sooner or later, to come up against mystery ; whether we believe or believe not in God, whether we accept creation as a fact, or, rejecting it, try to discover another way out, we are bound to find ourselves in an intellectual blind alley. And, to take only the lowest view of the matter, it is better and more sensible to put the mystery in its right place than in its wrong, better, that is, to put it on the side of God, who, from the nature of the case, is infinitely above our comprehension, dwelling in light inaccessible, than on the side of creatures, whom, since they are our kin, we can claim to have some right and capacity to understand. To put the mystery on the side of God does, at least, make other things understandable, and does introduce orderliness into the world we know; to deny God and divine mystery is to bring nothing but confusion and obscurity into the world, and to put a full stop to straight thinking long before it reaches its natural limits.

## §III: CHURCH'S TEACHING ON CREATION IN GENERAL

*The Old Testament*

HAVING thus defined and made as clear as we can what we mean by creation, we go on now to set forth what the Catholic Church teaches on this matter. And in the first instance we shall take the dogma of creation in the most general way, leaving its particular applications until later.

As has already been said, faith in God as the Creator of all things is not exclusive to the Christian religion. It had been held by the Jews from the earliest days of their existence as a separate people, and from them it passed on as the heritage of Christ's Church. But there is no need for us to undertake a searching examination into the teaching of the sacred Scriptures on this point. It is hardly too much to say that in every book of the Bible, from Genesis to the Apocalypse, the creation of all things by God is either explicitly or implicitly asserted. With regard to the Old Testament it is well to note that it is unwise to lay too much emphasis upon a particular phrase or a single text, as, for example, the first words of Genesis, " In the beginning God created the heavens and the earth," since the word in the original Hebrew text may not necessarily have the full force of the word as we understand it to-day. But when the whole context is taken into account, when the witness of the Old Testament is read in the light of our knowledge of other ancient religions and of Eastern mythologies, it becomes quite evident that the Hebrews had a clear and definite faith in God the Creator of all things.

In the ancient Eastern religious systems, and especially in the Babylonian, between which and that of the early Hebrews there are several lines of connection, there is found an essential element or a basis of dualism. That is, two original and primeval principles are posited as the necessary beginnings of things. These principles, under various names, represent good and evil, light and darkness, spirit and matter. There is conflict and war between the two, and it is only by victory, and a victory that is by no means absolute and complete, that the one principle is enabled to claim and to uphold his rights as the supreme God, to whom all are subject. In such a system of dualism, whatever may be its special characteristics and its accidental variations, there is no room for a First Cause who, in absolute independence, brings everything else into being, such as is required by the Christian teaching of God the Creator.

But in the Hebrews' sacred Scriptures there is no trace of any such dualism. Throughout them God is spoken of as supremely independent. He creates by his word without having to overcome the resistance of matter, he rules with sole authority with none to dispute his sway ; there is no indication of any primeval strife between him and any ruler of darkness. The earth, the heavens, men, the gods of the Gentiles must render him unquestioning submission ; there is no hint or sign of any power whatsoever that can for a moment claim the right of resisting or opposing him. The only possible foundation for such a consistent body of teaching is a firm belief in the dogma of creation by one only omnipotent God. A notable concrete example of this steadfast belief is afforded by the Book of Job. This book presents us with precisely that case which has always been the occasion of one of the strongest objections felt by many against the doctrine of an all-powerful and all-good Creator— the case, namely, of the just and God-fearing man who suffers all sorts of misery and evil, while God's enemies rejoice in prosperity and happiness. If God, being the Creator of all things, is the Lord of all, why does he allow such things to be ? This is the baffling question that has always troubled men. It is the same question, at least in principle, as was so often asked during recent years, and generally, it is to be feared, in a spirit of defiance ; if there be an almighty God, why did he allow the horrors of the War ? The answer given by pagan thinkers not professing a pure monotheism always involved some form of dualism. The root and origin of evil, they said, was to be found in the existence of an evil principle, antagonistic to God and putting a limit to his power and goodness. Such, in substance, whatever the varieties in presentation and explanation, was the current religious philosophy of the time. But of any sort of dualism the inspired writer of Job gives not the slightest indication. Philosophically his solution of the problem may not be wholly satisfactory, but from our present point of view it is excellent, for throughout he insists upon God's supreme power and lordship, and upon the fact that he is at liberty to dispose of all things as he will because he is the almighty Creator of all.

In the time of Jesus Christ this belief was so firmly established as *The New Testament* an article of the Jewish faith that there was no need for him explicitly to inculcate it. But it is to be found, even on a cursory reading of the gospels, as a necessary presupposition of much of his teaching. This is so little contested and so easily verified that we may well be excused any proof of it by actual quotation. When, however, the gospel began to be preached to the Gentiles who did not believe in one God the Creator of all things, it became necessary again to bring this truth to the front ; hence, St Paul, speaking at Athens to materialists and pantheists, gives it an important place in his discourse.[1] Whereas also in his earlier epistles, although the

[1] Acts xvii 18 ff.

doctrine is often mentioned, it is without any special emphasis,[1] in the later ones, the situation having changed, it behoved him to explain this truth more fully and carefully. Some false teachers, borrowing the fancies and speculations of the prevalent gnosticism, had begun to disturb the faithful by trying to explain the world by bringing in a multiplicity of semi-divine beings between God and creatures. Hence such passages as Col. i 15 ff., wherein the apostle lays stress upon the universality of God's creative act, from which nothing whatever is excluded, in the heavens or upon the earth, of things visible or invisible.

We may fittingly close this very brief summary of the teaching of the sacred Scriptures with the unequivocal and sublime witness of St John in the prologue to his gospel : [2] " All things were made by him, and without him was made nothing that was made."

*Tradition* Such being the clear teaching of sacred Scripture, and this doctrine being of so fundamental a character, it is not surprising that the Church should have made explicit profession of this faith in the earliest of her formularies of belief, the so-called Apostles' Creed. Scholars, however, are not agreed as to whether the words " Creator of heaven and earth " formed part of the creed from the beginning. The form given by the celebrated writer and translator of the works of the Greek Fathers, Rufinus, who died A.D. 421, omits them ; on the other hand, Tertullian, the African apologist and controversialist, in his work *The Prescription of Heretics*, written probably shortly before the year 200, includes them in what is an evident allusion to the creed as used at Carthage, and in all proba- bility at Rome, in the instruction of catechumens. " Let us see," he says (chapter xxxvi), " what she (*i.e.*, the Roman Church) has learnt, what she has taught. She knows one God, the Lord, Creator of the universe," etc. This would be decisive if we could be certain that Tertullian is quoting the actual words of the creed, but of that we cannot be sure. St Cyril of Jerusalem, in one of his famous *Catecheses* or instructions given to his catechumens, gives the text of the creed as used in his church, as follows, " We believe in one God, the Father almighty, maker of heaven and earth," and this instruction dates from about A.D. 325. These words, then, even if they had no place in the creed from the first, were certainly intro- duced into it at a very early date, and the occasion of their intro- duction would have been the necessity of definitely rejecting the errors of pagans, gnostics, and others who held materialist and pantheistic opinions.

*Manicheism* The third century saw a wide extension of Manicheism. This was a dualistic system according to which the world was produced by two eternal and more or less equal principles, light and darkness, the light being responsible for the spiritual world, which is good, darkness for the material world, which is essentially evil. This,

---

[1] *E.g.*, Rom. i 20, 25, xi 36 ; 1 Cor. viii 6, etc.      [2] John i 3.

of course, cuts at the very root of the Catholic faith, and as the rapid spread of the system had become a danger to religion, the Fathers assembled in the First General Council at Nicaea (A.D. 325) judged it expedient, in drawing up the profession of faith, to proclaim explicitly that God is the " Creator of all things, visible and invisible " —that is, of the material as well as of the spiritual world. Strange and absurd as Manicheism seems to us, it has proved a persistent and an alluring form of error, cropping up in one shape or another many times through the centuries, and not yet, seemingly, being wholly extinct. During the Middle Ages the Church had to fight against various manifestations of this perversity. So, for example, in the Fourth Council of the Lateran, held A.D. 1215, setting forth the true faith against the Albigensians and others, she amplified the older creeds, and declared God to be the " one principle of all things, the Creator of all things visible and invisible, spiritual and corporeal, who from the beginning of time, by his almighty power, created from nothing both the spiritual and the corporeal, that is the angelical and the mundane world of creatures, and finally human creatures, as if common to both worlds, being composed of body and spirit."

Finally, it became necessary for the Church once more solemnly *Vatican* to proclaim and define her faith against the false teachings of *Council* nineteenth-century atheists, materialists, and sundry sorts of pantheists. To a great extent the decrees of the Vatican Council are a repetition of that of the Fourth Council of the Lateran. There are some changes in the arrangement of the text, two or three points are left out as having no longer any bearing on the actual circumstances of the time, while some others, of great importance, are inserted. For example, God *alone* is said to be the Creator of all things, emphasis thus being laid on his independence of all help or instrument ; then the concept of creation is made more definite and clear by the assertion that God created all things from nothing, " according to their whole substance." Finally the decree brings in two fresh points of deep theological and spiritual import, in view of definite errors which had lately been propounded, and which, among theologians outside the Catholic Church, are now widespread. The first of these points is God's supreme liberty in creating, the second is the end he had in view in creating, which the Council defines to have been his own glory. These two points we must consider in some detail.

## §IV: GOD FREELY CREATED FOR HIS OWN GLORY

THE freedom of the will is one of the highest prerogatives of men *God not* and angels, a gift that distinguishes them fundamentally from the *constrained* brute creation, and gives them a real likeness to God himself. This *to create* freedom has various manifestations, or may be looked at from different points of view. Without going into details or discussing subtle matters that lie outside of our province, we may say that human free will consists in the absence of constraint, in that man is so master of himself that no one can force his will into action against his own inclination or resistance, and no one but himself can determine the direction in which he exercises his will. He has freedom of choice, firstly between action and inaction, or willing and not willing, and secondly between willing one particular object or another. There are, indeed, certain limits to this freedom, as there are to all created perfections, but to discuss these is beyond our scope. In so far, however, as it is a positive perfection, it is evident that it must be found in an eminent degree or mode, and without its human limitations, in God. The source of freedom must himself be supremely free. And since God is the First Cause of all things, which he created from nothing, it would only be labouring the obvious to spend time in proving that there was no constraint from without himself forcing him to create the world. What has no existence can exercise no pressure. Mere nothingness cannot constrain. This is common ground to all who believe in God the Creator.

But a further question arises which men have not found so easy to answer, and which, even when rightly answered, is by no means easy to explain. Granted that God be not constrained to create by any power external to himself, may it not be that his very nature, or to speak somewhat loosely, one of his attributes, such as his love, impels him to create? Or, if we shy at the word "impels," may we not at least say that by his nature there is within him such a strong essential tendency to manifest his power and goodness in creatures, that creation becomes a sort of moral necessity? Just as by divine necessity he exists, so by divine necessity he loves. Is there, then, anything in his divine nature which would make it incumbent upon his divine love to seek an object outside of itself, to look for an outlet for its overflowing infinity by bringing creatures into existence? Men of genius and piety have not been wanting who have answered affirmatively. Many non-Catholic Christians hold that there is some such necessity, while it is a common element in all pantheistic systems of philosophy. Hence the Vatican Council judged it expedient to define the truth in clear and explicit terms. It lays down that God created by a most free act of the will, and it anathematises those who assert that his will in creating was not free from all necessity, and who say that it was as necessary for him to create as it is for him to love himself. Further, the Sacred Congregation of the Holy Office in the year 1887 reprobated the opinion that God's love gives rise within him to any moral necessity for creating. Here, in passing, we may refer to the Essay *The One God* for further treatment of God's love of himself. It is enough now to point out that it is something wholly different from what is commonly known as self-love in man.

Catholic teaching, then, on this matter of God's absolute freedom in creating is clear. But it is not easy to give a clear and, at the same time, a reasonable and positive explanation of it. There is no difficulty, however, in establishing a negative proof. The ultimate reason lies in what will be found written in Essay III of this work about God's nature and attributes. God is sheer, infinite perfection in himself, possessing in himself complete and independent beatitude. Nothing is wanting to the fulness of his happiness. His love, his wisdom, his intelligence, find from eternity absolute satisfaction in the contemplation of his own perfection as he lives and loves, Three in One. But where there are perfection and happiness, full, final, unchangeable, absolute, nothing else can be necessary to their possessor. This is self-evident. If, then, God wills that something else besides himself should exist, it can only be by the supremely free act of his perfect will, uninfluenced by any sort of necessity arising from within his own nature.

We may look at the matter in another way by comparing, as the Vatican Council does, God's love for himself and the act of creation. The former is absolutely necessary, so much so that it would be true to say that if God did not love himself he would not exist. If, then, creation were equally necessary, it would also be true to say that if God were not to create he would not exist ; which would be to make the infinite depend upon the finite, the perfect upon the imperfect, and would so be self-contradictory.

Nor is there any moral necessity why God should create. Those *A false* who maintain that there is, often argue from the principle that love *analogy* is of its nature self-communicative, ever seeking an object upon which it may bestow itself. But God is love, the argument proceeds, infinite love ; hence there is in him a natural tendency to bestow himself upon objects other than himself, a tendency so strong, since he is perfect love, that if he were to withstand it and withhold himself from self-communication through creation, this would be some derogation from his perfection, and, in some way not easy to define, would constitute a blemish in his nature. The argument is specious and has deceived many. But it has two defects. It is founded on a false analogy drawn from rational creatures, and it neglects a fundamental Christian dogma. An examination of these two defects will show the insufficiency of the argument.

The false analogy lies in this : men are not only rational creatures, but also social beings. No man is sufficient unto himself, and every man is brother to his fellows. Hence men have towards one another mutual duties, to neglect which is sometimes a sin, at other times rather an imperfection. By virtue of these duties it is incumbent upon men to communicate to their fellow-men some, at least, of their own possessions, material, moral, and intellectual. Without the fulfilment of such duties human society—that is, natural human life—would become impossible. Yet I use the restrictive phrase "some, at least, of their possessions" advisedly, for man is not bound to give all he has. A very learned man, for example, is under no sort of obligation to communicate all his learning to others. If he does so he fulfils a free counsel of perfection, but if he does not it cannot be imputed to him as a fault.

But there can be no such mutual social obligations between God and merely possible but non-existent creatures, for there is no society wherein they can arise. God cannot possibly be bound by any sort of duty to enrich nothingness with existence.

Again, with man every exercise of any of his faculties is an additional, if accidental, perfection. Life is not stagnation, but action; to stagnate is to lose what one has, and finally to die. A faculty that is not exercised becomes atrophied. Conversely, to act is to acquire, and every time a man acts, even if he acts only to give to another, he really enriches, not only that other, but also himself; by giving he acquires, he grows in perfection. And this is one reason why he is called upon to give, why he falls short of his duty if he does not give, because, namely, he is under an obligation, put upon him by God, to tend to his own perfection. But the same reason cannot apply to God, who, being all perfect, cannot grow in perfection, and, being all sufficient to himself and in himself, cannot be enriched by another.

*The Trinity* Finally, as has been said, this argument takes no account of a fundamental Christian doctrine, the mystery of the· Blessed Trinity. If God were one person only, living in individual solitude and divine loneliness, it might be difficult to resist the contention that, being infinite love, he must seek an object to which to give himself. But as he is not one person but three equal persons the difficulty vanishes, since in the Trinity every tendency and every yearning of love is fully satisfied by the eternal, perfect self-communication of the Godhead from Father to Son and from Father and Son to Holy Ghost, and by the ever active mutual flow of infinite love between the Divine Persons.

*The best possible world* God, therefore, cannot lie under any sort of necessity, arising either from within or from without his own nature, to create. If he elects to create it is purely by an act of free choice. So far we have spoken only of what is called the liberty of execution, or executive liberty, the freedom of choice between action and non-action. We have now to consider another aspect of free will as it is found in men, and to ask whether it also can be attributed to God. Thus a man may deliberate as to whether he shall go to Brighton for the week-end or stay at home. Having decided, by an act of executive liberty, to go, he now deliberates upon a choice of ways, thus exercising what is called the liberty of specification. He may go by rail, road, sea or air. And if he decides to go by road he has still a wide choice of means before him and may hesitate between a motor-car, a horse, a bicycle, or his own feet. Finally he will choose that way of going which, in all the circumstances, seems to him to be the best, which most adequately meets his desires, his inclinations, his purse, his time, the end in view and so forth. Similarly with regard to God; having seen that, in creating, he enjoys full executive liberty, we have now to ask whether he likewise enjoys full liberty of specification. In other words, was God, having elected to create, in any way bound to create this actual world and this actual order of things, or could he have chosen another? Or, again, is this the best of all possible worlds, and was God therefore obliged to exert his creative energy on this, to the exclusion of any other? It might well seem that he was. For since it is the part of wisdom always to choose what is best and highest, or lapse from the rule of wisdom, and since God is perfect wisdom in whom no lapse is possible, it would seem to follow that he must of necessity create the best of all possible worlds.

Although this question is not of such theological and spiritual importance as the last, and although a full discussion of it would lead us into needless subtleties, it cannot be altogether neglected. We must first remark, then, that God is not only the efficient cause of the world, but also its exemplary cause—that is, he not only made it by his power, but he also made it according to the pattern existing in his divine mind, much as an artist produces a picture according to the pattern he has in his mind's eye. The world, then, is a reflection—faint, indeed, but faithful as far as it goes—of the divine mind, and so of God's nature and perfections. But these are infinite, and can therefore never be perfectly reflected or manifested. God's power likewise is infinite. Whence it follows that, however wonderful and great and apparently perfect a world may be created or even conceived, God's perfections are capable of a still greater and higher degree of imitation, and God's power is equal to the work of giving actual existence to such a still greater and more wonderful world. In this sense, therefore, the absolutely perfect world is a contradiction in terms. But if we look at the matter in another way our conclusions must be otherwise expressed. Taking a broad view of the universe and looking at it as a whole, and as a manifestation of God's goodness, power, and wisdom, it is impossible to conceive a world in which these could be more faithfully or fully expressed. In the first place, it comprises the only three possible classes of beings—the purely spiritual, the purely material, and man who is both material and spiritual. These three orders of beings exhaust the possibilities. Again, in each order we find a bewildering and marvellous range of degrees of perfection, from the lowest to the highest; in the material order from the simplest to the most complex, from the inanimate through all the grades of the vegetable and animal kingdoms, with uncountable differences and degrees and combinations of perfections. In men, though all have the same nature, there is yet a similar variety of capacities and endowments; and from the little, comparatively speaking, that has been revealed about the angelic kingdom we can deduce, with an approach to certainty, the existence therein of a like immense variety of degrees of excellence. It is clear that such a universe, constituted of such a multiplicity of differences combined in one vast harmony, is a fit reflection of God's perfections, corresponding worthily to his wisdom, power, and goodness. It is true that we can conceive of other creatures that he might have created: he might possibly have made a race of flying sheep, or a kind of water that would freeze at sixty degrees, or have created a race of green men as well as white and black and yellow, or have endowed Shakespeare with the military genius of Napoleon and the scientific genius of Newton. But after all these would have been but accidental differences, and it does not appear that they would have expressed any more clearly than does the actual world the infinite perfections of his nature. In fact, it is quite likely that some of these or similar possibilities, if translated into reality, might rather take from than add to the world's perfection, by disturbing its present ordered harmony. All this St Thomas puts very briefly in answering the question whether God could have created things better than he did.

"When it is said that God can make a thing better than he makes it, if ' better ' is taken substantively, this proposition is true. For he can always make something better than what actually exists. Moreover, he can make the same thing in one way better than it is, and in another way he cannot, as was explained in the body of this article [where the author distinguishes between essential and accidental perfections]. If, however, ' better ' is taken as an adverb, implying the manner of the making, thus God cannot make anything better than he has made it, because he cannot make it from a greater wisdom and goodness. If, however, it implies the manner of the thing done, he can make something better, because he can give to things made by him a better manner of existence as regards accidentals, not, however, as regards essentials." [1]

And again: " The universe, the present creation being supposed, cannot be better, on account of the most beautiful order given to things by God, in which the good of the universe consists. For if any one thing were bettered, the proportion of order would be destroyed, as if one string of a harp were stretched more than it ought to be, the melody would be destroyed. But God could make other things, or add something to the present creation, and then there would be another and a better universe." [2]

God, then, is supremely free, both as to creating or not creating, and, given the determination to create, as to the objects to be created.

[1] *S. Theol.*, I, Q. xxv, art. 6, ad 1.     [2] *Ibid.*, ad 3.

He is bound by no sort of necessity whatsoever. If we seek the sufficient reason for his choice of this universe rather than another, the only reasonable answer possible is that such was his good pleasure. In him his own will is the sole measure and standard of goodness in acting; whatever he does is good, just and simply because it conforms to that standard. But since that standard, being divine, is the highest possible, whatever he makes is made according to the best possible pattern, and hence is said to be formally the best thing possible. Such is the actual universe. Yet since the present universe does not exhaust God's mind and strength, another might conceivably be created which would surpass this in beauty, grandeur, and all that goes to the perfection of achievement, and which would, therefore, from the material point of view, be superior.

But this question disposed of, another and a cognate one at once *Why did* arises : Why did God create the world ? 'It was not from necessity ; *God create ?* yet a good and sufficient reason there must have been. The human intellect is so fashioned that, despite the efforts at persuasion of sundry philosophers, it r´ ises to accept pure chance, mere fortuit. ness, as accountinᵦ for anything. Almost as soon as its intelligence awakens to conscious life the child begins, in season and out of season, to ask why. The child's parents and teachers may often find its inquisitiveness embarrassing and inconvenient, but it is nothing but the recognition and the proclamation of the eternal principle that *Omne agens agit propter finem* (Everything that acts, acts on account of some end). The armchair philosopher, his intelligence perverted by years of misdirected speculation, may raise his voice in protest against the very idea of what he calls teleology, but it is the child with its insistent " why " and continual " what for " who is the mouthpiece of truest wisdom. And, indeed, no sooner do we look at things a little closely than we see that it is the recognition of this principle that lies at the root of all human progress in the sciences and arts of civilisation. It is because we realise that everything is ordained to some end or purpose that we want to discover what that is, and it is this desire that prompts all human investigation into the nature of the physical universe and all human ingenuity and inventiveness. Man only makes a tool or a new machine because he wants to do something with it, and he fashions it for that end.

As soon, then, as we begin to think upon the problem of creation, once we have decided that God made the world and made it impelled by no necessity, we are led to ask why he made it, what purpose he had in view. In answering this question we must carefully distinguish between two things that, though quite different, may be easily confused. The Catechism asks, Why did God make you ? and answers, God made me to know him, love him, and serve him in this world and to be happy with him for ever in the next.

This answer might, in part, be extended so as to include not only man, but all creatures, for all creatures are made to serve God according to their own proper ways and fashions, though men and angels alone are made to know and love him, and to be happy with him for ever.

But this is not the end of the matter. We can go further and ask: Why did God make the world for this end, what purpose had he in view in providing this destiny for the world? This is a very different question and brings into view a very different end. Let us illustrate it by an example. An artist paints a picture which he hopes to sell. The purpose or end of the picture is to represent a certain scene, and in so far as the representation is a faithful one and conforms to the canons of art—whatever they may be—the picture is a good one and has achieved its end. But the artist's purpose in painting it is by no means achieved if it remains hanging in his studio or is returned unsold from the gallery where he had exhibited it. He painted it to sell, to provide food and clothing for himself and family, and it is only when it is sold and the money is in his pocket that this end is attained. And to make the distinction clearer, and more applicable still to our present subject, we may point out that it does not matter, from this point of view, whether the picture achieves its end or not—whether, that is, it is a good or a bad picture—even if it be thoroughly bad ; so long as someone is so foolish or so undiscerning as to buy it at the artist's price, his end is gained.

The Catechism answer, then, as to the end of man (and by extension and adaptation of the world) tells us the end to which man is destined, and that is a matter with which we in this essay have no concern, but which is discussed in Essay IX. But it tells us nothing of God's ultimate purpose and motive in making the world with such a destiny, which is the question now at issue. On this point there is no chance of the instructed Catholic going wrong, for he has the Church's teaching defined in the Vatican Council to guide him. It is there laid down that God created the world " neither to increase nor to attain his own beatitude, but to manifest his perfection," and anathema is pronounced against anyone who shall deny that the world was created " unto God's glory." Given the firm Catholic teaching about God, who is " infinite in all perfection," which is the only teaching reasonable and satisfying, no other answer as to why he created the world is possible. God needs nothing, lacks nothing in himself to his perfect happiness. His infinite love and infinite intelligence are fully exercised and satisfied in the ineffable activities of his intimate life as a Trinity of divine persons. The happiness resulting from this exercise and satisfaction, even he, in his omnipotence, cannot possibly increase. He could not, then, create the world in order to attain or to increase his own happiness. The only end, therefore, he could have, was that the creatures whom he made, and to whom he gives existence and all their various perfections, which are in different ways and degrees reflections of and a sharing in his own goodness and perfection, should, by seeking him, and serving him, and reaching out to him and returning unto him, each according to its own powers and fashions, attain their own ends and so doing show forth his perfection and glory.

And here we may pause a moment to consider the practical application and consequence of this so simple yet sublime teaching. Some philosophers and moralists preach what seems at first sight not only a stern but a pure and selfless morality. They maintain that men should practise virtue without any regard to ultimate reward from God ; that this is the highest, indeed, the only true virtue worthy of man ; that to be good for fear of hell or hope of heaven is but selfishness disguised, or even a degrading servility. The ancient Stoics taught the same doctrine. It is a doctrine which, by its subtle flattery of man's natural pride, is seductive. It has an appearance of nobility that appeals to the man of upright mind, and it goes well with the spirit of independence. But apart from the fact that it will not work, except on a very small scale, since human nature as a whole is too weak to stand the strain, it is a doctrine that contradicts these fundamental truths that we have been considering. God is man's Creator, and his end in creating him is his own external glory, which consists in the manifestation of his divine perfections. The higher the gifts he gives to creatures, the better and more highly are his perfections made manifest. More power and goodness and wisdom are shown in the creation of one human soul than in the whole solar system, because it is a creation of a higher order and one nearer to God's own nature. But, as is shown elsewhere,[1] and here taken for granted, he gives man not only natural but supernatural gifts, the higher nature of sanctifying grace, which is a still more wonderful reflection of himself. And giving him this he means him so to use it that after death it will expand and blossom into the still closer approach to God, the still more perfect assimilation to him, which we call the beatific vision or eternal happiness, which is the highest possible manifestation of divine perfection, apart from the hypostatic union in Jesus Christ, that even the wisdom and power of God can devise and produce. The blessed in heaven are God's greatest glory.

It follows, then, that when a man leads a good life, practises virtue, spends himself in the service of others in the hope of thereby gaining heaven, he is acting not from a selfish motive, not simply to promote his own end, but also and truly to fulfil God's end in the most perfect way. He is acting for God's glory. His happiness is God's will, and his end is God's glory. And even if this ultimate and higher end is not always openly in view and explicit in intention,

[1] Essay ix, pp. 311 ff.

it is always implicit and effectually operative, since God has commanded us to seek the kingdom of heaven, and it is his will that we should wish to attain our happiness by promoting his glory. So we see how truly this Catholic teaching of God's supreme liberty in creating and of the end he had in view is at the base of all Catholic morality, asceticism, and the practice of sanctity; since, as a man becomes more perfect by repressing concupiscence and overcoming his passions, as he grows nearer to God and more like him by practising in an ever higher degree every kind of virtue, by so much the more does he make manifest God's perfections and give his Creator the glory due to him.

## §V: THE WORLD HAD A BEGINNING

*Connection with divine freedom*

ONE other point of Catholic faith remains to be noticed before we pass from this consideration of creation as a whole and in general to the treatment of the various kinds of created things. This is the question whether God created the world from all eternity, as he exists from eternity, or whether it had a beginning in time. It might seem at first that this is a question of a purely metaphysical character or of scientific interest, without any theological, moral, or dogmatic bearing whatever. What can it possibly matter to me whether the world has existed, in some form or another, from eternity or not? What bearing can it have on my life, provided that I acknowledge God as its Creator? Why should the Church go out of her way to define, as she has done, in the Fourth Lateran Council, and again in the Vatican Council, that the world is not coeternal with God, but that he created it in the beginning of time? Surely this should be left to the scientists to discover if they can, or to the metaphysicians to argue about as they will. In reality, however, though this matter may have no direct bearing on one's spiritual life, it is closely connected with questions that have, and so it possesses a real theological importance. The doctrine of the non-eternity of the world is intimately bound up with that of God's liberty in creating. For if he had created from some necessity arising from his own nature, the world must have been coeternal with him, since owing to his immutability such necessity would be eternal and eternally necessitating. But if he creates freely, simply from his own free predilection, then as he alone determines to create, and what to create, so also in his free determination lie all the circumstances of creation, among them being the moment of its realisation.

Again the theory of a world existing from all eternity has been invariably in the history of thought bound up either with some sort of Manichean dualism, or else with some kind of materialistic evolutionism, or with some variety of pantheism. Hence the Church has had at different times to condemn the error and proclaim the truth.

But although this clearly is the revealed truth, proclaimed, for *The diffi-*
example, by Jesus Christ himself,[1] it is a truth bristling with diffi- *culty of the*
culties, which, were it not for the gift of faith, might easily result *conception*
in doubt.  For according to Catholic teaching God is from all
eternity changeless, and not changeless inaction, but changeless
activity and life.  If, then, he is now actually creating, he must
have been so from all eternity or there would have been a change
in him ; and if the result of the changeless creative action is now
the world, the same must have been the result from all eternity,
or else you would have the same changeless action producing no
result for a period and then at some determinate instant beginning
to produce a result, which would be absurd and impossible.  Nor
does it seem to be any use to try to escape by saying that the world
is created by God, not in so far as he is divine power or divine
being, but in so far as he is divine will and freedom.  For after
all, these distinctions that we make between God's power and his
will, as between his justice and his mercy or any other attributes,
do not correspond with any real distinctions in him, in whom,
apart from the three Divine Persons, everything is supremely one
and undifferentiated unity.

The objection is undoubtedly serious, so much so, indeed, that
to try to solve it, at least in such a way that the difficulty disappears,
would be useless.  The most we can do is to point out wherein
the fallacy lies, and to show how the difficulty arises, in part from
comparing things that are not comparable, and in part from the
fact that it involves two ideas, of which one is beyond our understanding and the other beyond our experience.  It may help us
also if we first note how the argument used in the objection proves
too much, and therefore proves nothing at all.  For if it is applicable to the creation of the world in general, it must apply with
equal force to the creation of any individual thing—for example,
to the creation of each and every individual human soul, each one
of which is thereby shown to be eternal, which no Catholic and
few Christians of any sort would allow.  Or if the example seems
to be a begging of the question, consider instead the Hypostatic
Union of God and man in Jesus Christ.  This was an event which,
though not a creation, yet requires the direct exercise of changeless
divine power as much as creation itself.  Yet it took place, not
from eternity, but at a definite moment in time.  This consideration, however, does not take us very far.  It shows, indeed, that
the objection is invalid, but not only does it not help us to its solution, which as I have said is beyond us, but it does not even help
to show why it is beyond us.  We can, however, see why this is so,
and thus gain some relief, if not repose, for the mind, by a brief
consideration of the ideas involved in the objection.

One of them is wholly beyond our experience—namely, the *Time and*
*eternity*

[1] John xvii 5.

idea of the first beginning of all things. We see many beginnings of things, but all of them take place in already existent time. They are all accompanied by and surrounded by movements, by noting which we can place them in their order and date them; thus when we say that one thing begins on Tuesday and another on Wednesday, what we really mean is that these two beginnings are dated or measured by different stages in the relative motions of sun and earth, stages that we mark off as years, months, days, and so forth. Even if we could actually experience the absolute first beginning of a thing as distinct from its development from something already in being, such as the creation of a human soul, we should still be able to place it exactly in its time position, to put it in its proper place in relation to some movement that preceded, accompanied, and followed it. We should still be able to say, supposing we had instruments accurate enough, that up to the end of the twenty-seven hundredth part of a second after six o'clock on such and such a date the soul did not exist, but before the twenty-eight hundredth had gone by it was in being, therefore it was created in this twenty-eight hundredth of a second after six o'clock. But we cannot do this when dealing with the absolute first beginning of all created things. We cannot date it by working backwards on any evidence. Geologists trying to date a geological period have to be content with approximations covering thousands of years. And if we try to work back in thought and imagination we soon find ourselves groping. All we can do is to say that if we go back so many thousands or millions of years we come to a time when the universe was only a day old, or what would have been a day, if there had been the sun, working as it is now, to measure it, of which we cannot be sure. We can now work backwards through this day to its first hour, its first minute, its first second, and then we drop off into a blank which leaves us baffled. We cannot say that we come to the beginning of time and find it dated by a certain fixed point in eternity. We cannot say that God had existed for so many ages of eternity and then created the world. We are brought up dead against this idea of eternity, which is the second idea involved in the objection, and which is beyond our comprehension. Time and eternity are not two similar and comparable sorts of duration differing only in having and not having a beginning and an end. There is no ratio, no proportion, no standard of comparison between the two. Time consists in motion, it is the measure of motion according to succession; without things moving, and so moving as to be relative to each other in their movements, there can be no time. But eternity is without movement or succession, it cannot be split up into periods, it has no measure, it overrides and embraces all time, it has no past and no future, it is all and always present. In fact, there is no such *thing* as eternity in the same sense as there is such a thing as time; there is an Eternal, who is God, and eternity is a name we give to an abstraction when we wish to speak of God under the aspect of duration. And God is incomprehensible. We can see then why it is impossible fully to understand this matter of the creation of the world in time : it is because it is simply a special aspect of the whole question of the relation between God and the universe, the Creator and the creature, the Infinite and the finite, and that must remain a mystery, or God would be no God.

We have now reviewed the principal points of doctrine arising from an examination of the created universe taken as a whole. We must now turn to the creation of the various distinct kinds of things that go to make up the universe, and this will introduce us to sundry matters that are nowadays much discussed.

## §VI: THE DISTINCTION OF THINGS

ST THOMAS, whose arrangement we have been more or less closely *God the* following, prefaces his treatment of the creation of the various *author of the variety of* classes of beings by a brief enquiry, first into the authorship of the *things* multiplicity and variety that distinguish the world, and then into the cause of the great primary distinction between good and evil. This latter question, because of its complexity, will more conveniently be treated in the following essay ; the former will detain us but a very short while. In so far as we are expounding Catholic dogma and neither the free opinions cherished by private theologians nor, much less, the speculations of scientists or philosophers, all we need say on this point may be put under two or three heads. Firstly, that God is the immediate cause of the threefold division according to which the whole universe is classified under the material, the spiritual, and the composite. (As to the last class, namely men, a little more must be said later.) This is clear from the definitions of the Fourth Lateran and the Vatican Councils, and from other pronouncements of authority.

Secondly, that he is the author of all the different natural *Not neces-* varieties to be found within each of these three classes. But here *sarily the immediate* a distinction must be made. He is, of course, the immediate author *author* of the different grades of angels,[1] since each angel must of necessity be a separate, distinct creation. But it is no part of Catholic faith that he is in the same way the immediate author of all the multiplicity of variations, from the simplest elements of the inorganic world to the highest animals, that comprise the visible universe. It is not Catholic dogma that all of these, or any of them (with certain reservations, to be noted later, as to man), are the products of distinct acts of creation by God. In other words, the Catholic Church allows scope for the theory and the working of evolution.

[1] Essay viii is devoted to the angels ; to this readers are referred for a full treatment of this question.

But yet God is the author of all this multiplicity and variety, in the sense that, granting the truth, by no means proved, of such universal evolution, it still remains true that the development has been worked out along the lines intended and determined by God, in virtue and by means of the natural forces and tendencies implanted by him in the primeval matter which he created, under the direction of his all-pervading providence, and under the continuous impulse of his sustaining omnipotence, the withdrawal of which for an instant would mean the annihilation of all things.

Finally, it is also part of the Catholic faith that certain differences and inequalities now existing are not due to God's original plan and are contrary to what is called his primary intention. These are the differences that consist in some of the defects which are evil. Thus all the angels were created good, and the devils became bad solely by the free abuse of their liberty. So likewise it cannot be doubted that many of the purely natural evils that afflict the world are the result of human sin and of the sinful activities of men, and in this way, being evil, are not the direct outcome of God's creative action.

Provided, then, that he avoids such crudities of thought as are commonly denoted by such phrases as the struggle for existence, natural selection, etc., by which divine oversight and direction are generally meant to be excluded, the Catholic is free to think and to speculate as he likes on the question as to the immediate causes of the world's variety. If he is wise, he will confine himself to facts and evidence and go no farther in assertion than strict proof allows. But if he wishes to indulge his fancy, he may do so without sinning against the faith. This will become clearer from what is to be said in the next section. Meanwhile one more point arises for discussion here.

*Other worlds?*  It has become quite common to take more or less for granted the truth of the hypothesis of either the existence of other worlds in the solar system, inhabited by men like ourselves, or else the existence of other systems beyond the limits of the solar system, in one or more of which the conditions of the earth are repeated in all that concerns animal and human life. And from this unproved hypothesis the conclusion is drawn that, since traditional Christianity is essentially geocentric and looks upon the earth as the sole theatre of the Incarnate Word's activity and, indeed, as the only scene of God's revelation and dealings with men, it must be changed, or, to use the favourite modern word, restated, in order to bring it into line with the advance of astronomical science. Hence there is some theological interest in the question whether the world be one, in the sense of being unique. But for Catholics it is not of great importance, and hitherto the Church has had no occasion to speak upon the matter. Scientifically the existence of other inhabited worlds is purely theoretical. Revelation, so far as it has been made to us, concerns this world alone, neither including nor excluding any other but wholly abstracting from it. If it should turn out to be true that there is another world or twenty more, Christianity will not be affected in the least. If other worlds exist we know that they, like ours, must have been created by God and must be ruled by his providence; and whatever theory we may choose to apply to their human inhabitants, whether their spiritual history and experiences be similar to ours or not, we know that God will have provided for their needs, as he has for ours, in a manner befitting his infinite wisdom, justice, and love. More than this it is impossible to say. But, whatever be the facts, the Christian religion will need no " restatement," because it, as well as God's revelation in the Old Testament, concerns and affects this world alone. So no Catholic needs to be disturbed in his faith, whatever wonderful discoveries astronomy may yet make.

## §VII: THE STORY OF CREATION

WE come now to what many will probably look upon as the most *Mosaic cos-* important part of our task. We have to examine the story of the *mogony and* creation of the world, from the first chaos to the making of man, *physical science* as it is told in the beginning of the Book of Genesis. How is this story to be understood? How can it be reconciled with what is now known and accepted by all, Catholics as well as others, of the physical history of the universe, and especially of the earth, of the living things, vegetable and animal, that dwell on it? How can we pretend that there can be any real reconciliation between the Catholic doctrines of the inspiration and the inerrancy of sacred Scripture and the biblical story of creation when this is subjected to the test of scientific knowledge? Many Catholics, perhaps most of them, are prepared to accept it as true that there must be a reconciliation, that the theologians, at least, must know how to solve these difficult questions, and to acquiesce in leaving the matter to them, and not worrying themselves about it any farther. Such an attitude, while most creditable to their faith and their trust in the Church, cannot be satisfactory intellectually, and may often be dangerous to themselves and others. It is therefore necessary for us to deal with it in so far as it has any bearing upon Catholic doctrine. Though it still has its difficulties and is still a question of some delicacy, yet, happily, it is not so formidable by far as it would have been some forty or fifty years ago. On the one hand, the advance both of scientific knowledge and of biblical studies has put out of court certain ideas and theories that were wont to cause heated discussion; and on the other, the enlightened wisdom of Pope Leo XIII and his successors, in laying down the true principles of interpretation and in definitely settling some points, has made it easier for Catholics to defend the faith, removed sundry causes of domestic disagreement, and on certain matters enlarged the boundaries in which they may move freely without incurring suspicion of disloyalty to faith or Church.

*The problem*   The first thing to do is to state the problem as clearly and succinctly as possible. In the first chapter of Genesis the sacred writer tells the story of the creation of the world and all it contains. His narrative is divided according to the works done by God on each of six days. It may be thus analysed. First of all comes the primary work, the creation of heaven and earth in a state of chaos and darkness. Then comes the work of differentiation, in three divisions. The work of the first day is the creation of light, and its separation from darkness, day and night. The work of the second day is the creation of the firmament, which is called heaven, and the division of the waters beneath it from those above. The work of the third day is the gathering together of the waters and the appearance of the dry land, or the division of land and sea. To this the writer adds a kind of supplement in the production of plants, trees, and fruits.

After this comes the adornment and furnishing of the different parts of the world, with a similar threefold division. The work of the fourth day is the creation of the heavenly luminaries, the sun, moon, and stars, to rule the day and night and divide light from darkness. The fifth day sees the production of fish in the waters and birds under the heavens. On the sixth day are produced the various sorts of beasts and reptiles that people the earth, and finally man, male and female. The seventh day is consecrated to rest from labour.

No one can help admiring the sublime simplicity of this story. And the more we learn of the accounts preserved by other ancient people wherein are narrated the beginnings of the world, the greater by comparison appears the nobility of this Hebrew narrative as well as the purity of the religious teaching therein enshrined. Unfortunately, however, it does not seem to fit the facts as we know them or are slowly learning them. The most obvious discrepancy is, of course, the fact that the world, instead of being made and completely furnished in six days, must have existed for unknown ages before man appeared on the earth. Among other defects of the narrative viewed in the light of present knowledge we may note the creation of plants and trees on the third day ; and that of the sun, which is necessary to plant life, on the fourth ; the creation of light and its separation from darkness on the first day, four days before the creation of the sun and heavenly bodies, the source of light. Again, all forms of vegetable life are said to be created together on one day, the third, and similarly all animals on another day, the sixth, whereas science proves that the production of plant life extended through immense periods of time, and was to a great extent coincident in time with that of animal life. There are other points of disaccord which need not be specified.

On the other hand, the inerrancy, the objective truth of the *Inerrancy of* whole of Scripture and all its parts, is one of the fixed and traditional *the Bible* elements of Catholic teaching, reaffirmed more than once, and in strong terms, by the Popes during the past thirty years. Then, again, the Biblical Commission, specially constituted by the Pope to deal with difficult points of scriptural interpretation, and speaking with an authority which, though not infallible, no loyal Catholic will reject or contest, has laid it down that these early chapters of Genesis are truly historical in form and contents, and that we cannot hold that they narrate, instead of actual facts corresponding to objective reality and historic truth, either fables borrowed from old pagan mythologies and cosmogonies, or merely allegories and symbols propounded under historical form in order to teach religious or philosophic truth, or legends in part historical and in part fictitious, made up for the instruction and edification of souls.

This is more or less a translation of the second and longest of *Rule of* the series of eight decisions issued by the Biblical Commission in *interpretation* 1909. And when the Catholic has read so far, he will probably begin to feel that whatever chance there may have been of reconciling Genesis and modern knowledge, to say nothing of some theories which, though not certain, are at any rate highly probable, has wholly gone. He will perhaps begin to think that if he is to remain a faithful and obedient Catholic he will have to cut himself off from all sorts of modern scientific thought, to throw overboard the most widely accepted scientific explanations of things, and to live a life of intellectual stagnation in company with his few fellow-Catholics. But as he reads on he will see a little light breaking before him. He will find that he still has some liberty of interpretation in those places as to which there has never been agreement or definite teaching among the Fathers and Doctors, and that he is not bound to the literal sense where it is clear that this would not be reasonable. When at last he reads the seventh decree, the dawn will broaden into the full light of day and the way will lie clear before him. This decree runs as follows : " Since it was not the intention of the sacred writer to teach the inmost constitution of visible things, or the complete order of creation, in a scientific manner, but rather to give to his countrymen a popular notion, conformable to the ordinary language of those times, and adapted to their opinions and intelligence, we must not always and regularly look for scientific exactitude of language when interpreting this chapter." This is no new departure in Catholic methods of interpretation. It is merely an application of the principle laid down by Pope Leo XIII in his encyclical *Providentissimus Deus*, that the Holy Ghost, speaking through the inspired writers, did not wish to teach men the truths of physical science—the inmost constitution of visible things—since they are of no profit to their eternal salvation. Nor was Pope Leo an innovator in thus speaking, for he was but repeating the ideas and language of St Augustine. The sacred Scriptures, then, according to authoritative and traditional Catholic teaching, are not meant to be taken as books for the instruction of men in the physical sciences.

When it happened that the inspired writer had, incidentally, to touch upon such matters, to enforce or illustrate his teaching, to set it in a framework that should make a deeper impression upon his readers, or for some similar reason, he adapted himself to the level of their intelligence, he conformed his phraseology to their common (that is, their uneducated and often false) opinions, he took over their current modes of expression. Humanly speaking he had to do this or he would not have been understood by those whom it was his business to instruct, but in so doing he gives thereby no guarantee whatever that the expressions he uses, relating to the physical constitution of material things, correspond to actual physical reality. Such expressions are merely the vehicle of religious truth, rather than the proclamation of scientific truth. A good example occurs in the use of the current notion of the firmament, as we shall shortly see.

*An inter-pretation*

Guided by these principles, armed with their authority, and safe in the assurance which that authority gives, the Catholic can now proceed to the interpretation of this story of creation in such a way as to safeguard all that the Church teaches about the inviolable truth of sacred Scripture, without at the same time violating or contradicting any proved truth of the physical sciences. Among the different interpretations proposed in recent years by competent and approved theologians, I shall speak in detail of but one, since my object is to expound the Catholic faith, not the free opinions of theologians ; and the sole reason for introducing at all what is but an opinion of some theologians, is that so the reader may have at command, not only the principles he must hold, but also an example of their application in a matter that to some might prove disturbing.

According, then, to this interpretation, the sacred writer composed his narrative upon a plan chosen by himself. His main thesis is that the world and everything in it was created by God. This it is what he wished to impress upon the minds of his countrymen, so as to preserve them from the errors and fancies current among the surrounding Gentiles. To express this the more clearly and vividly he chose the ordinary popular division of the universe into three elements, the heavens, the waters, the earth. In each of these three parts he pictures the work of creation as proceeding by stages. The first stage is the creation of all three divisions in a state of chaos (vv. 1, 2). The second stage is the work of discrimination, which is realised in the heavens by the division of light and darkness ; in the waters by the separation of the higher waters from the lower, by means of the firmament, which was conceived as a solid canopy stretched across the heavens; in the earth by the segregation of the sea from the land; while this is completed by the production of trees and plants, which, as springing from the soil, were regarded more as an integral part of the dry land than as a mere adornment of it. He then takes the threefold division again and summarises the work of their adornment or furnishing: the heavens are filled with sun, moon and stars; the waters are occupied by fishes (and here he introduces the birds as the living ornaments of the air); while the land is peopled by all sorts of animals and finally by man.

So is completed the whole work, with its three main stages, each containing three secondary divisions, always in the same order— heavens, waters, earth. The second and third main stages comprise, therefore, six divisions, to each of which is assigned a day. Such an arrangement, with its evident striving after symmetry, though of course not impossible in reality, certainly appears highly artificial, and to be adopted by the writer with the practical aim of making a deeper and more lasting impression upon the minds of a people who, like children, could understand a picture-story much better than a scientific disquisition. As for the " days," the " mornings " and " evenings," they would be, on this interpretation, an element of the writer's artificial plan, chosen to exhibit creation as the type or model of the week given to work, followed by the repose of the Sabbath. They represent, therefore, six moments or impulses of God's creative activity rather than any definite periods of time. With this interpretation, all the objections brought against the Mosaic account of creation from the physical sciences collapse. As it is a religious document in popular language, with no scientific object, it contains no scientific teaching and cannot therefore contradict scientific truth. The creation of all things by God is not a truth of physical science, but of philosophy, as has already been noted. We can therefore, in accordance with the teachings of science, or, if we like, of mere scientific theories, rearrange the order of the development of the world and its forms of life. We can lengthen out the astronomical periods of the solar system and the geological periods of the earth's history to as many millions of years as we choose, and we shall not be contradicting Genesis. If we think that the evolutionists have proved their case, or even that they have gathered evidence enough to make it prudently tenable, we may hold that from the lowest protoplasm to the highest animals there has been a continuous progress and evolution, either gradually or with occasional leaps, and by the instrumentality of any natural means that we may prefer, and, upon one condition, we shall not be rebellious to the Holy Ghost speaking through the mouth of Moses. This one condition is that we exempt nothing and no process from God's creative and directive activity, and acknowledge him, working through the powers of nature which he has made, as Lord and Creator of all.

## §VIII: CREATION OF MAN

*Special importance of the question* So far as we have gone in our review of the work of creation we have taken no account of the origin of man. This question, of course, has a special importance of its own, and theological implications of no mean gravity. Also, its treatment needs particular care in view of the distinctions which must be made between man as a whole and his two component parts, body and soul, since the teaching of the Church is not equally definite about all the different points involved.

We proceed first to take the question of the origin of the first human couple, man and woman, leaving till later the little that needs to be said about subsequent generations. And as the aim of this essay is an exposition of Catholic faith, other aspects of the matter in hand will not be touched, except in so far as they are necessary to an understanding of the faith and its implications. In their own spheres philosophy and the physical sciences have much to say about man's origin, but our concern is not with them, except by way of occasional contact.

*Unity of man's nature* In view of the extreme looseness of language and thought among so many modern proponents of current theories, we must be careful to define our terms strictly. Speaking, then, of the origin of man, we understand man to be a unity, one substance, composed of two distinct and different elements, one material, the other immaterial or spiritual, commonly called body and soul. He is as much one substance as water or wood or a horse is one substance ; but there is an immensely greater difference between his two component elements, body and soul, than between the various different elements making water, wood, or a horse. All of these are material, and as such can be measured and counted and weighed, and are subject to all the laws that scientific investigators have discovered as ruling the whole material universe. But while man's body is akin with these, and is itself made up of the same material elements as they are, his soul is in a wholly distinct category and world. It has nothing in common with material things, nor is it subject to any of the laws which they must obey. It cannot be seen, weighed, or measured ; even its existence and its nature can be known by us only by the use of the power, seated in itself, of observing its operations in ourselves, and thence arguing to its being and character. All this we try to express by saying that it is non-material or spiritual. Yet these two disparate elements combine to form a real unity, man, as was laid down explicitly in formal philosophical terms by the Fifteenth General Council, that of Vienne, in A.D. 1312. I have insisted on this, only to make it clear that man does not and cannot exist until the soul indwells and gives human life to the body. Whatever origin or process of formation we may, for the moment, and by way of hypothesis, assign to body and soul, it must be remembered that, until the two come together and coalesce in one living unity and substance and being, there is no man. It is important to keep this in mind, as it has a bearing on the understanding of ecclesiastical documents and definitions which are always drawn up with strict regard to accuracy of phraseology.

As far, then, as concerns man, understood in this sense as a whole *Creation of* and one substance, the Church has spoken with infallible authority *Adam's soul* in the Vatican Council, besides making her mind known in other and less solemn ways. The Vatican decree lays down that " God created from nothing both sorts of creatures, the material and the spiritual . . . and then (*deinde*) the human creature, as it were partaking of both, being composed of spirit and body." This decree teaches that the creation of man was distinct from and subsequent to (*deinde*) that of the angels and the purely material world. It implies necessarily that the first man's soul, by which he was essentially and formally constituted in human nature, was due to a distinct divine creative act, by which it was drawn into being from sheer nothingness. This, also, is the evident teaching of the Holy Ghost speaking through Moses in Gen. ii 7 : " And the Lord God . . . breathed into his (*i.e.*, man's) face the breath of life, and man became a living soul." This first point, then, is clear and fixed : Adam's soul was created directly and immediately by God from nothing. This is as much a part of Catholic teaching as it is a truth of sane philosophy. To deny it would be to rebel against the Church's authority, as well as to reject the dictates of sound reason. For a Catholic there can be no question and no debate about the hypothesis or even the possibility of the development of Adam's spiritual soul from the non-spiritual animating principle or soul of any brute, however highly advanced in the scale of animal perfection. The theory of evolution taken universally, as embracing the development of the first man's soul from some non-human faculty of one of the higher animals, is out of court for the Catholic ; and far from feeling this a restriction of his intellectual and human freedom, he is grateful to the Church, which, by her authoritative pronouncements, keeps him to the broad highroad of common sense and saves him from aimless wanderings down all the blind alleys of human folly.

When, however, we go on to consider the origin of Adam's *Origin of* body we enter a region where the definite certainty that obtains *Adam's body* concerning his soul is lacking. This arises in part from the nature of the case, and in part from the nature of the available evidence. Clearly, the origin of man's body can have, of itself, no such grave theological and spiritual implications as are necessarily involved in the origin of his soul. That his body came into existence in this way or that is a matter of historical truth and of scientific interest, but whether it was this way or that has, in itself, no direct theological bearing. But the Church, though she can, as the sole authoritative interpreter of Scripture, determine the meaning of any passage dealing with historical fact or scientific truth, when it is necessary or expedient, in order, for example, to safeguard some religious truth involved in a statement of fact, yet has, by virtue of her divine commission, no direct interest in purely historical and scientific questions as such. When, therefore, such a matter arises the question to be decided comes to this : Does the Holy Ghost through the inspired writer teach clearly, and mean us to accept as revealed truth, that such an event actually took place, or that such an assertion is a scientific fact ? If he does, there is no more to be said, since God cannot err. But if there be any doubt as to whether that be his intention, then unless and until the matter is decided by the Church's divine authority, the Catholic is free, within the limits and subject to the conditions laid down to be observed in such cases, to understand the passage in the way that seems best. And so long as the Church gives no decision, diversities of interpretation and fluctuations of opinion are bound to occur.

What, then, is to be said concerning the origin of Adam's body ? In the first place, it is certain that by far the greater part of Catholic thought, both through the ages and at the present day, favours the opinion that Adam's body was produced immediately and directly by God's act. The reasons for this are obvious ; such seems to be the plain literal meaning of Gen. ii 7, " And the Lord God made man from the slime of the earth," and such an origin seems most fitly to accord with man's natural dignity and his supernatural destiny both of soul and body. And there can be little doubt, if any, that in the present state of our knowledge it is prudent and wise for Catholics as a body to retain this general and traditional opinion. For unless there be a prudent reason for so doing, it is rash to depart from a view which has commended itself to the minds of so many Christian generations.

In this instance no cogent reason exists. Far from it. For against this traditional view there stands nothing but the theory of evolution, as to which it cannot be too often repeated that, despite the claims of many of its supporters, it is still a theory only, having, indeed, some indefinite degree of probability, but no sort of certainty : while if we take it as covering all forms of animal life and so embracing the origin of the human body, the positive evidence in favour of it is, at present, so slight and feeble as to be negligible.

We might leave the question at that, but it may be useful to carry it a step further. It has often been asked if there is anything in the Church's teaching to prevent a Catholic from holding man's body to be a development from one of the higher animals, if this should ever be proved to be a scientific fact. If the question is put in this way the answer must, of course, be a simple No, for the teaching of the Church, being divinely preserved from error, can never run contrary to anything proved to be a fact, in any field whatsoever of human knowledge. The question, then, should be differently framed. Is there anything in the Church's teaching to prevent a Catholic from holding the said theory concerning the human body, and so to make it certain that this can never be proved to be a fact ?

The Vatican decree already quoted is by no means definite on this point. It does not say that Adam's body was immediately or directly produced by God from nothing, nor does it say anything about the process by which God fashioned it, or about the state or condition to which it had been brought, whether by direct divine agency or other means, at the moment when God breathed into it a living, human soul. As a consequence of this, and because the evolutionary hypothesis appealed to them, some few Catholic theologians set forth views on the origin of man's body more or less in agreement with current evolutionary theories. And, although in one or two cases writers had their works condemned or were called upon to retract their opinions, in no instance did it clearly appear that a condemnation, issued officially by one of the Roman Congregations, fell precisely on the point now under discussion—namely, that Adam's body was the term of a process of development, rather than the result of a special and particular divine creative or formative act.

The only other authoritative pronouncement is the decree of the Biblical Commission (No. 3) which forbids a Catholic to call in doubt the literal and historical sense of those passages in the first three chapters of Genesis wherein are narrated facts which touch the foundations of the Christian religion, among others mentioned being " the special creation of man, the formation of the first woman from the first man, the unity of the human race." We must see whether this decree has made any real change in the situation, to the extent of making it impossible for a Catholic to hold that Adam's body was the term of a process of natural, though God-directed, development, and that God took one of the higher animals and, by infusing into it a human soul, made it a man.

A Catholic evolutionist, recalling what has been said about the oneness of man's substance and the impossibility of man's existence until the soul indwells and vivifies the body, and claiming, as he is entitled to do, that ecclesiastical decrees which restrict liberty are to be interpreted strictly and narrowly, might contend that since this decree speaks of the creation of " man," and says nothing about his body, he is still free to hold that this latter was the result of an evolutionary process. Also he might argue that the literal historical sense of Gen. ii 7 is not absolutely certain, since first, according to the Hebrew, it does not read " God made man from the slime (or dust) of the earth," but " God made man slime (or dust) from the earth," which may be variously understood ; and secondly, that, whereas it is certain that not all animals were made immediately from the earth by God, yet Gen. ii 19 asserts that they were. Hence, invoking the seventh decree of the Commission that it was not the inspired writer's intention to impart scientific knowledge of the whole of creation, he may conclude that this passage about man is one of those wherein we are not to look for the accuracy of scientific language.

Whether such a position be reasonable, especially in view of the absence of any real scientific evidence in favour of the evolutionary descent of man's body, and of the many difficulties against it, is one question which, however, it is not within our province to debate. Another and quite distinct question is whether such a position is to be condemned as offending against, I do not say the Catholic faith, but against the loyalty and obedience owing to ecclesiastical authority as vested by the Pope in the Biblical Commission. All things considered, it would seem that the answer must be in the negative, and that unless and until authority should speak more clearly and definitely, freedom of opinion and discussion on this point are still allowable.

In other words, the Church gives us in this matter evidence of that truly divine prudence which characterises all her actions. When the faith is assailed she speaks promptly, decisively, clearly. When the matter in debate does not appear to imperil the faith, even though some among her children may scent danger, she waits. In her regard for man's dignity, she will not curb his intellectual freedom ; in her anxious care for the faith of the timorous or more sensitive souls she impresses upon all the necessity of single-minded loyalty to truth in research, of sobriety in language, and of the spirit of obedience to her authority.

*Origin of Eve's body* As for the production of the first woman's body, a few words will be enough. The decree of the Biblical Commission particularly mentions the " formation of the first woman from the first man " as one of the instances wherein the literal historical sense of sacred Scripture may not be called in question. The reasons are plain. Firstly, the literal interpretation of the passage is presupposed or confirmed in many other places in Scripture, as when St Paul, addressing the Athenians, says [1] that God " hath made of one, all mankind," or, writing of the relations of man and woman, reminds the Corinthians [2] that " the man is not of the woman, but the woman of the man."

Secondly, this truth has considerable dogmatic importance ; Catholic teaching about the sacrament of matrimony and about the intimate union of Christ and the Church is closely bound up with it, illumined and strengthened by it. Beyond this it needs

[1] Acts xvii 26.      [2] 1 Cor. xi 8.

only to be said that within the ambit of this literal meaning does not lie the " rib " from Adam's side, since the exact meaning of the Hebrew word used is doubtful.

Here, also, we may note that the Biblical Commission mentions *Unity of the* the unity of the human race as a point as to which the historical, *human race* literal sense of Genesis is not to be doubted. This is, if not actually a part of Catholic faith, at least an example of what theologians call dogmatic facts. That is, it is a fact so closely bound up with a defined dogma that to deny the one is to reject the other. Let it be allowed that from the time of Adam onwards there have been any men dwelling upon the earth who were not his descendants, and it becomes impossible to hold the Catholic dogma of original sin, or that of the Redemption embracing the whole of, and limited to, the race of Adam. But since the Church is the guardian of the faith, she clearly must have the right, which indeed she has often exercised, of authoritatively stating such matters of historical fact as are necessary for the holding or the defence of revealed dogmas of faith.

It may here usefully be added that the Church has defined *Antiquity* nothing with regard to the antiquity of man, or the number of *of man* years that have passed since Adam's creation. She does not guarantee or assert that the list of the early patriarchs, with their ages given in the Book of Genesis, is meant as a complete and mathematically accurate record, from which any certain conclusion as to the date of man's first appearance upon the earth can be drawn. In this matter an attitude of prudent reserve, which includes a willingness to accept proved facts but a determination to take a large dose of salt with all unproven theories, is that best fitted to the Catholic mind, temper, and tradition.

When we pass on to the origin and mode of production of the *Origin of* souls of all of Adam's descendants we come to a question the interest *each human* of which is now mainly historical. *soul*

Leaving aside such errors as that attributed to the great Origen, who held that all human souls, as well as all angels, were created simultaneously from the beginning ; and that promulgated by certain early heretics, who taught that they were some kind of emanation from God's own substance ; and that imputed to Tertullian, that the soul is, like the body, the result of generation, errors more than once condemned by the Church—we must say a few words about an opinion once somewhat widely held in the Church itself, and the subject of controversy between two such celebrated Doctors as St Jerome and St Augustine. The immediate occasion of the discussion was the denial of original sin by Pelagius and his followers. St Augustine, as the great champion of the faith, was forced into the investigation of the way in which original sin was handed on from father to son, and found himself faced with a difficulty. St Jerome, consulted by him, pronounced unequivocally in favour of creationism—that is, the opinion that each human soul is created directly and immediately by God, at the very instant of its infusion into the body, or more accurately, perhaps, that it is created *in* the body. St Augustine, though willing to be persuaded and, indeed, inclined to the same opinion, was not convinced. Since original sin is in the soul, he argued, if this is directly created by God, how can he be acquitted of, at least, part complicity in the production of sin ? Unable to solve the difficulty, he clung to the possibility of the theory that the soul of the child is produced by the parent's soul, not, however, by its own natural power, but by virtue of a special power given it by God. St Augustine's great authority gave to this opinion a longer life than its own worth deserved, but it was afterwards abandoned, and on two or three occasions when it has been revived, even in a modified form, the writers responsible have been required to retract. Consequently there is no doubt that, though not explicitly defined by the Church, the direct creation by God of each soul at the moment when the body is ready to receive it, appertains to the substance of the Catholic faith. But as to when this moment is, and at what stage of pre-natal development the body becomes vivified by the creation of its rational soul, is a question still open to free debate.

## § IX : CONSERVATION OF THE UNIVERSE

EVERYTHING, then, that is in the heavens or the earth, or in what may be other worlds or other systems beyond the stretch of human eye or human power to discover or investigate, was at some moment lost in a past beyond human calculation called by God's command into being out of sheer and absolute nothingness. In that instant the world began, and with it time and motion. From that instant this vast created world, under the impulse of the forces and activities with which God had gifted it, began to go forward and to change and develop until it became the world such as we see it and partly know it to-day.

But there is one conception of this world which, common enough even among Christians, we must most carefully avoid. We must not think of the universe as something analogous to a piece of machinery made by man. A clock-maker may make a clock, and having wound it up, leave it to go " by itself " for a week or a month. The world is not like that, differing from the clock only in size and complexity. It was not just " wound up " by God in the beginning and then left to go " by itself " for so many thousands or millions of years until it runs down and comes to a stop or has to be wound up again. God could not make a world like that. As it needed his creative omnipotence to call it out of nothing, so it needs, at every moment, his sustaining omnipotence to keep it from sinking back into nothing. God's power and activity are necessarily involved and exerted in every movement of every planet, in every vibration of the ether, in every breath that man draws and every thought he thinks, in every tick of that very clock that we speak of as going "by itself." The forces that move the world are his creation, the laws that govern them are of his making. This is the fundamental fact, let it be noted by the way, that makes miracles both possible and reasonable, since they are simply particular and striking examples of the Creator's power over and loving interest in his own work. This continuous and immanent activity of God in every phase and detail of the world's existence and life is as important and as necessary to bear in mind as creation itself. It is the complement and the correlative of creation. It enables us to realise that "the earth is the Lord's and the fulness thereof" (Ps. xxiii) as truly now and as completely as when "in the beginning God created the heavens and the earth" (Gen. i 1), and also it enables us to follow without fear all the speculations, and to accept without anxiety all the proved or to be proved conclusions, of science as to the course taken by the process of world development and the means used to attain the end.

There is, however, one all-important field in which the work of creation, in the strictest sense, did not end on any hypothesis as to world processes, when the material universe was called into being and started upon its voyage across the sea of ages. Every human soul, from Adam's down to the baby's of to-day, is, as it comes into being, the direct, immediate result of God's creative act, who at that instant calls it out of eternal nothingness. The human soul, when it begins to be, has no past, no previous existence in a state of potentiality, such as next year's plant has in this year's seed; there is no process of evolution behind it; it is something absolutely new. So that in this way the sum total of created being is still growing, and will go on growing until the number of the elect is filled and all generations of men are called to judgement. The human parents of a child are not the generators of his soul. This, which alone makes man to be man, is the work of God alone. Here is the profound truth underlying the whole of Christian morality, the truth that gives solid reality to the prayer Christ taught us, "Our Father, who art in heaven," the truth that alone makes to be true and gives sweetness and reason to that word of Jesus that otherwise would be harsh and unnatural: "He that loveth father or mother more than me is not worthy of me." [1] Only God could make such a claim, and God may make it only because he is our Creator, our Father, the only real author and immediate cause of our immortal soul.

B. V. MILLER.

[1] Matt. x 37.

# VII

## DIVINE PROVIDENCE

### § I : THE CONCEPT OF DIVINE PROVIDENCE

*General notion and definition*

HOLY SIMEON of old proclaimed the child Jesus to be a light to the revelation of the Gentiles who sat in darkness and in the shadow of death. How great was that darkness we know from the pages of contemporary secular writers. The Græco-Roman world at large was a temple of idols, in which men sought by degrading rites to placate a venal rabble of gods and goddesses. These deities, for the most part, were regarded by the masses as dread tyrants oppressing humanity from the security of the heavens, and by the leaders of religious thought as, at best, shadowy beings " content to sit aloft and watch the world go round." Many of the philosophers had abandoned themselves to crude materialism, or pronounced the world a cruel jest of Fate.

But it was not so within the narrow confines of Judea. There, and there only, the worship of the one true God obtained. For it was the peculiar glory of the Jews, throughout their chequered history, to have preserved upon the earth, amidst the surrounding corruptions of polytheism, the primitive concept of the one true God ; the all-loving Father " who provideth food for the raven, when her young ones cry to God, wandering about because they have no meat " ;[1] the personal God of Abraham, Isaac, and Jacob, who delivered Israel from the bondage of Egypt ; the great ruler of all nations, who brought the Philistines, the mortal enemies of the Jews, out of Caphtor, and the despised Syrians out of Kir.[2] It is, above all, his universal providence which distinguishes the God of Revelation from the heartless deities of the cultured heathen and the tribal gods of the untutored savage.

The word " providence " is derived from the Latin word *providere*, which means " to look before," " to make provision," " to take heed for the future." In its widest sense, then, providence pertains to the moral virtue of prudence, of which it is generally held to be the principal part, since the other two parts, remembrance of the past and understanding of the future, are merely its helpmeets in furnishing the grounds of decision. It is the aim of the prudent man to act circumspectly, in harmony with the dictates of right reason, so as to avoid extremes and attain to the golden mean. The first thing that a prudent man does is to co-ordinate his past experience and appraise the present situation

---

[1] Job xxxviii 41.  [2] Amos ix 7.

in the light of that judgement. His next step is to look forward and make provision for what is coming, according to his resources ; in other words, he orders things to an end in view. This ordering of things to an end is the precise function of providence.

Clearly, it involves the forming of a plan on the part of the intellect, and the carrying out of that plan on the part of the will. Since it entails the employment of both these faculties, it has been variously defined, sometimes from the standpoint of the intellect, and sometimes from the standpoint of the will. Thus, St Thomas Aquinas stresses the part played by the intellect when he says : " Providence is the divine reason itself, seated in the supreme ruler, which disposeth all things " ; [1] whilst St John Damascene emphasises rather the function of the will, when he defines divine providence as " the will of God by which all things are ruled according to right reason." [2]

There is no discrepancy here, but merely a difference of point of view. The first definition is from the more logical standpoint of the divine plan to be put into operation, the second from the more practical aspect of the actual carrying out of the plan. Briefly, however, we may define providence as the divine governance of the universe, in accordance with the solemn pronouncement of the Vatican Council : " God watcheth over and governeth by his providence all things that he hath made, reaching from end to end mightily and ordering all things sweetly." [3]

The Catholic Church teaches that the world in which we live, and of which we are part, is no mere plaything of some celestial order of beings, nor a work of such inferior worth that it has been abandoned by its architect, nor the mechanical product of impersonal evolutionary forces, nor yet the outcome of some aimless chance, but the ordered achievement of the Creator, who owes it to his own infinite wisdom so to direct and govern it that it may attain to the fulfilment of his divine purpose.

Providence, then, is simply the divine ordination of all created *The end* things to an end. But to what end ? Reason and revelation unite *aim of* in assuring us that the final goal, the ultimate end, to which all *Divine* created things tend, cannot be anything in the things themselves. *Providen* The objects of our daily experience are neither self-contained, self-sufficient, nor self-supporting. No created being is of such a kind that its non-existence is unthinkable, for the simple reason that no created being has a necessary grip upon existence. We may survey the whole universe without finding an entity which is in itself a sufficient reason for its own existence. Everything in Nature is at once the cause and the effect of other things. The greatest of created things at the highest provides only a partial explanation of anything.

[1] *S. Theol.*, I, Q. xxii, a. 1.
[2] *De Fid. Orth.*, i 3.  [3] Sess. iii, c. 1.

To suppose, then, that any one of these things, or the sum-total of them all, is its own end, the harbour, so to speak, of its own ceaseless quest, is about as sensible as, to borrow Aristotle's illustration, the supposition that the art of shipbuilding is in the timber of which the ships are made. Even unaided reason leaves us in little doubt that the final end of the great conspiracy of Nature must be the glorification of the Creator. Hence the Vatican Council has declared : " If anyone shall deny that the world was founded for the glory of God, let him be anathema." [1]

On this point the inspired writers of Holy Writ speak with no uncertain voice. " The Lord hath made all things for himself," says the author of the Book of Proverbs ; whilst in the Apocalypse of St John we read, " I am Alpha and Omega, the beginning and the end, saith the Lord God." St Paul declares that " of him, and by him, and in him, are all things." [2] The supreme purpose of all created things is set forth by the Psalmist in the verse, " The heavens show forth the glory of God." [3] The final consummation of the designs of divine providence is thus depicted by St Paul : " Afterwards the end, when the Christ shall have delivered up the kingdom to God and the Father . . . when all things shall be sub-dued unto him, then the Son also himself shall be subject unto him that put all things under him, that God may be all in all." [4]

*The glory of God*
It is, then, the function of inanimate Nature to manifest the glory of its maker ; much more, obviously, is this the function of animate Nature with its greater capabilities, ever-widening till we reach rational Nature itself, creatures endowed with intellect and will, mortals made in God's own image. It is the daily lesson of our lives that nothing created can ever fill the heart of man. Each and every one of us has at some time or other set his heart on the attainment of some one thing ; we have felt that if we could only attain to *that*, whatever it was, we should be perfectly happy. And, perhaps, we have had the good fortune to gain our heart's desire. If so, we have not been perfectly happy ; disillusionment has fol-lowed swift and sure ; we have discovered that, after all, it was not *that* that we wanted, but something else, and the ceaseless search begins all over again.

" We were made for Thee, O Lord," says St Augustine, " and our hearts are restless till they find peace in Thee "—restless as the river on its way to the ocean. From the infinite we came and to the infinite we tend. It is perfect happiness that man desires, a happiness which this world cannot give, the secure enjoyment of an unending bliss which cannot slip from his grasp, the everlasting possession of God.

However, it is not as though man's happiness were the all-important matter, and the enjoyment of God merely a means to

---

[1] Sess. iii, c. 1, can. 5.  
[2] Rom. xi 36.  
[3] Ps. xviii 1.  
[4] 1 Cor. xv 24-28.

that end. Far from it. Man's enjoyment of God in the Beatific Vision lies precisely in the knowledge that his union with God contributes to God's greater extrinsic glory. Hence says Holy Writ: "The Lord hath chosen thee this day to be his peculiar people . . . to make thee higher than all nations which he hath created, to his own praise, and name, and glory." [1] So, too, in the New Testament, St Paul writes to the Ephesians of God the Father, "who hath predestined us unto the adoption of children through Jesus Christ unto himself, according to the purpose of his will, unto the praise of the glory of his grace." [2] Again, the Apostle prays for the Philippians, that they may abound in charity and be filled with the fruit of justice "unto the glory and praise of God." [3] Finally the end and object of creation is admirably expressed in the salutation of the four-and-twenty ancients prostrate before the great white throne of the Almighty: "Thou art worthy, O Lord our God, to receive glory and honour and power, because thou hast created all things, and for thy will they were and have been created." [4]

In the Book of Job we read how, when the foundations of the earth were laid, the morning stars sang together and the sons of God shouted for joy.[5] This was the opening chorus of Nature's triumphant hymn of praise, which has been chanted unceasingly ever since throughout succeeding ages, to the accompaniment of the harmony of the spheres. In this mighty orchestra every created being plays its proper part, each in subordination to the whole, for there is no instrument too humble to contribute something of its sweetness to the melody of the divine symphony.

Service is the essence of order, and service is the badge of the creature. Man, it is true, is the lord of creation, to whom all else in this world subserves. He can harness the forces of Nature to do his will and contribute to his well-being, but, in accordance with the same law of service, he himself can find happiness only in doing the will of God and manifesting God's glory. This law of service is impressed upon man just as much as upon everything in Nature, "from the cedar of Lebanon to the hyssop that grows on the wall." The gradation of purpose in the ever-ascending scale of creation, from the lowest to the highest, was set forth in arresting fashion many hundreds of years ago by Lactantius, whose graceful style won for him the title of the Christian Cicero. Rhetorically he declaims: "The world was made that we might be born. We were born that we might know God. We know him that we may worship him. We worship him that we may earn immortality. We are rewarded with immortality that, being made like unto the angels, we may serve our Father and Lord for ever and be the eternal kingdom of God." [6]

[1] Deut. xxvi 18, 19.    [2] i 5, 6.    [3] i 11.
[4] Apoc. iv 21.    [5] xxxviii 7.    [6] *Institutiones divinae*, vii 6.

All created things in some way show forth the glory of their maker. Because of his own intrinsic, infinite perfection, God must necessarily do his own will. It is impossible to conceive God as necessitated by anything outside himself, for were he so necessitated, clearly he would be limited from without, and therefore not infinite. Consequently God must, through the immanent necessity of his own unbounded perfection, seek always his own glory—a fundamental truth which has been solemnly defined by the Vatican Council in the proclamation : " If anyone shall deny that the world was founded for the glory of God, let him be anathema."

Not that it is in any way possible to add to the intrinsic glory of that which is infinitely perfect. That glory was complete in the long silent years of God's eternity, so to speak, before the dawn of creation. But in the time-series which begins with the external fulfilment of the creative act there is an outward manifestation of that glory on the part of the myriad creatures which, in manifold ways, reflect the divine perfections. That extrinsic glory may be increased, may be made more manifest ; and it is precisely the greater revelation of that ever-varying glory which is the ultimate end of the universe. The work of his hands must necessarily fulfil the purpose which he has foreordained, for the counsels of the Eternal Father, which are coeval with himself, " reach from end to end mightily." [1]

## § II: THE ATTRIBUTES OF DIVINE PROVIDENCE

WE may perhaps best present the teaching of Catholic theologians with regard to divine providence if we consider separately the various qualities or attributes which they ascribe to it, and these we may classify under four general headings.

### 1. *Its Universality*

To Christian ears there is nothing novel about the view that God's providence reaches as far as his causality, that nothing is too vast, nothing too small, to escape his care. But there have been philosophers who have said of God what Herbert Spencer said of Nature, namely, that it cares nothing about the individual, but everything about the species.

This curious restriction of the workings of divine providence to the conservation of species bears a distinct family resemblance to the muddled metaphysic of the eighteenth-century Deists in this country. It will be remembered that they so stressed the transcendence of God as to banish him altogether from the detailed working of the universe which he had brought into being. He had, they insisted, made the universe, and then left it to run its own

[1] Wisd. viii 1.

course in accordance with the universal laws which he had imposed upon it at its creation, very much as a watch-maker leaves the watch to its own intrinsic resources.

In these contractile views of providence, both ancient and modern, there is always the underlying assumption that it is derogatory to God to act otherwise than according to heroic scale. The propounders of these theories appear to be of Cicero's opinion that " the gods are careful about great things and neglect the small." Not so the teaching of Christ, who said that not even a sparrow falleth to the ground without the Father.[1]

The highest grade of knowledge about anything is to know it, not merely in its appearances or in its effects, but in its causes. The man who can make a wireless set knows far more about wireless than the man who only listens in. The latter's knowledge is at best superficial, and cannot be compared with the causal knowledge of the man who is able to construct his own instrument. To know a thing in its causes is to know it in its constituent principles, to understand it in the very foundations of its being. Now, since God is the ultimate efficient and exemplary cause of all creation, it follows that he must have the most intimate and penetrating knowledge conceivable of each individual thing, in its very separateness, in the height of its dignity, or in the depth of its lowliness. For God made not only the rolling orbs of heaven, but also the tiniest flower that blows, so that to much of his handiwork we may apply the saying of Virgil, " It is labour bestowed on a trifling matter, but not trifling is the glory " (*in tenui labor at tenuis non gloria*). Indeed, Aristotle has remarked that the nature of anything is best seen in its smallest proportions, and truly the surpassing wisdom of the Creator shines forth with dazzling splendour from the meanest micro-organism.

*Apparent failures*
Huxley uttered a profound truth, more profound than he realised, when he declared that chance is only another name for ignorance. Nothing really happens by chance. Everything in the universe is directed by the all-comprehending divine intelligence to the ultimate end of glorifying God. The so-called irrationality of the universe, of which rationalists speak so glibly, turns out on examination to be more apparent than real. Indeed, it requires a peculiar type of mind to rule out providence on the sentimental ground that a beneficent God would not permit sparrows to be eaten by cats.

Do the devoured sparrows fail to attain their end ? It is necessary to distinguish carefully between the proximate or particular end of created things and their final or general end. The particular end may, and oftentimes does, fail to be fulfilled, but not so the general or ultimate end. The particular end of the vine is to bear grapes on every branch, but the gardener may prune away many branches

---

[1] Matt. x 29.

in order to get better fruit. The failure of the particular end here subserves a general good—namely, the provision of more nutritious food for man. And many a hard-hearted farmer has remained unmoved at the tragedy of the sparrows, declaring them to be pests which ruin his crops.

Nature itself checks its own prodigality for the good of the whole, by ruthlessly frustrating the particular ends of many of its most fertile products. Thus says Professor J. Arthur Thomson : " A cod has several millions of eggs ; if these all developed into codlings and these into cod-fish, there would soon be no more fishing, and that would be the end of the world. There is a star-fish called *Luidia*—and not a very common one—which has 200 million eggs. Huxley calculated that if the descendants of a single greenfly all survived and multiplied, they would, at the end of summer, weigh down the population of China. An oyster may have 60 million eggs, and the average American yield is 16 million. If all the progeny of one oyster survived and multiplied, its great-great-grandchildren would number 66 with 33 noughts after it, and the heap of shells would be eight times the size of our earth. ' Which is absurd,' as Euclid used to say when (according to Samuel Butler) he was tired of arguing." [1] It is obvious, then, that in many respects Nature is cruel only to be kind. The particular end must in many cases give way to the general, and there results a hierarchy of divine purpose, according to which everything in creation is directed to the ultimate end for which the universe was brought into being, the extrinsic glory of God.

*God's providence for man*

It is to be noticed, however, that in the adjustment of particular ends to general purposes, in the subordination of the good of the part to the good of the whole, man is not simply on a level with the rest of creation. He ranks above and beyond every other living organism in this cosmos, and immeasurably above the whole inorganic world. All other mundane things are fleeting as " the grass of the field, which is to-day, and to-morrow is cast into the oven." To man alone, of things of earthly mould, is vouchsafed a life beyond the grave, a conscious existence after the dissolution of the physical compound, a personal immortality. Throughout the eternity which lies beyond the portals of death, the immortal soul of man must glorify God ; either in his infinite goodness by union with him in the Beatific Vision, or eternally separated from him in hell, in vindication of his infinite justice.

Essential immortality belongs to God alone, but the soul of man is naturally immortal ; that is to say, the created nature of the human soul is such that it has not within it any principle of corruption, and we know from revelation that it is God's design to conserve the soul for ever according to its nature. The soul of man, then, has an absolute value, and not merely a value relatively to the

[1] *The Control of Life*, pp. 193, 194.

other finite things whose mutual limitation makes up the order of Nature.

It is impossible, then, that the good of man should be subordinated to the welfare of anything else in Nature. On the contrary, the universe and all that it contains are subordinate in purpose to the eternal destiny of man. Christianity assigns him his true place: midway between the extremes of Celsus and Protagoras. The former placed him on a level with the ant, contending that he never rises above the instinctive ingenuity of that insect, whilst the latter boldly declared that man is the measure of all things. The truth is that God made man a little lower than the angels, that he stands at the head of the hierarchy of the universe, as embodying its various perfections, a veritable microcosm. As the poet Herbert has it:

> " Man is one world, and hath
> Another to attend him."

St Thomas Aquinas points out that the providence by which God rules the world is like the providence by which a father governs his family, or a ruler directs a city or state.[1] The father administers everything for the benefit of his wife and children, whilst the ruler's supreme solicitude is for the welfare of his subjects. In both cases the providential care devoted to land, buildings, and business generally is subordinate to, and regulated by, the primary end in view. So, too, is it with God's providential care of the world; everything else is administered for the sake of man, on the principle that the closer the kinship of any created substance to the nature of God, the higher its position in the order of God's providence.

Now God is a pure spirit, and consequently spiritual substances approach most nearly to their maker. Such a spiritual substance is the soul of man. It is not, of course, an immaterial substance altogether independent of matter, as is an angel, since its especial function is to animate the material human body. In fact, it has an essential, a basic, relation to the body, which is not destroyed by the death and decomposition of that body. St Thomas Aquinas emphasises this point, insisting that to be strictly accurate in our invocation of St Peter we ought to say, not " St Peter, pray for us," but " O soul of St Peter, pray for us," since St Peter was, and will be again, soul and body in one unity. Nevertheless, the human soul in its essence is immaterial, and, in so far, a reflection of the divine nature and a seal of resemblance. Therefore is it at the head of all created things under heaven, an immortal being made in God's own image, to which all else ministers in the hierarchical scale of the universal providence of God.

---

[1] *De Veritate*, q. v, art. 2.

## 2. Its Immediacy

Furthermore, God's providence is not only universal, it is immediate. The Platonists of old distinguished a threefold providence, only one of which pertained in any way to the supreme deity. In this view, the guardianship over material things is relegated to the lesser divinities who circulate in the lower heavens ; the affairs of men are left to the slender mercies of demons, powerful beings of doubtful character betwixt the gods and mortals ; whilst only purely spiritual beings, in whom there is no admixture of matter, are deemed worthy of notice by the great God himself.

*Matter and spirit*

It is surely a significant fact that matter has been the despair, and sometimes the undoing, of every religion except Catholicism. Either it has been glorified and worshipped by the worldly-minded, or it has been degraded and despised by idealists. In pagan systems of philosophy and theology generally, matter was regarded as a flaw in the handiwork of the gods, the source and the origin of all evil ; and consequently from the outset Christianity was open to the charge of materialism.

Because the early Christians cherished the charred remains of the martyrs, they were scornfully described as " cinder worshippers." This, too, by the Epicureans, who thought it more spiritual to maintain that the soul of man is born with the body, grows with the body, and dies with the body. The Gnostics laughed the Christians to scorn for their belief in the resurrection of the body. Was it not the function of the spirit to purge itself of matter which is its shame ? And why, they asked, venerate the mangled bodies of the martyrs, since those bodies, in life and in death, were an ignominy, a hindrance, and a reproach to spirituality ? Similarly gibed the Manicheans. Just as they held that God is not great enough to overcome the devil, so, too, they held that spirit is not great enough to overcome matter, which is, and must be, for ever in all its forms and phases, ignoble. The Neo-Platonists, likewise, taunted the Christians with the unspirituality of their teaching, with the gross glorification of matter. The same charge is made against the Catholic Church to-day. It is objected that she is sacramentalist ; that she elevates material things—water, oil, bread, and wine— to be actual channels of grace to the souls of men ; that she venerates the relics of the saints, and indulges in spectacular rites and ceremonies.

But the fact is that she, and she alone throughout all the ages, has understood the great synthesis of spirit and matter. She sees that matter is not a flaw in God's handiwork, but a triumph of his power ; that spirit can and does glorify matter ; and she points triumphantly to the doctrine of the resurrection of the body as the crowning instance of spiritualised matter. And, therefore, in the Christian economy, it is not necessary to relegate matter and material things to the care of some demi-god. It comes within the scope of the immediate providence of the infinitely perfect Creator.

Nevertheless, there are certain intermediaries in the workings of *The angels in* divine providence, not because of any defect in God's power, but *Providence* because of the abundance of his goodness. St Paul describes the angels as " ministering spirits," and the Fathers depict them as assisting in the divine governance of the universe, as having charge of countries, provinces, cities, families, and individuals. But this guardianship of the angels is exercised in the carrying out of the all-embracing plan of divine providence, subject, as it were, to God's immediate supervision. The angels, like earthly kings and princes and rulers, are all part of the eternal design of God's providence, all powers and principalities sustained within the hollow of his hand.

However, it would seem as though God, through intermediaries, *Constant* governs the world from afar, after the manner of the lord of the *dependence of* vineyard mentioned in the Gospel, who let out the vineyard which *creatures* he had planted to husbandmen and himself went into a far country.[1] In interpreting this parable, the Fathers see in the absence of the master a reference to the fact that God no longer spoke to the children of Israel face to face ; for though with them he was no longer visibly present. So, too, though God may seem to us to have withdrawn himself from the actual governance of the universe, in reality this is not so. St Paul calls upon us to realise that God is " not far from every one of us : for in him we live, and move, and are." [2] He is present, though unseen, and present in such a vital way that our very continuance in being at every moment is dependent on him.

We are inclined to think of creation as a past benefit, very much as we think of a plaything of our childhood as something which was a boon to us then, but which has long since passed out of our busy lives. And yet, assuredly, creation is not static ; it is essentially dynamic and kinetic. It is a ceaseless act, for the work of conserving things in being is a prolongation of the act by which they were brought out of nothingness into being. " My Father worketh until now, and I work," [3] says our Blessed Saviour ; whilst in the Old Testament we read. " How can anything endure, if thou wouldst not ? or be preserved if not called by thee ? " [4] In the Psalms, the work of creation is depicted as going on uninterruptedly : " Thou shalt send forth thy spirit, and they shall be created : and thou shalt renew the face of the earth." [5]

Creation, then, in Holy Writ, is represented as a continuous act involving a direct divine influence on the very being of the creature, in such a way that, without this divine influence, the creature would simply cease to be at all. We are literally sustained in being at

[1] Matt. xxi 33.          [2] Acts xvii 27.          [3] John v 17.
[4] Wisd. xi 26.          [5] ciii 30.

every instant by the divine power and providence, without which we should lapse into sheer nothingness. We are as dependent on the act of God as the spinning celluloid ball in a shooting-gallery is dependent on the jet of water which keeps it revolving in position. If the jet cease for the fraction of a second, the ball drops ; if God's sustaining hand were withdrawn, we should collapse, literally, out of existence.

However, this sustaining influence is not a new act, or rather a multiplicity of new acts, on the part of God. He conserves things in being by a continuation of the same act by which he imparts being. The divine conservation is likened by St Thomas to the preservation of light in the atmosphere by a persistent influx from the sun. In the continuous execution of the plans of divine providence there is no change, no succession in the creative act itself, since it is eternal and immutable, though the verification of the creative act, which takes place in time, involves both change and succession in the created object. As the sun is the only source of light to this planet, so God is the only source of conservation to the universe. It is his immediate providence which sustains and governs all.

## § III : THE ATTRIBUTES OF DIVINE PROVIDENCE (*continued*)

### 3. *Its Certainty*

WE have seen that there are two essential parts of providence, the one pertaining to the intellect and the other to the will, namely, the plan and its execution. Obviously, providence is the more perfect according as its plan is the more far-reaching, and the more faithfully it is carried out. Now the plan of divine providence, since it is the eternal wisdom itself, must necessarily be the most perfect for the end which God has in view.

"The best-laid schemes o' mice and men gang aft agley," because of the failure of the mouse or the man to foresee what is going to happen, or because, though he foresees correctly, he cannot control the actions of other mortals or of other forces. But God's knowledge extends as far as the knowable. No thing that is, or ever was, or will be, or could be, is hidden from his ken. " Neither is there any creature invisible in his sight ; but all things are naked and open to his eyes," [1] and consequently his plan must be flawless, all-embracing, and perfect in its minutest detail.

Again, since God is the omnipotent first cause of all, it is impossible that any secondary cause should thwart the execution of his plan. Every action of every free agent in the universe has been

[1] Heb. iv 13.

foreseen, in all its consequences, by the "searcher of hearts and reins," [1] and duly taken into account in his eternal counsels. His providence, therefore, is certain, absolutely infallible, in its workings. This, however, does not imply that everything which happens under divine providence must happen of necessity.

Long ago Aristotle, on biological as well as on philosophical *Providence* grounds, laid it down that the nature of any being is the infallible *and freewill* indication of its end or purpose, and this principle has received the endorsement of many modern psychologists. Thus, William James's celebrated argument for the immortality of the human soul comes to this, that immortality is grounded in the structure of man ; in other words, that the nature of the human soul, being such that it has not within it any principle of corruption, is an indication that it is meant to survive the death of the body. In fact, it is difficult to see how anyone who believes in an all-wise God can think otherwise. God owes it to his own wisdom not to act against the grain of the nature he has established, but in accordance with it.

Consequently, if it be the nature of any created being to act necessarily and uniformly, as, for instance, water seeking its own level, God will order it according to that nature ; whereas, if it be the nature of a being to act freely, and therefore in erratic fashion, God will likewise order it accordingly. Failure to grasp this point has been responsible for many frivolous objections similar to that put forward by Cicero, who argues that if God foresees all things, then he ordains all things, and therefore are all things determined by inexorable fate. Consequently, there is no room in the world for free will ; everything happens of necessity.

To this difficulty St Thomas Aquinas replies tersely that it is not only effects that are foreseen by God, but also causes, and that God foresees free causes acting freely, and necessary causes acting necessarily; [2] and to the objection that self-determination on the part of the creature is incompatible with infallible knowledge on the part of God, he answers that God's knowledge of the future is not really *fore*knowledge at all, since to the eternal Mind all things are present. So long as a free act is considered as future, i.e. as contained in its free cause, it is indeterminate and incapable of being known with certainty. But God knows free acts not as future but as present, that is, as though they were actually happening before his eyes. "They are displayed before the divine gaze," he says, " according as they are when they are being actually performed." [3]

Again, it has been urged that the certainty of divine providence *Prayer* in its workings is a bar to the utility of prayer, at all events, to the prayer of petition. The objection takes the common form that if God has fore-ordained what is going to befall me in eternity, it

---

[1] Ps. vii 10.  [2] *Contra Gentiles*, III, 94.
[3] *S. Theol.*, I, Q. xiv, art. 13.

cannot make any difference whether I pray or not. Now, clearly, this objection regards prayer as a sort of irruption into the order already established by divine providence, a sort of attempt to upset God's eternal plan. Nothing could well be further from the truth. Prayer is a part, and a vital part, of the order established from the beginning by God's providence. Prayer is just as much a part of the order as are the winds and the waves and the weather. As St Thomas remarks, one might just as well exclude the effects of these everyday causes from the scheme of providence as exclude the effects of prayer.

If God from all eternity foresees that a certain man who does not pray will be damned, and so ordains it, we may rest assured that one reason for that fore-ordination is that God, equally from all eternity, foresaw that the man, in his perversity, would not pray. The oft-quoted line of Virgil, " Cease to hope that the gods' decrees are to be changed by prayer " (*Desine fata deum flecti sperare precando*), has no point when addressed to a well-instructed Catholic, for he at least hopes for no such impossibility. He prays in the sure knowledge that his prayers have been foreseen by God " before anything was, from the beginning," and that they have been taken into account, as it were, in the divine economy of his marvellous mercies and infinite love.

### 4. Its Uniformity

Finally, divine providence may be described as uniform in that it is in harmony with the laws of Nature. We have seen that God governs everything according to its nature, and so he is said to order all things sweetly.[1] Hence, says Henry Ward Beecher: " Providence is but another name for natural law. Natural law itself would go out in a minute, if it were not for the divine thought that is behind it."

*Miracles*    It is sometimes contended that the providence of a God who works miracles runs counter to the basic scientific principle of the uniformity of Nature. For practical purposes we may state the principle of uniformity thus : the same non-free agents acting in the same circumstances produce the same effects. In this statement the sameness is sameness of kind and not, of course, of identity. The same specific causes acting in like circumstances produce the same specific effects. The principle applies only to non-free agents, that is, to physical or natural causes, in contradistinction to the self-determining activity of human beings.

*The laws of nature*    Is not this order of nature violated by God when he works a miracle ? Has not Hume declared that " a miracle may be accurately defined as a violation of a law of Nature by a particular volition of the deity, or by the interposition of some invisible agent " ?

[1] Wisd. viii 1.

We may at once dismiss the invisible agent as a *bêtise* on Hume's part, since it does not require the erudition of Macaulay's schoolboy to know that a miracle can be worked by God alone. But the essential accuracy of this definition has been persistently questioned outside the narrow circle of professed rationalists and, of late years, even within it. Most theologians are at pains to explain that a miracle is not a violation of a law of Nature, but a sensible effect wrought by God beyond the ordinary course of Nature.

Now the effect of a divine action may well be beyond the scope of the ordinary powers of Nature, and yet not be a violation of the laws of Nature. For instance, accurate, detailed prophecy of remote future events is certainly beyond the ordinary mental powers of man, but by no means contrary to them. When Isaias foretold certain incidents in the Passion of our Lord, he was vouchsafed a vision of future events which were part of the eternal present to the divine intelligence. Surely in such case there is no violation of any law of Nature, psychological or physical. What happens is that, for the time being, the first cause uncaused supersedes a secondary cause, and produces a result beyond the power of the latter.

Mill, in his *Logic*, expresses the view that the laws of Nature ought to be stated as *tendencies* to uniform action. Thus, the law of gravitation in its most general form reads : " All bodies tend to move towards each other." Many causes other than miraculous intervention may prevent bodies actually exerting mutual attraction on each other ; but nevertheless the *tendency* remains. Or, again, take the thermodynamical law : " If one part of a body be at a higher temperature than another, heat tends to travel from the part at the higher temperature to that at the lower." It is sometimes a matter of vital importance, a matter of life and death, to prevent this law actually operating, but it is impossible to eradicate the tendency to operation. Clearly, the law which admits of no exceptions, which cannot be violated, deals with *tendencies*, with the natural properties of things, and not with their extrinsic effects. And the natural tendencies of all created agents remain unchanged, even when there is miraculous intervention. That intervention does not change the nature of any mundane agent, though it may suspend, alter, or increase, its normal external effect. The supreme cause operates in place of the subordinate cause.

Thus when God preserved the three youths from harm in the fiery furnace,[1] the flames still retained their tendency to burn matter ; in fact, they did burn the Chaldean ministers who stood close by. In the case of the youths, the tendency did not pass into action, because the operation of the secondary cause, fire, was in that case superseded by the action of the first cause uncaused, which is the cause of all else. It cannot be said that here there is a violation of the law of the uniformity of Nature. This becomes clear if we only

[1] Dan. iii 93, 94.

attend carefully to the wording of the law, which states that the same non-free agents acting in the same circumstances produce the same effects. Now, obviously, the fire of the furnace was not acting in the same circumstances when it attacked the Hebrew youths, who were protected by God, and the king's ministers, who were not. In the same circumstances, when there is no causal intervention, flames of fire will always consume human flesh ; but where the first cause of all intervenes, the circumstances are certainly not the same, and consequently the law does not apply. It is a case outside the law altogether. There is no violation either of the general law of the uniformity of Nature, which applies only in its proper sphere, or of any particular law governing the tendencies of any particular body, since those tendencies remain unaffected by miraculous intervention. And hence Huxley, in his *Essay on Hume*,[1] says : "The definition of a miracle as a violation of the law of Nature is in reality an employment of language which cannot be justified."

## §IV: PROVIDENCE AND THE EVILS OF LIFE

### 1. *The Nature of Evil*

*The difficulty* THE chief objection against the providence of God has always been drawn from the existence of evil in the world. It has taken many forms, from the classical dilemma of Epicurus, that Omnipotence could, and Benevolence would, have prevented evil, to the naïve question put by Friday to Robinson Crusoe, "Why does not God kill the devil ? "

During the Great War one frequently heard it said, and occasionally found it stated in print, that, when the war was over, there would be either no religion at all, or a completely revised and up-to-date religion, from which all idea of a benign providence would have vanished. It was felt by many noble-minded men that, at the crucial moment, Christianity had failed, and failed ignominiously. Why, we were asked, if God is infinitely good, did he permit that devastating war, bringing unutterable anguish to countless thousands, who had always striven to serve that God well and faithfully ? Christianity seemed to have no satisfactory answer to offer. In the blood-welter the forces of evil appeared to have triumphed.

And yet the war, with all its attendant horrors, was only the newest form of the problem of evil. War or no war, it is always with us. Even in the piping times of peace it stares us in the face daily from the columns of the newspapers : earthquakes, shipwrecks, train disasters, air tragedies, famines, pestilences—why does God

[1] P. 129.

permit these things, bringing so much sorrow and suffering in their wake ? Or, to come much nearer home, how is it that each one of us is called upon to endure so much misery from the cradle to the grave ? It has been well said that man enters this world with a cry of pain upon his lips and leaves it with a groan. Or, again, think of the thousands of hapless infants who are born into this world every day diseased, deformed, or mentally deficient, and thus sadly handicapped at the outset for the stern struggle of life. The evils are real enough ; they loom as a cloud of witnesses against the providence of God, darkening the heavens from view.

Every system of philosophy, every religion, that has ever existed from the dawn of creation down to the present day, has had to face the problem of evil, and try to triumph over it in its manifold guises. If we are really to grasp the problem, and perchance find a theistic solution wherein evil is reconciled with the providence of God, our approach to the problem must of necessity be through its philosophical and historical implications.

Talleyrand is reputed to have said that the purport of language is to conceal thought. This witticism seems to be particularly applicable to the language of philosophy. The difficulty is always to get at the thought at the back of the language, and certainly it is not lessened by the fact that each philosophical school considers it necessary to have a language of its own.

However, if due allowance be made for the peculiarities of expression of different philosophical schools, there is a striking unanimity amongst them with regard, at all events, to the *nature* of evil. It is thus possible for those who are poles asunder in their general outlook on " Nature, red in tooth and claw " to approach the problem of evil from a common standpoint.

It is, I think, universally admitted—in fact, it seems to be *Evil a priva-*evident—that evil is not a thing in itself, but rather a condition of *tion* a thing. It is impossible to have a bad chest, for instance, without first having a chest ; a moment's reflection makes it obvious that the badness is merely a condition of the chest. Furthermore, this condition implies the absence, rather than the presence, of something ; in this case, the absence of a sound state of lungs. For evil is essentially a negation, and not a positive entity. Even Schopenhauer, who made of evil not only an active, but a dominant, principle, when he came to a metaphysical analysis of it, defined it as a negation, or rather a privation, in the will which fails to attain its object.

In the last analysis, then, evil will always be found to consist in the privation of good, in much the same way that a shadow on the ground consists in the privation of light. The shadow cast by a great tree appears to be real enough ; it seems to occupy space, and to move from one place to another. Yet, obviously, it has no real existence of its own ; it merely marks the spots from which the rays of the sun are excluded by the tree. The shadow is, in fact, simply the absence of light.

*Pain*

So, too, evil, no matter how positive it may appear at first sight, is in essence the privation of good. Confusion arises from the fact that, in many minds, evil is identified with pain, which is most assuredly not a mere negation, but something very positive indeed. Yet, paradoxical as it may sound, pain is not in itself evil ; it is merely the evidence of the existence of evil. It is Nature's warning signal that something is amiss.

Consider, for instance, the pain of a troublesome tooth. The pain arrests attention, and goads one to seek relief from the malady of which it is only the symptom. To that extent, pain is positively good, and, furthermore, many writers, ancient and modern, have pointed out the compensating values attaching to pain. Oftentimes it has been the discipline of great souls, and the school of character and personality. By the general psychological law of contrasts, it enhances the pleasure of physical and mental well-being. Its alleviation affords opportunities for the practice of heroic virtues ; in fact, pain has much to its credit.

But my present point is that pain, so far as it is positive, ought not to be confused with evil. Clearly, in toothache, the evil, of which the pain is the evidence, is not something positive at all, but the absence of something that ought to be present, namely, the ordinary healthy functioning of the tooth. Cancer, too, with its accompanying agonies, is rightly regarded not merely as a positive malady, but as something very aggressive, greedily eating away the human flesh on which it fastens. Yet the evil of cancer consists ultimately in the absence of the proper structure of the flesh affected. Or take the case, oft-quoted during the war, of a bleeding wound full of shrapnel. The evil in the wound is not the excruciating pain, nor the shrapnel, nor the lacerated flesh, nor the life-blood gushing forth, but simply the absence in the flesh of the normal relationship of tissue to tissue which Nature ordains.

Evil, then, (1) is never a thing in itself, but a condition of a thing ; and (2) it is never positive being as such, but a privation of being. Hence it has been defined by St Thomas Aquinas as " the deficiency of some good which ought to be present." [1]

## 2. Classification of Evil

Shakespeare makes that wiseacre Polonius, who is all for nice distinctions, remind us that the drama is divided into " tragedy, comedy, history, pastoral, pastoral-comical, historical-pastoral, tragical-historical, tragical-comical-historical-pastoral, scene undividable or poem unlimited." What Polonius has done for the drama, others, with a mania for meticulous classification, have

[1] *S. Theol.*, I-II, xlix, a. 1.

done for evil.   To follow them is to lose oneself in a maze of words, so I will confine myself to the broad distinction of evil into physical, moral, and retributive.

Since evil is essentially negation, it follows that every deficiency, *Metaphysical* every privation, every limitation is in a way evil.   It is in this sense *evil* that the Scripture says : " None is good but God alone." [1]   Only the infinite, which knows no limits, knows no evil.   Every finite being, precisely because it is finite, is to that extent evil.   This is known as metaphysical evil.   But were there no evil other than metaphysical evil, there would be no problem of evil to harass us. " Metaphysical evil," says Harper, " is only called such analogically ; and, in this manner, is predicated of the limitation of finite Being. But, as this limitation is not a privation, but a simple negation, and is only called evil by an analogy of proportion, it is wisely disregarded." [2]   The problem is concerned chiefly with those privations which result in consequences disagreeable to man.   Man rarely suffers in silence, and so we hear a great deal of the problem of evil, but very little of the corresponding problem of good.

This fact was not overlooked by Hobbes, who remarked in satirical vein : " Every man calleth that which pleaseth, and is delightful to himself, good ; and that *evil* which *displeaseth* him." [3]

The problem of evil, thus considered, arises from the fact *Physical and* that, when the forces of nature impinge upon man, consequences *moral evil* unpleasant to himself frequently follow.   King Canute, seated on his throne at the water's edge, commanding the flowing tide to ebb, succeeded only in getting his feet wet.   The boy who stood on the burning deck did not live to tell the tale ; whilst we all know the very sad fate that befell the young lady of Niger who went for a ride on a tiger.   Moreover, when the established moral order is disturbed we have what Aquinas describes as " the evil of wrongdoing."   Then the suffering which the disturbance entails has the nature of a penalty, and is therefore described as " the evil of punishment."   One of the earliest lessons we learn is that if we violate the order of Nature, some one, usually oneself, must suffer.

Just as there is a physical order governing the mutual interaction of the forces of Nature, so, too, there is a moral order, a normative system of conduct resulting from the harmonious balancing of such impinging regulative ideas as justice and mercy, truth and humility, or, in the Aristotelian ethic, of such extremes as cowardice and rashness, prodigality and meanness.

It is universally admitted that there is a moral order, though *Moral evil* there are wide differences as to its nature, ranging from the inde- *and punish-* pendent morality of Kant to the utilitarianism of Mill.   However, *ment*

---

[1] Luke xviii 19.
[2] *The Metaphysics of the School*, by Thomas Harper, S.J., vol. i, p. 541.
[3] *Human Nature*, chap. vii.

in any system of ethics, an infringement of the accepted order is regarded as moral evil, the evil of wrong-doing, and it carries with it, in some way, the evil of punishment.

Now the Church has condemned the distinction between philosophical and theological sin, between an offence against one's rational nature and against God, as erroneous, rash, scandalous, and offensive to pious ears.[1] The teaching of Catholic theologians is that a morally bad act which violates the order of natural reason necessarily violates also the divine law. For, says Billot, "the dictate of conscience, essentially and from the very nature of the case, involves knowledge of the divine law as the source of moral obligation, and consequently it is metaphysically repugnant that a man who does not know God, or who does not advert to his law, at least in a general way, should have any consciousness of a morally bad act."[2] Actually and in practice there is no such thing as a purely philosophical sin which is not also theologically a sin. Where there is consciousness of a morally bad act there is consciousness of the transgression of the law of God. "The strength of sin is the law," says St Paul.[3]

The point is of great importance in considering the workings of divine providence, for it means that moral evil is always something which runs counter to the will of God. Consequently, that God should permit moral evil at all seems incongruous, and constitutes a special difficulty which we shall consider presently. Again, if moral evil is always an offence against God, and not merely against oneself, we begin to see the reasonableness of retributive, and not merely corrective, punishment for sin. By moral evil, then, we mean sin, which is defined by Billot, following St Thomas, as "a human act deprived of its due rectitude,"[4] its due rectitude comprising conformity with right reason and with the law of God.

We may classify evil, then, as physical, moral, and retributive. So far, in considering the nature of evil and its classification, we encounter no great difficulty; but as soon as we enquire into the *origin* of evil, and seek to find the cause, or it may be the culprit, responsible for it, we are wellnigh deafened by the din of contending parties.

### 3. The Origin of Evil

*Dualism*    1. Dualism is the earliest method of accounting for the existence of evil. In this system all things are classified as good or evil, and then traced along distinct lines to separate ultimate sources. Thus in Zoroastrianism, which flourished in the sixth century B.C., all good proceeds from Ormuzd, the infinite light and supreme wisdom, whilst all evil comes from Ahriman, the principle of darkness. We find the same dualistic conception in Manicheism,

[1] Denzinger, 1290.    [2] De Peccato, p. 27.
[3] I Cor. xv 56.    [4] De Peccato, p. 19.

in which the Father of Grandeur was held to preside over the realm of light, and the Father of Darkness over the realm of gloom. Each was supreme in his own domain.

In this way the problem of evil was dramatised, but not really faced. However, dualism escaped the necessity of attributing evil in any way to the god of light and goodness, and its convenient shelving of the problem of evil is held to have been one of the causes of the rapid spread of Manicheism in the third century of the Christian era. The advance of exact philosophical thought dealt a deathblow to all such fantastic theories of the origin of the world. Cultivated reason recognised the absurdity of the crude conception of two infinites. From the mere fact that each must have something that the other has not got, in order to differentiate them, it was recognised that one must be limited, and therefore itself to be accounted for. Hence the dualistic theory as to the origin of the universe, since it did not account for the origin, was abandoned.

2. But the abandonment of dualism does not necessarily imply *Pre-exist-* the acceptance of a monistic origin of the universe. Between *ence of souls* the two there is a pluralism which postulates a number of distinct and independent sources of being, variously described as souls, selves, or monads. No one of these is infinite. Each is struggling for fuller realisation and greater perfection throughout many successive existences. Consequently, pluralism is enabled to fall back on the theory of the pre-existence of souls when confronted with the problem of evil. The champions of pluralism never tire of telling us that they are free from the necessity of attributing evil, in any way whatsoever, to God. It is not he who originates evil propensities in the human soul, they say; these propensities are merely the result of misdemeanours in previous existences. The soul that suffers from physical or moral evil in this life is being purged of the delinquencies committed in an unremembered, but lurid, previous life.

So far, so good. But, for one difficulty which the theory of pre-existence removes, it creates a dozen others. Are we to suppose that, at the end of each terrestrial existence, the human soul is detained in a sort of vacuum till it can be born into a suitable body, as a member of just the right family, in all the appropriate circumstances for its future development, and for its adequate punishment on account of previous misdemeanours? And what is the use or meaning of it all, when the soul, in each successive existence, is blissfully unconscious of its pre-natal good or bad deeds? The best that can be said for metempsychosis, or the transmigration of the soul from one body to another, is that, like many another fantasy, it is incapable of philosophical disproof; surely no great merit in the entire absence of any positive evidence for such an elaborate attempt to render an all-ruling providence unnecessary.

On philosophical grounds alone most consistent thinkers have been driven into some form of monism, in the sense of a system which seeks for the origin of the universe and all that it contains, in a single principle. And at once the difficulty presents itself, that to that single principle, in some way, all evil must be traceable. This embarrassment is deftly evaded by those monists who regard the ultimate principle as impersonal being; but it will be found on examination that the non-theistic solutions to the problem of evil offered by materialists, idealists, and agnostics alike, are in reality merely restatements of the problem in esoteric terms. It is the old device of solving one difficulty by making another. Impersonal being, which is absolute, or unrelated, or unconditioned, or unknown, explains nothing, for the simple reason that it, above all else, stands in urgent need of explanation itself. To assign impersonal being as the cause of personal being is about as satisfactory as expecting water to rise above its own level.

#### 4. Attempts to Dispense with Providence

(a) Pessimism

As typical of modern methods of handling the problem of evil whilst dispensing with God and his providence, and at the same time as affording an excellent approach to our own theistic standpoint, we may consider briefly the rival practical solutions of modern pessimism and optimism.

Pessimism in its origin is neither Western nor modern. It was cradled in the East, long even before the days of Buddha, who first raised it to the dignity of a doctrine. " The thirst for being," says Buddha, " is the origin of suffering," and, moreover, there is no way of escape, but by ceasing to exist otherwise than in the impersonal state of Nirvana. Some three hundred years before Christ, the Greek philosopher Hegesias enunciated a proposition which has since become the fulcrum of elaborated systems of pessimism, the proposition that the sum-total of the pains of life outweighs its pleasures. Nor did he shrink from the practical consequences of his philosophy; he openly advocated suicide as the only gateway of escape from the evils of life, till Ptolemy ordered his school to be closed in the interest of public morals.

What subtle connection there may be between poets and pessimism we leave to others to determine, but we have it on the authority of a poet that " our sweetest songs are those that tell of saddest thought "; and, certainly, Heine, Leopardi, Byron, to say nothing of lesser bards, gave a message of persistent pessimism to modern Europe.

*Schopenhauer* But pessimism, as a metaphysical system, is the product of the modern German mind. It owes its origin to Schopenhauer [1] and its development to von Hartmann and Mailaender. During the

---

[1] A.D. 1770-1838.

first half of the nineteenth century Schopenhauer worked up and systematised the material which he had collected from Hindu religions and contemporary poets, and presented the world with the first attempt at a rational philosophy of pessimism.

Man he regarded as the outcome of a cruel cosmic process. Man alone is capable of fully appreciating the evils and miseries of life. More than that, man himself necessarily adds to them. The will-to-live, the primal instinct of life, is the eternal driving force at the back of all human activity. Because man wills to live under better conditions than his fellows, he becomes sober, chaste, honest; he finds it his best policy to be so. Hence all the natural virtues are directly traceable to this primal will-to-live.

But this same will-to-live is responsible also for the evils of life. It is precisely man's will-to-live, to live under the most advantageous conditions possible, that produces deceitfulness, dishonesty, hypocrisy, murder; in fact, the whole category of the vices. Good and evil alike are traceable to this will-to-live. But in Schopenhauer's contention the evil of life far outweighs the good, its pains outweigh its pleasures. The balance is all on the side of pain, of evil. It is the worst of all possible worlds.

Happiness is impossible until the cause of the evil, the will-to-live, is willed out of existence. The logical deduction from Schopenhauer's premises would be to abolish the will-to-live by the voluntary surrender of individual existence. Such, however, is not the conclusion of Schopenhauer. He rejects suicide, not as being in any way criminal, but merely as not solving the problem. " He who commits suicide," said Schopenhauer, " destroys the individual only, and not the species." The species is kept in existence by generation. It is generation that must cease. Men and women must cease to propagate their kind. Let the whole human race die out: therein lies the solution of pessimism, in the gospel of blind renunciation and abject despair. There will be an end of evil only when, as Swinburne has it, " this old earth will be a slag and a cinder, revolving round the sun without its crew of fools."

### (b) Optimism

In opposition to pessimism we have optimism. I do not mean the fallacious metaphysical optimism of Leibniz, who pronounced this to be the best of all possible worlds, on the abstract principle that there is a sufficient reason for saying so, in that the work of an infinitely perfect Creator must be perfect, not merely for its purposes, but, apparently, in its possibilities. Still less am I alluding to the roseate optimism of Hammerling and Pangloss, who seem to have enjoyed habitually the kind of generous outlook on life which most people experience only after a good dinner. Such views made Schopenhauer forget his manners and say : " I cannot here avoid the statement that to me *optimism*, when it is not merely the thoughtless talk of such as harbour nothing but words under their low foreheads, appears not merely as an absurd, but also as a really wicked way of thinking, as a bitter mockery of the unspeakable suffering of humanity." [1]

*Nietzsche*  I am speaking now of that philosophical system which, in direct opposition to the pessimism of Schopenhauer, hopes ultimately to stamp out altogether the evil which afflicts man : the optimism of Friedrich Nietzsche. [2]  He tells us that from his earliest years the problem of evil haunted him, until one day he came across a copy of Schopenhauer's work, *The World as Will and Idea*. It enthralled him.  Here at last was someone actually giving expression to the doubts and difficulties which had long surged in his own youthful mind.  Here was someone who had an answer to offer. Nietzsche caught the infection of Schopenhauer's enthusiasm only to realise in calmer moments that he was not satisfied with the latter's anæmic answer, and he himself determined " to blaze a new path."

It is not so much life, as power, that man craves, contended Nietzsche.  Life without the power to dominate others in some way would be a feeble thing, and therefore the real primal instinct of man is the will-to-power.

He agreed with Schopenhauer that life at best is but a melancholy adventure, but he would have none of Schopenhauer's renunciation.  He set out to become the prophet of defiance.

He impeaches Christianity with being a " slave morality," with preaching an ethic fit only for slaves, an ethic which extols mean qualities, such as obedience, humility, and chastity.  Away with it all, says Nietzsche ; let us have a " master morality," a morality fit for the lords of creation, who will do exactly as they please, guided only by the prudent caution of selfishness.  " The weak must go to the wall," says Nietzsche, " and we must help them to go."  Only the strong shall survive.  In the course of this process, continued through centuries, there will evolve the " superman " who will ruthlessly trample out of existence any evil that may threaten his own happiness.

Such is the solution to the problem of evil offered by optimism. It is, if possible, a worse solution than that of pessimism.  For where it touches the problem at all, it is only to widen it, by giving us more evils to account for, as witness the results of the Great War, which was assuredly brought about by the principles of " master morality."

[1] *The World as Will and Idea*, vol. i, p. 420.
[2] A.D. 1844-1900.

## § V: THEISM AND THE PROBLEM OF EVIL

### 1. *The Fall and its Consequences*

BETWEEN these pagan extremes of pessimism and optimism which are reflected in the practical lives of so many men of the world to-day, there is the time-honoured answer of theism, at its best and fullest as expounded in Catholic theology ; an answer which at least has made life liveable for countless thousands.

Both Schopenhauer and Nietzsche were of the earth earthy ; *Evil seen from* they never raised their eyes above the earth, never could. " Cease *God's stand-* to look beyond the stars for your hopes and rewards," says Nietzsche. *point* With their eyes fixed upon the earth, they sought to solve an eternal problem. Hence the dismal failure of both pessimist and optimist. The solution is not on the earth. It is precisely " beyond the stars " that man must look if he is even to understand the problem. From this earth we have not the point of view necessary to see evil as it really is in itself. We see it in so far as it affects us at the present moment. From a different point of view we would see it in a totally different light.

A beetle standing on a mole-hill regards every tiny speck of earth as a mountain, a huge obstacle to be surmounted. But a man standing alongside, with an enlarged vision of the whole country, sees the speck of earth in its true perspective. The beetle is too close to that speck of earth, too much harassed by it, to see it as it really is in itself. So, too, is it with us. We are like beetles on a mole-hill, too much taken up with the obstacle in our path to see it otherwise than as an obstacle.

A child regards many things as evil which in later life he recognises as having been good. From the point of view of the child it is evil that he must go to school, must obey his parents ; but from the point of view of the grown man it is good that he was made to go to school, made to obey. He is so convinced of it that he insists on his own children going through the same discipline.

From our point of view, evils, very real evils, surround us on every side. But there is another point of view : there is the point of view of the Creator who called all things into being and who watches over them. How the evils appear from that point of view we know not at present. And yet that is the only point of view that really matters ; the only point of view from which evil can be seen in its true character and in all its bearings. " For who among men is he that can know the counsel of God ? or who can think what the will of God is ? " [1]

But even with our present limited vision we can discern the wisdom of the workings of divine providence, and see at all events that man is largely the architect of his own misfortunes. A slight

[1] Wisd. ix 13.

taste of philosophy, says Bacon, may dispose the mind to be indifferent to the things of religion, but deeper draughts must bring
it back to God ; and, we may add, to the realisation that " he hath
made all things good in their time, and hath delivered the world
to their (men's) consideration, so that man cannot find out the
work which God hath made from the beginning to the end." [1]

*God does not
directly cause
evil*     In the first place, from the metaphysical standpoint, it is obvious
that God cannot be the direct cause of evil. We have seen that evil
is not a thing in itself, that it is not positive being, but something
privative. It cannot, therefore, be the object, or the term, of a
positive creative act. The result of such an act must necessarily
be positive being as such. Just as the sun in the heavens gives light,
whilst the shadow on the ground, the absence of light, is caused
by the intervention of some obstacle, such as a tree, blocking out
the rays of light ; so the infinitely good God is the direct cause of
things which are good, though these are able incidentally to do
harm to others. And hence the contention of the second-century
heretics, the Florinians, and the kindred view of some of the
Novatians, that God created things in themselves evil and was the
author of sin, came to be abandoned on purely philosophical grounds.

Again, it is clear that God does not directly intend evil as such.
In fact, no rational being can desire evil if it be apprehended merely
as evil. Whatever evil a man may desire, he does not desire it
except under some aspect of good. The drunkard is seeking to
drown his sorrows, to while away time, or to produce a feeling of
exhilaration ; the libertine is seeking pleasure ; the murderer is
seeking in some way to make smooth his own path in life. All men
are seeking happiness, though oftentimes they are much mistaken
as to what is happiness. Now God, the infinite intelligence, cannot
mistakenly apprehend evil as good ; he must needs apprehend it
as it is, as evil ; and therefore he cannot positively or directly will
it or intend it ; that is, will it or intend it under its formal aspect
of evil.

Nevertheless he can intend and cause physical evil as part of
the order of his providence, not precisely as evil, but as implied
in the more general good, or the good of the whole order, or the
good of man. Death, we are told, entered into the world by sin,
and the death of man is intended by God, not as an affliction, but
as a punishment for sin. " For God made not death, neither hath
he pleasure in the destruction of the living," says the author of the
Book of Wisdom. [2] Again, in the book of Ecclesiasticus, we read :
" Fire, hail, famine, and death, all these were created for
vengeance " ; [3] that is to say, they are intended by God as punishments for sin, and only under that aspect does he desire them.

*Man's
original
perfection*     God made not death. For, says St Paul, " by one man sin
entered into this world, and by sin death ; and so death passed upon

<hr>

[1] Eccles. iii 11.          [2] i 13.          [3] xxxix 35.

all men, in whom all have sinned." [1] The Christian revelation teaches that Adam was created, not in a state of pure nature, but in what is called the state of original justice ; that is to say, from the beginning his soul was endowed gratuitously by God with habitual or sanctifying grace, which raised him to a plane altogether beyond the human. Man by nature tends to God as his last end, as the creature tends to the Creator ; but sanctifying grace made him a partaker of the divine nature, and gave to him a supernatural end, namely, to see God as he is, face to face, and ultimately to be united to him as to an all-loving Father. Furthermore, man was enriched with certain preternatural gifts, that is, with gifts which did not altogether transcend his nature, but nevertheless were not essential to it. Thus, he was free from the dread of suffering and death, captain of his own soul, with his intellect unclouded and his will untrammelled by the motions of concupiscence.

Adam fell from that high estate, and fell as head of the race. *The Fall* Human nature in its entirety was represented in him, and in his fall we all fell. In consequence human souls, at their coming into being, are deprived of the sanctifying grace which they would have had if Adam had not sinned. With this deprivation of grace, technically known as original sin, went concurrently the loss of the soul's supernatural qualities, capacities, and rights. By his fall Adam and his descendants forfeited also the preternatural gifts of impassibility, felicity, and immortality of body, whereby he had been exempt from physical suffering, mental worry, and the dissolution of soul and body. Hence, says St Paul, " by one man sin entered into this world, and by sin death."

Our Lord and Saviour Jesus Christ has redeemed us from the *Redemption* bondage of sin, and restored us to the supernatural order, but there remain with us certain effects and evidences of the fall. The preternatural gifts of Adam have not been restored to us, and man is, as it were, wounded both in the clarity of his intellect and the strength of his will. Consequently, much of the physical suffering endured by man is traceable to the representative sin of Adam, and some of it to the actual sins of ourselves and others. Sin is the root of human suffering.

But though Christ has not merited for us a restoration of the preternatural gifts of Adam, he has made it possible for us to make ignorance, concupiscence, and the physical pains and penalties of sin the occasions of supernatural satisfaction and merit. On this point St Ephraem says : " Man inflicts chastisement in order that he himself may derive some utility therefrom. He inflicts punishment on his servants in order that he may be master of them ; but the good God chastises his servants in order that they may be masters of themselves." [2] Furthermore, the disabilities of human

---

[1] Rom. v 12.          [2] *Carmina Nisib.*, Ed. Bickell, 1866, p. 70.

nature which issue in death are at least salutary reminders that "we have not here a lasting city, but we seek one that is to come." [1]

Clearly, then, the ills that human flesh is heir to may become instruments of divine providence in making us "conformable to the image of his Son," [2] so that, having suffered with him, we may be also glorified with him. [3]

## 2. *Providence and Sin*

**God not the cause of sin**    With regard to moral evil, in its theological aspect sin, the Council of Trent has solemnly pronounced : "If anyone says . . . that God works evil as he works good, not merely permissively, but properly and for its own sake, so that the betrayal of Judas is the proper work of God just as much as the calling of Paul, let him be anathema." [4] There is abundant scriptural testimony on this point. Thus says the Psalmist, "Thou hatest all the workers of iniquity" ; [5] and the prophet Habacuc declares, "Thy eyes are too pure to behold evil, and thou canst not look on iniquity " ; [6] whilst in the New Testament we read, "Let no man, when he is tempted, say that he is tempted by God. For God is not a tempter of evils, and he tempteth no man." [7] In fact, as we have seen, a special difficulty arises with regard to the divine permission of moral evil, in that it can be perpetrated only by a rational being rising in revolt against the will of God ; so that moral evil would appear to be, in its very essence, a thwarting of the divine will which is said to govern the universe.

**He permits it**    Yet that God permits sin follows from the fact of his all-ruling providence. Nothing can happen apart from the will of God, that is, apart from either his positive sanction in the case of morally good actions, or his permissive tolerance in the case of morally bad ones. God permits moral evil in the sense that he does not impede it, though he prohibits it by his law. We can see several reasons for this negative permission.

In the first place, God is self-sufficient and altogether independent of the work of his hands. But, so far from being independent of creatures, he would be limited in his operations by the malice of human beings if he were constrained to prevent moral iniquity ; or, as some modern philosophers have not hesitated to say, he would be more or less perfect in proportion as he did prevent it. He would be a kind of limited progressive deity instead of the "Lord God almighty, who was, and who is, and who is to come." [8]

In the second place, it is the function of providence to preserve, and not to destroy, the nature of the thing that is governed. In the present actual order, whatever may be said of possible orders,

---

[1] Heb. xiii 14.      [2] Rom. viii 29.      [3] Rom. viii 17.
[4] Sess. vi, c. 6.      [5] Ps. v 7.      [6] i 13.
[7] Jas. i 13.      [8] Apoc. iv 8.

liberty of choice, even between good and evil, is of the nature of the freedom of the rational creature, and because of this very freedom it must needs be that scandals come.

Thirdly, from the beneficent comparison of good with evil, the morally good is rendered more desirable, just as the brightness of the stars is the more appreciated on account of the darkness of the night. In much the same way, the iniquity of man forms a background for the better manifestation of some of the divine attributes. Who does not see in the divine tolerance of sin the evidence of the boundless mercy and forbearance of God, " patient because he is eternal " ?

Finally, it does not pertain to divine providence to bring about the total exclusion of evil from the universe, but to order to some good end whatever evils may betide. In fact, St Augustine lays it down as a principle that God would not permit evil were it not for the consequent good. He says : " For the almighty God, who, as even the heathen acknowledge, has supreme power over all things, being himself supremely good, would never permit the existence of anything evil among his works, if he were not so omnipotent and good that he can bring good even out of evil." [1] The good which may appear to us to be only incidental to the permission of moral evil is in reality a constituent, and a very necessary constituent, of the order of divine providence. God permits moral evil in one case, in order that greater moral good may obtain in another. Thus, St Thomas points out, the wickedness of Nero led to the gaining of many martyrs' crowns.

Now it is obvious that he who perpetrates moral iniquity places himself on the level of the lower order of things which subserve to man's higher good. The sinner by the irrationality of his actions degrades himself to the plane of irrational beings, so that his evil actions become merely the means of bringing about greater good to other men. In this respect the sinner insists, as it were, on ranging himself, not with men, but with the brutes. But assuredly in some way goodness is begotten of his wickedness. It is precisely in the fact that out of moral evil comes greater good that we are to look for the basic reason of the divine tolerance of sin.

§ VI: SPECIAL DIFFICULTIES AGAINST DIVINE
PROVIDENCE

### 1. The Prosperity of the wicked

THAT God should allow the wicked to prosper and the just to be afflicted with calamities is considered by many men to be a special grievance against divine providence. And yet this difficulty was faced and answered in pagan times. Seneca begins his treatise

[1] *Enchiridion*, c. xi.

*De Providentia* with the old perplexing question : Why, if there be a providence, are good men buffeted by misfortune, whilst the baser sort go free ? And the Stoic philosopher answers in a vein which has won for him the title of the Bossuet of Imperial Rome. After pointing out the difference between maternal indulgence and paternal discipline towards children, he goes on to say that God in his great love for good men exercises towards them a measure of paternal discipline in permitting them to be assailed by adversity. In the school of adversity they are trained to spiritual hardihood. Do you marvel, he asks, that God, who so loves these men, and wishes them to attain to the best and the highest, should permit them to be so severely tried by ill-fortune ? For my part, I do not marvel, says this pagan writer, for the spectacle of noble men successfully combating evil is one worthy of the regard of the deity.[1]

It is too hastily assumed that the just receive more than their fair share of the slings and arrows of outrageous fortune. That pessimistic contention is by no means supported by facts. Famine, pestilence, and war are no respecters of persons, and are as likely to mow down the impious as the just. The available evidence tends to show that both good and evil fortune are distributed indiscriminately to the godly and the ungodly. As the Scripture has it, your Father who is in heaven " maketh his sun to rise upon the good and bad, and raineth upon the just and the unjust." [2] What happens is that our attention is more easily arrested by the sufferings of the just, since instinctively we feel that the unjust are meeting only with their deserts. But, as Seneca insists, all suffering is not in the nature of punishment ; it has its disciplinary and formative value.

Again, our calculus of pleasure and pain is a very defective one. It estimates only the things that appeal to the senses, and registers nothing of the just man's peace of soul amidst all his afflictions. This point, too, was grasped by the ancients. In answer to the question, Why do many adversities befall good men ? Seneca answers : No real evil can take up its abode with a good man, for contraries do not mix. Just as no raging torrents, nor storms of hail, nor the rush of many waters into the sea, can take away or appreciably lessen its salt savour, so the flood-tide of adversity cannot perturb the soul of the just man. Immovable he stands, making all things subservient to himself, stronger within than all else without.[3]

If this could be said of the honest pagan, what shall we say of the Christian who has in his soul the grace of our Lord and Saviour Jesus Christ ? His is the peace that passeth all understanding. He may be called upon to spend his life in poverty and, worse still, to see his loved ones bereft of the good things of this world ; but, after all, it was not the great God of eternal truth who, pointing to all the glories and splendours of the world, said, " All these will

---

[1] *De Providentia*, c. 2.     [2] *Matt.* v 45.     [3] *Op. cit.*

I give thee, if thou dost fall down and adore "; that was said by the devil, the father of lies. Or, it may be that we mourn the loss of one cut off in the flower of his age, by what is called an untimely death; listen to the inspired words of the wisest of men: " The just man, if he be prevented with death, shall be in rest. . . . He pleased God and was beloved, and living among sinners he was translated. He was taken away lest wickedness should alter his understanding, or deceit beguile his soul. For the bewitching of vanity obscureth good things, and the wandering of concupiscence overturneth the innocent mind. Being made perfect in a short space, he fulfilled a long time: for his soul pleased God. Therefore he hastened to bring him out of the midst of iniquities: but the people see this, and understand not, nor lay up such things in their hearts: that the grace of God and his mercy is with his saints, and that he hath respect to his chosen." [1]

It was Rousseau who said that if he had no other argument for personal immortality than the prosperity of the wicked and the adversity of the just in this life, it would be more than sufficient to convince him. Instinctively we feel that there is a life beyond the grave where the balance is adjusted. David confesses that he was sorely puzzled by the prosperity of the wicked till the Lord revealed to him their end. " I studied that I might know this thing, it is a labour in my sight," says the Psalmist, " until I go into the sanctuary of God, and understand concerning their last ends. But indeed for deceits thou hast put it to them: when they were lifted up thou hast cast them down. How are they brought to desolation? They have suddenly ceased to be: they have perished by reason of their iniquity." [2] Truly their prosperity is purchased at a great price. At best it is short-lived, for the day of reckoning fast approaches. We may take leave of this perplexing problem with the profound reflection set forth in the book of Ecclesiastes: " I saw under the sun in the place of judgement wickedness, and in the place of justice iniquity. And I said in my heart: God shall judge both the just and the wicked, and then shall be the time of everything." [3]

## 2. God's Tolerance of Evil

But, it is contended, God does more than merely permit the evil to exist; being omniscient, he must necessarily foresee the evil, and to foresee an evil which you can prevent and yet remain passive is in reality the same as positively to will it. We answer that the result may be the same, but that there is a world of difference between positively intending to do evil and merely allowing a natural chain of causes to produce its proper effect, even though that effect may be evil, not merely in the physical, but in the moral sense.

[1] Wisd. iv 7-15.     [2] Ps. lxxii 16-19.     [3] iii 16, 17.

Suppose, for instance, that an employer decides to give a bonus of ten shillings to each of his employees; and suppose further that he knows, not indeed with infallible certainty, but with a very high degree of probability, that one of his employees, X, will misspend the money in drink. Nevertheless, he gives the bonus to X, because X is one of his employees. X, having inherited a severe thirst and developed it by practice, does spend the money in drink, and through failure to report for work next morning is summarily dismissed. Whose fault is it that X is dismissed? Is it the employer's because he gave X a good gift which might have been put to an excellent purpose? Surely the culpability rests entirely with X, who abused the gift.

Similarly, God gives to each of us a good gift, the priceless gift of freedom. He knows, even with infallible certainty, whether I will choose good or evil. That infallible foreknowledge no more interferes with my real freedom than the conjectural knowledge of the employer interfered with the free action of the employee. If I am really free, as my consciousness testifies, I must in honesty place the culpability for an evil choice where it really lies : with myself. Having established a definite order in the universe, it is God's intention that that order shall take its course. It would be utterly unreasonable to expect special interventions of divine providence to avert natural consequences in the physical or moral order because they are unpleasant to man.

*Predestination*

At this point difficulties arise on the score that God positively predestines some men to glory, and permissively reprobates others. We have already formulated the general principles underlying the permissive action of God in allowing such evil as the damnation of the wicked. The reconciliation of the efficaciousness of divine grace, on the one hand, and the freedom of man, on the other, is a question which does not immediately concern us here.

St Thomas Aquinas keeps the question of predestination distinct from that of providence, pointing out that these questions differ in two important respects. In the first place, providence is concerned with the universal ordering of all things, whether rational or irrational, good or evil, to an end ; whereas predestination is concerned only with that end which is the principal one of the rational creature, namely, the attainment of eternal glory. The term predestination, then, applies only to men's salvation. In the second place, since not everything that is ordered to an end attains that end, there is a manifest distinction between the ordering and the attainment. Providence is concerned only with the ordering, and consequently by divine providence all men are as a matter of fact ordained to happiness ; but predestination is concerned with the outcome, or the issue, of the ordering, and therefore is restricted to those who actually do attain to heaven. Predestination fulfils the same function with regard to the attainment of the end that providence does with regard to the imposition of that end, for the fact that some men do attain to the Beatific Vision is not principally through their own powers, but by the aid of grace divinely bestowed.[1]

In the view of St Thomas, then, the problems of predestination pertain to a different order from that of divine providence. Such problems must be considered apart in the light of the workings of divine grace, and consequently lie outside the scope of this short essay. For a concise exposition of Catholic teaching on the subject of predestination we refer the reader to Essay XVII of this same work.[2]

Apart altogether from all questions as to the operation of divine grace, the further objection is raised that if God foresaw, even though he did not positively forewill, the damnation of the wicked, nevertheless, as an infinitely good God, he ought to have abstained from creating such souls. A little reflection, however, makes it clear that if God could be influenced in that way by a condition outside himself, the condition would be greater than he ; he would be limited, constrained from without, and therefore not infinite, and not God. It would be as though the damned soul, whilst still only a mere possibility, could defy the Omnipotent to create it.

As we have seen, God must of necessity do his own will. This *The free* necessity is part of his very perfection, just as it is part of his per- *homage of the* fection that he cannot sin. He might, of course, have created a *creature* world of intelligent beings in which there would have been no sorrow, sin, or suffering. Why he selected this world rather than innumerable other worlds without, at least, moral evil, we do not know, nor can we know till we attain to the Beatific Vision. And yet we have some inkling of God's providential purpose in his choice of this world. A world without sin would be a world without our present freedom, and a world without this freedom would be a world without love or, at all events, without the freely given love of the creature. When a doctor of the law asked, " Master, which is the great commandment in the law ? " Jesus said to him, " Thou shalt love the Lord thy God with thy whole heart, and with thy whole soul, and with thy whole mind. This is the greatest and the first commandment." [3] For the free rational creature is capable of giving to God a homage which transcends that of every other conceivable work of his hands. And it is precisely this freedom, this perilous gift, which may be so easily abused, which imparts to man's actions their supreme glory or their supreme shame. It is the noblest natural gift of God to man, so prized that Dryden has said of it :

> " And life itself th' inferior gift of heaven."

It is the love of the free creature, engaging every faculty of the rational soul, that the God of love desires. Love seeks to be

---

[1] See *De Veritate*, q. vi, a. 1 in corp.
[2] *Actual Grace*, pp. 610-612, 619-620.     [3] Matt. xxii 37.

requited, and it is written, "God so loved the world as to give his only begotten Son. . . ."

### 3. Eternal Punishment

But, it is urged, the infinite love of an all-provident God is not compatible with the doctrine of eternal punishment. As this difficulty is dealt with fully elsewhere in this work,[1] it will be sufficient here to indicate the main points in our reply.

1. The sin that consigns to hell is the deliberate uprising of the creature against the Creator, an act of malice perpetrated with full deliberation and free consent. God could no more pardon an unrepentant sinner than an earthly king could pardon an unrepentant traitor.

2. The eternity of hell is, as it were, a corollary to the doctrine of the immortality of the human soul. The soul of man, of its own nature, is immortal : that is to say, it does not in its essence involve any principle of corruption ; it cannot lose its individuality, as material things do, by the dissolution of its own parts, or of the parts of any composite substance on which it depends for existence. Thus, a wall ceases to be a wall when its bricks are scattered, and the colours of a soap bubble vanish when the bubble bursts. Not so the human soul. Of its own nature it tends to continue in being, in full conscious individuality, and we know from revelation that it is not God's intention ever to annihilate it.

If, then, a human soul leaves the body in a state of separation from God, it continues eternally in that state, because of its own natural immortality. It is not as though God specially endowed the soul with immortality in order to punish it for ever ; that conceivably might be regarded as the action of a fiend. But such is far from being the case. Man here and now is abundantly conscious of his personal immortality, and of the eternal destiny of happiness or misery that lies before him at his choice.

### Conclusion

Life and death are full of mysteries. "All things are hard : man cannot explain them," says Ecclesiastes.[2] But the fact that man cannot explain them does not mean that there is no explanation. It is an axiom of scientific method that unexplained facts are not to be taken as running counter to established principles. It would be execrably unscientific to suggest that, because certain unexplained facts seem to militate against an established principle, the principle should be called in question, or perhaps even abandoned. Obviously, an explanation must be sought which is in harmony with the known law. So, too, however perplexed we may be at the complicated evils of life, neither our perplexity, nor the evils themselves,

[1] See pp. 1200 ff.  [2] i 8.

constitute an argument against the already established providence of God.

Suppose, for instance, that a prisoner is on trial for his life. Day after day you read the evidence against him; day after day it gets blacker, till you can have no reasonable doubt but that he is guilty of the crime. However, we will suppose further that, on the last day of the trial, he successfully proves an alibi. He was not there when the murder was committed, and so he cannot possibly be guilty of the crime. Nevertheless, all the circumstantial evidence is dead against him, and not the ablest lawyer in all the land can unravel its tangled skein. Fortunately for the prisoner it is not necessary to do so, since his innocence is established beyond rebuttal.

So it is with the evils which seem to cry out against the providence of God. We know, can prove, that there is an infinitely good God, who neither slumbereth nor sleepeth while he keepeth Israel.[1] The fact that we cannot smooth out all the evils of life to fit in to our satisfaction, and harmonise perfectly with the providence of God, is no argument against that providence, any more than our inability to explain away the evidence against the prisoner proves him guilty of the crime. It is a convincing proof that man's intelligence is very limited, and beyond that it proves nothing. "Only this I have found," says Solomon, "that God made man right, and he hath entangled himself with an infinity of questions. Who is as the wise man? and who hath known the resolution of the word?"[2]

Though the problem of evil remain, to man on this earth, for ever inscrutable, the providence of God shines forth like the gleam of the gold or the flash of the diamond, even from out the wastage and the wreckage wrought by man. Notwithstanding the evils which do abound on every side, and which do afflict us, every healthy-minded man and woman is forced to see that the mighty universe simply teems with the evidences of the infinitely good God who has called it into being, not for our satisfaction, but for his own greater honour and glory.

RICHARD DOWNEY.

[1] Ps. cxx 4.    [2] Eccles. vii 30.

# VIII

## THE ANGELS

### § I: TRADITIONAL ANGELIC NATURE

THERE is in every treatment of Catholic thought, unless it be a rigidly technical treatise, that happy mixture of the certain, the extremely probable, and the moderately probable which constitutes a real philosophy, where conservatism and liberalism are congenially blended. Thus in the pages which follow all the things written down are not matters of faith, nor would it be possible in a short essay of this kind to affix a proper theological note to every proposition, distinguishing what is strictly of faith from the conclusions and happy inspirations of minds fond of the things of God ; but much edification and instruction can be derived from the sayings of theologians and preachers which are not *de fide*, but rather the legitimate speculations of minds habitually attuned to revealed truth.

*Angelology in Scripture*    Our first authority on the history of the angels, their lives and their natures, is found in Holy Scripture. There is a great oneness in the presentment of angelic character in the various books of the Bible, from Genesis to Apocalypse ; the angelic type never alters, we may even venture to say that it never develops as the divine revelation in other matters goes on and gains momentum from century to century ; what the angels do at Bethel they do also in the days of Christ, they " ascend and descend upon the Son of man." [1] Cherubim with " a flaming sword, turning every way, to keep the way of the tree of life " [2] are visions as formidable as any angelophany in Ezechiel or the Apocalypse. There is not, therefore, in our angelology that progressive revelation of a mystery which is the characteristic of our Christology ; the mystery of the God-man is revealed gradually to the minds of men ; not so that of the angels ; they are made completely manifest from the very beginning, and though, in the course of the centuries of the faith, angels show forth now one kind of activity now another, their essential behaviour is always the same. The fact is that our Scriptures never teach us anything about the spirits of the invisible world *ex professo*, they never narrate anything about them as a revelation of their mysterious existence ; the inspired writers take them for granted and mention them only in connection with human history, the history of the people of God, and the history of Christ. Nothing is more casual and unexpected than the mention of angels in every portion of the Scriptures ; you never know when to expect an angel ; there is no set of events of which you could predict with certainty that they

[1] John i 51.    [2] Gen. iii 24.

would bring an angel from heaven to earth. The same thing which at one moment is done through angelic ministry, at another time is left in its natural setting. Our Scriptures, then, may be said to accept the angelic world as a complete, self-sufficient, unaccountable power, which cannot itself be altered by the course of human events, but which may influence them whenever it pleases. Nor do the Scriptures distinguish clearly at all times between angelic intervention and divine intervention ; the heavenly visitant who is called " angel " passes at once into a rôle which is obviously divine. This is very remarkable in the oldest angelophany in the Bible—the angel whom we might call the angel of the family of Abraham ; the heavenly messenger who spoke to Agar, the slave-wife of Abraham, is at the same time angel and Lord of life :

" And the angel of the Lord having found her (Agar), by a fountain of water in the wilderness, which is in the way to Sur in the desert, he said to her : Agar, handmaid of Sarai, whence comest thou ? And whither goest thou ? And she answered : I flee from the face of Sarai, my mistress. And the angel of the Lord said to her : Return to thy mistress, and humble thyself under her hand. And again he said : I will multiply thy seed exceedingly, and it shall not be numbered for multitude." [1]

The clearest instance in Genesis of angelic, as distinct from divine, manifestation is perhaps the vision of Jacob :

" And he saw in his sleep a ladder standing upon the earth, and the top thereof touching heaven : the angels also of God ascending and descending by it ; and the Lord, leaning upon the ladder, saying to him : I am the Lord God of Abraham thy father, and the God of Isaac. The land, wherein thou sleepest, I will give to thee and to thy seed." [2]

There is no mention of angels in the great period before the flood, nor are they described as ministering to Noe in his peril ; the angelic ministry, as a ministry, begins with the history of the Jewish people. In the narrative of creation there is not the remotest mention of them, and that the evil spirit should be spoken of long before any other power of the unseen world shows clearly that the inspired writers never gave themselves any other task than the history of man and his vicissitudes. Spirits are not the theme of the Bible.

One might not unaptly compare the attitude of our Scriptures towards the spirits with their attitude towards those portions of the human race which are neither the Jewish nation itself nor the Christian Church. The peoples who are not the chosen race come frequently into contact with it, and are even meant to help the people of God in many ways ; the scriptural allusions to them are therefore very valuable from the historical point of view, and we learn a good deal about the non-Jewish peoples from the Bible, though that book is in no sense a history of mankind at large. In a similar way the inspired historians and writers, whilst dealing

[1] Gen. xvi 7-10.                [2] Gen. xxviii 12, 13.

with man's supernatural career on earth, have revealed to us much of the unseen world, but only incidentally, and in so far as it concerns man's eternal welfare. We must bear in mind this relative position of our angelology in the Scriptures, and not expect more than fragments of angelic history ; yet those fragments are precious and instructive in the extreme.

It would not serve the purpose of this essay to quote and explain all the various scriptural allusions to the spirits ; every reader can perform this task for himself. Broadly speaking, we may divide the references of Holy Writ to the angels into four classes—the *historical*, the *liturgical*, the *theological*, and the *prophetic*.

By *historical* angelophany I mean all those assertions found in the Bible that spirits did a work, bore a message, or lent their help to humanity from the time of Agar to that of Peter in his prison. These activities are narrated as ordinary historical events, and they are never concerned with angels in their multitudes, but only with them as individual spirits.

Then there are the *liturgical* allusions to angelic presence in divine worship ; the psalms abound in them, and the " sweet singer of Israel " professes to utter God's praises in the presence of the angels. The " multitude of the heavenly army praising God " at Christ's nativity may be considered under this heading.

As *theological* references those passages of the Scriptures may be quoted where the heavenly spirits are mentioned, not in connection with worship or missions, but as a portion of the supernatural world ; as when Christ is said by St Paul to be raised up on God's right hand in heavenly places above all principality and power and virtue and dominion,[1] when the same Apostle says that the Christian man has " come to Mount Sion and to the city of the living God, the heavenly Jerusalem, and to the company of many thousands of angels," [2] or when Christ himself says that he will confess the name of his faithful witness before the angels of God,[3] or that there is " joy before the angels of God upon one sinner doing penance." [4] The office of the guardian angels may also be considered as belonging to the theological aspect of angelology ; the Scriptures reveal to us a side of the spiritual world which is more than a transient mission, in our Lord's words : " I say to you that their angels in heaven always see the face of my Father who is in heaven." [5]

The *prophetic* allusions are numerous in the Apocalypse where angels are described as doing great things in the mysterious future ; but we have also some such prophetic references in the Gospels themselves, as, for instance, where Christ says that he will " send his angels and gather together his elect from the four winds, from the uttermost part of the earth to the uttermost part of heaven." [6]

[1] Eph. i 21.     [2] Heb. xii 22.     [3] Apoc. iii 5.
[4] Luke xv 10.     [5] Matt. xviii 10.     [6] Mark xiii 27.

If we take the trouble to make for ourselves a complete col- *General* lection of all the angelophanies of our Scriptures we shall easily gain *characteristics of angels in* an impression which might be called the traditional Christian sense *Scripture* concerning the angels. Their character, as I have already said, is clearly marked from the beginning and does not change ; their readiness to do God's bidding is as great as their power to perform it ; nothing can resist their will, and they never fail ; they are always spoken of as being God's own, and at no time is there any fear as to their future. They carry out the commands of God with un-flinching firmness when they are sent forth as the ministers of God's justice, and nothing diverts them from the course of apparent severity. They are standing in the fierceness of God's counten-ance, and yet the lowliest things of this earth are the objects of their attention, as when Raphael goes to the city of the Medes and finds Gabelus, giving him the note of hand and receiving from him all the money which was owed to Tobias.[1] The angels are never described as struggling with evil ; it is always overcome by the sheer might of their presence. From the scriptural account of them we learn that they know neither temptation nor suffering. As we study them we are transplanted into a world entirely different from our own—a world where spiritual wealth is the rule, and where moral or mental destitution is unknown. It could not be said that through all the angelophanies of the Bible we learn any-thing personal about any one of the angels. There is certainly a variety of those spiritual personages in our Scriptures—some are more important than others, some fulfil missions which are not entrusted to others ; but it could not be said that we learn much about these heavenly actors in the drama of the world, as we learn to love, to admire, to compassionate the human actors, like Moses or Elias or Paul, or, above all, like Christ himself. The angel who comes nearest to human sentiment is the angel who comforted Christ in his agony in the Garden : " And there appeared to him an angel from heaven, strengthening him. And being in an agony, he prayed the longer."[2] But even in this instance how divinely anonymous the heavenly comforter has remained. All this con-firms the truth of a remark already made, that the angels are not the principal theme of our Scriptures, but only an incidental one.

There is another most authentic source of information concern- *Angels in the* ing angelic life, angelic power, and angelic character—the Church's *Christian liturgy* worship, both in its sacramental and in its liturgical aspect. But there also we shall find the same features for which the Scriptures have prepared us, of spiritual aloofness on the one hand, and spiritual helpfulness on the other. The Church considers the spirits as her fellow-workers in the sanctification of the world, and her fellow-worshippers in the adoration of Christ. The Church's faith in the guardian angels is to be ranked differently ; this is not

---

[1] Tob. ix.  [2] Luke xxii 43.

so much an act of the Church as a dispensation of the Creator himself. What I mean here is this, that besides that universal guardianship of man by the angels—of which we shall speak later on—the Church makes use of the angels most freely in her sacramental and liturgical life. In her power of sanctifying visible things the Church seems to know no limit ; she calls upon God to send the heavenly spirits and cause them to dwell in the place which she has blessed, to bid them guard the object she has sanctified, to make good the promise she herself has given of protection from the evil one. The *Rituale Romanum* is most instructive from this point of view. The great blessings of the Church, which are, after all, merely an extension of her sacramental power, are extremely bold in their use of angelic intervention. If the Church blesses a bridge over a river, she confidently expects that an angel will be deputed to the keeping of that bridge. The Church prays God to join his angel to the chariot on which her blessing has been bestowed. The angels are called down into the house of the sick, into the home of the newly wed, into the rooms where Christ's little ones are being taught their faith and their letters. There seems to be no end to those angelic possibilities in the sense of the Catholic Church. Everywhere the evil spirits are driven away, and the good spirits are made to take their place.

In the Liturgy, properly so called, the angels play a great rôle. They are present at the Eucharistic Sacrifice ; one of the most mysterious and sacred prayers of the Canon of the Mass introduces an angel who has remained without a name throughout all the centuries during which the prayer has been recited :

"We most humbly beseech thee, Almighty God, to command that these things be borne by the hands of thy holy angel to thine altar on high, in the sight of thy divine Majesty, that so many of us as at this altar shall partake of and receive the most holy body and blood of thy Son may be filled with every heavenly blessing and grace."

At the beginning of Mass, Michael is among those holy ones to whom we confess our sins. When incense is burned over the offerings on the altar the intercession of Michael, "who standeth on the right side of the altar of incense," gives an additional aroma of sweetness to the burning perfumes. Then we have the glorious communion with the angels at every one of the Prefaces of the liturgical year :

"Through whom the angels praise thy Majesty, the dominions worship it, the powers are in awe. The heavens and the heavenly hosts, and the blessed seraphim join together in celebrating their joy. With these we pray thee join our own voices also, while we say with lowly praise : Holy, holy, holy, Lord God of Hosts."

Many other such evidences of the Church's faith in the presence of heavenly spirits round the Christian altar might be quoted from the Liturgies of the East and West. They are for us a very sure guidance as to the nature of our participation in the comity of the invisible nations of spirits. We are as sure of their co-operation, of their love for us, of their knowledge of us, as we are ignorant of the details of that mysterious intercourse. It may certainly be said that the kind of spirituality which the Scriptures and the Church have made their own is a most healthy and most serene contribution to man's spiritual inheritance.

## § II : HISTORY OF ANGELIC CULT

IF the spiritual character of the angels is well defined and clearly *In Scripture* marked in our Scriptures, the same thing could not be said of the way in which these mysterious beings are described for man's apprehension. There is no uniform way in the Bible of representing the angels. The most elaborate descriptions, such as the vision of the Seraphs by Isaias and the vision of the angel by Daniel, are completely baffling to the art of the painter. It is extremely difficult for us to visualise the scenes described so carefully by the prophets, as we are entirely without experience in such matters. The angels of the Resurrection and the Ascension are the most human presentments of the heavenly messengers : " And entering into the sepulchre, they saw a young man clothed with a white robe." [1] " And while they were beholding him going up to heaven, behold two men stood by them in white garments." [2]

The first point of interest, then, in the cult with which Christians have honoured the angels is precisely this attempt to make visible the unseen by giving a bodily form to the heavenly spirits. The earliest Christian representations of angels are concerned with the historic appearances, with those spirits who have fulfilled missions in the New Testament under definite names. Up to the fifth century no other angels are found represented in Christian art ; and these are given the ordinary human form, with their names in such proximity that there can be no mistake about their identity, just as in the case of the apostles and martyrs. About the fifth century we begin to find mosaics, paintings, engravings of angels generally, without a clear historic reference, and the distinctive symbolic sign becomes prevalent, the wings attached to the bodily frame. There is quite a chapter of religious development implied in this progressive adoption of wings for the heavenly spirits by the Christian artists of the earlier centuries of our era. We have in Isaias the first mention of wings in connection with spirits :

" In the year that King Ozias died, I saw the Lord sitting upon a throne high and elevated : and his train filled the temple. Upon it stood the seraphims : the one had six wings, and the other had six wings : with two they covered his face, and with two they covered his feet, and with two they flew." [3]

[1] Mark xvi 5.   [2] Acts i 10.   [3] Isa. vi 1, 2.

*Development of angelic art*

There is no clear evidence that the universal custom which has prevailed from Byzantine times of representing the angels with wings owes its origin to the vision of Isaias. The Seraphim as described by the great seer are one of the most difficult subjects to be materialised in art. The two-winged angels are a spontaneous creation of the Christian imagination which in this matter has followed the artistic tradition and intuition of the Western civilisations of earlier times. Nothing is more common in Greek and Roman art of the best periods than to give a pair of wings to a superhuman being. The divinity called Victory is invariably endowed with a glorious pair of wings, and so are innumerable genii. That Christian artists, of all shades of talent, should have pictured superhuman beings in the same way as that in which the pagans depicted them is no more astonishing than the circumstance of a hymn to Zeus being sung in melodies which are adapted to a Christian hymn, or of metres of pagan poetry being adopted by Catholic hymnologists. There are two instances of the classical art which have passed into the service of the angel worship which are especially striking. Genii or demi-gods are seen on ancient friezes and sarcophagi carrying the privileged ones of the human race to the ethereal spheres, and also weighing the souls of men in the scales of justice. In Christian art these two conceptions are commonplaces. Angels carry the elect to heaven, and angels weigh the souls of men in the final balances. The period of history when paganism was giving way finally to Christianity under the first Christian emperors is particularly interesting from this point of view. The Victory statues are often adorned with Christian symbols such as the Labarum, and genuine heathen medallions of Mercury have an entirely different signification when the word "Michael" is engraved upon them. Perhaps the owner of the art-treasure was loth to part with his gem, and had a Hermes Christianised into an archangel ! [1]

From the sixth century onwards the angelic type is fixed. With the exception of the Seraphim of Isaias, who have always been the despair of draughtsmen, angels are given asexual lineaments of body and their garments flow in dignified folds. The alternative forms of winged heads are expressions of beauty which is neither masculine nor feminine.

It was reserved to the latest renaissances, the baroque and the rococo, to lower the majestic type of the best periods of Christian art. Can the name of " angel " still be given to that host of nude figures in plaster or marble which people the continental churches from one end of Europe to the other ? It would be difficult to find any principle or justification underlying such handiwork on the part of Catholic craftsmen. The one reassuring thing about those periods of artistic extravagances is this, that at the very time when the artistic representation of the spiritual being was at its lowest,

[1] See *Dictionnaire d'Archéologie Chrétienne,* " Anges."

the theological schools of the Church produced some of the profoundest speculations on the nature and the might of the angels.

From the very nature of the case, acquaintance with the angelic *Development* world has not progressed as angelic art has progressed. We know *of angelology* of no more angels to-day than were known in the first century. Michael, Gabriel, and Raphael are the only authentic angelic names. In the first centuries there is often mentioned another angel, Uriel, even by the orthodox. He is invoked in some of the ancient litanies ; he is supposed to be the spirit who stood at the gate of the lost Eden, with the fiery sword. But the trilogy of Michael, Gabriel, and Raphael stands nowadays without any competitors.

Superstition there has been in the cult of the angels. In the old Egyptian fashion an angel was supposed to be the Keeper of the Tomb, and to make it inviolable. The Gnostics had their own angelic mysteries. To know the true names of the " Seven who stand before God " was a talisman. St Paul alludes to the perversion of a great truth which had already begun : " Let no man seduce you, willing in humility and religion of angels,[1] walking in the things which he hath not seen, in vain puffed up by the sense of his flesh." [2]

The intellectual development of the angelic cult in the Church has far exceeded the liturgical and the artistic developments. If art has been once or twice on the point of making the angels vulgar, of turning them into pixies, theology, mystical and speculative, has more than compensated for such a lapse. Angels have become for the Christian thinker a sort of minor infinitude, with endless powers of mind and will.

The great classic of angelology is a work whose probable date is the second half of the fifth century, called the *Heavenly Hierarchy*. It is a portion of the work of an unknown writer who goes by the name of Dionysius the Areopagite. In this book the writer takes for granted that classification of the spirits into nine choirs, and again into three triads within those nine choirs, of which much will be said in the following pages. Quite an original contribution of the author seems to be the doctrine of hierarchic illumination, of which there is no clear trace in the Scriptures. It is, however, a most happy and genial application to a special case of the well-established theological principle of the interdependence of creatures, and the oneness of the created universe.

The angelic manifestations narrated in the Scriptures are part *Christian* of the traditional Christian Faith and belong to the most authentic *angel-* history of the people of God. The question now arises whether *ophanies* such angelic manifestations belong to the normal life of the Christian Church in her mighty course through the centuries. It is evident that whatever angelophanies there may have been since the last

[1] *I.e.*, by affecting humility and religion towards angels.
[2] Col. ii 18, 19.

book of the Scriptures was written, such manifestations are to be considered merely as historical facts, not as things integral in any way to the *depositum fidei*. It is, of course, a matter of faith that the heavenly spirits are associated in one way or another with the life of Christians here on earth, as will be explained by and by in this essay. The question now asked is about miraculous angelophanies, such as Peter was granted when he was delivered from his prison; are there on record clear and undoubted interventions of heavenly spirits, under easily observable circumstances in the history of the Church?

There is certainly an *a priori* assumption in favour of such manifestations; it may even be said that they belong to the ordinary *charismata* of the Church. Spiritual phenomena that occurred in the primitive Church are characteristic of the normal life of the Church, as the primitive Church is the ideal Church.

It has been found as feasible, therefore, to write the history of angelic intervention as to write the history of martyrdoms and missionary expeditions. This task has been carried out with great care and perfect soberness of method by those princes of Christian hagiography, the Bollandists. In their *Acta Sanctorum*, under the date of September 29, the feast of St Michael the Archangel, they give an exhaustive survey of all the known angelophanies in Church history. The learned historians deal with age after age from the second century onwards, under titles such as this: " *Beneficia Angelorum saeculo quarto* " (" the benefactions of the angels in the fourth century "). Thus nothing is easier than to gain from the complete and critical studies of the Bollandists a general impression of the miraculous interventions with which the Christian people have been favoured in their long history.

The interventions of St Michael are considered apart in the *Acta Sanctorum*, and they differ slightly in character from the usual angelophanies of the Catholic Church. More than once, though not as often as might be imagined, Michael, the leader of the celestial hosts, helps the Christian warriors on the battlefield to gain a victory over adverse powers. Moreover, St Michael has two great shrines in Western Europe towards which kings and peoples have pilgrimed as they pilgrimed to the tombs of the Apostles. Mount Gargano, in Southern Italy, and Mount St Michel, in Northern France, have been true angelic shrines from the early middle ages; there the heavenly prince has been believed to distribute favours and receive the pilgrim with all the graciousness of a mighty lord.

If we examine now the other angelophanies, century by century, we are struck by their sobriety and their manifest humanness. Rarely, if ever, do we come across anything in history that is of a terrifying nature in angelic manifestations, nor do we find the angels taking part ostensibly in the great struggles of the Christian people. Even the Crusades, which would have been such a perfect setting for the scintillating intervention of heavenly hosts, are remarkably devoid of such glorious legends. Now and then a straggling battalion of Crusaders, athirst and discouraged, is led out from a hopeless wilderness by a mysterious stranger who disappears when the danger is past, but on the whole the angelic ministries, as narrated in Church history, are of a much more private, nay, intimate character.

Angels come and console the martyrs in their prisons, and even heal their wounds, like so many good Samaritans ; angels are seen taking care of the bodies of the Christian athletes, which the persecutor had thrown out to ignominious neglect ; angels feed the hermits, and manifest to the early monastic lawgivers what is wise and what is excessive in Christian asceticism ; they help the solitary to overcome his terrors at the sight of solitudes filled with evil presences ; they give warnings of the approaching death of some lonely servant of God, and they are seen carrying to heaven the soul of many a saint.

Quite early in ecclesiastical history we find the angels intimately associated with the Eucharistic mystery. They visibly assist at the sacrifice of Mass, they carry the sacramental Body of Christ to the solitary Christian who would otherwise have been deprived of that heavenly Food ; and—what is more striking still—in the very heart of Catholicism, in a well-peopled nunnery for instance, an angel is seen taking Holy Communion to a privileged soul as a mark of special favour. St Isidore, the ploughman, is helped in his humble work by angelic fellow-labourers ; and an angel girds the loins of St Thomas Aquinas with the mysterious *cingulum* of perfect chastity—a very remarkable attention in the life of the great doctor and thinker, for we do not read of heavenly intelligences whispering to him the secrets of Catholic theology. In the case of Thomas, the angelic ministry is of a much more intimate and personal nature. St Francesca is favoured with an almost constant vision of an angel, whose attention to his protégée is most minute in matters both spiritual and temporal. St Teresa sees angels carrying, as in triumph, the virginal body of one of her dead nuns ; and St Stanislaus Kostka, detained in the house of a heretic in Vienna, receives the sacred Viaticum at the hand of an angel. An angel brings a lump of sugar to the infirmarian of St Philip Neri, thus making it possible for the saint to be given the medicine of which he was so sorely in need. Angels are heard alternating with monks in divine psalmody in many a medieval abbey, when the brethren were in need of encouragement during the painful vigil of a cold winter night.

Such are the characteristic angelophanies we find in Church history. There is a sweet sameness about them in all times. May we not say that angels break through the veil of mystery and manifest themselves, not in order to frighten Christians and overawe them, but to smile at them with the smile of love and compassion ?

## §III: ANGELIC LIFE

OUR Scriptures are remarkably reticent as to the nature, the life, and the activities of those wonderful beings whom we call the angels. They show themselves to perform definite missions, to deliver messages, and they disappear as suddenly as they have come. The only trait which the Scriptures seem to distinguish clearly is precisely this agility of motion, this freedom from the trammels of space, and this also, no doubt, is the characteristic in angelic nature which is most attractive to the human imagination. Yet it would be an uncatholic thing to say that we are quite ignorant concerning the nature of the angels. Catholic theology has its own resources, and with regard to angelic existences it has arrived at certain conclusions, which in their outlines may be taken as expressing truth.

Christian thought is not satisfied with the merely ministerial rôle of the heavenly spirits; the angels are more than ministers and messengers, they are, above all, a portion of the universe, they are its noblest portion; and very early in the history of Christian thought we find the angels occupying a most important cosmic position. There is stability of power and life in the spirit world, and the angels are become great beings on whom the cosmos reposes as on solid foundations. This view is certainly adumbrated in the writings of St Paul when he speaks of Christ as being raised "above all principality, and power, and virtue, and dominion, and every name that is named, not only in this world, but also in that which is to come." [1]

*Pure spirits*    Our theology starts with the principle that angels are pure spirits, and whatever may be deduced from such a principle we may hold as being true. Perhaps we cannot go very far, yet when we find the best theologians writing voluminously on the subject of the angels we ought to admit that much can be said without extravagance of speculation. Some extravagance there may have been at times, as it may intrude into philosophy of every kind, but such excess nowise detracts from the merit of the labours of a sober genius like St Thomas Aquinas, to quote only one of the great and humble theorisers about the angels.

There is a conflict between Catholic art and Catholic theology in this matter. Catholic art gives bodily substance to the angels; it gives them physical colour, visible beauty; whilst it is the effort of Catholic theology to discard every element of materiality and visibility. We need only be reasonable in order to find peace in a contest that cannot be avoided. As we are now, in our mortal state, we cannot think in purely spiritual elements, we must have the aid of our phantasy, and the richest imagination will be the one to conjure up the most gratifying visions of heavenly messengers.

[1] Eph. i 21.

But we ought to know that the reality is very different, incomparably different indeed, and immensely more beautiful; we ought not to feel sad if we are told that our visions of angels, if we have such, do not represent the heavenly visitant in his native existence, but that he appears to us in the borrowed garb of imaginative impressions.

What, then, are the certain conclusions to be drawn from the principle that angels are spirits? The following statements may be taken as being widely accepted theorems concerning angelic existence :

1. Angels have a beginning, but they cannot perish; they remain everlastingly the same.
2. Angels are not subject to the laws of time, but have a duration measure of their own.
3. Angels are completely superior to space, so that they could never be subject to its laws.
4. Angelic power on the material world is exerted directly through the will.
5. Angelic life has two faculties only, intellect and will.
6. In the sphere of nature an angel cannot err, either in intellect or will.
7. An angel never goes back on a decision once taken.
8. The angelic mind starts with fulness of knowledge, and it is not, like the human mind, subject to gradual development.
9. An angel may directly influence another created intellect, but he cannot act directly on another created will.
10. Angels have free will; they are capable of love and hatred.
11. Angels know material things and individual things.
12. Angels do not know the future; they do not know the secret thoughts of other rational creatures; they do not know the mysteries of grace, unless such things be revealed freely, either by God or by the other rational creatures.

These theorems have reference to the natural state of the angel. But the angel has been elevated to the supernatural state, the state of grace, and concerning that state some other principles have currency amongst theologians; we must defer them to the subsequent section on Angelic Sanctity.

I think the enunciation of the aforesaid theorems is quite clear. Every one of my readers will understand what is meant by the phrases, though he may find it difficult to adjust such ideas to his ordinary way of thinking. The theorems here stated practically cover the whole field of theology; anything beyond this becomes subtlety.

From our Scriptures we know that amongst the angels there is a hierarchy—there are the greater, perhaps the immensely greater angels, and the lesser angels; but it would be temerarious, not to say foolish, to attempt an explanation of those differentiations in spiritual substances. Why is one spirit greater than another ? To this we can give no answer. We may say, of course, that a spirit is greater because his intellect is more powerful, because he grasps things in a more simple and limpid fashion, because he sees with one act of mind what other spirits of a lower order can only perceive by many acts ; but it is evident that this would not give the root of his greatness. The reason why he can thus comprehend and visualise is because his is a greater mind. Why is his mind greater ? Because his is a greater nature. But how is his a greater nature ? To this query there is no reply among the children of men. So our theology of the angels concerns itself with the general angelic features, not with their special attributes, and we know no more about the highest angel than about the lowest ; we give them the generic attributes which belong to all finite spiritual substances, the human soul alone excepted.

We may now say a few words in explanation of each one of the above theorems.

1. *Angels have a beginning, but they cannot perish ; they remain everlastingly the same.*

Spirits, like matter, were created by God's omnipotence out of nothingness ; they are no more a portion of the divine Substance than is a stone or a tree, but they resemble the divine Substance in a fashion that is immensely closer, so that by comparison they might be called divine, as God's likeness is in them in a manner in which it is not in other portions of his creation. We cannot say whether all the spirits that now exist were created at one and the same moment, or whether there were different creations. But no finite spirit could create another, and it is more in keeping with Catholic thought to say that God created all the angels together. The distance that separates the present moment from the creation of the spirit world is, of course, not calculable by time standards. Spiritual substance once produced by God cannot decay, it may do wrong in mind and will, but it always remains a perfect substance ; it does not change in its essentials, it does not deteriorate in its nature. We could hardly say that it is immortal, because the word immortality would not do justice to such permanence ; a spirit is simply unalterable, his changes are merely changes of thought and will.

2. *Angels are not subject to the laws of time, but have a duration measure of their own.*

This has been most beautifully expressed by Cardinal Newman in his *Dream of Gerontius*, and though the passage is often quoted it would be a neglect on my part to omit it here :

> " For spirits and men by different standards mete
> The less and greater in the flow of time.
> By sun and moon, primeval ordinances—
> By stars which rise and set harmoniously—

By the recurring seasons, and the swing,
This way and that, of the suspended rod
Precise and punctual, men divide the hours,
Equal, continuous, for their common use.
Not so with us in th' immaterial world ;
But intervals in their succession
Are measured by the living thought alone,
And grow or wane with its intensity.
And time is not a common property ;
But what is long is short, and swift is slow,
And near is distant, as received and grasped
By this mind and by that, and every one
Is standard of his own chronology.
And memory lacks its natural resting-points
Of years, and centuries, and periods."

Newman put into matchless language the technicalities of scholastic theology. Though angels remain for ever, we do not say that they are eternal. Eternity is the measure of God's existence ; it implies negation, not only of an end but also of a beginning ; it implies, moreover, immutability of every kind, even immutability in intellect and will : such immutability or eternity is possessed by God alone.

3. *Angels are completely superior to space, so that they could never be subject to its laws.*

Our reason assents to this theorem more readily than does our imagination. Reason tells us that a spirit, through the very definition of his nature, has nothing spatial in his composition. Movement, in the bodily, the mechanical, sense of the word cannot be predicated of spirits. They act, they exert power on material things, now at one point of the universe, now at another ; these acts or influences are successive, not simultaneous, but it could not be said that a spirit has moved or flown from one spot to another, he has merely exerted two different acts of power over objects that are mutually remote.

4. *Angelic power on the material world is exerted directly through the will.*

Angelic will-power is not only immanent, it is executive ; it can alter the things of the material universe by a direct contact or influence. Spirits can work signs and prodigies by making use of the powers of nature, though it could not be said that they can work miracles, in the proper sense of the word, such as the raising of the dead ; this would require divine power. Angelophanies, or apparitions of angels or spirits generally, may be explained through the power these lofty beings possess of acting on our sense-perceptions, and of giving us those mighty impressions of which we find instances in the Scriptures : " His body was like the chrysolite, and his face as the appearance of lightning, and his eyes as a burning lamp : and his arms and all downward even to the feet, like in appearance to glittering brass : and the voice of his word like the voice of a multitude." [1]

[1] Dan x 6

5. *Angelic life has two faculties only, intellect and will.*

With this theorem we banish from spirit-life every vestige of sense-life. Angels cannot be said to have imagination, passion, sentiment, all of which manifestations of life are essentially the modifications of organic life and sense-powers. This is what we mean by the very common expression " angelic purity." Angels are pure from all sensuality, not through virtue, but through nature. If there is sin in them it could never be, even in the faintest degree, sensual sin. Of such life we human beings have absolutely no experience, yet it is one of the very first conclusions we must admit when we state that angels are spirits. Attractive as the notion of angels has become to Christian imagination, there is no softness, no sentimentality, in true Catholic angelology.

6. *In the sphere of nature an angel cannot err, either in intellect or will.*

This may sound astonishing to our ears, for we hear much of the instability of all created things ; yet it follows directly upon the simplicity of spirit-nature. There cannot be in an angel any source of sin or error within his own sphere of existence, but he may sin and err in the mysteries of grace, as those mysteries are above him. Here again I must refer the reader to the sections on Angelic Sanctity and Spirit Sin.

7. *An angel never goes back on a decision once taken.*

There ought to be little difficulty in our admitting such a trait in the mentality of a spirit, for we admire such a characteristic even in man. There is this difference between obstinacy and strength of resolve in man—that obstinacy comes from narrowness of view, while strength of resolve comes truly from a wide grasp of a fact, of its circumstances, and its implications. The perspicacious man need not alter his views and decisions, because he has seen so clearly the true issues of a thing from the very beginning. Vacillation of purpose in man comes from a predominance of the sentimental element over the intellectual element. With spirits, as may easily be perceived, there could be no such source of weakness, no such hesitancy of purpose. At a glance they perceive a truth, either theoretical or practical ; they see all its aspects, all its consequences, and there are no lower powers in them that could act under impressions of a more mobile kind, and deflect their clear reason and their entirely spiritual will from its first course.

8. *The angelic mind starts with fulness of knowledge, and it is not, like the human mind, subject to gradual development.*

In this we have the profoundest difference between spirit intellect and human intellect. A spirit starts his existence fully endowed with all knowledge ; he is never a learner in the true sense of the word, as man is a learner. It may be said of an angel that he applies his knowledge to new objects, but he does not acquire ideas that were not infused into him by the Creator in the very making of him.

9. *An angel may directly influence another created intellect, but he cannot act directly on another created will.*

The former part of this theorem seems, at first sight, to contradict the last theorem, which said that angels never learn in the real sense of the word. Yet much of Catholic theology is taken up with the mutual illuminations of the angels—that one angelic mind illumines another angelic mind. The contradiction is merely apparent. Such influence as the theological term of illumination implies is not the teaching of the ignorant, but a communication of messages from higher spheres of divine commands for which the angelic mind is prepared, and to which it is attuned. Speaking colloquially, we may say that no angelic mind is ever taken by surprise by any communication that reaches it from the council chamber of God. Spirits, then, may act on each other's minds, but it is a sacrosanct principle with Catholic theology that God alone has power to act directly upon a created will. A creature may entice, may persuade, may tempt the will, but it can never touch it directly.

10. *Angels have free will; they are capable of love and hatred.*

Freedom of will is the very essence of ethical perfection, and angels have always been supposed to be ethically good. Love and hatred must be taken in their case, not in the sense of a passion, of a sentiment, but as representing either affinities or oppositions of a will which knows of no sensual attachments.

11. *Angels know material things and individual things.*

12. *Angels do not know the future; they do not know the secret thoughts of other rational creatures; they do not know the mysteries of grace, unless such things be revealed freely, either by God or by the other rational creatures.*

Our eleventh and twelfth theorems are clear by their very enunciation. Angelic knowledge is not only of abstract things, but of concrete things. The future free acts of created rational beings are not knowable to a created intellect. God alone contemplates them with infallible security of vision in the light of his eternity. For the same reasons which make it impossible for a spirit to act directly on the will of any rational creature we may say that the secret thoughts of the heart of man or the mind of a spirit are hidden, unless freely revealed by the one who thinks the thought. In every thought there is an act of will, because I think when I will and I think what I will, but the hiddenness of the will covers my very thoughts. The mysteries of grace are the decision, not of a created will, but of the will of God. *A fortiori* it will ever be far beyond a created spirit's ken to find out what God is thinking, unless God be pleased to reveal his thoughts.

## §IV: ANGELIC MULTITUDE AND HIERARCHY

THE idea of multitude has always been associated with heavenly spirits. Though in our Scriptures they are never shown in multitudes in the execution of work, they are always many when they are shown as praising God or as forming his Court : " And suddenly there was with the angel a multitude of the heavenly army praising God, and saying : Glory to God in the highest : and on earth peace to men of good will." [1] One angel is seen delivering the message of Christ's Nativity to the shepherds, but a multitude of spirits is heard to sing the praises of God. In the Book of Daniel isolated spirits are sent forth with great power, but when the Ancient of Days is seen by the prophet sitting on his Throne there is again multitude in the spirit world : " Thousands of thousands ministered to him, and ten thousand times a hundred thousand stood before him." [2] Thus, too, in the Apocalypse, four angels are seen " standing on the four corners of the earth and holding the four winds of the earth, that they should not blow upon the earth nor upon the sea nor on any tree " ; [3] but there is " heard the voice of many angels round about the throne, and the living creatures and the ancients (and the number of them was thousands of thousands)." [4] Again in the Apocalypse we see judgement being executed on the earth by seven angels, of whom each one holds a vial full of the anger of God, and successively, not simultaneously, they each pour out their vial upon the earth ; but when Christ comes forth in triumph he is surrounded by the armies that are in heaven : " And he was clothed with a garment sprinkled with blood, and his name is called the Word of God. And the armies that are in heaven followed him on white horses, clothed in fine linen, white and clean." [5]

*Meaning of angelic multitude*
From this we may gather that in scriptural thought spirit multitude has a special significance—we might call it the notion of society ; that the heavenly spirits are God's society, and that multitude refers not so much to the variety of external missions as to the variety of contemplation of God in himself. In other words, the concept of multitude in spirits is something very different from the concept of multitude in material things. Number is indeed a marvel of material nature ; even the human race has that astonishing factor of number : God has multiplied the children of men. St Thomas remarks wisely that with material things, man not excluded, number supplements the weakness of the species ; a species is saved from death, from disappearance, through its numbers, and the weaker the species the greater its numbers. It is evident that when we come into the spirit world the notion of number must take a different form, and when we say that angels are innumerable we mean something quite other than the

[1] Luke ii 13-14.  [2] Dan. vii 10.  [3] Apoc. vii 1.
[4] Apoc. v 11.  [5] Apoc. xix 13-14.

idea suggested if we say, for instance, that the pebbles on the shore
are innumerable. In material things number is rather a necessity
than a perfection, in spiritual things multitude means perfection,
and cannot mean anything else.

This point of theology is approached most satisfactorily if we
bear in mind what I have insinuated already—that in our Scriptures
spirit-multitude is always associated with the society of God, with
the praise and contemplation of his perfection. Spirits are multiplied for this very end, that the perfections of God may be reflected
more and more completely. If we take this as the starting-point
we shall readily see the beauty of traditional Catholic doctrine
which holds that spirits exceed in number anything that we know.
The whole idea of multitude is changed ; one angel reflects God's
glory in one way, another angel in another way, and multitude is
something very perfect for this precise reason that it is the image
of a perfection which is absolutely inexhaustible. Such ideas are
not connected with the numberless in the material world. We do
not find any special beauty in the " innumerables " of the physical
world, but the " innumerables " of the spirit world are expressions
of beauty ever more and more complete. So we find startling
theories held by our theologians—theories which sometimes do
not approve themselves to thinkers whose intellect is more the
servant of imagination than they would themselves admit. St
Thomas makes it one of the corner-stones of his angelology that
there are no two angels of the same species ; that there are no two
angels equal in nature ; that the angelic world constitutes an ever-
ascending progression of spiritual substances, each one higher than
the other. With this he maintains the traditional view that spirits
are innumerable, holding a principle which makes such a view quite
acceptable ; that it is the proper mission of the spirits to reflect,
in a created fashion, divine perfection ; that every spirit does so in
his own way ; and that an infinite ascending hierarchy of spirits
cannot exhaust the wealth of God's reflected beauty. Number has
become something very different in such philosophy from what it
is in the calculations of the physicist and the naturalist. It is a
thing of dignity, not a mere juxtaposition of beings side by side.
There are, I admit, a good many theologians to whom this view seems
too bold ; they would more willingly talk of brother angels, of many
spirits of the same rank, glorified and spiritualised human beings,
in fact, which constitute a heavenly nation. But I think a very little
consideration will show that imagination plays a large part in the
opposition to the great Thomistic angelology ; the angelic crowds
of a Fra Angelico are certainly crowds of brother angels, not hierarchies of spirits.

I ought to say that St Thomas had deduced his theory of
essential variation between angel and angel from the profounder
principle of spirit nature. As angels are not united with bodily

frames, the great metaphysician finds it impossible to distinguish between spirit and spirit, except on the grounds that they all differ as one species differs from another species. Put quite simply, the idea comes to this : that there are no two angels alike, nor any two angels of equal rank. This view is certainly very commendable from the metaphysical point of view, and, though it may in a way bewilder the imagination, it contributes towards a clearer understanding of what is meant by angelic multitude. It is not an endless repetition within the same plane of being, as is the case even with man ; it is, on the contrary, an ever fresh addition to the permanent and essential beauties of the universe.

*Hierarchy of angels*　　These considerations lead us on naturally to the treatment of hierarchy among angels. It is one of the best-established doctrines of Christian angelology that there is a diversity of hierarchic gradation among the heavenly spirits. Our Scriptures tell us the names of nine different angelic orders, usually classified in the following succession, beginning with the lowest hierarchy : Angels, Archangels, Principalities, Powers, Virtues, Dominations, Thrones, Cherubim, and Seraphim. These nine choirs are again distinguished into three orders, the impression having prevailed in Christian tradition that there is a certain community of nature, genius, and mission in these triple sets of spiritual categories. That kinship is usually expressed in three different affinities : Seraphim, Cherubim, and Thrones are associated together ; then Dominations, Virtues and Powers ; finally Principalities, Archangels, and Angels.

The first question one asks is this : is this ninefold hierarchy exhaustive, so that it may be said to describe the whole angelic world ? We cannot speak with certainty, yet it would seem that with the Cherubim and Seraphim we have reached the limits of the spirit world, for these sublime beings are constantly spoken of as the nearest unto God of the whole mighty creation. But no doubt this query is answered more completely if we can give a satisfactory explanation of angelic hierarchy itself. Certainly no theologian need admit that an angelic choir, say the choir of angels, is constituted of spirit beings of the same rank. A moment ago I said that some of the best theology holds that equality of rank is not possible amongst spirits, as each one is a hierarchy in the ever-ascending scale of beings ; we must, then, give to angelic hierarchies and orders a very wide meaning, nay, an indefinite meaning, and it would be again indulging our imagination if we made of those nine choirs nine different classes of spirits. The secrets which are revealed to us in those traditional names are just the few hints given to us of the glorious variety in God's spiritual world. To make of those names categories and exclusive partitions would be contrary to the intentions of the Spirit who whispered the great secrets. We are expected to multiply, not to divide, in our thoughts of the heavenly citizens. We should not divide them into classes, but we should be ready for endless varieties of spiritual splendours.

Hierarchy in the angelic world is not primarily a matter of grace, but a matter of nature. If angels differ in grace it is because they differ in nature, grace being granted to them according to the capacity of their nature ; such seems to be the more probable theological view. St Thomas is quite liberal in his treatment of the meaning of hierarchy and of the angelic orders within that hierarchy. He says that within the nine choirs we make three divisions on account of our imperfect knowledge, *propter confusam notitiam*, because we do not know more than the vaguest outline of their functions ; but did we know more clearly, then we should really see that every angel is in himself an order, because he fulfils a mission in himself, complete and not interchangeable. " If we knew perfectly the offices of the angels and their differences, then we should know that every angel has his proper office and his proper order in the universe, and this much more than any star, though it be hidden from us." [1]

We have only the vaguest hints as to the specific functions *Functions of* covered by those great names of Seraph, Cherub, Thrones, etc. *the various* In so free a matter doctors are allowed to differ. As a sample of *angelic orders* the speculations to which those holy names have given rise we may quote St Thomas who, in his turn, cites the words of the pseudo-Dionysius : " Let us then first examine the reason for the ordering of Dionysius, in which we see that . . . the highest hierarchy contemplates the ideas of things in God himself ; the second in the universal causes ; and the third in their application to particular effects. And because God is the end not only of the angelic minis-trations, but also of the whole creation, it belongs to the first hier-archy to consider the end ; to the middle one belongs the universal disposition of what is to be done ; and to the last belongs the application of this disposition to the effect, which is the carrying out of the work ; for it is clear that these three things exist in every kind of operation. So Dionysius, considering the properties of the orders as derived from their names, places in the first hierarchy those orders the names of which are taken from their relation to God, the *Seraphim, Cherubim,* and *Thrones* ; and he places in the middle hierarchy those orders whose names denote a certain kind of common government or disposition, the *Dominations, Virtues,* and *Powers* ; and he places in the third hierarchy the orders whose names denote the execution of the work, the *Principalities, Angels,* and *Archangels.*" [2]

Though it be commonly admitted, as we shall see in another section, that the lower order of spirits, called, with a more constant appropriation of language, the angels, are those spirits who watch over man, in fact, the guardian angels, we need not therefore hold that they are spirits of the same rank ; they differ essentially amongst themselves and there is only one spirit who may be truly called the lowest spirit. The guardianship of man by the angels is not so

[1] *S. Theol.*, I, Q. cviii, art. 3.    [2] *Ibid.*, art. 6.

much a matter of the personal dignity of the spirit as a matter of the influence he is pleased to exert on man. To an objector who would like all spirits, at least those within the same hierarchy, to be equal, on the ground that all men have an angel guardian, and that it would not be suitable that the guardians of beings so similar as men should themselves differ essentially, St Thomas answers that it is not truly a question of angelic essence so much as of angelic power. The results of that power are similar whatever the greatness of the spirit that exerts it.

It might be said that in many of the angelophanies narrated in our Scriptures the multitude of angels need not have been more than an impression on mortal minds of multitude when there was in reality no multitude. There is, however, an insistence on the number of spirits in the Bible narrative which it would be temerarious to represent invariably as merely a subjective impression on the minds of those men who saw the angels. There are, moreover, passages in the Scriptures which cannot be read otherwise than as meaning truly objective numerousness in the spirit world. Thus in the Epistle to the Hebrews the company of many thousands of angels is stated to be one of the elements of the Christian election : " You are come to Mount Sion, and to the city of the living God, the heavenly Jerusalem, and to the company of many thousands of angels." [1]

## § V : THE GUARDIAN ANGELS

It is a favourite theme with St Thomas Aquinas to represent the whole physical world as being entrusted by God to the keeping of the angels. The stars in their courses are watched by the mighty spirits ; nations are committed to the care of a heavenly prince, and there is no part of the universe which does not feel the breath of those whose mind beholds the countenance of God.

*General principle*  An all-pervading principle governs the theology of the spirit ministry—namely, an inferior thing in creation is invariably under the tutelage of a higher thing. To this great law there is no exception. The universe is held together with the golden threads of spirit power as well as with the coarser sinews of natural energy. As a principle in its vast and indeterminate form this doctrine is very beautiful, and we should not go beyond this generic outline of a great truth ; we cannot fill it up with specific facts and details, for the very reason that spirit power, however and wherever exerted, could not be observable in the physical order, precisely because it transcends the physical order.

One objection against this comprehensive theory of theology ought not to be made, that under such an hypothesis physical laws would become superfluous, as spirit activity and will would be the ruling elements of the universe. The theological theory of the

[1] Heb. xii 22.

universe leaves the physical theory completely untouched. It supposes merely that the wise Creator, who governs the material universe in accordance with the uniform laws of nature that he has made, makes use, in the application of those laws, of angels as intermediaries and executors of his plan. Nor ought we to consider those created activities of the spirits superfluous on account of God's omnipresent vigilance over his universe. God multiplies created power, not because he could not effect the result himself, but because it is a more beautiful universe which has a hierarchy of potentialities.

The last form, the ultimate application of that great principle *Angelic* is embodied in the sweet and popular doctrine of the guardian *tutelage of human beings* angels. Every human being is under the tutelage of a heavenly spirit, and this in virtue of a natural law. It is not at baptism, it is at birth that every child of Adam is handed over to the keeping of an angel. Great as is the Christian faith in the privileged state of those that are baptised in Christ, it never made the guardianship of the angel an exclusive privilege of the regenerate, but the unbaptised infant shares this divine provision with the baptised. Spirit guardianship of the human race belongs to nature itself. It is true that in the Gospels the angels of the children spoken of are the angels of children who have faith in Christ : " Their angels behold the face of my Father who is in heaven," [1] but Christian tradition has always been emphatic in admitting the universal guardianship of all men, because all men are, at least potentially, the children of God.

The question will be asked at once whether each human being *Nature of* has a separate angel, individually distinct from every other angel. *angelic* To such a query it would be quite impossible to give an answer, *tutelage* unless we had some authoritative teaching. The work itself of guarding man could not be such as to necessitate the presence of a separate spirit for every separate human being. One angel has power enough to watch over millions with undivided carefulness ; but the burden of opinion is in favour of individual angelic guardianship, not of collective protection. But for this we could give no other reason than that the will of God so ordered it. The protection of spirits must be conceived on entirely spiritual lines. No good purpose is served by false sentiment in a matter so holy. We could not say, with any vestige of truth, that the angel leaves his beautiful heaven for this dreary earth, to take charge of weaklings such as we are ; for there is no real departure from the glories of angelic life when a spirit assumes the tutelage of a lower being ; more truly the lower being enters into the sphere of activity of one special spirit, just as a planet is kept within the orbit of one special sun. As I have said already, the angelic guardianship of man by angels is only the last instance of the mighty tutelage of the spirit world

---

[1] Matt. xviii 10.

over the material world, with this difference, however, that free will comes into play where man is concerned. Here again we must not ask for precise facts, but must be satisfied with the general principle. We must start with the assumption that the human race has fared as it has fared up to now precisely because it has been under the tutelage of spirits—a tutelage which is constant, all-pervading, the most permanent element in the preservation of the human race. We might say, to make this point quite clear, that if the human race had not possessed the spirit tutelage its history would have been very different from what it has been; it would have been infinitely more dismal, though we cannot indicate the facts and events directly attributable to the spirits that watch over man. And what is said of the race is true of every individual human being; we must simply say that this life is what it is because he has been given at his birth into the keeping of an angel. Very few occasions in a man's mortal career can be traced to the immediate activity of his watching spirit; in fact, unless we are given a special revelation on the subject, not one event in life can be said with certainty to be the direct arrangement of the guardian angel. But we have much more: we have the assurance from our faith that we are being guarded; we have never known any other kind of existence; we might almost say we do not know what it is to be without an angel, just as we do not know what it is to be without the laws of gravity. There is this *a priori* certainty that if individual men are thus entrusted by the Creator to a mighty spirit their whole life is profoundly modified, whether they know it or not.

It would be a mistake to think that the guardianship of the heavenly spirits is given to man only as the result of prayer; it is given absolutely, as a final, unalterable dispensation of God's providence. This spiritual tutelage is meant above all things to keep the human race and human individuals in perfection of nature, and we may say without any exaggeration that the human race would have succumbed long ago to enemies, to deleterious influences, but for the ever-protecting, divinely directed activity of those benign powers. Prayer to the angels is, of course, an act of piety much to be commended and most fruitful, for it is in our power to make use of that great tutelage to an extent which varies greatly according to each man's good will; just as prayer to God, in another sphere, makes the divine Majesty more and more propitious, though it could not be said that God would have no thought of man unless man prayed. There is a providence on the part of God which is absolute and independent of man's good will. In the same sense there is a spiritual tutelage of the human race and of every individual being which transcends the vacillation of man's ethical state; the race is kept from destruction and internal dissolution for God's own purposes, we might almost say, in spite of itself. The sins of men are no signs that men are not guarded by good spirits, for, as

St Thomas says so well,[1] we can act against the good instigations
of the spirit that is outside us as we can act against the good instincts
that are within us. The good instincts remain as a great reality
in spite of our prevarication; so likewise the angelic inspiration
remains in spite of our voluntary deafness to it. Nor could it be
said that the spirits work in vain, even with those who are lost.
Not only are we to suppose, again with St Thomas,[2] that the most
perverted of men are kept from greater evils by their heavenly
guardians, but the evil committed by one man is kept in check by
those spirits of sanctity, lest it work havoc in other men.

This angelic guardianship is something natural, something
normal, as normal as the great powers of the physical cosmos. The
spirits have not received a mission to interfere with man's free
action; they have received a mission to save man from the results
of his own evil deeds as far as is compatible with the higher dictates
of God's justice. When an angel shows his protecting power
manifestly, as when he delivered Peter from the prison, you have a
miraculous intervention which ought not to be taken as the criterion
of the ordinary working of spirit tutelage. There can be miracles
of angelic intervention, as there can be miracles of divine intervention; but they are exceptions; God and his angels work unceasingly for man's welfare.

Illumination of man's mind is the most direct and most constant
effect of the angelic tutelage; according to St Thomas,[3] it is not
too much to say that the human race is kept in mental equilibrium
through the unceasing watchfulness of the good spirits. There is,
in spite of individual aberrations, a sanity of thought in mankind
which makes all men to agree on some universal principles. Would
it not be a beautiful thing to consider such unanimity as the result
of the supervision of the spirits? Certainly Catholic theology would
not be loth to encourage such a view.

Then there is that extremely important office of the protecting
angels to ward off the darkening influence of evil spirits. So far
we have been assuming that spirits are good, but Christian revelation does not allow such optimism to be complete; there are bad
spirits just as there are good spirits, as we shall see in one of the
following sections. An immense amount of angelic work for man's
benefit must be of the defensive kind; man could never know,
unless it were revealed to him, from what evils he has been saved.
The spirits fight for us to a great extent without our knowledge,
their mission is essentially one of guardianship of a lower being,
and it is carried out quite independently of that lower being's
participation or recognition. It is truly a trust, and the spirit is
responsible for the full discharge of that trust to the heavenly Father
by whom it was committed to him.

[1] *S. Theol.*, I, Q. cxiii, art. 1, ad 3.        [2] *Ibid.*, art. 4, ad 3.
[3] *Ibid*, art. 5, ad 2.

So far we have considered angelic guardianship in the life of nature, as one only of the great forces that keep the universe together ; but it is evident that we cannot separate man's higher and supernatural destiny from his natural life ; we are called to the kingdom of heaven, the angels see in us their fellow-participants in the graces of the Holy Ghost, and they have the additional mission of leading us to heaven.

In connection with this supernatural purpose of the spirit tutelage St Thomas makes a few wise remarks which, in a way, justify the common Catholic opinion that each man is under the protection of a separate spirit, that there is no disproportion between the ward and the guardian. Man's destiny being eternal happiness, it is not too much that it should be watched over by one whose nature is unchangeably great. Again, the secrets of grace are the greatest secrets, they are God's personal province, they are the dealings of the adorable Trinity, not *en masse*, but with individual rational creatures ; only God knows the graces that make up the predestination of the elect. It is not astonishing, therefore, St Thomas would say, that individual angels are chosen to watch over human souls which are treated with such preference by God himself. God has messages to communicate to an angel about a definite human being, which are truly the secrets of the divine counsel : " Are they not all ministering spirits sent to minister for them who shall receive the inheritance of salvation ? " [1] St Thomas has a good commentary on these words : " If we think of the last result of the spirit tutelage, which is the receiving of the inheritance, the angelic ministry is effective only in the case of those who receive the inheritance. Nevertheless, it is to be maintained that the ministry of the angels is not denied to other men, although in their case the ministry falls short of its final result, the leading on to salvation. Yet in their case also the ministry of the angels is not without its efficacy as they are kept from many evils."

## § VI: ANGELIC SANCTITY

*Natural perfection*

NOT once in the Scriptures, so full of angelic incidents, do we discover a vestige of moral imperfection in an angel, nor do we ever find that one is rebuked for anything that he does. The angels are perfect in all their ways. Angelic sanctity is, for us Christians, a self-evident fact. Our theology greatly helps our spiritual intuition, and starting from certain clearly proven principles it has uttered beautiful things on the purity of the angels and the eminence of their holiness. What we know concerning the nature of a spirit and what we know about grace stands us in good stead when we come to look at the lives of our heavenly brothers. As spirits they can never do anything by halves, they cannot be

[1] *S. Theol.*, I, Q. cxiii, art. 5, ad 1.

imperfect, they cannot act remissly, the whole energy of their intellect and will is given to every one of their movements in the ethical order—if one may speak of ethics in connection with spirits. Venial sin is quite unthinkable in angelic morality; it is easier for us to understand a total collapse of the angelic will than a partial deflection; a spirit may choose a wrong end, but he could not choose it with less than the whole impetuosity of his nature.

Bearing in mind the excellency of a spirit nature, our best theologians have said that, in its natural sphere, on its own plane, so to speak, a purely spiritual being cannot fail either in mind or in will, but it could fail with regard to things that are above it; in other words, with regard to the supernatural. This point we shall elaborate more completely when we come to speak of angelic sin; for the present let us feel happy in the thought that the angels have not in themselves any weakness, any temptation, any of that division between higher and lower motives which is found in us. They have not the conflicts of any kind of concupiscence, they have no doubts, they are not in danger of forming precipitate judgements; and all this in virtue of the very principles of their nature.

But it is a matter of Catholic faith that the spirits have been raised *Elevation to* to the supernatural order, that they received grace, and that they *supernatural order* possess sanctifying grace and the gifts of the Holy Ghost just like the Christian man here on earth. There is not in them the division between flesh and spirit, between a higher and a lower nature, but there is in them the division between the natural and the supernatural. They have been raised above themselves for a destiny greater than the spirit destiny; they are meant to behold God face to face in Beatific Vision—an end so lofty that no spirit, however excellent, is capable of it without a gratuitous infusion of those higher qualities called grace. Grace with the angels, then, could not be a medicine to heal the wounds of a fall, as it is with man to so large an extent, nor could it be a help to powers weak and anæmic in themselves—spirits have no wounds, spirits are never weak— but grace with angels is essentially the lifting up of a perfect being to a still higher plane, the initiation of a created mind into the secrets of the Uncreated Mind; and without grace even the supreme spirit would be incapable of that communion with God which constitutes the life of charity with the Father, the Son, and the Holy Ghost. So we have to assume at once that, with regard to the final and supernatural union with God, the spirits are in the same position as man. It may be said that spirits, both discarnate and incarnate, are equidistant from the final goal of Beatific Vision, and that the angels, equally with us, are in need of the grace of God to reach communion with him. There is, therefore, at once brought about, through the supernatural, a true community of condition between man and the spirits. Abysmal as may be the differences of minds and wills between man and spirit, and between the spirits themselves, the differences disappear, are as nothing, in presence of that true infinitude—the Vision of God. Just as in astronomy there are·no real differences when distances are said to be infinite ; the surface of our earth may appear extremely uneven to us who dwell upon it, there are the high mountains and the deep ravines, but looked at from the fixed stars such unevenness is as if non-existent.

**Trial of the angels**    Though there is a radical difference between the natural and the supernatural even in the spirits, it is the more common opinion that all spirits were created with the gift of grace in them already ; this would only mean that between the production of nature and the infusion of grace there was no time-interval, but there is always the profound and essential differentiation between the two elements, nature and grace. The spirits were not created in the clear Vision of God ; this was to be the goal towards which they had to aim, the reward of their fidelity ; they were created in grace outside the Vision of God, with the invitation to rise up to that supreme Vision ; they were created, says St Thomas, not in the heaven of the Trinity, but in the empyrean heaven ; from the one they were expected to ascend to the other. The *caelum sanctae Trinitatis* [1] is the heaven of the clear Vision of God face to face. The angels did not find themselves in that heaven to begin with ; they found themselves in that other heaven which may be called the supremest place of the natural cosmos, whilst the heaven of the Vision is that glorious kingdom which has been prepared specifically for the elect from the beginning of the world : " Then shall the king say to them on his right hand : Come, ye blessed of my Father, possess you the kingdom prepared for you from the foundation of the world." [2] We say that the angels merited eternal life as truly as man merits eternal life, through correspondence with that supernatural grace that was in them, for the spirits as well as man had their day of trial, they were wayfarers between their earth and their heaven, between the *caelum empyreum* and the *caelum sanctae Trinitatis*. These principles are certain. How long did their trial last ? Here we must leave imagination alone. Let us take it for granted that whatever element of duration there was in the angelic wayfaring it amounted in worth and spirit intensity to the value of the longest human life. Theologians would say that the first act of the angels was self-consciousness, the second act a full co-operation with the grace that was in them, and the third act the clear Vision or, shall we say, the flight from the *caelum empyreum* to the *caelum sanctae Trinitatis*. Only let us remember that centuries of human activity would pale before the energy of that single act of the spirits between creation and glorification.

**Grace proportioned to nature**    We have already spoken of the profound inequalities of the angelic natures ; we said that they were an ever-ascending hierarchy of

[1] *S. Theol.*, I, Q. lxi, art. 4, ad 3.     [2] Matt. xxv 34.

spiritual substances. The question arises, then, whether grace and the supernatural endowment were meted out to them according to the capacity of their natures, so that an angel of a higher grade in nature is also of a higher grade in grace and of a higher grade in glory. This we may readily grant: a Cherub is greater than an inferior spirit in all his endowments, both natural and supernatural. Human beings are all of the same nature, but they receive grace in a variety of measures ; some are given one talent, some five. We may say that with man nature is not the measure of grace ; let us ever bear in mind that one human being, Mary, the Mother of God, has received grace more abundantly than any other creature. With the spirits, however, there seems to be a fitness that grace should exactly follow the perfection of nature. Men, though of one nature, work with various intensities ; spirits, on the contrary, work at all times to the full extent of their energies, there can be no intermittencies, no relaxations, there can be no progress—in the human sense of the word—so it seems the wiser thing in theology to concede to the vaster mind and the vaster will an ampler manifestation of the counsels of God's supernatural order.

After these exact theorisings on angelic sanctity we could give our imagination free scope and let it enjoy the spectacle of that inexpressibly great holiness, but whatever we could imagine would fall short of the reality.

The vision of Isaias is the greatest imaginative presentment of angelic sanctity :

" In the year that King Ozias died, I saw the Lord sitting upon a throne high and elevated : and his train filled the temple. Upon it stood the seraphims : the one had six wings, and the other had six wings : with two they covered his face, and with two they covered his feet, and with two they flew. And they cried one to another, and said : Holy, Holy, Holy, the Lord God of Hosts, all the earth is full of his glory. And the lintels of the doors were moved at the voice of him that cried : and the house was filled with smoke. And I said : Woe is me, because I have held my peace ; because I am a man of unclean lips, and I dwell in the midst of a people that hath unclean lips, and I have seen with my eyes the King the Lord of hosts. And one of the seraphims flew to me : and in his hand was a live coal, which he had taken with the tongs off the altar. And he touched my mouth, and said : Behold this hath touched thy lips, and thy iniquities shall be taken away, and thy sin shall be cleansed. And I heard the voice of the Lord, saying : Whom shall I send, and who shall go for us ? And I said : Lo, here am I. Send me." [1]

There is, however, one aspect of angelic sanctity which we might *Obedience of* almost call its moral side : it is expressed generally as the obedience *the angels* of the angels—more truly it might be called their " order " ; that the spirits keep the order in which they are created, carry out the missions which are entrusted to them, that all their mighty activities are an unceasing dependence on God's will ; above all, that they accept the kingship of a nature lower than their own. They have

[1] Isa. vi 1-8.

not rebelled against the exaltation of the human nature in Christ Jesus, and the Catholic Church never ceases to speak of the Mother of God as Queen of the angels. This observance of the order established by God is the true angelic virtue, the one thing in which they might fail; it might even be called their temptation, and if the temptation be overcome, it is their victory. That there was some such victory is evident from more than one passage in the Scriptures; angels are considered as having come out of some great spiritual war triumphant in the moral order:

"And there was a great battle in heaven: Michael and his angels fought with the dragon, and the dragon fought, and his angels. And they prevailed not: neither was their place found any more in heaven. And that great dragon was cast out, that old serpent, who is called the devil and Satan, who seduceth the whole world. And he was cast unto the earth: and his angels were thrown down with him." [1]

Fidelity to God over a great, a mightily debated issue seems to be an essential portion of angelic sanctity.

## § VII: SPIRIT SIN

*Satan not created evil*

WHEN Christ speaks of the reward of the elect he represents it in the form of an invitation to take possession of the kingdom that had been prepared from the foundation of the world.[2] The chastisement of the wicked he speaks of as everlasting fire prepared for the devil and his angels.[3] This terrible penal arrangement is not said to be, like the gracious provision for merit, *a constitutione mundi*, from the foundation of the world. Satan and his followers were not created evil; there was no thought in God's first providence of an *ignis aeternus*. No Christian doubts the existence of evil powers in the spirit world, but no Christian considers those evil powers to be anything but a miscarriage, through the creature's act, of the Creator's first plan. There is no evil principle having, so to speak, an estate by itself; all evil is an apostasy of a being that was primarily good; all evil is a bad use of the good things of God.

It is an extremely difficult point of theology to explain sin in connection with spirits. If our Scriptures were not so full of the activities of evil spirits the temptation might arise to regard all wickedness as a human phenomenon. The sinfulness of man is a thing of daily experience; we can explain it through man's composite nature, through man's passions and difficulties; man is morally a sinner, as socially he is a savage; both sin and barbarity are patient of explanation. But how shall we arrive at any satisfactory explanation of spirit lapses? If we regarded spirits only as more agile forms of human beings, then we might give them passions and instincts whose workings, sooner or later, would entangle them in difficult positions. But spirits are perfect, at any rate those spirits

---

[1] Apoc. xii 7-9.    [2] Matt. xxv 34.    [3] Matt. xxv 41.

in which Catholic theology believes ; it is their very essence to be perfect in nature ; we cannot think of any sort of allurement which might deflect them from their path.

We might, as a first attempt at explanation, give this reason for a possible lapse in the spirit world : that spirits, since they are created beings, are finite beings, and that no finite being can claim absolute immunity from every possible error of mind or will. In this universality the principle may be considered as the remote cause of sin in all but God himself ; yet this does not work in Catholic theology as a cause of the fall of the angels, except as a most vague explanation. A spirit has no ignorances, has no weakness of mind ; his nature is so perfect that there is nothing for which he can wish or to which he can aspire ; though he is finite, he is complete in his sphere.

With great wisdom St Thomas has discarded every sort of motive *No spirit* for the angelic lapse that is not entirely spiritual, that savours more *can err in the* of imagination than of intelligence. He teaches with steady per- *natural sphere* sistence that no spirit in his natural sphere can transgress or err in any way. But if the spirit be taken, so to speak, out of his natural order and placed in another, a higher order—the supernatural order—then there is the possibility of a refusal ; the spirit may refuse to accept or to hold something that is above his order ; he may, in fact, rebel against the order of God. This is the only tenable theological explanation of the fall of the angels, and I must develop it more amply.

Through the supernatural a spirit is taken out of his sphere into *Rejection* a higher one ; but this higher sphere means essentially a community *of the* of life with all other spirits thus favoured ; it means community *supernatural* with lower spirits ; it means community with man himself. The *order* higher grace is indeed the more excellent gift, but it is also the more universal gift. The natural greatness of the angel is a glory which has no equal ; it is a singular perfection which is without a rival. A spirit may thus choose to enter into communion with the super- natural or to remain entirely in his own sphere, preferring his own natural excellency to the communion of the universal family of God. St Thomas says that some spirits chose the second alter- native ; they preferred their natural glory in its isolation to the community of the supernatural charity ; and this is the fall of the angels. It is pride—because they elected excellency without refer- ence to the more excellent good ; it is rebellion—because the Will of God was that they should accept the supernatural ; it is envy —not in the sense of the dark human passion, but in the sense of an opposition to a holy thing, the grace of God. All other sins must be taken more or less metaphorically in the case of the fallen angels. When it is said that Satan desired to be like unto God we could not take it as a reasonable view that he aspired to be as great as the divine Creator ; no spirit could be capable of such folly ;

but as St Thomas puts it : " In this wise did Satan wish unlawfully to be like unto God, because he desired as the final goal of happiness that which was within the power of his own nature, turning away his desires from the supernatural happiness which is obtained through the grace of God. Or it might be said also that if he desired as his last end that resemblance with God which comes from grace, he wanted to possess it through the power of his nature, not through the divine help according to God's order." [1] All this is very clear in a way ; it is opposition to the supernatural order which constitutes the *malitia angelica*, it is spirit rebellion. It is said sometimes that the mystery of the Incarnation was revealed to the spirits, and that their unwillingness to adore the God-man was their fall. This would only be another expression of the same doctrine that angels fell through a deliberate opposition to the supernatural, as the Incarnation is the highest phase of the supernatural.

*Effects of spirit sin*    So we may leave this matter in that wise moderation in which it was left by St Thomas : " In this way did the angel sin, because he turned his free will to his own good without reference to the (higher) rule of the divine Will." [2] The great theologian thinks that such a sin is compatible with complete knowledge of means and end, principles and results, and that such a sin can be found in a being devoid at his creation of all perverse inclination and of all passion. It is essentially a free election of a definite state, and it is an irrevocable election. All other perversities which are attributed to Satan come from this free election, for it is not a passive state of personal excellency which Satan has chosen, it is of necessity an active opposition to the higher order. Thus every other sin is truthfully predicated of the evil spirits, because with every means in their power do they wage war against the supernatural order ; they are the great disturbers of the divine order. Satan always sins, Satan is mendacious, Satan is a murderer ; and he incites man to the foulest sins, not because of any pleasure he himself could have in the works of the flesh, but because the works of the flesh render man unfit for the grace of God and exclude him from the supernatural order. It is quite in keeping with all we have said when we hear the Scriptures stating that it is Satan's chief occupation to deceive man, deceiving him in the most subtle manner and transforming himself into an angel of light. The difference between natural excellency and supernatural grace may be called a subtle difference, and man's great deception lies in this : that through the splendour of natural gifts he is led to despise the grace of God.

It is a simple consequence of all that has been said to maintain that the evil angels keep all their natural gifts without any diminution ; they even keep their order ; they remain in the state which they elected, yet they are banished completely from the supernatural order ; and as the supernatural order is the one which

[1] *S. Theol.*, I, Q. lxiii, art. 3.    [2] *S. Theol.*, I, Q. xliii, art. 1, ad 4.

must ultimately triumph, Satan and his followers are truly cast out into eternal darkness, into the fire which will be their prison for ever. They are darkened in their intellects with regard to the mysteries of grace, with regard to the counsels of God's free will, but not with regard to things which constitute the glories of the natural universe ; the knowledge of the natural universe is part of their very being, and they could not lose it without losing their identity.

In the foregoing considerations we have spoken as if the super-natural were offered to the spirits, when some accepted it and some refused. In the preceding section we said that the more probable opinion is that all spirits were created in the supernatural, so they were given no option as to its acceptance or its refusal. This, of course, does not alter the worth of the theological opinion. Though the spirits were created in the supernatural, they were free to remain in it or to forsake it, because it was something essentially added unto their spirit-estate, not something inherent in their very being. The demons are called apostate spirits, because they fell away from the vocation and the grace to which they had been called by the Creator ; they did not persevere in their supernatural election as did the good angels. It is obviously a thing self-evident in theology that when once a created spirit has been admitted to the clear Vision of God all falling away becomes impossible. The spirits that lapsed had never attained to that Beatific Vision.

## § VIII: EVIL SPIRITS AND MAN

It could not be said that the spirit tutelage, of which through a wise *Demons* dispensation of Providence man is the object, has a direct counter- *tempt by* part in the sad influences of the fallen spirits on the destinies of the *divine* *permission* human race. We are not in reality standing, as it were, between two spirits, a good one on our right and a bad one on our left ; this would be an exaggerated notion of the activities of the reprobate spirits among the children of men. The angelic tutelage is a divine ordinance, directly willed by God ; the temptations of the demons are not, of course, a divine ordinance, they belong to what is called the permissive providence of God ; he allows them, but he does not order them. With this reservation made, we may go very far in our belief in the reality of demoniac power in the world.

To begin with, we must bear in mind that whatever may be the explanation of the presence of the evil spirits on our planet, such a presence was not originally brought about by the sin of man. The devil tempted man when he was yet in a state of innocence ; the evil spirit was on this earth before human sin had ever been committed. Man's sins have strengthened Satan's position in this world, but it could not be said that they have created it. The presence of the Evil One on this earth in the days of man's innocence is an insoluble mystery.

*Evil spirits and material things*    Nothing is expressed more often and more explicitly by the Roman Church in her various exorcisms and blessings than the idea that evil spirits abide in material things, from which they are driven out by the Church's triumphant power of sanctifying and consecrating the visible elements which are the basis of human life. The human body itself may be the dwelling of an evil spirit : this might be called the silent occupation of this earth by Satan, a thing full of mystery and independent in its origin of man's consent to Satan's evil suggestions. But there is also the more manifest presence of these dark beings. It would be temerarious to belittle what the early Fathers said of the power of the demons in the pagan temples, in the idols, in the groves and caverns where heathen rites were performed. The demons were loud in their utterances through the mouth of the idols, and many are the incidents in early Church history which prove that the pagan nations were accustomed to exhibitions of unseen powers which could never be considered as powers of light. Then we have, through all the centuries of the Christian spiritual warfare, most authentic records of manifest activities of the demons. The servants of God are persecuted by fierce powers, visibly, physically, in open daylight, as it were. The best-known case in modern hagiography is the persecution which the holy Curé d'Ars suffered in his body from his spiritual adversaries.

*Temptation to sin*    The more recondite temptations of Satan which concern man's religious life hold a middle place between that silent occupation of this earth by Satan, and the tumultuous showing forth of his power in cases of possession or obsession. Satan tempts man to sin, not manifestly but secretly, in such a wise that it is not possible for man to discover whether an evil prompting comes from his own nature or from the suggestion of an alien spirit with a perverted will. Such discernment demands great spiritual gifts, one might even say it requires a special charisma which is given only to few. Indeed, it is not necessary for us to know whether an evil propensity is caused by an outside spirit, or is the result of our own evil inheritances ; the avoidance of sin is the one thing that matters, and that is always within our power, through God's grace and the assistance of the holy spirits. On the whole, it is more in conformity with Catholic tradition to consider the Christian, with his glorious spiritual armour, as being himself formidable to the devils rather than as living in fear and terror of those beings of darkness. " Give not place to the devil " [1] is an apostolic precept which reveals the true psychology of diabolical temptations in our spiritual life. Place is given to the devil through any voluntary deflection from the moral order ; the evil spirit enters into our life through those weaknesses of which we are guilty through our own carelessness. It is as if infidelity to divine grace could not remain a merely human

[1] Eph. iv 27.

affair, it has prolongations which man does not intend, but which are unavoidable consequences. We are, in the strong words of one of the Collects,[1] exposed to the diabolical contagion (*diabolica contagia*). The devil's influence on the human masses is no doubt much more powerful than the seduction of individual men, masses are more liable to suggestion, and all we know of mass-psychology makes us fear that, outside the Christian people, Satan's influence on mankind is a very real fact. The devils are, in St Paul's words, " the rulers of the world of this darkness." [2]  I do not mention here that kind of bondage to Satan in which mankind found itself through sin, and from which it has been released through the Cross of Christ, for this aspect of demoniac power belongs rightly to the mystery of Redemption.

Man's intercourse with the demons is a thing which has no *Human* counterpart in his relationship with the good spirits. With a good *intercourse* spirit we never hold any intercourse which is not perfectly in the *with devils* divine order, through the very definition of angelic sanctity. As demons are rebellious spirits, the question may pertinently be put whether it is in the power of man to get into touch with those wicked, but mighty ones, for some selfish end ; one would naturally ask : has the devil ever answered man when man has tried to approach him, and to hold intercourse with him ? Dark magic has always had a fascination for a certain class of minds, but no doubt most of its claims, if not all of them, belong to the realm of fables. Consulting the devil has always been held to be one of the darkest sins which man can commit.

Spiritism of the modern type is a more serious, a more alarming *Spiritism* matter. It does not belong directly to either angelology or demonology, as the modern spiritist claims to hold intercourse with disembodied human spirits ; however, there is a strong presumption that spiritistic phenomena, when they are not impostures, are things of evil origin ; viewed from that angle, spiritism is only a province of demonology. I am aware, of course, that all modern spiritists repudiate dealings with the dark powers of the unseen world. They claim a purity of intention in their efforts to get into touch with the invisible world, which, no doubt, is sincere in many cases. They say that they want to learn from the spirits the things of the spirits ; that they want to come into contact only with the holy ones on the other side. A spiritism thus refined is a most seductive thing, and to refute it, to show its illegality or its immorality, is not possible, to my thinking, apart from revelation, and unless we profess our faith in the guiding authority of the Church. All other arguments against spiritism are based on certain accidental, evil by-products of the practice, or they take for granted the very thing that has to be proved—that spiritism is an intercourse with fallen angels. We have here a first-rate instance of the

[1] XVII Sunday after Pentecost.                    [2] Eph. vi 12.

beneficent meaning of the guidance of a living Church; it enables us to see clearly, where so many are deceived and led in captivity by the spirit of error who transforms himself into an angel of light. Nothing is sadder than to see the numbers of well-meaning men and women who are held in thraldom by the fascination of contemporary spiritism, for we, as Catholics, know that they have become the playthings of the spirits who have been liars from the beginning. The circumstance that they are ignorant of the ethical perverseness of the practice does not in the least diminish its evil; they have become the victims of a terrible conspiracy of wickedness in high places, from which we escape unscathed through our loyalty to the guidance of the living Church. As for the Catholic who will not listen to that guidance in these most dangerous matters, I do not see that a merely speculative exposition of the evil of spiritism could possibly have any influence to save him from the worst excesses of unhealthy curiosity.

It may be said that the Catholic Church has her own spiritism, a thing full of health and life; it is her belief that every soul in the state of grace is in spiritual communion with every other soul thus privileged, and that this communion goes beyond mortal life. The Christian here on earth has a most intimate affinity with all elect spirits, angelic and human, in the world to come. The Church holds very definite and very practical views as to the mode in which spirits may approach each other. This profound doctrine is merely a part of the larger truth of the mystical Body of Christ; and we may add that deeper knowledge of the disembodied state into which the spirit of man enters at death will facilitate the intelligence of the Catholic standpoint. Readers may be referred to other portions of Catholic theology for these absorbing matters.[1]

## § IX: THE SOCIETY OF THE HEAVENLY CITIZENS

*Angels and man's eternal happiness* IT is evident by all the laws of spiritual life that angelic beings must be, in one way or another, a great element in the constitution of man's eternal happiness. The bliss of the elect will be essentially this—to possess all truth, to be in contact with all reality, to see all beauty. To see the angels, to behold them, must of necessity constitute a source of happiness greater than anything which the visible world could afford; in fact, it is the supreme created source of happiness; God himself, clearly seen in the Beatific Vision, being the uncreated source of happiness. To be with the angels, to see them in their glory, is a most legitimate desire in the heart of man, and the saints of God have often given utterance to such a longing. We must always keep alive within us that essentially Catholic principle of life, that the possession of the supreme Goodness, God himself, never destroys the appetite for created goodness,

[1] *Cf.* Essay xxxi, pp. 1118-1122.

but, on the contrary, enhances it ; to see God face to face produces in the minds of the elect a new capacity to see him in his creatures, and where is he seen to greater advantage than in the world of angels, which mirrors back, with an almost infinite power of radiation, the glory of the invisible God ? Moreover, through the communion of supernatural grace man is allied to the angels by the bond of charity, he is not a foreigner but he is a fellow-citizen. There will be this truest exchange of love between man and the heavenly spirits : man, besides beholding the angels in their glory, will hold intercourse with them as citizens of the same kingdom, as the children of the same Father. This intercourse with the heavenly spirits will be the last thing in created love ; greater love than that there could not be except man's communion with God himself.

There is, however, something deeper than this association with *Elect of* the angels in vision and love. This association would be possible *mankind to* if the whole human race—I mean the elect human race—remained *angels* in its own sphere, on its plane, lower than the angelic world. The human race could be considered as the boundary-line of the whole world of the elect and as its lowest portion. Yet such is not the traditional view of Catholic theology. There is quite a volume of opinion which considers man's association with the angels to be of a more intimate kind, and of a much profounder dispensation. The elect of the human race are believed to be assumed into the very hierarchy of the angels, into the ranks of the Cherubim and Seraphim and all the other orders ; the elect of the human race will not be only the outside fringe of the spirit world, they will, on the contrary, be shining stars in every one of the spirit planes. It is Catholic tradition that the elect of the human race are destined to take the place of the fallen spirits, to fill up the gap made by the apostasies of the rebellious angels. This tradition profoundly modifies man's relationship to the angels ; it puts him on a footing of equality with those mighty beings which is the most astonishing of all spiritual exaltations. We could not say with any degree of certainty whether all the elect of the human race are meant to take the place of fallen spirits, but it would seem that no doubt is permissible with regard to God's intention of filling the vacant places in the spirit hierarchies with human beings. God will multiply his graces, and prepare his saints with such power of predestination that not one of the high thrones of spirit life will be found vacant on the day of the consummation of his mighty plan.

That there will be more than mere association of men and angels in the glory of eternity is clear from our Lord's words in speaking of the elect at the resurrection : " Neither can they die any more : for they are equal to the angels and are the children of God, being the children of the resurrection." [1] This equality

---

[1] Luke xx 36.

means more than a mere similarity, it means a community of privilege which makes of the human elect and the spirit elect one society. This equality is entirely based on grace. Human nature will always remain what it is, vastly inferior to the angelic nature; but such is the power of grace that the inequality of nature is bridged over, and that an elect from the human race may truly become, in all literalness of language, the equal of the highest angel, and that consequently he will be vastly superior to other angels of lower rank.

In this matter, as in most of our philosophising on spirit-issues, we must be satisfied with the general principle; detail, from the very nature of the case, is not possible to us. Thus we do not know in what proportion the spirits fell or in what proportion they passed into the unchanging glory of the Blessed Vision; we do not know, either, with any degree of certainty, what direction that great cleavage in the heavenly world took when there was that sliding away from God of so many spirits. Did angels of every order fall away? Was there a preponderance of rebellion in any given hierarchy? Did many more fall in the lower than in the higher orders? Such questions cannot be answered with any degree of certainty. St Thomas is inclined to think that only a minority of the spirits fell away, because, he remarks wisely, to fall away is, in a spirit, against his nature, and things that are contrary to nature happen usually more by way of exception than by way of generality. It would seem, however, that the supremest spirit fell, and that this mighty prince of light was the cause of the apostasy of many. It is generally considered that Lucifer was that highest spirit who became the Prince of Darkness. We are not concerned here directly with demonology; our scope is a more consoling one. Whatever height a fallen spirit may have occupied in the scale of being, it is possible for the grace of God to raise man to that height, so that even the throne vacated by Lucifer himself may become the congenital inheritance of some holy human soul.

We need not maintain, of course, as already insinuated, that all human beings who are saved through the grace of Christ are meant to be raised to the angelic hierarchies. Cajetan,[1] the stern theologian of Reformation times, thinks that the children who die and are saved in virtue of baptismal grace, without any personal merit, will remain below the angelic order of election; they will be the true human race in its own setting; they will resemble the angels without being equal to them. Then again there are those human beings who will be absolutely superior, by the very laws of their predestination, to every angelic order; the blessed Mother of God is certainly one such creature.

The all-pervading principle is this: that grace is greater than nature, greater even than the highest spirit nature, and its scope is vaster than the vastest world.

[1] In *S. Theol.*, I, Q. cviii, art. 8.

As a confirmation of the doctrine of human substitution for the lost spirits we may quote St Paul's text, 1 Cor. vi 3 : " Know you not that we shall judge angels ? how much more things of this world ? " The Apostle evidently alludes to the great judgement at the end of time ; judgement will be given to the saints, and they will execute it, not only on this world, but even on the angels—the fallen angels, no doubt. This power of judgement would naturally presuppose, not only equality, but superiority of rank.

In the Western Church virginity is considered to be more particularly the angelic life amongst men, whilst in the Eastern Church the angelic life is more commonly identified with the renouncing of temporal possessions. The striving after higher perfection, after the angelic life in all its aspects, is, in Christian spirituality, a preparation for the higher ranks amongst the angels in the world to come ; the martyrs, also, are those who will be found worthy to have their names confessed by the Son of God before the holy angels. Whatever heroism there is amongst Christians in the days of their earthly pilgrimage it gives them a right to a reward which again is fitly expressed by the word " throne." " To him that shall overcome, I will give to sit with me in my throne : as I also have overcome, and am set down with my Father in his throne." [1]

ANSCAR VONIER, O.S.B.

[1] Apoc. iii 21.

# MAN AND HIS DESTINY

THIS volume already contains essays that speak of God and of the Angels.  Man and his Destiny come third.

This order was demanded by respect: for it would be unfitting in a work like this one to speak of God in any but the first place; and even the Angels, being of a nature so superior to man's, have a just claim to be approached before Man is.

Yet though this order be that of Nature, and indeed of time —for while God is in any case eternal, we hold that the Angels were created before man was—yet it is not the order in which we actually know things.  We are conscious of ourselves and of other limited objects before we know anything of God: time, experience and most probably some intellectual guidance are needed before we become aware that God exists, and that he must be thought of in such and such a way.  Still less are we directly conscious of the Angels; and though we might feel it very probable that such beings existed, and though we might shrink from the extreme arrogance of asserting that human nature exhausted all the possibilities of existence in itself, and though the fancy of every age of the world's history has proved how natural it is to surmise that the universe is peopled with invisible inhabitants, yet the Catholic knows that there are Angels because he is told so by the Authority he recognises as legitimate.  On the other hand, he knows, without the possibility of doubting, that he exists himself; and he observes that there are other beings like himself round about him; and while he is sure he is not numerically the same as they are, he cannot but class them along with himself under one heading—Man.

Indeed, at the root of all human philosophy is the double perception, that I exist, and that I am not the same as what surrounds me.  It is largely because I observe that I am not the same, and that I *clash* to some extent with my surroundings, resist them and am resisted by them, that I develop an adequate consciousness of my own existence: but this self-consciousness was involved in every act by which I became properly aware of other things, and the proposition, " I exist," is one of those few propositions which I cannot so much as deny without asserting it.

Now it is not long before a man begins to ask himself two questions—(1) *What* am I? (and generalising, What is Man?); and (2) What am I *for*? (and generalising, What is the Purpose of Man's Existence, if any?).

I am inclined to think that in the concrete it is the second of these two questions that most haunts mankind. Illogical as it may be to ask what I exist " for," till I have become clear as to what " I " am, men are quite apt to take themselves for granted, but by no means to take their destiny for granted. If you want to see a thoroughly haunted man, you will find him in the one who cannot see what he is " for," and is tormented by the surmise that he may not be " for " anything ; that life is quite pointless ; that there is no purpose anywhere ; that he is what he is owing to a mixture of fluke and fate, and that after a meaningless spell of irksome years he will relapse into the general stock of existence and be thrown up thence again, who knows why, who knows when, like a bubble in a scum. Few men have chilled me more than the one who said to me : " I work, because I suppose I've got to live. But what am I living for ? To work again to-morrow." That in itself is one of those sentences which, once heard, can never be forgotten. " I work, in order to live : I live, in order to work again to-morrow." It is horrible to an intelligent man to observe that everything in, say, the factory or workshop where he works has a *purpose*—windows ; ventilators—save himself. Do not say that he *has* a " purpose," that is, to do his particular bit of the total job. He knows that a hundred men could do it as well as he : it is not *he* as he that matters ; he could be dismissed to-morrow, and very often is, and forthwith replaced : he is a name, a number, a "hand." Hence he cannot see why *he* exists, and he resents it.

Now in an earlier essay it has been shown that God created man and all things else. It follows that man *was* created with a purpose, for God cannot act without one. God, it has been shown, is the perfect and ever active intelligence, and cannot therefore create unintelligently, nor in a moment of distraction. But to act without purpose is the very sign of unintelligence—the man who acts always without knowing why, is off his head : the one who does so intermittently may be charitably supposed to be " in the moon " unless he does it too often, and then you begin to have your doubts even about *him*. Moreover, God cannot create man for a purpose which man cannot sufficiently *know* (for you cannot do what you have no sufficient knowledge of), nor for one which, however well he may know it, he cannot possibly carry out. For it would be un-wisdom of the worst, to make a man for a purpose, and forthwith render the carrying out of that purpose impossible. God cannot thus contradict himself. And finally, this purpose cannot be a mean or petty one, let alone a bad one, for the Infinite Goodness cannot purpose anything evil, nor even mean. Therefore, even before we begin this essay, we have the right to assert that there lies before Man, and before each man, a Destiny that he should aim at fulfilling, that he can fulfil, and that will prove to be a high and noble one.

I need but add here that what God purposes should be accomplished, he wishes to be accomplished : and when his wish concerns an intelligent creature such as man is, God makes his wish known to him, and this amounts to " calling " him. Therefore you may at once declare that man, and each man, has a " vocation " and must have. But since man depends wholly upon God, he is under a total obligation to God, and therefore not only will it be good for him to obey God's call, but he *ought* so to obey it, and would do wrong were he consciously to neglect or to defy it. But since upon the fulfilment of his vocation depends the whole of his well-being and his happiness, his non-fulfilment of it implies his ill-being and his misery. And finally, since God does not and cannot create a " world " chaotically, but creates within it an order (and indeed it is " order " that makes it into a " world "), and calls men to play their part in perfecting that order, it follows that if man does not fulfil his vocation, he introduces disorder into the world in general, and into human society in particular. Therefore it is of extreme importance both for each man and for society at large that God's purpose should be fulfilled. Social misery and dislocation, as well as personal woe, attend upon its non-fulfilment.

All this you might deduce merely from reading the foregoing essays : I wish now to get closer to the subject by studying man himself and in himself.

## § II : DUAL UNITY IN MAN

THIS is not an essay of general philosophy, nor even of psychology, but one that is meant to explain in what way the Catholic Church looks at man's destiny. Still, a minimum of explanation must be offered as to what she holds that man is ; and enough ought to be stated to show that this is not out of keeping with what man, without any appeal to outside authority, is conscious that he is.

*The evidence of consciousness*    Whatever else a man may think about himself, he is conscious of himself as *urged* interiorly to certain things. He experiences the urge to preserve himself—to extend himself—to reproduce himself. For my part, I consider all these " urges " to be aspects of one and the same vital impetus or force : but it is convenient to think of them as three. Quite without argument, the living creature feels the necessity to eat—to drink—to defend itself by throwing up its arm and so forth when attacked. But it does not want just to remain as it is : it tries to be *more*—it tends to " get," to possess. And when it has got a thing, it so identifies the thing with itself, that its possession becomes somehow part of itself—one says one has " extended one's personality " over this or that. If someone takes away what is mine, I feel that *I* am what is attacked and injured. I need a certain amount of outside apparatus to be, even, my proper self. Finally, there is the urge towards self-reproduction :

a man feels deep within him that alone he is incomplete : it is not " good " for man to be alone : he requires a mate, and the natural result of this association of two lives is a child, and a home. When I am alive, living with wife and child in a home, then the fulness of my human nature has been acquired. In any case, then, you observe that man is imperfect at first : he strains *towards* something : he has a destiny.

I next observe that all these urges or instincts admit of a " too much " and " too little." As a rule it is the " too much " that is noticeable. A man may allow his instinct for self-preservation so to master him that he cannot stop himself eating, though he knows that the food he likes is bad for him in large quantities—and if " gluttony " in this sense is on the whole observed in older men, so that the goutier an old man is, the more he is sure to want to eat rich foods and to drink port, the instinct for drink does not wait for old age before it starts to be a nuisance in very many lives. Quite young men may let themselves become unable to resist so much as the smell of drink, when the door of a public-house they are passing swings open, but in they go. Others cannot resist the craving to get, to take. The glittering trinket fascinates them, and they pocket it. If you are poor, this is called stealing. If you are rich and important, they call it kleptomania ; if you are a politician, it is called " extending your sphere of influence." But it comes back to the fact that you cannot now keep your hands off things, be they yours or not. And everybody knows how the sexual urge can so increase within a man as to make him, as they say, a sexual maniac. All this means that instincts can get out of hand, and may master you instead of serving you : you may become their victims and their slaves.

But now—what is this " you " who should master and who may succumb to instincts ? Are not your instincts " you " ? Part, at any rate, of you ? It is *I* who want to eat, to get, to mate. Am I then two " *I*'s " ? No. I say : " *I* must not let *myself* eat sugar when *I* have diabetes ; drink the fifth, tenth, fifteenth glass that I should like to : fall in love with Mrs. So-and-So." " *I* must not let *myself* . . . ."

I see then very clearly that I am somehow double—there is in *Sense and* me something which is " I " which yet has not to allow something *thought* else, which is " I," to act always according to the instinct of the moment, but must say to the " instinctive self "—" No. Not just now : later. Not so-and-so—someone else. Not so much : not so little : not like that : not at all ! " This at least suggests that the element in me which gives these orders is the more important, the more dignified and to-be-attended-to, of the partners.

Now—still speaking roughly and without entering into details or subtleties—I can observe that this " instinctive self " resides in, or quite simply *is* my body. Nothing will ever induce men *to* think that they haven't got bodies. I shall always say : " My head aches : my back hurts : I have sprained my ankle." And so far as instincts go, this is where they reside. It is my body that requires food and drink : clothes and material comfort : the sexual life. And it is *not* a bodily thing that tells my body to do what it doesn't want to and not to do what it does want to—*e.g.*, to get up and dress when " I " want to stay in bed : not to drink another glass when " I " want to drink another. Say I am honestly very thirsty, and it is hot, and beer is accessible. Left to itself, my instinctive " I " would fling itself on that drink and swallow it and be unable to act otherwise. But a *thought*, as we say, occurs to me—" I know beer makes me sleepy : my business rival is just coming to discuss a plan—I shall need all my wits about me. I daren't risk drinking." I still am thirsty : the flagon still is handy : I none the less don't touch it, for a thought has intervened. And if there is still something " material " about a business rival, a sleepy brain, and a financial transaction, you can think of something still more " abstract "—for example, that the beer isn't mine and that it would be stealing to take it and that stealing is wrong. The notion, then, of wrong, attended to, judged more important than bodily pleasure, used as a motive, comes in to check my bodily instinct and its natural sequel—action. I already begin to see pretty clearly that these two elements that make me up—these two coefficients—are, one of them bodily, one of them not. Examine them now a little more closely.

Here is my body with its senses and instincts. It sees, tastes, touches particular objects—round, square, red, blue things : hard or soft things : sweet or sour things. It hears a shout, a whisper, first one sound and then another. Also it is my palate and my tongue and my throat that are soothed or disgusted with food : and it is my system of internal organs that have to deal with the food when I have eaten it. It is my body too that exhibits the cravings I have mentioned, especially that of appetite for what suits it, and shrinking from what harms it. When a fly flicks up to my eye, I blink without waiting to argue about it : a baby makes by instinct for its mother's milk and cries if it cannot get even that which it does not know it wants.

Now how different is my " mind." *Thought* can do all sorts of things that are just the opposite to those which the body does. I can think, for example, of " circle," which is an entirely abstract notion, and one which you never find realised in the concrete. You can have a small white round biscuit : a middling-sized black round gramophone record : a large green round bowling-green : but " circle " is neither white nor green nor black, nor two inches nor two miles across : it has nothing to do with size, colour, weight —you could destroy all round objects in the world, and your notion of " circle " would remain for ever as true as it for ever has been true. You realise at once that you cannot cut off a yard of thought : nor weigh out an ounce of thought : not even have a coloured thought, whatever people may say about red rages and feeling blue. In other words, there is something in me which by nature deals with individual concrete things, and something else which by nature deals with universal abstract things—ideas.

Further, this latter element is what sees *order* among things and even puts it there. For example, so far as the actual paint goes, which catches my eye, a portrait is merely a number of daubs alongside of one another. My mind holds them together into a " unity," an order, a whole. And it is the mind of the artist that has seen to it that the daubs be put down not haphazard (as if he had thrown several pots of paint at a canvas), but in an order. And when an artist looks at a view, he invariably, for such is his peculiar sort of mind, pulls it about in his thought till it makes a " picture," falls into proportions. If he paints it, he will alter the masses of shadow, or intensify lights, and even change the disposition of the buildings somewhat, till a kind of rhythm is established. Critics then cry out : " But that is not *like* Piccadilly," or the Pyramids, or whatever the scene may be. " No," answers he, " but it's better. It's less lop-sided : it makes a better *picture* so." He has added *order*. Similarly, what you hear with your ear is simply a number of sounds that beat upon it : it is your mind that puts them together into a shape, a tune. A tune is for the ear what a pattern is for the eye. Words, so to say, meaning nothing when taken separately, have been put together so as to form a meaningful sentence for the mind, and by means of the mind. Not that everybody's mind is equally good at doing this—most people who listen to music have to leave out almost everything in order to retain the " tune " : often that is all they so much as listen for : the musician perceives and enjoys the harmony as well as the melody : he sees deep, as well as " along " : he not only follows the music as it flows, but delights in the sheer flow, the curving rhythmic changes.

So far we have thought of " instincts " as proper to the body, and so in a strict sense they are. But people often call any " appetite," or urge, or natural tendency, an " instinct." This breeds confusion, for not all " appetites " are instinctive in the physical sense. First and foremost, our *power* of knowing has the *appetite for* knowing. From sheer inquisitiveness up to an ardent and most pure desire for truth, I experience in myself the desire to *know*. In a moment I shall qualify this, for you can hear phrases spoken like : " Don't tell me : I don't want to know ! " But then you will observe that you fear a piece of knowledge that would practically interfere with something you want to do. On the whole, people don't like being ignorant.

When I say " I know," I mean that I have appropriated by my mind a thing that *is*. I cannot even say, with any real meaning, that I know a thing that *isn't*: I can be mistaken, and think that a thing is so and so when it is not: but I cannot desire to make a mistake—I always mean to get at what a thing really is, unless, of course, it interferes with me, as I said, and then I bluff myself. Hence I want to strike an agreement between my mind and a thing. When I do know a thing, I have, first, reached a *fact*: I know the fact. And second, I have enriched my mind to that extent—it stood neutral to the fact before I knew it; there was no active harmony established between my mind and the fact. When I know it, there is. So I can say that my mind has an appetite for " truth," and by truth I shall mean, that a fact exists, that I have turned my mind to it, and have adapted my mind so as to lay hold of it in accordance with what it *is*. So I can say, for example, That is a rose —a real rose—a *true* rose. And I have a real and *true* idea of what a rose is. My mind does not misrepresent the rose.

However, living as we do, body-souls, we can normally only *get at* the rose, or any other object, by way of our senses: we have to " see " it with our eyes, and very likely augment our method of reaching it by smelling it and even touching it. I have a much " truer," more adequate idea of a rose when I have not only seen its shape and colour but savoured its fragrance and felt its velvety softness. Even if someone describes a thing to me that I have never seen, such as a Feather-Snouted Yak, they have to help me out by saying that a yak is (or isn't) like a goat, and I presumably remember what feathers and snouts are like, and add this knowledge in with what my informant has administered to my pictorial imagination. So while I can truly know a rose, and even a yak, I know them as my senses supply them to me. I am grateful to my senses for doing so, though they cannot do it always very successfully, as when, for example, I catch my first sight of a yak in a densish mist. But at times the senses actually interfere with our ideas, as when we try to " think " a " circle," and cannot help " imagining " it (as we saw) like *a* round thing, which it isn't and never was or will be. But even so, the senses assist us a little by providing the vague floating image which helps us to rivet our attention. But when you come on to conceptions like that of the fourth dimension, the invasion of sense-imagery is a sheer disaster: what more fatuous than the *drawings* of " fourth-dimensional " objects that you sometimes see inserted into articles on that subject ? Similarly, and most of all, the senses are no suitable instrument in any way for knowing God himself, whom even the purest idea cannot adequately represent.

Hence we must say that the normal way of knowing, at least in this sort of life which we are living and about which we are talking, is to " pick up " some object by means of our senses, and forthwith, by the sheer natural power of the mind, to get a " true idea " of it, which " true idea " is nothing less than the mind itself adapted to the thing known. Thus we are right to say that by means of our idea of the thing, we know the thing. The upshot of all this is, that the mind wants to " know," and is healthy and happy when it is knowing, and when it is knowing properly, that is, adapting itself successfully to what the object of its knowledge really is. The well-being, then, of our mind is its Knowledge of Truth.[1]

But you observe that that which knows also wills. The will *Will* too is a sort of appetite. But not just any appetite—not one, for example, that in no way involves and presupposes knowledge. You cannot strictly speaking *will* what you do not know. In fact, it exhibits its action best of all in *choice*—when it acts, as we say, freely. I *select* one of two or several objects of which my mind takes stock. Short of that, I may even know no more than this —that I lack something : that I am in need of something. Then my vague appetite goes forth in quest of it knows not what exactly, save that whatever it is, I need it. Moreover, it is chiefly for the sake of clearness that I thus mark off the " will " from " knowledge " : for my will can quite well stimulate my mind to enquire further—" I want something so much, that I am sure that it exists : look for it ! " or again, it can check my knowledge—it can make me yield assent to something that I desire, even though I half know that it will not be good for me ; and it can prevent my attending to what I fear may turn out to be true, and objectionably so. But in all these ways of behaving there is always a certain amount of knowledge that comes first. I may not know a fact, but I may suspect that it is there, and be pretty sure that I could find out if I hunted. But the introduction of that word " good " gave us a hint. It suggested that though in a sense I am bound to like pleasant things, I am not bound to *will* them. I choose very many things in which the pleasure is but incidental. I may like taking exercise, but I would take it even if I did not like it, because I have decided that it is good for me. I am resolved to do, and in fact do, things I simply loathe, because I hold that they are right, and that I ought to do them. (And that word *ought* gives us another hint that we shall take in a moment.) On the other hand, my feeling that a thing is pleasant, or hateful, may quite dominate my will, so that I yield to the pleasant action or shirk the painful one, hating myself for succumbing all the while. Nay, so far are such actions from being connected with knowing, that they may involve forgetting. I am insulted : I " see red " : I forget everything else—nay, I " forget myself "—and I kill the man.

[1] For the sake of clearness, I want henceforward to call that thing which is associated with our body so as to form a " person " (an " I "), the *soul* : in so far as it is engaged in thinking and knowing in its normal way, I want to call it " the mind " : that which it is in itself, is *spirit*. This, I repeat, for the sake of clearness, and not meaning to discuss the *relation* of " thought " and " will," as " faculties," to the " soul." By " faculties " I mean " *powers*."

The process of choosing seems really to be this—I become aware of two or more facts : if neither attracts me—interests me—I pass them by. If only one of them attracts me, I cannot but attend to it until I see a reason for attending to the other, and then I may direct my attention to *that* one. But if they both attract me equally, and for just the same reason, my tendency is so to hesitate as to stay paralysed and do nothing with regard to either. But if one attracts me for one reason (*e.g.* that it is pleasant) and the other for another (*e.g.* that it is good), my mind can bring itself so to attend to the one, that the other practically fades out of sight, and the attraction of the former becomes stronger. Then it will turn from being an idea into being an ideal, and it will no more be a mere attracting force, but a reasonable motive. Then I choose it. Yet even so, not inevitably. I still have the consciousness that I can pause, and not yield to the motive. It is, on the whole, in this negative power of *not yielding* that I catch myself acting " freely."

Notice then that the real source of the difficulty of " free will " arises from my using the imagination, and imagery drawn from the material world, by means of which to examine and explain the activity of what we have seen to be essentially non-material—spiritual. I cannot but picture my " mind " as a light I turn on to an object. I turn it on to this object rather than that, or on this " feature " in one object rather than on that. But then, *why* do I so turn it ? Inevitably ? or because I choose to ? The problem gets pushed one stage further back. Then I think of an attractive object as " pulling " me towards it. I allow one object to pull me harder than the other. But have I then not already made a choice ? Why did I do so ? Inevitably ? Or freely ? Put it thus : In order to choose X rather than Y, I must see X as more desirable, or good, than Y. But why do I so see it ? Because I attend to it. But have I chosen to attend to it ? If so, why ? Apparently because I see a reason for attending to it, and choose to give that reason priority. Observe then that so long as you try to " picture " the process of a free choice, you will always fail. For you will always be introducing metaphors drawn from weights and physical forces, and will never do more than get confused by applying these to the spiritual thing that the soul is.

You will be far better advised to rely upon two facts—one is, your personal consciousness. Nothing will induce you, or has ever really induced anyone, to believe that all your actions are sheerly automatic. Many of them may be : indeed, you can " attend " to this or that fact so hard, that far from being able to choose, you cease to be able so much as to pause, and are swept to the thing that is tugging at you, and whose " tug," by the very fact of attending to it, you have increased. However, there is always a residuum of activity in your life for which you know quite well you are responsible, for which you deserve reward or punishment, praise or blame. And this radical fact of self-awareness—awareness of self as responsible—clears itself up when you tie it down to the special awareness of " I *ought.*" Not only that I *can*—*e.g.*, choose tea, or choose coffee—but, that I *ought, e.g.* to get up and not stay in bed. If you think this out carefully, you will see that you simply cannot reduce " I ought " to meaning " I must." Even if you speak of " moral compulsion," it is not coercion and inevitability. If I " ought " I *can* and I *need* not. Nor certainly is " I ought " the same as " it would pay." For often it doesn't. Nor yet, as " people expect of me " ; for often I " ought " to do things that people either will know nothing about, or, may even object to my doing. Finally, " I ought " does not mean that *I* impose an obligation on my *self.* For did it mean merely that, well, the authority that imposes a command, can abrogate it. By " I ought " I imply then two things—an Authority that has the right to impose an obligation on me, and freedom in myself to disregard it if I choose. It is not here the place to prove that in the long run the source of such Obligation must be God,[1] but so indeed it is.

With these two irresistible data of our consciousness the whole world is obviously and ever has been in accord. So true is this, that not one of those very few theorists who argue that we are in no sense free, can behave for five minutes as if they were not, nor treat anyone else as if they were not. A " determinist " will refuse absolutely to be treated as a machine ; and will not dream of bringing up his child as if it were a machine. And even a naughty child knows it isn't a machine. When you tell it to do so and so, its characteristic answer is : " Shan't ! " It asserts its wicked little will against you. It just *won't,* and its joy is in its " won't ! " [2]

It remains then that we have the power, and the obligation, of choosing what is for our good, when we see it so to be.

### §III: MATTER AND SPIRIT

IT is worth noticing that already we have got, I think, quite clearly the idea that there are two interacting elements in man ; if I have presented the instincts rather as in conflict with thought than as merely differing from it, that is because in *conflict* the idea of *contrast* is more obvious.

[1] See Essay iii, pp. 84-85, 87.

[2] I might add that a confusion arises sometimes, owing to people thinking that free-will implies that you can act *without a motive.* We have not said that ; but, that you are not forced instantly to act according to even the stronger motive. And again confusion arises owing to its being thought that we suggest that all human acts are as a matter of fact " free." I suppose there are very few fully free acts in a day of life ; and many that are not free at all. Much *is* automatic ; much is impulsive ; much is very largely just instinctive.

I have now to speak of this thinking element as such, and in doing so, I shall be forced to repeat parts of what I have already said : but in view of the immense importance of the subject, this does not matter in the least.

*Properties of matter*

Unless we are prepared to deny that " matter " exists at all we must study it, and we must do so by way of those qualities through which it becomes accessible to physics and to mechanics. These are, on the whole : Extension, configuration, mensurability ; molecular intervallation, elasticity, compressibility, divisibility ; ponderability (according to surfaces, density and volume) ; and inertia, displacement, acceleration (in regard to movement).

The human body is manifestly then material. Moreover, " sensation " and " feeling " (we use these words, at first sight identical in meaning, as referring to more, or less, localised effects —you have the " sensation " of being burnt in your tongue when a dish is unexpectedly peppery : you may have the " all-over-ish " " feeling " of " not being quite so well ") are activities of living *matter*, which, because it is living, does not for that lose the properties of matter, but has them in its own *way* merely. After a sense has been occupied with its proper object for some time, it grows *tired* and can no longer function readily. Sensation then and feeling are states of the whole organism in general and of special parts in particular, and not merely of brain or nervous system. It remains that they are material, and belong to a material subject, *i.e.* the body. I add, that they at least share in the general determinism of matter : given the proper stimulus, they cannot, normally, *but* react ; and they do so in response to the actual interior state of the organism, its movement, tone, and impressions, and also, in regard to its physical action and reaction connected with other material bodies. Even sense " appetency " or bodily instinct and emotion, correspond normally to sense-perception and to feeling, and are limited therefore to the material organism.[1]

Now we have already suggested that when we are aware of a thing, we are not only experimentally aware of *it*, but also of the fact that we are aware. There is an " over-knowledge." I know that this is a red-hot coal, and that I have burnt myself with it and that I am hurt. Being hurt is not the same as the coal ; and knowing that I am hurt is not the same as being hurt. A reviewing faculty exists, higher than what it reviews, which recognises and

[1] It does not follow from this that sense-activity occurs in isolation from the rational life, of which we shall speak in a moment. It has already been insisted that man is a whole, and, speaking of what is normal, his activity is *total*. I feel so and so, and think so and so concomitantly : I think so and so, and experience emotion. A whispered word can make me faint ; and a scent can revive memories that fill me with sorrow or delight. But it will be seen, once more, that the sensation of scent *is* not the thought, nor even the sadness or delight. Nor does the sensation turn into the thought.

assesses and correlates sensations and other things. "I touched that coal : that is why I am burnt and suffering : this is bad for my hand—it will be sore—and most unfortunate because I am booked to play at a concert to-morrow."

We have already seen that none of the properties of matter, *Immateriality* such as those enumerated above, can be applied to these thoughts *of the knowing self* or to any thought. I cannot cut an inch off my thoughts about my finger, though I can burn an inch off my finger, and so forth. Correspondingly, what is proper to thought cannot be said about matter. The "idea," which is the primary product of intelligence, not only has *not* the properties above mentioned as belonging to matter, but *has* "meaning," which matter as such has not got. What it "means" involves mind-play upon it. The mental act, moreover, of seeing "relations" between ideas, lies outside the scope of matter, and so, in fact, does the power of seeing relations between material objects. If I see two men, all that I do see is "two men" : it is my mind that "relates" them as father and son or even as bigger and smaller. And when it comes to inter-relating two ideas, I see better still that I see them as two and yet make them co-exist. The two operations issuing into two ideas can yet be brought under a single operation, "thinking them together" and not merely in succession, and seeing in one single glance their *relation* as similar or different.

It is worth stating at once that this cannot take place in matter, which consists of "part outside part" and is susceptible only of *succession* in its modifications. The mind which can be aware of two things simultaneously and of their relation, is, therefore, to be called "simple." This is here a technical word meaning, precisely, that a substance that is thus simple has no parts outside parts. The mind then is in substance and in kind different from the body, which is material.

No single judgement, classification, distinction or inference can be made without involving this substantial simplicity of the mind, for, not only have the two or more ideas to co-exist, but I have to be able to think one in terms of the other—for example, the man George, as King, and as Fifth and so on. I must see these two ideas at the same time in one "medium." Did my mind consist of parts outside parts, as matter does, I could not do this.

Still more does reasoning involve the "immateriality" of the intelligence which reasons. For I either pass from a general idea to a particular one, *e.g.* impurity is evil—therefore adultery is : or, from a particular one to a general one—men are part body ; therefore they must be classed as animals. But an *idea* cannot fall under the senses or the cognisance of any material thing whatsoever. The thinking mind must retain its identity of consciousness throughout the operation, and yet be able to modify itself as it forms the new ideas without any intervention or stimulus external to itself. But the inertia of matter renders such immanent activity impossible. The mind thus seeing the meaning of the relation of two ideas, involves not only its knowing the two ideas each with its meaning, but also forming within itself further ideas concerning them which are not actually there in the data supplied to it.

Personally, I see the immateriality of the knowing self best from the fact of self-consciousness. I not only am conscious of this and that, but I am aware of that very consciousness as *mine*, as " I-conscious." It is obvious that the *subjective* aspect—the *I*-knowing—is not given to me by those objects that are not I. That would contradict their identity. So the notion of Self arises from what is *not* those objects, and yet in some sense has become identical with them. *I am my ideas.* I do not merely mirror them to myself. I am they, and they are I. No material object is, or can be, thus *self-aware. No* form of " relation " is given by sense-perception, and least of all, this most intimate and impressive of relations—of one's own acts to one's own nature. The power here involved is therefore of a quite different order from that of the senses and of matter. Perhaps in the act of choice is the identity of one's acts with one's self revealed with supreme cogency. Even when I see my motives to be interior to me—my self, in short, presenting certain " final causes " to my self, I still have the power of *self-direction* which is excluded from matter by reason of its " inertia."

*Spirituality of the soul*   If you reflect upon this characteristic of " simplicity "—of existing *not* so as to have " parts outside parts "—you will see that so to exist is to be indestructible. For from what does the destructibility of a thing emerge ? From its being composed of parts. A blow from outside can shatter it : a force acting from within can explode it. In no other way can it cease to exist, unless, of course, God withdraws his sustaining power. An object therefore can be destroyed by being reduced to its component parts ; that, then, which is not composed of parts provides no starting-point for its destruction. Therefore the immaterial, " spiritual " element in man is imperishable—for I prefer to reserve the word " immortal " for religious considerations later on.

It is true that this order of ideas is an abstract one, and approached with reluctance and difficulty by one who is not accustomed to thinking in that sort of way. It does not therefore follow that it is a bad way. And even those who do not apply this sort of thinking to this sort of topic, constantly apply it to others—for they theorise. Even when they deny the immateriality of the mind, they are exercising *reason* when they offer " proofs." Yet, again, nothing is more common in the periodical discussions about the immortality of the soul than to observe sentimental reasons being given for the belief that it *is* immortal, such as : " Surely we shall see those whom we loved once more ? " or, " surely the Beautiful, the Noble and the True are Eternal Values," whatever that may mean. And other reasons given against it are no less sentimental, and indeed are more so, being most decidedly not intellectual : such as, " I see no trace of two principles, material and spiritual, in the brain ": " When I alter the brain, I alter thoughts ; therefore when the brain crumbles, thought ceases altogether ; there is nothing left to survive." It is *because* the soul is immaterial—spiritual (to put the word positively)—that no scalpel ever will discover it. The scalpel, a material object like the brain, can deal *with* the brain ; and the brain, a material object, contains material elements proper to itself, and will not reveal the spirit any more than the analysis of a wire as such will reveal the electricity with which it is electrified —and even that is not a very good comparison, since after all electricity is, ultimately, in the same order of existence as the wire is.

Still, an *electrified* wire may be compared to the *animated* body, which is then " I." The electricity does not run through the wire like water through a tube ; it is not even in the wire as water is in sponge, or air in lungs. Still, there it is, and it works ; and if you modify the wire, you modify the way in which the electricity is able to work in and through it ; and no one has begun to say anything whatsoever against the immateriality of the soul when they have said that by stimulating or injuring some part of the brain they have altered your powers of thinking. Of course. They have made one of the two human coefficients more, or less, apt to co-operate in the total activity of the self.

It merely remains to say that while we can quite easily say negative things of the soul—that it is immaterial, and therefore non-spatial, and indestructible—it is obviously harder to describe it positively, precisely because all our language is drawn from what is reached through our senses, and necessarily keeps the qualities of its starting-point—as, when I say " I *see*," meaning " I understand." Yet we can say that spirit is self-conscious, produces ideas, sees their meaning, relation, value, becomes all things without losing its sense of personal identity, is itself in all its acts, recognises at once its limitations and its possibilities. While then it finds no adequate solution to the problem of the universe within itself, it craves to solve it, and asks therefore to pass beyond the prison of material things and to profit by its imperishable nature. Yet even so, and seeing that its explanation of things scarcely less limited than it is itself must needs be but a partial explanation, it cries aloud for communion with that Being to which it must ultimately be related in order even to exist, a Being not discernible by sense, nor exhaustible even by intelligence, yet containing in its independent Existence the adequate explanation of all that it is not. Finite Reality was that which first evoked thought ; and finite reality is thus seen to lead, inevitably, towards the Infinite

Reality, source and end of the finite, and Alpha thus and Omega of all existence.

*Unique nature of man*

Without going any further, we can see how mysterious and unique a thing is Man. At times he might seem to us almost a richer nature than that which the Angels are : for they are un-mitigated spirits, just as a stone is matter and nothing more ; man, however, includes in himself matter and spirit too. I could not, however, admit that this is so, for, if there is space, I shall have to show that association with " body " does quite as much to cramp and interfere with the full and free action of man's spirit, as it does towards supplying it with material for thought. But already we can admire the richness, at any rate, of God's creative action, which leaves no unbridged gulfs in his Universe, but has linked spiritual with material in the person at any rate of man. One more, and only one, Union of a *personal* sort remains to be exhibited by Divine Revelation—that of God and Man in the Person of Jesus Christ. But that is not for this essay. I might, however, suggest that the whole of God's action can be contemplated by us as tending to more and more perfect unions. God is no schismatic : he binds the separate together in Communions each more marvellous than what went before : and though the Universe itself is never to be one *person*, and though men are not to be one person with God, yet already you are finding a hint as to their destiny—one of perfect harmony not only within themselves, but with all that is, and indeed, through the God made Man, with God.[1]

## § IV: SUMMARY OF PRECEDING

BEFORE concluding this part, I must point out that Man experiences in himself an instinct quite as profound as any that we have men-tioned—that which prompts him not to live in isolation : which urges him to form groups : to fulfil himself in a " society." Man, to use the old phrase, is a " social animal." We all recognise that the complete hermit is somehow abnormal. We recognise that certain actions are bad most obviously because they destroy the links that knit society closely together and make thus for its well-being and permanence—lying, for example, not to insist on murder or adultery. The supreme form that society will take for each man is the State ; and while on the one hand we see that " treason " makes a man an " outlaw " or at any rate is regarded as the worst crime of which he can be socially guilty, we also see that if a State, as expressed in its Government or its Chief, has become such as really to prevent the mass of the citizens, or even their great majority, from developing their lives properly and being able to live suitably as individuals, it has ceased to be a true State at all, and should

[1] The concept of " spirituality " will be found more fully explained in Essay iii. See pp. 101 ff.

disappear. I cannot here embark on the discussion of when, for example, revolution is permissible : suffice it to say that the citizen does not exist for the sake of the State, but the State for that of the citizen, and for that very reason must take the greatest possible care of that perfect human unit which the family is. Of families the great unit of the State is composed. Anything that injures the family, rots the very texture of Society. You may therefore say that the individual man or woman finds, in normal circumstances, his or her perfection in the family : and families that are right and happy so compose the State as to make it a good State, and to derive yet more strength, stability, and general well-being from their mutual association within that State.

We see then that whatever else may prove to be the destiny of Man, it is one that must take cognisance of his body, his mind, his will, and his aptitude for " social " life, and, what is more, of the fact that there is in him somewhat that survives physical death, so that all his bodily life, his use of ideas, and of his will and its choices, and of his life as member of a family and as a citizen, lead up to the producing of a thing that shall pass into a further way of being *in good condition.*

Hence to me, the eternal fascination of human nature consists largely in this—that it is one, yet manifold ; complete, yet growing, and ever changing without losing its identity ; unique in its position, yet with an infinity of attachments in this direction and in that —driving its roots to the very depths of material existence, yet flinging its shoots and tendrils high towards things that are wholly spiritual ; adjusting itself, that it may be the more permanent ; yet shielding itself and retreating ever into the secret recesses of personality, that never may, never can, be shared ; uniting itself with one, with a score, with a million individuals, yet never fusing itself even with one, let alone with the race in its entirety ; a thing manifestly of time and place, yet peering over into unfathomable futures, and reaching into worlds beyond all systems of unimagined suns.

Thus, you behold man standing up on the surface of the earth and striding over it, hunting its beasts and living on their flesh and on the plants, and increasing thus his bones and blood and his muscles. He seems so solid, so one with the other solids of existence, with all that you can see and taste and handle and make no mistake about. And then you suddenly find that you are thinking of man in his maturity, of healthy man, of well-developed man, and are forgetting the helplessness of his babyhood, and (what the Greeks, who loved the body, did so detest and passionately shrink from) the fallings-to-pieces of old age. You realise that the prime of bodily life is a laboriously achieved and swiftly passing hour ; that there have been growing-pains, stresses and strains, and that generally man notices his strength, and seeks to enjoy the gifts of the body, most when they force themselves on his attention by their unreliability.

Since then the most solid-seeming turns out to be beyond all else most wraith-like, you half expect the paradox to verify itself, that the most unsubstantial, the invisible, unseizable thing, thought, vision, the "dream that cometh through the multitude of the business," will prove to be the strongest thing of all. You turn then from the flashing glowing limbs to that which after all alone appreciates so much as the pleasure of bodily life—for without thought you would not know you were alive, nor be conscious even of pleasure.

## Note on Geocentricism

It is often asserted that the whole medieval way of thinking about *man* has been destroyed beyond hope of repair by the discovery that our planet, the Earth, is not the material centre of the Universe. We are constantly being told that our earth is but a whirling grain of dust, one among millions of millions of such grains. How, then, we are asked, can anything very dignified be perceived in human nature ? And anyhow, the medieval notion of man's being the crown of creation, and of all things else having been created for his sake, must be once and for all abandoned.

Those who write this are, first of all, victims of their imagination as never the medievals were ; and further, have but a faulty knowledge of history, philosophical and theological ; and finally, are guilty of logical lapses in their reasoning. For (1), medieval thinkers were never so silly as to suppose that man was great in origin or in destiny because he lived in a place that was centre of the universe : it was because they saw that man, being part spiritual, was intrinsically great, that it seemed appropriate to them that his domicile should hold even physically a central position among places where there was no reason to suppose there were any inhabitants at all. But (2), they are not to be supposed to have been the *victims* of such a notion, as they would have been if they had held that anything *depended* on a mere physical centricity of the earth. That would have been to succumb to the vulgarest of illusions, one, that is, of the imagination. But the thinkers who worked out the theory of, say, transubstantiation were the very last persons to succumb to the imagination, since the exclusion of all imaginative data is the most obvious of prerequisites if anyone is even to begin to understand the dogma—and discussion often shows that non-Catholic controversialists are quite unable to grasp what Catholics mean by transubstantiation because, precisely, they are unable to divest themselves of their imagination, and persist in thinking that Substance means a lump of something. Medieval writers surrounded their doctrine with all sorts of imaginative decoration, but they never confused the two, any more than our

Lord did, when he described heaven in terms of feasting. And (3) even if there are "inhabitants" on *e.g.* the planets, even we are able to perceive that they are not " men," since human life could not be lived on gaseous Jupiter or frozen moon and so forth. But that our Universe is densely "populated" by beings other than men, which indeed far outstrip men in natural dignity, the Christian tradition has always maintained, and tells of spiritual beings manifold in grade of excellence—indeed, St Thomas was perfectly prepared to admit (by way of a quite different line of reasoning) that every "angel" or "pure spirit" was a species in itself! So since the Christian religion does not even profess to exist save for *man's* sake, and to tell us more about *man* and his destiny and how he should achieve it, and since the centre of that religion is Christ who was *Man* and upon *this* earth, the earth most certainly is and ever must be the physical centre of the Christian's universe, and, for him, everything else lies round it. Of what may exist upon other planets or in the stars, and what wonders God may work there, we know nothing at all, save the general truth that through the Second Person of the most Holy Trinity God wills to establish a communion between himself and all that he has created. Enough for men that they live upon this earth, are what they are, and achieve what they were created for by means of Jesus Christ, true God and true Man. There is indeed a singularly beautiful poem by the late Mrs. Alice Meynell on this very subject. Neither the geocentric theory, then, nor the heliocentric theory, have anything whatsoever to do with the view we take of Man, nor ever had.

## § V: GOD THE END OF MAN

WE have, so far, considered Man as it were in himself, examining the constituents of nature, albeit these displayed themselves forth-with as *tending* to this or that (truth, good, social life, etc.). We are now able to think of him as it were from God's end, and thus to perceive more clearly man's destiny. Everything that exists is so interlocked, interactive, that just as it has been impossible even hitherto to speak about what man is, without insisting upon that towards which he is tending, so now it will be impossible to speak of what God means that man should become, without assuming all that we have said as to what man already by nature *is*.

*Evidence of order in man*

We can at any rate see this—first, that man is made on a certain *plan*; that he grows. Even his body grows, though save in cases of violent abnormality a man does not grow eight foot tall nor exist under eight inches long. But the very fact that we can call a dwarf or a giant abnormal, proves that there is a *norm*—a set of natural limits within which a human body develops and establishes itself. The human mind appears at first sight not to have any such limits for its growth; for you can always learn more and more. But this is a confused way of looking at the facts; for, however much the human mind can always go on acquiring knowledge and thereby growing, it is always the same *sort* of knowledge that it gets, namely, limited ideas which are always associated in some way with a physical coefficient, and we shall have to say this even when the soul has become discarnate after physical death; for, say Catholic theologians, it always has and retains an aptitude and even an appetite for association with " body," whereas an angel never has any such thing. Hence " man " lives within a certain " order " of nature; it is " out of order " that he should be an imbecile, and he cannot struggle out of his co-natural limits and *be* an angel. If you throw a heap of stones down on the ground, however much you may go on chucking stones on to the top of it, the group has no order within itself, though it can *enter into* an intellectual " order " with regard to its surroundings, like a cairn, for instance, which I can build " in order to " show the way to travellers over a fell-side, or even, " in order to " remind them that someone has died there. It then enters into the " order " of cairns and is not a mere haphazard heap any more. But I can put order into and among the very stones that I thus place one on the top of another, so as for example to produce a house by means of them: then the building definitely enters into the order of architectural stonework. Indeed, I can pick and choose the *kind* of order with which I infuse the stonework, and I have not merely a column, but a Doric, Ionic, or Corinthian order of column-work; I can put stones together so as to make a building, and a building which is a cathedral, and a cathedral which is Gothic, and a Gothic cathedral which is Early English, Decorated, or Perpendicular according to the " order " of architecture I am using or creating.

Therefore it is seen what God's making man " according to plan " means—man has a certain structure within himself, and he is meant to fit in with a plan that God (to use human language) has in his mind. Again, there is a certain " order " within man —all that is in him is disposed so that each part " sets towards " each other part, and all conspire so as to make a " whole," and yet man himself exists " in order to " other things, is what he is that he may fit in with other parts of God's far greater scheme, and *is* in order that he may *become*, and so become as at last adequately to *be*.

*Man made for God*

Now God cannot possibly make or do anything save, in the last resort, for his own glory. What does that mean? I neither can nor need go into details here, since the nature of God has been spoken of elsewhere.[1] But God cannot have any *end* outside himself, since he would then be subordinated to that end, and God

[1] Essay iii.

is the crown of all that is, and the summit as well as the source of all Order whatsoever. " From him are all things, and unto him, and in him they all of them subsist." Yet, in this no " selfishness " is to be discerned ; for created things *are* God's exterior glory, just by being what they should be. Therefore man, at his most perfect, is a marvellous exterior Glory given to God. More than anything in our world, man is " in the image, in the likeness " of God, for among all things of which we are aware, man *knows*, and is *free*. But when man is at his most perfect, he is in his *best* way of *being* ; but happiness is nothing else than the conscious-ness of well-being. Therefore when Man is most truly giving glory to God and fulfilling the final end of his existence, he is at his happiest. So God made man to *be* happy.

We have then first of all to say that *God* made man what he is in *order* that he may *become* perfect in his " order " or " line," and reach thereby his happiness and give the perfect glory to his Creator.

Hence God, in creating man, wished that a perfect harmony should exist, first of all, between the body and the spirit that unite to make up man. Such perfect harmony between the body with its instincts and the soul with its power of knowing and choosing, was brought about by the " gift of integrity," a " preternatural " gift of which more will be said in another essay.[1] Moreover, he willed that man should continue to be body-soul. Hence in Catholic dogma the assertion of the resurrection of the body is included.[2] When my body dies, my soul survives, and survives, as I said, with an aptitude for reanimating flesh. The moment God's omnipotence reunites them, the complete man, " I," is there once more. Such, we are taught, is in fact our destiny—to be once more and for ever truly man and nothing else whatsoever—perfected man.

Next, God created us to use our most noble possession, our intelligence, in the best way of all, that is, upon the noblest object, that is, upon himself. *Man made to know God.* Hence the knowledge of God is at the root of our true happiness, for after all you cannot love nor enjoy that of which you are quite ignorant ; and the destined happiness of our race is always, in Scripture, stated in terms of this true knowledge —The earth is full of the knowledge of the Lord as the waters cover the sea—This is Life Eternal, to know thee, the only true God. This, once more, is a topic which is officially treated in other pages ; it is not for me here to prove that we *can* know God at all, nor, by means of what intellectual mechanism, so to say. I will but emphasise one fact of experience, as I believe it to be. At the bottom of modern irreligion, but also, of modern forms of religion itself, lies—I most definitely hold—an often unconfessed conviction

[1] See Essay x : *The Fall of Man and Original Sin.*
[2] See Essay xxxiv : *The Resurrection of the Body.*

that you cannot and do not really know God at all. In this country, where everyone in some way believes in God, it occurs to no one that you can prove his existence or anything else about him. Nothing seems to astonish a convert more than what you are able to tell him and to show to him about God. Perhaps this is partly due to our national temperament: we hate abstract reasoning, and we have been taught to distrust all authority in religion. But a piece of reasoning is, most definitely, authority, for it may bring us to a conclusion that we do not like, or that anyway we do not " feel " to be true.

But if the Englishman does not " feel " a thing, he is lost. Not long ago a whole series of books on " Faiths " was published, of which the authors were explicitly exhorted not to make any mere catalogue of the articles of their creed, not to adduce arguments on its behalf, but to inform an inquisitive public what their creed " Meant to Them ": " I *do feel* . . . May one not feel . . . ? "— which has a psychological or personal interest, but is, religiously, quite the least important fact that you can know. I may be interested to hear that Prof. X., Lady Y. (the earnest social worker), the Rev. Mr. Z., the novelist A., the film-actress B., and a football international C. " do feel " about God—I can even thank God, in my heart, that they are occupied with him at all: but all this implies that my only way of knowing anything about God is by way of studying the impressions of my fellow-men, and that I cannot win any quite certain knowledge of him at all, which can and must survive even in hours when I do not feel anything whatsoever towards or about him, just as (to use a brutal example) a newly married couple continue to love one another, not to insist on the fact that they continue to know one another, even when, on their honeymoon, they are both being sea-sick and are not feeling anything whatsoever about one another. It must most definitely be stated that this uncertainty about God is sub-human, and not what is intended for mankind ; and that the kind of cult of uncertainty that you often see to-day in sophisticated persons, is due, perhaps, at its very best, to a Zulu-like timidity of any close contact with God, and a confusion of reverential awe with indecent familiarity, but also, at its frequent worst, to a real fear of finding yourself too compromised—too committed to consequences—should you have to acknowledge that you knew certain things about God " for sure." It might demand of you certain ways of behaving, based not upon your " feeling them to be right," but upon your knowing that they *are* right, little as you enjoyed that knowledge.

To be honest, feeling (if it is to exist at all) should as a rule be itself a consequence ; and an habitual association with certain ideas about God does generate very often a profound and quiet contentment which is far more substantial, abiding, and productive than gusts of spiritual emotion are. Truths about God that seem at first sight to be abstract and chill, like those of his Eternity, his Unchangingness, his Omnipresence, and of course his All-power, All-wisdom, and All-goodness, are able to produce in the soul, even here and now, a very deep happiness. So even the intellectual knowledge we can already gain concerning God, leads us very far towards our true End, which is, as I said, so far as it regards ourselves, Happiness.

I am very far from saying that God cannot or does not impress the knowledge of himself upon human minds in all manner of ways. But I am saying that since the human mind is made by him to know Truth, and can know much about himself, it ought to do so, and is not fulfilling its end if it does not, nor providing man with that happiness which God means him to have. And I will even add a practical conclusion, which is, that children *ought* to be taught about God, assimilating, first, the *conclusions* of right reasoning about him, till they can begin to assimilate the reasoning itself. But in any case and by whatsoever method be judged best, they ought to be *taught*, for, why should the human mind be expected to succeed in this matter all by itself, if no one dreams that in any other department of knowledge it will succeed without due training ? I repeat, the mere fact that people say : " A child ought to be allowed to choose its own religion " (when no one would say the same about its food, its dress, or its education in " lay " topics), or " no particular view ought to be taught in schools—the child's mind must not be put into a religious strait-jacket "—this sort of language proves that people do not really think you can know anything for certain about God, but that one person feels this way, another person that, and no one has the right to quarrel with either. Yet it is strictly true to say that it is far more certain that God exists, and is what Catholic theology says he is, than that two plus two make four. Because God is the source of that truth, as of every subordinate and created truth.

Next, God is the only true end of the *will*. I mean, one chooses *Man made* things because they seem " good." I don't mean that one may *to love God* not choose a thing that one knows very well to be bad for one—but one chooses even that because from some narrowed standpoint it seems somehow to be good ; *e.g.*, one knows that another glass of wine will be bad for one in an hour's time ; but at the moment it seems pleasant and " good " for the satisfying of one's sensual appetite, which indeed it is. Even if a child does what in all but every way is " bad " for it, and by sulking, for example, knows that it is merely hurting itself and will be refused a treat it very much wants to have, and " cuts off its nose to spite its face," it still is giving itself a queer satisfaction at the moment, even if it be nothing else than making its parents miserable or annoyed. We ought therefore to desire and to choose always the fuller, richer, " better " good, in so far as we can ; and we become able to do so *by* doing so. The best good is what God sees to be best; and since there is nothing better than himself, we ought always to aim at choosing him, and we do so by acting according to his "will," for in choosing thus, we are choosing *his* choice.

*Doing the will of God*

The first step in this direction is never to choose what we know to be in opposition to God's will, for this is simply to oppose our wills, *i.e.* ourselves, to what is God himself, that is, to Truth and to Life—that is, to slay ourselves out of reality—to divert ourselves away from our only true "end," and to "come to nothing." The next step is positively to do whatsoever we know that God commands us to do, for this is in keeping with God's own nature, and therefore we approximate ever more closely to him who is the absolute Good and source of good and happiness. Then we ought to try to find out those things which are not actually commanded by him, but which in one way or another we know that he loves and prefers. No doubt it is in part because this is so hard a thing to do, God being invisible and unimaginable, that he wills us, as Christians, to contemplate himself in the person of Christ, who has made God manifest to us. But we are not speaking for the moment of the Christian Revelation; and even without it, there is possible for us a real love of God and adhesion to him, for to choose ever what God wills marks a "love of preference," carrying with it an austere joy, devoid maybe of those "pathetic" experiences, those sympathies, which the study of the human life of Christ can hardly fail to arouse in us. But it is worth always remembering that no emotion, however sublime or tender or noble or pitiful, no ecstasy, however marvellous, *is* God. I am not actually, at such moments, "feeling God," but experiencing results in myself—why, in my very nerves—that may be the overflow into those semi-physical regions of a spiritual union with him. It may indeed be much better for me to experience no such emotions: for I continually tend to attach importance to them; to think myself good when I have them, and to become attached to *them*. But that would be to make idols of them, and to remove my spiritual eye from its true object, and to fasten my will to what is not God at all.

*Duty of social religion*

Finally, God wishes me to tend to him as to my last End *socially*, since my nature, made by himself, is "social." From the outset, it has been known that I am "my brother's keeper." That is to say, putting it at a minimum, that along of what I *am*, I "influence." I am all the while influencing my surroundings. If I am dislocated, as within God's plan, I put all with which I am in contact "out of joint"; what is rotten, rots. If, on the other hand, I am moving ever towards my Centre, my magnetism draws others with me towards it. All "social" workers should remember this. They endeavour might and main to bring men in closer contact with one another; but they try ever to do so by shunting them, so to say, towards each other upon a vast circumference. As likely as not, thus to push one nearer to a second, is merely to push him further from a third. But if I try to " set towards " the Centre, and to carry others with me towards It, necessarily all these disparate items move nearer to one another too. Such is the good Communion between men that Communion with God necessarily produces.

I think that it becomes at once clear how grateful we should *God the* be to God for telling us so clearly the way to Truth, to Right, and *solution of* to Union. The believer in God, even though he be not a Christian, *man's problems* ought I think to see that any plan for social unification, or pacification, or amelioration, is second-rate and partial, if not bound to fail, if the origin and end of all reality be disregarded. Once you can *start* from God, you already possess the foundation for all fraternity and equality and liberty, for which you will find no adequate foundation if you just examine human nature as it *is*. You must see it as what it is meant to be, and that towards which it tends, no less than that which starts from the One most Perfect God. And when you can be certain about God, you are emancipated from much fumbling and guessing and speculating, and also from the paralysis of scepticism, and again from the fatuity of succumbing to the intellectual fashion of the hour. You need no more be guilty of the snobbishness of trying to keep " up to date," or " in harmony with modern thought." God is neither in date nor out of date. I have no reason to suppose that " modern thought " is more right than any other thought. For, after all, modern thought is what most people think at the moment, or more probably what a group of people who like to imagine that they are leaders of thought are thinking at the moment. But it has constantly occurred in history that the thought of a certain epoch has been less good than that which went before. Thought in our eighth century was not so good as that of our fifth century ; and that of our eighteenth century incomparably less good than that of the thirteenth. God's Truth is timeless, and we are able, as we have seen, to participate more and more in it. Even in this part, then, of life, we find more peace and happiness in knowing God than in any amount of material research or discovery.

Moreover, it is goodness on God's part if he chooses to let us know what is right and what wrong. " Religion " is not a mass of arbitrary taboos. God is not playing a cat's part, on the look-out for wretched mice, to seize and worry them. We are able to find sign-posts on our path : we are able to distinguish what *is* path. We are shown the precipice, and the morass. Hence we can move with safety and rapidity. I cannot imagine anything more silly, or, at its worst, more conceited, than to announce that you are going to carry a difficult thing through without any help. What people would describe as the behaviour suited to an unlicked young cub, fresh to his job in business or in civil service, coming out with his own ideas and impressions and methods and regarding his predecessors as old fogies or reactionary, is quite often recommended as the ideal way of approaching the part of life that concerns the most enormous issues imaginable. " Think your own thoughts : obey your private conscience : express your Self." Granted, if you are so sure that your conscience is instructed sufficiently ; that your ideas are as true as they are original ; that you possess a self worth expressing, and not one that it would be more decent to keep discreetly veiled for a time, until it has grown a little—until the days of awkward wrists and ankles and gawky foal-like limbs be just a little passed, and some spiritual elegance be discernible in you. . . . Where a self-expression is modest and diffident, tentative and most ready to ask advice, well and good. And the best advice is God's.

It will have been observed that hitherto I have not appealed to Catholic doctrine as such, or as authoritative (which, for us Catholics, it is) to recommend what I have said about the nature of man, or of God, or about the relation in which man stands to God. It is not even necessary so to appeal in order to decide that the human soul is indestructible. Alone the notion of the " resurrection of the body " needs such appeal. It follows quite clearly from what I have said that the soul, on separating itself from the body, stands in a relation to God which is substantial—I mean, either it is thinking what God thinks and choosing what he wills, or it is not. If it is not, it is either totally alien to God in these matters, or partially so. Possibly human reasoning cannot *prove* that the soul is irrevocably united with God once it is totally so at all ; nor yet that it can totally exhale itself, so to speak, in an irrevocable act of alienation from God. Still, we can see that human reason is in no way conflicted with, if we find further reason to assert that the soul which leaves the body in complete union with God, stays for ever thus united ; or that the soul which has absolutely willed its own separation from the Truth and Right of God, remains for ever thus dis-united. It is hard for human thought to arrive at an " always," " never," " wholly." What we can very easily imagine, and would most naturally assume, is, that souls leave the body in as mixed a state as they have been while united with the body—for is not ordinary experience entirely on the side of men being mixtures ? And if the soul leaves the body, mixedly good and bad, may we not find it easy to suppose that in the " next world " it pursues its course of degeneration or improvement ? As a matter of fact, Catholic doctrine will be wholly on the side of improvement. Unless a soul has so completely expressed itself in an anti-God act, bad as its state may be, it yet is destined to improve. A word upon this below ! At least we can see that the destiny put before man by God is the perfect union of the intelligent soul with the Source of Truth, and of the soul's free will with God as Source of Right and Good itself. And since there is no reason to suppose that God will ever annihilate a soul, we can see that the proper destiny of a soul is to endure for ever, thinking what God thinks, loving what he loves, and therefore united with him in intelligence and will, and happy beyond words in consequence. This is caught up into the Church's doctrine and no part of it is denied, but all of it is expanded as shall now be explained.[1]

## § VI: THE SUPERNATURAL LIFE

WE now pass into quite a different world—that of the Christian *The life* Revelation and of Catholic Religion. I hope that it has been per- *of grace* fectly clear that in what I have written so far, I have not appealed to authority of any sort—whether scriptural or ecclesiastical. I have only alluded to these, if at all, as sanctioning or corroborating what intelligence is able, unaided, to discover, save indeed in the note concerning re-incarnation. There exists, however, the Christian Revelation. This Revelation contains, as St Paul says, precisely what " eye hath *not* seen, what ear hath *not* heard, and what it hath not so much as entered into man's heart to conceive." We are told things that we not only do not, but cannot, find out by ourselves. And one of these is, that we are to be made to live by a life essentially higher than this our co-natural human life— a supernatural life, which God always intended for us, so that our true end is a supernatural end, such that we can neither earn nor merit it, nor most certainly be " improved into " it, by any mere

---

[1] The doctrine of successive reincarnations can neither be proved nor disproved philosophically. That a soul requires further education after physical death, to accomplish in it the perfect assimilation in thought and will to God, is intelligible and usually true. But nothing can show that this occurs by means of such new unions with a body. The arguments usually adduced are, that certain people " remember " that they were this or that in a previous " incarnation." Such claimants are anyhow very few ; and if they " remembered " that they had been Cleopatra's scullery-maid as often as they " remember " they have been Cleopatra, they might carry more conviction. That you " feel you have been here before," or take sudden likes and dislikes to people you have never seen before, goes on distance as an argument. Nor do inequalities in birth or condition demand that we should see in them the consequences of behaviour in an earlier life. For the mere fact that so and so is in bad material conditions, viewed as uncomfortable, has nothing to do with his moral or spiritual state : to suggest that the poor have less chance of becoming " good " than the rich, and are therefore paying for pre-natal sin, is rebutted by the fact that they are often much more good than the rich. Finally, since no one is conscious of his previous state, if any, there has been a moral snap in personality, and the continuity would be purely mechanical. Hence I, who now am living, would be perfectly right to resent paying for the misdemeanours of Julius Caesar, assuming I had once been he. Catholic doctrine, however, forbids us to entertain the notion of successive incarnations.

development of our human nature and its constituents, as a wild-rose may be developed into a garden rose.  The gift of this super-natural life has therefore to be a free gift from God, for which reason it is named " grace," or the " life of grace," for *gratia* means a " free gift."

*Immediate*   No discovery of scientific men has ever shown what was not
*vision of God* alive turning into a living thing, nor even a vegetable into an animal, still less, an animal turning into a man.  Were an animal to turn abruptly into a man, this would be due to a life *above its nature* being infused into it.  It would have been given, from the point of view of an animal, a " supernatural " life.  You might ask, then, at once, whether I suggest that Man, when a super-natural life has been given to him, is no more *man* ?  Does he shift right out of his " species " ?  I will answer forthwith that he does not.  He is and will remain *man*, though supernaturalised.  How can this be ?  Because, as you will see, the first result of his " super-naturalisation " is, that he *knows* God in a way in which man, by his own natural forces, cannot know him.  But observe—man *is* constructed *to know*.  A stone is not constructed so as to grow— a plant is not constructed so as to feel—an animal is not constructed so as to know at all.  For a stone to grow, for a plant to feel, for an animal to know intellectually, a totally new *sort* of element, of constituent, would have to be inserted into it.  In the case of man, the power of knowing is already there.  He is already a spiritual being.  But he knows only by means of ideas.  Even in his dis-carnate state, when ideas will not reach him by way of his senses, he would still know what he knows by means of ideas and of reasoning.  True, the reasoning would be much more rapid, and his intuitions much more complete, than they are at present.  But in no case would that be verified of him, which St Paul asserts concerning the Christian's state in heaven—" At present," says St Paul,[1] " I see as by means of a mirror, dimly—but then, face to face.  Now I know in a fragmentary way, but then, I shall know even as I am known."  He means, that I know God, now, by means of ideas, and even, ideas derived from creatures of which I first have knowledge :  but in my destined state, I shall contemplate God *immediately*.  Now, I know only *truths about God* :  then, I shall know " as I am known "—that is, directly and by contempla-tion.  He does not mean that I shall know God comprehensively, as God knows me comprehensively—for so to know God would mean that I had an exhaustive knowledge of God :  but he means that I shall know God without any *medium* between me and him, even as he requires no interposed ideas in order to know me.  We shall, therefore, " see God as he is,"[2] and for that reason, says St John, we shall be " like him," no more with that likeness and in that image which is inevitable in those who are spiritual creatures,

---

[1] 1 Cor. xiii 12.          [2] 1 John iii 2.

as we are, but to those to whom power has been given to become, from children of men, " sons of God " ; [1] who not only are named such sons of God, but truly are so,[2] who have been born not from human marriage merely nor by desire of man, but of God—who have been " born anew "—born a second time, and, this time, supernaturally.[3]

Hence, because there is a new and supernatural life in us, we shall " see God," and because we see him that new life, already fully constituted in us by grace, will spread and triumph and reveal itself within us and assimilate us, so far as our human nature can admit of such a thing, to God himself, having been made " partakers," says St Peter,[4] " of the Divine Nature."

The actual history of the gift of grace is related, we have *The Fall and* recalled, in other essays. Here I have but to say that the Church *Redemption* teaches that this gift was given to our first father, Adam, yet given to him under condition, and held by him precariously. A moral command, of which he was sufficiently conscious, was imposed upon him, upon the fulfilment of which depended his retention of that supernatural gift—since God will not force even his best gifts on man's free will. Adam disobeyed, and was deprived of grace, and of those preternatural gifts of immortality and " integrity "—or interior harmony of all the constituent elements of his nature—that were the suitable complement of grace. This was the Fall. Because however Adam stood not for himself alone, but for us, and was truly the Head of the human race, and because we were " incorporate " in him, therefore we too in him were deprived of that supernatural life that God meant us to possess, and " in Adam, all died." We are therefore conceived and born deprived of somewhat that we were meant to have, " in Original Sin," to use the technical phrase. In some way, then, or another, this Original Sin had to be made away with—Death had to be slain —were we to live again supernaturally, and attain the true end for which we were created. We regain our life by being incorporated afresh in a Second Adam, a Second Head to the human race—that is, in Christ, who being true man *can* be for us, as he is in himself, the first of all men, and who, being God, has in him no participated life merely, but the very source of life itself. Hence, if a man be *in Christ*—behold ! a *new creature* : [5] and on this theme, were it here in place, we could linger very long. But, as I have said, its proper place is in another essay, and all that I have to do here is to insist with a minimum of development, but sufficiently clearly, that the triumph in man of this supernatural life is his only true destiny in the full sense, and that for which God created him, *The modern* and that into which he redeemed him. *reaction to*

Experience has taught me that the paragraphs I have just written *this doctrine*

[1] John i 12.     [2] 1 John iii 2.     [3] John i 13 ; iii 3.
[4] 2 Peter i 4.     [5] 2 Cor. v 17.

are those which the " modern " non-Catholic Christian will above all others dislike.  I had occasion not long ago to repeat their contents in a society composed of several modernist clergymen, of science-professors, and of undergraduates.  It was interesting to observe the several reactions of my listeners.  The younger men had nothing to say against this supernatural presupposition of my actual subject, which was sacrifice.  Young men and women, I suppose, not least to-day, have an appetite for life, which is a very healthy asset and symptom !  They " take kindly " to any suggestion that they may have more life even than they have.  They see that should the Catholic doctrine of supernatural life be proved false, men simply stand to lose.  They lose a whole *sort* of life.  A whole world of vitality is shut to them.  All that they can do is to improve what they have got, and in a human earth-lifetime, you cannot as a rule get very far with that, and a generation taken as a whole most certainly does not get very far.  Therefore, among the very sensible questions that they asked and criticisms that they made— all of which I was delighted to see were to the point, which was more than could be said of most of the rest—no sign was noticeable of dislike for the notion that God could thus infuse a supernatural life into man, and indeed they appeared to welcome the possibility of its being true.  So far has the genuinely modern generation, when it thinks at all, travelled from the old materialist days of, say, 1880.

There was a time when it was the fashion positively to exult if it could be argued that nothing spiritual existed at all.  Materialism is now a system grimy with disuse, and rationalism hardly less " dated."  Not that a system need be the worse for being unpopular at the moment, as I shall say very soon.  But our modern generation is showing that the race, in history, has been right when it has refused to think that matter is everything and that there is no mind, and even, that a quite fatuous conceit is needed for a man to assert that there *is* nothing higher than human thought, or even, that if there is, men are for ever and totally shut out from coming into any contact—having any dealings—with it.

A representative of scientific anthropology suggested that whatever might be the possibility or desirability of a supernatural life, its " history " as I had outlined it was manifestly impossible, if research failed to show any sign of things having happened like that, and if, in fact, it displayed man as having struggled upwards from a low level, and not as descending from a high one.  I had to ask the elementary question, first—what *could* research of the kind that he and his companions most properly went in for, display to him ?  He had to examine ancient bones.  Even if the entire series of skeletons could be produced from the first " man " down to his own father's, what would that tell him about even the mental dispositions of those men ?  Nothing at all.  No analysis of our physical structure will tell us about our mind, any more than the analysis of printer's ink upon a page will tell us of the music in the musician's mind, close though the link be between what the musician thinks and what he prints. Further, since the whole doctrine of the supernatural life *is* supernatural, how should a study of nature *expect* to tell us anything about it ? At least, no study of nature can show us its *impossibility*.

The speaker was prepared to acknowledge the justice of these considerations, but also, that being unable to make use of any method other than the observation of concrete facts for the formation of his theories, and being unable (though he should not have been) to reach by that road any clear belief in the existence or nature of God, he naturally could not understand a belief like that in Supernatural Grace, which involves a very definite belief in God and his power of entering into and acting within his universe on his own conditions, so to say.

But the attitude taken by the clergymen was far the most significant and I may say discreditable, though they were eminent men in their departments. They merely uttered lamentations to the effect that " all this kind of thing " was so " alien to modern thought —so remote from up-to-date interests "—the very words " grace, sanctification, original righteousness " and so forth, had long ago become meaningless to them. It was necessary to insist, first of all, that their difficulties arose from an inability to achieve a clear and intelligible notion of what *God* was. They had, certainly, given up any attempt to reach a *reasonable* idea of God—an idea obtained along the intelligible lines that are explained in the essay in this volume which discusses the Existence and the Nature of God, and how we know them. Therefore they were reduced to impressionism, and, since men's feelings may quite likely differ from generation to generation, they were right, up to a point, in trying to observe what men are " feeling " about God to-day. But, they far outstripped the legitimate gifts of observation, when they assumed that what men are feeling to-day is necessarily better than what they felt a generation or a century or nineteen centuries ago. I have already insisted that every sort of thought has at some time or other been " modern " and up to date ; but that there is not the slightest grounds for assuming that it has always been better than what preceded it. And apart from all this, there was a grave begging of the question in what they said. For, *does* " modern thought " coincide with what the intellectual laboratories of Oxford and of Cambridge produce ? Most certainly not. It is true that in any case I cannot imagine what " modern thought " *is*, for the only general characteristic I can observe about it is, confusion. But it is impertinence to suppose that the ordinary man cannot think, and that only professors in their studies do so. There is a deal of robust and honest thought outside such places, and indeed, I have felt regularly that the mental air there is exhausted, and I have sought intellectual bracing in very different haunts. Indeed, I had to say, then and there, that the two best definitions of Art had come to me, first, from St Thomas Aquinas in the thirteenth century, and, from a gentleman who described himself as a Street-Corner Bruiser in a mining town. . . .

*Revelation*    But to sum up this parenthesis. While we hold that Thought, ancient or modern, is quite capable of reaching the certainty that God exists, and that he created us, and has perfect power over us, and while we might even surmise that he could raise us to a supernatural way of living, we could never know that he had done so, or even meant to do so, save by revelation. Hence neither anthropological research nor any other kind of study of material facts will ever begin to show us anything one way or the other about this, nor can sheer intellectual deduction prove it to us. It is, I repeat, an affair of revelation. If God has not revealed the matter to us, well and good : if he has, his revelation is true eternally, and fashions do not alter it. It is for us to adapt our minds to God, and not to adapt God and his message to the preferences of our minds.

*Some of the*    What remains to be said is far more a matter for meditation
*implications*  than for explanation. I recall that we are taught that into us God
*of the life of* wishes to infuse a supernatural life, of which the eternal conse-
*grace*         quence is that we " see God face to face," and thereby love him supernaturally, for the very fact of contemplating the Infinite Beauty makes the purified soul to love It—and no soul could thus contemplate It unless its purification had already been accomplished. But, says St John, " we shall be *like* him, for we shall see him as he is." Love *assimilates* : and since we cannot assimilate the eternal and immutable God to ourselves, the likeness fulfils itself in us, who see him without the shadow of falseness in our minds, and adhere to him without any defection in our will being any more allowed. Therefore in his Presence we shall taste for ever the fulness of joy.

Catholic dogma fears no consequence of this principle of our supernatural union with God. Indeed, Scripture anticipates the deductions of dogma, and there is little left for the theologian to do but to fit the assertions of Scripture into their several places in his scheme., Thus, for example, united with God, we are united with that One God who is the Most Blessed Trinity. To the essay on that Mystery we refer our readers. Enough to say that while what God does, he does in his most simple Totality, yet there is this activity or that which can be " appropriated," as they say, to each several Person. We have told how the Fatherhood of God is as it were re-enacted in our favour, owing to our new manner of filiation—I mean, we are now adopted into so lofty a position as his sons, that we become truly brethren of his Sole-

Begotten. Incredible prerogative—God actually adopts us into a position hitherto held by him alone who is the Eternal Son by nature. And since he is Son, and we now are sons, we are brothers with him, and also co-heirs with him, co-heirs of his own glory. And, through our entry into his Church, we are also supernaturally incorporated into him, and are in him, and he is in us. Finally, we are taught that although God, by his very immensity, is ever wholly " in " us, now, by virtue of our new supernatural union with him, the Holy Spirit of God dwells in a special way within us, so that our very bodies are become " temples of the Holy Ghost."

We are, then, to be associated in a special way with the whole Most Blessed Trinity, and are united thus inevitably with whatsoever else is united with It. Inanimate nature, and living yet non-human creatures, are united with God after their several kinds ; and other human creatures besides ourselves are no less united with him. Therefore with all these are we " in union." In what way, precisely, will the *communion* between them and us be effected ? There is little need to speculate on that. At any rate we can see that it would suffice if we contemplated them, and loved them, as God sees them, and loves them—as they are " in himself." In him we shall see love, and meet all these good things radiant with the qualities that *he* sees to be theirs, as *he* intends them to be. And how far more rich our understanding of them, and more intimate our love for them, than when we merely saw and tried to love that travesty of themselves that things at present, in this low world of imperfection, are !

This essay must have appeared very abstract, especially in its last part, to those who are not accustomed to " endure as seeing him that is invisible." [1] Indeed, the Catholic is often attacked on the grounds that he shifts the centre of gravity of life into the " next world." Hence, it is argued, he will not take trouble over improving the sad conditions that prevail upon this earth. It is curious that other critics of the Church are fond of calling her " worldly," "·opportunist," " materialist," and so forth ; and indeed it is true that objections lodged against her cancel one another out, for it is quite impossible that she should really be so many contradictory things simultaneously.

This is not the place, I think, to sing the praises of the Church's history of beneficence among men. Enough to say that though it is perfectly true that our " conversation is in heaven "—that is, our proper and full life will be hereafter, and our life here below has to be ordered in view of this fact—yet precisely because of that we are, first, able to be happy even in the hardest of earthly circumstances, even as " for the joy set before him," Christ " endured the Cross, despising the shame," and even as Saints and Martyrs have displayed to the very eyes of men their joy in the midst of suffering ;

[1] Heb. xi 27.

and second, inspired to help our brothers in life's struggle, with motives of unique strength because they are all the more our brothers seeing that we all possess that title because of Christ, which is far better than the dubious consideration of our equality and fraternity as sons of Adam. Moreover, we who are Christians have the most explicit of injunctions from our Lord, that we should work on behalf of our fellow-men for his sake. Again and again I have been told that nuns, who regard their entire service of their fellow-creatures as vocational, are the only ones who can, as a class, be enduringly patient and self-forgetful in their toil. Allowing for exaggeration here, we at least may say that they who *can* regard themselves as working for Christ and with him, ought to be able to do a thousand times more and better than they who have to tread their rough and lonely path, with its myriad disappointments, upon the dry bread of mere philanthropical ideals, or social theories or hopes. Therefore we dare to say that how supernatural soever we judge man's destiny to be, Catholics will not be found wanting in the simple honest works of " corporal mercy," nor on the whole are they, and perhaps among them only is to be found, on a general scale, and enduringly, the lofty practice of *heroism*.

*Summary*

God created men therefore for a purpose. That purpose is, that men should become their true selves, as he sees and intends them, and thereby give him glory, and be happy.

This happiness is therefore not merely an affair of the years we spend on earth, but shall endure so long as we do ourselves, that is, for ever, since, if God shall not let our soul lapse out of existence, it cannot of itself cease to exist.

None the less, this destiny, and this happiness, do not concern our soul only, for Man is not merely soul. He is also body, and in him body and soul are so joined as to make one *person*—a unit complete yet twofold—not a gross amalgam, nor yet a mere container and contained. It is *man* therefore whom God makes for happiness.

All then that God has made, he has made according to a plan —a plan already realised, so far as a man is a man at all, and to be realised hereafter, since a man grows and only tends to become what God means him, when perfect, to be.

In order then to become this, man has to live according to certain rules ; else, he spoils himself. He must therefore respect, yet subordinate his body, and govern it according to reason, and by free choices. His mind too must ever seek to know, and to know truth ; just as his will must ever perfect itself by choosing and adhering ever more and more constantly and closely to what is Good.

Thus man shall pass into his eternity, the consummate Man, the perfect success that God intends, and already we see reasons for expecting that somehow he *will* continue to be man, and not change into some discarnate spirit only. He can also see that it may be at least possible so to spoil himself as to become waste product—the total unsuccess.

But God has done more than equip man with reasoning powers, able to reach to these certainties and these surmises. He has given him a revelation.

This revelation tells him over again, and with divine authority, many things that his reason already has told him, such as all those truths that we have just recalled ; also, it confirms certain surmises of his, such as, that he *will* for ever be truly man, body-soul ; and that there *can* be total ruin in store for him, alongside of complete success. God also reveals certain definite rules for success, and indicates certain mortal dangers.

However, God also reveals truth that no reason might discover, no guess descry. He tells us that the co-natural union of our minds and wills with himself is to be raised to a supernatural level—our whole human life is to be supernaturalised, so that whatever happiness would by nature have been ours, shall be enhanced not only in quantity or intensity, but in kind. This is to be done for us through the Grace of our Lord Jesus Christ, with whom we may be, if we but will, incorporated so as to live by his life, and in him to " see God," and, in him, all that *is* in him.

Hereby the perfect Communion establishes itself. The Bread of God is kneaded, and gives life to the world : the Vine has blossomed, has reddened into clusters, and of that Wine God himself shall drink. The House is built ; the Temple becomes perfect from foundation up to roof ; the Body lives, and the Marriage of Christ is consummated. From heaven the New Jerusalem descends, and clothes the earthly Sion that becomes all the world, and that which is in us now in germ—that secret Grace that is ours—manifests itself as Glory, and thereafter " our joy no man taketh from us."

C. C. MARTINDALE, S.J.

# X

# THE FALL OF MAN AND ORIGINAL SIN

## § I: ADAM BEFORE HIS FALL

THE study of the dogma of the fall of man and its corollary, original sin, is interesting from many points of view. If we look at its first beginnings at the dawn of human history, and its echoes or analogies or counterparts, whichever they be, that are found in the traditions, myths, and legends of many ancient peoples, we are led into a vast field of research in which, of late years, many scholars of eminence have busied themselves, and where, only too often, imagination and the desire to justify preconceived theories have taken the place of argument and sound reasoning upon sure evidence.

If we confine our attention to the course of the dogma within the Church, we are introduced to some of the greatest names in the Church's story, and to some of the movements and controversies that have cut the deepest traces across her history. The Pelagians, in the fifth century, struck at the very roots of the supernatural life and religion, but though their fundamental heresy was concerned with grace, their denial of original sin, which of necessity followed, became one of the pivotal points around which controversy ranged, and afforded the Catholic champion, St Augustine, matter for much thought and many writings.

In the sixteenth century the Protestant religious leaders did not, indeed, deny the doctrine of original sin—many of them, in fact, exaggerated it ; but while they kept the sound form of words, they understood them in a new way, and the nature of their doctrinal content was altered and degraded. Since then the process of disintegration has been carried to its logical end, especially of late years, under the influence of the theory of evolution. This, in its extreme form, necessitates the biblical story of Adam and Eve being looked upon as a myth, or at best, as a piece of mere folk-lore, enshrining some spiritual truths. Consequently, while many Protestants deny the doctrine of the fall altogether, others, less bold, less logical, but more ingenious, retain the old phraseology, but interpret it in the sense of a lapse or a series of lapses in primitive and brutelike man's struggle towards higher things. We have even been told, in all seriousness, that the fall was a " fall upwards." Original sin, then, becomes nothing but the deep impress of man's animal nature upon his slowly dawning spiritual consciousness.

To meet these adversaries is the apologist's task, not ours. Our aim is much more modest. We have to take for granted the Church's authority and her interpretation of the sacred Scriptures given into her care.  Upon this sure foundation we have simply to build an edifice of doctrinal exposition and explanation, setting in view what the Church means by and teaches in the dogma of the fall and original sin, and gathering together and explaining, as best we can, its various theological consequences and implications.  The task is not without its difficulties ; it should not be without some interest to those who have an appreciation of the things of faith, and it may have some small apologetic value as showing the utter reasonableness of the Catholic teaching, both in itself and in its close relations with other fundamental articles of Catholic belief.

To understand man's fall we must know whence he fell and what his condition was before he fell.

The tradition of a golden age at the beginning of man's history *Tradition of* is widespread ;  recent investigations have shown it to be almost *a golden age* universal among the races, nations, and tribes of men throughout the world.  The existence of this tradition might, perhaps, be taken as evidence in favour of the Christian belief in man's original state of innocence and happiness, since the trend of historical research is to show that there is always some foundation of fact for ancient, deep-rooted, and widespread traditions.  But even if we allow the fullest possible weight to this piece of evidence, it amounts to very little, for the tradition, varying from race to race and tribe to tribe, is so much overgrown and corrupted by fable, myth, and legend that the core of truth, even if it could be with certainty discovered and determined, would be too slight and vague to be of any real use.

We have, however, a surer and purer source of information. *The* Just as the story of the creation told in the Hebrew sacred writings *scriptural* is far superior in its noble purity and religious simplicity to the *narrative* complicated and often immoral myths and legends preserved in the books of other ancient peoples, so likewise does the biblical account of the primitive happiness of the first man and woman surpass all the legends of a golden age which the traditions and folk-lore of other nations have handed down to us.

It is not for us to vindicate the historical character of this narrative against the view, so widely prevalent outside the Church, that it is simply another, even if a superior, piece of ancient folk-lore.  As to the method of interpretation, something has been said in Essay VI, *God the Creator*.  Here we need only note the decision given by the Biblical Commission in 1909 when deciding certain questions about the historical character of the first three chapters of Genesis.  The third question was " whether in particular the literal, historical character can be called in question when things are narrated touching the foundations of the Christian religion, such as among others . . . the original happiness of our first parents in a state of justice, integrity, and immortality ; the command laid upon man by God to test his obedience ; the transgression of the divine command through the persuasion of the devil under the appearance of a serpent ; the fall of our first parents from that primitive state of innocence ; and the promise of a future Redeemer ? " The answer is in the negative.

*Original state of first parents*

It is therefore to this inspired record, guaranteed by the Church's authority, and confirmed by many other parts of sacred Scripture, that we go as our principal source of information for all that concerns man's state when first God had breathed into him the breath of life. This decree of the Biblical Commission says that, according to the literal, historical sense of the record in Genesis, our first parents before their fall were endowed with the three qualities of justice, integrity, and immortality. What these were and how exactly they are to be understood we must now examine.

*Supernatural grace*

We need not here, however, say much about the first, though it is quite the most important, for it is fully explained in other essays.[1] It is only necessary to note that the word *justice*, as here used, means first and principally the supernatural gift of sanctifying grace, which raised Adam to a higher state and nobler dignity, which put him into a relationship of real friendship with God in this life, and gave him the pledge of eternal happiness in the closest union with him in the next.

But of the other two qualities mentioned we must speak at greater length. These, immortality and integrity, are called preternatural gifts. This term is used to show that, although these qualities did not belong to Adam by virtue of his human nature, and were no part of that bodily and mental equipment necessary to his being and life as man, and although, therefore, they were bestowed upon him of God's sheer benevolence, as something over and above his purely human faculties and capacities, yet they did not put him, as grace did, into a different and altogether higher order of existence. They gave him additional and greater perfection without raising him above the purely human level.

*Immortality*

We take first the gift of immortality. " And he (God) commanded him, saying : Of every tree of paradise thou shalt eat : but of the tree of knowledge of good and evil thou shalt not eat. For in what day soever thou shalt eat of it, thou shalt die the death."[2] Then in the next chapter, after Adam had eaten of the forbidden tree, God lays upon him the punishment of his sin, a life of hard toil to be ended by death ; " for dust thou art and into dust thou shalt return."[3] Whence it is clear that death was positively the penalty of Adam's sin, and that if he had not sinned he would not have had to die. He was made to be immortal. This was the traditional belief of the Jews. As a modern writer well puts it : " This penal sense of death colours all that the Old Testament says

[1] See especially Essays ix and xvi.
[2] Gen. ii 16-17.
[3] Gen. iii 19.

of man's end. It is in its thoughts where it is not in its words. It is the background of pathetic passages in which the immediate subject is the misery or the transiency of life, rather than death itself. It gives to the thought of death, as it is expressed, for example, in the 90th Psalm, and to those lamentations over man's frailty and the grave's rapacity which recur in the Psalter and the Prophets, in Ecclesiastes and in Job, a meaning and an elevation which such things have not in ethnic literatures, the best of which know death only as a thing of nature, and know it not in its relation to sin and to the wrath of God." [1]

St Paul's clear teaching on the matter, in the epistle to the Romans, is well known to all, and, as we shall have to deal with it later, his witness need not be quoted here. More than once the Church has had occasion to define her faith upon this subject against heretical errors, notably in the Council of Trent, where in Canon I, Session V, they are condemned who deny that Adam by " the offence of this prevarication incurred the wrath and indignation of God, and therewith death, with which God had previously threatened him." In other words, had Adam not sinned he would not have died ; made to be immortal, he brought death upon himself as the punishment of his sin.

Closely connected with this gift of immortality was that of *Impassibility* impassibility or freedom from pain and suffering. It is the common teaching of theologians that Adam enjoyed this privilege, but it is not a part of Catholic faith, for it has neither been defined by the Church, nor is it explicitly taught in the sacred Scriptures. It is, however, easily deduced from the sentence passed by God upon Adam and Eve after they had sinned. In this matter all exaggeration must be avoided. It is not necessary to suppose that Adam was wholly incapable of feeling pain ; the possession of impassibility simply means that he was secured against all those pains and evils which are, directly and indirectly, the consequence of sin, ignorance, and folly.

Theologians commonly also hold that Adam was endowed with knowledge infused by God, and not acquired by the exercise of his human faculties. Here also a warning against exaggeration is not out of place, for some, indulging their love of ingenious speculation, have credited him with possessing an all-embracing wisdom. Scripture gives us no explicit information on this point, and the Church has decided nothing. But from general principles it may be safely concluded that, at the moment of Adam's creation, God infused into his mind the knowledge which, though he had had no chance of acquiring it for himself, was necessary to enable him to lead a properly ordered human life. More than this it would, perhaps, be unwise to assert. Undoubtedly also God endowed him with excellent mental faculties and powers of observation, by

[1] Salmond, *Christian Doctrine of Immortality*, p. 197.

*Integrity*

which he would be able to equip himself quickly with all necessary and convenient knowledge.

The other preternatural quality mentioned in the Biblical Commission's decree as belonging to Adam before his fall is of even greater importance than the gift of immortality. Theologically it is called integrity, which, first and foremost, consists in the total absence of concupiscence. In modern English concupiscence is generally understood as applying only to fleshly desire; it is usually restricted to that field wherein it is most violent. But in theological language the word is of much wider application. It indicates any and every motion or impulse of the lower, the sensitive and imaginative, faculties or appetites of man's nature that is not under the perfect rule and dominion of his higher faculties, reason and will. All our faculties and appetites, even the lowest, are from God and are good in themselves. They tend naturally to find satisfaction in their appropriate acts, and this tendency in itself is good. Above all man's sensitive faculties stand his reason and will, his noblest natural endowments, which should govern and direct all his actions if he is to live rightly and worthily as a man. In the possession of these lies essentially his human dignity, by these he is raised immeasurably above all the lower animals. As his highest faculties they have the natural right of dominion over the lower elements of his nature. Experience, however, proves that this dominion is by no means absolute. Our sensitive and imaginative faculties are so quickly and so strongly excited to action that, even when they do not overcome the rational will and lead it captive, as too often happens, they can be dominated and regulated by it only with much effort and often painful striving. "For I do not that good which I will, but the evil which I hate, that I do. . . . For to will is present with me, but to accomplish that which is good, I find not. For the good which I will, I do not; but the evil which I will not, that I do. . . . I find then a law, that when I have a will to do good, evil is present with me. For I am delighted with the law of God according to the inward man; but I see another law in my members, fighting against the law of my mind, and captivating me in the law of sin that is in my members." [1]

This unhappy state so vividly pictured by St Paul is called the state of concupiscence. Every impulse of man's lower nature not in accord with the dictates of his reason and the urge of his will is a manifestation of concupiscence; it is a proof of the two-sidedness of his nature not yet brought into a perfect oneness or wholeness of activity—a proof, that is, of the absence of *integrity*.

Adam, before his sin, did not suffer from concupiscence; he was gifted with integrity. Although this has not been explicitly, in so many words, defined by the Church, the Council of Trent

---

[1] Rom. vii 15-23.

clearly presupposes it when, in the fifth canon on original sin, it says that concupiscence is sometimes called sin because it arises from sin and inclines man to sin ; whence it follows that before there was sin in Adam there was no concupiscence in him.

This is very simply and delicately expressed in the second chapter of Genesis. Eve, fresh from God's creative hand, is presented to Adam, " and they were both naked and were not ashamed." Shame arises when a person is overcome by an enemy whom he ought to have conquered, or when the danger of defeat just escaped has brought him a lively sense of his unworthy weakness. So the inspired writer in noting that Adam and Eve were not ashamed, despite their nakedness, wishes to indicate that they felt no undue, disordered impulse of the strongest of sensitive appetites, that their reason and will held such complete and easy rule that they felt no weakness and had no cause for shame. But having sinned, as we read a little farther on, they at once experienced the sense of shame, caused by the unruly urge of passion, and covering their nakedness, tried thus to lessen the danger to which they now felt themselves exposed.

To prevent misunderstanding, we may add that, in exempting Adam from concupiscence, we by no means deny to him the enjoyment of all the pleasures of sensitive life. St Thomas,[1] indeed, teaches that, in his state of innocence, he enjoyed these even more than we do, since his natural faculties were purer and therefore keener. But the whole of his sensitive life and activity was in complete subjection to the rule of his reason.

Such, then, was the condition of our first parents when they came from the hand of God. They were in a state of supernatural grace, they were free from all concupiscence, and they were not subject to death. These three points belong to the deposit of faith, guaranteed by the Church's authority. Further, it is common theological teaching, though not a part of Catholic faith, that they were free from all pain and suffering, and possessed some measure, impossible to determine, of divinely given or infused knowledge.

About their material circumstances, their culture and civilisation, we know practically nothing. The Bible seems to show that they led a life of great simplicity, God's bounty supplying all their needs with but little trouble on their part. But however interesting this question may be to our human curiosity, it has no theological importance. From this point of view all we need to know is that they were capable of leading a really human life, however simple.

Now a question arises with a direct bearing upon the doctrine, *Preternatural* to be expounded later, of original sin. We have seen what Adam's *gifts* condition was at the beginning of his life, but, although we have spoken of his endowments as supernatural and preternatural, in so doing we have been guilty, in reality, of begging the question, for

[1] *S. Theol.*, I, Q. 98, a. 2, ad 3.

we have not determined whether these endowments did really and of right belong to him as man, or were something given to him over and above his natural due. The question is both important and delicate. Its importance, which will become clearer as we proceed, lies in this that, if Adam's endowments, as already described, were natural, then, since by his sin he lost them both for himself and for us, it will follow that man's nature now is intrinsically and essentially vitiated by being deprived of some elements originally proper to it ; it will therefore be in itself an evil thing. This is, in fact, the position taken by many of the early Protestant theologians, and later maintained by the Jansenists. If, on the other hand, these endowments were something given to Adam over and above all that went to make up his full manhood, then it follows that, in spite of their loss, human nature remains complete, in essence unimpaired by original sin, intrinsically whole and good in itself.

The delicacy of the problem lies in determining with accuracy what is meant by the word *natural*, and by its correlatives, supernatural and preternatural. Some little has already been said, but more careful definition is now necessary. The word *natural* has many meanings. It would be but a waste of time to enquire into most of them. We shall confine ourselves to the strict theological sense in which theologians use the word when treating of this present question, and of all matters touching the doctrine of grace. And for the sake of clearness and brevity we shall speak of man alone among all creatures.

It is clear that man, to be man, to answer to the idea of man eternal in God's mind, must be made according to a certain definite pattern. He must consist of body and soul, and must be endowed with certain faculties, capacities, and powers. All these are his natural constituent elements, properties, and possessions, and in their sum make up a complete human nature. Further, to keep him in life and to give due play to his powers many other things are necessary. He cannot live without food and air, for example ; these, therefore, though not a part of his being, though external to him, are yet natural to him, a part of his natural surroundings and requirements. Again, the powers that God has given him as elements in his nature, especially his intellectual powers, are of such vast stretch and grasp that, to provide them with enough to work upon with some sort of satisfaction, a whole universe of almost immeasurable immensity, complexity, beauty, ingenuity, intricacy, harmony has been created by God for his dwelling-place and workshop. All this created universe is man's natural environment and inheritance, and all that he can do with it and all his discoveries in it are his natural achievements and attainments. So, to take an example, though countless millions of men have lived full human lives without being able to fly, flying is quite natural to man, since it has come about by the application of his own innate powers to the material objects and forces of the created world.

But by the exercise of these same powers without any outside help he can rise still higher, soaring above the created world to the Creator himself. He can gain an extensive knowledge of God and his nature and conceive for him a real love. That this is possible to man's unaided natural powers—at least, as regards the knowledge of God—was defined by the Vatican Council.

Taking into consideration, therefore, all these points, we conclude by defining as natural to man all that goes to his making and being, all that is possible to his unaided powers, all that is necessary for the due and sufficient satisfaction and activity of his innate appetites and faculties. With this in mind we can answer the question put above.

The truly supernatural character of grace will be found fully explained elsewhere.[1] Now it is enough to note that the Church teaches that, while God could have left Adam with his own natural powers to work out his own natural end by the unaided exercise of the powers, he did in fact destine him for an end infinitely beyond the reach and exigencies of these powers left to themselves. This end was an unending life of perfect happiness, produced by immediate union with and direct sight of the very being of God, by the beatific vision, as it is called in Catholic phraseology. And for the preparation for and meriting of this supernatural end God gave Adam a new nature and life, the supernature and supernatural life of sanctifying grace. Beyond this we need not go, but shall confine our attention to the gifts of immortality and integrity.

Adam's immortality was, in reality, only potential, not actual —that is, it was something that would have been given to him if he had observed the conditions accompanying God's promise of it, but of which he was deprived owing to his failure to observe them. This is fairly clear from an attentive study of the second chapter of Genesis, where it is explicitly stated that the fruit of one tree will bring death, and implied that the result of eating of the other, when God should allow it, would be unending life. Therefore, while death was truly the penalty for Adam's sin, it was a penalty that consisted in not giving a conditionally promised additional privilege, but not in taking away something already held by natural right. Death, therefore, was Adam's natural lot ; immortality was not natural to him. So we find that when Michael du Bay, a theologian of Louvain, taught that " the immortality of the first man was not a free gift but his natural condition," this teaching was condemned by St Pius V in 1567.[2]

As St Augustine well expresses it : " It is one thing not to be able to die, as is the case with some beings (viz., the angels) whom

[1] Cf. Essays ix, xvi and xvii.
[2] Denzinger-Bannwart, Enchiridion Symbolorum, No. 1078.

God created ; but it is another thing to be able not to die, which was the way the first man was made immortal ; his immortality came from the tree of life, not from his natural constitution. He was mortal therefore by the condition of his animal nature, but immortal by the free gift of his Creator." [1]

Yet immortality cannot be called strictly supernatural, for it does not raise man's life to a level above itself, but only prolongs it, in its own order, along the line of duration. Hence it is called by theologians a preternatural gift.

The preternatural character of Adam's freedom from concupiscence is not, at first sight, so clear. For it would seem that, in a state of sinlessness, there ought to exist perfect harmony between the various elements of man's nature, and that the lower ought to be in complete subjection to the higher. But, without going deeply into the psychology of the matter, we may point out that concupiscence is a natural effect of man's dual nature, of his having two kinds of appetites, sensitive and rational. Between the objects of sense and of reason there must often, of necessity, be opposition, and since the sensitive faculties and appetites are directly, easily, and strongly excited and stimulated by external objects, it comes about inevitably that they begin to act without the co-operation or the consent of the reason, and that sometimes they act so forcefully as to put the reason to great stress before it can impose its power of control. Concupiscence, therefore, is a natural concomitant of man's composite being, and integrity a special and free gift of God, but preternatural and not strictly supernatural, as it does not raise man's nature above itself to a higher level of being or action.

This happy state in which our first parents were created, and which we have been describing, did not continue. Instead of enjoying this blissful condition of life, when Adam dwelt in God's intimate friendship, untroubled by pain or sorrow or the assaults of concupiscence or the doom of impending death, man is now born into sorrow, lives in suffering, is overwhelmed with concupiscence, sins much and often, and even with death and the threat of damnation hanging over him, finds it hard to remember God, to live in his presence and to love him. Whence comes the change ? Only revelation can enlighten us, and we have now to see what it teaches.

### § II : ADAM'S FALL

IN treating of Adam's fall various points must be carefully distinguished. First we must establish the fact of his sin, determine with accuracy, as far as possible, in what it consisted, and enquire how he came to commit it. Then we must consider what effect his sin had upon Adam himself, and finally we shall have to see how it affected his posterity. In this section we shall treat of the fact, the nature and the motive of Adam's sin.

---

[1] *De Genesi ad litteram*, Bk. vi, ch. 15.

That it belongs to the Catholic faith, as defined by the Church, *The sin of* that Adam sinned, is too well known to need any elaboration. But *Adam* we have to enquire what exactly this means. Two conditions are necessary for there to be a sin against God. The first is that there must be a command imposed by God, whose authority and right to command are supreme ; the second is that he who is bound by this command must deliberately and consciously transgress it. The narrative of Genesis makes it quite clear that in Adam's case both of these conditions were fulfilled. God imposed upon him the command to abstain from the tree of knowledge ; Adam deliberately broke the command, and so sinned. But the fact of his sinning, which stands out so clearly, raises some interesting matters which, though not affecting directly the substance of the faith, will help to put it in a reasonable and easily acceptable setting.

In the first place, we may note that, according to many accredited theologians and exegetes, it is not necessary to understand in a literal sense the prohibition against eating the fruit of some particular tree. We may take it, without offence, as a vivid but symbolical way of representing God's command which may have been of some wholly different character. But, on the other hand, there is no good reason compelling us to give up the literal acceptation of this narrative. Since God wished to try Adam by testing his obedience, by laying upon him some positive command over and above the natural law, it seems a matter of indifference what form the command should take or what thing should be commanded or forbidden. And in view of the conditions of Adam's life, it seems altogether suitable that the prohibition should fall upon the fruit of some one tree among the many whence he gained his sustenance. Then, inevitably, the question suggests itself : Why should God wish to impose such a prohibition upon him ? If he had been left with nothing but the natural law to obey, it would have been much easier to avoid sin. Why did God make obedience harder ?

It is evident that God's prohibition put a limit to Adam's liberty *Reason of* and narrowed the range of his lordship over the rest of the visible *divine* creation. This points the way to the answer to our question, for *prohibition* it was most fitting that man, so splendidly endowed and ennobled by God, should make some offering, some sacrifice of what he had received, as an acknowledgement of his indebtedness to God for all he had, and as a sign of his ready obedience and entire submission to his Creator. And what better sacrifice could he offer than that of his will and his freedom ? God therefore laid this command upon Adam, with the condition that disobedience would bring about the loss of those supernatural and preternatural gifts that had been bestowed upon him, which implies necessarily that obedience would have meant their retention until the time should have come for him to be taken from this world into the life of heavenly glory. There was, therefore, an implied pact or covenant between God and Adam, the observance of which by Adam was a grave obligation, for God's will is the highest law, and it was his will that Adam should pass from this life into the beatific vision ; he was therefore bound to keep those means which God had given him for the attainment of that end, to wit, sanctifying grace and its concomitants.

*Possibility of sin in Adam*

Turning now from the command to its transgression, we are faced with another and a more difficult question. How came it about that Adam, in all the circumstances of his holiness, his happiness, his spiritual and intellectual clearsightedness, his intimacy with God, could possibly sin ? The question has intrigued enquirers for ages. Many answers have been given, and if none is wholly satisfactory, some are much less wise and cautious than others. It is of no use to make Adam's sin consist in any act involving the insurgence of concupiscence, for, as we have seen, this had no place in him. This consideration at once disposes of many answers that have been suggested, and at the same time cuts away the ground from all those who attack and ridicule the faith because of the disproportion between the price of an apple and eternal life. Again, we shall not go far towards a solution of the problem if we look at Adam's sin as simply a matter of ordinary morality, as a mere disobedience, for in view of his perfect moral state and unclouded spiritual perception, it is more than hard to understand how he could, in such a simple case, have fallen. We must go deeper.

*Nature of Adam's sin*

The first thing to note is the intrinsic possibility of sin. This, as is explained elsewhere, is a necessary accompaniment of the possession of freewill in the absence of the vision of God face to face. Then also, Adam was in a state of probation, and therefore, with God's permission, subject to temptation by Satan. His position was one of wonderful dignity and nobility. He had no equal upon the earth, none even to come near him in power and honour and endowments. All living things were subject to him. He was lord of all. But he was not supreme. God was above him, and God had restricted his freedom of action by forbidding him to touch one tree. Then to him came Satan, speaking through the serpent, and asking why he did not eat of that tree.

" Why should so noble a being as you suffer such a restriction upon your liberty ? Eat of the tree, break through the bonds imposed upon you, let your freedom be unfettered. Become as God yourself, knowing all things and daring all ; be subject to no one, have no master ; be lord of yourself, serving none other." In some such way, as the sacred writer himself indicates, the temptation entered into Adam's mind. There is in it no insurgence of concupiscence, no mere simple disobedience to a moral precept ; but there is the sheer rebellion of mind and will against the ultimate supernatural claims and rights of God. It is the elementary conflict between the natural and the supernatural, which must always be possible to created freedom, until all its capacities and desires are fully extended and satisfied by the immediate possession of the Infinite Good in the beatific vision.

Let it be noted that this explanation in no way goes against the scriptural narrative, which is almost wholly confined to outward things, whereas we have tried, following St Thomas,[1] to go below the surface. We may still marvel at the apparent ease with which Adam fell, but we must remember that only the outlines of the position and circumstances have been revealed to us. If we knew more of his life during the time preceding the fall, how long it lasted, more of the actual circumstances of the temptation and of Satan's subtle and persuasive arguments, much that now puzzles us might become clear. Meanwhile we accept the fact on God's authority, and pass on to examine the effects produced in Adam by his sin.

### § III : ADAM AFTER HIS FALL

THE Council of Trent sums up under one canon the Catholic teaching *Loss of grace* about the immediate effects produced in Adam by his sin, to wit, that he lost the sanctity and justice in which he had been established, that he incurred the wrath and indignation of God, and thereby death, likewise captivity under the power of the devil, and that both as to soul and body he was changed for the worse.[2] That Adam lost his holiness and justice is too clear to need any long demonstration. It is at the root of the whole of Catholic teaching on the Redemption. One of the themes running all through St Paul's epistles is that Jesus Christ, the second Adam, died to regain for us what the first Adam had lost, and that through his redemptive and re-creative work we are revivified by sanctifying grace, and become, by adoption, the sons of God. This is what the second Adam won for us ; this is what the first Adam lost.

And, indeed, such a loss is easily seen to be inevitable. Adam's original condition of holiness constituted a special relationship with God. He was destined to a supernatural end ; he was given the means of attaining it ; he was given, that is to say, a higher life principle in his soul, sanctifying grace. This higher life, now here on earth, and still more, of course, its perfection in the next world, postulates and implies conformity between man's mind and will and God's, for it consists in the close union of the soul and the soul's activity with the divine life. But where there is disunion of wills there can be no oneness of life. Adam, therefore, by putting his will in opposition to God's, deprived himself necessarily of this union with and sharing in the divine life, which is sanctifying grace. By his sin he also lost his preternatural gifts of immortality and

---

[1] *S. Theol.*, II-II, Q. 163, art. 1 and 2.
[2] Session V, can. 1.

integrity.   The threat of death was over him, to fall if he disobeyed God.   The natural law of death was conditionally suspended ; but as the result of his sin it was allowed to work itself out, the conditional promise of immortality was cancelled, and death came into the world ;   " by one man sin entered into this world and by sin death." [1]

*Loss of immortality*   Here we may be forgiven a reference to an objection which of recent years has become a common one.   It is urged that St Paul's teaching about the origin of death is clearly erroneous since science has proved that death stalked through the world for countless ages before man appeared on the earth.   It is hard to believe that such an objection can be seriously made.   Those who bring it are, as a rule, ready enough to find an acceptable interpretation of any passage of Scripture, even at the risk of distortion, if it will agree with their theories, or if the literal sense offends their own susceptibilities.   The only reason for not using some like indulgence here would seem to be that they are only too well pleased to be able to attack the inerrancy of the Bible.   For to the unprejudiced reader it is evident that the only world St Paul is here thinking about is the world of men.   His subject is sin and grace which affect men only ;   he is outlining the spiritual history of mankind, and therefore the only death he speaks of is the death of men, not that which is the lot of all the brute creation.

*Loss of integrity*   The biblical story of the fall makes it equally clear that Adam lost his integrity or freedom from concupiscence.   We have already, in describing his endowments, said enough about this to dispense us from any further elaboration of it.

The Council of Trent mentions also, as an effect of Adam's sin, " captivity under the power of the devil," but it will be more convenient to deal with this in another section and to go on now to a matter of greater difficulty.

*Human nature as such unimpaired*   Did the effects of Adam's sin reach beyond his supernatural and preternatural gifts and penetrate into the very core of his human nature so as to spoil and vitiate, to poison and infect, the substance of his being ?   We are speaking of the direct and immediate effects of his sin, not of those which might, conceivably, have followed from a long course of indulgence in sin if he had not at once repented, as Catholic tradition supposes him to have done.

Certain enactments of some early Church councils, as well as the Council of Trent, seem, at first sight, to teach that it was so. For example, the second Council of Orange, held in 529 to combat Pelagianism, lays down in its first canon that " anyone who holds that Adam was not wholly, that is, both in body and soul, changed for the worse, but that his liberty of soul remaining uninjured, his body alone was made liable to corruption, is deceived by the error of Pelagius and contradicts Scripture " ;   and again, in the eighth

[1] Rom. v 12.

canon, it speaks of the will being vitiated. The Council of Trent, as we have seen, speaks, at the end of the canon describing the effects of his sin, of the " whole Adam, both as to body and soul, being changed for the worse." Theologians commonly, in summing up this teaching, speak of Adam being deprived of his supernatural, and wounded in his natural endowments.

The right interpretation of these decrees is a matter of the greatest importance, for it has serious consequences. We may first of all, for the sake of completeness, set aside an extreme opinion which no Catholic could ever hold, but which was the position taken by Luther, Calvin, and Jansen, and is still set forth in some Protestant formularies. The foundation of this opinion is the denial of the reality of sanctifying grace as a supernatural gift and the consequent assertion that Adam's condition, before his fall, was purely natural. After his fall, therefore, it will follow that his nature was intrinsically depraved and corrupted, and a thing evil in itself. This is a fatal and truly horrible teaching. It means that every human act is of itself and in itself evil. It makes man to be a sink of moral corruption by nature. Natural virtue becomes impossible, and unregenerate man can do nothing of himself but sin. Needless to say, the Church has more than once condemned this doctrine, which is a blasphemy against God's goodness. But even among those who fully admit the Catholic teaching about the supernatural character of Adam's original state, traces of this Protestant and Jansenist poison are sometimes to be found. There are those who, while, indeed, keeping clear of the heretical errors just mentioned, yet speak of man's nature having been in some way positively infected, and possessing in itself a positive and natural inclination to evil. Various explanations are given as to how this comes about and in what it consists. It will be enough to speak of one. It has been suggested that Adam, in sinning, produced some sort of cataclysmic disturbance in the depths of his hitherto harmonious being, a disturbance that upset everything, clouding his intellect, weakening his will, and violently inflaming his passions, so that even his restoration to grace was powerless to restore his shattered natural forces. The only comment that needs to be made upon this suggestion is that it is imaginary and improbable. There is no trace of authority for it, and when we recall that, to fall, Adam had to commit but one sin and not a whole series going on for months or years, and that his sin, being in the intellectual order, was unaccompanied by any violent movements of concupiscence, it cannot be conceded that it produced such a far-reaching, deep-going disturbance of his whole nature, in both body and soul, as this theory requires.

The truth of the matter is both simpler and pleasanter. Adam indeed lost, by his sin, all his supernatural and preternatural gifts, but did not lose anything belonging to his nature as man. All the

elements, properties, and endowments that constituted his manhood he kept intact and unspoilt. So also the human nature that
he handed on to his children was perfect in its kind, having in it
no natural defect or infection or evil inclination that can be looked
upon as the direct result of his sin.

*The language of the Councils*  It may appear that this does not do full justice to the decrees
of Orange and Trent, or even that it is a flat contradiction of them.
As regards the decrees of Orange, an examination of their historical
circumstances will dissipate the apparent contradiction. The
Pelagian heretics, against whom they were directed, denied that
there is any difference between Adam's state before his sin and that
in which we are born. His state, they said, was purely natural,
a state of subjection to death, concupiscence, and suffering. Adam's
sin, they also contended, was a purely personal matter, entailing no
consequences upon his children except in so far as they are apt to
follow his bad example. It is also to be remarked that, in the course
of this controversy, both Catholics and Pelagians always considered
Adam from the historical, not from the philosophical, point of
view ; in other words, they took him as he really was, without
distinguishing between his actual condition and the hypothetical
condition in which he would have been if God had given him nothing
beyond his merely human endowments, if he had been created in
the state of pure nature, as theologians call it. This distinction
was a refinement of later theological thought, unused at that time.

Now the Catholics, while condemning the Pelagians' tenets,
used their language, and basing themselves always on the comparison between the historical Adam before his fall and the same
man after his sin, found no difficulty in saying that, through sin,
the whole man in both body and soul was changed for the worse,
suffering injury to his liberty and the vitiation of his will. In thus
decreeing they did not mean to affirm that he was any the less a
complete and perfect man than he had been at first ; they only
wished to make it clear that man in a state of sin is, in every way,
a much less perfect being, especially when looked upon as a voyager
to heaven, than man in the state of original justice and sanctity.
The continuation and conclusion of the decree confirm this interpretation, and show that the Fathers of the council simply wished
to emphasise the incapacity under which Adam lay, after his sin,
to perform any " salutary act," that is, any act which would positively help him along the road to heaven.

Moreover, a little thought will show how deeply the deprivation
of the gifts in question affected Adam's human nature in its entirety,
and thus will justify the language of the conciliar decree. Though
they were not natural to him, yet they were seated and rooted deep
in his nature, in his soul ; they were an adornment and perfection
of his whole being, raising him to a higher level, giving him new
capacities, and setting up a perfect harmony between all the elements

of his nature. Therefore their loss, while not depriving him of any natural perfection, while leaving his manhood intact and unspoilt in itself, yet left it without all those added ornaments and graces which gave it such strength and beauty.

If we turn from the decree of Orange to that of Trent, which, as far as concerns this particular point, but repeats the phrase used in the earlier council, we find confirmation of our interpretation in the explanation of the words given by a theologian who took a leading part in the formulation and discussion of the Tridentine doctrinal decrees, to wit Dominic Soto, whose comment runs thus : " Man is said to be wounded in his natural endowments. For since it belongs to man's nature to act according to reason, which he is prevented from doing by sensuality, the gift of justice, by repressing sensuality, perfected man in his nature, by removing the obstacle preventing him from acting according to reason, as is natural to man. So therefore the privation of this supernatural gift was an injury and a wound inflicted upon his nature, in so far as it left man defenceless and open to the attacks of the devil, the world, and the flesh, so that he could not always act as nature meant him to do. It is as if, it being a man's nature to walk straight, he had a dog tied to him pulling him this way and that ; then anyone controlling the dog would perfect the man in his natural endowments, and anyone removing the control would, in the same way, injure him. And this is how we are to understand the first canon of the fifth session of our synod (viz., the Council of Trent), where, dealing with the effects of original sin, it lays down that, because of it, we have incurred captivity under the power of the devil, and that the whole Adam and therefore we also have been changed for the worse both as to body and soul. Whence it follows that a man with original sin alone upon his soul, and free from the habits contracted by actual sins, has no greater propensity towards the objects of sense than he would have in a state of pure nature." [1]

We conclude, then, that Adam's sin did not deprive him of any of his purely natural endowments ; after it, as before, his manhood was intrinsically whole and perfect.

A further difficulty now meets us. When we repent after sinning and are taken back into God's friendship, we recover every-thing—grace, virtues, merits—that we had lost by sin. Why cannot the same be said of Adam, if, as Catholic tradition believes, he did penance for his sin and was forgiven ? If grace was given back to him, why were integrity and immortality withheld ?

As regards immortality the answer is at hand, implied in what *Connection* has been said above. He was promised immortality conditionally, *of integrity* if he kept God's command. He was only potentially immortal, *with grace* subject to a condition that affected one act alone, and not any others that might follow. Hence this one condition being unfulfilled,

[1] Dom. Soto, *De Natura et Gratia*, Bk. I, ch. 13.

his loss of the promised gift was final ; repentance could not recover it for him. But this argument does not apply to the gift of integrity which he actually possessed ; some other reason must be sought. This is found in the very nature of sin and in the special circumstances of Adam's sin. Sin (we refer to mortal sin only) is essentially an act of the will which perversely turns away from God, seeking its full satisfaction and final good elsewhere. Any sin is incompatible with the presence of sanctifying grace in the soul, but it does not necessarily affect all of man's spiritual powers or therefore drive out all his supernatural virtues, some of which may have their immediate seat in the unaffected powers, and may exist apart from grace. So, for example, the virtue of faith is not destroyed by every mortal sin ; it is seated immediately in the intellect and is destroyed only by that sin whereby the intellect turns away from God, the sin of unbelief. Similarly our other and lower natural faculties are not directly affected by every sin. Hence repentance, which means the rectification of the will and of the particular faculty affected by the sin, and its consequence, forgiveness, restore to us all that the sin had lost us.

But let us now take the case of a man who, through long indulgence in some sin, such as drunkenness, has contracted a strong, habitual inclination towards it. The act of repentance restores him to grace and rectifies his will, in the purpose of amendment, with regard to that sin, but it does not take away his inclination towards it. Putting right his will does not put right the habit acquired by his lower appetite, and he has a struggle in front of him before the inclination is overcome and he regains balance and control. So in this case, repentance does not restore all that is lost by sin ; it does not restore the right inclination of the appetite perverted by the habit of sin, because this inclination, set up by repeated acts, affects a part of his nature which is not wholly within his will's controlling power. Similar principles apply in Adam's case. Integrity is evidently not a necessary accompaniment of grace, but in him it depended upon grace, so that losing the one by sin he lost the other. But there is no intrinsic reason why getting back the one should mean getting back the other. Adam could rectify his will by repentance, which involves by God's benevolence the restoration of grace ; but integrity, or its contrary, concupiscence, is not a thing within the power and control of his will, but something affecting the impulses and movements of his sensitive appetites under the stimulus of external objects ; hence the rectification of his will in repentance did not involve the restoration of integrity. God could have given it back to him, but we need not investigate the reasons why he did not ; it is enough to have shown why its restoration was not involved in Adam's repentance. Before going on to discuss the transmission of original sin, a little more must be said about the effect produced in Adam from a special point of view, which has some bearing upon questions to be treated later.

In one way or another all the evils suffered by Adam after the fall were the punishment of his sin, even though some of them were not caused by any positive action on God's part, but were simply the result of the withdrawal of his non-natural endowments. Thus the insurgence of concupiscence was the natural result of the loss of integrity. God did not put concupiscence into Adam as a positive punishment; he took off the special brake that he had provided, and natural laws were allowed to have a free course.

But the matter must be looked at from another angle also. Sanctifying grace was not merely a favour given to Adam to keep or to throw away as he pleased. He was under a strict obligation to keep it, because it was the necessary means to the fulfilment of God's design in his regard, the necessary means to the attaining of the end which it was God's will that he should reach. Therefore the rejection of it was in itself sinful; the loss of sanctifying grace was not only the consequence of his sin, not only the penalty of his sin, but also in itself had its share in the guilt of sin. The same is true, in due proportion, of the loss of integrity. In itself this gift is morally indifferent, in the sense that it is not a virtue (just as its opposite concupiscence is not a vice or a sin, as was explicitly defined, as regards those who have been baptised, by the Council of Trent), but in tendency, or what may be called intention, it is decidedly and positively moral, since through the perfect harmony it sets up between man's lower nature and his higher, and the easy and full dominion it gives to the latter over the former, it removes all the perils of temptation arising from the senses and so makes sin much less easy. It was, consequently, a means, subsidiary indeed, but highly important for the attainment of the end set before Adam by God, and he was therefore under strict obligation to preserve it. Further, its loss exposed him to the grave and proximate danger of falling into many more sins, and for this reason also its rejection, just as that of grace, was in itself sinful.

This line of reasoning, however, will not hold if applied to the loss of immortality, which did not share in the nature of a sin, but was exclusively a punishment. In the first place, as we have seen, Adam did not actually possess this gift; it had only been promised him conditionally. Secondly, it is morally a thing wholly indifferent, both in itself and in its implications and bearings. To be immortal is certainly a great privilege, but to be subject to death cannot be a fault. Death is not, even indirectly, a moral evil to be avoided, as is the absence of grace, and likewise, in its way and measure, the absence or loss of integrity. Subjection to death, then, unlike the loss of grace and integrity, was exclusively the penalty of sin, but not, in itself, partaking of the nature of sin. And, we may note in passing, this consideration will help us to understand why our blessed Lady, though conceived immaculate and free from concupiscence, though placed, as far as these two endowments are concerned, in the same exalted position as Adam had been before his fall, was yet not made immortal. The presence in her soul of original sin would have been a moral blemish, so also would have been the existence of concupiscence in her nature, by reason of its close connection with sin, whereas subjection to death is wholly outside the sphere of morality.

## §IV: ORIGINAL SIN IN ADAM'S CHILDREN

So far we have confined our attention to the results of Adam's sin as they were personal to himself. We have now to consider its consequences as they affect all his descendants, always excepting, of course, Jesus Christ himself and his immaculate mother, Mary.

The Church's teaching, which we have to expound, is contained in the 2nd, 3rd, 4th, and 5th Canons of the Fifth Session of the Council of Trent. For our purpose in this section the 2nd Canon is the most important. Herein it is decreed that they incur anathema who assert " that Adam's sin wrought injury to himself alone and not to his posterity; that he brought upon himself only and not upon us also the loss of sanctity and justice which he had received from God; or that he . . . transmitted to the whole human race death and bodily sufferings alone, and not sin which is the death of the soul."

*Act of sin and state of sin*    First of all, a few words of preparatory definition and explanation. Theologians define sin as a turning away from God, our last end, and seeking our end in some created good. We are speaking of mortal sin, which alone is sin in the full sense of the word. This is an abstract or formal definition. In concrete terms sin is any act (and *act* includes words, thoughts, and omissions) whereby man, by violating the divine command and rebelling against God's will, turns his back on God. This is actual sin. The act, however, which may be the work of but a moment, passes, but it has brought about a state of the soul which persists. It has expelled grace from the sinner's soul. Graceless, he is in a state of aversion from and hostility to God. His soul, deprived of its supernatural life, is spiritually dead. He is in a condition of moral disorder; he has left the path to heaven and set his feet on the road to hell. This state is called the state of habitual sin. A warning against possible confusion is here necessary. In ordinary colloquial English habitual sin generally means something quite different; it denotes some sinful act committed so often that it has become an acquired habit; so we speak of an habitual liar or drunkard. We are using the term now in its closer theological sense, as meaning the permanence or fixity of a condition of sinfulness, which results from the committal of any one sin. This condition of habitual sin persists, until the sinner, helped and urged by actual grace, repents, puts himself right with God, whether in the sacrament of Penance or otherwise, is received again into God's friendship, and made holy by the renewed in-pouring of sanctifying grace into his soul.

As we have seen, Adam was put into the supernatural order and *All men born in state of sin* enriched with many gifts, with sanctifying grace, integrity, and potential or conditional immortality. By his sin he lost all these and, though he repented and recovered grace, it is Catholic teaching that, as the result of his sin, all men, except Jesus Christ and his blessed mother, are born without these gifts, which, but for Adam's sin, they would have possessed, born,[1] therefore, subject to death and concupiscence, and deprived of grace.

This condition in which we are born is contrary to God's primary intention with regard to man, it is a state of privation, and, considered in its totality, is called the state of fallen nature or of original sin. It is clear that all the elements of this state are not of equal importance, or equally pertinent to the essential constitution of original sin, and later on we shall have to discuss their relative values.

Our immediate task is to set forth the fact that we are born in this state, and that it is, in fact, the consequence of Adam's sin. Since the aim of these essays is mainly expository and explanatory, it is not for us to set out and examine in full the scriptural proof of the dogma of original sin, or to follow its unfolding from the first indistinct indications of it in some of the Old Testament writings, to its clear and definite formulation by St Paul. We cannot, however, pass over in silence St Paul's witness to this dogma, and his emphatic and clear exposition of its fundamental importance, although this must be well known to all Catholics.

The relevant passage is from the 12th to the 21st verse of the *Romans v.* fifth chapter of the epistle to the Romans. Let us look for a moment at the setting of this passage. In the first four chapters the Apostle treats at length of man's justification, showing that it cannot be brought about by doing the works prescribed in the law of Moses, but that Christ's grace is necessary. In the sixth chapter he begins to speak about the life of man after his justification and his progressive sanctification if he lives according to the spirit of Christ. The fifth chapter forms a kind of bridge connecting these two parts and is itself divided into two distinct portions. In the first half he shows how justification, acquired by the grace of Jesus Christ, is of itself a sure pledge of salvation and is the way that leads to future glory. Then from the twelfth verse onwards he gives a sort of historical explanation of all that he has already said about justification, and so makes it of universal application. Few passages in St Paul's writings are more vivid and dramatic than this, with its continual swing and movement from one extreme to the other, its repeated contrasting of opposing hostile forces, sin and grace, life

---

[1] A partial exception must be made in the case of St John the Baptist, " conceived " being substituted for " born."

and death, Adam the sinner, Christ the saviour, and its joyful celebration of the final triumph of grace :

" 12. Wherefore as by one man sin entered into this world, and by sin death ; and so death passed upon all men in whom all have sinned. 13. For until the law sin was in the world ; but sin was not imputed when the law was not. 14. But death reigned from Adam unto Moses, even over them also who have not sinned after the similitude of the transgression of Adam, who is a figure of him who was to come."

So runs the Douai version of the first three and the most pertinent verses of the passage. This, however, does not give the full force of St Paul's words as they stand in the original Greek. In verse 12, for example, the words " in whom " should, according to the most probable interpretation, be replaced by " because " or " in that " to get his real meaning. Thus he says that death came upon all men because all sinned. And how they sinned is clear from the argument that he at once goes on to state, which, though faulty, perhaps, in construction, is cogent in its demonstrative force. There was sin in the world from the beginning, but it was not imputed—that is, it was not imputed unto death ; until the law of Moses was enacted there was no positive law among the Hebrews, none at least with divine sanction, making any particular sin punishable with death ; and yet during this time death reigned and exercised dominion over all, even over those just men who did not imitate Adam by committing personal, actual sins.

So, to put it briefly, the argument runs thus : Death is the penalty of sin ; death afflicts all men, therefore all have sinned ; but not all men have committed personal sins ; therefore the sin under which all labour, and for which all suffer death, is the sin that all committed when Adam sinned. As his death made all men mortal, so likewise his sin made all men sinful.

So far as this particular point is concerned the rest of the passage adds nothing to the argument. St Paul does not explain how Adam's sin has come down to us, or how we can be said to have sinned, in any true sense, through or in his sin, or what exactly this sin of ours consists in, or several other points that depend upon or result from this teaching. The elucidation of these questions was to be the work of the Church and her doctors and theologians in later ages ; before, however, we turn our attention to these matters, we may briefly consider the fact of the existence of original sin in all mankind from another point of view.

We have, so far, been looking at this doctrine from the point of view of revelation alone. We wish now to ask what, if anything, human reason has to say about it. It is, of course, evident that reason cannot prove directly that the soul of a newly-born infant is deprived of sanctifying grace, and is in a state displeasing to God, a state of sin. This can be known by faith alone, in much the same way as, for example, the real presence of Christ's body in the Eucharist. But in a more general way has reason anything to say in the matter ? Can the human reason, unaided by the light of divine revelation, deduce from man's history and present condition that the race is in a fallen state, that there has been some primeval moral catastrophe, which has so affected all mankind that the whole race is oppressed by its weight and subject to its consequent penalty ?

Many have answered affirmatively. Looking round upon all *Critique of* the evils that afflict mankind and fill the world, they have concluded *argument* that there is no adequate explanation of this terrible state of things *from reason* except that afforded by the dogma of original sin. The best-known exposition of this view in English is, probably, the one given by Cardinal Newman. " To consider the world in its length and breadth, its various history, the many races of man ; their starts, their fortunes, their mutual alienation, their conflicts ; and then their ways, habits, governments, forms of worship ; their enterprises, their aimless courses, their random achievements and acquirements, the impotent conclusion of long-standing facts, the tokens so faint and broken of a superintending design, the blind evolution of what turn out to be great powers or truths, the progress of things, as if from unreasoning elements, not towards final causes, the greatness and littleness of man, his far-reaching aims, his short duration, the curtain hung over his futurity, the disappointments of life, the defeat of good, the success of evil, physical pain, mental anguish, the prevalence and intensity of sin, the pervading idolatries, the corruptions, the dreary hopeless irreligion, that condition of the whole race, so fearfully yet exactly described in the Apostle's words, ' having no hope and without God in the world '—all this is a vision to dizzy and appal, and inflicts upon the mind the sense of a profound mystery, which is absolutely beyond human solution.

" What shall we say to this heart-piercing, reason-bewildering fact ? I can only answer, that either there is no Creator, or this living society of men is in a true sense discarded from his presence. Did I see a boy of good make and mind, with the tokens on him of a refined nature, cast upon the world without provision, unable to say whence he came, his birthplace or his family connections, I should conclude that there was some mystery connected with his history, and that he was one of whom, from one cause or another, his parents were ashamed. Thus only should I be able to account for the contrast between the promise and the condition of his being. And so I argue about the world : *if* there be a God, *since* there is a God, the human race is implicated in some terrible aboriginal calamity. It is out of joint with the purposes of its Creator. This is a fact, a fact as true as the fact of its existence ; and thus the doctrine of what is theologically called original sin becomes to me almost as certain as that the world exists, and as the existence of God." [1]

[1] Newman, *Apologia pro Vita sua*, ch. v.

In much the same way Pascal argues.[1] Both he and Cardinal Newman set out the argument in quite a general way. Others, wishing to strengthen it, come down to particulars and details ; some, by appealing to physical and moral evils indifferently, try to prove that the discord, confusion, pains and wickedness of the world cannot be reconciled with the notion of a good, wise, and omnipotent God, except upon the hypothesis of some great primeval catastrophe which upset everything ; others, for the material of their argument, bring up moral evil alone, in so far as it results from concupiscence, and insist upon its universal and almost complete dominion over mankind, with the resultant enormity and universality of human malice. If for no other reason than the genius and just renown of those who have sponsored them, these arguments cannot be lightly dismissed. But they all seem to lie open to one fatal objection which robs them of real demonstrative power. When we recall that immunity from death, suffering, and concupiscence was a gratuitous privilege added to human nature and not a constitutive part of it, it becomes impossible to say with certainty that human evils and miseries cannot be wholly explained by purely natural causes, that they are not the result of the ordinary action and interplay of simple human and natural passions and tendencies, without postulating some far-off fall from a higher state, some aboriginal break with the Creator's purposes.

The argument, then, is not absolutely conclusive ; it is, however, by no means valueless. It is a strong confirmation of the truth of the revealed dogma, and shows that this is the most satisfying solution of the riddle of human affairs. On this point, as on others, St Thomas speaks with that caution and prudence characteristic of him, his conclusion being that, if we take into account divine providence and the dignity of the higher part of human nature, it can with great probability be shown that the evils afflicting mankind are of a penal nature, whence it can be gathered that the human race is from its origin infected with some sin.[2]

Now that we have established the bare fact of the existence of original sin, derived from Adam, in all his children, many questions at once confront us. What is the precise nature of this sin and how can it be called sin, in any true sense of the word, seeing that it does not depend upon the individual's free will ? How can it be handed down from father to son ? How can its existence and results be reconciled with God's goodness ?

The pivotal question is the first, to which our next section must be given.

[1] Pascal, *Pensées*, sect. vii.
[2] *Contra Gentiles* (Engl., *God and His Creatures*), Bk. IV, ch. 52.

## §V: THE NATURE OF ORIGINAL SIN

THIS is a matter on which Catholic theologians have differed among themselves, a matter as to which there has been a progressive elucidation of the content of divine revelation, and wherein the defined teaching of the Church still leaves some little room for speculation.

St Augustine was the first great theologian who was called upon *St Augustine* to deal specifically and in any detail with the nature of original sin.[1] His treatment, however, was far from being systematic, and his thought is so elusive that, even to-day, though his doctrine has been closely studied by many, there is no general agreement as to what he really held. According to some authorities he thought that original sin consisted in unruly concupiscence, especially sexual concupiscence, and it must be admitted that there is much in his writings to support this opinion. Others, however, acquit him of so crude and almost materialistic a conception, and maintain that he taught that original sin lay rather in the guilt or imputability of concupiscence, in so far as, all men being morally contained in Adam, all human nature being morally summed up in his, it follows that the whole race of men is not only subject to concupiscence, but also shares in the guilt attaching to the existence of concupiscence. As we have seen, the existence of concupiscence in Adam is to be imputed to him as a sin, since his rejection of integrity was sinful. St Augustine, then, would have it that this guilt is shared by all men, and constitutes the original sin. This is probably the truer interpretation of St Augustine's thought.

In the succeeding centuries most theologians followed more or *Protestant* less faithfully in St Augustine's footsteps ; but, though something *exaggerations* was done towards clearing away the uncertainties, it was left to St Thomas to find in this, as in so many other difficult matters, the true way of reconciliation between revelation and the demands of sound reason. With the coming of Protestantism in all its many forms, the whole dogma of original sin became once more the subject matter of attack, denial, and controversy. Some of the Protestant theologians attenuated its importance and its effects, others exaggerated them beyond all measure, even going so far as to say that human nature was wholly corrupted and free will destroyed. The spread of these errors made it necessary for the Church to define her teaching somewhat more accurately than had hitherto been done. In the decrees of the Council of Trent, therefore, the following points are made clear : Man's primitive holiness and justice have been lost, and to all of Adam's descendants have been transmitted both bodily death and sin, which is the death

[1] Perhaps a partial reservation should be made in favour of St Irenaeus, but as his teaching on the question had no influence upon later doctors, he may here be neglected.

of the soul ; [1] original sin is not caused by our imitating Adam's sin, but is produced by natural propagation—that is, it is not actual sin, yet it is proper or personal to each soul ; [2] it is heretical to say that through baptism it is merely covered up or not imputed, for it is utterly taken away. Concupiscence, however, remains, which, though sometimes called sin, is not sin really and strictly speaking, the name being given to it because it arises from and tends to sin. [3]

A few years later the condemnation of certain propositions extracted from the writings of Michael du Bay of Louvain made it clear that original sin is to be taken as voluntary with respect to the free will of Adam in whom it began.

These definitions are not complete, nor are they meant to be ; they were not intended to cover the whole ground, but were framed simply in view of the particular errors then current, as is usually the Church's way in defining her teaching. But they give us a solid foundation, upon which, by the application of approved principles, and by a faithful following of St Thomas in particular, it is easy to build a positive explanation without fear of going astray.

The enquiry into the exact nature of original sin demands close attention ; the matter is by no means as simple as it may seem ; it is, on the contrary, somewhat subtle, and it behoves us to speak with a nice appreciation of phraseology and care in the use of words. But any trouble will be well repaid by the better and deeper understanding of the truth, by the enhanced appreciation of the reasonableness of the Catholic doctrine, and the clearer view of the harmonious agreement between its various parts.

*St Thomas*    St Thomas, then, whom we take as our guide, begins his exposition of the subject by laying down the evident principle, that nothing can be included under the concept of original sin except what is derived from the sin committed by Adam as head of the human race. [4] But in his sin, as in every other, there are two elements to be taken into account : the first is the turning away from God, our last end, and the direct result of this is the loss of sanctifying grace ; the second element is the undue and inordinate cleaving to some created, lesser good in place of God, and to this element corresponds the introduction of concupiscence. Hence we find both of these elements existing in all Adam's posterity. By a process of reasoning which we need not follow in detail, he goes on to show that the deprivation of grace is the more important element, the distinctive, determining, or, in scholastic language, the formal element, while concupiscence is secondary, complementary, and participates in the nature of sin only under the influence of the former element ; in scholastic speech, it is the material or quasi-material element. It will make this clear if we suppose, for a moment, that Adam had been created in a state of grace, but yet,

[1] Can. 2.        [2] Can. 3.        [3] Can. 5.
[4] *Quaest. Disp. De Malo*, iv, a. 2.

at the same time, subject to concupiscence. Then his sin would have deprived him of grace, but would not have *introduced* concupiscence, as this was already present. In that case concupiscence would not have been a constituent element in his sinfulness, because it would not have been influenced, determined, brought into existence by the sinful act entailing the loss of grace.

Finally, since there can be no sinfulness where the element of willing is altogether absent, St Thomas proceeds to show how the loss of grace in us, and the presence of concupiscence, can be said to be voluntary. Here he invokes that principle, so dear to St Paul, that governs the whole economy or dispensation of the spiritual relationships of men in the fall, the redemption, the Church, the communion of saints, and, indeed, is nowadays coming to be more and more clearly recognised as the connecting thread of all human affairs, the principle of the physical and moral and spiritual solidarity or oneness of all mankind.

Upon this principle, Adam sinned not merely as an individual, but as the moral head and spiritual representative of the whole race ; when he rebelled it was all mankind that, through the rebellious will of its head, refused obedience to God, and thus it is this relationship of our dependence upon Adam, and this alone that brings us, born without grace and with concupiscence, under the category and denomination of sinners, in a real and proper, though evidently a very special, sense. And so we come to the definition of original sin, which, according to St Thomas, is the culpable privation of original justice (the word " justice " including both grace and integrity), the culpability, so far as it affects us, being due to the fact that it results from the act of our moral and spiritual head and representative.

Some later theologians, striving after an even greater accuracy of expression, leave out the element of concupiscence (the loss of integrity), and so define original sin as the privation of sanctifying grace, whereby we are averted from God, our supernatural end, and which is, in a way, voluntary in us by reason of our dependence upon Adam. It would be wholly out of place to look more closely into the comparative merits of these two definitions. The trained theologian will appreciate the difference between them and will see wherein one may, perchance, serve better than the other for the solving of subtle objections against the Catholic dogma ; but without a doubt both are satisfactory as enshrining and guarding the substance of the dogma.

In this connection it is interesting to note what was done at the *Proposed canons of Vatican Council* Vatican Council in 1870. Had the Council been able to finish its labours, cut short by the Italian invasion of Rome, it had been intended to include among the definitions of doctrine some on the subject of original sin, in view of a fresh crop of errors that had sprung up. The canons or decrees had been drawn up, examined, revised and amended by the committee of theologians appointed for the purpose, and were ready to be submitted to the fathers of the Council in full session. They have, of course, no conciliar authority, but they have the authority attaching to the representative body of theologians who framed them, and, judging from what happened in the case of other decrees that were actually approved and issued by the Council—for example, those on the Pope's infallibility—we may conclude that these on original sin do represent, in substance, what would have become defined dogma had circumstances allowed. The relevant canons are as follows ! Canon 4 : If anyone shall say that original sin is not truly and properly a sin in Adam's descendants, unless they, by sinning, actually consent to it, let him be anathema ; Canon 5 : If anyone shall say that original sin is formally [1] concupiscence itself, or some physical or substantial disease of human nature, and shall deny that the privation of sanctifying grace is an essential constituent of it, let him be anathema. [2]

In the explanatory notes accompanying these canons it is set forth that the fifth is directed against those who, holding various and discordant opinions, agree in denying that the privation of sanctifying grace enters into its essence ; and it is then noted that the canon does not define that the essence of original sin is nothing but the privation of grace, but that this privation does enter into its essence. [3] This is stressed in another annotation which recognises that among Catholic theologians there are different ways of defining the essence of original sin which quite safeguard the dogma, and again asserts that the only intention of the canon is to define that the privation of grace does belong to that essence. [4]

The primary essential element of original sin is, therefore, the deprivation of sanctifying grace, while, according to St Thomas, a complementary element is the deprivation of integrity, or, speaking in positive terms, the existence of concupiscence.

*Further explanations*  It now remains to be seen how this state of deprivation in which we are born, this loss of original justice, can be said to be sinful, displeasing to God, and morally evil, or in other words, how it can, as it exists in us, be brought under the denomination of voluntary ; for otherwise it cannot in any true sense be called sinful, since sin is essentially a matter of free will. Some little has already been said when expounding St Thomas's doctrine on the essence of original sin, but we must now enquire more closely into it.

To solve this question we must go back to the beginning when God bestowed original justice upon Adam, so that by considering the conditions upon which it was given, we may the better under-

---

[1] *Formally*, a word of common occurrence in scholastic theology, which may be rendered here as " precisely identical with."
[2] *Collectio Lacensis*, vol. vii, col. 566.
[3] *Ibid.*, p. 558.      [4] *Ibid.*, p. 549.

stand the results flowing from its loss. Or it would be truer to say that from the known results we can come to a knowledge of the original conditions of the gift, since these are, at the most, implied and not explicitly stated in Holy Scripture.

Original justice, then, was not given to Adam for himself alone, but given to him for all men ; it was not just a privilege personal to him, but was a gift to all mankind, who potentially were in him and were, in the future, to derive their human nature from him. So it was to have been passed on to all through the channel of natural generation, in the sense that, according to the divine plan, it would have been given to all men as the inevitable but supernatural consequence of their coming into human existence by way of natural procreation. The state of grace, with all that it implies, was to have been mankind's inheritance, on condition that it had been preserved by Adam, who was thus put into the position of the official and, as it were, the juridical head and representative of the whole human family. This is clearly implied by the Council of Trent [1] when it rejects and condemns the opinion that Adam's loss of the holiness and justice that he had received from God was his loss alone, and not ours also, for he could not have lost it for us unless he had also received it for us, as a sacred trust and inheritance to be handed on to us.

Now it must be noted that this divine dispensation or arrangement depends upon God's positive ordinance ; it does not result from the very nature of things. There is nothing in the nature of grace to make the universality of its distribution dependent upon the oneness of the human race ; had God so chosen, he could have raised every individual to the state of grace from the moment of conception, without taking any account of what Adam had done, of whether he had sinned or not. As Creator of both nature and grace he has supreme and unfettered liberty in all his dealings with men on either plane. Hence by giving Adam this power of handing on grace to all men or of cutting it off from them he gave him a special privilege and responsibility ; he constituted him the head and representative of all mankind in a new way, in the spiritual order, the order of grace ; he set up another and new kind of unity and solidarity between Adam and all his children. Adam became the human spring whence grace was to flow and pass through the whole human stream. Yet, at the same time, this new, high office of his, though strictly supernatural and dependent upon God's special ordinance and positive dispensation, was based and raised upon Adam's natural office as the fount and spring of human nature ; it was closely connected with it, and may even be looked upon as the same office raised to the supernatural order. As all men were seminally in Adam from the point of view of their human elements and nature, so it was God's dispensation that they should all be in

[1] Session VI, can. 2.

him, as a river in its source, with regard to their supernatural endowments. Hence Adam's probation or trial and his reaction to it were matters of the greatest moment to all his children. If he had proved staunch and faithful he would have been confirmed in his high office as the human source of supernatural life for all mankind. There would have been no need for the " second Adam," Jesus Christ, to have been installed in that office. But as he failed under trial, the office was taken from him, and he became, instead of the supernatural spring of life, the natural source of death, of both body and soul, for all men.

We see then, that, by reason of Adam's representative character, and on account of the supernatural unity and solidarity established by God, between him and all his posterity, when he was put on trial, it was the whole human race that was being tested, and all mankind that was found wanting. It was not simply the will of an individual, isolated man that rebelled against God, but a will that represented and acted in behalf of the whole human family.

Thus original sin, as it is in each one of us, is voluntary, not indeed by any act of our personal will, but through the act of the " family will," [1] through our relationship of spiritual dependence upon and solidarity with our first, divinely appointed, supernatural head and representative Adam. This explanation may seem, at first sight, to be far-fetched, or to be merely an arbitrary theory concocted in order to escape the difficulties caused by a harsh and unreasonable dogma. It is, in fact, strictly scriptural. It is implied in all that St Paul says about the fall and the redemption. His epistles are full of this idea of moral unity and solidarity, on the one hand, between Adam and his posterity, on the other, between Jesus Christ and his members or brethren. We have already seen how his incisive words, " For all sinned " [2] can refer only to the sin that all committed in Adam ; again he writes : " For by a man came death, and by a man the resurrection of the dead. And as in Adam all die, so also in Christ all shall be made alive," [3] where he invokes the same principle to explain the whole dispensation of the fall and the redemption.

The same explanation was given by the theologians who framed and annotated the decrees and definitions which were to have been submitted to the consideration of the Vatican Council. " In this form of the definition," they write, " three things are to be noticed : (a) what is said to belong to the essence of original sin is not a mere negation, the absence of sanctifying grace, but is the privation of grace, that is, the absence of that sanctity which, according to God's ordinance, ought to have been found in all Adam's descendants, inasmuch as God raised the whole human race to the supernatural

[1] As St Thomas calls it, the *voluntas naturae*, the will, not of the person, but of humankind taken collectively.
[2] Rom. v 12.          [3] 1 Cor. xv 21-22.

order of grace, in its source and head, whereas now all are deprived of grace. But this privation (b) neither does nor can exist without a fault committed by free will; this free will, however, is not that which is personal to each individual, but the free will of the head of the whole human race, of Adam himself, who, sinning, lost not only that grace which belonged to him personally, but also that which, according to God's plan, would have been passed on to all his children. Hence Adam's sin was the sin of human nature and becomes the habitual sin inhering in all who, by carnal generation, share in the nature derived from Adam. . . ." [1]

It was necessary to treat of this rather subtle matter at some length because it forms the centre and core of the whole dogma of original sin from the explanatory point of view. The points to be remembered are these : original sin, as it is in each individual, is not an actual sin but an habitual sin or a state of sin ; the free will concerned in it is not the free will of the individual, but the free will of the head of the family or race, in so far as Adam was appointed the family or race representative in the supernatural order ; and therefore the individual is not responsible personally, for through no fault of his own is he a member of the family despoiled by its father's sin of its supernatural privileges. These points being established, everything else follows almost as a matter of course.

## § VI: TRANSMISSION OF ORIGINAL SIN

THE question of the transmission of original sin from generation *Theological* to generation presents no great difficulty once its nature has been *development* settled, but it is interesting from the point of view of historical theology. It is a good example of the way in which, with the progress of time and the incidence of conflict and discussion, the meaning of some revealed doctrine grows clearer, though in substance and reality it has been firmly believed from the beginning. From the very first the Church taught that all the children of Adam are born in a state of enmity with God and need to be reborn and cleansed in the Sacrament of Baptism. The whole dogma of original sin is bound up in this belief, but, as is clear, it is implicit only. It was but gradually that the implications were worked out, and that many points of truth, hitherto hidden or unheeded, began to be seen clearly. During the first four centuries the process of development had already gone some way, but the Pelagian controversy in the fifth did more to carry it forward than anything that had hitherto happened. But even this did not bring full enlightenment, one point upon which there was still some obscurity being that of how original sin is passed on from generation to generation. The ante-Pelagian fathers had stressed, even to exaggeration, the act of generation as the medium of transmission ; some of them, indeed, seem

[1] Acta Conc. Vaticani, *Collectio Lacensis*, vol. vii, col. 549.

to regard it as the true effective cause of original sin. The Pelagians put the question in a new light. The soul, they said, is spiritual and, therefore, cannot be produced by the physical act of generation ; neither can a father transfuse or pass on some of his soul to his son, for being spiritual, it is indivisible. The soul, then, must be directly created by God. So far the argument is sound, but, because they had a wrong notion of original sin, they drew a false conclusion, for they said to the Catholics : " If the soul is created in a state of sin, as you contend, God must be the author of the sin, a blasphemous doctrine that no Christian can hold. Therefore, you must give up your false dogma of original sin."

*St Augustine's difficulty*

St Augustine felt the force of the objection which has its full effect to-day upon those who hold erroneous opinions upon the nature of original sin. He could not see a good way out of the difficulty, and consequently against his instinctive inclination and his better judgement, could not bring himself to accept without reserve the teaching that each soul is immediately and directly created by God. He hoped that some justification could be found for the theory of traducianism, according to which the father exerts a real causative and productive efficiency in the production of his son's soul. His letter to St Jerome on the subject [1] proves both his painful hesitation on the point and his profound intellectual humility ; whatever his preferences might be, and however great the difficulties entailed by the truth, he would accept it whole-heartedly. The real cause of his difficulty lay, of course, in his imperfect understanding of the nature of original sin. This problem had not yet been worked out to its final solution. Though St Augustine, probably, did not hold that original sin is identical with concupiscence, as he has often been accused of doing, though he did not conceive of it as some positive poison infecting the soul, yet he was overmuch inclined to look upon its positive aspect, and over-estimated the part played in it by concupiscence. But if we bear in mind the definition that has been given and its explanation, the difficulty that bothered him disappears and the transmission of original sin through the act of generation is easily understood.

*Explanation*

It is a result of mankind's solidarity, physical and spiritual, with Adam. We are burdened with original sin only in so far as we are one family with Adam as our head and representative. His headship in the supernatural order is founded on and co-extensive with his physical headship, and therefore affects all those and only those who are descended from him by physical generation. Or, again, original sin is not a matter of the individual's will, but of the " family " will, the representative's will ; it partakes of the nature of sin only in so far as it is derived from Adam. But every-thing derived from him comes to us by the way of physical genera-tion whereby human nature is handed on from father to son. Hence

[1] *Epist. S. Augustini*, 166.

original sin, just as every other human inheritance, comes to us by this channel. This is not to say that the act of generation is the efficient cause of the existence of original sin in the individual. That act is not the efficient or productive cause even of the existence of the child's soul.[1] All it does is so to dispose the material body, to put it into such a condition that, according to the divinely established laws of nature, it calls for and, if we may be allowed the word, necessitates the creation of the soul by God. But this soul, good and, indeed, a perfect thing in the natural order, is deprived of that sanctifying grace which it ought to have had, according to God's original but conditional design ; instead of being supernaturalised, as it ought to have been, it is a purely natural thing ; at the same time, and owing to the same cause, the whole human being, body and soul, is deprived of the gift of integrity, which it ought to have possessed, and, therefore, subject to concupiscence. But all this comes into effect when, and only when, the complete human being comes into existence, which is the result of the act of generation. This act, then, is the vehicle of the transmission of original sin.

After all that has been said, it is hardly necessary to enter upon *Answers* the process of argument by which God is defended against the charge *to some* *objections* of injustice commonly made against him in this connection. If original sin were a positive thing made or created by him, the charge could not be met ; but such an hypothesis is blasphemous. Again, if original sin lay in the deprivation of something belonging, of right, to man's nature, even though this natural right be God's gift, the accusation could be sustained. But since it consists in the deprivation of something to which man has not the shadow of a claim or right, of something that is farther above his own capacity of attainment, farther beyond the stretch of his own faculties to reach, than even reason would be above the powers of the lower animals, the deprivation, to wit, of sanctifying grace, the bottom drops out of the charge altogether. God chose to give this supernatural gift to man out of the abundance of his love. His decision was unfettered, divinely free. Similarly, therefore, he was completely free to make the conditions upon which the gift should be given, kept, and handed on. In the supernatural order, it cannot be too often repeated, man has and can have no rights against God, no claims upon him ; God can have no duties towards man. On his side it is all a matter of free bestowal ; on ours of undeserved receiving. Even our merits, real as they are, are not ours in principle, but come from God's grace through Jesus Christ. Therefore there can be no question of injustice arising out of the existence and transmission of original sin, because this is a matter concerning the supernatural order of grace, wherein God's freedom is above all measure and understanding. Many Catholic writers, in dealing with this question, use as an illustration the example of a king who,

---

[1] See Essay vi, pp. 211-12.

out of pure benevolence, raises one of his lowest subjects, an unlettered, unknown peasant, to the highest and most honourable position in the kingdom, with the promise that, should he prove himself faithful and deserving, his honours and estates will be confirmed to his heirs for ever, while, on the other hand, the consequence of unfaithfulness will be the reduction of himself and them to the lowly condition wherefrom he had been raised. Put to the test, the ungrateful subject fails and rebels against his king. As a result he is stripped of all his possessions, and not only does he sink back to his former state of poverty and misery, but he and all his children, as long as men keep the remembrance of his history, lie under the stigma and disgrace of ingratitude, rebellion, and treason. As far as it goes the illustration is good; it shows that no accusation of injustice against God can be upheld, but it is only an illustration, and, like all analogies between the human and the divine, falls far short of being an adequate picture of the reality, since there can be no true measure of proportion between the highest worldly position and the divine, adoptive sonship conferred by grace. We have now to see what effects are produced in us by original sin, first as regards this present life, then as far as the future life is concerned.

## § VII: EFFECTS OF ORIGINAL SIN

*Loss of grace* THE first effect of original sin, as regards this present life, is, of course, the loss of sanctifying grace with all therein involved, to wit, the loss of the theological and moral virtues and the gifts of the Holy Ghost. Although this loss, as we have seen, is of the very essence of original sin, it may also, from another point of view, be regarded as an effect.

The canon of the Council of Trent [1] which defines the Catholic teaching on this point, indicates that the deprivation of grace has two aspects : it has the nature of sin in so far as it is an aversion from God, and the nature of a penalty in so far as we are thereby left bereft of the power and means of attaining the final end to which we were destined.

*Loss of preternatural gifts* The second effect is the loss of the preternatural gifts, namely, integrity, immortality, and freedom from pain and suffering. The Council of Trent clearly defined that subjection to death is the result of original sin, but does not speak in such explicit terms about the loss of integrity. Since, however, as seen above, it says that concupiscence " comes from sin," it implies, clearly enough, that Adam's sin is responsible for the loss of integrity, and this is the unanimous teaching of all theologians.

*Wound in man's nature* As for the other gifts bestowed upon Adam, their loss is included under the general phrase that " the whole man, both in body and soul, suffered a change for the worse." This loss of the pre-

[1] Session V, can. 2.

ternatural gifts is often spoken of as a wound in man's nature. A wound is cut in the body, a severance of parts or tissues which ought to be united, thus creating disunion and disorder and preventing the proper functioning of the parts affected. Similarly by original sin the perfect harmony and unity, that originally reigned throughout the various levels of man's nature, are broken, with the result that his different faculties, especially his higher powers of will and intellect, cannot work with that ease and sureness and peace that otherwise would have been theirs.

These effects had to be mentioned here, even at the cost of some *Captivity under Satan* repetition ; but after what has already been set down about them there is no need to say more. There is, however, another effect that must be more fully explained. The Council of Trent speaks in two places of " captivity under the power of the devil " as being the result of Adam's sin.[1] Modern thought, so called, cannot abide the idea of a personal devil, and to its votaries the Tridentine doctrine will appear absurd ; many Catholics, even, are a little shy of such teaching, and few, perhaps, realise all that it means. Yet the New Testament is full of it : " Know you not, that to whom you yield yourselves servants to obey, his servants you are whom you obey, whether it be of sin, unto death, or of obedience, unto justice," [2] and, " By whom a man is overcome, of the same also he is the slave ; " [3] it is, indeed, but one special aspect of a universal natural truth and law.

God, in creating the world, established it as a vast hierarchy of beings, according to a plan of an ascending scale of natural dignity and perfection. From inanimate beings we rise through the different degrees of living things to man, who is supreme among material creatures. Above man is the world of pure spirits, the angels, who, according to Catholic teaching, are divided into choirs according to the varying degrees of their natural dignity. Above all, infinitely transcending all, is God. Now it is the general law of nature that power and dominion correspond with natural perfection and dignity. Every being has some sort of natural dominion over those lower in the scale of perfection, and may make use of them to serve its own lawful ends and convenience. So we may use the lower creatures, animate and inanimate, for our own good, as our servants. We have natural rights over them. These rights are not unlimited, and may be abused. It is, perhaps, impossible to determine the exact limits of this dominion, but as to its real existence there can be no doubt. Similarly in the angelic world, according to Catholic theology, the higher angels exercise a certain empire over the lower, in many ways, as St Thomas sets forth at length in his treatise on the angels.

Finally, the angels, by virtue of their higher place in the scale

[1] Session V, can. 1, and Session VI, cap. 1.
[2] Rom. vi 16.          [3] 2 Peter ii 19.

of natural perfection, have certain natural rights of dominion over their inferiors—men, brutes, and lifeless creatures. How far this empire extends we cannot say ; of course, it does not destroy man's autonomy, but there is no doubt of its existence as a natural corollary of the hierarchy of things. The story told in the Book of Job is an illustration of it.

*Natural empire of Lucifer*

Consider, now, the angels who rebelled and fell. They were shut out from the supernatural kingdom, but there is no reason whatever to suppose that they suffered any loss or hurt in their natural qualities and endowments. They kept all their wonderful natural gifts of intellect and power, their natural dignity and superiority, and therefore, likewise, their natural rights of dominion, over the lower creatures. And if we accept the common teaching that Lucifer was one of the very highest of God's angels, it follows that his natural empire is of immense power and extent. But another factor in the ordering of things has here to be taken into account. The angels had not been left in their natural state, but had been raised to the supernatural plane, becoming sharers in God's life and glory. Hence when Lucifer was cast down he lost all his natural rights of dominion over those of the lower angels who remained faithful, since the least of those who are in the supernatural order is superior in dignity and perfection to the highest of them who are possessed of natural gifts alone. Satan was despoiled of his kingdom. He suffered a further and greater rebuff to his dignity when man was created and raised by grace to the supernatural plane. Here was a creature who, by all the laws of nature, should have been a lowly subject in Satan's kingdom, yet who, through God's magnificent generosity, had been raised above him and set upon a height of dignity and perfection which he could envy but never reach. Lucifer the proud, " the prince of this world," [1] found himself humbled, deprived of his natural rights, forced to take a lower place even than man; so far beneath him in the hierarchy of nature. No wonder that he tried to recover his lost empire. Against the faithful angels all assaults must, of necessity, be vain, but man was still open to attack, and when attacked, succumbed. But we must not confuse the issue. This first struggle was purely a battle between the natural and the supernatural. It was not a conflict of good and evil in the merely moral or ethical order. Satan wished to rob man of his supernatural dignity and to pull him down to his purely natural level, so as to enrol him in the ranks of his own subjects. The attack was successful ; Adam, for himself and his children, rejected the supernatural, proposing to be his own end and his own ruler, chose the merely natural, fell to the lower level, and so doing, came once more beneath the empire of Satan, who recovered his natural rights over him as an inferior being, which man's elevation to the supernatural

[1] John xii 31.

level had taken away from him. Herein lies the basis of man's captivity under the devil's power. It is but the working of a general natural law.

But God's goodness was not defeated. The Redeemer was appointed and, by his merits, drawn upon in advance, mankind was again raised to the supernatural order, and Satan once more despoiled of his natural rights of empire. While, however, man's fall was actually universal, affecting every individual, the redemption, though universal in principle, does not become individually effective until the individual is incorporated with Christ, until Christ's merits are applied to him personally, and sanctifying grace is thus infused into his soul. Being born, then, without grace and subject to the universal effect of Adam's fall, he is born a citizen of the natural kingdom only, where Satan still has and wields his rights and powers of empire. He is born a subject of the devil. In essence, therefore, this subjection to Satan is a quite natural thing, resulting from the natural superiority of angelic to human nature. There is still, however, a reservation to be made. It is true that Christ's redemptive merits are not actually applied to the new-born child until, in baptism, he is incorporated with Christ. But Christ died for all the members of the human family into which the child is born ; Christ wishes all to be saved ; the child, therefore, is included in the all-embracing supernatural destiny of mankind ; if not actually, he is already potentially supernaturalised, and it would seem to follow from this that God does, in fact, curtail to some extent Satan's natural rights of empire. Besides, since the infant is not yet capable of using his reason and will, since they are beyond the influence of his nascent imaginative faculty, in the stimulation of which Satan's power over men principally lies, his dominion over the child is almost wholly, if not quite, passive and ineffectual ; he cannot produce in him any actual evil effects or sinful acts. We need not here enquire into the consequences of this captivity, either in infants or adults, which is set forth in the essay on the angels. It is enough to have established its reality and to have shown that it means that the child, until its rebirth in baptism, is enrolled under Satan's flag and subject to his natural dominion. Hence, when the priest, in the prayer of exorcism before baptism, admonishes Satan to " go out and depart " from the child, he is not indulging in ecclesiastical rhetoric or repeating the tags of ancient superstition ; he is speaking the language of stark realism. Whence it is easy to understand the desire of the Church that children should be baptised as soon as possible, to put them beyond Satan's power, and enrol them in the supernatural kingdom of Christ.

So far we have been considering the effects resulting from original *Fate of* sin, as regards this life. We have now to see what effects it will *unbaptised* have upon the soul's destiny in the next life. For the sake of clear- *infants* ness we shall take the case of the soul that passes into the other world, unstained by actual sin, but yet still burdened with original sin. Though some who come to the full use of reason may die in this condition, which is a matter of dispute among theologians, it is evident that the question principally concerns children who die without baptism, and in view of their immense numbers, it is of great practical interest and importance. Opponents of the Church, neglecting her authoritative pronouncements and the general and current teaching of her theologians, are given to seizing upon some opinion held by St Augustine or some other early father, to putting this individual view forward as representative of Catholic doctrine, and then denouncing this as harsh, inhuman, and incompatible with God's loving mercy.

We do not deny that some of the early fathers or later theologians may have spoken about this matter in terms of exaggeration, or held opinions that to us seem harsh and unreasonable, especially when they were excited by the denials of heretics, with whom controversy was often violent and bitter, and led, not seldom, to overstatements on both sides. Notwithstanding the reverence due to these earlier champions of the faith, and the authority and prestige rightly attaching to their names and teachings, it must be borne always in mind that no father and no doctor is infallible ; and where the Church has spoken, or even shown the bent of her mind, it is not only our right but our duty to throw over even an Athanasius or an Augustine, if his teaching is not wholly at one with hers.

On this present question the Church has had occasion to make clear certain points of her faith, sometimes when issuing conciliar decrees, sometimes when publishing condemnations of erroneous doctrines. In the Council of Florence, A.D. 1439, which effected a short-lived reunion between the Church and the schismatical Easterns, she included as an article of her creed the affirmation that " the souls of those who depart from this life, either in actual mortal sin or in original sin only, go down at once into hell, there however to suffer disparate penalties." In 1567 Pope St Pius V condemned a number of propositions taken from the writings of Michael du Bay of Louvain ; among them is one asserting that the unbaptised child, attaining the use of his reason after death, will actually hate and blaspheme God and set himself against God's law. In 1794 Pius VI condemned a great many of the errors propounded by the Erastian synod recently held at Pistoia in Tuscany, among them being the " doctrine that rejects as a Pelagian fable that part of the lower regions (generally known as the limbo of infants) in which the souls of those dying in original sin alone are punished with the pain of loss (i.e., the beatific vision) without the pain of fire. . . ."

From these pronouncements we draw the following conclusions : unbaptised children are deprived of the beatific vision of God, which is man's true final end ; this is a part of the defined Catholic faith.

It is certain that they neither hate nor blaspheme God nor rebel against his law, and it is, at least, most improbable that they suffer from the fire of hell or any sort of positive, sensible pain ; while, on the contrary, it is most likely that their state is one of true peace and natural happiness. The dogma of faith is clearly contained in Christ's words to Nicodemus : " Unless a man be born again of water and the Holy Ghost, he cannot enter into the kingdom of God," [1] and is, also, the direct theological consequence of all that has been said about the nature of original sin. This consists primarily in the privation of sanctifying grace, which is the principle of divine sonship, and, hence, the necessary condition for entry into God's eternal kingdom. The beatific vision is the full flowering of grace ; when the soul in grace is freed from the bonds of flesh and cleansed from its lesser impurities and from the debts it owes to God's justice, it passes naturally into glory. Where, however, the bud has not formed no flower can bloom.

On the other hand, there is no ecclesiastical authority for the opinion, now almost universally rejected, that the child who dies unbaptised suffers any pain of sense, that is, any positive punishment such as is inflicted upon those who die with unforgiven, actual, mortal sins upon their souls. On this point Catholic doctors and theologians have not always been in full agreement among themselves. St Augustine, for example, held that such children would suffer some sort of positive pain, though he admitted that he did not know how or what, and was, as a rule, careful to add that it would be of a kind very light and easy to bear. He was followed by many in the West, whereas the Greek fathers, generally, were inclined to the view that these children suffer nothing except the pain of loss or deprivation of the beatific vision. The theological reason for this opinion, which is now held by all, is clearly explained by St Thomas : " The punishment," he writes, " bears a proportion to the sin. Now in actual sin there is, first, the turning away from God, the corresponding punishment being the loss of the beatific vision ; and secondly, the inordinate cleaving to some created good, and the punishment corresponding with this is the pain of sense. But in original sin there is no inordinate cleaving to created good, . . . and therefore it is not punished by the pain of sense." [2]

From this follows our third conclusion, to wit, that it is most probable that the state of unbaptised children in the next world is one of peace and natural happiness. Since they do not suffer any pain of sense, and since they do not hate God or set themselves against his law, the only thing that could trouble their peace or spoil their happiness would be a sorrow or anguish resulting from the knowledge of the supernatural happiness for which they were intended, but which is for ever lost to them. Some eminent theologians, as St Robert Bellarmine, have held that they do

[1] John iii 5.  [2] *Quaest. Disp., De Malo*, v, a. 2.

suffer in this way. Apart from the authority of some of the fathers, their main reason for thinking thus is that the child will see and understand his loss and therefore grieve over it. St Thomas, however, denies this and his reasoning seems conclusive.[1] It is based on the truth, fundamental in Catholic theology, that grace and, therefore, the possession of the beatific vision, which is the final culmination of grace, are absolutely and in the strictest sense of the word supernatural. They not only exceed man's natural powers of attainment, but also and equally his natural powers of knowing. It is impossible for a man to know, by natural reason alone, without the help of revelation and the gift of faith, that his final happiness consists in the immediate sight and possession of God. Consequently unbaptised children, not having received the sacrament of faith, have not the supernatural knowledge, without which they cannot know what they have lost. Hence their loss causes them no anguish of soul.

Although these considerations may bring some little consolation to the Catholic mother grieving over the fate of her child who has died unbaptised, they will not relieve the weight upon her conscience, should hers have been the fault, or free parents from the obligation to have their children baptised as soon as possible, since there is no measure or proportion between the natural happiness that will be their lot in limbo, and the inconceivable felicity of heaven, of which man's carelessness may so easily deprive them. Moreover, it must be clearly understood that the child dying without baptism is definitely lost. He is not in some midway state between salvation and damnation. He was made for one end only, a supernatural end ; and failure to reach that, whether the fault be his own or another's, is complete failure, is eternal loss, even though unaccompanied by the positive tortures of a soul that has wilfully damned itself.

*Conclusion*       To conclude this short study of the fall and original sin, we may call attention to the fact that the whole of it is based upon the truth and the reality and the supernatural character of sanctifying grace. Without this the fall becomes a myth and original sin an absurdity. Consequently, since the most fundamental error of Protestantism is its denial of the reality or its grievous misunderstanding of the nature of grace, Protestant theology is always hopelessly at sea and at loggerheads with itself when dealing with original sin.

Again, the dependence of the dogma of the fall and original sin upon the reality of grace at once puts this dogma into its place among those that are essentially mysterious. It is beyond the power of our reason fully to understand it, or even to prove its existence. This we know only by revelation. But once it is accepted it makes nearly everything else clear. The fall explains the life and death of Jesus Christ, and the whole sacramental system. Without

[1] *Quaest. Disp., De Malo*, v, a. 3.

original sin the Church, which is the permanent means established by God to make good the damage done by Adam's sin, would be a useless encumbrance, and without the Church religion, in the full meaning of the word, would soon flounder and disappear. And even the history of the world, especially that of the chosen people, can only be properly understood in the light of this dogma. Mysterious, then, as it is, it is lit up and made easy of belief by all around us, by everything that touches us most nearly ; unpalatable as it may be to our natural taste, it is sweetened by its necessary connection with all those things that are our greatest joy in this world and our only hope for the next.

B. V. MILLER.

# XI

## JESUS CHRIST, GOD AND MAN

### §I: INTRODUCTORY

AN essay so small upon a subject so vast as " Jesus Christ, God and Man " seems to require a few preliminary words to define its scope. This is the first of four essays in the present volume devoted to the theology of the Incarnation, and its object is to explain, so far as space will permit, the doctrine of the hypostatic union, that is, the admirable union of the human and the divine nature in the adorable Person of our Lord Jesus Christ.   For this is the fundamental truth regarding our holy Redeemer, and if this is denied or misconstrued all else that is said of him must be either false or inadequate.

Christ is the model of manhood, he is the exemplar of every human virtue and perfection, he is the man who has been loved and reverenced more than any other since the world began.   But his human nature is perfect because it is the humanity of God himself ; his love has won all hearts because it is the human love of God.   He is the Man of Sorrows, he stands out in history as the Sufferer. Well could he say through the mouth of his prophet, " Attend and see if there be any sorrow like unto my sorrow " ; [1] there could be no other such sorrow because there could be no other human nature so sensitive and so perfect, none with such capacity for suffering as the humanity which God had made his own.   He is our High Priest and Redeemer.   But he could have been neither, unless he were both God and Man.   By reason of his very Person he is the ideal Mediator between God and men ; being man he can offer sacrifice to God ; and because he is God his sacrifice is of infinite value.

The hypostatic union, therefore, is the foundation of the whole of the Catholic teaching about Christ.   In fact, so dominated are Catholic theologians by the vital importance of this fundamental truth that they have been accused of emphasising the divinity of Christ at the expense of his true manhood.   " Although the Church theoretically maintains the humanity of Christ side by side with his divinity," wrote Sabatier, [2] " the latter inevitably absorbs everything. The traditional Christology is incurably docetist ; so much so that from this point of view it has become practically impossible to write a serious life of Jesus Christ."   How little this accusation is justified may be seen from several monumental works on the life of Christ which have appeared in late years from the pen of Catholic

[1] Jer. Lament. i 12.
[2] *Esquisse d'une philosophie de la religion* (Paris, 1897), pp. 179-180.

scholars,[1] and also from the two immediately succeeding essays in which an account is given of the human life and experience of our Saviour. If the Church jealously safeguards the true divinity of Christ, she is no less intransigent upon his real humanity ; for the one no less than the other is revealed by God, the one no less than the other is essential to the work of the Redemption.

Comparatively little space will be devoted in the present essay to the purely scriptural basis of our faith in the divinity of Christ, in the first place because for those who accept the gospels as the inspired word of God, as all Catholics do, it is enough to read a few pages of the gospel of St John to be persuaded that Christ is truly God, and secondly because the faith of the Church on this point becomes luminously clear as we follow the Christological controversies of the first six centuries. The Catholic Church has ever re-echoed the profession of faith of St Peter, the rock and foundation upon which she is built : " Thou art the Christ, the Son of the living God " ; so that the dogmatic letter of Pope Leo I (449), in which the dogma of the hypostatic union was defined in precisely the same terms in which theologians teach it to-day, was acclaimed by the Fathers of the Council of Chalcedon with the cry : " Peter has spoken by the mouth of Leo."

To the history of these controversies more particular attention will be paid, since the study of them will enable us to understand the exact meaning of the famous dogmatic definitions of the Church on the union of the two natures in the one person of Christ. The fuller appreciation of all that is involved in the hypostatic union will lead us to consider its consequences as far as they concern the Person of the Word Incarnate, and in particular the preternatural and supernatural perfections of his human nature.

The theme is profound—for we are dealing with a mystery —and the manner of treatment must accordingly reflect something of the abstruse character of the subject. " So then, let our human weakness sink under God's glory, and ever find itself inadequate to the exposition of the works of his mercy. Let our thoughts fail, let our minds be at a loss, let our utterance fade ; for it is good that we should feel how imperfect are even our true thoughts concerning the majesty of the Lord." [2]

§II: GOD WITH US

CHRISTIANITY has been defined as the religion of the Fatherhood *The Father-* of God ; and, properly understood, the definition is perhaps as *hood of God* good as any that could be given. Even a superficial reading of

[1] *E.g.* L. Fillion : *The Life of Christ*, tr. (Herder, 1928-30), 3 vols. ; Archbishop Goodier : *The Public Life of Jesus Christ* (Burns Oates and Washbourne, 1930), 2 vols.

[2] St Leo, Serm. 11, *de Passione Domini.*

the Gospels leaves the predominant impression that God is the Father; and St John himself seems to regard this as a suitable summing up of the Christian revelation when he says, " No man hath seen God at any time. The only-begotten Son who is in the bosom of the Father, he hath declared him." [1]

But the definition is one which needs explanation. An entirely inadequate conception of Christianity would restrict the revelation of Christ to the bare statement that God is the provident Father of all his creatures, and in particular that he has a special care for the human race. If this were so then Christ would have added little to what was already common knowledge among the Patriarchs of the Old Testament, or indeed to what the human reason is able, even without revelation, to discern. The Jews, who knew their Scriptures well, could have found in any one page of their sacred books abundant evidence of the providential care of God for the chosen people of Israel, and the author of the Book of Wisdom speaks clearly enough of the wisdom of God that " reacheth from end to end mightily and ordereth all things sweetly, [2] ordering all things in measure and number and weight " ; [3] for " he made the little and the great, and he hath equally care of all." But the revelation of Christ concerning the Fatherhood of God is a mystery " which in other generations was not known to the sons of men " ; it had been " hidden from eternity in God, who created all things " ; [4] it is a " wisdom which is hidden, which God ordained before the world, unto our glory." Hence when St Peter made his profession of faith in Christ, saying : " Thou art the Christ, the Son of the living God," Christ answered him : " Blessed art thou, Simon Bar-Jona, because flesh and blood hath not revealed it to thee, but my Father who is in heaven." Thus the apparently simple statement, that God is the Father, has a meaning unspeakably profound. Let us try, with all reverence, to penetrate it.

*Christ the natural Son of God*    It is clear, first of all, that Christ presents himself as standing in a unique relation to God his Father. Already St Augustine had acutely remarked that he never places himself on a level with the rest of mankind by addressing God as " our Father." [5] He refers to God as *his* Father, and when he has occasion to associate himself with us he seems careful to preserve the distinction between our sonship and the much higher relationship in which he himself stands to God. [6] What that relationship is emerges clearly from numerous passages of the New Testament : he is the only-begotten of the Father. " God hath sent his only-begotten Son into the world, that we may live by him " ; [7] formerly God had spoken to men through the prophets, now he spoke in his son ; [8] formerly

[1] John i, 18.                     [2] viii 1.                     [3] xi 21.
[4] Eph. iii 5, 9.              [5] *In Joannem*, tr. 21, 3.
[6] See Matt. xxv 34 ; xxvi 29 ; Luke xxiv 49.
[7] 1 John iv 9.              [8] Heb. i 1-2.

he had sent his " servants," and these had been mocked and spurned, now he sent " his own most dear son," whom he thought they might reverence.[1] He sent him that he might reveal the Father to mankind ; for he alone had seen the Father.

It was an axiom with the Jews that no man could see God and live. "No man," says St John, "hath seen God at any time ; the only-begotten son who is in the bosom of the Father, he hath declared him." [2] The consequence is evident : Christ is God. He is the Son of God in the strictest sense of the word, the Son of God because he has received the divine nature from the Father by eternal generation. "All things," he says, "are delivered to me by my Father. And no one knoweth the Son but the Father, neither doth anyone know the Father but the Son and he to whom it shall please the Son to reveal him." [3] The Father and the Son have an intimate and exclusive knowledge of each other, a knowledge which can be imparted to others only by a special favour. Christ could not have expressed more clearly his claim to be God ; for none but God can see God as he is.

Christ, then, is the son of God by nature ; and he came to reveal to us the Father, whose sons we are by adoption. "Behold," says St John,[4] "what manner of charity the Father hath bestowed upon us that we should be called and should be the sons of God. Dearly beloved, we are now the sons of God, and it hath not yet appeared what we shall be. We know that when he shall appear we shall be like to him, for we shall see him as he is " ; or, according to St Paul, "then I shall know even as I am known." [5] We are the sons of God by adoption, partakers of the divine nature, as St Peter calls us, because we are destined by divine supernatural favour to enjoy that vision of God which is naturally proper to God himself alone. Christ is shown to be the only-begotten son of God, not merely a partaker of the divine nature, but truly and essentially God, because he enjoys this intimate and intuitive knowledge of the divinity as his own natural right. *Our adoptive sonship*

This then is the meaning of the divine Fatherhood which Christ came to reveal to us : the true and only-begotten Son of God, the second Person of the Blessed Trinity, assumes our human nature that we may be made partakers of his divinity ; the divine life, which is in the Word incarnate in all its fulness, is communicated to us through his humanity ; God's own Son lives and dies as man in our midst in order that we may become co-heirs with him of eternal life, adopted sons of God by a real participation in that divine nature which is his by eternal generation. This association of mankind with Christ in his filial relation to the Father, and yet this contrast between his natural filiation and our own adoptive sonship, may truly be said to constitute the essence of the Christian revelation.

[1] Mark xii 1-12.  [2] John i 18.  [3] Matt. xi 27.
[4] 1 John iii 1 *seq.*  [5] 1 Cor. xiii 12.

*Christ truly God*

In the light of Christ's divine sonship strictly so-called the mysterious announcement of the Angel Gabriel to his blessed Mother becomes luminously clear : " The Holy Ghost shall come upon thee and the power of the Most High shall overshadow thee, and therefore also the Holy that shall be born of thee shall be called [1] the Son of God." [2] No wonder then that her cousin Elizabeth hailed her as blessed among women, humbly confused by the honour of this visit from the " mother of her Lord " ; no wonder that the Precursor himself, though yet unborn, is constrained to give testimony to the presence of the divine Messias by leaping in his mother's womb. We may also note as particularly significant the fact that the first spoken words of Christ related in the Gospel are a reference to his divine Sonship—" Know you not that I must be about my Father's business ? " [3]—and that his public life begins with a most solemn revelation of his unique relationship to the Father : " This is my beloved Son, in whom I am well pleased." [4] Hence he justly claimed a love and a reverence due to God alone ; [5] since he is eternal he lived before the time of Abraham ; [6] he has power to forgive sins by his own authority, a power which the Pharisees recognised to be divine. [7] Being the Son of God he spoke with authority, no longer merely conveying a message from God, as the prophets had done, " Thus saith the Lord," but making laws in his own name : " I say unto you " ; he had power to perfect, and if necessary even to set aside as obsolete, the prescriptions of the Old Testament ; he is greater than David, he is Lord of the Sabbath. Nor did the Jews misunderstand his claim. They knew well that he was calling himself God. " Art thou then the Son of God ? " asked Caiphas ; and when Jesus answered that he was indeed, he was accused of blasphemy and regarded as worthy of death. [8] This was the reason why from the beginning they had sought to kill him. It was not because of his works that they took up stones to cast at him, but for blasphemy, and because being a man, he made himself God, [9] and " because he said that God was his Father, making himself equal to God." [10]

His disciples, too, had well understood their Master's teaching. " Being in the form of God," says St Paul, [11] " he thought it not robbery to be equal with God, but emptied himself, taking the form of a servant, being made in the likeness of men, and in habit found as a man." The same Apostle in his epistle to the Colossians gives us a sublime description of the person and prerogatives of Christ. Having called him the image of the invisible God, the first born of all creatures (*i.e.* born before all creatures), he continues, in a

---

[1] A hebraism for " shall be."      [2] Luke I 35.
[3] Luke ii 49.      [4] Matt. iii 17.
[5] John vi 29-47 ; xi 26 ; xiv 1 ; xiv 21-28 ; xvi 7-13.
[6] *Ibid.* viii 52-56.      [7] Mark ii 1-12.      [8] Luke xxii 67-71.
[9] John x 30-33.      [10] *Ibid.* v 18.      [11] Phil. ii 6-7.

passage so magnificent that any commentary would but weaken its force : " In him were all things created in heaven and on earth, visible and invisible . . . and he is before all, and by him all things consist." [1]  The opening words of the epistle to the Hebrews are reminiscent of the first chapter of the Gospel of St John, so explicitly do they affirm that Christ is God : " God . . . in these days hath spoken to us by his Son, whom he hath appointed heir of all things, by whom also he made the world.  Who being the brightness of his glory and the figure of his substance, and upholding all things by the word of his power . . . sitteth on the right hand of the majesty on high.  Being made so much better than the angels, as he hath inherited a more excellent name than they.  For to which of the angels hath he said at any time, ' Thou art my Son, to-day have I begotten thee ' ? "

But most clearly of all speaks St John, the disciple whom Jesus loved.  It was to prove that Christ was God that he wrote what we know as the fourth gospel.  " These things are written that you may believe that Jesus is the Christ, the Son of God, and that believing you may have life in his name." [2]  His account of the life of Christ opens with words very similar to the first words of the book of Genesis.  But whereas the author of the Pentateuch was concerned only with the origin of created things, St John speaks of the timeless origin of the Word, born of the Father from all eternity : " In the beginning was the Word, and the Word was with God, and the Word was God."  When the universe came into being he, the Word, already was, for it was through him that all things were made.  He came forth from God into the world as the light into the darkness, to reveal the Father to mankind and to enable men to be born again as the adopted sons of God, raised by God's favour to be brethren of Christ, the only-begotten of the Father.  Such is the theme of the prologue of the fourth gospel ; such is the theme throughout : " The Word was made flesh and dwelt amongst us."

But he who proclaims himself so clearly to be God is un-*Christ truly* doubtedly also a man.  He is conceived and born of a human *man* mother.  We see him now as an infant, now as a young boy, growing in stature and in wisdom.  He grows to manhood, living in subjection to his parents.  We see him finally as a grown man ; he is truly a man, subject to the ordinary laws of human life ; he is hungry and eats, he is weary and rests, he is sorrowful and weeps, he suffers and dies.  In all things he behaves as a man ; he is a man.  St John, who is so solicitous to show that Christ is God, is no less emphatic concerning the reality of his human nature.  The Apostles had touched him with their hands, they had seen him with their eyes ; they knew that he was a man.[3]  And they knew also that he was God.

[1] i 15 *seq.*          [2] xx 31.          [3] 1 John i 1.

God with us ; Jesus Christ, God and Man. This is the mystery of the Incarnation.

## §III: DENIALS AND DEFINITIONS

THE doctrine of the Incarnation as stated above is a stupendous truth, but its formulation contains no words that may be called technically philosophical. Equally simple is the language of the Apostles' Creed in which we profess our belief in Jesus Christ, the Son of God, who was crucified and died for us. And so indeed the dogma of the Incarnation was expressed during the first two centuries of the Christian era. The early (or Apostolic) Fathers, in teaching this, as the other doctrines of the Church, use the terminology of Scripture. It was only when, with the rise of heresy, it became important to emphasise now this and now that aspect of the truth, that the dogmas of the faith were formulated with greater technical precision.

*Gnostics, Manicheans, Docetists*    Of the first heresies concerning the Person of Christ we already find mention in the New Testament. These errors take the form either of denying the true humanity of Christ or of rejecting his true divinity, and in either form they had a more or less continuous history during the first four centuries of the Christian era. The Gnostics, and later the Manicheans of the second and third centuries, held that matter was essentially evil, the product of the god of evil. For this reason they denied the resurrection of the body and also the possibility of any association of God with matter. Evidently to such the idea of a divine incarnation was repugnant. In the endeavour to make a compromise between Christianity and their philosophical tenets they taught that Christ had not a real body, but merely the appearance of a body, thus reducing the whole of Christ's human life to a pretence ; hence the name given to these heretics, the Docetists (from δοκεῖν, to appear). St Paul is probably referring to early advocates of this view when, in his second epistle to Timothy,[1] he speaks of the followers of a false science that merits not the name, and insists upon the mediatorship of the *man* Christ Jesus. The epistles of St John also contain clear references to these early opponents of the Incarnation. " Everyone," he says, " that confesseth not Jesus in the flesh is not of God." [2] Hence the emphatic opening of his first letter : " What we have seen with our eyes and touched with our hands of the word of life . . . that which we have seen and heard we declare unto you."

Docetism was refuted later in turn by St Irenaeus, Tertullian, and St Augustine. Tertullian, in particular, wrote a complete work, *De Carne Christi*, against the docetism of the Marcionites.

*Ebionites*    But more dangerous and more long-lived were the heresies that denied the divinity of Christ. A Jewish sect, the Ebionites,

---

[1] vi 20.    [2] 1 John iv 3 ; *cf.* 2 John 7.

held that Christ, the son of Joseph and Mary, was a great man indeed, but yet a mere man. The spirit of God, they said, descended upon him at his baptism, raising him to the dignity of adopted son of God. It was against this heresy that St John wrote his Gospel to prove the divinity of Christ, and it is to this sect that he refers in his first epistle as the antichrist who denies that Jesus is the Son of God.[1] Certain Jews who set the angels higher than Jesus are refuted by St Paul in his epistle to the Colossians, and the same are probably in his mind when, at the beginning of his epistle to the Hebrews, he extols the majesty of Christ above all the categories of the heavenly spirits : " To whom of the angels hath he said at any time, ' Thou art my son, this day I have begotten thee ' ? "

This error appeared again in Rome at the end of the second *Adoptionists* century under the name of Adoptionism, associated with the names of Theodotus the Currier and Theodotus the Banker. Here too the champion of orthodoxy was Tertullian, who in this connection has given us a treatise on the divinity of Christ, *Adversus Praxean*. In fact it is in this work that Tertullian provides the first attempt at a technical formulation of the mystery of the Incarnation : " We see plainly the twofold state, which is not confounded, but conjoined in one Person, Jesus Christ, God and man. . . . Forasmuch as the two substances [2] acted distinctly each in its own character, there necessarily accrued to them severally their own operations and their own issues." [3]

A similar doctrine to that of Theodotus—but with a more im- *Paul of* portant outcome—was taught in the East by Paul of Samosata, *Samosata—* Bishop of Antioch (*c.* 260). The mention of the see of Antioch *Antioch and* makes it opportune at this point to call attention to the two great *Alexandria* theological schools of Alexandria and Antioch, which played so important a part in the Christological controversies of the fifth century. The school of Antioch was characterised by a spirit of rigid adherence to the letter of Scripture and by the tendency to view theological problems from a positive standpoint. Thus the Antiochenes approached the study of the Person of Christ from what we may call the historical angle. Christ was portrayed in the Gospels as being God and as being also man ; hence they tended to insist upon the distinction of the two natures in Christ. The Alexandrian spirit, on the other hand, was mystical and speculative, and the theologians of that school were inclined to stress rather the unity of Christ than the distinction of his two natures. The exaggeration of these tendencies led respectively to the heresies of Nestorianism and Monophysism. Paul of Samosata, then, taught that Christ was a man, but a man in whom the mind of God

---

[1] ii 22, 23.    [2] " Natures," we should say.
[3] Ch. 27. Note the similarity between this passage and the famous Dogmatic Letter of Leo the Great. *Cf.* p. 373.

—the Logos—dwelt in a special way; if he is called God it is only by reason of his intimate union with the Word of God. This doctrine, condemned in a synod of Antioch (267-268), is important because it was the prelude to Arianism which denied the divinity of the Word.

The end of the third century and the beginning of the fourth were occupied with the great Trinitarian heresies, into which we cannot enter here, except to remark that the Christological problem could not be precisely formulated or solved until the Catholic doctrine of the Trinity of Persons in God had been put beyond misunderstanding. It was obviously premature to discuss the exact relation of the human nature to the divine nature in Christ until the divinity of the Word was vindicated against heretics. With the Council of Nicaea in 325 this was done, and the arena was thus cleared for the great Christological controversies of the fourth and fifth centuries.

*Diodore*

We may conveniently resume our study of these with Diodore, Bishop of Tarsus (378), founder of the second great school of Antioch. Anxious, in accordance with the Antiochene tradition, to safeguard the integrity of the two natures in Christ, Diodore, as far as we are able to gather from the fragments of his works that remain, accentuated the distinction between Christ's humanity and divinity to the point of separation, so that for him God is one person and Christ another. These two were intimately united, indeed, but only as God is intimately united with a creature in whom he dwells as in a temple and in whom he works his will. The influence of Paul of Samosata is manifest. Nevertheless it is only fair to remember that other influences were at work. The school of Alexandria at the same time had a leader whose exaggerations in the opposite sense Diodore justly reprobated, namely, Apollinaris, Bishop of Laodicea (360).

*Apollinaris*

The teaching of Apollinaris is typical as showing the excesses to which insistence upon the unity of Christ could lead. It seemed to him that if the human nature of Christ was admitted to be complete it must constitute a human person distinct from the Person of the Word. One would thus, he argued, be reduced to the heresy of Paul of Samosata, now renewed by Diodore of Tarsus, that Christ the son of Mary was one person and the Son of God another. The only way, he thought, of saving the unity of Christ was to admit that his humanity was incomplete, lacking in some essential element which the Word, by uniting himself with it, would supply. He therefore taught that Christ lacked an intellectual soul,[1] the place of this being taken by the second Person of the

---

[1] Arius had taught that the Word took the place of a human soul in Christ. But Apollinaris differed from Arius inasmuch as he distinguished three elements in man : body, soul, and spirit, *i.e.* intellect. The last-named is proper to man and this, according to Apollinaris, was lacking to the humanity of Christ.

Blessed Trinity. Hence while Diodore sacrificed the unity of the Person of Christ to the integrity of his two natures, Apollinaris had recourse to the mutilation of his humanity in order to save the unity of his Person.

These two opposite excesses, that of Diodore and that of Apollinaris, led subsequently to the two famous heresies of Nestorianism and Monophysism. It may not, however, be out of place here to remind the reader that these men were, as far as we know, sincerely groping after a precise statement of the scriptural truth that Christ is both God and man. Neither school, Antiochene or Alexandrian, set out with the professed object of denying either the integrity of his human nature or the unity of his Person. It was no doubt their honest endeavour to safeguard both ; but the fact is that in seeking for an expression of the truth they fell into heresy.

More famous than Diodore was his pupil, Theodore of Mopsuestia *Theodore* (392-428), who synthesised and developed the theory already outlined by his master. True to the Antiochene tradition, he emphasised the reality and the completeness of Christ's human nature. The humanity of Christ was united to God, he said, because God dwelt therein as in a temple. In Christ God had put his complacence, and in him willed to accomplish all things ; and since Christ was the temple of the divinity he shared with God the honours of divine worship. Nevertheless, in spite of the exuberant terms in which Theodore extols the union of Christ with God, it remains that Christ and God are two different persons ; God was in Christ, but Christ was not God.

Throughout this controversy it is the so-called " communication of properties " that is the touchstone of orthodoxy. If Christ was one individual who was truly God and truly man, then the properties and activities of either the human or the divine nature might with equal truth be attributed to him. If God truly became man, while remaining God, one might say of him that God died on the cross, that he was born of the Virgin Mary, that Mary was the mother of God, that Christ, who was passible and mortal according to his humanity, was omnipotent, eternal, the Creator of all things, according to his divinity. Now it was precisely here that the Christology of Theodore failed. He refused to admit that Mary was Theotokos—Mother of God. The same acid test revealed the heresy of his still better known disciple, Nestorius.

This man, with whom the heresy we have been describing is *Nestorius* historically always associated, became Patriarch of Constantinople in the year 427. In the following year he made known his views on the Person of Christ when he defended one of his priests, Anastasius, who in a sermon had refused to Our Lady the title of Mother of God. It was the teaching of Theodore of Mopsuestia publicly proclaimed, and it caused a great stir in Constantinople, where both clergy and laity soon became divided into two parties.

*St Cyril of Alexandria*      St Cyril, Patriarch of Alexandria, now entered the lists against Nestorius, and an acrimonious dispute followed which culminated in the condemnation of the latter at the Council of Ephesus in 431. It is beyond the scope of this little essay to describe at any length the intrigues that preceded, accompanied, and followed the Council. Some modern historians have tried to show that Cyril was actuated chiefly, if not solely, by motives of jealousy in his opposition to Nestorius ; the latter being represented as the champion of orthodoxy, unjustly persecuted by his powerful rival at Alexandria. But a sober consideration of the documents leads one inevitably to the conclusion that, while the antagonism between the rival sees cannot be overlooked as a factor in the situation, nevertheless Nestorius was definitely unorthodox, while Cyril, despite some inexactitudes of expression—not unnatural in view of the vagueness of current terminology—stood for the traditional teaching of the Church on the Person of the Word Incarnate.

*Terminology*      It is impossible to form anything like a just estimate of the merits of this monumental controversy without some understanding of the terms used by the participants. In fact the vagueness of the language of either side contributed in no small measure to the prolongation of the dispute. The words used nowadays by the Catholic theologian in formulating the dogma of the Incarnation have a definite meaning, so that, to the Catholic at any rate, it is clear enough what is meant when it is said that in Christ there are two natures and one person. Not so to the Greek of the fifth century. He did not possess even the clear Greek equivalents of " nature " and " person." The difficulty of terminology had already been acutely felt in the discussions on the Trinity, in which it had been necessary to find words to express the unity of the divine essence or nature on the one hand, and the Trinity of divine persons on the other. Four words were available : οὐσία, φύσις, ὑπόστασις, πρόσωπον. After a great deal of discussion it was agreed to use the word *ousia* to indicate the one divine essence and to reserve the word *hypostasis* for person. The word *phusis* (nature) was little used in connection with the Trinity. The word *prosopon*, the exact Greek equivalent of the Latin *persona*, was for a long time suspect, since it had been used by the Sabellians in an unorthodox sense ; [1] but eventually it was accepted as the equivalent of *hypostasis*. For the purposes of Trinitarian doctrine the rough and ready distinction made by St Basil between *ousia* and *hypostasis* served well enough. The essence, he said, is that which is common to all the individuals of a species, while the person adds to the essence the individual characteristics that distinguish them one from another. But the explanation is superficial, and its inade-

---

[1] The Sabellians used the word in the etymological sense of a mask, or character, and said the one person was called Father, Son or Holy Ghost according to the activities he exercised in relation to creatures. See Essay iv, p. 114.

quacy became apparent when applied to the Christological problem of two concrete natures subsisting in one person.

Nestorius said that in Christ there were two φυσικὰ πρόσωπα, two physical persons, but only one πρόσωπον ἐνωσεως, one person of union. What did he mean? Apparently, that so far as their physical reality was concerned the human nature and the divine nature in Christ were distinct. This, of course, was perfectly true. But what did he mean by the "person of union"? The person of union, for Nestorius, had a particular name: "Christ," and was simply the man Christ, considered as endowed with the special indwelling of God. Hence Mary, he said, was *Christotokos*, Mother of Christ; to call her *Theotokos*, Mother of God, was to confuse the natures and to make Mary the mother of the divinity.

On the other hand, Cyril of Alexandria made frequent use of the word *phusis*, nature. His axiom was: "The incarnate nature of the Word is one." Nestorius said that this was simply the heresy of Apollinaris; and surely enough it was, if Cyril had used the words in the sense in which Apollinaris had used them. But by *phusis* or nature Cyril did not mean what Apollinaris meant, nor what we mean by nature. When Cyril said that the incarnate nature of the Word was one he meant that Christ was one concrete individual, God and Man, which of course was perfectly orthodox. Why, then, did he not say that Christ was one person who had two natures? Simply because there were no words which were quite unequivocal to indicate person and nature. If he had said "one *prosopon*" he would not sufficiently have distinguished his doctrine from that of Nestorius, who also, but in his own sense, admitted one *prosopon* in Christ, namely, the *prosopon* of union, by which God dwelt in Christ as in a temple. Hence Cyril, to indicate that the union of divinity and humanity in Christ was in the substantial order of personality, used the word *phusis*, and spoke of a "physical union" as opposed to a moral union. "A physical union," he explains, "that is, a true union, . . . a union according to hypostasis." [1]

But it is easy to understand why Nestorius, and many others, took exception to the language of Cyril. To speak of a physical union of the two natures in Christ was to lay himself open to the accusation of holding with Apollinaris that the two natures are merged in one, and that the human nature of Christ was not complete. He found it necessary on this account to justify himself and to explain the sense in which he used these equivocal phrases.

This being so, the real discussion was centred upon a point *Theotokos* which is really a consequence of the unity of Christ's person, that of the divine Motherhood of Mary. Here Cyril was on firm ground and here the heresy of Nestorius became manifest. It was vain for the latter to declare that to admit the Divine Motherhood

[1] *Apol. pro xii cap.* (P.G. 76, 332, 405.)

of Mary was to make Mary the mother of the divine nature. What Cyril insisted was, not that Mary had given birth to the divinity —that would be absurd—but that the same individual, the Word, who was born eternally of the Father according to the divinity, was born in time of the Virgin Mary according to his humanity. It was precisely this that Nestorius denied, and his denial of Mary's divine Motherhood showed him to be unorthodox on the Incarnation.

*Ephesus— "Symbol of Union"*

Nestorius, then, was condemned and deposed from his see by the Council of Ephesus. John, the Patriarch of Antioch, for some time defended Nestorius, but two years later he was reconciled with Cyril, and the agreement of Alexandrians and Antiochenes was recorded in the " Symbol of Union " of 433. In this document the Antiochene contention that the two natures of Christ, human and divine, were complete and unmingled was embodied, while the Alexandrian solicitude for the unity of the person of Christ was fully satisfied by the statement that one and the same individual who was born eternally of the Father according to the divinity was the son of Mary according to his humanity, and the right of Mary to the title of " Mother of God " was explicitly acknowledged.

*Monophysism*

The exaggerations of what we may call the " separatist " school of thought had been condemned and the unity of the person of Christ was vindicated. But not everybody was yet satisfied. There was still no terminology sufficiently exact to exclude all misunderstanding. It has been seen that Cyril had spoken of one nature in Christ, and although this expression had been excluded from the " Symbol of Union " and Cyril, for the rest, had used it in an orthodox sense as meaning one person in Christ, yet some of the disciples of Cyril were not so orthodox as their master. Among these was Eutyches who, by his indiscreet zeal and ignorance, gave rise in the year 448 to a further doctrinal dispute, regrettable no doubt for the peace of his contemporaries, but providential inasmuch as it led to that amplification and exactness given to the formularies of belief which made all further equivocation impossible.

Eutyches refused to admit that the body of our Lord was consubstantial (of the same nature) with ours, or that after the union in him of human and divine natures it was legitimate to speak of *two* natures. Whatever may have been the inner belief of the simple old monk, the refusal to admit that Christ had a body like ours gave rise to suspicion since it left room to doubt whether, according to such a view, there had been any real Incarnation at all. As for his rejection of the phrase " two natures," he said, Cyril had spoken of one nature, and he did not intend to depart from the teaching of his master. It was the old difficulty of terminology again.

*Leo I*

Without considering the various phases of the new heresy of Monophysism, it is sufficient to note two things : first, that just as Nestorianism represented the *reductio ad absurdum* of the Antiochene tendency to separate the natures, so Monophysism is the heresy involved in exaggerating the unity of Christ. Cyril had said " one nature " and had been orthodox in meaning ; the Monophysites said " one nature " and were unorthodox, because they meant that the two natures were merged into one. The second important thing about Monophysism is that, on appeal being made to Rome to settle this further dispute, the Dogmatic Letter of Pope Leo I was written, a letter afterwards adopted as the rule of faith by the Council of Chalcedon in the year 451.

This famous letter is important by reason of its wonderful precision of language. While in the East there had been the verbal misunderstandings which we have described, the theologians of the West had been but little troubled with such difficulties. We have seen that the Latin terminology was already clearly defined at the beginning of the third century with Tertullian, who already speaks of a " twofold state, not confounded but conjoined in one Person Jesus Christ." Thanks to this early crystallisation of the dogma, theologians in the West were little affected by the Christological controversies which divided the East for well-nigh a hundred years. Clear thinking, clearly expressed is the keynote of Pope Leo's letter : " The properties of the two natures being safeguarded and being united in one person, majesty took upon itself humility, power weakness, eternity mortality ; and to pay our debts an impassible nature was united to a passible one, so that one and the same mediator of God and men, the man Jesus Christ, might on the one hand die and on the other be immortal. . . . Each nature keeps what is proper to it, and just as his divine condition does not destroy his human condition, so his condition of servant does not diminish his divinity."

Little else remained to be done in the Councils of Chalcedon *Councils of* (451) and Constantinople II (553) than to consolidate the advance *Chalcedon* already made, by enshrining in an official formula the terminology *and Con-* *stantinople II* upon which agreement had been achieved. The following extracts from their decrees need no commentary. From the Council of Chalcedon : " In accordance with the teaching of the holy Fathers we all profess our faith in one and the same Son and Lord Jesus Christ, perfect in his divinity, perfect in his humanity, having a rational soul and a body,[1] consubstantial with the Father according to the divinity,[2] the same consubstantial with us according to his humanity, ' in all things like as we are except sin ' ; born before all ages of the Father according to the divinity, and the same in these last days born of Mary the Virgin Mother of God for us and for our salvation ; one and the same Christ the Lord and only-begotten Son *in two natures* without confusion, change, division or separation, the difference of the natures being in no way suppressed by their union, but the proper manner of existence of each being safeguarded, while each nature is united with the other *in one person*

[1] As against Apollinarianism.   [2] As against Arianism.

*and hypostasis.*" [1]  From the second Council of Constantinople :
" If any one understand the one hypostasis of our Lord Jesus Christ
as if it might mean several hypostases and therefore attempt to
introduce into the mystery of Christ two hypostases or two *prosopa*,
saying that the two prosopa thus introduced are one according to
dignity and honour and adoration, as Theodore (of Mopsuestia)
and Nestorius in their madness wrote ; calumniating the holy
Synod of Chalcedon as if it had used the words ' one hypostasis '
in this impious sense ; and does not rather confess that the Word
of God was united to flesh *according to hypostasis*, and that on this
account his hypostasis or prosopon is one, and that in this sense
the holy Council of Chalcedon confessed the hypostasis of our Lord
Jesus Christ to be one, let such an one be anathema."

## §IV:  ONE PERSON

*" Person "
and
" Nature "*

THE doctrine of the Incarnation as revealed to us in Scripture may
be stated in these simple terms : Christ is one individual who is
both God and man.   The Council of Chalcedon defined that Christ
is one person who has two natures, united by a hypostatic union.
The second formulation of the mystery contains nothing more than
the first ; it merely states the same truth in technical and precise
terms.   But although the terms nature and person may have a
particular philosophical connotation, the Fathers of the Council
of Chalcedon in defining the dogma of the hypostatic union had
not in mind any esoteric meaning to be attached to them : the words
were used in their popular sense.

What they meant when they said that Christ was one person
may be clearly seen from the controversies which led up to the
definition.   They meant that he is one individual, one subject of
attribution ; and this is the meaning that we ordinarily attach to
the word.   When we speak of a person we mean a complete existing
rational [2] being who has his own distinct individuality, incommunicable to others ; one to whom we attribute his own actions,
saying that *he* thinks, *he* sits, *he* walks, and so on.   This " selfness "
or personality we understand to be absolutely incommunicable ;
and it is here, perhaps, that we reach the essential element of personality.   The sense of being alone when I am in mental distress,
the feeling that " I must work this out for myself," that nobody
can possibly understand my difficulties, these are but evidences
in my consciousness of that splendid, yet in many ways awesome,
isolation from every other individual of my species which constitutes
my personality.

[1] As against Monophysism and Nestorianism.
[2] The name " person " is reserved for rational or intellectual beings.
An irrational or inanimate individual is called by the generic name of
" individual," philosophically a " hypostasis," or *suppositum*.

The word nature, too, has a definite meaning in popular usage. The nature is that which makes a thing *what* it is ; it is that composite unity of substances, qualities, and powers by means of which a person acts in a particular way, and in consequence of which he belongs to a particular category or class of being. Now ordinarily a complete existing human nature is a human person. But the Council of Chalcedon defined that there is an unique exception to this rule in the case of the humanity of Christ which, although it is complete and existing, is nevertheless not a human person. The humanity of Christ was from the very first moment assumed, appropriated, by the second Person of the Blessed Trinity, so that Christ is a divine Person, having two natures, a human nature and the divine.

It can hardly be stressed too much that the doctrine of the *The hypostatic* union thus defined is nothing more than the revealed *hypostatic* doctrine of the Incarnation : " The Word was made flesh." It is *union* not the fruit of human speculation upon the revealed word of God ; it is not a theological conclusion ; it is itself a divine revelation. Hence the hypostatic union precisely as such can never be the subject of debate among Catholic theologians. Upon this all Catholics are, and must be, agreed : that the human nature of Christ, though real and complete, does not constitute a human person distinct from the Son of God ; that the one person of Christ is the divine Person of the Word who, subsisting eternally in the divine nature, in the fulness of time took upon himself a human nature and thus is both truly God and truly man.

But the theologian is not content to stop here. In his legitimate *Theological* desire to enter more deeply into the meaning of the divine mysteries *theories* by applying to them the principles of human reason, in order to show that although these mysteries are beyond our comprehension they are not contrary to reason, he analyses the ideas which are used in the formulation of revealed truth, thus arriving at what the Vatican Council calls " a most fruitful understanding of mysteries." Hence Catholic theologians, while admitting, as in duty bound, that the humanity of Christ is not a human person, proceed further to inquire the reason why. What is lacking, they ask, to this humanity, the presence of which would make it a human person ? What does the Word supply in this mysterious union so as to make Christ a divine Person ? What, in other words, precisely constitutes personality ? Three questions, clearly, which are really one ; put in the first two forms the question is theological ; in its last form it is purely philosophical. And as the answer given to the third question varies, so also different answers are given by theologians to the other two.

Since the problem of personality is primarily a philosophical one it does not belong to the theologian as such to attempt to solve it. Nevertheless the Catholic philosopher is not entirely free to solve it as he wills. Suppose, for example, that he forms the opinion—for the rest an erroneous one—that what constitutes personality is the human soul; there have been philosophers who have held this view. Even apart from the metaphysical objections to the theory, such a position is impossible for the Catholic as a theologian, because it would lead him logically to the heresy of Arius concerning the person of Christ. Holding as a Catholic theologian that the humanity of Christ lacked what was necessary to make him a human person, he would be forced to the conclusion that Christ had no human soul and that the place of this was taken by the Word; this is exactly what Arius taught. Or, if as a philosopher he held that the human intellect is the essential element in personality, as a theologian he would logically be an Apollinarist, holding that Christ lacked a human intellect, the place of this being supplied by the divine Logos.

Hence the answer given to the philosophical question is by no means a matter of indifference to the theologian. He cannot accept a philosophical view of personality which is irreconcilable with the dogma of the Incarnation. In fact a moment's thought will show that, if the truth of the hypostatic union is to be safeguarded, the constitutive element of personality must be sought outside the nature itself. Any philosophical theory identifying the notion of person with that of nature, or making some element of the nature (such as intellect, will, consciousness) the essential constituent of personality cannot but have disastrous results in Christology. And the reason is that Christ has a perfect and complete human nature, and yet is not a human person. Whatever it may be, therefore, that the Word supplies to the humanity of Christ to make him a divine person, it is certainly not a part of his human nature.

That this distinction between nature and person is crucial in the matter of the hypostatic union was felt strongly by the Fathers of the Vatican Council, who, in view of certain errors current in Germany in the nineteenth century, had prepared the following draft for a definition on the mystery of the Incarnation: " Just as in the holy Trinity three distinct persons subsist in one nature, so in Christ, on the other hand, one person subsists in two distinct and different natures. Therefore, in accordance with the teaching of the Fathers all must understand that the notion of essence, substance, or nature is by no means to be confused with the notion of hypostasis, subsistence [1] or person, lest one be led into making the statement—manifestly subversive of the sacred dogmas—that there are as many persons as there are intellectual or—to use the modern expression—conscious natures." [2]

[1] The Latin equivalent of hypostasis.
[2] It is important, however, to notice that the above statement enjoys no greater authority than that of the theologians who formulated it. It is a theological statement upon which all Catholics are agreed; but, since it was never discussed or embodied by the Council in its published decrees, it is not as such an article of faith.

But within the just limits set by orthodoxy theologians enjoy freedom of discussion. Some content themselves with the theory that the humanity of Christ was prevented from being a human person by the very fact that it was assumed by the Word. A human nature is a person, they maintain, if it is not assumed by another ; but the humanity of Christ was assumed by the Word ; therefore it is not a human person. But this explanation, it is urged, fails to explain anything. The question is precisely why the humanity of Christ was capable of being assumed, why, in other words, it was not incommunicable. To answer that in fact it was assumed, or communicated, seems equivalent to evading the point at issue. If, as these theologians maintain, the humanity of Christ possessed the whole reality that is required to constitute it as a human person, it is difficult to see why it actually lacked human personality. Hence others, dissatisfied with this theory, have seen the need of postulating some real complemental entity which, added to the nature, makes it a person, and have held that personality consists in what they call a " substantial mode " distinct from the nature, which has the effect of rendering the nature complete in itself and incommunicable. Others, finally—and with these the writer is inclined to agree—find the constituent of personality in the real act of existence which is the connatural complement of every created nature or essence.

It has been pointed out elsewhere [1] that " the universe and the minds of men are composite, for in them essence and existence are not one, but are two distinct (though inseparable) principles. . . . The distinction between ' essence ' and ' existence ' in the universe (whether considered in part or whole) is no invention of the human mind, but, like all other real distinctions, is objective in things themselves. Observation makes us aware that things not only have existence, but over and above existence they have each also a distinct fabric of a given kind which we call their nature or essence. Existence tells us *that* a thing is, while knowledge of its essence tells us *what* a thing is. To know *that* a thing exists is very different from knowing what particular nature it consists in. Consequently we always think of things and persons as *possessing* existence rather than as constituting it."

Hence, according to this commonly accepted view, an individual nature receives that incommunicability which is characteristic of the hypostasis or person from its own act of existence, an activity distinct from the nature as such. Why is the human nature which I possess incommunicable to any other individual of the same species ? Precisely because I exist, because this nature of mine has the act of existence which is its natural complement. If, therefore, a human nature were without its own connatural existence it would not be a human person. And this was the case with the humanity of Christ which, having all that is required for the perfection of humanity

[1] Essay iii, *The One God*, p. 79.

—body, soul, and faculties—even as we have, existed not by its own connatural act of existence, but by the infinite subsistence of the second Person of the Blessed Trinity, who thus communicated to that human nature a divine Personality. Christ, therefore, is a divine Person because that in him which constitutes personality, namely, the act of existence, is not human but divine.

*The mystery remains*

But whatever may be the solution of the metaphysical problem of personality, the hypostatic union still remains a mystery, a truth beyond human comprehension. That a human nature should not possess its own connatural human personality is a fact which transcends the order of nature ; that upon this humanity should be bestowed a divine Personality is a sublime and ineffable condescension of God to our race ; and no theologian by his speculations intends or hopes to explain the hypostatic union as if it were a natural phenomenon. All that he is able to do is show that, since the concepts of nature and person are distinct from each other, there is no evident contradiction involved in the revealed truth that God has made a created nature his own, by uniting it to his own Person. Whatever be his method of showing this, whether he favour the theory of " mere assumption," or of the substantial mode, or of substantial existence communicated to the humanity of Christ, in common with every other Catholic, theologian or layman, learned or unlettered, he bows in humility before the mystery of a God who unites a human nature to his own Person in order, through that lowly nature of ours, to raise us up to a participation of his.

*The " communication of properties "*

The first important consequence of the hypostatic union is what is known as the " communication of properties." The person is the subject of attribution ; hence it is to the person that the nature and all the properties and activities of the nature are attributed. But Christ is one person who has two natures. It follows that to him may be rightly attributed either the human nature or the divine nature, and the properties and activities of each. We may say with equal truth that Christ is God and that he is man, that he is the Creator and that—according to his human nature—he is finite. Hence also concrete names signifying one nature may be predicated of concrete names signifying or referring to the other ; thus, God is man ; the Eternal died upon the cross ; God was born of the Virgin Mary ; Mary is the Mother of God. It will be noted that only concrete names may be used in this way ; and the reason is evident, for only concrete names indicate the person in whom the two natures subsist. Abstract names signify the nature—or properties of the nature—" abstracting " from its existence in a given individual or person. Thus while it is true to say that Mary is the Mother of God, it is false to say that she is the Mother of the divinity. It has been seen in the previous section how the whole discussion between Cyril and Nestorius centred in the title of *Theotokos* given to Our Lady. Whatever might be the meaning attached by either side to such words as nature, person, or hypostasis, here was an infallible means of testing the orthodoxy of Nestorius. Were Christ and the Word the same person or two different persons ? In answering this question it was possible to dissemble ; but with regard to the divine Motherhood of Our Lady all equivocation was impossible. If this were admitted, then Christ and God were evidently recognised to be one and the same individual, the same person, the same subject of attribution.

From the fact that Christ is one Person, God and man, it follows *Christ not* also that he may not be called the adopted son of God. He is God's *the adopted* own son. A heresy arose in the eighth century called Adoptionism,[1] *Son of God* which consisted in asserting that Christ, admitted to be the natural son of God according to his divinity, was nevertheless his adopted son according to his human nature. This doctrine was condemned by Pope Hadrian I in the year 794. The truth is that in no sense can Christ be said to be the adopted son of God. If Christ, the Word Incarnate, is the natural son of God, born of the Father from all eternity, God cannot adopt him, because to adopt is to elevate to the condition of sonship one who by nature does not possess that status. This form of Adoptionism is thus seen to be a thinly veiled compromise with Nestorianism.

Logically connected with the doctrine of the hypostatic union *Worship due* is the obligation of paying to Christ divine worship. If Christ is *to Christ* God, then we must adore him ; the conclusion is evident. What is perhaps less obvious is the duty of paying divine cult to the human nature of Christ : less obvious, because to worship the humanity of Christ would seem at first sight equivalent to worshipping a creature. However, it should be noted that theologians distinguish between what they call the material object and the formal object of worship. By the material object they mean the person to whom worship is rendered, by the formal object, the excellence or the perfection in the person which is the motive of the honour paid to him. Clearly, when we worship Christ we worship his whole person, the Word Incarnate, God and man. It is not because he is man that we adore him, but because he is God ; nevertheless we do not dissect him, we do not separate his humanity from his divinity in order to adore the latter alone. " The incarnate Word of God," says St Cyril,[2] " since he is the one Son of God, is to be adored, not apart from his flesh, but together with it, just as in honouring a man we honour his soul together with his body." Likewise St Athanasius :[3] " Although the flesh (*i.e.* the humanity of Christ) regarded separately is a part of created things, yet it has become the body of God. Thus we do not divide this body from the Word to adore it, nor when we wish to adore the Word do we separate

---

[1] To be distinguished from the Adoptionism of the third century to which reference is made above, p. 367.

[2] *Apol. contra Orient.*, 8.      [3] *Ad Adelphium*, 3.

him from his body ; but mindful of the words ' The Word became flesh ' we recognise as God the one Word incarnate. Who then will be so foolish as to say to the Lord : ' Depart from thy body that I may adore thee ' ? " Theologians express this truth technically when they say that the humanity of Christ is part of the material object of divine worship, while its formal object is the divinity.

Hence devotion to Christ is not devotion to a mere man, it is the worship of the Word Incarnate, and that worship embraces all that is in him, all that is united with his divine Person. It is here that the wisdom of God's merciful dispensation becomes especially apparent. God became man, in the words of the beautiful Preface for Christmas, *ut dum visibiliter Deum cognoscimus, per hunc in invisibilium amorem rapiamur,* " that while we know God visibly we may be led to the love of things invisible."

*The devotion to the Sacred Heart*
This doctrine has an important application in the popular devotion to the Sacred Heart of Jesus. The Jansenists in the synod of Pistoia (1794) attacked this practice on the ground that to worship the human heart of Christ was to give divine honour to a creature. Pope Pius VI in condemning the Jansenists indicated the dogmatic truth which underlies the devotion to the Sacred Heart ; for he accused the Jansenists of " detracting from the pious and proper cult which the faithful pay to the humanity of Christ." In paying divine honour to the Sacred Heart of Jesus the faithful do nothing more than worship the Word Incarnate, with special reference, however, to his humanity, and indeed to that part of his humanity —his Sacred Heart—which custom regards as chiefly affected by human emotions and consequently uses as the symbol of love. " The faithful adore the Heart of Jesus," says Pope Pius VI (*l.c.*), " considered as the heart of Jesus, that is, as the Heart of the Person of the Word to whom it is inseparably united, just as the body of Christ was adorable when for three days it lay dead in the tomb, unsevered and unseparated from the divinity." [1] The object of devotion to the Sacred Heart, therefore, is the physical heart of the Word Incarnate considered as the symbol of his human love for God and for mankind. In addition we adore that human love itself, for it is the human love of the Word Incarnate, the sacred love with which he loved Mary and Joseph, the merciful love that converted the Magdalen and Peter, the love that poured itself out in pity upon all that suffer, the heroic love for mankind that knew no limit, the love of him who " having loved his own who were in the world, loved them unto the end."

The popularity of this devotion among all faithful Catholics is in fact a sign of their unfailing adherence to the traditional faith of the Church in the unity of the divine Person of Christ. For the Catholic Christ is not merely a great moral teacher, not merely a

---

[1] The same may be said of the living soul of Christ in Limbo.

lovable man, not merely a man who lived in the closest possible union with God; he is God himself. The human perfections that we admire in him and strive to imitate are the human perfections of God, the sympathetic understanding, the human lovableness which has attracted men in all ages to follow him and, if need be, to die for him, have their seat in the heart that has won all hearts, in the human Heart of God himself.

## § V: TWO DISTINCT NATURES

SINCE the hypostatic union is essentially supernatural, there is *Athanasian* no union in nature with which it can properly be compared. *Creed* Nevertheless, as it is only by comparison with the natural that we are able to form any conception of the supernatural, the Fathers have made use of various analogies in order to illustrate what can never in this life be adequately understood. Of these the best known and most striking is certainly that of the union of body and soul in man. "Just as rational soul and flesh are one man," we read in the Athanasian Creed, "so God and man are one Christ." In man body and soul are two (incomplete) substances substantially united to form one person; likewise the humanity of Christ and the divinity are substantially united to constitute one person. But, like all analogies, this must not be pressed too far. Body and soul in man indeed constitute one person, but they form one nature too; whereas in Christ the human nature and the divinity remain distinct and physically unaltered by each other. Thus to exaggerate the analogy used in the Athanasian Creed would be to fall into the error of Apollinaris or of Eutyches.

The Incarnation involves no change in the Godhead. In God *Kenotic* there is no change or shadow of alteration. Hence when St John *theories* tells us that the Word became flesh he does not mean that God was changed into man; he can only mean that God, remaining truly God, became truly man also. "Man was raised up to God," says St Augustine; "God did not descend from himself." [1] It has been suggested by some non-Catholic theologians that the Word in becoming man abdicated his divinity for the period of his life upon earth, or at least voluntarily deprived himself of those divine attributes which he found to be incompatible with a truly human experience. The Catholic Church has always resisted such an idea. She has ever strenuously maintained the reality of Christ's human nature against the Docetists; but she is no less emphatic in asserting his perfect and immutable divinity. In the words of St Leo: "Each nature keeps what is proper to it, and just as his divine condition does not destroy his human condition, so his condition of servant does not diminish his divinity."

[1] Ep. 136.

The words " condition of servant " show that St Leo has in mind the famous text of St Paul in the epistle to the Philippians : [1] " Who being in the form of God thought it not robbery to be equal with God, but emptied himself, taking the form of a servant, being made in the likeness of men and in habit found as a man." Now it is to this text that appeal is made by the supporters of the " kenotic " theory above mentioned. The words, " emptied himself," they claim, can only mean that God deprived himself either wholly or partially of his divinity. And in this, they say, God has given us the most sublime example of humility, inasmuch as he has vouchsafed for our sakes to strip himself of his divine omnipotence. The metaphysical difficulties in the way of this doctrine are, they admit, insuperable, but these are more than counterbalanced by its moral value.

Such a doctrine, however, is quite inadmissible ; and no statement can have any moral value if it is a contradiction in terms. However useful it may appear—and the moral utility of the doctrine is, to say the least, debatable—that God should cease to be God, the necessary Being cannot change his nature. The words of St Paul, therefore, must be so interpreted as not to contradict the evident truth that God is immutable. The following paraphrase, perhaps, better renders the meaning of the original text : " Christ, while he was in the form of God, that is, while he had the nature of God, did not regard his equal rank with God as something to be jealously guarded, but he deprived himself of this, taking the form (or nature) of a servant, so that he appeared externally to be nothing more than a mere man." The second Person of the Blessed Trinity was willing to forgo the external honour which man owed to him as God, being content to appear in the eyes of the world as if he were not God, but merely a man. God deprived himself, therefore, not of the divinity, but of the outward marks of honour due to his divine nature, which was hidden from the eyes of men.

But if God loses nothing by his ineffable union with the humanity of Christ, still less is his divine perfection increased thereby. God incarnate is not greater than God, considered simply as God. One may be inclined, perhaps, by a process of mathematical addition, to think of the Word Incarnate as being in sum of reality more than God before the Incarnation. The truth is that, far from any perfection accruing to the infinite essence of God by his union with humanity, it is the human nature which the Word assumed that is raised to an infinite dignity. But at least, it may be urged, God acquires a new relation to finite reality, inasmuch as he is now united personally to a human nature, whereas formerly he was not. To which it may be answered that the divine relation to finite reality involved in the hypostatic union is no more an increment of divine perfection than the act whereby God creates the universe. The

[1] ii 6-7.

whole change is in the creature; the Creator is eternally changeless. We may apply to the humanity of Christ what St Augustine says of the relation of creatures to God in general: "Without God thou wouldst be less; if thou art with God, he is not the greater on that account. He is not the greater because of thee; but thou without him art less." [1] Hence instead of saying that God formerly was not united to a human nature, but now is united to it, it is more accurate to say with St Thomas that "the humanity which formerly was not united to the divinity now becomes united thereto." [2]

Another difficulty needs to be faced. It is shown in the Essay *Incarnation* on *The Blessed Trinity* that in God "everything is common to all *proper to* three Persons of the Blessed Trinity with the exception of those *the Son* properties which are radicated in the relative opposition between the Persons." [3] Thus all the operations of God in regard to creatures are common to Father, Son, and Holy Ghost. How then is it true that the Incarnation, or the assumption of a human nature, is peculiar to the second Person of the Blessed Trinity? The answer is seen if we distinguish a twofold aspect of the hypostatic union. This may be regarded actively, that is, as a divine operation whereby God creates a human nature and unites it to a divine Person; and in this sense the work of the Incarnation is common to all three Persons of the Blessed Trinity. But it may also be considered passively, that is, in its term, inasmuch as the divine Personality is communicated to the human nature assumed; and in this sense the Incarnation is proper to the Son of God, since he alone made that humanity his own by giving to it his own distinct Personality. To illustrate this point the Fathers use the analogy of three men combining to clothe one of themselves. As St Thomas puts it: "The three Persons operated to unite humanity to the one Person of the Son." [4]

The hypostatic union, therefore, does not change the nature *A true* of God. But nor is the humanity of Christ physically altered by *human* the divinity to which it is personally united. The human nature *nature* receives personality indeed; but it has been shown that what constitutes personality as such is something distinct from the nature—in the view of the writer, the act of substantial existence —and this does not change the nature to which it is united. The humanity of Christ, therefore, is in all essential respects similar to our own; Christ became "in all things like as we are, except sin."

The Docetists denied the reality of the body of Christ; they held it impossible that God should be intimately associated with anything material, which they conceived to be essentially evil. In addition to refuting the false presupposition of the Manicheans

[1] *In Joannem*, tr. xi.
[2] *S. Theol.* III, Q. 1, art. 1, ad 1.
[3] Essay iv, p. 137.
[4] *S. Theol.* III, Q. 3, art. 4.

concerning the origin of matter, the champions of Christian orthodoxy insisted upon the axiom that God assumed our nature in order
to save it, and that consequently whatever he did not assume he
did not save. The reality of Christ's body was re-asserted later
against the Monophysites in the Council of Chalcedon and in the
Dogmatic Letter of Pope Leo, where we read that "in order to pay
our debt an impassible nature was united to a passible one, so that
for the sake of our salvation there might be one mediator of God and
men, the man Christ Jesus, who on the one hand was able to die,
and on the other hand was immortal."

The Church was no less prompt to reject the error of the Arians
who denied that Christ had a human soul, and that of Apollinaris
who denied him a human intellect. It was vain for the latter to
claim that the place of the human soul was taken by the Word.
Such a substitution is impossible ; God cannot become a part of
the nature of man ; the result of such a combination would be
monstrous, a being who is neither man nor God. But of the human
intellect of Christ we shall have more to say in the following section.

*The human will of Christ* It would seem superfluous, when once it has been stated that
the humanity of Christ is perfect in all essentials, to emphasise the
fact that he had a human will. Yet there were some in the seventh
century who denied this. Just as the Adoptionism of the eighth
century was an attempted compromise with Nestorianism, so this
heresy of Monotheletism was a faint-hearted concession to Monophysism. The Monotheletes argued somewhat after this manner :
if in Christ we admit two wills, the human will and the divine will,
we must admit that the will of Christ as man was not the will of God,
and that the one was contrary to the other ; but Christ is impeccable ; therefore in Christ there can have been only one will, the
will of God. The argument is not conclusive. It does not follow,
if there are two wills in Christ, that they must be contrary to each
other. Christ himself has told us that he came not to do his own
will but the will of the Father who sent him ; his whole life was
one of constant submission to the will of the Father. Physically
in Christ there were two wills, although morally speaking there
was but one, because the human·will was in all things subject to
the divine. If he had no human will his humanity would have
been an inert instrument in the hands of the divinity ; without a
human will all his submission to the will of the Father—" Not my
will but thine be done "—would have been an hypocritical pretence.
If he had no human will he had no human virtue, he had no merit,
his death was no free-will offering, the Cross is void and we are still
in our sins. Christ, therefore, had a human will as well as his divine
will, but these were not contrary to each other. In this consisted
his obedience unto death ; his human will was perfectly free, but
through grace it was ever in perfect conformity with the divine
will.

To say that in Christ there are two natures is equivalently to *Human and* profess a duality of operations in him ; for to every nature corres- *divine* ponds its proper operation. One and the same divine Person, *activity* the Word Incarnate, performed through his human nature all those operations which are proper to man, while as God he remained for ever in the ineffable exercise of his divine life and activity. Yet although these operations are physically distinct from each other, the oneness of the divine Agent lent to the whole complex of his human and divine activities a wonderful unity and coherence. All his human operations were under the complete and unfailing control of his holy will, even those wayward emotions which in us are so often an occasion of sin. He was angry, but there was no sin in his anger ; his heart was filled with love for men, but in his human emotion of love there was none of that selfishness that so often mars the perfection of human friendship ; he wept for the sorrows of others, but there was no despair in his grief ; his sensitive heart was cut to the quick by the betrayal of Judas, by the desertion of his friends in his hour of need ; he shrank from physical suffering and from death. But not for a moment did his will allow itself to be led by his emotions ; he was ever captain of his soul. Holding all his human activities in complete subjection, his human will was none the less itself completely, though freely, subject to the will of the Father. Thus there is a true sense in which we may speak of *one* operation in Christ, namely, by reason of the complete sub-ordination of the whole of his being and activity to his own divine will. In fact it seems to have been an undue insistence upon what we may call this moral unity of operation in Christ that led to the heresy of Monotheletism.[1]

One further point remains to be explained before we conclude *Theandric* this section. The Fathers and theologians of the Church use the *actions* expression " theandric operations." What does this mean ? It does not mean that any action of Christ is a mixture of the human and the divine ; this would be equivalent to the error of the Mono-theletes, and the expression was used by them in that sense. But

[1] It was for his failure to make a definite and unequivocal pronouncement on the subject of two wills and operations in Christ that Pope Honorius I was condemned. The third Council of Constantinople (680-681) condemned him as " following the false doctrines of heretics " and for " confirming the impious dogmas of Sergius " of Constantinople, who was the leader of the Monotheletes. But, as is well known, an Oecumenical Council has validity only inasmuch as it is confirmed by the Pope, the head of the Council, and therefore the condemnation of Honorius is to be understood in the sense in which it was approved by Pope Leo II, who wrote as follows : " We anathematise the inventors of this error . . . and also Honorius who did not shed lustre upon this apostolic (Roman) Church by the doctrine of apostolic tiadition, but allowed this immaculate Church to be stained by a false betrayal." Hence Honorius was anathematised for a practical rather than a dogmatic error, because he failed to condemn a heresy when he should have done so. For a fuller treatment of this controversial question see Dom Chapman : *The Condemnation of Honorius* (C.T.S.).

as used by Catholics it means primarily those actions of Christ in which both his human nature and his divine nature took part. So when Christ worked a miracle his action was strictly theandric. His divine nature was the principal cause of the miracle, while his humanity co-operated as an instrument.[1] In a wider sense all the human actions of Christ may be called theandric, *i.e.* both human and divine, human by reason of the nature from which they proceed as their principle, divine by reason of the hypostasis or Person whose actions they are. It is for this reason that theologians point out that the human actions of our Redeemer, though they are finite from a physical point of view, are nevertheless of infinite dignity since they are the acts of God himself, and that therefore any act of the Word Incarnate would have been sufficient to save the world from sin.

### APPENDIX ON MODERN ERRORS

Such is the Catholic doctrine of the two natures in the one divine Person of Jesus Christ. What we shall have to say subsequently is but a consequence of this portentous fact that Christ is one individual, God and man. But before we proceed to consider these consequences it may not be out of place to give some account of modern erroneous views concerning the Incarnation, not with a view to refuting them—that is not the object of the present essays—but in order that Catholic doctrine by contrast may stand out with greater clearness.

It is significant that all those who, since the Reformation, have departed from the traditional lines laid down so clearly in the Councils of Chalcedon and Constantinople (II), have—at least equivalently—fallen into one of the two heresies of Nestorianism or Monophysism. Certain among the followers of Luther invented a doctrine known as Ubiquitarianism. Having rejected the Catholic teaching concerning the real presence of the body and blood of Christ in the Eucharist, and faced with the necessity, under pain of parting company with the whole of Tradition, of admitting some sort of presence of Christ in this sacrament, Chemnitz and other Lutherans taught that some of the properties of the divinity were communicated to the human nature of Christ, in particular the attribute of ubiquity. In this manner, they said, the human nature of Christ, since it is everywhere, is present also in the Eucharist. Evidently this is to confuse the two natures. It is true that the communication of properties is one of the consequences of the hypostatic union. But this does not mean that the properties of one nature are communicated to the other. It is one thing to attribute to the *one Person* of Christ the properties and activities of both the human and the divine natures ; but it is quite another to predicate divine

[1] See below, p. 397.

attributes of the human nature and vice-versa. The basis of the communication of properties is not the confusion of natures, but the unity of Person.

The philosophy of Descartes in the seventeenth century, and to an even greater extent the critical system of Kant in the early nineteenth, resulted in a secession from what we may call the philosophy of substance. It came to be held by nearly all who were outside the current of the Scholastic philosophy that the " thing in itself," the substance, as distinct from phenomena, was unknowable. In fact the very existence of substance came later to be denied. Nothing exists, it was held, but the modifications which we experience either within ourselves or from without. What we call substance is nothing else than the sum of the qualities, activities and modifications which we perceive. Hence for most modern philosophers outside the Church the person is simply consciousness, " a series of feelings " as Stuart Mill called it, " with a background of possibilities of feeling."

Gunther attempted to reconcile this view of personality with the Catholic dogma of the hypostatic union. In Christ there is a human consciousness and a divine consciousness ; but he is only one person, he said, because the human consciousness was absorbed by the divine. Rosmini explained the unity of the Person of Christ by supposing that his human will which, according to him, is the dominant factor in personality, completely abdicated the government of his humanity in favour of the divine will to which it was completely subject. In either case Nestorianism is the evident consequence. Ontologically there would be two persons in Christ, a human and a divine, and they would be united only by some psychological or accidental function.

The fact is that neither consciousness nor will *constitutes* personality. Consciousness is the apprehension of the self, it is not the self. The will is an indication of the presence of a personality ; ontologically the person is the existing rational substance which thinks and wills. Both the above views have been condemned by the Church because neither is reconcilable with the Catholic doctrine of the hypostatic union.

At the present day all Christians—thus excluding rationalists who, like the Arians and Adoptionists of old, regard Christ as a mere man—admit that in Christ there is a divine as well as a human element. Outside the Catholic Church, however, nearly all are on common ground in rejecting the definitions of Ephesus and Chalcedon, relics, they say, of an effete philosophy. They are thus reduced to the necessity of combining these two elements in Christ in terms of the modern psychological conception of personality. It is precisely here that non-Catholic Christologies fail.

It cannot be too much emphasised that the Incarnation was not revealed to us by God in philosophical terms. It is not as if

God, after the manner of the Delphic oracle, had propounded a riddle to mankind : " Christ is one person having two natures," so that philosophers in the ages to come might discuss the meaning of the words person and nature, and thus arrive at some understanding of what the divine oracle meant. If this were so the meaning of God's revelation would change from age to age, subject to the vagaries of the human mind as it invented now one, now another signification of the words person and nature. It was this modernist conception of the development of Christian doctrine that was condemned by Pope Pius X, and this is the reason of the chaos of modern non-Catholic thought as it endeavours to " re-state " the doctrine of the Incarnation according to the requirements of present-day research. No development of the philosophy of personality, however much more it may teach us concerning the person of Christ, can ever change the meaning of the simple statement : the Word was made flesh. The Gospel story represents Christ as being God, and as being also man. It was found convenient in the course of time to state this truth by saying that Christ is one person having two natures. Other words might have been used to express the same truth, as long as they did not distort it. The criterion to be applied is not : What is the philosophical meaning of personality as I use the word, but : What did God reveal ? If, therefore, any conception of personality, when applied to the doctrine of the hypostatic union, is seen to destroy the truth of the simple statement that Christ is truly God and truly man, then the hypostatic union understood in terms of that philosophy is not the revelation that God has committed to his Church.

The more advanced, or Modernistic, school among non-Catholics tends to attenuate the divine element in Christ. God is in Christ, according to these theologians, very much in the same way as he is in any holy man or prophet. God, they say, has expressed himself in Christ as perfectly as it is possible for God to express himself in a creature. But however superlative the terms used to describe the intimacy of the union between Christ and God, it remains, in this theory, that Christ and God are distinct individuals. This teaching does not differ materially from that of Nestorius.

Others are more careful to safeguard the divinity of Christ, but they are fatally handicapped in their praiseworthy endeavour by their psychological conception of personality. Obsessed with the idea that a person is constituted as such by his consciousness of his individuality, and faced with a human consciousness side by side with a divine consciousness in Christ, they have been forced, in order not to admit two persons in him, to merge the one consciousness in the other, or—as others put it—to make one continuous with the other. But whatever be the process of identification it is inevitable that one of the two is in some way absorbed or suspended. It is here that the kenosis enters as an essential element of their Christology. It is clear, they say, that Christ is truly man ; his human consciousness is written large on every page of the New Testament. But many of the divine attributes are irreconcilable with a truly human consciousness and experience. Hence the Deity was temporarily suspended, not indeed essentially, but in some of its attributes, in order to render possible a truly human experience. Evidently these attempts to re-interpret Catholic doctrine in the light of the modern philosophy of person issue only in a form of Monophysism. In the Catholic conception of the hypostatic union Christ has two consciousnesses, a human consciousness which is a property of his humanity, and a divine consciousness which is identical with his divinity. To merge them would be to confuse the two natures.[1] Each nature operates in the manner proper to it. Neither absorbs the other, neither interferes with the activities proper to the other, and yet both are united in the one divine Person of the Word made flesh.

That such a mysterious union of two natures in one person should give rise to psychological problems of a unique order is to be expected, and the Catholic theologian is not surprised or disappointed if he is unable to solve them. The Incarnation is a mystery, a truth which apart from divine revelation we could never have known and which, even when we know it, the human mind is unable to fathom. But the fundamental mystery of the Incarnation is not psychological but ontological ; the primordial mystery concerning Christ is not so much what he knows or feels about himself, but rather what he is in himself, namely, true God and true man. With this fact in mind the Catholic theologian, guided by revelation, approaches with reverence the study of the human soul of Christ. He knows from the beginning that he cannot hope to explain by the principles of natural human psychology the unique complex of perfections that adorn that soul ; he is content to be wise unto sobriety. He asks himself the question : What is certain concerning the soul of Christ ? If truths which are certain appear to contradict each other, he knows that the contradiction is merely apparent ; so he proceeds, with a full realisation of the limits of his knowledge not only concerning God but also concerning the psychology of human nature, to try to harmonise them. If he fails in his reverent attempt to understand, he does not cease to adore him in whom are hidden all the treasures of the wisdom and the knowledge of God.

§ VI: FULL OF GRACE AND TRUTH

HOLINESS, in the ordinary acceptance of the word, means voluntary " Sub-
adherence to God, the sovereign Good. Hence God, who infinitely stantial "
loves himself, is infinitely holy and the source of all holiness in holiness of
creatures. We call holy those men and women who entirely and Christ

[1] How Christ is humanly conscious of his divinity is shown below, pp. 393-394.

voluntarily devote themselves to God, who seek perfectly to conform their lives and actions to God's holy will. But there is a holiness which, as distinct from this holiness of operation, may be called static or substantial holiness, and this we attribute to a creature that is closely connected with God or with divine worship. Thus the person of the Pope is holy or sacred, whatever may be the goodness or otherwise of his moral life, precisely by reason of his office which consecrates him in a special way to God. In this sense even inanimate things—buildings, vessels, and other objects used for the worship of God—are called holy or sacred.

If any creature that is intimately associated with God may on that account be called sacred, it is clear that the humanity of Christ in this sense is infinitely holy. Nothing could be more closely united to God than the human nature which he has made his own, which is anointed with the divinity itself, which is joined with God in the substantial order of personality. This is the fundamental reason of the reverence which, apart from the consideration of any moral goodness or human virtue in Christ, we owe to his sacred humanity. To that humanity, as has been said, we pay the cult which is due to God alone. The hypostatic union confers upon the human nature of Christ an infinite substantial holiness.

*His fulness of grace and his impeccability*   This substantial holiness of the humanity of Christ is the root and foundation of his impeccability and of what we may call his dynamic sanctity. It is unthinkable that sin should besmirch the beauty of the soul which God has made his own. From the law of original sin, evidently, the human nature of Christ was exempt because he was not born by the natural process, his body being formed in the most pure womb of the Virgin Mary. But not only could he not inherit sin, he could not commit it. The hypostatic union requires that all the operations of the assumed human nature should be attributed to the divine Person of the Word ; we should therefore have to say, if Christ could sin, that the Word Incarnate, as man, is able to offend God. The repugnance of such an idea, if it is not metaphysical, is at any rate absolute. If God assumes a human nature, that humanity must be not only sinless but impeccable.

But human holiness is something more than the mere absence of sin ; it is a positive supernatural perfection. Elsewhere in these essays [1] it is shown that man has been raised to a destiny immeasurably above his nature, that in addition to his natural life he is called upon to live a supernatural, divine life which during our period of probation upon earth consists in sanctifying grace, and in heaven reaches its consummation in the beatific vision. By this grace we are made partakers of the divine nature, adopted sons of God and heirs to eternal life. Hence to be holy, to be pleasing in God's sight, means to possess this divine life of grace, and since Christ is

[1] See Essays ix, xvi, xxxv.

the source of all grace he possesses it in all its fulness. "We saw his glory," writes St John, "the glory as of the only-begotten of the Father, full of grace and truth . . . and of his fulness we have all received, grace upon grace."

Sanctifying grace in the soul of Christ "may be conceived," says St Thomas Aquinas, "as resulting from the hypostatic union as light proceeds from the sun." [1]  Christ is God's own Son.  As God he possesses the divine life not merely by participation but essentially by reason of his eternal generation from the Father. Will he not then, as man, be made a partaker of the divine nature ? If to us, whom he has predestined to be conformable to the image of his Son, God has given grace so that we are made his sons by adoption, capable of meriting in God's sight because we are no longer merely his servants but his sons and his friends, surely then upon the human soul which he has made his own he will shower every most precious gift that will make it pleasing in his sight, and especially sanctifying grace by which his human nature is made to partake of the divine life.   For, although the hypostatic union raises that human nature to an ineffable dignity, although it confers upon it a substantial sanctity which is rightly said to be infinite, yet the assumption of humanity as such brings about no physical change in the human nature assumed ; it does not make it a partaker in the divine life, unless there are infused into the human soul those finite habits, sanctifying grace together with the supernatural virtues, which are the principles of supernatural operation.

Christ, therefore, has sanctifying grace.  He possesses it in his soul, not as the physical resultant of the hypostatic union, but as that to which, being God's only-begotten Son, he has an hereditary right : "We saw his glory, as of the only-begotten of the Father, full of grace. . . ."  Hence the important consequence, that he possessed that grace in all its fulness from the very first moment in which he was conceived in Mary's womb.  We receive grace by baptism, thus becoming adopted sons of God, and by hard striving are able to merit an increase of it.   Christ, even as man, is the natural son of God, and therefore from the beginning of his human life he received that fulness of grace which it was fitting that God's human soul should have.  When, therefore, we are told that he increased in grace [2] we must understand this development, says St Thomas, "in the sense that he worked more perfectly according to the progress of his age to show himself truly man in all that regards God and in all that regards man."

With sanctifying grace are inseparably connected the infused *Virtues of* virtues, theological and moral, and so too it was in the soul of Christ. *Christ* But with his human virtues I have not to deal here, since they are fully described in another essay.[3]  I have only to remark that those

---

[1] *S. Theol.* III, Q. 7, a. 13.          [2] Luke ii 52.
[3] Essay xii, *Jesus Christ, the Model of Manhood.*

virtues must be excluded from the soul of Christ which are incompatible with his impeccability and with the extraordinary perfection of his state. Hence, in the first place, there is no room in his soul for the virtue of repentance, since he had, and could have, no sin of which to repent. Nor could he possess the virtue of temperance, so far as it is concerned with the repression of disordered desire, since concupiscence, the effect of original sin in us, could have no place in him. Finally, Christ had not, properly speaking, the virtues of faith or hope. We believe what we do not see ; we hope for what we do not possess ; but, as will be seen below, such was the perfection of the soul of Christ that from the first moment of his human existence he enjoyed the beatific vision, seeing the Godhead face to face, and delighting in undisturbed possession of the sovereign Good. The gifts of the Holy Ghost, too, were in the soul of Christ in all their fulness, rendering the whole of that delicate supernatural organism an apt instrument upon which God with his actual grace played that symphony of celestial melody and harmony which is the life on earth of the Word Incarnate.

*The human knowledge of Christ*

We come now to the study of a subject which is full of difficulty : that of the human knowledge of Christ. The difficulty does not arise formally from the fact that Christ, as well as being truly man, is also truly God. When once it has been understood that the two natures exist side by side, unconfused, in the same person, it follows as a necessary and obvious consequence that in Christ there is a divine knowledge identical with his divine nature and a human knowledge which is an inseparable property of his humanity ; and as the natures are unconfused, so there can be no confusion of his divine knowledge with his human knowledge. The one does not take the place of the other, as Apollinaris suggested, nor is the one absorbed or in any way limited by the other, as those would have it who uphold the kenotic theory. If there were any such substitution, intermingling, or absorption, then indeed the difficulty would be insoluble ; in fact, as we have seen, any such theories totally destroy the truth of the Incarnation. The real difficulty arises, not from the confusion of one knowledge with the other, but rather from the extraordinary supernatural perfections with which, in consequence of the hypostatic union, the human intellect of Christ was endowed. Natural psychology, or the study of the natural operations of the human mind, is already sufficiently complex, but when we have to include in our study types of knowledge of which on earth we have no experience, then the difficulty of the subject is immeasurably increased. In the human intellect of Christ we have to consider the knowledge that was natural to him as man, the infused knowledge with which he was preternaturally endowed, and his beatific knowledge, whereby during the whole of his life on earth he saw God face to face.

*Acquired knowledge*

That Christ had natural human knowledge, few since the time

of Apollinaris have dreamed of denying, the tendency outside the Church to-day being rather to deny that he has any other. For the rest, St Luke tells us that he advanced in wisdom and, unless all the questions that he asked of others and the surprise that on some occasions he showed are to be treated as a mere pretence, we must needs admit that Christ acquired knowledge by natural experience even as we do. His senses and his intellect were essentially similar to ours, and there appears no reason why they should have been denied their normal exercise. On the contrary, if Christ had not the natural use of these faculties it would be difficult to understand why he should have possessed them. Thus the country, the village in which he was reared, the home in which he received instruction and education from his holy Mother and St Joseph, the environment, racial, physical, and social, in which he gradually grew to manhood, all these had, in the all-wise Providence of God, their influence in the formation of his natural character and outlook, a natural character which, it is important to remember, is a necessary substratum for the perfection of supernatural virtue which makes Jesus Christ the model of perfect manhood. For it is no less true of Christ than it is of us that the supernatural perfects nature, but does not destroy it.

But if it would be erroneous to say that the human knowledge *The Beatific* of Christ was in no way subject to development, it would be still *Vision in* more seriously wrong to restrict that knowledge to what he could *Christ* learn by purely natural means. It is the teaching of the Church, not indeed explicitly defined by any Pope or Council, but enshrined in the unanimous consent of all theologians, that the human intellect of Christ, in addition to knowledge naturally obtained, was supernaturally endowed with the beatific vision of God. The faithful, with that instinct for divine truth which is a sign of the constant presence of the Holy Spirit in the Church, have felt that the fulness of grace which befits the humanity assumed by the Word requires that he should possess the divine life, not merely in its incipient stage of sanctifying grace, but in the perfection of its ultimate development, to wit, the beatific vision ; that if we, who are but God's adopted sons, must pass through a time of probation that we may be found worthy to enter into our inheritance, he, who is the only-begotten of the Father, must possess that divine heritage from the moment in which he first had a human nature ; that he who is to lead us to beatitude must himself be already in enjoyment of it ; that the human mind which God has made his own should not be debarred by any veil from looking upon the Godhead with whom it is hypostatically united.

Can we suppose that he " that was the true light that enlighteneth every man that cometh into this world," that he who gave witness to what he had seen, walked in the relative darkness of faith ? Christ, as man, knew that he was God ; he knew that with his human nature the second Person of the Blessed Trinity was hypostatically united, and his knowledge of the hypostatic union and all that was involved in the mystery of the Incarnation must have been perfect and complete. Consciousness of personality is an immediate perception of self, and the only way in which the human intellect of Christ could have had intuitive knowledge of his divine personality was by seeing God face to face. Even the infused knowledge that is given to the angels could not give him a full understanding of the mystery that so closely touched his own personality. Christ as man knew that he was God because, being truly and in the fullest sense the son of God, with his human mind he saw God " as he is."

Wayfarers on this earth, we see God as he is imperfectly reflected in the finite works of his hands. The blessed in heaven, on the contrary, see creatures as mirrored in the essence of God, the first Cause of them all. Thus Christ by his beatific knowledge not only sees God but in God he sees also all creatures that are, have been or will be ; he sees the whole created universe of which he is appointed heir and king ; he sees the innermost thoughts of all men, of whom he is the Judge, he sees the salvation or—alas—the damnation of the souls of which he is the Redeemer ; in a word, although, his human intellect being finite, he cannot exhaust the divine intelligibility, he knows all things that in any point of time have existence. Add to this the infused knowledge which, according to the common view of theologians, Christ also possessed, and we may well understand how St Paul could speak of Christ as one " in whom are hidden all the treasures of wisdom and knowledge." [1]

That God should thus have lavished all his most precious gifts upon the human nature which he had assumed is what we should have expected. In fact theologians lay down as an indubitable principle that the soul of Christ is endowed with every perfection, natural or supernatural, which a human soul is capable of receiving. As the king honours his spouse, so God has delighted to honour the soul to which he has indissolubly wedded his divine Person. Small wonder, then, that the soul of Christ is impeccable ; for he who sees God face to face can find nothing in creatures to diminish his loyalty to the sovereign Good ; well might the wise men of the synagogue be confounded by the questions and answers of the boy of twelve, and those who heard his discourses say among themselves, " Never did anyone speak as this man " ; for Christ spoke to them in human language the truth that he derived directly from the vision of God, who is infinite Truth itself.

*No ignorance in Christ*     Hence the faithful have ever refused to admit in Christ as man ignorance concerning any matter pertaining to his person or office. It is true that some of the Fathers in their controversial writings

[1] Col. ii 3.

against Arianism said that Christ, who was omniscient according to his divine nature, was ignorant according to his humanity.[1] But it should be borne in mind that in these cases the human knowledge of Christ was not the question directly at issue. The Arians, who held that the Word was not God but a creature, pointed to certain texts of the Gospels where it is stated that Christ grew in knowledge, or that he asked questions, or that he was ignorant of the day of judgement, as showing that the Word is not omniscient and therefore not God. Catholics found an easy reply to such arguments in attributing such development and ignorance to his human intellect.

But when in the sixth century the question of Christ's human omniscience was explicitly raised and ignorance attributed to the human intellect of Christ by the sect of Agnoëteş, such a contention was rejected as impious and contrary to Catholic tradition. Suffice it to quote these words of St Gregory the Great, written to St Eulogius, Patriarch of Alexandria : " I write to your Holiness to tell you what I think of your book against the heretical Agnoëtes, and also to explain my delay. . . . In your teaching against these heretics there is much that I admire and nothing that displeases me. . . . So perfect is the harmony between your teaching and that of the Latin Fathers that I see, without surprise, that the Holy Spirit is the same in spite of the difference of language." [2]

The chief difficulty, of course, was the famous text : [3] " Of that day or hour no man knoweth, neither the angels in heaven, nor the Son, but the Father." Space does not allow of an enumeration, still less of a discussion of the various explanations of this text given by the Fathers in order to reconcile it with the traditional doctrine of the omniscience of Christ.[4] It is sufficient for our present purpose to remark that their very attempt to make such a reconciliation is a proof that they regarded it as uncatholic to attribute ignorance to Christ. *Difficulties: The day of judgement*

The first difficulty presented by the co-existence in Christ of these three types of knowledge—natural or experimental, infused, and beatific—is that, given the third, the former two would seem to be superfluous. It is a difficulty, but not a very serious one. If Christ *His human experience*

---

[1] *E.g.* St Athanasius, *Or. contra Arianos*, III, n. 37.
[2] *Epist.* Bk. X, Ep. 39.     [3] Mark xiii 32.
[4] Of all the explanations proposed the following seems to the writer the most satisfactory. Christ often disclaims powers, which he really possesses, inasmuch as it does not pertain to his mission to use them. Thus he says that he has not come to judge the world (John xii 47) ; although elsewhere he says that the Father has given him all judgement (*ibid.* v 22) ; that it is not his to grant that one may sit on his right or on his left in the kingdom of heaven (Matt. xx 23), although this is indeed the right of the Judge of all mankind. In the same sense he denies that he, the Son, knows the day of judgement ; it is not among the things which he has come from the Father to reveal. *Cf.* John viii 26, 28 ; xiv 10 : " The words that I speak to you I speak not of myself."

had possessed only beatific and infused knowledge his natural powers of intellect would have remained inoperative, and the whole of his natural human experience as depicted to us in the gospel-story would have been fictitious. Nor is his infused knowledge super-fluous, since this gives to his natural intellect a preternatural per-fection which otherwise he could never have acquired. It is true that the first two types of knowledge did not add to the sum of what he already knew in contemplating the essence of God, but, mysterious as the whole of this supernatural psychology must ever remain, even we are able to appreciate that to know a thing in three ways is better than to know it only in one. Nor did this superior know-ledge render his human experience nugatory or merely apparent. He truly advanced in wisdom, adding experience to experience, he learned obedience through the things that he had suffered, he truly wondered at the faith of the humble as he was shocked by the incredulity of the Pharisees. In his natural human life nothing was abnormal, for, again, grace perfects nature but does not destroy it.

*The Passion*     More formidable is the mystery of Christ's Passion. It is not for me to describe his sufferings : bodily torments, emotional sorrows, mental distress and pain beyond all human conception, sufferings which were increased by the very perfection of his knowledge. A picture of them is drawn in another essay.[1] But how, if Christ really enjoyed the beatific vision during the whole of his human life, can he have suffered these unspeakable torments ? Surely, if we admit that the soul of Christ was delighted with the possession of the sovereign Good, all the sufferings of which we read in the gospels must have been a pretence, or at any rate must have been considerably alleviated by his beatific knowledge.

The incompatibility of his joy with his very real suffering is but apparent. The beatific vision is a purely intellectual operation, and even our own experience tells us that spiritual joy is not in-compatible with intense bodily pain. It is true that in us physical pain may eventually occasion such spiritual exhaustion that the joy of the mind begins to fade, but this is due to the fact that none of our spiritual operations is entirely independent of the body ; the human mind cannot work without the co-operation of the brain. The beatific vision, however, is entirely independent of bodily organs, and the joy of the mind in the contemplation of God is unruffled by the torments that the body may endure. Have we not seen heroes suffer tortures for an ideal and rejoice in their pain ? Was not the face of St Stephen transfigured by spiritual joy while in his mangled body he suffered still ?

Even the more refined torments that the imagination begets may co-exist with the joy of the mind, because here again the suffering is in the sensitive or emotional part of man, and thus may leave the spirit undisturbed. Hence Christ was able to be supremely happy

[1] Essay xiii, *Jesus Christ, Man of Sorrows.*

in the contemplation of the divine essence and yet, although he accepted his Passion willingly and with joy, to feel all the shrinking horror that a sensitive nature must experience at the thought of suffering and death to come, an emotional stress to which he gave utterance in his prayer to his Father : " If it be possible, let this chalice pass from me ; yet not my will but thine be done."

But more grievous far than all this was the mental torture that he felt when he thought of the sins of mankind, of the many souls for whom his Passion would be in vain, of the friend that had betrayed him to death, of the false friends that would betray him until the end of time. Here was a sorrow that sorely afflicted his spirit, and yet he was ever filled with a spiritual joy that no sorrow could abate. It is here that we reach the heart of the psychological mystery of Christ. Are we not perhaps too venturesome when we seek to analyse the mysteries of his spirit ? Our human loves, our human joys and sorrows are but puny affections when compared with the beatific love, the superhuman joy and the unfathomable sorrow of the Redeemer. But it is only by looking into our own hearts that we are able to see some reflection of the great heart of Christ. There is no purer love, no love more unselfish than the love of the mother for her child. Yet a mother will give her only child to God with joy, a joy that is not abated by her very real pain at the thought that she may never see her child again on earth. Does this perhaps help us to understand that the sins of mankind, which so grieved our Redeemer in his agony, could yet be a subject for intense rejoicing as he contemplated in the beatific vision the mercy of God for sinners and the infinite wisdom whereby he draws good even out of evil ? That his pain at the neglect and scorn of many had its counterpart in the joy and consolation that many others would give him by offering themselves in reparation ? That his every torment added to his joy, that he delighted in his sorrow, because he suffered for love of us ? I end this subject on a questioning note, for none may dare to say that he has solved the mystery of Jesus Christ.

＊    ＊    ＊    ＊    ＊    ＊    ＊    ＊    ＊

Of one more perfection of the soul of Christ a few words must *Miraculous* be written, namely, his miraculous power. It is a commonplace *power* with the Fathers to speak of the humanity of Christ as the " organ," or the instrument, of his divinity. The principal author of miracles, evidently, is God, who alone is able by his omnipotence to supersede the forces of nature. But history attests that on many occasions God has used instruments to bring about these marvels, either to authenticate a message to mankind [1] or to manifest the sanctity of the miracle-worker. Greatest of all wonder-workers, however, is Christ, both by reason of the number of his miracles and their

[1] See Essay i, *Faith and Revealed Truth*, p. 13.

extraordinary and varied character, and by reason of the permanence of this miraculous power in his human nature. I say that this power was habitual in him, not in the sense that it was a property of his human nature but that, unlike others whom God has from time to time used as the instruments of his omnipotence, Christ was able, in virtue of the power constantly communicated to his human nature by God, to work a miracle whenever he wished.[1] As to its extent St Thomas thus expresses the traditional view : " He had power to bring about any miraculous change which might be directed to the end of the Incarnation, which is to renew all things in heaven or on earth." [2]

*The grace-giving humanity of Christ*  More marvellous still than this power of working miracles is the power of sanctifying the souls of men which both Scripture and Tradition assert to have been inherent in the humanity of Christ. Thus, as a proof that he had worked the invisible wonder of forgiving sin, he worked the visible miracle of curing a man's bodily infirmity,[3] and the woman who had anointed his feet was privileged to hear from his lips those comforting words : " Thy sins are forgiven thee." [4] Hence it is too little to say that Christ merited grace for us through his humanity. He does more than this ; he is also the efficient instrumental cause of our sanctification, inasmuch as God uses this sacred humanity as the instrument for infusing grace into our souls. It is in this that our condition differs from that of the just under the Old Testament. They received grace in view of the merits of Christ who was to come ; for those who preceded his coming Christ could not be other than the meritorious cause of sanctification. But for us who live after him his humanity is also the instrument by means of which that grace is produced in us ; and it is for this reason that the Council of Ephesus calls the flesh of Christ " life-giving." It was the source of supernatural life to those who, like St. John, saw him with their eyes and handled him with their hands ; [5] it is the source of grace to all men who still receive of his fulness. " To give grace or the Holy Spirit," says

---

[1] *Cf.* Matt. viii 2-3. The permanence of this miraculous power in Christ is compared by some theologians to the habitual power of consecrating the Eucharist possessed by the priest.

[2] *S. Theol.* III, Q. 13, art. 2. To this miraculous power also belongs the complete control that Christ possessed over his own life. He died because he willed to die ; not only in the sense that he offered himself voluntarily to his executioners, but that, even when his physical weakness had reached the stage at which naturally he must have died, he was able, had he so willed, to keep himself in life. " I lay down my life that I may take it again. No man taketh it away from me ; but I lay it down of myself, and I have power to take it up again " (John x 17-18). Hence also Christ as man was the (instrumental) cause of his own resurrection, although its principal author was his divinity. Thus we read in the Scriptures both that God raised Christ from the dead (*e.g.* 1 Cor. xv 15) and also that Christ raised himself (John ii 19).

[3] Matt. ix 2-6.          [4] Luke vii 48.          [5] *Cf.* 1 John i 1.

St Thomas,[1] "belongs to Christ as God authoritatively (*i.e.* as principal cause); but it belongs to him also as man to give grace as an instrument; for his humanity was the instrument of the divinity; and therefore the actions of that humanity were salutary to us, causing grace in us not only by way of merit but also by a certain efficiency (*i.e.* as an efficient instrumental cause)." During his life on earth Christ exercised this instrumental causality in respect of grace directly through his human nature. Now, however, it is communicated to the sacraments which he has instituted. "The principal efficient cause of grace," to quote St Thomas again,[2] "is God himself, to whom the humanity of Christ stands in the relation of conjoined instrument and the sacraments as separate instruments; hence salutary virtue flows from the divinity of Christ through his humanity into the sacraments."

It is significant that our study of the humanity of Christ should have brought us finally to the mention of the sacraments; so true is it that the sacramental system, since it is but the continuance of the divine economy of the Incarnation, is essential in Catholic doctrine and practice. For the centre of that system is one Sacrament of unique excellence, the sacrament which is the source of the sanctifying power of all the others, because it contains the life-giving humanity of the Redeemer: the sacrament of the Body and Blood of Christ himself.

In speaking of the Eucharist, which he proposed to institute, Christ uses words which I cannot but quote here, because they seem to sum up in a wonderful way the whole purpose of the Incarnation of the Son of God: "As the living Father sent me, and I live by the Father, so he that eateth me the same also shall live by me." Christ lives by the Father according to his divinity, because he has received the divine nature by eternal generation. But he lives by the Father also according to his humanity, for his soul is filled with sanctifying grace, which is nothing else than a participation in man of the divine nature and of the life of God. Sent by the living Father to bestow that life upon us, the Son of God through his human nature pours out into our souls the grace which he possesses in all its fulness, and in order that the source of grace may be accessible to all men in all ages he institutes a Sacrament under the form of food and drink, wherein his life-giving humanity is truly, really and substantially present, so that by eating his flesh and drinking his blood all men may live by Christ as he lives by the Father, with that supernatural life of grace which is a participation of the divine life of the Blessed Trinity.

And so we have returned to the point from which we set out. Christianity is the religion of the Fatherhood of God, from whom

---

[1] *S. Theol.* III, Q. 8, art. 1, ad 1.     [2] *S. Theol.* III, Q. 62, art. 5.

all Paternity in heaven and earth is named. Father from all eternity of his only-begotten Son, God has willed through the humanity of his Incarnate Son to raise up to himself other sons, sons by adoption and co-heirs with Christ of eternal life, sons "who are born, not of blood, nor of the will of the flesh, nor of the will of man, but of God."

## EPILOGUE

### CHRIST THE KING

THEREFORE Christ is King. "A child is born to us and a son is given to us, and the government is upon his shoulder, and his name shall be called Wonderful, Counsellor, God the Mighty, the Father of the world to come, the Prince of Peace. His empire shall be multiplied, and there shall be no end of peace. He shall sit upon the throne of David and upon his kingdom; to establish it and strengthen it with judgement and with justice, from henceforth and for ever." [1] Christ is King, not only as God, but as man also. He is King, not only by reason of the perfection of his humanity, not only because he has purchased us as his people by redeeming us; he is King because he is the Word Incarnate. "He has dominion over all creatures," says St Cyril of Alexandria, the great champion of orthodoxy against Nestorius,[2] "a dominion not seized by violence nor usurped, but his by essence and by nature." As God he is the eternal Lord and Creator of all; becoming man he received from his Father the royal dignity as the rightful attribute of his human nature; for it was only fitting that a manhood joined in unity of Person with the Godhead should be "appointed heir of all things";[3] it is his birthright as the Word Incarnate to receive the homage of all creatures. Hence the whole of creation hails his advent with the cry of the Psalmist:[4] "Lift up your gates, O ye princes, and be ye lifted up, O eternal gates; and the King of Glory shall enter in."

G. D. SMITH.

[1] Isaias ix 6-7.
[3] Heb. i 2.

[2] *In Luc.* x.
[4] Ps. xxiii 7.

# XII

## JESUS CHRIST, THE MODEL OF MANHOOD

### § I: INTRODUCTION

1. *England and Jesus Christ*

IT is fortunate, it is very much more, that in this country, to the present day at least, whatever vagaries our religion has gone through during the last four centuries, men generally have clung to the belief in the reality and divinity of our Lord Jesus Christ. England may have broken away from the common faith of Christendom, but she has not yet broken away from the common faith in Christ. She may have split up into many divisions, Catholic and Protestant, Protestant and Nonconformist, Nonconformist and one knows not what, but always there has been a rallying round the Name which is above every name, always there has been a willingness to bend the knee before it. While in other countries history has witnessed the formation of the most determined hostile camps against it, and determined war waged to overthrow it, among ourselves we have had little more than individual voices raised, and these for the most part have not known what they did ; usually they have uttered little else than echoes of what has been already heard abroad. With all our differences, with all our indifferentism, England has always been, and still is, essentially Christian ; even our Modernism, when it finds itself bringing into question the belief in Jesus Christ and what he stands for, looks at itself with not a little unrest and hesitates to draw conclusions.

This is particularly marked in the attitude of the British mind towards the Bible. At times, especially in the nineteenth century, we have been overwhelmed by German learning, or Dutch analysis, or French brilliance ; we have indeed produced some kind of imitation of them all ; but always in the end we have recovered our feet, and by far our best, certainly our most lasting, work has been done in defence of the sacred text and all that it contains. We have had no Strauss or Renan ; we have no Tübingen school ; our higher criticism, such as it is, if really our own and not merely borrowed from elsewhere, has gone steadily in favour of the Bible and of our Lord Jesus Christ as he is therein portrayed. If at any time a writer has denied any of its contents, its miracles, or its supernatural element—at least, until these days when Modernism has come to shake the foundations of all faith—such a man has been more condoned as an eccentric, or pitied as one prejudiced, or feared as a danger, than followed. He has never formed a lasting school ; he has never even founded a new rationalism ; his permanent influence on English religious thought has been, almost without exception, virtually none.

What is true of Great Britain in general has its reflection in the British Catholic mind. Before the unhappy sixteenth century, if we may judge from the spiritual literature of that time, our fore-fathers were marked by a deep devotion to the person of Jesus Christ and his Mother. In those days poets and play-writers gloried in singing for the people the praises or the sorrows of Mary and her Son, or in setting them in all their attractiveness upon our village stages. If we had not ascetics of the same type as Italy or Spain, we had our anchorites and hermits and recluses, who were never tired of repeating the holy Name of Jesus to many tunes. Men went out to battle with the Blessed Sacrament in their breasts, their women stayed at home and worked chasubles and vestments for the holy sacrifice ; when there was peace, and leisure for other things, they spent their time and their means multiplying every-where across the land homes for Jesus Christ, the Son of God, and dedicating them to his Mother.

Nor is the modern Catholic mind very different ; it easily responds to the names of Jesus and Mary. It seems to know them personally ; witness its devotion to the Sacred Heart, its ever-increasing love of the Blessed Sacrament, seen especially in frequent communion, in the processions of Corpus Christi, in the practice of the Forty Hours now universal, and, on Mary's side, in the love of our Lady of Lourdes. It is seen in the type of our pictures and statues, in our books, in our hymns ; no one who watches the devotion of our faithful in their churches can doubt their conspicuous veneration and love for the sacred humanity of our Lord Jesus Christ. Our poorest and least instructed may be ignorant of many things, but, if their faith has not been sapped by the blight of circumstances, to them Jesus is a real fact, whom they know, and in whose hands they can safely trust themselves, whatever lot this world may mete out to them.

It is therefore with no little relief that, in writing for English readers on a subject of this kind, one feels oneself entitled to set aside for the moment all controversy concerning the New Testa-ment or the Person of Jesus Christ. In doing so we have little fear of being accused either of shirking difficulty or of making use of premisses which are unwarranted. From the beginning the destructive schools have found many of their chief opponents among our own scholars ; these have done their work so well that it still stands the test of keen attack, and upon it we may rely. To English students as a whole the Gospels are both genuine and credible ; if, until this generation, there has been a tendency to err, it has been rather on the other side, the side of over-literalness, finding too much in the human words and forms of Scripture, reading into them more than they were meant to contain.

## 2. *The model of perfect manhood*

We may assume, then, the truth of the Gospels ; we may assume, as established elsewhere in these essays, the reality of Jesus Christ, truly man, truly God ; it will be enough for us here to dwell upon the human character of him who is both God and man, and to show how in matter of fact this character has revealed itself to be that of the Perfect man. Indeed, we may limit ourselves still further. It will be enough to confine ourselves to that aspect of his character which concerns us men who follow him ; what belongs to him in his higher aspects, as Prophet, as Redeemer, and the rest, may well be left to another Essay which treats of him as God and Man. Here we look for the Model of Manhood and no more.

Many philosophers in the past, many novelists and poets in more recent times, have attempted to describe for us the perfect man. From the very nature of the case their descriptions have differed one from another ; while, perhaps, all have been good so far as they have gone, none has been able to include in his description the whole idea of man's perfection. For man is limited and finite ; he cannot conceive in his mind an ideal which contains in itself the whole scope of perfection, not though his vision confines itself to the plane of nature alone. And even if he could, when he comes to describe it, he can do so only in the limited terms of his own imagination and language. He will speak from his own experience of himself, especially his own shortcomings, from his knowledge of and insight into other men, possibly from the ideal picture which his imagination has conjured up after the sordidness of real life has been eliminated. But in every case it will be his own vision and perspective, his own point of view, which will be expressed ; true, noble, complete, perfect in its degree, but nevertheless with the confining limitations and lacunæ which human nature cannot escape. In fact or in fiction, in history or in drama, the altogether perfect man does not exist ; if he did, if he were in all things and always perfect, he would be something more than human.

So we say, speaking of ourselves and of one another, of all men as we know them, of all men as they have been described by others ; the knowledge of this truth leads us to judge not that we may not be judged, to forgive as we would be forgiven, to see not the mote in our brother's eye, being only too conscious of the beam within our own. Human nature, because it is human nature, is faulty. And yet we are compelled to make one exception. There has lived in this world one Man in whom, if he is taken wholly, no fault whatsoever has been found, who has shown himself in all things perfect, whose accurate picture, moreover, has been handed down for us all to study ; the impossible has been done before our eyes. The more closely the portrait is examined, and the more in detail the character is revealed, so much the more is this amazing fact found to be true ; and that not only by followers who love his Name, and may therefore be predisposed to see in him " the most beautiful of the sons of men," but by unbelievers also, who would look on him with cold eyes, unenthusiastic in his cause, what they would call unprejudiced and scientific, and yet would be honest and sincere. They have scrutinised Jesus, the Carpenter of Nazareth, and have found him to be " the Lamb of God," " the King of Israel." They have listened to and sifted his words, and have acknowledged that " never did man speak as this man spoke." They have weighed all his deeds and have declared that " he hath done all things well." They have compared him with others and have concluded : " We have never seen the like." They have looked for a charge against him and have owned with Pilate : " I find no fault in this just man." They have pierced his heart, and what they have found there has made them confess : " Indeed this was the Son of God."

This conclusion, however vague in its final expression, we may well be justified in claiming as the glorious outcome of the long-drawn battle which a century and more has seen waged round the name of Jesus Christ. Whatever adverse and less enlightened criticism may have attempted in the past, whatever specious science may attempt to-day, sober scholarship all the world over comes more and more to acknowledge this at least—not only the full fact of Jesus Christ as the Scriptures give him to us, not only that he stands out pre-eminently the greatest man this world has ever seen, but also the further fact that he is so great, so complete, so universally perfect, as to be unique, in some sublime sense more than ordinary man either is, or could be, or could ever of himself fashion in his mind. Students have naturally looked for limitations, and have found none ; some have assumed shortcomings, and others have proved their assumptions to be contrary to the facts. They have searched for the shadows corresponding to his established virtues, and have found them not to be there ; powers and gifts which in other men do not co-exist are discovered united in him. He is undefinable ; limited though he may be because of his humanity, still we cannot fix the limits ; if we try to lay hands on him, if we say that because he is this therefore he is not that, he slips through our fingers and escapes us. No one quality can be ascribed to him as characteristic to the exclusion of another ; he possesses them all ; the ideal which man of himself cannot so much as imagine has been found in him in real life. We live in an age of discoveries, but no discovery of our time has been more momentous, more epoch-making, than this.

### 3. Points of view

It is not that we have discovered anything we have not known before ; fortunately for the world the knowledge of Jesus Christ never has been and never can be lost. Rather it is the angle of vision which may be considered comparatively new. From the days of St Paul it has been well understood that Jesus Christ, the

true Son of God, since he chose to become man, could not but be
Perfect Man ; since he came for man, for man's redemption and to
be man's model, he could not but be man's perfect model.   Given
the Godhead and the truth of the Scriptures, there was only one
light in which those Scriptures could be read by the Fathers and
the early Church, and that was " the Light which was the life of men,
the true Light, which enlighteneth every man that cometh into this
world."   But in our own time the tendency has been to begin at
the opposite extreme ; to argue not from the Godhead to the
Manhood, but from the Manhood to wherever the argument might
lead.   It was a course inevitable for those to whom God had come
to have little or no meaning, who were therefore compelled to
investigate the facts of history as historic facts alone, incapable of
being anything more.   Since the Sonship of God to them meant
nothing, the truth had to be read and interpreted by them in the
absence of that guiding light ;  and though, even in that darkness,
the picture obtained of Jesus Christ has been of surpassing human
beauty, yet has it fallen far short of the whole.   By way of contrast
and example, compare the Life of Jesus Christ by Ludolph of Saxony,
written in the fifteenth century, and the Life by Renan in the nineteenth ;  the Life by Ludolph still lives, while that by Renan, with
all its charm, has been long repudiated, by none more than by his
own disciples.

The same tendency has been followed, and seems now to be
increasingly followed, by another school.   To this school God is
indeed a great reality, but it has made so much of the kenosis, the
" emptying-out " of the God-made-man, as virtually to assume
that Jesus, if he is rightly to be understood, must be studied as
being man only, prescinding entirely, or almost entirely, from his
divinity.   To this school would seem to belong an ever-growing
number of English Protestant writers to-day.   To it the Jesus of
history must be considered apart from the Jesus of faith ;  where
history records a fact, that fact must be understood as man by his
experience understands it and no more.   In this restricted light
much of necessity has been distorted.   Jesus Christ, considered
as man and man only, whatever might lie hidden in the background,
forced into the mould of other men, has rendered disconcerting
conclusions.   Many words and actions and events in the Gospels
have been surrendered ;  their riddle can only be read when his
own full light has been turned upon them.   And yet, even to this
school, in spite of its assertion of his ignorance, his groping to the
discovery of himself, and other limitations put upon him, he stands
out as a perfect being, unique, more than man.

But in this simple exposition of the Catholic mind, or rather
let us say of one single aspect of the Catholic mind, in regard to
Jesus Christ, there is neither room nor need for controversy.
Except perchance by way of confirmation, we need not dwell upon

the opinions of others. We stand on sure ground, we walk along paths that have long been well-trodden, and from whatever goal men of goodwill set out, they arrive in the end at the same centre. Jesus Christ, being God, is also as Man the Model of Perfect Manhood ; Jesus Christ, being Man, is found to be more than man, is found to be what he declared himself to be, the true Son of God made truly man, yet remaining one with the Father. In this way the revelation grew upon those who first learnt to read the Carpenter of Nazareth ; when they had read him, then the overwhelming truth took hold of them, and in the light of the Godhead the Manhood became more manifestly clear. Thus does the one truth reflect upon and clarify the other ; the Light that is the Life of men is the Word made flesh, the Word made flesh is the Light of the world, whose " glory we have seen, the glory as it were of the only-begotten of the Father, full of grace and truth."

§ II: A GENERAL BACKGROUND

1. *A first impression*

WHEN we read the four Gospels with attention, one thing at least must strike us of their respective authors—that is, the conviction deep down in them all that every word they wrote was true. There is no attempt to emphasise what they have to say, as will one who narrates the naturally incredible, or who is eager to convince either himself or his audience ; miracles are told with the same simplicity as other events ; in dealing with the central figure they pass from the sublime to the commonplace with disconcerting ease. But in regard to that central figure this has a wonderful effect ; it is alive ; it walks out of its surroundings and stands apart ; it detaches itself, it would seem, from its own generation and walks through all ages, belongs to all time.

Before any attempt is made to draw out the features of this portrait, it will be well, for the sake of a background, to look at the life of Jesus as a whole. Of the earliest phase little need be said : that phase of miraculous promise, of " good tidings of great joy " and yet of humble infancy, of that combination of joy and sorrow, adoration and subject helplessness, submission to the Law and yet supremacy, command and obedience, which at once prepares us for the paradoxes, the seemingly impossible contrasts, which mark his whole career. The period closes with his first recorded words : " Did you not know that I must be about my Father's business ? " (Luke ii 49). They are the motto of his life.

Until he was thirty years of age all we are told is that " he was subject to them " (Luke ii 51) ; that " he grew and waxed strong, full of wisdom, and the grace of God was in him " (Luke ii 40) ; and that he " advanced in wisdom, and age, and grace before God and men " (Luke ii 52). At the age of thirty he came down to the

Jordan, a sinner it would have seemed among sinners, to be baptised by John. From the Jordan he again passes out of sight into the desert ; not only will he be accounted a sinner among sinners, but, like every sinner, he will be tempted even as they.

So completely is this willingness to be unknown and unnoticed a part of his nature, that not until he is revealed by John, and not until some followers of John of their own accord come to him, does he make the least effort to be found. But as soon as they come, then follows a quick response. They are welcomed as dear companions ; by mere contact with him they are stirred with an enthusiasm they had never known before ; instantly they go away and bring others to him ; the fascination captures them all, and they long to be with him always. And he rewards them ; he takes them with him into Galilee ; before their eyes he turns water into wine ; back he comes with them to Jerusalem, and again before their eyes he drives out the buyers and sellers from the temple ; they learn from the beginning what he can do, what power over things and men is behind this Carpenter of Nazareth. They have begun in love, they are at once led on to faith and trust.

Nevertheless, so long as John the Baptist is in the field, Jesus is content to bide his time and wait ; not until the Precursor is taken and clapped into prison does he show himself before the world. But when that deed is done, then he begins to move. With a daring that defies all opposition, of Pharisees and doctors of the Law, of Herod and all his myrmidons, of ignorant Galilæans and all their prejudices, of dwellers in Jerusalem and all their bigotry, he comes out boldly and proclaims that the Kingdom is at hand, and that he, Jesus, is the messenger sent to found it. From this moment he moves quickly and surely. There is no hesitation in his method, no drawing back because of opposition. His own men of Nazareth reject him, and at once he calls others to his aid ; the people of Capharnaum accept him, and he pours out upon them all he has to give in a very torrent. Pharisees set themselves to catch him in word or deed, and before their eyes he proves his power, not only of healing, but of forgiving sins. This first outburst of authority carries all before him ; men look on and ask themselves : " What thing is this ? What is this new doctrine ? What word is this ? For with authority and power he commandeth even the unclean spirits, and they obey him and go out " (Mark i 27 ; Luke iv 36). " And all the multitudes were astonished and filled with fear, and wondered and glorified God that gave such power to men " (Matt. ix 8 ; Mark ii 12 ; Luke v 26).

Endurance of friends, equal endurance of enemies ; forbearance, silent and ignoring, with those who knew no better, encouragement, gentle, cheerful, happy, fascinating, to those from whom he hoped for and expected more ; equally considerate to rich and poor, learned and unlearned, sophisticated citizens of Judæa and narrow country-folk of Galilee, Pharisees and publicans, rulers in the city and lepers on the road, disciples and strangers, believers and harsh critics ; intimate with all but depending on none, appealing to them to believe in him, but not despondent if he failed, giving all he had to give if they would but receive it, inviting all, refusing none, striking friends and rivals dumb by his lavish and unconditional generosity ; and when abused for the gifts he gave, never closing up his hand, sparing himself in nothing, though he knew that the seed he sowed fell on stony or thorn-choked soil ; and underneath, like a thundering, awful, underground torrent, a life apart and independent, of prayer and spiritual understanding that could not be ruffled by the gales and storms upon the surface—such is an impression of Jesus in the first and most active, yet perhaps the least self-revealing, period of his public life.

### 2. *To the confession of Peter*

So he prepared the ground. Then up on the hill behind Capharnaum, after a whole night spent in prayer—" And he passed the whole night in the prayer of God " (Luke vi 12)—he called to himself his Twelve Apostles, choosing " whom he would himself " (Mark iii 7-19 ; Luke vi 12-19), and no man should interfere or deny him. It was an act of high command ; it was followed by that momentous sermon, the charter of the new kingdom, the challenge thrown down in his own name to all the world (Matt. v 1-7, 29). This again was confirmed by deeds of singular mercy : by praise and reward of a pagan's faith (Matt. viii 5-18 ; Luke vii 1), by singular pity for a widowed mother's tears (Luke vii 11-17), by the befriending of a " woman in the city, a sinner " whom no self-respecting man would touch (Luke vii 36-50), by permitting that women should come with him, to help him in his need (Luke viii 1-3).

And yet it was not all victory. Indeed, at every turn he met with disappointment. Already from the first, by the Jordan in Judæa, suspicion and jealousy had hunted him out ; now in Galilee he was not to be left alone. His rivals could not do what he did ; therefore must he be proved a deceiver. He went about doing good ; therefore must he be stopped : " And they were filled with madness ; and they talked one with another, what they might do to Jesus " (Luke vi 11). He spoke " as one having authority " ; therefore he was a blasphemer : " Who is this who speaketh blasphemies ? " (Luke v 21). The miracles could not be denied ; therefore in them must be found ground for accusation. He did them on the sabbath day, and thereby broke the sabbath (Matt. xii 9-14 ; Mark iii 1-6 ; Luke vi 1-11) ; he did them by no human power, and thereby proved that he was himself possessed : " This man hath Beelzebub, and casteth out devils by the prince of devils " (Matt. xii 24 ; Mark iii 22).

And to some extent, as must always be the case, the people were influenced by these insinuations of their leaders. They, too, began to wonder and to doubt. From this time we see him turning more and more away from them, as they turned more away from him. He still has deep compassion for them, for they are lying " like sheep that have no shepherd " (Matt. ix 35-38 ; Mark vi 6) ; he still lets them crowd about him, and jostle him in the streets (Mark v 31 ; Luke viii 45) ; but he knows that not on them can the Kingdom be founded. He must attend more and more to the Twelve. To them apart from henceforth he gives special instructions (Matt. xiii 11 ; Mark iv 11 ; Luke viii 10) ; for them alone he works special miracles, stirring them to ever more faith (Matt. viii 23-27 ; Mark iv 35-41 ; Luke viii 22-25) ; filling them at once with awe and confidence (Matt. viii 28-34 ; Mark v 1-20 ; Luke viii 26-39) ; before them allowing his simple, childlike affection to appear in the midst of his weary disappointment (Matt. ix 23-26 ; Mark v 35-43 ; Luke viii 49-56) ; endowing them with his powers and sending them forth that they may learn in practice the work to which they have been called (Matt. x 5-15 ; Mark vi 7-13 ; Luke ix 1-6).

They went out over Galilee while he remained at home. They preached ; they worked wonders in his name ; they came back happy men. They came to him like children to one who understood them, and told him all that they had done ; they rejoiced with him and he rejoiced with them (Mark vi 30 ; Luke ix 10). In spite of the gathering of the gloom about him, in spite of the threats and warnings which of late had been coming from his lips, he had not lost, he never lost, that inward peace and fascination and familiarity by which those about him were made glad. Never throughout his life does Jesus lose this trait. If he is roused to anger, the next instant proves that he is always controlled ; if he is stung to the quick, however he may show that he feels it, there is never any change in his heart. Once only, at the end, in the Garden of Gethsemani, does the cloud seem to enclose him altogether ; but even then his will is bent to the will of his Father, and he can face his death with calm.

The first period, of wonders and success, had led up to the choosing of the Twelve and the Sermon on the Mount ; the second, of reaction, had been marked by the instruction of the Twelve apart from all the rest. He would close it with a new high-water mark. He drew his best apart into the desert ; there he fed them, five thousand men, beside women and children ; he stirred their zeal till they called him " the Prophet," and would hail him as their king ; in the plain of Genesareth, by a yet more lavish outpouring of miracles, he deepened the impression ; then, when they at last professed their allegiance as they had never professed it before, he gave them the one test of all ; he offered them his flesh to eat, and his blood to drink. And at this last moment they failed him ; in spite of all they had received, in spite of all they had promised, they

failed him. " M..ny of his disciples, hearing it said : This saying
is hard, and who can hear it ? " (John vi 61). And " after this,
many of his disciples went back, and walked with him no more "
(John vi 67).

Jesus left Capharnaum with a saddened heart ; we do not hear
that he ever set foot in it again. He had made the one great offer
for which all these months he had been preparing, and it had been
rejected ; the one offer which, had they but shut their eyes to their
own questionings and accepted the truth of him that was all truth,
would have revealed to those men the wealth of power and love
and generosity which was within their grasp, and which was more
than belonged to any mortal man to give. He left the place ; he
left Galilee ; he went out of the land of the Jews into pagan Tyre
and Sidon. For months he wandered abroad, keeping the Twelve
continually with him, giving to them in this alien land an utterly
new outlook on life. Since the mission on which he had sent them
through Galilee there had been a long respite : miracles a few,
and they were less spontaneous than before ; preaching very little,
and that with a continued note of warning ; avoidance but not fear
of his enemies, for when he met them he defied them to their faces ;
prayer and solitude in abundance ; all the time a deepening upon
them of personal influence, in familiarity along with dignity, leaving
through these hot summer months the seed he had sown to grow
within their hearts. More and more he had confined himself to
them ; at length the time came when their faith, too, must be finally
tested.

" And it came to pass in the way, as he was alone praying, his
disciples also were with him, and he asked them : Whom do the
people say that I am ? Whom do men say that the Son of man is ? "

They gave him an answer which now concerned him little. Then
he asked :

" But whom do you say that I am ? Simon Peter answered
and said : Thou art Christ, the Son of the living God " (Matt.
xvi 13-16 ; Mark viii 27-29 ; Luke ix 18-20).

It was enough ; at last, by a single man on earth, with the light
of the Father from heaven, he had been discovered and owned for
what he was. There and then, upon that man, the Church of God
was founded ; henceforth it mattered little what Pharisees or doctors
might say or do. His work was now assured ; now he could march
on boldly to his death.

### 3. *To Palm Sunday*

With the confession of Peter the manner of Jesus seemed completely to change. At once he cut short his wanderings into foreign
lands. He returned into Galilee ; on Mount Thabor, to reward
them for their faith, and to prepare them for what was yet to come,
he showed to three of them a shadow of his Godhead. For a month

or thereabouts he still hung about the upper province. But he seemed no longer to care to preach. He no longer busied himself with miracles ; instead he took means to hide himself away, content only with deepening the faith of his Twelve, strengthening them for the great ordeal that would soon now be upon them.

Nevertheless, how little after all did these poor men from Galilee understand ! In many places we are reminded of their ignorance, even at this late hour (Mark ix 32) ; patience and forbearance he had to show them to the end, perhaps more at the end than in the early days of hope and promise. Nor only to his own ; he had to show it also to his enemies. One might say that the rest of his life is but a continued manifestation of unwearied patience and long-suffering to all who came within its range. On the Feast of Tabernacles he marched again into Jerusalem. Let his enemies do what they would, he stayed there all the time, moving in and out of the Temple as he pleased. He came again for the Feast of Dedication ; in the intervals he remained for the most part in the neighbourhood, in Judæa or Peræa, for any of his foes to meet him who chose. The atmosphere is heavy with storm ; his death is continually on the lips of men ; more than one attempt is made to take him ; we need to bear all this in mind if we would understand aright the depth and warmth and all-enduring patience of his last appeals.

" If any man thirst let him come to me and drink " (John vii 37).

" I am the light of the world. He that followeth me walketh not in darkness, but shall have the light of life " (John viii 12).

" I am the good shepherd. The good shepherd giveth his life for his sheep " (John x 11).

" I am the good shepherd, and I know mine, and mine know me " (John x 14).

" Come to me, all you that labour and are burdened, and I will refresh you. Take up my yoke upon you, and learn of me, because I am meek and humble of heart ; and you shall find rest for your souls. For my yoke is sweet, and my burden light " (Matt. xi 28-30).

With language such as this Jesus fought his great campaign against his bitterest enemies in Jerusalem, only a few months before he died. It was the forgiveness of " seventy times seven times " put into practice. Such enduring forbearance could never have been invented ; the whole story teems with emotion, the man who speaks has his heart full. Incredible bearing of abuse and insult and trickery, understanding sympathy with friends and foes, quick response to any least sign of recognition, fascinating imagery linking his words with all around him, firm, consistent assertion of the truth that seemed to compel belief, exact interpretation of the past, clear and unflinching vision of the future, seeing at once both death and victory, beneath it all peace and assurance and strength in the knowledge and love and intimate union with the Father—all this was evident to all, and portrayed a soul so perfect as to be more than human ; his enemies even better than his friends knew what it implied.

With this last cry, one might almost say, the portrait of Jesus for our present purpose is completed. It is strong as a tower, yet delicate as a feather ; yielding as a blade of grass to every breath of wind, yet firm as a rock before the heaviest wash of water. For the rest the evangelists, among them chiefly St Luke, are content merely to touch in the lights and shadows, all in keeping with this last impression. For instance, soon after this, down the highroad from the city a lawyer asks him what is the great commandment of the Law, and he is made to answer his own question, that it is the love of God and the love of one's neighbour. He asks who is his neighbour, and he is given that perfect story of the Good Samaritan (Luke x 25-37). It is at this time that we find him accepting hospitality from two simple women of Bethania (Luke x 38-48) ; at this time that he is found alone in prayer, and by his example makes others long to pray like him (Luke xi 1-13) ; at this time that he sees a poor, aged woman bent double, and puts unasked his gentle hand upon her, and makes her stand up straight (Luke xiii 10-17). While the enmity about him grows ever more bitter, while he is compelled to become ever more emphatic in his retort, nevertheless precisely at this time, and it would seem precisely in proportion, does his tenderness of heart reveal itself, in the parable of the Lost Sheep (Luke xv 1-7), and of the Prodigal Son (Luke xv 11-32), in his weeping over the tomb of his friend Lazarus, and his raising him to life (John xi 1-46), in his healing of the ten lepers, and his expression of regret that only one came back to thank him (Luke xvii 12-19), in the parable of the Pharisee and the Publican (Luke xviii 9-14), in the welcome he gave to the little children and their mothers (Matt. xix 13-15 ; Mark x 13-16 ; Luke xviii 15-17), in the love he showed to the young man who fain would follow him : " Jesus looked on him and loved him " (Matt. xix 16 ; Mark 17 ; Luke xviii 18), in the hearty, even merry greeting to the publican Zacheus (Luke xix 1-10), last of all in the defence he made of the woman who poured out upon him of her best (Matt. xxvi 6-13 ; Mark xiv 3-9 ; John xii 1-11).

### 4. *To the Passion*

That last scene ended all ; the rest was but the conclusion of the tragedy. In the triumphant Procession of Palms he told the world that he was its Master (Matt. xxi 1-11 ; Mark xi 1-11 ; Luke xix 29-44 ; John xii 12-19); on the next day, when again he cleansed the Temple, he told the priests and the doctors of the Law that he was their Master too (Matt. xxi 12-17 ; Mark xi 15-19 ; Luke xix 45-48). For two days more he came into their midst and let them gather round him ; he permitted them to harry him with bickerings and questions, as they had never harried him before ; with a power at once noble and crushing he silenced them every one, so that from that time forward they dared ask him no more questions (Matt. xxii 46). Then with an eloquence that is unsurpassed he pronounced upon them their doom (Matt. xxiii 1-39). With that he passed out of the Temple, never to enter it again ; on the hillside of Olivet he warned his own of the evil days that would be (Matt. xxiv 25 ; Mark xiii ; Luke xxi 5-36) ; he retired to Bethania, and there he hid himself away, preparing for the last great surrender.

In what follows, though through it all the character of Jesus is seen as it is seen nowhere else, we must be content to move quickly. It was paschal time, the last of his life, and a place must be found in which he might celebrate it ; like the King he was, the Son of David proclaimed on the Sunday preceding, though on other nights he had yielded to his enemies and fled the city, on this night he would choose, for this ever memorable ceremony, a noble mansion in the noblest quarter of the town, under the very walls of Annas and Caiphas, and not a soul should deny him (Matt. xxvi 17-19 ; Mark xiv 12-16 ; Luke xxii 7-13). When the hour arrived he would go up with his own, and to them alone he would reveal the secret of his heart ; this last bequest he would leave to them before he died, the key to all that had gone before, and to all that was to come after.

" Before the festival day of the pasch, Jesus knowing that his hour was come, and that he should pass out of this world to the Father, having loved his own who were in the world he loved them unto the end " (John xiii 1).

He sat down with them at table ; restlessly he rose and washed their feet ; his heart fluttered at the remembrance that in spite of all he was to them, and of all they were to him, one among them would betray him, another would deny him, all would desert him in his hour of need. Still he would not stay his hand ; for them he had never before stayed it, he would not do it then. Instead, even to them, even at this hour of utter disappointment, he would surpass himself in generosity. He gave them his flesh to eat ; he gave them his blood to drink ; he gave himself to them for all time, that they might eat him and drink him when they chose, and, when they chose, give him to be food and drink to others. He gave as only God could give, and that only the God of utter love (Matt. xxvi 26-29 ; Mark xiv 22-25 ; Luke xxii 19, 20).

Love and service, mastership and lowly submission, we have seen them manifested all through his life, but never more conspicuously than now. Sensitive agony because of desertion, overwhelming gratitude because of the least recognition, sadness unto death because of failure, encouragement because of the certainty of victory beyond, all these lights and shadows play upon his soul during all that supper night ; but always in the end love conquers, and always to these men, no matter what they may then be, no matter what they may soon do, there is nothing but hope and ehcouragement, and love and sympathy poured out. They will be separated from him, but let them not mind ; he will not leave them orphans, he will come back to them. They will be scandalised in him, but let them not mind ; he has prayed for them, for Simon in particular, and all will yet be well. They will be hated by the world, but let them not mind ; the world has hated him before them. They will be persecuted by men, to put them to death will be deemed a duty, but let them not mind ; he himself has overcome the world, the prince of this world is already conquered.

Even that is not enough. Such consolation is only negative, and Jesus can never stop there. They are his own, he loves them to the end, they must partake of his reward. " With a strong cry and tears " he makes to his Father a further claim, and it is based on an argument which no man but he, none but the Son of God made man could make.

" I have glorified thee on the earth : I have finished the work thou gavest me to do " (John xvii 4).

He had lived a perfect life ; the Manhood had corresponded with the Godhead ; while other men had to learn : " Forgive us our trespasses," he could with truth say this only of himself, and because of it could ask of his Father what he would. And what did he ask ? For himself nothing, for them everything. That these his own should be preserved from evil ; that they should be made one among themselves ; that they should be for ever one with him ; " that the love wherewith thou hast loved me may be in them, and I in them " (John xvii 26).

That was the final goal. We take that last expression of his soul and look back, and in the light of it all the life of Jesus is aglow with a new significance. This is his Kingdom, as he himself esteems it ; for this he has laboured all the time ; to satisfy his own outpouring love for men, to win their love to himself, to stir within them a love for one another such as mankind has never known before.

## § III: JESUS CHRIST PERFECT IN HIMSELF

### 1. The human limitations of Jesus

" IT behoved him in all things to be made like unto his brethren, that he might become a merciful and faithful high priest before God, that he might be a propitiation for the sins of the people. For in that wherein he himself hath suffered and been tempted he is able to succour them also that are tempted " (Heb. ii 17, 18).

" For we have not a high priest who cannot have compassion on our infirmities : but one tempted in all things like as we are, without sin " (Heb. iv 15).

" Who in the days of his flesh, with a strong cry and tears, offering up prayers and supplications to him that was able to save him from death, was heard for his reverence. And whereas indeed he was the Son of God, he learned obedience by the things which he suffered " (Heb. v 7, 8).

" It was fitting that we should have a high priest, holy, innocent, undefiled, separated from sinners, and made higher than the heavens " (Heb. vii 26).

In these and many other passages of the later New Testament we are shown how the real humanity of Jesus Christ, with all its limitations and weaknesses, remained impressed, after he was gone, upon the minds of his first disciples. When the whole picture had been completed, then, and then only, they saw the significance of all its parts. Then at last they realised the meaning of that lowliness and meekness which in his lifetime, especially at the latter end, had tended to be to them a scandal. They understood at last the purpose of the Child lying helpless in the manger at Bethlehem, dependent on the care of a mother and foster-father, flying in fear from his enemies ; of the Boy growing up among other boys, " in wisdom, and age, and grace before God and men," at Nazareth, and plying a carpenter's trade ; of the Man standing as a sinner among sinners at the Jordan, on that memorable day when they first met him, waiting his turn to be baptised by John.

They knew at last why, like other men, even more than other men, he underwent the fire of temptation ; why he hungered and thirsted, and endured fatigue of body, and was weary and slept. They knew why he showed so simply the affections of his sensitive nature, sympathy for suffering on one side, indignation with injustice on another, tenderness at one time with weak human nature, at another firmness stern and unflinching, love of friends and denunciation of enemies, childlike expression alike of joy and pain, of gratitude and of disappointment, overflowing thanks when men gave him cause for consolation, grief unto tears in face of loss. Even after he had died, and had risen again, they saw why and how he had been so eager that his own should recognise him once again for what he was, truly man, and not a disembodied spirit ; letting them embrace his feet (Matt. xxviii 9), speaking with a plaintive voice that could not be mistaken (John xx 16), eating before them (Luke xxiv 30), bidding them to handle him (Luke xxiv 29-43), coming down to any condition they might lay down in order that they might be convinced (John xx 27).

In another way, again, now that all was over, they saw the complete and perfect human nature of Jesus manifested. It was in his full submission to God the Father. The will of the Father—that was for him the beginning and the end. To carry out that will was his life's work (John v 19), to preach his commission was his allotted task (John viii 28) ; the mind of the Father was above all things else (Matt. xxiv 36), the wish of the Father was the final goal (Matt. xxiv 39). He would seek no glory but such as should redound to the glory of the Father (Mark v 19 ; John viii 49, xiv 13) ; upon the Father he would lean and depend for everything. With the Father he would constantly unite himself in prayer (Luke vi 12, ix 18, 28 ; etc. ; Matt. xiv 23), thanking him alike in joy and in sorrow (Luke x 21 ; John xi 1-46), when things were hard appealing to him (John xii 27), often for his miracles seeking his assistance (Mark vii 34 ; John xi 38, 41). In all the story of the end submission of the real human will of Jesus to the will of the Father in heaven is continually repeated, from the prayer against his own petition in the Garden (Matt. xvi 39), till on Calvary are heard first the cry of desolation (Matt. xxvii 46), then the last word of all, with which in fullest confidence he gives his soul into his Father's keeping (Luke xxiii 46).

Without any doubt, therefore, Jesus had impressed upon those who had lived most intimately with him the fact of his human limitations. So much was he a child to his mother that she could never speak to him nor treat him as other than her own son ; complaining to him when he did what she could not understand (Luke ii 48), putting the needs of others before him (John ii 3), seeking him out when trouble threatened him (Matt. xii 19), when he died claiming a mother's place by his suffering body (John xix 25). Neighbours had known him only as the carpenter of Nazareth, and the impression never left them. His fellow-villagers despised him because he was just that, and therefore could not be more (Luke iv 16-30). Publicans and sinners could presume so much upon their acquaintance with him as to invite him to sit with them at table (Matt. ix 9-17) ; women realised his needs and were glad to follow him and help him (Luke viii 1-3). Crowds could knock up against him in the streets (Mark v 31), could hold him hemmed in among them so that he must needs be rescued from them (Mark iii 21), when he said what seemed to them absurd could openly jeer before him (Matt. ix 24). Friends could blame him when he let himself be hustled to and fro, and say he was becoming mad (Mark iii 21) ; could warn him against impending danger which his seeming imprudence provoked (Matt. xv 12) ; could contradict him to his face (Matt. vi 22) ; even when he was transfigured before them could come to themselves and discover that, after all, he was "only Jesus" (Matt. xvii 8). They could wrangle in his company, forgetting that he was there (Mark ix 33) ; they could offer him wise counsel as to what he ought to do (John vii 3, 4) ; they could take it upon themselves to decide who should come near him and who should not (Matt. xix 13, xx 31) ; in his very presence they could complain of those who honoured him in ways which he accepted, but which did not suit their fancy (Matt. xxvi 8). If intimacy and familiarity may prove how completely Jesus was a man among men, then on every page of the Gospels we have the evidence in abundance.

2. *The sinlessness of Jesus* : (i) *The witness of friends*

To men living so intimately with him, especially to those with whom he dwelt habitually, at whose board he ate, by whose side he slept in their cottages upon the floors, whom he kept with him in all his journeys, it was inevitable that as man he should be well known. What, then, is the account they give of him ? We are often told that " No man is a hero to his valet," and by that we are given to understand that familiarity discovers weaknesses even in a hero. Yet what do we learn from the intimates of Jesus Christ ? From the day when the sinless John the Baptist acknowledges him to be far more sinless than himself (Matt. iii 17), and pointed him out to all as the spotless Lamb of God, who would take away the sin of the world (John i 36), there is never the slightest deviation. Simon, a year later, shows the impression that has deepened in him when he cries : " Depart from me, for I am a sinful man, O Lord " (Luke v 8) ; and on that occasion, as on so many others, he spoke for the handful of men who had reason to know him best. He chose them apart from all others, and they clung closely to him ; he gave them himself as an example, and as such they studied him in every detail ; he called them his brothers and sisters, and they were beside themselves with joy. They do his work for him ; they are tested concerning their fidelity ; others may abandon him, but again Simon sums up the impression of them all : " Lord, to whom shall we go ? Thou hast the words of eternal life " (John vi 69).

A little later, and it has grown deeper ; once more Simon speaks for his companions. " Thou art the Christ, the Son of the living God " (Matt. xvi 16). It is the height of their confession of faith, but it is founded on their knowledge of the perfection of the man of whom they spoke. And there were deeper things to follow ; from henceforth they studied him more closely as the model for their lives ; " Come to me," had now grown into " Learn of me," and they felt the justice of the claim. They saw his infinite for-givingness, and asked how many times they were to forgive (Matt. xviii 21). They watched him often in prayer, and asked him that they might be taught to do the same (Luke xi 1). He told them to forgive as they themselves would wish to be forgiven ; he taught them to pray every day that their sins might be condoned ; by word he taught them that which he could not teach them by example. The nearer he comes to the end the more are they compelled to remark on the two striking features of his life : on the one hand his bold condemnation of evil-doers, on the other his never-ceasing sympathy for the weak, and the sinful, and the down-trodden, and the contemned. They say very little ; after the confession of Peter at Cæsarea, less than others do the Apostles express their feelings and beliefs ; but the impression is unmistakable : their Master is the Master indeed, who had the word of God, was the beloved of God, and taught more by example than by precept, and who by his utter truth won all to himself. He was wholly true, he was wholly to be trusted, he was wholly worthy to be loved : " Lord, thou knowest that I love thee " (John xxi 16).

But if the Apostles said little there were others about them both more voluble and more demonstrative, and the evangelists quote their words and describe their actions with evident approval and delight. In every case it is the homage paid to the utter genuineness of their Master that delights them. The learned Pharisee Nicodemus knew to whom he was speaking when he said : " Rabbi, we know that thou art come a teacher from God " (John iii 2) ; no less did that poor woman of Samaria, a little later, a creature at the opposite extreme, who after one conversation could go away and say : " Is not this the Christ ? " (John iv 29). The Roman soldier in Capharnaum had learnt much of this Jew before he could submit to pray : " Lord, I am not worthy that thou shouldst enter under my roof " (Matt. viii 15) ; as well as the woman, the sinner in the city, before without any conditions she could lay at his feet the whole of her miserable burden (Luke vii 36-50). When the multitude cried out with enthusiasm, " He hath done all things well " (Mark vii 37), clearly they spoke of more than miracles ; it was more than miracles that made the common people of Jerusalem say to one another in the streets : " He is a good man " (John vii 12), and use this as an answer to his enemies, who tried to seduce them.

So we may go on ; as the clouds thicken the Light of the world seems only to become more manifest. The mother's heart that cried out in the crowd : " Blessed is the womb that bore thee " (Luke ix 27), proclaimed what a good mother's instinct is quick to discern ; so too was it with the ever-growing believers in Judæa, who in response to the abuse of his enemies fell back on the evidence of the Baptist, confirmed by what they themselves had seen : " John, indeed, did no sign, but all things whatsoever John said of this man were true " (John x 41, 42). The infants that ran to him and clung about him on the road up from Peræa, and the mothers that so easily committed them to his care (Matt. xix 10-15), the women who gladly entertained him in their homes (Luke x 38), the young men fired at the sight of him to be themselves great and true and noble (Matt. xix 16, xx 20), the publicans and sinners, men who had accepted their fate, but who needed from him no more than a look or a word to find their whole lives changed (Luke xix 1-10), all these and more, coming from so many varied angles, are witnesses more eloquent than any declarations of the crystal clearness of his life.

At the end of all, this is made only the more conspicuous. When remorse compels his betrayer to confess, in the sight of his destroyers : " I have sinned in betraying innocent blood " (Matt. xxvii 4), they cannot contradict him ; tacitly they confess that what he says is true. When the wife of Pilate warns the Roman governor : " Have thou nothing to do with this just man " (Matt. xxvii 19) ; when Pilate himself in feeble self-defence declares : " I am innocent of the blood of this just man " (Matt. xxvii 24) ; when on the cross the criminal hanging by his side defends him with the words : " This man hath done no evil " (Luke xxiii 41) ; when, after he is dead, the guard beneath the gibbet sums up all he has witnessed in the sentence : " Indeed this was a just man " (Luke xxiii 47) ; we know something of the minds of those about him at the moment when of all times in his life it was most essential that he should be thought guilty.

Hence it was that after he had left this earth, when Peter, for the first time, stood before the people of Jerusalem to give his witness, it was natural and easy for him to speak to them of Jesus as " the Holy One and the Just " (Acts iii 14) ; it was natural for him, before such an audience, to sum up his life in the single phrase : " Jesus of Nazareth : how God anointed him with the Holy Ghost and with power, who went about doing good " (Acts x 38). When later he wrote to his neophytes he could best so describe him : " Who did no sin, neither was guile found in his mouth. Who, when he was reviled, did not revile : when he suffered, he threatened not, but delivered himself to him that judged him unjustly. Who his own self bore our sins in his body upon the tree " (1 Pet. ii 22-24). And again : " Christ died once for our sins, the just for the unjust " (1 Pet. iii 18).

Precisely the same is the evidence of the other Apostles ; they dwell, not upon his wonder-working, not upon his preaching, but upon the surpassing, positive sinlessness of Jesus. Thus St John sums up his Master and his work : " You know that he appeared to take away our sins : and in him there is no sin. Whosoever abideth in him sinneth not ; and whosoever sinneth hath not seen him nor known him " (1 John iii 5). The same he puts elsewhere in another form : " My little children, these things I write to you that you may not sin. But if any man sin, we have an advocate with the Father, Jesus Christ the just " (1 John ii 1). So much does the disciple whom Jesus loved make of the spotless innocence of his Beloved. And akin to it is the single sentence of St James, the " Brother of the Lord " : " You have condemned and put to death the Just One : and he resisted you not " (James v 6).

### (ii) The witness of enemies

All this and more we have from those who were his friends, who were won by him, or at least were not disposed to stand against him. But there were other eyes than those turned upon him : eyes that looked, not merely for any flaw in word or deed, but for any pretext whatsoever, for any show of evidence, whether true or false, which might be turned to his destruction. We find them first in Judæa, their suspicions roused and their machinations working before he has yet begun to move (John iv 1). We find them next in Galilee, early in his public life, combining with Herodians whom otherwise they would have scorned to know (Mark iii 6) ; later, in Judæa, Pharisees and Sadducees join hands to catch him in any way they can. In the streets of Jerusalem, after their manner, in the hearing of the people, they boldly say : " Thou hast a devil " (John vii 20) ; " We know that this man is a sinner " (John ix 24) ; but when they are asked to specify their charge it is shamefully little that they can rake together. Three times at least Jesus challenged them to frame an accusation. " Why seek you to kill me ? " he asked them in the Temple court at the last Feast of Tabernacles (John vii 20) ; and a little later : " Which of you shall accuse me of sin ? " (John viii 46). Again in the same place at the Feast of Dedication, four months only before his death : " Many good works I have showed you from my Father. For which of those works do you stone me ? " (John x 32). In the Garden of Gethsemani, when at last they seized him, there is more than rebuke, there is overwhelming evidence in his favour which could not be denied in his simple words : " Are ye come out as it were against a thief with swords and clubs ? When I was daily with you in the temple, you did not stretch forth your hands against me " (Luke xxii 52, 53).

In spite of these searching eyes kept incessantly upon him from the beginning to the end of his career, and in spite of the challenge with which he confronted them, what did these experts in duplicity find ?

" What sign dost thou show, seeing thou dost these things ? " (John ii 18).

" Therefore did the Jews persecute Jesus because he did these things on the sabbath " (John v 16).

" Is not this the son of Joseph ? And his mother, do we not know her ? " (Luke iv 22).

" He blasphemeth. Who can forgive sins but God only ? " (Mark ii 7).

" Why doth your master eat with publicans and sinners ? " (Matt. ix 11).

" This man, if he were a prophet, would know surely who and what manner of woman this is that toucheth him, that she is a sinner " (Luke vii 39).

" This man casteth not out devils but by Beelzebub the prince of the devils " (Matt. xii 24).

" How came this man by all these things ? Is not this the carpenter, the son of Mary ? " (Mark vi 23).

" How can this man give us his flesh to eat ? " (John vi 53).

" Thou hast a devil " (John vii 20).

" We know this man whence he is : but when the Christ cometh, no man knoweth whence he is " (John vii 27).

" Doth the Christ come out of Galilee ? " (John vii 41).

" Search the Scriptures and see that out of Galilee a prophet riseth not " (John vii 52).

" Thou givest testimony of thyself ; thy testimony is not true " (John viii 13).

" Do not we say well that thou art a Samaritan, and hast a devil ? " (John viii 48).

" Now we know that thou hast a devil " (John viii 52).

" This man is not of God, who keepeth not the sabbath " (John ix 16).

" Give glory to God. We know that this man is a sinner " (John ix 24).

" We know that God spoke to Moses : but as to this man, we know not whence he is " (John ix 29).

" He hath a devil and is mad. Why hear you him ? " (John x 20).

" For a good work we stone thee not, but for blasphemy ; and because that thou, being a man, makest thyself God " (John x 33).

" What do we, for this man doth many miracles ? " (John xi 47).

" It is expedient for you that one man should die for the people, and that the whole nation perish not " (John xi 50).

" Do you see that we prevail nothing ? Behold the whole world is gone after him " (John xii 19).

The series wearies us. His enemies themselves were weary of this vain repetition of empty phrases. On the last day of his public teaching they were compelled to change their tactics.

" And they sent to him their disciples, with the Herodians, saying : Master, we know that thou art a true speaker, and teachest the way of God in truth. Neither carest thou for any man : for thou dost not regard the person of men " (Matt. xxii 16).

It is no wonder, then, that at the end, when at last they have him at their mercy, they must deliberately seek false witness, they must deliberately garble and twist his words, that they may have wherewith to accuse him even among themselves (Mark xiv 55) ; before others they must conclude with assumptions they could never attempt to prove : " If he were not a malefactor, we would not have delivered him up to thee " (John xviii 30) ; and after he was dead and buried, and as it seemed could no longer speak, they must still emit their slander : " That seducer " (Matt. xxvii 63).

This, then, was all. Never before or since has any man been subjected to so keen a scrutiny, never has hatred been so watchful, so determined to destroy ; and yet this was all. Any trifle would have sufficed, an imprudent word however true, a hasty deed however justified, a look, a gesture that could have indicated a hard or bitter mind ; yet not so much as a trifle could be found. Jesus Christ ! Weighed in the balance and found perfect, tried in the severest furnace and found to be purest gold !

## (iii) *His witness of himself*

But now, upon all this, we have a further evidence, which at once puts Jesus on another plane from that of other men. It is the witness he gives of himself. Whatever else he was, on the evidence alike of friends and enemies, he was true, he was sincere, he was transparently genuine : indeed, it was his utter genuineness that in the end was the final proof to his friends, to his enemies was their despair. As then with others who are true, when he speaks of himself he must be heard. And what does he say ? Other men and women have been holy ; a few by the grace of God have been preserved in simple innocence from childhood to old age, and on that account alone have been treasured as the jewels of our race ; but no man, save only Jesus Christ, has dared to claim holiness and innocence as belonging to himself from his very nature. No saint, however confirmed in grace, has ever ceased to own himself a sinner, or to be in constant fear of his own rejection. " I chastise my body," says St Paul, " and bring it into subjection, lest while preaching to others I myself may become a castaway " (1 Cor. ix 27). And more pertinently St John : " If we say that we have no sin, we deceive ourselves, and the truth is not in us " (1 John i 8).

Very differently, as we have seen, does the same saint speak of Jesus Christ. " If we confess our sins, he is faithful and just, to forgive us our sins, and to cleanse us from all iniquity " (1 John i 9) ; and when he so emphatically marks the contrast he does but repeat that which Jesus, again and again, implicitly at least declared of himself. He came to the Jordan and was baptised with sinners, but not until he who baptised him had expressly proclaimed him to be more sinless than himself (Matt. iii 14). He ate and drank with, and permitted himself to be called the friend of, publicans and sinners, but never did he allow, and never did they pretend, that he was one of them (Matt. ix 10). He taught men to pray that they might have their sins forgiven ; but it was always in the second person, never did he unite himself with them in that petition. For them he said : " Thus, therefore, shall you pray : . . . Forgive us our trespasses," and in that he included all men ; but for himself : " Father, the hour is come. . . . I have glorified thee on the earth. I have finished the work which thou gavest me to do. And now glorify thou me, O Father, with thyself " (John xvii 4, 5).

So in practice does he make a sharp distinction between himself and other men. But he does it also explicitly. In the Sermon on the Mount, in very marked words, he speaks to his hearers : " If you, being evil, know how to give good gifts to your children," carefully separating them from himself (Matt. vii 11). By the well of Samaria he says to his disciples : " My meat is to do the will of him that sent me " (John iv 34), a first lesson in their understanding of him. Before the Jews in the Temple he is most emphatic :

" He that speaketh of himself seeketh his own glory : but he that seeketh the glory of him that sent him, he is true and there is no injustice in him " (John vii 18).

" And he that sent me is with me : and he hath not left me alone. For I do always the things that please him " (John viii 29).

" Which of you shall convince me of sin ? If I say the truth to you, why do you not believe me ? " (John viii 46).

" If I glorify myself my glory is nothing. It is my Father that glorifieth me, of whom you say that he is your God. And you have not known him : but I know him. And if I say that I know him not, I shall be like to you, a liar. But I do know him and do keep his word " (John viii 54, 55).

" If I do not the works of my Father, believe me not. But if I do, though you will not believe me, believe the works : that you may know and believe that the Father is in me and I in the Father " (John x 37, 38).

Add to this his words in the Supper room.

" The prince of this world cometh : and in me he hath not anything " (John xiv 30).

So he speaks of himself, but his actions are yet more eloquent. In his attitude to evil of any kind he assumes a position which he only could assume who is conscious of being its absolute master. His very name has this significance ; it is given because " He will save his people from their sins " (Matt. i 21). He is first announced by the Baptist as " the Lamb of God, who taketh away the sin of the world " (John i 29), as just before he had been declared from heaven to be one in whom God " was well pleased " (Matt. iii 17). From the first he is the avowed enemy of sin, who will drive it always before him, will conquer its kingdom, will bid its master begone (Matt. iv 10) ; never for an instant will he be subject to it or fear it. In whatever form it appears he denounces and defies it (Mark iii 28) ; in his own name he lays down fresh standards concerning it : " I say to you " (Matt. v 18, etc.). On the other hand, when the guilty soul comes penitent before him, he forgives us by his own right (Matt. ix 2 ; Luke vii 48 ; John viii 11) ; nay more, he hands on to others the power to forgive sins in his own name. Devils declare his independence of them : " What have we to do with thee, thou Holy One of God ? " (Mark i 24) ; they cringe before him and appeal to him, as to one who is wholly their Lord (Mark v 10). John had described him as one whose wand would be in his hand, and who would sift the chaff from the grain (Matt. iii 12) ; he himself declares that he is the Judge of sinners (Matt. xxv 31), he will reward and he will punish (Matt. xxv 46).

As the end draws near the claim grows ever more prominent. His last days witness, as it were, a struggle in his soul between justice and mercy towards those who offended his Father, but for himself there is never a shadow of doubt or fear or apprehension.

In the Garden he takes upon himself the iniquity of us all ; for man he is " made sin," and as such he suffers. When at last he comes to die he does not, like other men, pray for forgiveness ; he prays only that others may be forgiven : " Father, forgive them, for they know not what they do " (Luke xxiii 34). In him there is no repentance ; for him that would be untrue ; instead, when another repents, even from the cross, he exercises his prerogative : " Amen, I say to thee, this day thou shalt be with me in paradise " (Luke xxiii 43). There is desolation, but there is no remorse in the cry : " My God, my God, why hast thou forsaken me ? " (Matt. xxvii 46). It is answered by the last word of all : " Father, into thy hands I commend my spirit " (Luke xxiii 46).

---

NOTE.—This is not the place in which to discuss at length the question of the sanctity of Christ. For clearly, when we speak of his sanctity, we speak of that which belongs to him as God as well as Man ; and here we are concerned with that which belongs to him as Man alone, as the Model of Manhood. We have seen that he did not sin ; we might go on to show—were we studying him in all his perfection we would go on to show—that he was incapable of sinning : " Holy, innocent, undefiled, separated from sinners " (Heb. vii 26). Nor would that be all. It would remain to be shown that in virtue of the union of the human soul of Jesus with the Word of God, sanctity, holiness came to him as of his very nature ; he was not only sanctified by grace, as other men are sanctified, he was sanctified as being the incarnate Son of God : " The holy one which shall be born of thee shall be called the Son of God " (Luke i 35).

One reminder, however, we must not omit. It has been shown in the Essay *Jesus Christ, God and Man* (pp. 390 ff) that Jesus, the source of all grace, is himself full of grace. " And we saw his glory, the glory as of the only-begotten of the Father, full of grace and truth . . . and of his fulness we have all received," says St John (i 14). We must therefore not think of the human perfections of Jesus otherwise than as the manifestation and fruit of the fulness of supernatural life that is in him. So St Luke tells us that " Jesus advanced in wisdom and age and grace with God and men " (ii 52).

## § IV: JESUS CHRIST PERFECT TOWARDS MEN

### 1. *An example : The Sermon on the Mount*

" AND it came to pass when Jesus had fully ended these words, the people were in admiration at his doctrine. For he was teaching them as one having power : and not as the scribes and Pharisees " (Matt. vii 28, 29).

There are points in the story of the Gospels when the figure in the centre seems to rise out from its surroundings, when the reader's vision expands, when in that vision that central figure seems to occupy at once, not only all that period of years during which it lived, but the whole of this world's history :

" Jesus Christ, yesterday, and to-day, and the same for ever " (Heb. xiii 8).

At one of these points, in a summary such as the present, we may do best to study him ; though in consequence many other details may be lost, though we may miss that variety, and universality, and all-embracing sympathy of soul which the whole story portrays, still by so doing we may hope to catch the more essential details, from which we may judge of the rest.

Such a point we have at the conclusion of the Sermon on the Mount. It is comparatively early in his public life. Hitherto he has confined himself, for the most part, in and about Capharnaum. By generosity overflowing he has won the hearts of the people ; by personal contact he has stirred the enthusiasm of his disciples ; now the moment has come for the more formal opening of the kingdom. For an hour or more that morning, on the mountainside that runs up behind the little town, Jesus has been speaking and the people have listened ; they have listened in silence, and the fascination of his words has carried them out of themselves. For an hour or more that single voice has been pouring itself out, and has lifted them above their sordid surroundings, into a world where sorrow has been turned into blessedness (Matt. v 3) ; has given them new joy and courage in the good tidings that after all they are of some account in the eyes of their Father (Matt. v 16) ; has freed them from the bondage of the Law, making it a glory to brave things yet harder than the Law had ever enjoined (Matt. v 21) ; has given them a new understanding of sin, till innocence, and truth, and simplicity, and forgiveness, and loving-kindness, and charity have shone out as the real honour of mankind (Matt. v 44) ; has given the noblest possible ideal for life and character, even the ideal of the Father God himself : " Be you therefore perfect, as your heavenly Father is perfect " (Matt. v 48) ; has taught them to pray, to speak to that Father, in terms that can never be forgotten (Mark vi 9) ; has cut through all hypocrisy and brought to perfect light the genuine truth of the soul (Matt. vi 16) ; has shown them where absolute confidence can reach, higher than the flight of the birds of the air, lower than the grass beneath their feet (Matt. vi 26) ; has defined and vindicated true justice, which is also mercy, and equality, and meekness (Matt. vii 1) ; and though what has been said has ended on a note of warning, still has it been with joy, and hope, and love unutterable in the air (Matt. vii 24).

He has said all this, and he has said it in their own language. Never once has he needed to go beyond their own vocabulary, the vocabulary of that Galilæan countryside, their own ideas, their own surroundings, to teach and to illustrate his teaching ; they have caught and understood every word. As on a former occasion, speaking to poor working men at their street corner, he had made use of their patched clothing, their bottles and their wine, to bring home to them the truth of the Kingdom (Matt. ix 16), so now he has caught hold of the things about him and them by which to teach them the word. He speaks of their everyday joys and sorrows, (Matt. v 3), the salt of their everyday meal (Matt. v 13); the village perched up there on the hill above them (Matt. v 14); the candle-stick in the window-sill (Matt. v 15); their daily conversation with its oaths and loose language (Matt. v 22); their daily bickerings before the local judge (Matt. v 25); their household quarrels (Matt. v 33); the local thief (Matt. vi 20); the local borrower of money (Matt v 42); the sun now beating down upon them (Matt. v 45); the rain which had but recently ceased for the season (*ibid.*); the pompous display of religion in the streets (Matt. vi 2); their daily toil and their daily wages (Matt. vi 19), carefully stored and hidden away in their money-bags at home, the rust and the moth which were a constant trouble (*ibid.*); the raven at that moment hovering above them (Luke xii 24); the flowers flourishing abundantly around them (Matt. vi 28); the green grass on the plain with all its rich promise (Matt. vi 30); their food, their drink, their clothing, their need of daily sustenance (Matt. vi 31); the ditch over there between the fields (Luke vi 39); their dogs (Matt. vii 6); their swine (*ibid.*); their fish and their eggs (Matt. vii 9); the stones on the hill-side with the danger of snakes and scorpions beneath them (*ibid.*); the gate in the wall hard by (Matt. vii 13); their sheep and the wolves they knew only too well (Matt. vii 14); their vines and their fig-trees (Matt. vii 16); their thorns and thistles (*ibid.*); their fruit trees good and bad (Matt. vii 19); their house of detention (Matt. vii 23); last, down there below on the lake-side, a cottage that has fallen to ruins in a storm, and another that stands secure (Matt. vii 24).

## 2. *The speaker and the people*

He has spoken to them in their own language. He has said what he has said in the language of their lives. He has seen them in their poverty. He has seen them broken and weighed down by cruelty and injustice and misunderstanding, and has blessed them for it all; he has blessed them for it and has poured soothing oil into their wounds (Matt. v 11). He has listened to them in their heated quarrels, a brother against a brother, and has given them the means of reconciliation (Matt. v 22). He has noticed their proneness to coarse vices and has forewarned them (Matt. v 28); he has heard their loose talk, their ribald oaths, their cursing that has led to other abuses, their rising hatred one of another with revenge to follow as an imagined duty, and has pulled them up with a word that has swept all rancour aside (Matt. v 37). He has watched them at their prayer, in their almsgiving, during the fasting season, and has warned them against mere outward show (Matt. vi 3). He has compassionated with them in their daily cares, their anxiety for their daily bread and their daily clothing, their eagerness to hoard their daily earnings, their eyes keenly watching the tradesman's scales in the bazaar, and has boldly and assuringly lifted them above it all (Matt. vi 33). He has weighed the love of father and son, of friend and neighbour, and has accurately gauged how far they can be tried (Matt. vii 11). He has gazed on the good workman and the negligent, and has judged the value of their work (Matt. vii 26). He has lived their lives, he is one of themselves, he knows them through and through, their good points and their bad points, and he loves them; in spite of all, he loves them and gives them all this.

And yet on the other side, while he remains but one among them, how much above not only them but all others does he claim to be ! With an assurance such as no man, no, not even any prophet before him had ever ventured to assume, he pronounces blessing upon them (Luke vi 22); with the might of a monarch he pronounces woe on others (Luke vi 24). He speaks as of his own authority : " I am come to fulfil " (Matt. v 17) ; " I say to you " (Matt. v 22) ; " I tell you " (Matt. v 20). Who is this who so speaks of himself ? He quotes Moses and the prophets, and sets up himself and his new doctrine as something that shall transcend them all (Matt. v 19). He gives them commands beyond those of the Law, boldly contradicting those of scribes and Pharisees (Matt. v 20), yet promises rewards of which neither Law nor Pharisees have ever dreamt : " Your reward shall be great " (Matt. v 12) ; " You shall be the children of the Father " (Matt. v 45) ; " Your heavenly Father shall repay you " (Matt. vi 4). He takes it upon himself to teach all men how to pray, how to commune with Almighty God, and God he boldly calls his own Father and theirs. He speaks of this Father as of one with whom he is personally familiar, tells them of his providence and care for them as of something with which he is intimate, of his mercy as of a characteristic trait, of his perfection as an ideal towards which they themselves, as being sons, might hope to aspire (Matt. v 48). He speaks of the Kingdom of heaven as if it were his own, promises it to whom he will (Matt. vii 20), strange things indeed he adds about the value of his word and the keeping of it, as if the very being of men and of the world depended on it (Matt. vii 23).

Still with it all there has been no arrogance, no sense of false assumption, not a single word that has not rung true ; assurance, yes, and certainty, and dignity, and grandeur of ideal, but no arrogance. Truth has sounded in every word he has said, human truth, the truth that lies at the root of all that is best in man, to which the heart of man instantly responds ; bravery in face of trial (Matt. v 11), moral courage to its last extreme (Matt. v 44), which has sent a thrill of honour and glory tingling through the veins of all who have heard him ; at the same time a lowliness, a submissiveness, a contentment, a joy in whatever might befall, which has made the most crushed life noble. And with it has gone a gentleness of touch upon the most sensitive of suffering, a compassion that has entered into, and condoned, and lifted up, and made bright again the most downcast and the most sinful ; an understanding of the love of friend and enemy, and the extremes to which it would venture ; a love of the Father, an unquestioning surrender to the Father, a familiar dealing with the Father, as became a well-loved son, a simple reliance on the Father, tender and human as that of any child, even while he sat there master of them all, strong as adamant.

Thus inevitably from the words he said did these people come to gaze at and think upon the man who said them. All gazed at him ; all alike were drawn to him ; none of any kind were omitted. The little children gazed open-mouthed, and under the spell forgot their mothers whose arms were around them (*cf.* Matt. xix 13) ; the mothers gazed and for the time forgot their children. Old age bent double leaning on its stick looked up at him where he sat upon his stone and was stirred to new life (*cf.* Luke xiii 11) ; youth with its dreams looked, and was fascinated, and longed to do great things (*cf.* Matt. x 17). Ignorance, stupidity, listened and rejoiced that it heard what it could understand (*cf.* Matt. xiii 11) ; learning, cleverness listened, and was weighed down with the burden of thought that it bore away (*cf.* Matt. xix 10). Men in high station came, with intent to test him, and stood before him paralysed, feeling the force of his every word (*cf.* Luke x 37) ; crawling men of low degree and stricken down sat on the edge of the crowd, and knew no less that the message was for them (*cf.* Luke xiv 25). Innocent, true souls were there, and came away rejoicing, spurred to yet more truth of life and sacrifice (*cf.* Matt. xx 21) ; guilty souls, shameless hearts, felt their guilt the more, yet through it all were able to brush away the tears of despair, and look up with hope such as they had never known before, and love revived within them, the love that came out from and went back to that Man (*cf.* Luke xv 1).

### 3. *The people and the speaker*

Who was he ? What was he ? What should they think of him ? How should they describe him to themselves ? What portrait of him should they bear away, stamped upon their hearts ? They gazed and gazed, speechless and entranced, longing to enter into his soul. They saw the fire of zeal flashing from his eyes, flying from his words like sparks from iron, yet never a shadow fell upon the patience, the patience without limit, revealed in his face. They bowed before the grandeur, the nobility, the fervour for the truth, and for all that was best in men, yet did they recognise the lenient condoning, the gentle indulgence and compassion where they failed. They felt the holiness, the earnestness, the seriousness of purpose that compelled to silence, yet with it all was there a brightness, a gaiety of heart, a cheerful vision, a pouring out of blessing and reward that made all life a sheer joy. They were awed by his extolling of prayer, and of self-surrender, as if nothing else were of moment, yet alongside was a knowledge of the active things of life which only experience could have taught. They were lifted up by the sight of a greatness of soul, and of outlook, and of ideal, and of endeavour that might have paralysed them, were it not for the deep lowliness and union with them every one, that made them feel he was their servant even while he was their Master ; and along with him all things were possible (Matt. xix 26), they could do all things in him that strengthened them (Phil. iv 13).

They looked at him and they saw much that lay beneath. There was determination that never looked aside, that never for a moment flinched or hesitated, never bent or swerved, pressing on to a goal straight before it ; yet was it ever gentle, ever considerate, ever forbearing, taking poor weakness by the hand, lifting up the fallen, carrying the cripple on its shoulder. There was energy, action, daring to rush forward that carried all before it, yet none the less never losing self-control, always composed, always at peace within itself, a sense of quiet reigning all around it. There was hatred of everything evil, indignation, wrath, condemnation, fire and death, death undying, meted out in fierce anger against it ; yet never did a sinner feel himself condemned or his hope extinguished, but only knew that forgiveness, and love, and warm pressure to a warm heart awaited him if he would have it. There was a keen sense of justice, justice idealised, justice defended, strict justice without favour, yet was the hand that dealt it out soft and tender and soothing. There was passionate love of truth, truth that feared nothing, truth open and outspoken, to saint and sinner, to selfish rich and to sensitive poor, to men in high places and to those downtrodden ; yet for them all an attraction they could none of them resist, a sincerity that forestalled opposition or resentment. He was tolerant and he was stern ; he bent to the weakest, yet he stood up like a tower ; he yielded, yet he held his own ; he was a mountain of strength, yet a mother could not be more gentle ; he was lost like a child in the arms of his Father, yet was he ever fully conscious and master of himself. All this was uttered in every word he spoke, was expressed in every look and gesture. Who was this man ? What was he ? They longed to know him more, and they did not know that the longing within them was the first-fruit of love.

For indeed throughout his address love and love only had spoken all the time. Nothing else could have given such insight into the souls of other men ; nothing else could have fostered so great a craving to bless, and to give, and to receive back, and to make secure.

There was love for the poor, for the meek and lowly, for the sorrow-ful ; love for the hungry of heart, for the merciful of heart, for the clean of heart ; love for the makers of peace, and for those who failed to make peace and therefore endured persecution ; love on the other side for the rich, and the happy, and the contented, warning them against false security ; love for them all, both the motley crowd before him, and the chosen Twelve who stood around the throne where he sat. Indeed, for these last he had special affection ; they were his own, the salt of the earth (Matt. v 12), the light of the world (Matt. v 13), the Apostles that were to be. For them in particular he had come ; he had chosen them, he was living for them, soon he would die for them, and for them would rise again from the dead. With them he would always abide, with them and with all who would have him, the Lover of each, longing for each, speaking to each the same winning words he had just spoken on that mountain-side, the bosom friend of every hungry soul and its complete satisfaction, if only it would come up the hill and look for him, and find him, and listen to him, and lose its heart to him, as he had already lost his own to it. In the light of all that came after, it is not too much to say that this was the Jesus Christ men saw as he spoke to them on the mountain-side.

"And it came to pass when Jesus had fully ended these words, the people were in admiration at his doctrine. For he was teaching them as one having power : and not as the scribes and Pharisees."

## § V : A SUMMARY CONCLUSION

### 1. *Equality with men, yet sinlessness and truth*

IN the last sections we have been content to look at Jesus Christ as he reveals himself in but one scene of his life. To complete the picture, and to prove its entire consistency, it would be necessary to go through all the Gospels, and to draw out each chapter in at least the same detail. But this would be a work of many volumes ; nay, as St John says, " the whole world would not be able to con-tain the books that should be written " (John xxi 25).

But, instead, can we bring together our impressions of this Model of Perfect Man, so as to distinguish him from other men ? Can we say what are his special, individual features ? We cannot ; intensely individual as he is, easily known and recognised, never-theless, as has been already said, the more we try to fix him down, to appoint limitations, to declare him to be this and not that, so much the more does he elude us. On the other hand, the more we appreciate and see, the more he grows upon us, till any description of him seems a mere shadow of the truth, wholly inadequate.

For how shall we define him ? We watch him from the beginning coming down from Nazareth to the Jordan, one among a multitude, differing from none ; or if there is a difference it has been only this, that he has been so like, not simply to all men in general, but to every man with whom he has come into contact. From that moment to the end on Calvary he has never lost this equality. His office of preacher has not destroyed it, his working of wonders has not set him on a pedestal apart ; whatever men, in moments of enthusiasm, have said of him, they have never been able to resist this intimate union and equality of Jesus Christ with every man he has met. They have been struck with awe, yet have they remained familiar ; they have proclaimed him a prophet, " the prophet," and have wished to make him their king, yet they have continued to press upon him in their streets ; they have called him the Son of God, and almost in the same breath, when he spoke, they have contradicted and corrected him (Mark viii 32).

Nevertheless, by a strange paradox, as the life expands it grows upon us that in one thing at least he has differed from others ; nay, in this one point he has claimed for himself an abiding difference. No matter how otherwise he has been weak and has been humbled in body and in soul like other men, no matter how much he has been tempted, yet never could friend or enemy, when it occurred to them to search, find in him anything that so much as partook of the nature of an evil deed. He has known sin and its dread significance as other men have not known it ; he has hated it as other men could never hate it ; he has set himself to destroy it, to " save his people from their sins " (Matt. i 21), as the first great mission of his life ; boldly he has invited every man to come to him, that he may remove their evil, and that they may then begin really to live (Matt. xi 28), and no man has accused him, on this account at least, of arrogance.

And this is his next characteristic. Really Man, equal with each and all ; sinless Man, the implacable enemy of sin as man's one and only evil ; out of these there rises up that utter truthfulness which is stamped on his whole nature, on his every word and deed. Men meet him, and read him through, and know at a glance that in him there is no guile. Women, even of that pitied class that is most bitter and disillusioned, come in contact with him and at once put themselves wholly in his hands. They hear him speak, and though he does not prove or argue, though he asserts on his own authority and no more, yet do they know that what he says is true. They watch him, in public and in private, working miracles and submitting to be fed, preaching to the ignorant poor and refuting learned Pharisees, and in everything, with everyone, the most convincing proof of all is his utter genuineness ; in nothing is there affectation, or mere show, or double-dealing, or self-seeking, or pose, or sham, or arrogance of any kind. He hates hypocrisy ; above all, when it struts and slithers in high places. From first to last, in every circumstance, he lives his life simple and true ; when later he claims to be " the Truth, the Way, and the Life," not only is no one found to contradict him, but all listen to him as if the claim he made were in harmony with what they had seen and experienced.

### § 2. *Universality : In understanding, sympathy, word, action*

Thus, by his meekness and equality with each and all, by his sinless sincerity, by his transparent truthfulness, does Jesus make his way into the hearts and affections of men. The sinless find in him quick recognition and response, sinners no less quickly find in him their cure. The truthful hear in their own hearts an immediate echo to every word he says, an immediate understanding of every deed he does ; the untruthful, by a kind of instinct, at once recognise in him a mortal and unyielding enemy. But to all alike, enemies or friends, there is always the same understanding displayed, the same open frankness and simplicity. Whatever his enemies may say or do to him, before his face or covertly behind his back, his consciousness of utter truth prevents him from re-taliating, from any counter-machinations, from any the least attempt to overreach them, or ever to treat them otherwise than as fellow-men. However his friends may fail or disappoint him, he endures. If one is weak and unfaithful, he will wait for him to rise : " Thou being again converted confirm thy brethren " (Luke xxii 32) ; if those he trusts are not to be relied upon, still will he find cause to thank them : " You are they who have stood with me in my temptations " (Luke xxii 28) ; if his enemies have their way and do him to death, still will he seek excuse for them : " Father, forgive them, they know not what they do " (Luke xxiii 34). No matter who they are, he understands them better than they under-stand themselves ; the timorous he could fill with courage : " Fear not, henceforth thou shalt catch men " (Luke v 10) ; the repentant he could fill with the joy of friendship : " Be of good heart, son ; thy sins are forgiven thee " (Matt. ix 2) ; even the unrepentant traitor he could still call " Friend ! " (Matt. xxvi 50).

Universal understanding such as this is the mother of universal sympathy. He seems unable to meet a crowd but he " has com-passion on them " (Matt. ix 36) ; whenever the people gather about him, in Galilee, in Decapolis, in Peræa, in Judæa, he must yield to them and give them all he can. And to the fascination of it they respond ; among high and low, good and bad, educated and ignorant, young and old, men and women, Jew and pagan, goodwill wherever it is found no sooner comes in touch with him than it knows that it is understood, is met more than halfway, and that on its side it knows him. We sometimes hear of men with what is called a genius for friendship ; we see others who look on the power of making friends as the highest ideal of a man. In Jesus such a genius was something immediate; by those who had eyes to see, either he was at first sight known and loved, or he was known and hated.

Nowhere is this universal understanding of and sympathy with men made more manifest than in his teaching. He condescends to the lowest level of life as it is lived about him; he rises to the highest subtleties of the most sophisticated Pharisee. For his illustrations he chooses the experiences of the humblest cottager (Luke xiv 8), or he follows the millionaire merchant abroad (Matt. xxv 14), and goes into the houses of kings (Luke xvii 20). When it so suits his purpose he uses language which the dullest yokel may understand (Luke xvi 19), or it will be that which shall confound the most enlightened doctor of the Law (Matt. xix 3); sometimes, with noble irony, he will speak so that while the ignorant can take his words, their meaning is hidden from the wise (Matt. xiii 24); he will rejoice with those who rejoice (Mark vi 31), with those who lament he will break down in sorrow (John xi 33). He will praise (Matt. viii 10), and he will blame (Mark viii 33); he will meekly submit (Luke iv 30), and he will be stirred with indignation (Matt. xii 31); he will appeal (Luke xiii 34), and will threaten (Matt. xxiii 13); he will bless (Matt. xxv 34) and he will curse (Matt. xxv 41); with an ease that can come from no training, his language will express every phase of thought, will respond to every humour, and that with such perfection that all literature finds no parallel. It is not only eloquence, it is utter truth that speaks, and in a manner utterly truthful, with the result that what men hear, unpretending, unaggressive, unpremeditated, spontaneous, is found to be the most perfect oratory, the most perfect use of human language that the world has ever known.

As it is with his words so is it with his actions; in like manner does he adapt himself to all men without distinction. Universal as he is in understanding, universal in sympathy, it is inevitable that in his outpouring of himself he should be no less universal. His miracles are worked for all alike, for strangers as well as for friends, good men and evil, rich as well as poor, deserving and those who had no claim; though he declares himself to be sent " for the lost sheep of the house of Israel " (Matt. xv 24), and though his disciples believe that this is his only mission (Matt. xv 23), yet when poor pagans appeal to him he must make exceptions, in Galilee (Matt. viii 13), in the country round Tyre (Matt. xv 28), among the mountains of Decapolis (Matt. xv 29). He gives himself to all who seek him (Matt. xv 32); he dines with any who invite him: now a group of publicans in Capharnaum (Matt. ix 10), now a more fastidious company in Magdala (Luke vii 36), now simple women in Bethania (Luke x 38), now cautious Pharisees in Judæa (Luke xi 37). He is as much occupied with one as with a crowd, whether that one be a ruler in Israel (John iii 1), or a derelict woman in Samaria (John iv 7), or a loathsome beggar in Jerusalem (John v 6).

At a moment's notice he is ready to receive a willing candidate (Matt. xix 16), or, if need be, he will wait for months and even years (Matt. xxvi 50). Time seems to matter little to him, distance is not considered (Matt. iv 23); circumstances that might well make others pause with him are ignored. Men may laugh him to scorn, but he goes on doing good (Matt. ix 24); they may refuse him admission to their village, and he meekly proceeds to another (Luke ix 53). He will live in the midst of struggle (Matt. xxiii 53), as well as in the house of peace (Luke x 38); he is as much at home on the steps of the Temple as with simple people in Bethania. Though he never ceases to be " Master and Lord," yet is he always among men as " he that serveth " (John xiii 13); so much so that by a chance word we hear that he " has not where to lay his head " (Matt. viii 20).

### 3. *Strength and independence*

On the other hand, this universal understanding, this universal sympathy and familiarity with men, never degenerates to weakness. His utter sincerity, when it speaks, makes men " astonished at his doctrine, for his speech was with power " (Mark i 27); his strength in action makes them ask one another : " What thing is this ? What is this new doctrine ? What word is this ? For with authority he commandeth even the unclean spirits, and they obey him and go out " (Luke xxi 36). Though at one time the multitudes " pressed upon him " (Luke v 1), " so that he could not go openly into the city " (Mark i 45), yet at another he would so overwhelm them that they " were astonished, and were filled with fear, and wondered, and glorified God, that gave such power to men, saying : We have seen wonderful things to-day ; we never saw the like " (Mark ii 12 ; Luke v 26). Though to his own he is lavish in kindliness and service and consideration, though he will seek any excuse to condone their shortcomings, yet when there is need he will rebuke them with a sternness which they can never forget, when they would contradict his prophecies of failure (Mark viii 33), when they were jealous (Luke ix 46), when they would lose patience with those who opposed them (Mark ix 38) ; when they showed ambition (Matt. xx 20) ; when they were unforgiving (Matt. xviii 21) ; when they made little of the devotedness of children (Matt. xix 14).

Thus do his utter truthfulness and simplicity enable him to ride far above every inducement to weak indulgence ; they make him immune from any danger of yielding to false glamour and hollow devotion. They may call him " a great prophet," and he just passes up the village out of sight in the evening twilight (Luke vii 16) ; they may hail him " the prophet that is to come into the world," and wish to make him king, but he slips away from them all into the mountain for his evening prayer (Matt. xiv 23). His disciples may say : " Indeed thou art the Son of God," but he knows exactly the value of their words, and when at last they have grasped their full meaning. When men cry before him : " Hosanna to the Son of David," he is not deceived ; in the midst of their hosannas he sits still, and weeps over the doom that is coming (Luke xix 41).

No less does this utter truth and sincerity make him independent of those who would thwart him. He watches them gathering in numbers about him, and he does not change (Matt. xxi 23) ; he reads the questionings within their hearts, which they have not the courage to speak openly, and he answers them (Matt. ix 4) ; what they would conceal among themselves he brings into the light of day (Luke xii 2). They criticise his deeds or the deeds of his followers and he corrects them (Matt. ix 14) ; to catch him in his speech they ask him subtle questions, and he gives them their reply (Mark xii 13). While he does not conceal his contempt for their meanness and their falsehood (Matt. xv 7), while he warns others against the evil of their ways and example (Mark iv 24), none the less does he deal out to them unlimited patience and forbearance ; let one of them speak the truth from his heart and at once he is approved and encouraged (Mark xii 32). In all the pictures of the character of Jesus there is no feature more astonishing than this constant, unflinching endurance of his enemies, his constant entrusting of himself into their hands, even after he has been compelled to confute them (Luke xi 17), publicly to denounce them (Matt. xv 12), to put them to shame before their own disciples (Mark xii 15), to defy them in their own courts (John vii 28), to call them to their faces " hypocrites " (Matt. xxii 18), to warn the people against their example (Matt. xxiii 2), and his own against their falsehood and deceit (Matt. xvi 6). In spite of all this, he would continue to go to them ; to none does he make more fervent appeal ; the last days of his life are devoted wholly to them. And they in their turn would continue to come to him ; the fascination drew them, they would invite him to sit with them at table (Luke xi 37) ; at times one or another among them would break out and acknowledge that indeed he was the speaker of truth (Mark xii 32).

## 4. Prayerfulness and other virtues

But to those who lived close beside him it was not difficult to discover the secret of this independence. He was with men and among them, but in a true sense he was not of them ; while he lived their life to the full, and "bore their sorrows and carried their griefs " more than they carried them themselves, nevertheless, within him and all about him, for those to see who were familiar with him, there was another life and another atmosphere far more real and far more intense than anything this earth had to give him. It was his life of prayer, and with it as a consequence his constant preference for solitude. His friends soon learnt to respect his hours of prayer in the morning and evening (Mark i 35); when they awoke at dawn and he was not among them they knew where they would find him (Mark i 36). After sunset he had regular places for his prayer (Luke xxii 39); when he went apart to spend a night in prayer (Luke vi 12), they would understand and let him go; if he would take them they would readily go with him (Luke ix 28). Often whole days would pass by, and days would grow into weeks, and he would do apparently nothing. Crowds would gather round him and he would retire from them to pray, up the mountain-side (Luke vi 12), or into desert places (Luke v 16); they would become enthusiastic and wish to make him king, and he would fly " into the mountain alone, to pray " (Matt. xiv 23). Or they would desert him and he would not seem to mind; in the morning his friends would find him lost in prayer (Luke xi 1). During all his long tour, extending to months, outside the borders of Palestine there is no record of a single sermon preached or public demonstration made; his time would seem to have been spent in continual prayer. He is at prayer among the hills of Decapolis when the people find him out (Matt. xv 29); it is after prayer, a few days later, that he asks Simon the momentous question: " Whom do you say that I am ? " (Luke ix 18).

Such was the fact, which those who lived with him soon understood, and accepted, and in their feeble way aspired to imitate (Luke xi 1), and which this Man of utter simplicity and truth never made an effort to conceal. The atmosphere of prayer, the retirement apart from men, the personal dealing with the Father at all times, these were the features that most struck those who were most with him. God the Father the beginning and the end, and therefore all that came between; the will of the Father, and that alone, giving everything else its significance, every success, every failure, everything we do and are; this was his only perspective, and its constant repetition, not so much as a doctrine to be taught but as a truth to be assumed, runs through his life from first to last. " I must be about my Father's business " (Luke ii 49). " My meat is to do the will of him that sent me " (John iv 34). " As the Father hath given me commandment, so do I " (John xiv 31). " Heavenly Father, I give thee thanks " (John xi 41). " Father, save me from this hour " (John xii 27). " Father, not my will but thine be done " (Luke xxii 42). " I have glorified thee on the earth, I have finished the work thou gavest me to do " (John xvii 4). " Father, into thy hands I commend my spirit " (Luke xxiii 46). " As the Father hath sent me I also send you " (John xx 21). The life of the soul expressed in these and many more successive cries is unmistakable.

We must come to an end. Hitherto we have marked certain outlines which may help to distinguish the character of Jesus as it revealed itself among men; when we endeavour to descend more to details, when we ask ourselves what were his particular virtues, we are unable to proceed. He had no one virtue in particular, because he had them all; and he had them in so perfect a balance, so part of his very human nature, that they passed by unnoticed among men. And this we say, not because, knowing who he was, the Son of God made man, we believe that it must have been so, but because it is written in the actual portrait of the Man as the evangelists have drawn it out for us. We mark the virtues of other men, and we see them to be reflections of the same in him; we go to the theologians, and we find that what they teach of the virtues finds its best illustrations in his life. Whenever he himself speaks of virtue we know, and the men who listened to him knew, that the model of it all was to be found in him. Thus he enumerates the Beatitudes, and as he does so he draws a picture of himself; in the rest of the Sermon on the Mount he speaks of forgiveness and innocence, of simplicity in speech, of generosity, of forbearance, of hidden well-doing, of prayer, of trust in God, of contempt of earthly things, of mercy in judgement, of fidelity; and all who hear him see him to be a model of all that he demands. He declares himself to be the exemplar for all men, not in this virtue or that, but in that which is fundamental to all virtues: " Learn of me, because I am meek and humble of heart " (Matt. xi 29), and not a voice is raised in protest; the whole tenor of his life is proof enough that what he says is true.

## 5. Love

But at the last, for to us it is evident even more than it might perhaps have been to those who thronged close about him, the virtue which in him was the source of and the key to all the rest was his unbounded love. Love was at the root of his universal understanding and his universal sympathy; love made him pour himself out on all the world; what attracted men to him, what made " all the world go after him," and that though they did not know it, was the fascination of his love. Love as he taught it was a new thing in the world; love as he practised it has made the world another place, with him and his interpretation of it it became indeed " a new commandment," however ancient might be the words in which it was set. When later the Apostles looked back, and pieced the whole picture together, it was this tremendous love of Jesus that grew upon them, swallowing up all the rest: " Having loved his own who were in the world, he loved them unto the end " (John xiii 1). The memory of this was their abiding consolation and encouragement for all time, both to him that could call himself " the disciple whom Jesus loved," and to him who could remember that he had one day made a last profession of love for his Master and it had been accepted (John xxi 15).

To illustrate this, even inadequately, it would be necessary to pass again through the whole life of Jesus upon earth; for love reveals itself on every page, consistently the same however different in its manifestation. But on this very account there is no need to say more ; if ever in the world love has been associated with the name of any man upon this earth it is with the name of Jesus Christ. When St Paul endeavoured to express him to himself he could only sum him up by speaking of his love (Rom. viii 35-39) ; when since his time fathers and doctors and theologians and saints have tried to do likewise, they have one and all ended on the same theme. Or conversely, when St Paul speaks of love in detail and would endeavour to describe to the people of Corinth this new power that has come into the world, he can only keep the Model before his eyes ; when he has ended, what has he done but portray one aspect of him ?

> " Jesus is patient
> Is kind
> Jesus envieth not
> Dealeth not perversely
> Is not puffed up
> Is not ambitious
> Seeketh not his own
> Is not provoked to anger
> Thinketh no evil
> Rejoiceth not in iniquity
> But rejoiceth with the truth
> Beareth all things
> Believeth all things
> Hopeth all things
> Endureth all things "

(*Cf.* 1 Cor. xiii 4-7).

True, the description is inadequate ; the picture given is rather negative than positive ; but as with God we can more easily say what he is not than what he is, so is it in our effort to describe even the human love of Jesus Christ. St Peter, it would seem, can do no better, for he says :

> " Christ also suffered for us
> Leaving you an example
> That you should follow his steps
> Who did no sin
> Neither was guile found in his mouth
> Who when he was reviled
> Did not revile
> When he suffered
> He threatened not
> But delivered himself
> To him that judged him unjustly "

(1 Pet. ii 21-23).

If St Paul and St Peter can scarcely speak of Jesus and his love in anything but negatives ; if the former by the simple thought,

> " The Son of God loved me
> And gave himself for me "

(Gal. ii 20),

is struck dumb, how can anyone else in this world hope to describe him or it ?   It is enough to use the words of Jesus himself.

" Greater love than this no man hath, that a man lay down his life for his friends " (John xv 13),

and to realise how completely he has fulfilled this in himself, not on Calvary alone, but in every moment of his days on earth, and even to this day in heaven :

" Always living
To make intercession for us "

(Heb. vii 25),

" With us all days
Even to the consummation of the world "

(Matt. xxviii 20).

✠ALBAN GOODIER.

# XIII

## JESUS CHRIST, MAN OF SORROWS

### §I: INTRODUCTION

1. *Man and Sorrow*

IN the previous essay it has been seen how Jesus Christ has shown himself to men as the Model of Manhood. Nevertheless in that study, except as it were in parentheses, one aspect of that Model has been passed over ; and that in a true sense the most important aspect. For we cannot think of man in this world without thinking of him in contact with suffering ; living in the midst of it, enduring it within himself, when need be going forth to face it, taking it not only as the lot of man, but as one of man's distinguishing features ; seeing in it something which in a peculiar way belongs to him apart from all other creatures of this earth, something which he knows to be in the end his glory and his crown.

To enter into a discussion concerning the presence of suffering and sorrow in the life of man would serve no useful purpose here. In the ancient world it was for ever in the minds of men, to pagans a doom, to the Israelites an atonement ; though to both there was everlasting hope in the fact that sorrow was, as experience proved, always the close companion of greatness, and strength, and nobility, and virtue. This was the constant theme of ancient tragedy. In the Old Testament it grows as time advances, from the questionings of Job to the definite solutions of the Son of Sirach ; suffering an evil, suffering an evil out of which comes good, suffering justified because of its fruits and because of those whose lot it is to bear it.

For us let it be enough to take the facts of life as we find them ; and these, or some of these, are not only that suffering and sorrow have always been and always are with us ; not only that human nature itself recognises them as in some way a gift, an atonement for evil done, a means of rising from our dead selves to higher things ; but, on the other side, that suffering and sorrow bring out from man that which is best in him, which could be brought out in no other way ; develops him to his highest point of perfection, as by no other means he could be developed. In the end, as everyday experience proves to us, it is by the standard of suffering, by the power to endure, to stand up to misfortune, when duty or love calls to be ready to meet it, that man is most inclined to judge and reward his fellow-man.

That which man suffers, silently, willingly, generously, is that which, when discovered, wins the regard, the esteem, the love of others ; indeed, what else do we mean by the phrase, " to be a man," than to be ready to face suffering when it comes ? Readiness to suffer beats down all opposition ; its acceptance is taken to condone much that might otherwise be amiss. When we have nothing else to say of any man, let us but show that he has suffered much, and willingly, and for a cause that has been worthy of his manhood, and at once other things are passed over. It may indeed be a hard saying ; in daily life we may shun it, and seek every means to avoid it ; that is only to acknowledge that suffering is suffering, it does not deny that the bravery to face it is a gift than which man, as man, holds none greater. When we dream our dreams of youth we may put before it many other ideals ; but we know very well, and youth itself knows well, that there is no ideal to compare with the power to suffer, no matter under what form suffering may appear. To be able to suffer is to be a man ; to accept it when it comes is to be noble ; voluntarily to choose it for a worthy cause is to be a hero ; heroism has no other definition.

## 2. Jesus Christ and Sorrow

All this, it is obvious, must come within the scope of an ideal of manhood ; indeed, it must be its whole background, giving a meaning to whatever else is said. If, then, we see in Jesus Christ the Model of Manhood, this, too, will be conspicuous in him, and that in its highest form ; the Model of Man will in some way be the Model Man of Sorrows. And it is so. We speak not only of the Passion, though that alone, its cause, its course, and its issue, voluntarily undergone, for no other reason but that other men might be the gainers, their burden shouldered that they might be set free, would of itself suffice to win for him, *par excellence*, the title of the Ideal Man of Sorrows. But we speak also of his whole career ; of all that life which, from the day when he came among men to the end, was one of self-annihilation and subjection,[1] of injustice and mental agony, of contempt and failure and lonely struggle against ingratitude and hatred, of interior trial whose mere shadow, flitting from time to time across the surface, gives us no more than an idea of that which was endured within.

We speak, moreover, of one who alone of all men had no occasion to suffer ; who, from the very nature of his being, knew what suffering and sorrow were more than any other man could know them ; who from the very first foresaw all that was to come to him, and yet at every step deliberately chose it for himself ; who at any given moment might have said, with more than justice on his side, that what he had thus far endured was enough and the rest would have

[1] Phil. ii 6.

been spared him ; who, nevertheless, in ways we can see for ourselves and in ways we cannot hope to discover, took into his soul
every barb of sorrow that was hurled at him, every grief that it falls
to the lot of man to bear.

We say we cannot hope to discover the full extent of the sufferings
and sorrows of Jesus Christ. For we are dealing with one who was
not only man but was also God ; what was the consequence of that
union on his capacity for suffering, who shall attempt to describe ?
True, as God he could not suffer ; but as man, as God-man, set to
bear the sorrows of men and to carry their griefs, he must have been,
and on the evidence of Scripture was, a subject for suffering beyond
all means of ours to measure. The knowledge and foreknowledge
it implied ; the knowledge of evil, natural and supernatural, in itself
and in its consequences, in regard to God and in regard to the evil-
doer, man ; the foreknowledge of all that was to come, making all
suffering, his own and that of others, always vividly before his eyes ;
the ever-present realisation of the Father, what we dimly guess at
when we speak of the Beatific Vision, and yet in some mysterious
way the brighter light causing the blacker darkness, till his soul was
" sorrowful unto death " ; the fine-wrought nature, of body, and
mind, and soul, belonging of necessity to him who was God-man
—all these considerations, and there are many more, can be but
touched upon, yet do they open out vistas of suffering which must
make, whatever any man may say, a mere shadow of the truth and
no more. From time to time a saint has been given the grace to
see and realise, and the sight has drawn the blood from his own
body, and opened wounds in his hands, and feet, and side ; the
rest of us can but look on, content with the little we may learn,
knowing very well that the whole of the truth is as the ocean to the
running brook.

Still, leaving all this aside, we have more than enough for our
purpose. Confining ourselves to just that which human eyes can
see and no more, to just that which Jesus Christ endured on the
plane of other men, we shall still find in him the Ideal Man of
Sorrows ; ideal in that which he endured, insomuch as none endured
more ; ideal in the way he endured it, so that not one drop of the
chalice was permitted to escape him ; ideal in the motive which
prompted him ; ideal in the full deliberation with which he bore
it all to the end ; ideal, last of all, in the fruit his suffering has borne,
both in the merit of his sacrifice and in the example he has given
to mankind. The merit of his sacrifice we may leave to another
essay in this volume ; [1] we may rather dwell on the Man of Sorrows
as such, and what his life of sorrow has meant here and now. That
because of the sufferings of Jesus Christ this world has become
another place no one who has eyes to see, certainly no Christian,

---

[1] See Essay xiv.

will deny ; Christianity itself, with its standard of the cross, and its civilisation ranged around the cross, is the abiding confession of this truth.   However much in real life human frailty may induce us to pass him by, still in matter of fact the Christ in whom we believe is Christ crucified ; and crucified, not on Calvary alone, but from the first hour of his life in Bethlehem.   This is the Jesus Christ who has won the hearts of men in all ages, who has stirred them to great things, who has poured himself out over all the world and wherever he has reached has transformed it.

## § II : THE MAN OF SORROWS IN HIS LIFE

### 1. *Beginnings*

" He was in the world, and the world was made by him, and the world knew him not.   He came unto his own, and his own received him not " (John i 10, 11).

ON many accounts these two sentences may be taken as the text of the Gospel of St John.   After many years of reflection, after a generation and more of the new Church's life, this is the summary impression left upon him of his Master's sojourn in the world, this is the side of it which he deems most worthy of remembrance by the children who are to come after him.   Again and again during the course of his Gospel he comes back upon the same thought, now in his own words and comments, now in the words of our Lord Jesus Christ himself.   Underneath all else that happened, underneath whatever other sufferings there might have been, this unending agony was always gnawing at his heart, that he came among men, and men from first to last refused to know him, that he gave himself without reserve to those nearest to him, and they would have nothing to do with him or with what he had to give them.

St Luke, though he begins his Gospel with quite another object in view, soon is compelled to reveal the same colours in his picture. At first he is filled with all the glory of the Incarnation ; nevertheless, even as he tells the story of it, he cannot conceal the tremor of her who " was troubled " at the angel's salutation, who " pondered " what it might portend, who in the end accepted with submission her anxious destiny, surmising well enough much that it would imply :

" Behold the handmaid of the Lord, be it done to me according to thy word." [1]

Nor can he hide the background of privation, and suffering, and distress in the scene of the Child's first coming into the world :

" And she brought forth her firstborn son, and wrapped him up in swaddling clothes, and laid him in a manger : because there was no room for them in the inn." [2]

[1] Luke i 38.          [2] Luke ii 7.

At the outset, in the midst of all the joy of the story, St Luke has to own it : Jesus Christ, the Son of God, of whose kingdom there was to be no end, was born on the roadside, a homeless outcast, the shivering child of a tramp or little more.

There follows the Circumcision, the first blood-shedding of the Child, the price of the name he was to bear, the foreshadowing of the further price that must one day be paid that the promise contained in that name might be completely fulfilled. Immediately after is recorded the prophecy which at once puts the Gospel of St Luke on the same plane with that of St John. It would almost seem that in spite of himself Luke is forced to set the future suffering and rejection of Jesus in the forefront of his picture :

" And Simeon blessed them and said to Mary his mother : Behold this child is set for the fall and for the resurrection of many in Israel, and for a sign which shall be contradicted. And thy own soul a sword shall pierce, that out of many hearts thoughts may be revealed." [1]

In perfect harmony with these is the Gospel of St Matthew. No sooner has the Evangelist introduced his subject, recording the genealogy,[2] and the anxious doubting of the foster-father,[3] than he passes at once to the first scene of terror and ill-foreboding —the coming of the Magi, the proved understanding of the priests and their first rejection of the light, the craftiness and enmity of Herod, the massacre of the innocents, the lonely, homeless wandering of the Holy Family in Egypt.[4]

Thus did Jesus Christ come into the world, each step marked with suffering and sorrow, and it would seem with needless sorrow, that might easily have been avoided, ending in a cruel orgy of blood. When it is all pieced together, one asks oneself whether any other child has been born into the world under circumstances quite so tragic. With blood so smeared across the first page of his history, and that the blood of helpless infants, with first impressions those of an exile hiding from the hand of death, it was inevitable that in after years he should have blood and death constantly before his eyes. When he grew up, and among the hills of Nazareth reflected on the cruel fact that his birth had occasioned the murder of so many children and the misery of so many mothers, we can understand in part the natural source of that deep sympathy for children and mothers which marked him till his own death upon the cross. The prophecy of Jeremias, fulfilled thus early in his childhood, could never cease ringing in his ears :

" A voice in Rama was heard, lamentation and great mourning ; Rachel bewailing her children and would not be comforted, because they are not." [5]

---

[1] Luke ii 34, 35.  [2] Matt. i 1-17.  [3] Matt. i 18-25.
[4] Matt. ii 1-18.  [5] Matt. ii 18.

## 2. *Nazareth*

For one in sympathy with the hidden life at Nazareth it is not difficult to understand the agony of the long waiting. Thirty years of any life is a long time ; by the end of it the glamour and hope of youth has in great part disappeared. But in a country village such as Nazareth, under such drab conditions as those which he encountered, the glamour is stillborn, and the years drag on into featureless maturity. The monotony of that life ; the companionship of men who saw and could see nothing, whose horizon was confined to the rough village street that crawled up that hillside, who understood and were fixed to understand less than nothing, whose narrow prejudice could never tolerate that any man from among themselves should rise above their own level ; the coarse familiarities, the boorish manner, the galling condescensions, the patronising, the rough language of men blinded with their own conceit ; the work among men with whom gratitude was evidently a thing unknown, who could take as of course and without remark, as though it were their right, the service of one who gave lavishly ; who could find a cause of complaint in the fact that he gave with the same lavish hand to others than themselves—this was but the everyday atmosphere in which he lived, and which for twenty long years never varied.

And on his own side, as his later history revealed, the quick, sensitive, responsive nature, alive to every touch of joy or pain ; the insight, deeper than that of any man, into the souls of other men, so that nothing lay hidden from him, no falsehood, no scheming, no treachery, no sin ; the sympathy with another's sorrow that came of self-forgetfulness, and overflowed on every soul about it ; the service freely rendered, the spontaneous generosity ; the keen longing to do good and the agony because he was not allowed to do it—all these must be brought into the picture if we would estimate aright the human endurance of the thirty years.

This is no mere conjecture, it is no abstract consideration of what must or might have been ; it is more than confirmed by the events that followed. Nazareth, in the esteem even of other Galilæans, was nowhere ; and a man from Nazareth was nobody. Not only have we no mention whatever of Nazareth, either in Old Testament history or in any contemporary document ; not only have we proof of the profound contempt for the Nazarene among his neighbours—

" Can anything of good come out of Nazareth ? " [1]

—the Nazarenes themselves made it clear enough what manner of men they were, what esteem they had of one another. When at the beginning of his public life Jesus came back among them bringing the good tidings :

[1] John i 46.

" They rose up and thrust him out of the city : and they brought him to the brow of the hill whereon their city was built, that they might cast him down headlong. But he, passing through the midst of them, went his way." [1]

Again another time he came to them, after they had had more opportunity to learn. His miracles they could not deny ; his teaching they tacitly acknowledged ; this only they could not endure, that he should be only a Nazarene, no more than one of themselves.

" How came this man by all these things ? And what wisdom is this that is given to him, and such mighty works as are wrought by his hands ? Is not this the carpenter, the son of Mary, the brother of James and Joseph, and Jude, and Simon ? Are not also his sisters here with us ? And they were scandalised in regard of him." [2]

Another sign we have yet later. His very kindred were, many of them, no more appreciative than the rest. To them, after all his labours, he was little more than a prodigy, a nine days' wonder, a conjuror who might take a turn at a village fair or city festival. When towards the end of his life he delayed his journey to Jerusalem :

" His brethren said to him : Pass from hence and go into Judæa, that thy disciples also may see the works which thou dost. For there is no man doth anything in secret ; and he himself seeketh to be known openly. If thou do these things, manifest thyself to the world. For neither did his brethren believe in him." [3]

These, then, were the kind of people with whom he had lived from childhood, who were called his kindred ; and this was all the impression he had made upon them, even he, Jesus Christ !

" And he wondered at their unbelief." [4]

" No prophet is accepted in his own country."

" The enemies of a man are those of his own household."

" Blessed is he that shall not be scandalised in me." [5]

When Jesus spoke thus, he spoke from grating experience. Though he was the Son of God, though he was the son of Mary, though he was of the house of David, he had little to boast of in most of his kindred and connections.

### 3. Capharnaum

Jesus left Nazareth. He came to Capharnaum by the Lake of Galilee, and there took up his abode, so that later it could be called " his own city." Here for a few brief months we are given the impression that he had some superficial success and consolation. He called followers to him, and they responded. He worked miracles in abundance among the people, and they were carried away with enthusiasm ; indeed, it would seem that their devotedness, so thoughtless, so hollow, so self-centred, so boisterous, so

---

[1] Luke iv 29, 30.    [2] Mark vi 2, 3.    [3] John vii 3-5.
[4] Mark vi 6.    [5] Luke vii 23.

little considerate of him and of his common needs, soon became a burden to him, and he had to escape it—

" So that they could not so much as eat bread." [1]

" So that he could not go openly into the city, but was without in desert places." [2]

" And he retired into the desert and prayed." [3]

Nevertheless the little consolation he might have had from this oppressive but well-meaning crowd was soon taken from him. Scarcely has the period of miracles and teaching begun than we hear of :

" Pharisees and doctors of the law sitting by, that were come out of every town of Galilee, and Judæa, and Jerusalem " ; [4]

men prepared to misinterpret and take scandal from every word he said :

" Who is this that speaketh blasphemies ? " [5]

to carp at everything he did :

" But the Pharisees and scribes murmured, saying to his disciples : Why do you eat and drink with publicans and sinners ? " [6]

" Why do the disciples of John fast often, and make prayers, and the disciples of the Pharisees in like manner, but thine eat and drink ? " [7]

" Behold thy disciples do that which it is not lawful to do on the sabbath days." [8]

" And the scribes and Pharisees watched if he would heal on the sabbath day ; that they might find an accusation against him " ; [9]

men ready to ascribe any motive to him, rather than own the patent truth :

" He hath Beelzebub, and by the prince of devils he casteth out devils." [10]

" Behold a man that is a glutton and a wine drinker, a friend of publicans and sinners " ; [11]

men, last of all, who, when nothing else would serve, must seek any means to be rid of him :

" And they were filled with madness " ; [12] " and the Pharisees going out immediately made a consultation with the Herodians against him, how they might destroy him." [13]

Such are passages to be found in the earliest accounts of his preaching by the Lake of Galilee. Death at Bethlehem, death at Nazareth, death at Capharnaum, always and everywhere hatred unto death—this is the atmosphere in which from the beginning Jesus lived, and worked his miracles, and preached the kingdom of the Father.

[1] Mark iii 20.  [2] Mark i 45.  [3] Luke v 16.
[4] Luke v 17.  [5] Luke v 21.  [6] Luke v 30.
[7] Luke v 33.  [8] Matt xii 1.  [9] Luke vi 7.
[10] Mark iii 22.  [11] Matt. xi 19.  [12] Luke vi 11.
[13] Mark iii 6.

Nor was this all ; it was not even the worst. The enemy he knew how to treat ; it was the failure of his friends that cut deepest. At first the people of Capharnaum and its neighbourhood were all enthusiasm ; very soon they went their own way. It was not long before he had to complain that " hearing they would not hear, nor would they understand." [1] A very little later they have become so familiar as to laugh him to scorn when he speaks. [2] Yet a little more and there came the great rejection :

" After this, many of his disciples went back and walked no more with him " ; [3] and from that day we hear no more of the crowds in Capharnaum. On the contrary, he is exiled from the place ; he is compelled to go abroad. When next the name of the town is on his lips, it is uttered from a pierced heart :

" And thou, Capharnaum, shalt thou be exalted up to heaven ? Thou shalt go down even unto hell. For if in Sodom had been wrought the miracles that have been wrought in thee, perhaps it had remained unto this day. But I say unto you that it shall be more tolerable for the land of Sodom in the day of judgement than for thee." [4]

### 4. *Jerusalem*

When we pass from Galilee to Judæa, the opposition from the first is yet more manifest. In Galilee it had arisen, for the most part, from ignorance, and dullness, and the contempt that is mere stupidity ; perhaps, too, in Capharnaum, from selfishness and blind guidance ; in Jerusalem men were not ignorant, they were not dull, their enmity was founded on suspicion, which soon, as the truth became more manifest, inevitably developed into hatred. Already we have seen its foreshadowing when, thirty years before, the priests and elders had used their knowledge of the Scriptures only to foster Herod's evil mind, not to guide themselves to Bethlehem ; now, when as a full-grown man Jesus appeared in their midst, it was war to the death from the beginning. He came and cleansed the Temple court of its buyers and sellers ; he was asked for his authority and he gave a sign, the sign of his death and resurrection. Thus, at his first encounter with them, he showed his enemies that he was well aware how the contest would end.

As it began, so the bitterness continued. On the occasion of another festival he came into the city again. At the Probatic Pool he healed the cripple-beggar. The poor man had lain there, day in and day out, for nigh on forty years ; therefore he must have been known as a kind of institution in the place. But what came of the healing ?

" Therefore did the Jews persecute Jesus, because he did these things on the sabbath " ; [5]

---

[1] Matt. xiii 10-17.    [2] Luke viii 53.    [3] John vi 67.
[4] Matt. xi 23, 24.    [5] John v 16.

and when he made an effort to enlighten them, and spoke in his defence :

"Hereupon, therefore, the Jews sought the more to kill him, because he did not only break the sabbath, but also said God was his Father, making himself equal to God." [1]

His answer is not one of rejection. It is the first of those patient, compassionate, all-enduring appeals which throughout his life characterise his language, above all in his visits to the Holy City.

"You will not come to me that you may have life." [2]

"I am come in the name of my Father, and you receive me not : if another shall come in his own name, him you will receive." [3]

Never for a moment did the sky clear in Jerusalem ; and yet Jerusalem was the apple of his eye. On the contrary, it grew ever darker. If in Nazareth he "wondered at their unbelief," and "he could not work many miracles there because of their unbelief," much more was this true of Jerusalem. In fact, we have a detailed account of only two, and both of these are told us because of the yet greater persecution they entailed.

We need not pursue the subject further ; whenever he appeared the story was the same, aggravated only by constant attempts upon his life. It is enough to hear him at the end, more distressed because of what Jerusalem was doing to him than, it would seem, at all the rest besides. Outside the city in the latter days we hear him crying :

"Jerusalem, Jerusalem, thou that killest the prophets and stonest them that are sent to thee, how often would I have gathered thy children as the bird doth her brood under her wings, and thou wouldest not ? Behold your house shall be left to you desolate." [4]

A short time after, he rides into the city in triumph. But again his pierced heart bleeds.

"And when he drew near, seeing the city, he wept over it, saying : If thou hadst known, and that in this thy day, the things that are to thy peace : but now they are hidden from thy eyes. For the days shall come upon thee : and thy enemies shall cast a trench about thee, and compass thee round, and straiten thee on every side, and beat thee flat to the ground, and thy children who are in thee. And they shall not leave in thee a stone upon a stone : because thou hast not known the time of thy visitation." [5]

§ III: THE MAN OF SORROWS IN HIS TEACHING

1. *To men in general*

ON a background such as this the life of Jesus was lived. It might be easily expanded to other places : to the wanderings in enforced

---

[1] John v 18.   [2] John v 40.   [3] John v 43.
[4] Luke xiii 34, 35.   [5] Luke xix 41-44.

exile through Tyre, and Sidon, and Decapolis ; to the journeys through Peræa, where he was warned that Herod sought to catch him ; through Samaria, where the Samaritans would refuse him shelter ; through the other parts of Judæa, where, more than ever as the time advanced, his enemies followed him and " watched him," so that for the people's sake he had to turn upon them. When, then, he came to speak of suffering and trial, everyone who heard him knew that from his own experience he had a right to speak, and that what he uttered was the expression of his very soul.

This is one of the fascinations of the Sermon on the Mount. What is taught in that sermon might well have been given in many other ways : with command, as a rightful lord and master might have given it ; with threats and sanctions, as might a promulgator of laws, even as Moses had done before him, or as John the Baptist had foreshadowed him ; with cold aloofness, as might an independent ruler of his people. But it was not an independent, it was a feeling and fellow-suffering soul which prompted the opening of the Sermon with the Eight Beatitudes : blessing the poor, by one who was himself acquainted with dire poverty ; for the meek, from him who was of all men the meekest, and could claim meekness as specially his own ; for the mournful, for the hungry after justice, from him who was weighed down by the cruelty and injustice of men all about him ; for the merciful and forgiving, a new thing, as he taught it, in those days ; for the clean of heart from him who, on that very account, knew and felt more than others the shamefulness and horror of sin ; for the makers of peace ; last of all—and this is dwelt upon —for those who suffered persecution. In the conclusion of the series of blessings there was the ring of victory, as of one who had himself already endured and won through :

" Blessed are ye when they shall revile you, and persecute you, and speak all that is evil against you, untruly, for my sake : be glad and rejoice, for your reward is very great in heaven. For so they persecuted the prophets that were before you." [1]

This note, once triumphantly sounded, rings through the whole discourse ; at intervals the heart that has suffered breaks out, and always the refrain is the same. It is a constant warning against the bitterness that may come of long-endured cruelty, a constant reminder of the reward that awaits sorrow patiently borne.

" But I say to you, not to resist evil : but if one strike thee on thy right cheek, turn to him the other. And if a man will contend with thee in judgement, and take away thy coat, let go thy cloak also unto him. And whosoever will force thee one mile, go with him other two." [2]

Are such admonitions taken from the life and personal experience of him who uttered them ? Knowing him as we do, we are entitled to believe they are ; without that confirmation they would

[1] Matt. v 11, 12.  [2] Matt. v 39-41.

have been of little weight ; and if they are, what singular light they throw on the days that are hidden from us, at Nazareth, in Capharnaum, in Judæa ! Had he been so meek as this ? So contemned as this ? When, then, he had come back to Nazareth as a teacher, we may understand a little better why the people of the town " were scandalised because of him."

Listen to him a little further on :

" I say to you, Love your enemies : do good to them that hate you, and pray for them that persecute and calumniate you : that you may be the children of your Father who is in heaven, who maketh his sun to rise upon the good and bad, and raineth upon the just and the unjust." [1]

He who said that had himself been hated, had himself been calumniated, had known it and had felt it, and had looked elsewhere for strength to bear it.

Or again :

" Be not solicitous, therefore, saying : What shall we eat ? or, What shall we drink ? or, Wherewith shall we be clothed ? For your Father knoweth that you have need of these things." [2]

He who said that, and all that went before it, had himself shared and endured the squalid poverty and want that stalks through every Eastern town and village like a skeleton in rags. By experience he knew what it meant, and his hearers knew that he knew it. In this as in all things else he was one with themselves ; therefore they accepted the relief he offered them.

" And it came to pass, when Jesus had fully ended these words, that the people were in admiration at his doctrine. For he was teaching them as one having power "—let us say, as one who knew —" and not as the scribes and Pharisees," [3] who, from their own experience, at least, had been careful not to know or learn. In this light, throughout his great discourse to the people, did the Man of Sorrows reveal himself, the Man of others' sorrows as well as of his own, of others' sorrows because they were his own.

## 2. *To the Twelve in particular*

Jesus chose his Twelve. For a time he kept them with him, that by word and example they might learn of him ; soon he sent them out to preach the Kingdom, and to be witnesses in their turn. Before they parted, he delivered to them an address for their guidance. If the Sermon on the Mount revealed a heart that felt with the sufferings of men in general, much more did this address show sympathy for those who were destined to suffer for his cause. But it did much more ; now a new vista was opened out to them. It taught them to look suffering in the face, to brave it, to seek it, to love it, even to find in it their joy and their glory, and the true measure of their success. The whole address rings with a note almost of

[1] Matt. v 44, 45.    [2] Matt. vi 31, 32.    [3] Matt. vii 28, 29.

defiance ; and the defiance is based precisely on the fact that he has suffered before them, he their Master and Model, the model Man of Sorrows.

" The disciple is not above the master, nor the servant above his lord. It is enough for the disciple that he be as his master, and the servant as his lord. If they have called the goodman of the house Beelzebub, how much more them of his household ? " [1]

Let us notice the illustration which the Master uses. To have been called that name had stung, and the agony of it had stayed ; otherwise he would scarcely have recalled it.

But what were some of the sufferings that he would bid his disciples defy ? Before, he had blessed the poor in spirit, making them content with their lot ; now, he spoke of a poverty far more complete, of a spirit far more independent, of poverty that should be a glory :

" Freely have you received, freely give. Do not possess gold, nor silver, nor money in your purses, nor scrip for your journey, nor two coats, nor shoes, nor a staff." [2]

Before, he had spoken of meekness that would endure ; now, his meekness was aggressive :

" Behold, I send you as sheep in the midst of wolves. Be ye therefore wise as serpents and simple as doves." [3]

Before, he had promised comfort to them that mourn ; now, he spoke of no comfort, he made courage to face whatever trouble might come its own sufficient reward :

" Beware of men. For they will deliver you up in councils, and they will scourge you in their synagogues. And you shall be brought before governors and before kings for my sake, for a testimony to them and to the gentiles." [4]

Before, he had spoken of persecution from men as the price of a great reward ; now, he spoke of hatred as a settled thing, as part of the lot that would be theirs, a sign that would be upon them always, and would never be taken away :

" And you shall be hated by all men for my name's sake. But he that shall persevere unto the end, he shall be saved." [5]

It was a stern if glorious lesson, and it was long before the Twelve learnt it. Nevertheless, after he was gone, the day did come when its full light dawned upon them. One day it would be written of them :

" And they, indeed, went from the presence of the council, rejoicing that they were accounted worthy to suffer reproach for the name of Jesus." [6]

Nor did he stop there. Soon he took yet a further step. In the Sermon on the Mount he had promised blessing to those that suffered ; later, in his sermon to the Twelve, he had encouraged

---

[1] Matt. x 24, 25.    [2] Matt. x 8-10.    [3] Matt. x 16.
[4] Matt. x 17, 18.    [5] Matt. x 22.    [6] Acts v 41.

his own to find joy in suffering for the simple reason that he had suffered before them ; later again, after the foundations of the Church had been laid in the confession of Simon Peter, he hailed suffering, and bade men hail it, as the hall-mark by which alone his true disciples would be known :

"And calling the multitude together with his disciples, he said to them : If any man will come after me, let him deny himself, and take up his cross daily, and follow me.  For whosoever shall lose his life for my sake and the gospel shall save it.  For what shall it profit a man, if he gain the whole world, and suffer the loss of his soul ? Or what shall a man give in exchange for his soul ? "[1]

And in the meantime, as he thus strengthens his teaching to them, so does he speak more emphatically about himself.  It is just before this time that he begins that series of prophecies :

"From that time Jesus began to show to his disciples that he must go to Jerusalem and suffer many things from the ancients and scribes and chief priests, and be put to death, and the third day rise again."[2]

Henceforward the two ideas are never very far from his mind : on the one hand the cross that awaits his followers, on the other the still heavier cross which he would carry before them.  Mark the swinging of the pendulum, first to himself and then to his disciples :

"But while all wondered at all the things he did, he said to his disciples : Lay up in your hearts these words, for it shall come to pass that the Son of man shall be delivered into the hands of men."[3]

"And they were in the way going up to Jerusalem ; and Jesus went before them.  And they were astonished, and following were afraid.  And taking again the twelve, he began to tell them the things that should befall him, saying : Behold, we go up to Jerusalem, and the Son of man shall be betrayed to the chief priests and to the scribes and ancients.  And they shall condemn him to death, and shall deliver him to the Gentiles.  And they shall mock him, and spit on him, and scourge him and kill him : and the third day he shall rise again."[4]

Then it swings back to his own :

"Come to me, all you that labour and are burdened : and I will refresh you.  Take up my yoke upon you and learn of me, because I am meek and humble of heart, and you shall find rest to your souls. For my yoke is sweet and my burden light."[5]

"I say to you, my friends : Be not afraid of them who kill the body and after that have no more that they can do.  But I will show you whom you shall fear : Fear him who, after he hath killed, hath power to cast into hell.  Yea, I say to you : Fear him.  Are not five sparrows sold for two farthings, and not one of them is forgotten

---

[1] Mark viii 34-37.  [2] Matt. xvi 21.  [3] Luke ix 44.
[4] Mark x 32-34.  [5] Matt. xi 28-30.

before God ? Yea, the very hairs of your head are all numbered. Fear not, therefore : you are of more value than many sparrows." [1]

### 3. *The Last Supper*

One more discourse we have in which the Man of Sorrows revealed himself, and that is by far the most important of them all. It was at the last farewell, the supper with the Twelve. With the experience of his life behind him, with the Passion looming up immediately before him, and the further passion beyond, which these men would one day have to undergo, it was inevitable that again he should revert to the old subject—the place of suffering in life, in his own life and in theirs.

They sat down to the Supper. Almost at once there arose among the Twelve a quarrel. They were concerned about their respective seniority ; so little even then did they realise the meaning of that last assembly, or the soul of him who, for the last time, sat at table with them. But he had patience with them. He had endured from them so much before, their uncouth manners, their petty ways, their frowardness, their spirit of contradiction, and then again their shrinking cowardice, their dullness of understanding, and with it their self-assertion ; he had endured so much already, he would not surrender them now. They had, indeed, been bought at a great price, and he would not be angry with them now. In a new way he would settle their dispute, and at the same time teach them a lesson. Before, when they had quarrelled on this precise subject, he had taught them by setting a child before them, and making him their model ; now he sets himself, he annihilates himself once more, he washes their feet as any slave might wash them. Henceforth let them dispute, not who shall be first, but who shall be the last among them. [2]

Thus peace is restored, and he begins to speak his message of farewell. But he cannot proceed, there is one in their midst whose presence seems to paralyse his tongue ; not until that man has gone out into the darkness is he able to say what he would. [3] He institutes the Blessed Sacrament ; lavishly, as one who knows no limits in his giving, he bestows on them his own body and blood. They are unworthy, what does it matter ? This is no time for laying down conditions. Let them have him all ; let them eat and drink him ; let them take him and, when they like, give him away to others. [4]

Almost immediately, as if that act of generosity had exhausted him, a reaction begins to set in. He speaks of their coming desertion ; that very night those Twelve, to whom he had given so much, who were so much to him, would leave him. They might not believe him ; they may protest ; but he knows better. In a few hours

[1] Luke xii 4-7.    [2] Luke xxii 24-30 ; John xiii 1-20.
[3] Matt. xxvi 21-25 ; Mark xiv 18-21 ; Luke xxii 21-23 ; John xiii 21-35.
[4] Matt. xxvi 26-29 ; Mark xiv 22-25 ; Luke xxii 19, 20.

from now one will have betrayed him, and he will permit it ; another
will deny him, and he will pass it by and overlook it ; every one of
them will be scandalised in him and forsake him, and he will treat
them, now and after, as if it were not.    Instead he will find excuse
for them ; he will see in it all a fulfilment of prophecy and no more.
So far as he is able, he will take the blame ; since he is to be so
humiliated in their eyes, how can they be expected to stand by him ?

"For I say unto you, that this that is written must yet be fulfilled
in me : And with the wicked was he reckoned." [1]

"With the wicked was he reckoned !" It would come to that.
At the beginning he had stood to be baptised among sinners, but
there John, at least, had known him.    He had submitted to be
tempted as no man was tempted, but in the end Satan had confessed
him "the holy one of God."    He had forgiven sins, and had been
called a blasphemer for it ; but he had vindicated his honour.    Other
sinners had come to him, and he had stooped down to them ; but
though men had taunted him with being their friend, they had
hesitated to make him one of them.    Later they had ventured.
"We know this man is a sinner," they had said ; but he had silenced
them by the more defiant question : "Which of you shall convince
me of sin ?"    In all his life, whatever else men had said or done to
him, this, at least, had been kept secure ; they had not touched,
however they had tried, the honour of his good name.

But now this, too, was to go.    "He who knew no sin was made
sin" ; so one day would an apostle describe him.    At last his
enemies would call him "a malefactor," and he would not contradict them ; his own would see him treated as such, and he would
offer no resistance ; worst of all, his oneness with sinful man would
now press him down with all its fell significance.    When we human
creatures try to fathom what this means we are lost in darkness ;
we know remorse, we know fear, we know our contempt of ourselves,
we know indignation, we know sadness, and contrition, and the
agony of repentance ; but we see only as in a glass after a dark
manner.    What would the agony be if we saw sin as it is in itself,
as Jesus Christ saw it ?    It is here, more than anywhere else, that
we should look for the Man of Sorrows, yet it is precisely here that
human vision fails.    Jesus Christ "made sin" ; we know not
what we say, but we know that in comparison with this, all the other
sorrows of all his life were the merest trifles.

But for the moment he must lay the thought aside.    Soon it
will come back upon him in all its force and will crush him "even
unto death" ; now it is enough that he has said what he has said,
showing that the shadow of it hangs over him.    During the remainder of the Supper he has other work to do ; he must think
more of his own than of himself ; he is troubled by the thought of

[1] Luke xxii 37.

their coming sorrow, and he must set himself to prepare them for it. It is his third great lesson. At first, as we have seen, in the Sermon on the Mount he had blessed those who suffered ; later, in the sermon to the Twelve, he had filled them with his own courage ; now he would inspire them with the joy of it, that joy that it alone could give, in that by its means they would be drawn nearer, ever nearer, to himself. Thus as he speaks, while giving them assurance, we feel him giving a like assurance to his own quivering soul.

" Let not your heart be troubled. You believe in God, believe also in me." [1]

" Have I been so long a time with you, and have you not known me ? " [2]

" I will not leave you orphans. I will come to you." [3]

" Peace I leave with you, my peace I give unto you : not as the world giveth, do I give unto you. Let not your heart be troubled, nor let it be afraid." [4]

" These things I have spoken to you that my joy may be in you, and your joy may be filled." [5]

" Greater love than this no man hath, that a man lay down his life for his friends." [6]

At this point he looks back. He has spoken of love, of that love which alone has made him give and give, and suffer and suffer on, which will make him give and suffer till no more is left. Had he no more to say it would have been enough ; for he has just summed all up in the remark that the greatest love is love unto death. But there is the other side. He has given love, and what has he received in return ? Had it been nothing at all, that would have been bitter ; but it had not been nothing. He had received hatred, hatred positive and malicious ; it is much for us to realise the fact, that from first to last Jesus Christ had been faced with men who positively hated him, and that here at the end the thought burns through his heart. He dwells upon it ; he reads his own life in its light ; he sees that on his account his own will be hated with him. What can he do to save them from the agony he has gone through but give them his own companionship in it all, show them that the hatred will come to them, not on their own account, but because of him ?

" If the world hate you, know ye that it hath hated me before you. If you had been of the world, the world would love its own : but because you are not of the world, therefore the world hateth you. Remember my word that I said to you : The servant is not greater than his master. If they have persecuted me, they will also persecute you : if they have kept my word, they will keep yours also. But all these things they will do to you for my name's sake : because they know not him that sent me. But that the word may

---

[1] John xiv 1.  [2] John xiv 9.  [3] John xiv 18.
[4] John xiv 27.  [5] John xv 11.  [6] John xv 13.

be fulfilled which is written in their law : They hated me without cause." [1]

This, then, was the picture his life presented to him as he looked back upon it on that last night. Love unto death on the one side, hatred unto death on the other ; love giving its all, hatred flinging the gift away ; love in the end taking on itself the burden of its enemy, hatred flouting love because of the burden of which itself was guilty.

But he must come back to his own and the lives that were to be theirs. What he had said of himself had been said for a purpose ; it would prepare them for what might be their own fate. On it he must build their encouragement now ; later they would find it more than encouragement.

" These things have I spoken to you that you may not be scandalised. They will put you out of the synagogue : yea, the hour cometh that whosoever killeth you will think that he doth a service to God." [2]

" But because I have told you these things, sorrow hath filled your heart." [3]

" But I will see you again, and your heart shall rejoice, and your joy no man shall take from you." [4]

Once more, and for the last time, the pendulum swings. The mention of his love for men has made him think of their hatred for him ; the mention of his fidelity to his own reminds him of their coming infidelity to him. It is his last remark ; it seems almost to escape him. But he quickly recovers ; on that note he will not end ; his last word shall be one of encouragement and strength, for he has much yet before him.

" Behold, the hour cometh, and it is now come, that you shall be scattered every man to his own, and shall leave me alone : and yet I am not alone, because the Father is with me. These things I have spoken to you, that in me you may have peace. In the world you shall have distress : but have confidence, I have overcome the world." [5]

§ IV: THE MAN OF SORROWS IN HIS DEATH

1. *The Immediate Preparation*

" BUT some of them went to the Pharisees, and told them the things that Jesus had done. The chief priests, therefore, and the Pharisees gathered a council and said : What do we, for this man doth many miracles ? If we let him alone so, all will believe in him, and the Romans will come, and take away our place and nation. But one of them, named Caiphas, being the high priest that year, said to

---

[1] John xv 18-25.  [2] John xvi 1, 2.  [3] John xvi 6.
[4] John xvi 22.  [5] John xvi 32, 33.

them : You know nothing. Neither do you consider that it is expedient for you that one man should die for the people and that the whole nation perish not." [1]

In this passage is signalled the coming of the Passion proper. It contains in it a note of cruelty such as we scarcely find, certainly not so deliberately expressed, in any other place in the Gospel story. " It is expedient ! " Jesus has just raised Lazarus to life : this is inconvenient to Caiphas ; therefore " it is expedient " for Caiphas that Jesus should die. He " hath done many miracles " : this is inconvenient to the chief priests and Pharisees ; therefore for them as well " it is expedient " that he should die. He has won many to believe in him ; if he is left alone he will win them all : this is inconvenient to the politicians ; therefore " it is expedient " that he should die.

But not on any of these grounds can he be condemned ; what is expedient may not be just ; but with a little cleverness it may be justified ; therefore another pretext must be found. What that pretext might be mattered very little. A word that he had somewhere uttered could be twisted to their purpose, an action could be interpreted in any sense they chose, a motive could be invented. To none of such arguments is there any real answer, to reply to them is often only to make oneself the more suspect. All, then, that was wanted was a formula, a specious premise ; the rest would follow in due course.

The President of the Council was equal to the occasion ; he had not administered justice all these years for nothing. But first, before they sought a ground for accusation, he must satisfy the tender consciences of these just men that they were right. He gave them a proof, worded according to the strictest logic. Of two evils we should always choose the less. *Atqui*, that one man should die is an infinitely less evil than that the whole nation should perish. *Ergo*, in this case we should choose that one man should die. No, not only were they justified ; to carry out this policy was the plain duty of men who had been entrusted with the welfare of the people.

Thus by a pretentious syllogism was Jesus Christ fore-condemned. It is the syllogism by means of which more injustice has been justified, particularly among " good " men, than by anything else in the world. The men who were capable of framing and yielding to such arguments were incapable of any other. They were incapable of seeing the truth, even that elementary truth that one may not do evil that good may come of it ; the end does not justify the means.

Therefore for a time Jesus left them. As at Capharnaum, almost a year before, he had been respected, so now in Jerusalem the final decision was made. With a broken heart he could only

[1] John xi 46-50.

contemplate the doom. He retired to Ephraim ; thence he made a farewell tour of the country he had loved and for which he had laboured ; on the day of Palms he rode again into the city, to vindicate the truth and face the end. During the days that followed, while on the surface he proved his power in the sight of his enemies as he had never proved it before, underneath there is felt, beyond possibility of escape, an unspeakable agony, as of a love and friendship offered, and rejected, and trampled underfoot. St John tells the story of the parting in his own characteristic way. While the other Evangelists are anxious to champion their Master before his enemies, John throughout it all keeps his eyes upon the Man of Sorrows. Before the last time he leaves the Temple he hears him cry aloud :

" Now is my soul troubled. And what shall I say ? Father, save me from this hour." [1]

It is an anticipation of Gethsemani. And as at Gethsemani, so here, he hears him as it were recover himself :

" But for this cause I came unto this hour. Father, glorify thy name." [2]

After which, with renewed courage, he is able to proceed :

" Now is the judgement of the world : now shall the prince of this world be cast out. And I, if I be lifted up from the earth, will draw all things to myself. Now this he said, signifying what death he should die." [3]

## 2.  *The Passion.*

When we come to the actual story of the Passion, what better can we do, for the purpose of this study, than just recall the facts as they occurred ? They speak for themselves, better than anyone can elaborate them ; by their own intrinsic evidence they prove their truth ; by their dead weight alone, for any who can and will endure it, they tell more forcibly than any added words can make them. Much in the Passion we cannot hope to understand ; the very description, the effort to realise what the description means, leaves us amazed, bewildered, almost stupefied. Much comes to us as through a mist ; we dimly catch the meaning, we scarcely dare to do more, though we see how much there is beyond which we do not reach. The more we make ourselves ponder—for the effort has to be made—the more we find there is to be discovered, even if we go no further than through the simple narrative as the Gospels give it to us. Book after book has been written, by student and by saint, each one, it may be, adding something more to our knowledge and understanding, and yet we are well aware that the mine is not and cannot be exhausted ; there will be fresh ore in it to the end.

[1] John xii 27.          [2] John xii 27, 28.          [3] John xii 31-33.

For instance, what meaning are we to give to those opening words of St Matthew :

" He began to grow sorrowful (λυπεῖσθαι) and to be sad (ἀδημονεῖν) " ? [1]

Or to those of St Mark :

" He began to fear (ἐκθαμβεῖσθαι), and to be heavy (ἀδημονεῖν)"?[2]

Or to the words of both :

" My soul is sorrowful (περίλυπός) even unto death " ? [3]

Whatever may be the full meaning (and that we shall never know), we have here before us Jesus Christ, a broken Man, broken as those who knew him had never seen him before, overwhelmed by grief—for what ?—so that he would gladly die to be relieved of it ; stunned with amazement and fear—at what ?—so that he seems all but paralysed ; driven to what we would call distraction —by what ?—so that he appears no longer to know which way to turn.

Or what is the meaning, such that we can form any adequate conception of it, of that " chalice " and its contents of which Matthew, Mark, and Luke all speak, and which appeared to him, even to him whose love made suffering welcome, something too much to be endured ? Or of that agony which made him pray the longer, and which needed that an angel should be sent to support him ? [4] Or of that sweat of blood which fear and alarm forced through the pores of his body, flowing in such abundance as to run down to the ground ?[5] We look at all this and know that we are in touch with that which cannot be measured by any standards of our own ; human as it is, human and therefore finite, yet it is suffering far beyond the power of any man to fathom, much less to experience in himself. Saints and mystics and theologians have given us various interpretations ; they are all, perhaps, right, but none of them, not all of them together, have reached to the bottom of the ocean. That the Son of God should have " become sin " ; that the Lamb without stain should have taken on himself all the sins of all the world ; that, now, in some mysterious way, he should appear to stand " reputed with the wicked "—this was surely at the root of all the sorrow, of itself enough to make death welcome, a chalice whose contents the holiest might well petition that he might not be compelled to drink.

But the truth, as we have said, includes every explanation ; it includes very much more ; human nature grows weary, turns away from the scene and welcomes sleep beneath the olive tree. The sorrow is such that the Son of God must perforce endure it alone ; no other human being is equal to it ; as he stood alone in the past, much more now must he continue.

The agony is over ; but it is only the preliminary to more.

[1] Matt. xxvi 37.    [2] Mark xiv 33.
[3] Matt. xxvi 38 ; Mark xiv 34.
[4] Luke xxii 43, 44.    [5] Luke xxii 44.

" Jesus, knowing all that was to befall him "—St John once more is careful to remind us of this. He knew what was coming ; at any moment he might have prevented it ; he could have stricken those men down, he could have asked his Father, and he would have given him legions of angels ; but he would not. Every step in the Passion was an act of deliberate acceptance ; St John, and St Paul after him, can never let this single fact escape from their minds. " Christ loved me, and gave himself for me." " He was offered because he himself willed it."

Then follows the betrayal ; by such a man, the most trusted of all his inner circle, to whom, moreover, he had given warnings in abundance ; in such a way, the way of most intimate familiarity, abusing a privilege that few indeed could claim ; to such people, who needed no traitor to put him in their hands, for had he not been among them every day ? Under such circumstances that through all time that traitor and that crime have been taken as a byword for the basest deed that ever man could do to fellow-man.

" Hail, Rabbi ; and he kissed him." [1]
" Friend, whereto art thou come ? " [2]
" Judas, dost thou betray the Son of man with a kiss ? " [3]

To the astonishment of his disciples the deed of treachery succeeded. On other like occasions Jesus had passed through the crowd, but this time men laid hands on him and he submitted. Was his power, then, gone ? Was there no further hope ? What could they do but run away ?

" The hour cometh, and it is now come, that you shall be scattered every man to his own, and shall leave me alone." [4]

They bound him ; they dragged him down the hill and up the other slope to the southern gate. They brought him to the court of the heartless Sadducee, Annas, who sat in solemn state with his priests, and his elders, and his scribes about him. What was there to be enacted could be nothing else than a thing of form ; long since the sentence had been passed. And this, too, Jesus knew. He knew that he must be condemned, and must be condemned with all the forms of justice. Long since had these men decided on it ; hatred unrelenting had sealed his fate, policy had invented the manner of it. Hitherto a mysterious something had kept him out of their grasp ; now that something had suddenly deserted him ; he was wholly at their mercy, and they could wreak on him what vengeance they would—vengeance for the way he had defied them from the first, vengeance for the rebukes he had bestowed upon them in their own Temple court, vengeance for the warnings he had given men against them, vengeance for the condemnation he had publicly pronounced, vengeance for all he had taught and they did not, vengeance for all he had done and they could not,

---

[1] Matt. xxvi 49.
[2] Matt. xxvi 50.
[3] Luke xxii 48.
[4] John xvi 32.

vengeance, above all, for what he had claimed to be, and by irrefutable argument had proved it.

But, of course, it must not appear to be vengeance ; what they
would do must be done with all the forms of justice.· It must be
made manifest to all that they were right ; he must be put in the
wrong ; and since not one of his deeds could be brought up against
him, his words must be adduced, must be turned and twisted, and
misquoted, and taken from their context, and so made to mean
what they would have them mean.  In the last resort this is always
a safe method of conviction ; when nothing else will serve one can
quote a victim's words, by a shadow of an accent alter their whole
meaning, say that he said them, or that someone said that he said
them, and then put upon them any interpretation one may please.
" The devil can quote Scripture to his purpose."  No man ever
yet spoke anything but malice can turn it, if it pleases, to its own
ends.  It is a safe device ; it has the peculiar advantage that however cruel and unjust the inference may be, yet the fact cannot be
denied ; having so much of truth about it, it is the cruellest of lies.

So, in the first instance, was Jesus Christ condemned : condemned out of his own mouth ; condemned by his own people ;
condemned by those who knew that their evidence was hollow,
their inference utterly untrue, their sentence a base travesty of
justice.  On that very account, that they might support themselves in their mockery, as men will, they were driven to submit
him to the greater shame.  True justice is always merciful ; consciousness of wrong is always cruel.

" And some began to spit on him, and to cover his face, and to
buffet him, and to say unto him : Prophesy !  And the servants
struck him with the palms of their hands." [1]

Nor is this all that he must endure " in the house of them that
loved him " ; his prophecy concerning Simon Peter is yet to be
fulfilled.  It is done within his sight and hearing.  Simon disowns
him, declares that he does not know him, confirms the declaration
with an oath—the one man who, if he would, might have said a
word in his favour.  He does this in such a place, on such an
occasion, at the taunt of a mere servant girl ; after all that had
been done for him, after all that he himself had promised, in spite
of the repeated warnings he does it.  He does it in spite of his
love, for that Simon still loved his Master cannot be doubted ; on
that account it was a deeper wound than had been the treachery of
Judas.  Jesus heard it ; heard it from the lips of Peter :

" And the Lord turning looked on Peter." [2]

And that was all.  But what had the denial meant to him ?

He is thrown into prison for the night, left to the mercy of his
gaolers.  If before his judges they could strike him in the face

---

[1] Mark xiv 65.          [2] Luke xxii 61.

and be countenanced, what might they not do now that they had him to themselves ? And he let them do what they would.

Next day he must die ; the Passover that was to follow would not allow these scrupulous men to wait longer. Once again, as before, the formalities of justice must be gone through. He must be handed over to the civil arm ; Roman as well as Jew must be made partaker of this act of universal shame. So they fettered him again ; they dragged him through the crowded streets, through the main thoroughfare of the city. What better proof than this could be given to the rabble of Jerusalem that the man they had begun to revere was an impostor ? He who could not save himself, how could he be a saviour to others ? The beggar said to have been healed in the north of the city, the man born blind cured in the south, who now would believe such old women's tales ? And Jesus knew ; knew what men would infer ; knew the bitter anger and resentment that must rise up on every side against him ; and he endured it all.

They reach the house of Pilate ; he is handed over to the Pro-curator ; his own Jews surrender him to Romans. He is pursued with accusations ; what they are matters not at all ; so long as it will influence the Gentile, anything will serve. He is malefactor, this has no pretence of evidence ; [1] he destroys our nation ; [2] he forbids men to give tribute to Caesar ; [3] he says he is Christ the King.[4] Truly a jumble of charges ; a jumble of falsehoods founded on the faintest semblance of truth ; just the confusion of accusations, inconsistent, haphazard, yet leading steadily to their goal, which determination to destroy alone could have brought together, and which, because of their sweeping generalities, it would have been impossible to refute.

But for just the same reason the shrewd, unbelieving Roman knew their hollowness. " He knew that for envy they had be-trayed him." But Jesus was a Galilæan, a despicable Galilæan ; then to Galilee's ruler he should go for sentence. From Pilate he is dragged again through the streets to Herod ; to Herod, the son of that Herod who had sought his life as an infant; Herod, the crowned king of sensuality, the murderer of John the Baptist, who could be quelled by a dancing girl's sneer ; who in his moments of remorse had trembled at the thought of this Jesus, lest he might be his victim John risen from the dead ; who at other times, when the passion for revelry was on him, had long wished to have him in his hands that he might see his miracles ; who by this Man himself had openly been called " that fox." Before such a man Jesus stood ; by such a man he suffered that he should be judged, with the laughing court around him of ribald men and women, to whom vice the most degrading was their open profession, their very life. Jesus stood before them, and he needed not have stood

---

[1] John xviii 30.  [2] Luke xxiii 21.  [3] *Ibid.*  [4] *Ibid.*

there ; he endured the loathsome sight and let them laugh ; though once he had bidden Satan himself " Begone ! " these men he permitted to do their will.

Herod, that man of moods, was now in the mood when he was glad to have Jesus at his mercy. He would make this conjurer perform before him ; he would make him do his tricks to save his life. But it was of no avail. He spoke to him with civility ; he spoke to him with threats, but

" He answered him not a word." [1]

And since Jesus would not turn his court jester, Herod would make him his court fool.

" And Herod with his army set him at nought, and mocked him, putting on him a white garment, and sent him back to Pilate." [2]

One reflection on this scene we must make. All this time, Herodias and her daughter, where were they ? The blood of the Baptist was still red upon their hands ; because of that crime they hated everyone, because of him they hated this Jesus ; they hated him the more because of the fear his name had roused in their lord and master. That they were present at this scene seems only too likely ; may we not be sure that their laughter, shrill, hard, loud, triumphant, hideous, provocative, was not the least of the agonies of shame that Jesus endured in Herod's hall ?

And " he answered not a word."

What follows in the story of the Passion is nothing but the sheerest brutality. The refinements of cruelty are over ; regard for even the external show of justice is gone ; when Pilate, for his own sake, and for the honour of the Roman eagle, would preserve an appearance of law and order, he must be howled down. Let man play with the trappings of justice long enough, and the day will come when he will throw them all aside, when injustice will become a boast and a glory. Let him play with falsehood, and one day he will take pride in his powers of deceit. He will take pride in his powers of deceiving even himself.

So was it on this occasion. Barabbas or Christ ? That Barabbas was guilty no man would venture to deny, that Jesus was guilty not a soul believed ; therefore let him be put to death, let Barabbas go free ! How shall he be put to death ? If he were a blasphemer, as some said, then he should be stoned ; but they had attempted that before, and had failed. This time they must not fail. He was in hands that seemed able to hold him ; therefore by those hands let him die. Let him be bled to death, drop by drop, hanging on a cross.

But his executioners demurred.

" You have presented unto me this man, as one that perverteth the people ; and behold I, having examined him before you, find no cause in this man, in those things wherein you accuse him. No,

---

[1] Luke xxiii 9.      [2] Luke xxiii 11.

nor Herod neither. For I sent you to him, and behold, nothing worthy of death is found done by him. I will chastise him therefore and release him." [1]

" I will chastise him therefore " ! The logic of the conclusion ! Step by step in this story of horror the gross injustice of every deed is manifest and acknowledged. When men persist in evil usually they will not think ; or if they will, they justify themselves in what they do. With the murderers of Jesus it was not so. Let the Evangelist tell what follows in his own few words. He is unwilling to dwell upon its details ; he will tell the simple fact and have done with it.

" Then the soldiers of the governor, taking Jesus into the hall, gathered together to him the whole band ; and stripping him they put a scarlet cloak about him. And platting a crown of thorns, they put it on his head, and a reed in his right hand. And bowing the knee before him, they mocked him, saying : Hail, King of the Jews ! And spitting upon him, they took the reed, and struck his head." [2]

St Mark adds to this the one other detail :
" When he had scourged him." [3]
It is confirmed by St John :
" Then therefore Pilate took Jesus and scourged him." [4]

The scourging of Jesus was, as we have seen, part of his deliberate sentence ; the crowning and the mockery were a piece of wanton cruelty, at the hands of men whose profession trained them to be cruel, whose amusement was sought in the sight of cruel deeds, who found in one another an incentive to ever greater cruelty, in whom the sense of pity had long been dead, if it had ever lived in them at all.

Pontius Pilate could not but have known what was going on in the courtyard behind him. But he did not move. If the Victim died beneath the torture, let it be so ; in this way, at least, his problem would be solved. Slaves often perished by a like accident ; his own reputation would be saved ; and one life more or less, what would it matter ? But Jesus would not die beneath the lash ; then the condition to which he had been reduced might serve the Procurator's purpose. One so tormented, so tortured, so disfigured, that he could scarcely any more be called a man, would surely win the pity of the mob ; contempt for their Victim, if nothing else, would modify their hatred. One so beaten, a helpless mass of bleeding flesh, could no longer be called a danger to the people ; the very sight of him would be enough.

" Pilate therefore went forth again and saith to them : Behold, I bring him forth unto you, that you may know that I find no cause in him. Jesus therefore came forth, bearing the crown of thorns

---

[1] Luke xxiii 14-16.  
[2] Matt. xxvii 27-30.  
[3] Mark xv 15.  
[4] John xix 1.

and the purple garment. And he saith to them : " Behold the man ! " [1]

Rather : " Behold what once had been a man ! Behold a worm and no man ! Behold the Model of all Manhood ! "

But even this device was of no avail. He had reckoned on hatred as he knew it, of man for fellow-man ; he had not reckoned on hatred such as this, of man for the Son of God. At the sight of him they cried out the more ; he must be crucified ; so long as God made man walked among them on this earth, hatred would never be appeased.

"And their voices prevailed." He was clothed once more in his own clothing ; for the third time that morning was this singular humiliation done to him, and with it, for the third time, the wounds upon his body were opened. It was to be done to him yet again before that day was over. They took him down the steps into the street ; the heavy wood was put upon his shoulder ; up and down the rugged streets he dragged it, with two " other " malefactors in his company, at the end identified with sinners no less than during his whole life, more now at the end than it had ever been before. He had come to save his people from their sins ; he had been baptised among them ; he had eaten and drunk with them ; he had submitted to be called their friend ; he had welcomed their love and had returned it ; he had invited them to come to him ; he had gone after them, at what cost to himself ! He had forgiven them their sins ; on their account he had endured obloquy ; he had asked them to take his yoke upon them, to carry his cross, and had promised that it would be sweet, his burden would be light. Now in return he carried theirs, the whole weight upon him of all their misery, the shame and guilt flung at him like mud from the passers-by. He ascended their cross with them, was nailed hand and foot to it instead of them, that they in their turn might ascend and be nailed to his with him. " Jesus Christ, and him crucified." A fitting death-bed after such a life ; yet also a fitting throne for the Man of Sorrows. " I, when I shall be lifted up, will draw all things to myself." [2]

## § V : THE MIND OF HIS DISCIPLES

### 1. St Peter

THE most casual student of the first Epistle of St Peter cannot but be struck by the prominent place which the sufferings of his Master have in the mind of the Prince of the Apostles. The Peter of the Epistles is a very different man from that Simon who, in the early days, in his ship on the Lake of Galilee, fell at the feet of Jesus and bade him depart from him, for that he was a sinful man ; very different from him who, in the height of his enthusiasm, would

[1] John xix 4, 5.  [2] John xii 32.

rebuke his Master and say that suffering and death should never
be his lot ; or from him again who, on Mount Thabor, found it
good to be there and looked for nothing more.   Now everything
is changed.   He no longer fears ; the Man of Sorrows has become
an ideal, an inspiration, a support whom it will not be hard to follow
even unto death ; Jesus Christ crucified means to him now more
than Jesus Christ transfigured.   When he sets out to guide his
people, when he would encourage them in the midst of their hard
days, this is the motive and the model he holds up constantly before
them—the suffering of Jesus Christ, not in his Passion only, but
throughout his life, and the manifest fruit it bore.

Thus, when speaking to his Jewish converts, he looks for the
link between the old and the new, and he finds the only key to the
prophecies of old in the sufferings of him who fulfilled them :

" Of which salvation the prophets have enquired and diligently
searched, who prophesied of the grace to come in you.   Searching
what or what manner of time the Spirit of Christ in them did signify,
when it foretold those sufferings that are in Christ and the glories
that should follow." [1]

He looks from the past into the future, and finds man's inspiration in him who has been rejected, precisely because he has been
rejected :

" Rejected indeed by men, but chosen and made honourable
by God." [2]

He sets before them an ideal ; it is no other than Jesus Christ,
not hanging on the cross, but bearing his cross from day to day :

" For this is thankworthy, if for conscience' sake towards God
a man endures sorrows, suffering wrongfully.   For what glory is
it, if, committing sin, and being buffeted for it, you endure ?   But
if doing well you suffer patiently, this is thankworthy before God.
For unto this are you called : because Christ also suffered for us,
leaving you an example that you should follow his footsteps.   Who
did no sin, neither was guile found in his mouth.   Who, when he
was reviled, did not revile : when he suffered, he threatened not :
but delivered himself to him that judged him unjustly.   Who his
own self bore our sins in his body upon the tree ; that we, being
dead to sins, should live to justice : by whose stripes you are healed." [3]

Next, Peter would encourage his disciples to live up to that
ideal ; and again his encouragement is only this, that so Jesus lived
and so he died.

" Christ therefore having suffered in the flesh, be you also armed
with the same thought : for he that hath suffered in the flesh hath
ceased from sins : that now he may live the rest of his time in the
flesh, not after the desires of men, but according to the will of God." [4]

Furthermore, he would offer them a reward.   He does not forget

[1] I Pet. i 10, 11.          [2] I Pet. ii 4.
[3] I Pet. ii 19-24.          [4] I Pet. iv 1, 2.

that he himself once said : " Lord, we have left all and followed thee ; what reward, therefore, shall we have ? " But he has learnt much since then ; and now his reward is the joy we shall have in having shared in the suffering of his Master, when at last his glory is revealed :

" Dearly beloved, think not strange the burning heat which is to try you : as if some new thing happened to you. But if you partake of the sufferings of Christ rejoice that, when his glory shall be revealed, you may also be glad with exceeding joy." [1]

Last of all, he speaks of the witness to this as belonging to his special mission :

" Who am myself an ancient and a witness of the sufferings of Christ, as also a partaker of that glory which is to be revealed in the time to come." [2]

## 2. *St Paul*

St Peter has put the Passion and sufferings of Jesus before his individual followers as their inspiration, their consolation, their model, their encouragement, in their daily lives ; St Paul, as is his wont, looks at them more with the eyes of the universal Church. Already in his first Epistle he sees in the sufferings of the cross the bond of common fellowship for all :

" For you, brethren, are become followers of the churches of God which are in Judæa in Christ Jesus : for you also have suffered the same things from your own countrymen, even as they have from the Jews : who both killed the Lord Jesus and the prophets and have persecuted us, and please not God, and are adversaries to all men." [3]

With the same thought in his mind, that suffering with Christ creates fellowship with one another, when later he has to blame the Galatians, his accusation is that they have failed to stand by the banner of the cross ; for himself, to mark the contrast with them, he seeks for no other honour than that of having been loyal to it :

" O senseless Galatians, who hath bewitched you that you should not obey the truth : before whose eyes Jesus Christ hath been set forth crucified among you ? " [4]

" Christ hath redeemed us from the curse of the law, being made a curse for us, as it is written : Cursed is everyone that hangeth on a tree." [5]

" God forbid that I should glory, save in the cross of our Lord Jesus Christ : by whom the world is crucified to me, and I to the world." [6]

In the Epistle to the Corinthians this attitude becomes much more emphatic. Not only, as before, is loyalty to Christ crucified his special glory, to him Christ crucified is everything. In that

[1] 1 Pet. iv 12, 13.  [2] 1 Pet. v 1.  [3] 1 Thess. ii 14, 15.
[4] Gal. iii 1.  [5] Gal. iii 13.  [6] Gal. vi 14.

consummation is summed up all the revelation that has come to man from God ; it is the whole content of all his own preaching ; anything else, by comparison, is of no value whatsoever ; mystery as this may appear to those who do not see, it is nevertheless the truth, and to understand it is the highest wisdom. Let us not forget that St Paul, here as in all his epistles, keeps within his vision this world as well as the next ; he is a statesman as well as a champion of the Gospel ; in combined passages such as these one sees the marvellous consistency of the Apostle's mind, holding to the same idea and principle in the midst of much that may appear wandering and disconnected.

" For the word of the cross, to them indeed that perish, is foolishness : but to them that are saved, that is to us, it is the power of God." [1]

" We preach Christ crucified : unto the Jews indeed a stumbling-block, and unto the Gentiles foolishness : but unto them that are called, both Jews and Greeks, Christ, the power of God and the wisdom of God." [2]

" I judged not myself to know anything among you, but Jesus Christ : and him crucified." [3]

" We speak the wisdom of God in a mystery, a wisdom which is hidden, which God ordained before the world, unto our glory : which none of the princes of this world knew. For if they had known it, they would never have crucified the Lord of glory." [4]

So he writes, with an emphasis almost of defiance, laying down his foundations before he justifies himself in the eyes of his quarrelsome and not too loyal neophytes in Corinth. They have turned against him ; they have cut him to the quick ; let them not think that this in any way puts him and his doctrine in the wrong. It does nothing of the kind ; it does but prove that he is one with his Master.

But when the misunderstanding is over, and they have been reconciled, and peace has again been restored, then he writes in quite another strain. Not only now is the cross of Christ his glory ; that he had said while his Corinthians were still inflicting sorrow upon him. It is also the very cause and source of his joy ; and the greater has been his sorrow, so much the greater now is the joy he reaps. Let them not be troubled because of all they have done ; in it all he has the more contentment, because by it the lesson of the cross has been the more thoroughly learnt. And he will show them why ; though before God we are everyone sinners, yet in Jesus, and by the cross of Jesus, we are now all justified and free. In his life he became as one of us, shouldering our crosses, carrying our griefs ; thus he has made us one with him, our cause has become his cause, and in return he has bestowed on us all his own riches.

---

[1] 1 Cor. i 18.  [2] 1 Cor. i 23, 24.
[3] 1 Cor. ii 2.  [4] 1 Cor. ii 7, 8.

The lesson of the Apostle is characteristic; in the midst of their repentance he makes his Corinthians rejoice, and that by reason of the very fault that they have committed; it is the lesson of his perfect charity.

"As the sufferings of Christ abound in us, so also by Christ doth our comfort abound." [1]

"Him, who knew no sin, he hath made sin for us: that we might be made the justice of God in him." [2]

"You know the grace of our Lord Jesus Christ, that being rich he became poor for your sakes: that through his poverty you might be rich." [3]

In the great dogmatic Epistle to the Romans the Apostle has yet another point of view. In Christ we are redeemed and freed from the bondage of the law. But, it occurs to him, men may ask, was it necessary, seeing Jesus Christ was God, that redemption should be won at such a cost? Strictly necessary, he answers, no; but when we take into account the love in the heart of him who paid the price, yes. Such a love would have no half measures; it would give full measure and flowing over; down in the depths as man was, it would pay the fullest price to lift him to the highest.

"For why did Christ, when as yet we were weak according to the time, die for the ungodly? For scarce for a just man will one die; yet perhaps for a good man some one would dare to die. But God commendeth his charity to us: because when as yet we were sinners according to the time, Christ died for us." [4]

Since the price has been paid so lavishly, with so little desert on our part, then he asks himself how we are to benefit by it to the full. The answer to him is clear; as by the cross we have received it, so in the cross we shall profit most by it. Likeness to Christ, in his life and in his death, gives us likeness in sonship and in glory.

"If sons, heirs also; heirs indeed of God, and coheirs with Christ: yet so, if we suffer with him, that with him we may also be glorified. For I reckon that the sufferings of this time are not worthy to be compared with the glory to come, that shall be revealed in us." [5]

Thus he rises to the ever-memorable climax, the conquest that has come with the love of the Man of Sorrows:

"Who then shall separate us from the love of Christ? Shall tribulation, or distress, or famine, or nakedness, or danger, or persecution, or the sword? (As it is written: For thy sake we are put to death all the day long. We are accounted as sheep for the slaughter.) But in all these things we overcome because of him that hath loved us. For I am sure that neither death, nor life, nor angels, nor principalities, nor powers, nor things present, nor things to come, nor might, nor height, nor depth, nor any other

[1] 2 Cor. i 5.   [2] 2 Cor. v 21.   [3] 2 Cor. viii 9.
[4] Rom. v 6-9.   [5] Rom. viii 17, 18.

creature shall be able to separate us from the love of God which is in Christ Jesus our Lord." [1]

Such is the victory the Man of Sorrows has won. If, by his death, death itself has been conquered, so by his sorrow, sorrow has been turned into joy, failure has become triumph, wounds are an eternal glory.

In the Epistles of the Captivity, as might well be expected, yet a further aspect is put before us. The main work of St Paul has now been done ; this " vessel of election," who was to " carry my name before the gentiles and kings and the children of Israel," and who was to be shown " how great things he must suffer for my sake," [2] had faithfully carried out his task ; now, as it were, in reward for his labour, lying bound in his Roman prison, he sees and is filled with the realisation of the mystical body of Christ. Of that body Jesus is the head, we human beings are the members ; from him life flows down to us, likeness to him comes now to have a new significance. We live, no, not we, but he lives in us ; and merely because his life is ours, we only wish to know how that life may best express itself, how he may best reproduce himself in us. Hence the new tone in which he speaks henceforward of the cross ; he no longer urges with encouragement ; it is enough that he should state the likeness and leave the matter there.

" Be ye therefore followers of God, as most dear children : and walk in love, as Christ also hath loved us and hath delivered himself for us, an oblation and a sacrifice to God for an odour of sweetness." [3]

" Husbands, love your wives, as Christ also loved the church and delivered himself up for it." [4]

This, in those times, was new doctrine indeed.

" Let this mind be in you, which was also in Christ Jesus : who being in the form of God, thought it not robbery to be equal to God : but emptied himself, taking the form of a servant, being made in the likeness of men, and in habit found as a man. He humbled himself, becoming obedient unto death, even to the death of the cross." [5]

" I, Paul . . . who now rejoice in my sufferings for you and fill up those things that are wanting of the sufferings of Christ, in my flesh, for his body, which is the church." [6]

" And you, when you were dead in your sins and the uncircumcision of your flesh, he hath quickened together with him, forgiving you all offences : blotting out the handwriting of the decree that was against us, which was contrary to us. And he hath taken the same out of the way, fastening it on the cross." [7]

---

[1] Rom. viii 35-39.　　　　　[2] Acts ix 15, 16.
[3] Eph. v 1, 2.　　　　　　　[4] Eph. v 25.
[5] Phil. ii 5-8.　　　　　　　[6] Col. i 24.
[7] Col. ii 13, 14.

### 3. *The Epistle to the Hebrews*

The Epistle to the Hebrews must needs be taken apart ; in it, and most explicitly, the sufferings of Jesus are given their most significant place with regard to men. Those to whom it was addressed were indeed in great trouble. Persecution had broken over them ; there was nothing but failure and destruction everywhere ; they had reason to ask themselves what could be the meaning of it all. If Christ had come to save the world, to give it a new life, why this continuous failure, this living death ?

The Apostle knows what they are feeling and is full of sympathy. To comfort and strengthen them he plays throughout upon three themes ; that so Christ had suffered before them, and that therefore by suffering they were made like to him ; that through suffering he had conquered ; that the fact of his suffering and glory was their sufficient encouragement and joy. In the first place, by his Passion and death, the oneness of the Saviour with the saved is secured ; in the Passion, on this account, the Saviour and his work are made perfect.

" We see Jesus, who was made a little lower than the angels, for the suffering of death, crowned with glory and honour : that through the grace of God he might taste death for all. For it became him, for whom are all things and by whom are all things, who had brought many children unto glory, to perfect the author of their salvation, by his passion. For both he that sanctifieth and they who are sanctified are all one. For which cause he is not ashamed to call them brethren." [1]

Being thus made one with man, not only is he himself made the perfect Saviour, not only is he a perfect high priest, but he has become, through experience of sorrow of his own, a high priest and advocate merciful and faithful.

" Wherefore, it behoved him in all things to be made like unto his brethren, that he might become a merciful and faithful high priest before God, that he might be a propitiation for the sins of the people." [2]

On this account, we may live in the sure hope, not only that we are redeemed, but also that he who has redeemed us, having given us so much and at such a price, will continue to give us all that he can give.

" Having therefore a great high priest that hath passed into the heavens, Jesus the Son of God : let us hold fast our confession. For we have not a high priest who cannot have compassion on our infirmities : but one tempted in all things as we are, without sin. Let us go therefore with confidence to the throne of grace : that we may obtain mercy and find grace in seasonable aid." [3]

This high priesthood, as Jesus himself many times declared, was

---

[1] Heb. ii 9-11.    [2] Heb. ii 17, 18.    [3] Heb. iv 14-16.

not his own assumption, but was the appointment of the Father. Of himself as man he stood among men ; of himself he suffered like other men ; of himself he prayed with men, taking their guilt upon himself though he would have none of his own ; in their midst he was the accepted high priest, and in the hearing of his prayers, in the merit of his sufferings, in the acceptance of his sacrifice, their prayers and sufferings and sacrifice were made acceptable.

"Who in the days of his flesh, with a strong cry and tears, offering up prayers and supplications to him that was able to save him from death, was heard for his reverence. And whereas indeed he was the Son of God, he learned obedience by the things which he suffered. And being consummated, he became, to all that obey him, the cause of eternal salvation : called by God a high priest according to the order of Melchisedech." [1]

Not only is he the high priest ; he is also the sacrifice. And in that he offered himself, of his own accord and with full knowledge, elected to suffer and to die, and in that now in heaven he continues to renew that offering, therefore there was and is no need that the sacrifice be made more than once.

" For Jesus is not entered into the Holies made with hands, the patterns of the true : but into heaven itself, that he may appear now in the presence of God for us. Nor yet that he should offer himself often, as the high priest entereth into the Holies every year with the blood of others : for then he ought to have suffered often from the beginning of the world. But now once, at the end of the ages, he hath appeared for the destruction of sin by the sacrifice of himself. And as it is appointed unto men once to die, and after this the judgement, so also Christ was offered once to exhaust the sins of many." [2]

From the consideration of this sacrifice and all that it has entailed, deliberate, entire, more awful than man can conceive, rendered yet more unfathomable by reason of the person of him, the God-man, who has endured it, the writer concludes to the great heinousness of sin. Since Christ has done all this, how much greater now must the evil of sin be !

" A man making void the law of Moses dieth without any mercy under two or three witnesses : how much more do you think he deserveth worse punishments, who hath trodden underfoot the Son of God and hath esteemed the blood of the testament unclean, by which he was sanctified, and hath offered an affront to the Spirit of grace ? " [3]

Hence the author draws to his final glorious conclusion. Let Jesus be to us not only the high priest and sacrifice, but also the model. He who has endured so much, and has proved the value of endurance, he is a worthy example for us all. Nay more ; since he was of all the most beloved, then to be beloved is to be marked

[1] Heb. v 7-10.    [2] Heb. ix 24-28.    [3] Heb. x 28, 29.

by suffering and sorrow. The lesson has been taught beyond a doubt ; we have but to take it to heart.

"And therefore we also . . . laying aside every weight and sin which surrounds us, let us run by patience to the fight proposed to us : looking on Jesus, the author and finisher of faith, who, having joy set before him, endured the cross, despising the shame, and now sitteth on the right hand of the throne of God. For think diligently upon him that endured such opposition from sinners against himself : that you be not wearied, fainting in your minds. For you have not yet resisted unto blood. And you have forgotten the consolation which speaketh to you, as unto children, saying : My son, neglect not the discipline of the Lord : neither be thou wearied whilst thou art rebuked by him. For whom the Lord loveth, he chastiseth : and he scourgeth every son whom he receiveth." [1]

And much more to this effect. As we read we recognise the source of that resistance unto death which then and ever after has formed the most glorious page of the Church's history. For them, indeed, teaching such as this was very living. The Epistle to the Hebrews is the charter of the martyrs ; and it is written with the blood of Jesus, the Man of Sorrows.

### 4. St John

Let us end as we began, with St John, the disciple whom the Man of Sorrows loved, and who, in the light of love and sorrow, read with greatest accuracy the heart of his Master. " He ought to have suffered often from the beginning of the world." [2] Can this sentence from the Epistle to the Hebrews be the source of that emblem which dominates St John's Apocalypse ? The Lamb of God—the Lamb that was slain—the Lamb that was slain from the days of Moses—the Lamb that was slain from the beginning of the world—the blood that " is being shed " for many unto the remission of sins ; we seem to see growing in his vision the glory of the Lamb whose light enlightens heaven.

" And the city hath no need of the sun, nor of the moon, to shine in it. For the glory of God hath enlightened it : and the Lamb is the lamp thereof." [3]

In his Gospel we have heard John's repeated lamentation, that " He came unto his own and his own received him not." At the moment when the greatest dereliction was looming up he has recorded the assurance of the Master that " sorrow shall be turned into joy " ; now when we come to his final word it is one of triumph, and the triumph is that of " the Lamb that was slain from the beginning of the world." [4]

" And I saw : and behold in the midst of the throne, and in the

---

[1] Heb. xii 1-6.  [2] Heb. ix 26.
[3] Apoc. xxi 23.  [4] Apoc. xiii 8.

midst of the four living creatures, and in the midst of the ancients, a Lamb standing, as it were slain." [1]

" And they sang a new canticle, saying : Thou art worthy, O Lord, to take the book and to open the seals thereof ; because thou wast slain and hast redeemed us to God, in thy blood, out of every tribe and tongue and people and nation." [2]

" The Lamb that was slain is worthy to receive power and divinity and wisdom and strength and honour and glory and benediction." [3]

As are the triumph and glory of the Lamb, so is the triumph of those who follow him. The lesson has been taught and learnt ; all things have been made new ; as with him, so with them, with them because of him, the cross and all it stands for, suffering and sorrow and distress, have become an ideal, not a doom, to which mankind has learnt to rise. The curse of life has been conquered ; men have found the way " to rejoice that they are accounted worthy to suffer something for his sake " ; and in that rejoicing have wrested from death its victory, have deprived it of its sting.

" After this, I saw a great multitude, which no man could number, of all nations and tribes and peoples and tongues, standing before the throne and in sight of the Lamb, clothed with white robes and with palms in their hands." [4]

" And he said to me : These are they who have come out of great tribulation and have washed their robes and have made them white in the blood of the Lamb. Therefore they are before the throne of God : and they serve him day and night in his temple. And he that sitteth on the throne shall dwell over them. They shall no more hunger nor thirst : neither shall the sun fall on them, nor any heat. For the Lamb, which is in the midst of the throne, shall rule them and shall lead them to the fountains of the waters of life : and God shall wipe away all tears from their eyes." [5]

At the beginning we have heard John lamenting ; here at the end we hear him rejoicing ; we understand now the source of that courage which he inspires in his children, when in his Epistle he bids them lose all that they may gain all.

" Wonder not, brethren, if the world hate you." [6]

" In this we have known the charity of God, because he hath laid down his life for us : and we ought to lay down our lives for the brethren." [7]

Thus does John interpret the cross of Jesus Christ as the key to life, on earth and in heaven ; the source of all that is noblest and best in man, the mark above every other of that very civilisation which man has been bold to call Christian. *In hoc signo vinces.* " In this sign shalt thou conquer."

---

[1] Apoc. v 6.　　　　[2] Apoc. v 9.　　　　[3] Apoc. v 12.
[4] Apoc. vii 9.　　　　[5] Apoc. vii 14-17.
[6] 1 John iii 13.　　　　[7] 1 John iii 16.

Of a truth, then, the Man of Sorrows is also the Man of Joy ; he has fulfilled his prophecy in himself. He is, moreover, the Man of Victory. Without the cross of Christ what would this world be ; what would be the value of eternity ? With the life and death of Jesus Christ a new thing has come into the world, a new standard by which all things are judged. He has declared a new doctrine, and by his life has proved it : that suffering and sorrow are not the curse of man, but his privilege ; that he who would do the greatest things is he who can endure the greatest ; that only by suffering and sorrow can the evil of life be overcome ; that the life of trial is the life which, by its first and noblest instinct, human nature most reveres, because it is most like his own. He " came not to destroy but to perfect " ; nowhere more is it manifest than here. Human nature measures worth by suffering ; it esteems in proportion as it sees the brave endurance of sorrow ; and Jesus Christ has taken this truest trait in man, has purified and made it perfect, has identified it with himself, has given it back to man to be his abiding ideal in this world, has lifted it up with himself into heaven and there has enthroned it, " the Lamb slain from the beginning of the world." We understand the better now why, when he rose from the dead, he was careful to show that he retained in his hands and feet and side his precious wounds, carrying them with him as trophies to his place by the right hand of the Father, " ever living to make intercession for us."

✠ALBAN GOODIER.

# XIV

## CHRIST, PRIEST AND REDEEMER

### §I: INTRODUCTORY

THE Redemption is a fundamental doctrine of the Catholic Church, and references to it are to be found in many of the Councils and formularies of the Faith. In the Council of Trent, for instance, there is explicit mention of it in several decrees. That on original sin declares that Adam, having transgressed the command of God, forfeited the gift of holiness and justice which he had possessed, and the whole human race was involved in the same loss. Death came into the world as the consequence of sin, the death of the soul, and the evil plight of mankind was remedied by one means alone —namely, the merit of the one mediator, our Lord Jesus Christ, who reconciled us to God in his Blood.

The decrees on Justification and the Sacrifice of the Mass make explicit the manner of this mediation. The God of mercies and of all consolation sent Jesus Christ his Son in the fulness of time that he might redeem both the Jews and the Gentiles. God gave Christ to be the propitiation for our sins and the sins of the whole world. It behoved that another priest according to the order of Melchisedech should arise, our Lord Jesus Christ. He offered himself up once on the altar of the cross to the Father, and by means of his death won for us an eternal redemption.

Two conclusions follow immediately from the reading of these passages. The first is that the doctrine of Christ as Priest and Redeemer cannot be isolated from the other doctrines of the Faith. They are all of a piece, and hence the doctrines to be exposed in the following pages presuppose what has already been treated in other essays in this volume, principally the essays on Original Sin, Grace, and the Incarnation. The second conclusion is that the doctrine of the redemption is independent of any theory of sacrifice based on history or philosophical analysis. The teaching of the Church on sacrifice and priesthood has for its basis the inspired word, especially the Epistle to the Hebrews. We know that Christ was a priest, that he offered himself as a propitiatory victim to the Father, and that the shedding of his blood was the salvation of the world.

Nevertheless, as St Paul himself compared the priesthood of Christ with other priesthoods, and illustrated his sacrifice by reference to other sacrifices, it is not superfluous for the theologian to begin with an analysis of the meaning of sacrifice in general and to use that analysis in his interpretation of the sacrifice of Calvary.

477

Not that the meaning of Calvary is dictated by any particular theory of sacrifice, but the method is better adapted to give a setting to the dogma and to show the harmony and logic of its implications. The chief objection to such a method is that the meaning of sacrifice is controverted, and it may be thought that a writer who adopts one view is doing so at the expense of another, and taking sides when it is his duty to be impartial. On the other hand, the reader must suffer if nothing is said about the nature of sacrifice in general. Hence, in the following pages, I have attempted to set down the general constituents of sacrifice without determining which is to be considered the principal in the Christian sacrifice. The conclusions do not lead on inevitably to any one particular theory of the sacrifice of the Mass ; that issue is not prejudged, and, to repeat, the redemptive character of the Lord's act is not derived from any theory but from the teaching of the Church, Scripture and Tradition.

## §II : SACRIFICE AND PRIESTHOOD

*Meaning of sacrifice* THE meaning and nature of sacrifice have been within recent years the objects of close study. Various theories and definitions have been proposed, some of which have had to be abandoned, either because they did not cover all the facts or because they rested on inadequate conceptions of God and man. The chief difficulty has been to find some common feature in all the multitudinous forms which sacrifice has taken. Sacrifice is essentially a religious act ; in fact, it is almost always the central act of a cult, and as religion is universal in time and place, the sacrificial rite has had as many vicissitudes as religion itself.

The simplest and quickest method to arrive at a definition is to argue from the importance of sacrifice in all religious worship. Religion is comprised in reverence and worship or adoration, and it would seem as if sacrifice were nothing more than the expression in a definite form of this emotion and inclination. Mankind always brings its wishes or emotions to completion in an outward act, in a straightforward or symbolical expression. Goodwill to friends is expressed in gifts. Joy in feasting, sorrow in beating of the breast or some similar action. Now in his relations with God man is filled with awe and he is aware to some extent of God's rights and claims. This experience expresses itself spontaneously in a special form of homage, and homage is made concrete in that again special form called sacrifice. Just, then, as we react in certain definite ways in the presence of fellow human beings, or of sorrow or injustice, so too all men confronted with God tend to behave in a definite manner ; they bow down and offer gifts in sacrifice. Were this the place, it would be interesting to try and show how strong an argument could be built inversely from the fact of sacrifice to the existence of God. The relevant point for the moment is however this : that sacrifice is identical with the spontaneous act of homage paid by man to God ; it is that homage expressed in the offering of a gift. Not that we are bound therefore to hold that this form of homage is a purely human device. It would appear that sacrifice is part of the original revelation. Besides the sacrifice being a natural expression of man's nature, it is also the revealed will of God.

Now the history of religions shows us that the primary conception of God, if never completely lost, can nevertheless be covered over with human fancies and human passions. The primitive and simple conception is almost lost in anthropomorphic mythologies ; the pure idea, which needs high religious experience or philosophic abstractions to keep it integral, easily splits up into deities of one particular virtue or even vice, and is brought down and imaged in some sensible object or place. Correspondingly, the sacrifice takes on a local colour and expresses human feelings and ideas. There are many gods : some to be fed, some to be placated : they are kindly and ready to bless harvests or marriage or battle, or they are cruel and require human victims. So low, indeed, may the religious worship fall that it blends with superstition and magic. But beneath all the superstructure which human savagery and childishness have imposed on the religious act, there is to be discerned the basic tendency to pay homage to a supreme being. There are, moreover, other characteristics which are so common as to serve as a clue to the nature of sacrifice. In form, for instance, there is always the presentation or offering of a gift—and this is always the essential feature ; this presentation is a public act, usually in the name of the community, and being public and social the act has a ritual, which grows increasingly solemn and sacred from interference ; and lastly, there is the odd and often ignored fact that the gift or votive offering is prepared to be consumed as a meal, though the meal is not the essential part of the sacrifice. The motive which appears to underlie this preparation of a meal seems in the crudest ritual to be that the gods, like men, are pleased at being entertained ; but it should be observed that in this motive a far higher conception is latent, which gradually becomes explicit. In most of the more debased motives we can in fact discover concealed the highest, and they may fitly be distinguished as petition, thanksgiving and propitiation, all attached to the impulse to pay homage.

We have, then, three main motives all based on homage expressing *Propitiation* themselves in the ceremonious offering of a gift, which, if its nature permits, is prepared as food. One word is necessary as to the motive of propitiation. Not all even of the Jewish sacrifices are propitiatory ; nevertheless, the sense of guilt seems rarely to be altogether absent, and perhaps the imagery of a cruel God is nothing but a perversion of the anger which God is thought to feel towards sinners.

When the expiatory note is dominant, then commonly the offering is a victim, and some symbolic act, such as blood-letting or slaying, is part of the ritual. By custom and language the word sacrifice has come to be used as almost synonymous with slaying or mactation, but it should be noticed that in many sacrifices there is no such action present, or at least manifestly present.

*Union with God*

In the higher stages of religion the cruder forms of sacrifice disappear, but the essential rite of homage remains ; and in that motive all that is best in natural religions expands. The worshipper begins to see that his acts are symbolical of his own inward state, that the offering given to God represents the fact of his own dependence and his duty of obedience and dedication. The nature of God is better understood, and the end and ideal of man unfold themselves as both the service of God and simultaneously the enjoyment of God by union with him. That is, homage is not only a duty but also a method of approach ; worship is directed to God and lifts the worshipper up ; and God rewards the worshipper by friendship. And so now we can enlarge the idea of sacrifice by saying that it is an act of homage which furthers union with God, one's Maker and Last End ; and the way that this is done is through the offering of a gift which symbolises interior oblation, and perhaps repentance as well. The gift is sanctified and made holy with God's holiness, since it passes into his possession, if it is accepted by God. His acceptance passes, so to speak, through the gift to the offerer, and the alliance or friendship is ratified by the eating, not by God, but by the worshipper, of what is holy with God's holiness. Sacrifice has thus shown itself as a mode of mediation between God and man.

*Mediation*

It is in this mediation that the function of the priest is properly seen. In the religions of many primitive peoples the priest is often a sorcerer and magician as well. But even these accretions serve to bring out the office of priesthood, for they suggest a human being who has superhuman powers and closer relations with the God ; and the priest is a kind of mediator between his fellows and the Supreme Power. He is generally representative, a patriarch or head of a clan or a king, as in Polynesia and in parts of Asia and among the American Indians. He is a man specially chosen out by the Eskimos and Kafirs. He is always a guide and a mediator, the go-between, who can propitiate God or bring special favours on the worshippers. As usual the clearest example is to be seen in the Old Testament, where Moses acts as leader from on high to the Israelites and ascends to Mount Sinai and communes with God, and the priests of Aaron act as representatives of the people before God. The priest therefore is the representative of all, chosen out for his excellence to act as mediator between God and man. We have now all that is required to understand the priesthood and the sacrifice of Christ.

§III: CHRIST AS PRIEST OFFERING SACRIFICE

THE Council of Ephesus (A.D. 431), embodying the words of St Paul *The doctrine* to the Ephesians, " Christ hath delivered himself for us, an oblation *outlined* and a sacrifice to God for an odour of sweetness," [1] declared : " For he offered himself up for us as an odour of sweetness to God the Father.   Hence if any one say that the Divine Logos himself was not made an High Priest and Apostle, let him be anathema."   The same declaration is to be found in the well-known passage from the twenty-second session of the Council of Trent, and it is abundantly confirmed by the witness of Scripture.   The classical statement of the priesthood of Christ is to be found in the Epistle to the Hebrews, where the sacrifices of the Old Law are compared with the sacrifice of Christ, the High Priest, and great emphasis is laid on the propitiatory nature of his sacrifice.

Now, as Christ is said to be the great High Priest, the pattern of all others, we should expect to find all the characteristics of sacrifice and priesthood previously described embodied in his office and act ; and this expectation is fulfilled.   He is the Elect, not of man only but of God ; he is a King, a representative not of the Jews merely, but of all mankind, and he is the one Mediator.[2]   Moreover, this act of sacrifice is accomplished in a ritual oblation of a gift, which is immolated and becomes the food of those who worship and accept Christ's sovereignty and gospel.   The motive, lastly, is one of homage which contains in it reverence for God the Creator, expiation for sin, petition and, finally, love and thanksgiving which bring union and holiness.   Two characteristics are, however, specially in evidence, and these two are excellently expressed in the one word Atonement.   There is expiation for sin by the shedding of blood, and that blood is the seal of a new covenant in which man is in a special and supernatural way united through the Victim with God himself.

Such, then, is in outline the doctrine of the sacrifice of Christ *Types in* as Priest and Victim.   We must now fill in the picture.   According *the Old* to Catholic teaching the Passion of Christ was the one great medi- *Testament* ating sacrifice in which Christ was both High Priest and Victim. This dogma has been denied by non-Catholics who profess to see in the suffering of Christ nothing but an example of high moral worth, but the history of the Jews, the express statements in the New Testament, and the very nature of Christ's passion are overwhelmingly clear in their evidence.   We have in the Old Testament the record of the sacrifices of Abel, Noah, Abraham, and Melchisedech, which point to a more perfect sacrifice of which they are the types. Type and prophecy are seen again in the story of the Exodus, when, we are told, a lamb was eaten with unleavened bread and blood

[2] 1 Tim. ii 5 and Heb. ix 15.

sprinkled on the lintels and side-posts and the Feast of the Passover instituted. In the twenty-fourth chapter we read in connection with the promulgation of the Law that Moses " took the blood (of sacrifice) and sprinkled it upon the people and said : This is the blood of the covenant, which the Lord hath made with you concerning all these words." But the favourite type of the sacrifice and priest to come is, to the author of the Epistle to the Hebrews, Melchisedech. He says that " no one takes the honourable office of High Priest upon himself, but only accepts it when called to it by God as Aaron was. So Christ also did not claim for himself the honour of being High Priest, but was appointed to it by him who said to him, My Son art thou : I have to-day begotten thee ; as also in another passage he says, Thou art a priest for ever, according to the order of Melchisedech." And he goes on a few verses afterwards to repeat, " For God himself calls him a priest for ever, according to the order of Melchisedech," and gives in a later chapter a short account of the sacrifice of this Priest-King of Salem, and proves from the difference between his priesthood and the Aaronic priesthood the perfection of the new covenant instituted by him, of whom God said, " The Lord has sworn and will not recall his words, thou art a priest for ever." All the old sacrifices were inferior to the new unique sacrifice and but types of it. Christ it was who " once for all entered the holy place securing an eternal redemption, and he is the mediator of a new covenant, in order that, since a life has been given in atonement for the offences committed under the first covenant, those who have been called may receive the eternal inheritance which has been promised to them." These inspired words state clearly the priesthood of Christ, and they are full of significance as unfolding to us the meaning of the Redemption.

*The fulfilment*

The words of Christ himself are equally definite, though a treatment of them will be deferred till the sections on the Redemption ; and his behaviour in the Passion is throughout one of Priest and Victim. On the eve of it, he said : " For them do I sanctify (or dedicate) myself " ; [1] he goes through a ceremonial rite which recalls the great sacrifices of the past ; he blesses and offers a prayer of thanksgiving ; he speaks of the shedding of his blood in a new covenant which ends the former covenant initiated by Moses in the sprinkling of the blood of sacrifice ; and he gives the Apostles to understand that this is the true Pasch, and that he is the Lamb of God who takes away the sins of the world. He gives his life freely, but, if we follow the suggestive explanation of some theologians, he becomes sorrowful after he has surrendered himself as Victim. The mandate of God lies heavy upon him in the Garden, and he can no longer draw back. " He is offered because it is his own will," and " He is led as a sheep to the slaughter." The Jews take away his life by crucifying him and " the Lord laid on him

[1] John xvii 19.

the iniquity of us all." But by laying down his life for sin " He sees a long-lived seed," [1] because God accepted the sacrifice and exalted him ; and so he " swallowed down death that we might be made heirs of life everlasting." [2]

These texts from Isaias bear out exactly what has already been laid down as constituting the nature of sacrifice. There is a High Priest and a Victim, and that Victim is offered to God and through a bloody immolation. The sacrifice is visible and public ; the priest is representative, " the King of the Jews," as his enemies called him with an irony they did not perceive ; and, finally, the Victim is a propitiation, and a symbol—on him is laid our iniquity, who in the sequel is to be the food of a new life. In the Epistle to the Hebrews all these constituents are mentioned, and what is more, the relative importance of these constituents and their relation one to another can, without great difficulty, be deduced from the inspired account. " Every High Priest," we are told, " taken from among men, is ordained for men in the things that appertain to God, that he may offer up gifts and sacrifices for sin " ; [3] and later on, the same definition is given : " Every High Priest is appointed to offer gifts and sacrifices." [4] The High Priest, therefore, is chosen out to be a representative, and the choice is made by God himself. " So Christ did not glorify himself that he might be made High Priest, but he that said unto him, My Son art thou. . . ." [5] He was, moreover, " holy, innocent, undefiled, separated from sinners . . . who needed not daily to offer sacrifices, first for his own sins and then for the people's, for this he did once in offering himself." [6] The manner of his sacrifice was therefore by oblation, the oblation of a gift which was himself, and this gift was also a sin-offering, " being once offered to exhaust the sins of many," [7] " by a merciful and faithful High Priest . . . that he might be a propitiation for the sins of the people." [8] This offering, therefore, was sealed in death and in a ritual replacing that of the old covenant with its sprinkling of blood. In the ninth chapter the ritual connected with the Tabernacle is compared with that of Christ who " by a greater and more perfect Tabernacle . . . and by his own blood entered once into the Holies, having obtained eternal redemption." Moses sprinkled the blood, and similarly Christ through his blood, " by one oblation hath perfected for ever them that are sanctified." [9] Hence there is the consummation of the sacrifice in a new covenant, whereby " we have a confidence in the entering into the Holies by the blood of Christ, a new and living way which he hath dedicated for us through the veil, that is to say, his flesh. . . ." [10]

The sacrifice of Christ, therefore, to sum up, contains an oblation of himself as a sin-offering. It is therefore a propitiatory

[1] Isa. liii 10.    [2] I Pet. iii 22.    [3] v 1.
[4] viii 3.    [5] v 5.    [6] vii 26-27.
[7] ix 28.    [8] ii 17.    [9] x 14.    [10] x 19, 20.

sacrifice with the shedding of the blood of the victim. That blood cleanses the world, and because the sacrifice is acceptable to God a new covenant of friendship is struck in which the worshippers are sanctified. Such, in terms of sacrifice, is the account given by the inspired writer of the Atonement or Redemption. The final purpose of Christ's action, symbolised in his Priesthood and offering of himself as a Victim in obedience to a divine plan, must now be explained in the second part, the Redemptive character of the Passion and death of Christ.

There remain, however, several questions connected with the Sacrifice of Christ which have had to be put on one side till the truth and nature of that sacrifice had been established.

*Origin of Christ's priesthood*

The first of these regards the origin and exercise of the priest-hood of Christ. The majority of Catholic theologians hold that the ordination of Christ coincided with the union of the Word with flesh.

But this possession from the first moment of his life of the priest-hood does not necessarily mean that Christ was offering sacrifice always and without interruption. There is one school of theologians which asserts this. For them the Sacrifice of Calvary is only the consummation, or seal, of a life which has been sacrificial throughout. The view may appear to provide a solution for many of the difficulties felt by theologians in explaining the Mass, and it has for its support certain texts from the Epistle to the Hebrews. But it has against it, in the opinion of many, that the meaning of sacrifice is stretched very far when we have to group together under one head the Passion and the marriage feast at Cana ; and as the sacrificial act of the Redemption has been placed by dogmatic decisions of the Church principally, if not exclusively, in the death of our Lord upon the Cross, it is wise not to lay too much stress on the uniformity of all the actions of our Lord. The theologians of this school teach indeed a difference of degree between the importance of Calvary and the preceding acts of Christ the Redeemer, and further-more they admit that the sacrifice is visible and ritually expressed on the Cross. Their view is therefore tenable, though to many it does not appear entirely satisfactory. Sacrifice is usually, they say, an outward sign of an invisible self-offering. Our Lord, it is suggested, being God as well as Man, had no need for this outward expression of his obedience and self-surrender to the Father's will. This, while true, does not, however, cover the purpose of Christ's sacrifice. He was the Son of Man and representative of men before God. It is doubtful, therefore, whether the nature of his sacrifice could have been exhibited without some outward acts which would declare that he was the Lamb of God taking away the sins of the world and the High Priest of that world making oblation in its name to God.

For these, then, and other reasons most theologians distinguish between the office of Christ as Priest and that readiness to offer himself as a victim in whatever way the Father should ordain, and the actual accomplishment of the redemption on the altar of the Cross.   On the Cross the sacrifice which began on the eve of Good Friday was consummated.

One difficulty, however, rises out of this mediatorship.   Christ *Priest and* is both God and Man and he is Priest and Victim.   How, it may *Victim* be asked, can " these things be " ?

The answer will be understood if we recall that Christ is God, that he is Man, and that he is the God-Man.[1]   As God he is the recipient of Sacrifice, because it is the Trinity which is worshipped and propitiated in Sacrifice.   Some theologians, indeed, regard the Father, the first Person, as the acceptor of the sacrifice of the Cross, and the words of Trent, Christ " offered himself unto God the Father," and certain texts in the New Testament seem to support the view.   But generally the expression used at Trent is taken to be one of appropriation, a term explained in another essay, which means shortly that certain actions common to all three Persons are attributed by convenience and analogy to one Person above the others.   The expression in this context is, however, still more simply explained by the fact that Christ is regarded there as the God-Man, " the one mediator of God and men, the Man Jesus Christ."   However mysterious and above reason this conjunction of the natures in one Person must ever remain, it does allow for the possibility of God using manhood as a propitiatory gift, endowing it with his own personal merit, and so combining the representative and the pleasing and holy.   If Christ had been the Word and no Man, then he could not have been a Mediator, for there would have been nothing between himself and the Father save a distinction of personality.   If he had been but a Man, again mediation in the strict sense would have been impossible, because the gulf between sinful man and God would not have been bridged. The mysterious conjunction of two natures does, however, resolve the difficulty ; and as long as the mediation is assigned to One who does not lose anything of the Godhead by being Man, nor anything of his Manhood by being God, we can understand how Christ though God can offer sacrifice to God.

The difficulty arising out of the identity of Priest and Victim in the redemptive sacrifice is still less serious because there is no obvious inconsistency in a priest becoming a victim of his own sacrifice.   As our Lord had both roles and alone could discharge the debt as representative, it is fitting that he should be both offerer and offered.   If, indeed, the office of the priest entailed the slaying of the Victim, then the difficulty would be serious indeed, but it

[1] *Cf*. St Augustine, *De Civ. Dei*, x 20, where the solution followed in the text is given.

was the Jews who shed his blood : our Lord did not take his own life.

*Last Supper and the Passion*　　There are two other points which demand explanation before we can pass on. The first is concerned with the relation of the Last Supper to the Passion. The subject belongs really to the essay on the Holy Eucharist, and so a brief statement must suffice here. Catholic theology is quite definite in holding that the description of the Last Supper is clearly sacrificial. The parallels with the Passover and the sacrifice of Melchisedech, quite apart from the direct evidence of the words and actions of Christ, suffice to prove this. But its precise relation to the Passion is a matter of dispute. All agree that we must look first of all to the Cross. There is the scene of the Redemption and all else must be subordinated to or fitted in with that. But while some regard the Last Supper as part of one enduring act of sacrifice which reached its consummation in the death on Calvary, others make the latter the one absolute sacrifice and relate the Last Supper to it as another but relative sacrifice. That is to say, our Lord, in view of the one redeeming act, instituted a rite which would be a memory of it and enable his followers to share in it by a mystic or real immolation accomplished in the words pronounced over the bread and wine. In that way Calvary would remain the one sacrifice, with the Last Supper and the Mass subordinated to it as a relative sacrifice. The unity of the sacrifice would thus be one of subordination or dependence.[1] Others, on the contrary, deny that the Last Supper can be divided from Calvary so as to make a sacrifice within one sacrifice. They maintain that the various elements of a true sacrifice are made apparent each in its own proper place, and the Last Supper and Calvary are one. The oblation of the victim is exhibited in the evening, a rite instituted to perpetuate the offering, and without a break the sacrifice goes on till it is manifested in the dying glory of Christ on the Cross. Both interpretations of tradition are allowable, and the Church has not decided in favour of either.

*Eternal Priesthood of Christ*　　There is one other question which is so important as to merit a long explanation, and it concerns the eternal priesthood of Christ. Much is covered by this phrase. The Epistle to the Hebrews speaks of " the everlasting priesthood of Christ," whereby he is able " to save for ever them that come to God by him ; always living to make intercession for us. For it was fitting that we should have such a high priest . . . who needeth not daily . . . to offer sacrifices . . . for this he did once, in offering himself." [2] St John, again, in the Apocalypse described Christ as a Lamb slain but living, as one clothed as a victim who makes men priests unto God. So clear is the testimony of Scripture as to the ever-continuing priesthood of Christ that it can be called a dogma of the

[1] Billot ; *De Sacramentis*, I, pp. 604-605 (Rome, 1924).
[2] vii 24-27.

Faith.  But the precise manner in which Christ now and for ever exercises that priesthood is not so clear, and there are differences of view.  We may put aside first of all the view of the Socinians who so exaggerate the doctrine of the heavenly sacrifice as to refuse to admit any earthly sacrifice at all on the part of Christ.  Among Catholic theologians two tendencies have been marked.  The Protestant emphasis on the heavenly sacrifice has led the majority of Catholics to emphasise the sacrificial character of the Mass, and to pass lightly over the doctrine of the eternal priesthood apart from that.  This omission has had for effect that in many modern theological books the full meaning of the Resurrection and the Pauline doctrine of Christ's living intercession have been left to some extent undeveloped.  Christ is pictured as still in the Garden of Gethsemani, as subject to grief and waiting on the acceptance of his Father ; and no difference is made between the Risen Christ with his work consummated and Christ in the agony of its accomplishment.  Under such a conception the significant doctrine of our Lady as the great suppliant of her Son in the Mystical Body of the Church, of which he is the Head, is missed.  Some even minimise the priesthood of Christ so much as to suppose, like Lugo, that after the end of the Eucharistic sacrifice on earth, the priestly function of Christ will cease.

The other tendency is marked by a strong, and as some would *The heavenly sacrifice* think a too extreme, opposition to this.  Our Lord in his risen life in Heaven continues to perform actively the functions of a priest.  The manner in which Christ does this is explained variously.  Thalhofer holds that our Lord is ever renewing that act of obedience which led to the Passion, and this interior submission is sufficient for a sacrifice because the wounds of that Passion continue to manifest the will of Christ.  A number of French theologians go further, and the latest statement of their view can be found in the massive work of P. Lepin.  Despite small differences, P. Condren, Cardinal de Bérulle, M. Olier and P. Lepin are at one in holding that Christ in Heaven continues for ever to make an external and visible offering of his sacred body, but whereas on Calvary that body was destroyed in death, in Heaven it is annihilated, so to speak, in the radiant devouring glory of the divine life.  The two schools have this in common, that a sacrifice is being actively offered in Heaven ; but whereas the German theologians deem an interior act of homage ever renewed to be sufficient, P. Lepin introduces a new external offering and a new form of immolation.

A third view lays great emphasis on the eternal priesthood of Christ, but denies that a new positive sacrificial act of Christ is required to ensure the continuation of that priesthood.  According to this interpretation, our Lord was sacrificed on Calvary ; " he died for our sins, and he rose again for our justification." [1]  That

---

[1] Rom. iv 25.

is to say, the Victim was slain, and the Victim was accepted by God in the sign of the Resurrection. " For which reason God also hath exalted him and given him a name which is above all names." [1] Once accepted the Victim belongs entirely to God and remains sacrosanct—that is, invested with the holiness of an object which is a possession of God and pleasing to him. At the same time it continues as a pledge of the new covenant of friendship with God and man, a constant reminder, a kind of incorruptible relic or reliquary. But furthermore, as Christ was both priest and victim, his priesthood is not only ratified by the acceptance, but priesthood and victimhood are merged in one, so that the offering of the great sacrifice continues so to speak in the everlasting appeal of that Lamb slain but alive, dead but still speaking. There is no need for a new offering, no need for any new act, because the Priest is the Victim most pleasing to God, and the state of that Victim is one never-ending pontifical appeal. Therefore " being consummated he became to all that obey him the cause of eternal salvation, being called by God a High Priest according to the order of Melchisedech." [2]

To put this in another way, Christ the High Priest rising from the grave carried with him the spoils of victory, his own Body, and ascending into heaven presents himself as the sacrificial Mediator between God and man. As St Augustine reminds us : the Passion of Christ the Lord, the words of the Lord, the offering of the saving Victim, the holocaust acceptable to God, is the sacrifice of the evening. " That evening sacrifice he made in the Resurrection a morning gift." This adjective of the " morning " brings out the part of God the Father in accepting the sacrifice. Our Lord's offering was not for himself but for mankind, and as he was the representative priest, so he was the representative victim, expiating and propitiating. If then that sacrifice be accepted, the blessing will flow from and through him to all the world, and hence we may say that his priesthood or his mediating function will be confirmed in the acceptance and be his eternal title ; he will be seen, as it were, lit up in the glory of the divine light, a priestly figure sure in his mediation. And as he is the Victim, that mediation is the gift of his own glorified body to those whom he has rescued from death. The two rôles, therefore, of active and passive priesthood harmonise in a wonderful unity. His priesthood continues but he need never exercise it again after the Resurrection, for the sacrifice has been successful, the Victim is given over to God, and as he, the priest, is the Victim, the sacrifice continues for ever in the everlasting presence at the right hand of the Father of a Victim, whose wounded glory embraces priesthood, propitiation and life to those who are redeemed through him.

To make this conception still more clear, we may compare the fulness of Christ the Redeemer with the fulness of the Godhead.

[1] Phil. ii 9.    [2] Heb. v 3-10.

As God is so rich in possessions that he cannot receive increase and is therefore stabilised in an immobility which is at the same time unruffled activity ; and as that activity manifests itself in giving —for good squanders itself (*est diffusivum sui*) and of the fulness we have all received—so Christ now is fixed in the full glory of his priesthood and has no need to continue an active offering of himself or renew the one redemptive sacrifice. And so far from this unchanging state denoting loss, it spells fulness, and with fulness comes the gift of himself to mankind in the Holy Eucharist, and the communication of that priesthood to the race of men with all the redemptive blessings which attend such a giving.

This view has been developed at some length, because, whatever its intrinsic merits may be, it serves excellently to bring out the nature of the Redemption. Christ continues his priesthood in heaven, but without the need of any active offering or immolation of himself. His presence in heaven as the accepted and risen Victim is sufficient to constitute his eternal priesthood. " Jesus entered into the Heaven itself that he may appear now in the presence of God for us." [1] " For his intercession consists in this that he perpetually exhibits himself before the eternal Father in the humanity which he had assumed for our salvation : and as long as he ceases not to offer himself, he opens the way for our reception into eternal life " (Gregory the Great). The Resurrection therefore and the Ascension are the final stages in the sacrificial act of Christ. The Preface of the Mass tells us that our Lord " by dying destroyed our death and won back life by his rising." The end of the redemptive sacrifice was attained when God raised Christ from the grave. The death of Christ was indeed the cause of our salvation, but the fruit of the victory is seen in the glory which descends upon the victim in the Resurrection and in the translation of that victim in the Ascension to the place of honour at God's right hand ; and as the purpose of the sacrifice was the giving of divine life to man, the glory communicated to the representative is transmitted through him to all who worship in his name. Thus we are back at the essential constituents of sacrifice : offering, external manifestation, the passing of the victim from the worshipper's into God's possession, and the acceptance of that sacrifice by God and the return made. It now remains to work out this sacrifice of Christ in the theology of the Redemption.

### §IV: CHRIST THE REDEEMER

" FOR there is one God : and one mediator of God and men, the *Mediation* man Christ Jesus who gave himself a redemption for all." [2] In *and* these words St Paul sums up the Catholic doctrine. The word *Redemption* mediation may be used as synonymous with redemption, though

---

[1] Heb. ix 24.                    [2] 1 Tim. ii 5.

the implications of the two words are distinct. By mediation is meant an action which serves to reunite or reconcile two alien or opposing objects or powers. The Mediator will belong to both. When, then, it is used of Christ it means that he, the God-Man, was able to reconcile men with God. How he did this is not expressed so well in the word as in the equivalent " redemption " ; for mediation might suggest that Christ was a kind of intermediary in nature half-way between the divine and the human. Such a conception, which is to be found in certain philosophies and cults, is far from that of the Catholic Faith. And here the word redemption brings out the meaning ; Christ who is fully divine as well as fully human, and therefore not an intermediary filling up a gap, can perform some action which will create a friendship between God and man. Hence by his nature he is the one Mediator, and by his action he wins atonement.

The action then which determines more exactly the mediatorship of Christ is the Redemption, and the Church has defined this at the Council of Trent : " If anyone say that this (original) sin of Adam is taken away by any other remedy than the merit of the one Mediator, our Lord Jesus Christ, who hath reconciled us to God in his own blood . . . let him be anathema." These words, which recall the words of St Paul in the letter to the Colossians, " in him it hath well pleased the Father that all fulness should dwell : and through him to reconcile all things to himself, making peace through the blood of his cross," [1] bring out three points. First, our Lord is the one Mediator ; secondly, the cause of offence, namely original sin, is taken away ; and lastly, it is taken away on the Cross. The conclusion, then, to be drawn is that whatever sacrifice be offered in the Christian dispensation, and whatever priesthood may exist, they are not independent of Christ's mediation, but rather tributaries of it ; and again for a proper notion of the Redemption we must go to the Sacrifice of Calvary.

*Redemption and sacrifice*

It will be well then always to keep in mind, in the study of the Redemption, its sacrificial character, and to elucidate the meaning of the Redemption by what has already been furnished by the analysis of sacrifice. Otherwise there is the danger of a one-sided statement or of the over-emphasis of some image or analogy. As we shall see, even the very word redemption has led to false problems and difficulties, and there is always the temptation present to reduce the mysterious and divine operations of God to terms which serve only if their relative inadequacy or analogical character be kept in mind.

*Reparation and restoration*

As stated in the dogmatic utterance of the Council of Trent, the story of the Redemption begins with original sin, and ends with the Sacrifice of the Cross. The full account of original sin cannot

[1] i 19-20.

be given here.[1]  Suffice it to say that for redemption, reparation
for sin and a restoration into the supernatural life were both required.  The two parts are conjoined in the sacrificial act of Christ,
who " was delivered up for our sins and rose again for our justification " ; [2]  " Blotting out the handwriting that was against us
. . . And he hath taken the same out of the way, fastening it to the
cross." [3]  The first stage in this divine plan is seen in the Incarnation.  He took a human nature and so identified himself with
the cause of mankind and was able to plead as its representative.
As its representative the victim offered up was slain, and thus human
nature was purged of its evil vicariously.  The offering being of
infinite worth was accepted by the Father and reconciliation made.
Thus through the merits of Christ we are redeemed.  Those whom
Christ represented were privileged to share his honour and status
of friendship with God and even to partake of the very life which
he possessed.  This is the restoration of the supernatural order in
Christ.

Such is a bare outline of the interrelations between God and
man in the Redemption, but there are many points which need
elucidation.  Theologians like to go back and ask why God chose
this special way of redeeming man.  The creation of man and the
end of natural happiness do not raise any special problem ; nor
again does the generosity of God in willing to give man a greater
happiness than that which his nature required.  The extent of that
generosity is indeed beyond the highest hope, and we know of it
only through Revelation ; man was to become like God so far as
that is compatible with the continued existence of finite personality.
He was to see God face to face, that is, see him as he is and be
therefore an inmate, so to speak, of the intimate life of the Blessed
Trinity.  But now the plan of God was frustrated by the exercise
of man's freedom (we need not enter here into the question of
God's antecedent and consequent will).  And it is here that Catholic
theologians raise questions and attempt to answer them from what
they know, by revelation, of God's ways.  Was the Incarnation
for instance always a project of the divine bounty, or was it chosen
as a step towards redemption ?  Again, why was it that the Second
Person, the Word, became Flesh, and was it in any sense necessary
that he should suffer and die to win atonement ?

What first can be laid down with absolute certainty is that God *Necessity of*
was in no way strictly obliged to redeem mankind.  Throughout, *Redemption*
the action of God in the Incarnation and Redemption is on the plane
of the supernatural—that is, it is the manifestation of the free unmerited divine love.  A free gift had been offered and refused at
the beginning of man's history.  Whether that gift would be restored depended entirely on God's mercy.  The loss was man's own

---

[1] See Essay x.          [2] Rom. iv 25.          [3] Col. ii 14.

fault, and the original sin and all other succeeding sins have their proper and fitting effects and punishments, and in the working out of the effects of sin God's justice is made manifest. Therefore the Redemption is a free act and not necessary. But then comes a second question : if God forgives, is the sacrificial act of Calvary —in other words, the Redemption, as we understand it—the sole means of forgiveness ? The question has only to be put in this form for the answer to appear immediately. Forgiveness is a divine act and the act of one who is wronged. An injured person is free to forgive in the manner he likes, and God with his creatures can choose in his infinite freedom to lay down the conditions of forgiveness and to appoint the kind of satisfaction he requires. Therefore the Redemption of Christ is not the one possible mode of reconciliation. God might have sent forth a declaration of forgiveness through Moses from Sinai, or demanded some form of sacrifice, or again any one act of Christ would have been sufficient in a sense to repair the wrong. But while this is so, theologians add another clause. On the assumption that a proper proportion be observed between sin and satisfaction, guilt and atonement, they hold that only the infinite satisfaction and merit of Christ, the God-Man, are sufficient to atone for the infinite guilt contained in the sin of a creature against God. Therefore in the redemption of Christ alone can we find the full rigour of justice, as well as, we might add, the supreme act of love on the part of Christ, both as God in his becoming man, and as man giving himself in complete self-surrender to God.

But though necessity is excluded, the theologians are ready to admit the supreme fittingness of the Incarnation of the Second Person of the Blessed Trinity. It was fitting that it should be the Son of the Father, the Word, who should be the Son of Man, and that Christ even as God should be able to speak of his Father in Heaven and all that accompanies the tender revelation of the Godhead, and that by appropriation it should be the Father who raised him from the grave to cover him with glory. The Incarnation, besides, served to make manifest to man the visible image of the Invisible, and as man, owing to his composite nature, learns better by experience than by abstractions, such a revelation was just in accordance with his needs.

*Scotists and Thomists* As to the relation between the Incarnation and Redemption and their priority in the intentions of God there has been a long dispute between two of the famous schools of theology, the Thomist and the Scotist. St Thomas had inclined to the view that the Word would not have been made flesh had man not sinned. In favour of the Thomist view it is argued that in Scripture the sin of our first parents is given as the motive of the Incarnation, and the mind of the Church is expressed in its cry of *felix culpa*, which merited so great a Redeemer. The Scotists, on the other hand,

and with them Suarez, maintain that there is no proportion between the sin and copious redemption of the Son of God. They can point, too, to the Pauline doctrine of Christ as the centre and final end of all creation, " for whom are all things, and by whom are all things." Clearly the question can never be decided with absolute certainty. The Scotist view is, perhaps, the more attractive, but it has to face the fact that in Paradise Adam and Eve enjoyed the supernatural life without any stated reference to the mediation of a God-Man. That does not, of course, exclude the possibility that, even so, creation would have been recapitulated in Christ.

### §V: THE MEANING OF THE REDEMPTION

So far the Redemption has been described in terms of sacrifice, and it has been suggested that the best way to approach what is called vicarious atonement is from the aspect of Christ as Priest and Victim. Now it remains to make clear what exactly Christ accomplished by the Redemption, and as the subject lends itself to many misconceptions, it is best to begin with what is certain. The Council of Trent asserts that " if any one say that this sin of Adam is taken away by any other remedy than the merit of the one Mediator, our Lord Jesus Christ, who hath reconciled us to God in his own blood, being made unto us justice, sanctification, and redemption . . . let him be anathema." And again, " The causes of the justification are as follows : the final is the glory of God and Christ and life eternal : the efficient is God in his mercy, who freely washes away and makes holy : the meritorious is the beloved only Son, our Lord Jesus Christ, who when we were enemies, because of the exceeding charity wherewith he loved us, merited justification for us by the most Holy Passion on the wood of the cross, and made satisfaction for us to God the Father." Lastly a doctrine of the Reformers is explicitly condemned in these words : " If any one say that men are justified, either by the sole imputation of the justice of Christ, or by the sole remission of sins, to the exclusion of grace and charity which is diffused in their hearts by the Holy Ghost . . . let him be anathema."

In these passages there is a clear statement that the Redemption accomplishes something objective—that is, we cannot restrict it to the benefit of Christ's example, or even to a legal imputation of justice. Some real change is secured by our Lord's act ; men are liberated from sin, and by the grace of God and the charity of the Holy Ghost are made one with Christ and God. Again the motive of love on God's side as dominating the whole transaction, is made manifest, when our Lord is said to merit justification and to make satisfaction ; he does this not for himself but for others. Not that our Lord became in some mysterious way guilty of sin. He, the sinless one, endures the penalty attached to sin. No one can be

*Redemption objective : merit and satisfaction*

guilty of sin save the sinner, but besides the guilt there is the punishment due to sin, and another may (under certain circumstances, to be stated later) take upon himself the punishment and make satisfaction on behalf of the guilty person. The degree of satisfaction required is measured by the guilt, and that guilt is measured partly by the character of the offence, partly by the character or dignity of the person offended. *Lèse-majesté* deserves a more severe punishment than an offence of a similar kind against one's neighbour. Hence as St Thomas says : " A sin committed against God partakes in a manner of infinity, through its relation to the infinite majesty of God ; for an offence is the more serious, the greater the person offended." [1]

In Holy Scripture the act of Christ as Redeemer is quite clearly set out by Isaias, and the actual word, redemption,[2] is found with the meaning of a deliverance gained by a kind of ransom.[3] That the idea of a ransom is bound up with the use of the Greek word is clear and is confirmed by the alternative word " price," [4] and this ransom or price is always understood to be the blood of Christ shed for us. " Behold the Lamb of God who taketh away the sin of the world," [5] and again, " For you were bought with a great price " ; [6] " You were not redeemed with corruptible things . . . but with the precious blood of Christ . . . ." [7] But while this idea of redemption as signifying a ransom or price is essential to an understanding of the work of Christ, that work is so profound and rich in its connotation that we must beware of pressing any image too far. St Paul, for instance, multiplies images and aspects ; the effect is to convince his readers of the super-eminent wisdom and charity of God, but the actual relation of part with part, of aspect with aspect, is not made at all easy.

*Subjective view of Redemption*

The duty therefore of the Catholic theologian is to safeguard and make clear certain definite features of the Redemption and to try and control the statement of the doctrine by one or more dominant conceptions. At one period of Christianity, as we shall see, writers emphasised the aspect of ransom, at others those of satisfaction or substitution ; while throughout the history of Christianity the love of God and of Christ in the Redemption was naturally prominent. Each one of these aspects was as an aspect true, but each could be exaggerated into a distortion. After the fifth century and until the Reformation there was less fear of error because a sufficiently clear conception of the supernatural governed all speculation, and with a proper understanding of that cardinal doctrine the objective nature of the Redemption is almost certain

[1] St Thomas, *S. Theol.* 3a, Q. 1, art. 2, ad 2.
[2] Lev. xix 20 ; Exod. xxi 30, etc. ; Matt. xx 28 ; Mark x 25 ; etc., etc.
[3] λυτροῦν, λύτρωσις, ἀπολυτροῦν, ἀπολύτρωσις.
[4] τιμή.        [5] John i 29.
[6] 1 Cor. vi 20.        [7] 1 Pet. i 18.

to be safeguarded.[1]  But with the Reformation a different conception of grace and justification came in, and the tendency outside the Church since then has gradually grown to leave out the aspects of ransom and satisfaction and to concentrate alone on the love and example shown by Christ.  The old ideas are put aside as crude and unworthy of God.  A ransom, so it is thought, which justifies without any reference to the ethical factor, is too like magic to recommend itself.  For many non-Catholics the value of Calvary consists in this, that Christ has shown the perfect example of self-sacrifice, and we are invited by the spectacle of one giving his life for others to go and do likewise in the spirit of Christ.  A variant on this view is that Christ reveals the love of the Father, who is always willing to forgive and to have us as his children.  Whereas the old view of sacrifice made God into a tyrant demanding satisfaction, or at best into a harsh judge who requires a payment of the last farthing : on this interpretation we have a new revelation of the goodwill and mercy of God.

The fatally weak point in this explanation is its omission of the objective character of the Redemption ;  for, as non-Catholics as well as Catholics admit, St Paul cannot be interpreted as meaning only a redemption through love and an example of self-sacrifice. Nevertheless it is right in emphasising the motive of love, because the aspect of ransom or substitution is not by itself complete.  But to remove those elements and give an alternative such as has been described is a very human expedient, betraying the characteristic failure of religions outside the Catholic Faith to appreciate the supernatural.  The Catholic solution relies on the principle that God is giving man something which is so much above his worth and powers that, though it may demand man's co-operation, it is to some extent independent of him.  And just as holiness to a Catholic does not mean just a private devotion to Christ with the fruit of increased moral perfection, but a being lifted up by grace into a union with the Holy Trinity in Christ, so in the Redemption the transaction provides for this possibility and means a free gift of God to the race of forgiveness and grace through its one mediator and representative Jesus Christ.

This then is the first act to be recognised about the Redemption, that it is a supernatural event above private loves and aspirations, however much it may include them.  Next, as a supernatural event premeditated and brought about by divine wisdom, we may expect it to be so complete and rich in significance as to contain in an epitome what we more easily think of piecemeal or under various aspects.  We may be forced to use analogies which, though inadequate, may represent truthfully what happened.  There are degrees, certainly, in the value of such analogies, and there may be one

---

[1] Abelard is an exception, and his theory is very like that of many modern writers.

standpoint which is superior to the others. Now in the history of the dogma of the Redemption we do find these analogies and aspects, and they each and all serve to bring out its meaning. It will be well, so as to miss as little as possible of the richness of the doctrine, to give a short account of them and the explanation they afford.

*Various aspects of Redemption: ransom*

They can be classified into the aspect of Ransom, the aspect of Substitution, and that of Satisfaction. Worthy of mention, however, though it falls outside this classification, is the tendency, especially noteworthy among the Alexandrine Fathers, to speak of the Incarnation as the source of man's deification. There is an obvious connection between the two, and if the end of the Redemption be prominent in the mind, the intermediate stage between the assumption of human nature by God and the elevation of human nature to a share in the Godhead may for one cause or another be omitted. This does not mean that the doctrine of the Cross is made void ; for their apologetic purposes it was sufficient to enlarge upon the text that the Word was made flesh and that from his fulness we have all received.

The analogy of ransom or price rests upon Scripture. As mentioned above, the Greek word connotes deliverance or salvation, and there is a frequent use of it in this sense in the Old Testament. In St Paul it was a favourite image, and undoubtedly he has in mind the traditional Messianic force of the word. " You were bought with a great price " ; " Christ has ransomed us from the malediction of the law " ; " God sent his Son . . . to ransom those who were under the law " ; " Christ was given as a ransom for us." Throughout his writing the price is always the blood of Christ, but we are not told to whom the price is paid, and in fact the idea of compensation to another is absent. He speaks indeed of our being slaves to our sins and vices, and being delivered from all sin. The idea here is that we are in a state from which we cannot rescue ourselves, a state of enmity with God, into which we have put ourselves and one which is very unfortunate. Then legitimately the image may be pressed to this extent, that the blood of Christ pleads to God on our behalf and makes God propitious. In this sense we are ransomed. By sin God is offended, and the consequence is misery to self and, so far as it is possible, self-destruction. St Paul, when he cried out " who shall deliver me from the body of this death," [1] expressed a truth which all men feel partly as an effect of the Fall and partly on account of their own sins, past or present. A Deliverer comes who frees us from ourselves and from the effect of sin in our human nature and reconciles us with God. He pays the price, and the consequences of sin are worked out in him as representative, as the supreme embodiment, of human nature. That is to say, the mystery of Christ's assumption of human nature

---

[1] Rom. vii 24.

and sacrifice is expressed in part, if not perfectly, in the image of ransom ; and hence that image is appropriate and just.

But once it is taken out of its context and pressed, it presents a distorted picture of the Redemption. The price is paid as a compensation to one whose captives men are, and the slave owner is taken to be the Devil. Some of the Fathers, Origen, St Basil, and St Jerome, at times adopt this mode of speaking. Our Lord pays the price to the Devil, or as it is sometimes put, Christ outwits the Devil by allowing him to prosecute his death. In another version the Devil is said to have gone beyond his due right by causing the death of the Innocent One, and for this outrage he received not payment but punishment. Such ideas seem very bizarre, but it is easy to see how rhetoric or misplaced attention to what appeared logical could produce the phantasy. The exaggeration does not mean that the Fathers who wrote in such a way missed the meaning of the Redemption, no more than occasional exaggerated statements nowadays about the devotion to the Sacred Heart imply a radical misconception of the doctrine contained in the devotion. A deep spiritual doctrine can be explained in terms of varying appropriateness, and it is always difficult to distinguish in such terms the relevant and the irrelevant, the strictly analogous and the merely metaphorical. In the Middle Ages, for instance, Christ was spoken of as a King, and the title is significant and true, but feudal conceptions could easily be stretched too far, and a false logic would then lead to an image of Christ more repellent than attractive.

Nevertheless, sin is a captivity and some explanation can be offered of the phrase, the rights of the Devil. Our Lord speaks of the Prince of this World and of his power, and if we take a number of texts of Scripture at their face value, then there does seem to be an ascription of certain powers to Lucifer. There is a problem here, the solution of which falls outside the scope of this essay, because some explanation is needed of why the Devil should be the archenemy of mankind and permitted to trouble mankind to such an extent. It may be that, like other angels, Lucifer had from his creation some one destiny and function (it is of the very nature of an angel to have one mission or function, according to St Thomas), and that function may have been bound up with the lot of mankind. The loss of God's friendship would then still leave him his natural function but perverted. How far such an explanation would allow of his having rights in a very loose sense of that term, we must leave here undetermined.[1]

A similar mingling of the true and the incomplete is seen in the *Substitution* aspect of Substitution or Vicarious Punishment. In this view the idea of ransom passes into that of Christ as our substitute. His precious blood is our price and more than our price, because the

[1] See Essay x, *The Fall of Man*, pp. 353-355.

shedding of it represents what we deserved. His death is in place of our death, his suffering in place of our punishment. Now undoubtedly there is a truth contained in such statements, because the language with a slight change is the traditional Catholic language, and we all use it when we wish to speak of the Sacrifice of the Cross. But again it is not the full truth. If instead of using " in the place of," the holders of the view had written " on behalf of," their version would have served well. The Latin language with its preposition " pro," and the English use of " for," tend to confuse what St Paul kept quite distinct. The death of Christ for him is " *for our sake*," " *on our behalf*," [1] and not " in our stead " ; and if his words do imply some kind of substitution, it is a substitution based on an intimate union of Christ with us, and not on a mere exchange.

This meaning and the implications of St Paul's view will be developed later. It is mentioned here to bring out the resemblance between it and the representation of it, which is also partly a misrepresentation, under the form of an exchange or substitution of the innocent for the guilty. Those who support this latter theory do so on the ground that expiatory sacrifice generally takes the form of the offering of a victim in place of the guilty persons. They regard the ritual of such sacrifice as marking this transposition. An innocent victim is chosen, the priest lays his hands upon it in token of the substitution, then its blood is shed, and the blood signifies the life of the offerers which is then made over to God. Evidence to support this explanation is sought in the Jewish sacrifice, and the scapegoat is regarded as the best illustration.

This interpretation of expiatory sacrifice needs to be supplemented by other aspects. Taken independently it may hold good of certain primitive sacrifices where religious worship is debased by the intrusion of magic. But it does not do justice to all the features of Jewish sacrifice, and it is worth noting that in the example of the scapegoat which best suits the view there is no slaying or shedding of the blood of the victim. When then this aspect is converted into a rigid theory of our Lord's sacrifice, great caution is needed. Its exponents suggest that our Lord, like the scapegoat, suffers in place of man and endures all the penalties which, if he had not taken the place of man, man would have suffered. Now, as was said, there is a truth imbedded in the theory, and many outside the Church are under the impression that the theory without qualification contains the whole Christian and Catholic doctrine of the Redemption. Hence many minds have been turned away scandalised. Not without some justification they regard the conception of God contained in the view as indefensible. We have no longer the " Our Father " of Christ but a pagan God who maltreats the innocent because his lust for punishment must be sated.

---

[1] ὑπέρ not ἀντί.

And even if the justice of God, as it is claimed, demand the punishment either of the guilty or the guiltless, there is far too great an insistence on that justice as distinct from the divine mercy. This quality of mercy is everywhere present in the Christian theology, and the Christian God is no Rhadamanthus who ruthlessly condemns the innocent to suffer in place of the guilty. It should be added that the theory does not work out, because the death of Christ ought, if it is a substitute for the death of man, to procure a release for all mankind from the penalty of death.

The aspect of substitution, therefore, if pressed, cannot be maintained as a complete explanation of the Redemption. Undoubtedly there are traces of it at least as a theory among certain of the Fathers, but almost always the theory is an exaggeration of what is straightforward and accurate. As was said above, the theory needs only a small but important emendation to be wholly right, and it is because the meaning of our Lord's sacrifice was never lost in the tradition of the Church that the somewhat ambiguous statement of it in terms of vicarious suffering has always been intelligible and, when properly understood, accurate.

The immaturity of both the above theories led to a more *Satisfaction* sophisticated explanation when theology first began to be scholastic. This explanation is what is called the theory or aspect of Satisfaction, and its author was St Anselm. As might be expected, St Anselm avoids the crudities inherent in the preceding views, and starts with the premiss that sin is an offence against God. Now since sin against God is an infinite wrong, and since the honour of God must needs be vindicated, only Christ the God-Man could repair this wrong, appease the justice of God, and save mankind from the fate in which sin involved them. Hence the Redemption of Christ is morally necessary, and Christ by his willing acceptance of Calvary makes abundant reparation, manifests the justice of God, and obtains propitiation and redemption for all mankind.

There are several points to be noticed in this view. First, the factor of our Lord's willing obedience and self-oblation come into prominence, so that there is no question of a mere balance of punishment and satisfaction; and with this addition part of the harshness in former views disappears. Secondly, the emphasis laid on God's justice is certainly part of the doctrine of St Paul. Man must learn the nature of God and the nature of sin also, and these lessons are taught best by the exercise of full justice where sin has been committed. Thirdly, the substitution and satisfaction *motifs* are modified by the resetting of Christ's action in a large plan. Man must perish or be saved by a God-Man—Christ is the God-Man, he makes infinite satisfaction voluntarily, and his merit is appropriated by mankind.

The faultiness of the view lies in this, that it is still too rigid, too coloured by legal ideas. God is not bound to enforce an infinite satisfaction. If that is given by Christ, there must be some special motive attending his voluntary act. Again it is not clear why and how Christ, who is innocent, offers satisfaction for the guilty and transfers the merit which is his to those to whom it does not belong. Once again, therefore, we have a truth recognisable, indeed, in the form in which it is expressed, but nevertheless imperfectly expressed and therefore open to serious misinterpretation.

*Synthesis through (a) charity*
The worst exaggerations of the theory of substitution are to be found in Protestant writings and were the cause of that reaction which has taken the form of denying any objective factor in the Redemption. The Redemption is the appeal of love and nothing more. Such a formula is far too narrow for Catholic tradition and, as was said, is irreconcilable with the clear teaching of St Paul. The Redemption is for him a supernatural transaction which involves a change of status. But this objective fact does not exclude love, and so it is perfectly legitimate to try and co-ordinate all the various aspects under the *motif* of charity, so long as the supernatural character of the Redemption is kept intact. St Paul indeed always falls back in the last resort on the agency of love when he wishes to enter more deeply into the mystery of the Redemption. Isaias had already told the Jews that God loves with an eternal love, and St Paul in his letter to the Romans develops this same thought. When we were ungodly, Christ died for us. Whereas scarcely will one die even for a just man, yet when we were as yet sinners God showed his charity towards us.[1] But there are certain laws which must accompany such an unmerited gift as the supernatural life. That gift makes us children of God and as such it is essential that we should be docile and make a return of filial love. We must recognise the generosity of God who makes himself our Father, since that predestination is " to the praise of the glory of his grace."

The prelude then to the drama of the Redemption lies in the refusal of man's first representative to give God obedience and filial love. This refusal has certain consequences which are worked out by St Paul, especially in the Epistle to the Romans, and these consequences can be viewed conveniently from man's side and from God's side. Since mankind has been blind to the super-abounding charity of God and, instead of making a return of filial love, preferred the natural, we might expect a providence which educated man to recognise and appreciate the supernatural *as a gift*. This providence takes two forms : the majority of men are made to learn humility or at any rate the bankruptcy of the natural by being left to a degree to their own devices. This is the story of the Gentiles. They are not favoured like the Jews. The nemesis of the first refusal works itself out in their history ; they learn by bitter experience how evil a thing it is to have relied on themselves

[1] Rom. v 6-9.

instead of God ; and in the darkness they yearn for a great light.
" Because that, when they knew God, they have not glorified him
as God or given thanks : but became vain in their thoughts. And
their foolish heart was darkened. For, professing themselves to
be wise, they became fools." [1]  But the bitter experience has for
its effect that the Magi look for the King of the Jews, and the
Gentiles are more ready for the good news than the chosen people.

The Gentiles learn then by a law of consequences the value of
God's gift as a gift, and any incitement to pride and self-sufficiency
has been removed by the loss of integrity which brought a realisation of weakness of mind and will.   One race however, the Jews,
is selected in order to show the way back to God ; it is educated
gradually by the revelation of a moral code of natural law and by a
religion which is only partially supernatural.   The religion enforces
obedience to God.   " The Lord saith. . . ."  Repentance and
sorrow with strict punishments to leave no room for misapprehen-
sion are part too of the education, and lastly the worship is embodied in a sacrifice, which shatters the illusion of self-sufficiency.
The act of oblation symbolises homage and the surrender of ourself
to God.   It is the preamble to that gift which will be the sign of
true filial love, the offering of Calvary.

On man's side then the consequences of the rejection of the
supernatural are seen, as the ninth to the eleventh chapters of the
Epistle to the Romans explain, in the experience of loneliness and
the folly of self-satisfaction, and secondly in the long and necessarily severe training of the race which is chosen to prepare the way
back to the supernatural.   Throughout, the plan is governed by
love, and God uses the rod of punishment to drive in a lesson which
was essential for appreciation of the duties and privileges of supernatural love.

On God's side love, as it was said, is the prevailing motive.   As
all-holy his rejection of sin is automatic and necessary.   The Old
Testament speaks of him too as angry, and St Paul uses the same
language.   What is all-holy cannot be unaffected by sin, and God
would not be seen God by us were not his attitude towards evil
described under the term " anger."   Nevertheless St Paul generally
uses the future tense when he describes God as angry in the strict
sense, and at other times he is thinking more of the anger of a parent
who corrects in order to educate, or he is setting forth the natural
law and consequence of sin as falling under the disapproval of the
Author of nature.   For St Paul it is always the charity or the wisdom
of God which comes to the fore in the long run.   God's love edu-
cates and gives the initiative to a return from man's side.   Even
before the Incarnation the hope of the supernatural is restored
because a title to sonship is given which some day will bring those

---

[1] Rom. i 21 and 22.

who have faith to the enjoyment of eternal life in Christ. But what God will not do is to give back the inheritance before the lesson is learnt. For that reason the law cannot give life; it is but a pedagogue, and all have to experience the absence of the supernatural, "that no flesh may glory before God."

The full measure of God's love however is not made clear till the coming of Christ. "For God so loved the world, as to give his only begotten Son: that whosoever believeth in him may not perish, but may have life everlasting." First, Christ gave the finishing touches to that long education which was so necessary. He proves first of all the truth of God's friendship, and his attitude to the Father is the sublime pattern of what filial friendship should be, the friendship which man had refused. His food is to do the will of his Father; he does not snatch at an equality of honour with God. He is therefore the exact opposite of all that self-sufficiency which had stood in the way of the original divine design.

But he is not only the supreme example and the last and most perfect teacher sent from on high to make smooth the way back. He is himself the Way and the Life. He is a man and he is the first man who is able to give true filial love to the Father—that is, to adopt the attitude which is requisite for a gift to be given which will be appreciated as a gift. So striking indeed is this spirit of loyalty and love to the Father that it stirs up the hatred of the Jews. They, face to face with Christ, display the same vice which had brought about the loss of the supernatural life. They cannot accept a life which tells them that their self-sufficiency is wasted, and that all they have and are must come not from themselves but from the grace of God. The consequence is what the writer of Wisdom had foretold: "He is grievous unto us, even to behold: for his life is not like other men's, and his ways are very different. . . . Let us see then if his words be true, and let us prove what shall happen to him: and we shall know what the end shall be."

But this is not the whole story, and to complete it we must return to the partial aspects of the Redemption and to the motives of sacrifice. To make clear, however, what is necessarily difficult, the main points so far established must be repeated. God's action throughout is governed by love. He offers at the beginning of history a gift which far transcends the due of human nature. One condition is necessarily attached to it. Man must recognise the gift as a gift: God's love, that is, must be met by an attitude which is filial, selfless, trusting, full of hope and charity. Man refused the gift and preferred to be self-centred. The gift then is taken away, but the subsequent history of God's dealings with mankind shows God at work to remove the spirit of self-sufficiency, in order to give back the gift in the plenitude of Christ. The coming of Christ is the second great manifestation of God's charity. He completes the education; as God he shows the divine love for man;

as man he offers God that filial spirit, which is required for the supernatural gift, and is the model which others therefore must copy. St Thomas, when he treats of the question whether the Incarnation was necessary for the redemption of the human race, gives a series of exquisite quotations which illustrate the purpose and love of Christ : " God so loved the world that he gave his only begotten Son . . ." (John iii). " What else is the cause of the Lord's coming than to show God's love for us. . . . If we have been slow to love, at least let us hasten to love in return " (St Augustine). " Man's pride, which is the greatest stumbling-block to our clinging to God, can be convinced and cured by humility so great " (St Augustine). " Learn, O Christian, thy worth, and being made a partner of the Divine nature, refuse to return by evil deeds to your former worthlessness " (St Leo).

In these and many other passages St Thomas either in his own (b) *Solidar-* words or by quotation, lays emphasis on the motive of love, when *ity* he speaks of the Incarnation. But when he is resolving the question of the Redemption he makes the motive more determinate by introducing a further idea. This idea is the representative character of Christ or what may be termed the principle of solidarity. Now the theories already discussed fall short of the whole truth, but they one and all rely on the truth of Scripture that Christ died for us, he is our ransom, he is our substitute, he offers vicarious satisfaction. St Thomas subsumes all these theories in one profound conception, and in this conception he is faithful to St Paul. In the Second Epistle to the Corinthians St Paul writes : " The love of Christ presseth us : seeing that, if one died for the sake of all, then all were dead. And Christ died for all : that they also live may not now live to themselves, but unto him who died for them and rose again." [1] The meaning is that Christ is our representative and that there is such a close unity between his actions and those of humanity, that humanity is associated with him in his death and shares the triumph of his resurrection. Christ is the new Head of humanity, and so intimate and organic is his union with men that in some mysterious way, known best to love, his actions are our actions. As the Epistle goes on to show : " The Christ, that knew no sin, he made sin for us : that we might be made the justice of God in him." That is, our Lord is the representative of humanity, the second Adam undoing the work of the first Adam. His death and resurrection are our death and resurrection, our purgation and new life. We are incorporated in him, and because of this solidarity, his sacrifice is our sacrifice, and the fruits of that sacrifice our fruits. " He was delivered up for our sins and rose again for our justification." [2] " Being justified freely by his grace,

---

[1] In the Greek here and in the other texts quoted, I follow the interpretation of Prat, *La théologie de St Paul*, vol. ii, pp. 241 ff.

[2] Rom. iv 25.

through the redemption that is in Christ Jesus, whom God hath proposed to be a propitiation, through faith in his blood, to the showing of his justice, for the remission of former sins." [1]   Many similar passages might also be quoted ; in fact all the sayings of St Paul about the Resurrection, about the mystical Body and incòr-poration, about our being a new creature in Christ and living with his life, are nothing but expansions of the same doctrine.   It is admirably summarised in the second chapter of Ephesians.   " But God (who is rich in mercy) for his exceeding charity wherewith he loved us even when we were dead in sins, hath quickened us together in Christ " (convivificavit nos in Christo). [2]

St Thomas quotes this text, and in the questions which treat of the Redemption time and again he returns to the motive of the love of God and the principle of solidarity.   Elsewhere he brings to the fore the view that the example of the filial and perfect love of Christ proves God's love for mankind, and is the ideal which mankind had refused.   Christ is the tutor.   The Passion of Christ is the most suitable method of the Redemption because " by it man learns how much God loves man ; and by it he is incited to that return of love in which the perfection of our human salvation consists. . . .

" Secondly, because by it he gave us an example of obedience, humility, constancy, justice and the other virtues displayed in the Passion. . . . Thirdly, because Christ by his Passion not only freed man from sin but merited for him justifying grace and the glory of beatitude, as will be explained later." [3]   In the later explanation we find first that " Christ out of his love and obedience in suffering offered to God something greater than the repayment demanded for the whole offence of the human race " ; [4] and he goes on a little later : " As the head and members are as it were one mystical person, so the satisfaction of Christ belongs to all the faithful as to his members." [5]   And in another place " grace was given to Christ, not only as to a single person but in as much as he is the Head of the Church." [6]   And again : " The satisfaction of Christ has its effect in us in so far as we are incorporated in him, as members with the head." [7]   The whole doctrine is admirably summed up in the forty-ninth question.   " I reply that the passion of Christ is the proper cause of the remission of sins in a threefold way : first as an incitation to charity because, as the Apostle says in Romans v, God commendeth his charity to us . . . ; but by charity we gain pardon for sins . . . : secondly the passion of Christ causes the remission of sins by mode of redemption : for as he is our head, by his passion, which he bore out of love and obedience,

---

[1] Rom. iii 24.
[2] Eph. ii 4.
[3] S. Theol., III, Q. xlvi, art. 3.
[4] S. Theol., Q. xlviii, art. 2.
[5] Ibid., ad 1.
[6] Ibid., art. 1.
[7] S. Theol., Q. xlix, art. 3, ad 3.

he freed us as his members from sin, as it were by the price of his Passion. . . ." [1]

No less clearly is the same doctrine embodied in St Thomas's view of merit. Merit is almost the favourite word of the Church in its Councils and decisions when treating of our salvation through Christ. When then St Thomas puts to himself the question whether Christ's Passion brought about our salvation by way of merit, he answers as follows : " As stated above, grace was bestowed on Christ, not only as an individual, but inasmuch as he is the Head of the Church, so that it might overflow into his members ; and therefore Christ's works are referred to himself and to his members in the same way as the works of any other man in a state of grace are referred to himself. But it is evident that whosoever suffers for justice' sake, provided that he be in a state of grace, merits his salvation thereby. . . . Consequently Christ by his Passion merited salvation, not only for himself, but likewise for all his members." [2] That is to say Christ did not die instead of us or in our place, but on our behalf, because he was mystically one with us. His merit is our merit, " in the same way as the works of any other man are referred to himself."

The doctrine therefore of St Thomas is the fulfilment of the other theories and the replica of that of St Paul. Ransom, substitution, vicarious atonement are nothing but images of the mystery of incorporation ; the dominant motive of the Redemption is love, and it is love which is the efficient cause. We are far therefore from any mechanical or semi-magical theory, but we are far also from any mere subjective redemption. St Thomas lays stress on Christ as an example. He is the pattern of filial obedience, but this behaviour of Christ embodies the supernatural attitude and passes into an act which wins for us an inheritance once lost. He wins for us this redemption by the love shown in the Passion. He is not just a substitute, but One wholly man though also wholly God. As representative man he shares with those who possess human nature, just as he dies as their representative. The charity of his death is, however, supernatural : it has a divine quality, and as St Thomas says, it far outweighs the offensiveness of man's sin. Hence the reward is proportionate, and the reward passes from the representative to those represented, from the Head to the members. The principle of solidarity, therefore, explains how one can die and merit for another, and it contains all that was true in the other theories without their inconveniences.

There still remain two points which need further elucidation. Does this theory answer completely what is demanded in Scripture by the term " satisfaction," and secondly why is the Redemption accomplished precisely by the passion and blood of Christ ? The

---

[1] *S. Theol.*, Q. xlix, art. 1.          [2] *Ibid.*, Q. xlviii, art. 1.

first question St. Thomas answers by saying that "Christ satisfied not indeed by giving money or anything of that kind, but by giving what was the greatest of all, himself, to wit, for us, and so the Passion of Christ is called our redemption." [1] And in a later passage, he says : " So great a good was the willing suffering of Christ, that on account of this good being found in human nature, God was appeased for all the offence of the human race, so far as those are concerned who are conjoined to Christ the sufferer in the manner declared before."

But this does not explain why Christ suffered such grievous pain and gave his life on Calvary. Other reasons must be sought and they are readily forthcoming. It might be said that the Passion was just a consequence of all that had gone before, in the sense which the passage already quoted from the book of Wisdom indicates. But really there are many reasons on account of which it behoved Christ to suffer. It marks, as St John said, the perfection of love. "A greater love than this no man hath. . . ." Our Lord could not have shown in a better way the extreme to which his love both for the Father and for mankind was prepared to go, and no one can say that God has stinted his love or been reckless of his creation when he contemplates the figure of the God-Man on Calvary. The reward, too, is proportionate to the charity poured out—*copiosa redemptio*. And the risen life of Christ which his members share has all the glory of the sacrifice to make it rich with blessings. Moreover, there is this fact which could not have been realised without the unforgettable scene of Christ in agony and forsaken even by the Father. Sin is a hateful thing, an offence against the holiness of God with consequences which are inevitable and eternal. The real meaning of sin can only be brought home fully to the superficial intelligence of men by a picture of the natural consequence of it worked out in One of themselves. The charity of God would remain dark without this glimpse of his justice.

Throughout this account the attentive reader will have noticed how concordant the doctrine of Incorporation is with what was said in previous sections about sacrifice. To make everything clear, then, it will be well to recapitulate the Redemption in terms of our Lord's sacrifice and priesthood.

*Redemption and sacrifice* Sacrifice is the natural and spontaneous reaction of man in his relation with God. He expresses his dependence and desire for communion with his Maker and Final End by an act which exhibits homage, the offering of the best he has, and by an eating of the oblations. The object offered passes from being profane into something sacred, something belonging to God, if accepted by him, and in a special manner associated with him. This fundamental notion of sacrifice takes usually a special form when the worshippers

[1] *S. Theol.*, Q. xlviii, art. 4 ; Q. xlix, art. 4.

are conscious of sin and wish to make expiation. Here repentance has to precede union, and the repentance is seen in the treatment of the offering. It is made to suffer, its blood is shed, and the blood symbolises the expiation and wins atonement. It must be observed that the propitiatory element does not oust that of union. The latter is always present, and as culture grows the symbolism of the ritual becomes more and more pronounced. The external act is the symbol of love and self-surrender. That is why the definition of St Augustine, quoted by St Thomas, is an accurate as well as ideal statement. " A true sacrifice is every work which is done that we be made one with God in a holy society, being referred that is to that attainment of the good, in which we can most truly be happy."

The part of the priest in the sacrifice is to be the representative of the whole people. He acts in its name. The victim offered is generally something which can serve for a repast. The higher its worth the greater the sacrifice, and the victim should be something very closely associated with the lives of the offerers. The repast at the end is the consummation of the sacrifice already offered and admits man into the society of God.

Now after the Fall mankind not only lost the supernatural life, but lost it by sin. Hence a pleasing sacrifice would have to be propitiatory—that is, inclusive of two elements, expiation and re-union. It must further be made by one who represented human nature as such and gave to God a love which would be filial and supernatural. This double work Christ accomplished. He was the representative of mankind, the Word made flesh, and this communion with the children of men enabled him to offer in their name, to suffer on their behalf, to merit for them and share his reward with them. But he was also by nature a mediator, because, human though he was, he could offer God a supernatural love willingly : " Christ offered himself in his Passion for us : and this fact that he voluntarily endured the Passion was most pleasing to God, since it proceeded from the highest love : hence it is clear that the Passion of Christ was a true sacrifice." [1] Love therefore is the motive of the sacrifice, and decides the issue between God and man, and be-cause the Priest and Victim were one, were the identical God-Man and representative of human nature, human nature dies to the old Adam in the blood poured out and is restored in the new Adam, the risen Victim. Thus the sacrifice is propitiatory, the offering is the most precious conceivable, and the love the highest because the offerer offers himself even to the giving of his life. " He hath de-livered himself for us, an oblation and a sacrifice to God for an odour of sweetness." [2] " But now in Christ Jesus, you who some time were afar off are made nigh by the blood of Christ. For he is our peace

---

[1] *S. Theol.*, III, Q. xlviii, art. 3.   [2] Eph. v 2.

who hath made both one, breaking down the middle wall of partition, the enmities, in his flesh." The acceptance of this sacrifice is seen in the Resurrection. The blood with which we were redeemed becomes the food of the worshippers, the all-holy food which incorporates us into the life of Christ and so into a supernatural union with God.

The restoration therefore of humanity by God is achieved through the sacrifice of the Redemption. God becomes incarnate—represents human nature as priest and victim, offers to God willingly a sacrifice of supreme love, goes down to a death which is mystically ours, propitiates God for sin, and restores us to communion with the life of God by giving us to eat of the victim of the sacrifice, his own risen and glorified body and blood.

*Note on the freedom of Christ and his obedience*    There is a well-known problem connected with the obedience of our Lord about which I have said nothing above. The quotations given both from St Paul and St Thomas suffice to show that the obedience and love of Christ gave to Calvary its overflowing redemptive power. The emphasis which our Lord laid on his willingness to obey has, however, led certain theologians to the belief that God had laid a strict command on our Lord to die on the Cross. The inconveniences of this view are obvious. It is difficult to reconcile with the equally emphatic declaration of our Lord that he gave his life freely, and it suggests, at least at first sight, a harsh doctrine of God, as it seems to make Christ not a victim of love but a hostage demanded and penalised. The only legitimate solution must come in the admission both of obedience and freedom, because the New Testament makes it clear that both virtues were exercised by Christ. But, this granted, there are still several different solutions possible. For a reasoned discussion of these it would be necessary to bring in and discuss several complex doctrines concerning predestination and foreknowledge and their influx on the action of Christ. Suffice it here to say that God did not doom Christ to a grievous death. But any of the following alternatives are permissible. Christ the Son of God in concert with the Father out of his great love for mankind assumes the rôle of Saviour, and that in a way which shall manifest God's wisdom, justice and charity. Throughout his life he shows filial obedience to the will of his Father and most lovingly embraces the Cross. Or, in the foreknowledge of God, it is seen that if Christ were to offer to God that filial attitude, which Adam had rejected, and so be both a pattern of obedience to man and a child after God's own heart, then he would be rejected by the Jews. Our Lord accepts the consequences and by his blood makes the redemption still more plentiful. This view, if elaborated, fits in well with what has been said above ; and the comparison which St Thomas cites from St Paul is confirmatory : " As by the disobedience of one man the many were made sinners, so by the obedience of one man were the many justified."

It must be added that further on in the same article St Thomas seems inclined to interpret strictly the precept which Christ received from God to die. A third view, which differs slightly from the second but in many ways is only a further determination of it, may be stated as follows : There are two kinds of laws, positive laws of God and natural precepts. Christ received no positive command, but as man he was subject to the natural laws, which prescribed the duty of suffering for truth and justice. Christ had to be obedient to the law of death and all that might be involved in it. But furthermore Christ before the Passion offered himself as a Victim to the Father. After that offering there was no room for choice. He was dedicated to God, belonging to him as one without any will of his own. This latter point, as can be seen, fits in admirably with the sacrificial character of the atonement.

The three views mentioned do not exhaust the possible solutions ; other theories can be found in any of the larger textbooks of theology.

## §VI: THE EFFECTS OF THE REDEMPTION

CATHOLIC theologians, in order to bring out the perfection of Christ's atonement, describe it as adequate, rigorous and super-abundant. By adequate is meant that the sacrifice of Calvary is sufficient of itself by its own intrinsic merit to counterbalance the evil of sin. The infinite dignity of Christ as the God-Man gave to his actions an infinite value, and when we add to that natural dignity the love and obedience shown in the sacrifice of the Passion, the truth of the assertion seems sufficiently obvious. It was a great price, a mighty ransom, no less than " the precious blood of Christ as of a Lamb unspotted and undefiled." [1]

*Atonement adequate, rigorous, superabundant*

Rigorous when used of the Redemption means that Christ gave satisfaction even in terms of the most rigorous justice. The conception is legal, and theologians have some difficulty in working it out in all its details, but almost all are agreed that the debt of sin is more than fully paid by the Blood of Calvary, and it is paid by One who has identified himself with mankind and acts and suffers as its representative by virtue of the principle of solidarity.

Lastly the merit of the Redemption was superabundant. St Paul writes that " where sin abounded grace did more abound," [2] and the proof is evident in that the dignity of the person of Christ gave an infinite worth to even the least of his actions.

As our Lord was the representative of mankind, it is clear that he died for all. Through Adam's sin death came into the world, and the second Adam repaired the evil by a death in which we all mystically share. This does not mean, however, that without further

*Christ died for all*

[1] I Pet. i 19.    [2] Rom. v 20.

ado all are destined for heaven. Though the Redemption is objective there is nothing mechanical about it. The change of status required for man to pass from his natural state disordered by sin into one of sonship with God was beyond his power, and therefore the redemptive act of Christ is to that extent independent of human meriting. But in the very redemptive act Christ acted as Head of the human race, and gave back love to God freely. Therefore the will to share as a member with the Head, to belong to him freely is needed for the Redemption to be efficacious, and the closer one is united to that Head the more does one participate in that Redemption. Our Lord died for all : " He is the propitiation for our sins : and not for ours only, but also for those of the whole world." [1] " Who gave himself a redemption for all," [2] but belief in him is necessary. " And not for them only do I pray, but for them also who through their word shall believe in me." [3] Therefore against the view of certain heretics the Church has defined at the Council of Trent that " God hath proposed Christ as a propitiator, through faith in his Blood, for our sins : and not for our sins only, but also for those of the whole world," and nevertheless it has also been the constant teaching of the Church that it is possible to refuse the mediation of Christ, or depart from unity with and in him, and so forfeit one's salvation.

*Redemption and the Resurrection*      The aspect of sacrifice brings out this fact prominently. The essential element of sacrifice is the offering, and in the sacrifice of Calvary the offering is the Victim of Calvary. We have been saved by the death of Christ, but we are bound, if that Redemption is to have any meaning for us, to join in the oblation, offering ourselves in union with the representative High Priest and Victim in order that we may enjoy the fruit of the sacrifice. The fruit of the sacrifice is the supernatural life centralised in Christ, the risen Victim, given back to us as the food of life. This being so, it is not difficult to see the place of the Resurrection in the Redemption. Too often it has been neglected. Certainly it is the decisive evidence for the Christian faith, and, as St Paul cries out, unless Christ be risen our faith is vain. It is also true, as St Thomas says, that it is an emblem of hope, and Christ our Lord is the example of the new life to us. But the profound meaning of the Resurrection is by no means exhausted by such reasons. Sacrifice, we know, does not reach its full complement without the acceptance of God and the sign of that acceptance in the meal. Not that the meal is the sacrifice, for the essence consists, as already said, in the oblation. That oblation in the redemptive sacrifice is expressed completely and finally in the death of Christ. Moreover, as Christ was innocent

---

[1] 1 John ii 2.      [2] 1 Tim. ii 6.

[3] John xvii 20. Belief must be interpreted in the Catholic sense. The actual manner of incorporation is shown in other Essays in this volume, on the Sacraments and the Mystical Body.

and God as well as man, this sacrifice could not but be pleasing to the Father. The acceptance therefore is the complement of it and not intrinsic to it. But when all this is said the actual mode of acceptance remains profoundly significant for two reasons. The first is that Christ received a new honour impossible otherwise ; he became a victim risen from the dead—a victim who is the ever-lasting medium between God and the worshippers. And secondly, as the sacrifice was offered for mankind, the Resurrection signifies the risen state of those who will to be incorporated in him. Now, as stated in an earlier section, there are two sides to the Redemption —the rescue from sin and the exaltation of man into the supernatural order. Sin is washed away by the blood of Christ on Calvary, and symbolically the old life dies with Christ. At the Resurrection when our Lord rises in freshness of life we rise symbolically with him, and walk with him in newness of life. The Redemption takes effect, and the Holy Spirit is sent. In the Resurrection therefore, taken as inseparable from Calvary, and considered best under the light of the risen Victim, all the effects of Redemption are contained—Baptism, Faith, the Holy Eucharist, and the Church, the mystical Body of Christ.

All these features of Catholic life are treated in another place, and it is sufficient here to have shown their connection with the Sacrifice of Calvary. All the dogmas indeed of the Catholic faith fit together into a marvellous whole—so marvellous indeed that their union is a proof in itself of the divine origin of the Christian religion. But it should be observed that, so far as the Redemption is concerned, the easiest and most fruitful way of approaching it is through the priesthood and sacrifice of Christ.

In conclusion, therefore, we can return to the majestic language *Summary* of the Epistle to the Hebrews : " But Christ, being come an high priest of the good things to come, by a greater and more perfect tabernacle, not made with hand, that is, not of this creation : neither by the blood of goats or of calves, but by his own blood, entered once into the Holies, having obtained eternal redemption. For if the blood of goats and of oxen . . . sanctify such as are de-filed, to the cleansing of the flesh : how much more shall the blood of Christ, who by the Holy Ghost offered himself unspotted unto God, cleanse our conscience from dead works, to serve the living God ? And therefore he is the Mediator of the new testament : that by means of his death for the redemption of those transgressions which were under the former testament, they that are called may receive the promise of eternal inheritance." [1]

Sacrifice then is both the will of God as known by revelation, and the spontaneous expression of man's mind and will towards God. The creature is bound to adore, and without compulsion

[1] ix 11 ff.

he declares his utter dependence on his Maker by the ritual offering of gifts. As he comes to a deeper knowledge of himself and a better understanding of the nature of God, he realises that his gestures and acts have symbolised not only the homage of a servant, but the longing for holiness—the longing, that is, for union with his final end. In the very realisation of this, however, he is conscious of the infinite distance between the divine holiness and his own frail humanity and of the further defilement of that humanity by sin. Vainly then he tries to cross the intervening space by sacrifices which symbolise the detestation of sin in the ritual of blood-letting. The symbol is there, but not the reality. The sacrifice indeed is the natural language of mankind, and the symbol expresses the language of the psalmist : " Wash me, Lord, yet more from my iniquity, and cleanse me from my sin." And if Divine Providence had only been concerned with forgiveness and a moral righteousness, such a sacrifice might have sufficed despite the disproportion between the offence and the reparation. But God in his superabundant charity had more far-reaching designs : he sent his only-begotten Son to be the Sacrificer and the Sacrifice. All the cries of humanity now pass into one voice, and a new High Priest is beseeching God with many pleas ; all the symbols of sacrifice are subsumed in one Victim, who is the symbol of man's sin but a real human victim of flesh and blood. Hence it is that the descendants of Adam, who carried always with them the memory and stain of his disobedience, are slain mystically in the representative but real Victim on Calvary. The blood of Christ is the redemption of the world. But now the fruits of sacrifice are seen and the charity of God made manifest. Christ is the High Priest of good things to come. Though in all things save sin most like to man, though clothed in the form of a servant, he was also God, and as the God-Man his sacrifice was most pleasing to the Father. His act was most propitious ; it was motived by supreme love and obedience, and the reward was consequently proportionate and divine. Christ the representative becomes the new Adam, and whereas the children of Adam suffered through him, so now the children born of Christ gain through him. They walk in a newness of life, in the company of One who, being God as well as man, gives to them a share in his Godhead, and their sacrifice becomes one of thanksgiving, the propitious offering of the one eternal Victim, and a communion with his Flesh and Blood.

M. C. D'ARCY, S.J.

# XV

## MARY, MOTHER OF GOD

### §I: MARY, VIRGIN MOTHER OF GOD

CARDINAL NEWMAN has reminded us in a famous sermon that *Our Lady's* "the Glories of Mary are for the sake of her Son." So it is that *Divine Maternity* when we come to consider the revealed truths which our religion teaches us concerning our Lady we realise that they are what is known as *secondary* in the counsels of God. This is in no way to disparage their interest and importance ; it is merely to state the obvious fact that from whatever angle we may look at the Blessed Virgin she is never really the centre of the picture. The artist may depict her alone, but she is not alone—whenever we turn our eyes to her, inevitably we think of him whose Mother she is. She points men to her Son, before whom she kneels in adoration as her Lord and Saviour. No more than any other creature can she be blessed for her own sake independently of him. Her blessedness is the direct consequence of her nearness to him, who alone is Blessed in himself from endless ages. Her whole life—in a unique sense her very existence—can only be rightly viewed in relation to Another, since she was created for this one purpose, to be the human Mother of God made man. Pre-eminently of her it is true that "her life is hidden with Christ in God."

This is the meaning of Blessed Grignion de Montfort when he tells us that our Lady is *The Relation to God.* Mary is the link which "refers" (or brings) God to man, and joins man (above all the Christian man) to God. When the Holy Spirit overshadowed her she became the point of contact between the human and the divine. To reach her heart heaven bent down to earth and in her Motherhood earth was raised to heaven.

The primary truths of religion concern God in himself, in his Unity of Being and Trinity of Persons—God the Father, the Son, and the Holy Ghost. They refer to his infinite perfections (known as the divine attributes) ; to the work of creation, redemption and sanctification of men ; to the Incarnation of the everlasting Word, his death upon the Cross, his Resurrection and Ascension, his session at the right hand of the Father ; to the life-giving, co-equal, co-eternal Spirit, who, on the day of Pentecost, came to dwell with the Church of Christ, guiding her into all truth according to the promises of God.

The central and primary truth of Christianity (that is, of belief not only in God the Father, but also in Jesus Christ our Lord)

is the fact that " the Word was made flesh and dwelt among us." [1]
This is the mystery or secret, " hidden from ages and generations," [2]
until it was " manifested " on earth when, first the shepherds and
then the kings, first the simple and then the learned—wise men
from the gorgeous East, but also wise men from the open fields—
adored in a stable, wrapped in swaddling clothes, the Lord of all.
" They found the child," as Christians without number, in every
age, have found him since, " with Mary his Mother." [3] And so
it has come to pass that all the truths of our faith (secondary though
they are) concerning the incomparable dignity and privileges of our
Lady are the great safeguards and witnesses to the primary truths
of the Gospel, which, in their setting, shine with a light and splendour
such as could hardly encompass the bare statement of transcendental
facts, were it to stand alone without any comment or concrete
illustration. For example, it is easy to say : God is the Supreme
Being, self-existing, Creator of all things in heaven and on earth.
Easy even to say : Christ is God, without exciting much interest
or opposition. Certainly in our day and generation there would
be nothing sensational in any such statements ; they have been
made continuously in England for more than thirteen hundred years.
But say : Mary is the Mother of God, and people are startled and
quick to set to work questioning in their minds. They face realities.
They think.

I once heard Cardinal Manning state that John Bright told him
that he had heard this sentence, " Mary is the Mother of God,"
repeated in the course of a sermon preached in Rome, and that for
twenty years afterwards he was turning over these six short words
in his mind almost every day, and often during the night, asking
himself what exactly the preacher could have meant by them. They
were unfamiliar to him and grated harshly on his ear—indeed,
excepting among Catholics, they had hardly been spoken in our
midst for four hundred years. Yet they are nothing more than the
affirmation of the elementary, primary Christian truth, that Jesus
Christ is God, and that Mary is his Mother. Yes, the proposition,
Mary is the Mother of God, is the safeguard and witness of that
other proposition upon which all our religion depends : Jesus,
Mary's Son, is God.

" Because the children are partakers of flesh and blood, he also
himself in like manner hath been partaker of the same." [4] By his
merciful act of taking flesh and blood God came into immediate
contact with his Mother. He became her Son. She is " Mary, the
Mother of Jesus," Mary, " of whom was born Jesus." To believe
this is the very touchstone and criterion of the Christian Faith.
" Nowhere doth he take hold of the angels ; but of the seed of

---

[1] John i 14.     [2] Col. i 26.
[3] Matt. ii 11 ; Luke ii 16.     [4] Heb. ii 14.

Abraham he taketh hold." [1] " Of the seed of Abraham," that is, of Mary. She is the Mother of Emmanuel, God with us—not the Mother of his body merely, nor most certainly the Mother of his human soul, but *his* Mother—in the same way that our mothers are not the mothers merely of our bodies, and most certainly not the mothers of our souls, but *our* mothers. Even so, is Mary *his* Mother—and he is God—God made man for us men and for our salvation. It is obvious that she who was born in the course of the world's history in the same manner as all other women have been born, is not the Mother of the Godhead which is from eternity, but neither is she the Mother only of the manhood. Her Son is a divine Person. She is the Mother of Jesus, of the Eternal, of him who, living from all eternity, in the fulness of time was born of her at Bethlehem in the human nature which he had deigned to unite inseparably to himself. Simply, she is the Mother of God.

Saints and Doctors of the Church in East and West have vied with one another in proclaiming Mary's praises—we can read the beautiful and touching tribute of their devotion in a long line of witnesses to the tradition of Christendom concerning the wonder and excellence of Mary's Motherhood, from the time of Ephrem the Syrian in dim antiquity, to Alphonsus Liguori living almost in our own days ; but no poet, no theologian, no Christian mystic has ever uttered words that may approach in sublimity the simple words of the holy Gospel—" Mary, the Mother of Jesus." The creature has given birth to her Creator. This is the foundation of all her privileges, this is the one outstanding fact in the world's long history. We date from before Christ or from after Christ, that is, before or after Mary bore her Lord as his Mother. Here is the very centre and heart of our religion. It is the fruitful summary of the Faith.

For a full statement of the Catholic doctrine concerning the one Person and the two natures (divine and human) of Christ, I must refer my readers to Essay XI in this volume. Suffice it here to recall that the one Person of Christ is divine, the second Person of the Most Holy Trinity, who, God from all eternity, assumed a human nature, body and soul, at a definite moment of time, when the Holy Spirit overshadowed the Virgin of Nazareth. This union of two natures in the one divine Person of Christ is called the hypostatic (or personal) union. It is the mystery of the Incarnation of God ; it is also the mystery of the divine Motherhood of Mary.

This most sacred article of Christian belief was enshrined in the document known as the Apostles' Creed, which by the common consent of the learned was in its origin the baptismal profession of faith required of catechumens in the Roman Church from the days of the Apostles Peter and Paul. " I believe in God the Father . . . and in Jesus Christ his only Son our Lord, who was conceived by

---

[1] Heb. ii 16.

the Holy Ghost, born of the Virgin Mary." It was " the Lord of glory " who was crucified under Pontius Pilate.[1]

We know that St John in his extreme old age wrote his Gospel, and especially its opening passage, to confute those who already were making a division between the everlasting Word of God and Jesus Christ the Son of Mary. " In the beginning was the Word, and the Word was with God, and the Word was God. All things were made by him, and without him was made nothing that was made. And the Word was made flesh and dwelt among us." [2]

The Word became Mary's Son, and the Word was God.

Let us listen to St John once more :

" That which was heard from the beginning, which we have heard, which we have seen with our eyes, which we have looked upon and our hands have handled, of the Word of Life . . . ; that we declare unto you." [3] Again, " Try the spirits if they be of God. . . . Every spirit which confesseth that Jesus Christ is come in the flesh is of God. And every spirit that dissolveth Jesus is not of God." [4] Our Lord Jesus Christ is God, and he is come in the flesh, born of Mary of Nazareth. As St Paul writes, he was " made of a woman." [5]

With this teaching impressed upon the hearts and minds of the faithful, having been handed down from the beginning by the Apostles of Jesus Christ, both in their writings and by word of mouth, we can imagine the consternation and even horror with which men listened to the teaching, first of Paul of Samosata and subsequently in the fifth century of his disciple Nestorius, Bishop of the great See of Byzantium, preaching in his cathedral church, that our Lady was not rightly called Mother of God, but only Mother of Christ, who was only a human person, with whom the Word united himself as to an organ or temple of the Divinity. This was in effect to divide or " dissolve " Christ, for on this hypothesis there were two Christs, the divine Christ who was not the Son of Mary, and the human Christ who was. It contradicted the doctrine of the Holy Scriptures, as interpreted by all antiquity. The title " Theotokos " (literally God-bearing, in Latin *Deipara*, or *Dei Genitrix*, that is, Mother of God) had been given explicitly to our Lady by practically all the great Fathers who had preceded the denials of Nestorius ; by, amongst others, Origen, Methodius, Athanasius, Basil, Epiphanius, great and illustrious names. It was " in possession." This teaching of Christian antiquity was expressed by St Sophronius of Jerusalem when he wrote : " God became incarnate, not by uniting to himself flesh already formed and a pre-existing soul, for the flesh and the [human] soul of Christ were brought into existence at the very moment when the Person of the Son of God received them into his Unity. His flesh was not flesh before it became the Flesh of the

---

[1] I Cor. ii 8.  [2] John i 1-14.  [3] I John i 1-3.
[4] I John iv 1-3.  [5] Gal. iv 4.

Word; from the moment when it was animated by a reasonable soul, it was the body and soul [that is to say, a perfect human nature] belonging to the Word, who is God, since it did not receive its existence in itself but in him." [1]  Julian the Apostate bore striking testimony to this teaching of the Church when he wrote as a reproach that Christians were accustomed to call a creature—Mary of Nazareth—the Mother of God.

This is the Catholic faith in the Incarnation, that God became man, the Son of Mary.

Directly the Pope had been informed by St Cyril of Alexandria of the false doctrine of Nestorius, he condemned it by his supreme authority. Not content with this he summoned a General Council (the third œcumenical) to meet at Ephesus. This Council deposed Nestorius and solemnly defined the truth that the title " Theotokos " should be given to our Lady, since, through the operation of the Holy Ghost, she had conceived and given birth to God when he assumed human nature in her virginal womb. [2]

The decree of Ephesus was confirmed by Pope Sixtus III, the successor of St Celestine, the Pope who had first condemned Nestorius and summoned the Council. Thus was the divine Motherhood of Mary, the safeguard of the belief in the unity of the Person of God made man, upon which the whole superstructure of our religion depends, asserted for all time by the supreme authority of the Apostolic See and of the assembled bishops of Catholic Christendom.

We read that there were no bounds to the enthusiasm in Ephesus when the decision of the Council was made known proclaiming the integrity of the ancient faith. St Cyril tells us that the people had waited impatiently all day long the result of the deliberations of the assembled bishops. When all was over and Nestorius had been deposed from his see, Cyril writes : " When we came out of the Church we were led back to our lodgings by the light of torches, for it was already night. Women walked before us carrying censers smoking with incense. The joy seemed almost delirious. Everywhere bonfires were alight. Thus did our Lord show his almighty power to those who would have robbed him of his glory." [3]

Our Lord glories in being the Son of Mary. This is the title he gives to himself, " The Son of Man."

Not only is our Blessed Lady the Mother of God. She is the Virgin Mother of God. This union of virginity with motherhood is the crown of Mary's dignity. On this mystery the great St Bernard *Her perpetual virginity*

---

[1] Letter read and approved in the Third Council of Constantinople (680-681).

[2] Though at first Nestorius had refused the title of Theotokos to our Lady, in the end he admitted that it might be tolerated, but in his own heretical sense " because the temple which was inseparable from the Word was born of her," not because she is the Mother of the Word, that is of God.

[3] P.G. lxxvii 137.

in his sermons on the glories of the Virgin Mother, full of the love of Mary gives utterance to his wonder and admiration.

We read in the Holy Scriptures that there is a song that only virgins shall sing in their heavenly home. They, we are told, " follow the Lamb whithersoever he goeth, for they were purchased from amongst men, the first-fruits to God and to the Lamb." [1] On this St Bernard writes : " No one will doubt that this song shall be sung by her who is the Queen of Virgins, and that in this singing she will take the lead. But it seems to me that, besides this song in which all the virgins join with their Queen, there is another more sweet and more sublime with which she alone shall gladden the City of God. No one else, even amongst the virgins, shall be found worthy to utter the melodious modulations of this second song. This is a right which belongs to her alone, who alone amongst virgins rejoices in being a mother, and in being the Mother of God. But she does not glory in herself, rather only in him to whom she has given birth. She glories in the Lord who has made himself her Son, and who, having prepared a singular glory for his Mother in Heaven, willed also to endow her on earth with a singular grace whereby, in an ineffable manner, she might conceive and bring forth without prejudice to her virginity. For the only nativity worthy of God was that which made him Son of the Virgin, as the only motherhood worthy of the Virgin was that which made her Mother of God." [2] And again : " ' The Angel Gabriel,' says the Evangelist, ' was sent to a Virgin ' ; that is, to one who was a virgin in body, a virgin in mind, a virgin who had sealed her virginity by vow ; such a virgin as the Apostle describes, ' holy in body and in spirit '—to a virgin not newly discovered to be such, nor discovered by chance, but chosen from eternity, foreknown and prepared by the Most High for himself, guarded by angels, shown to us by the Patriarchs under types and figures, canonised from afar by the prophets." [3]

All Catholics will feel the truth of this great Saint's words, that, if God were to be born as a Child upon the earth, no manner of birth would have beseemed him save that which made him Son of a mother who was also a virgin.

St Proclus, a Patriarch of Constantinople and disciple of St John Chrysostom, writes : " Unless his Mother had remained a virgin her offspring would have been only a man, and the mystery of the birth would have disappeared. But if after her childbearing Mary remained a virgin, how shall he not be God and the mystery be unutterable ? " [4] In the same spirit St Thomas Aquinas says : " In order that the body of Christ might be shown to be a real body, he was born of a woman ; but in order that his Godhead might be made clear he was born of a virgin." [5]

---

[1] Apoc. xiv 4.     [2] *Super " Missus est," Hom. ii* 1.     [3] *Ibid.*
[4] *Oratio in laudibus S Mariæ.* This discourse was placed as a preamble to the Acts of the Council of Ephesus.
[5] *S. Theol.,* III, Q. xxviii, art. 2.

In this matter we have not been left merely to our own sense of the fitness of things. The testimony of the Holy Scriptures is express. It is also detailed. The wonderful first chapter of St Luke's Gospel was devoted by the evangelist to " a narration of the things which have been accomplished amongst us "—that is amongst the early disciples of Christ. He tells us that already they had been " instructed " by those who were eye-witnesses of these events. In order that they might be further assured of the " verity " of all they had been taught, St Luke " diligently attained to all things from the beginning," [1] and wrote his Gospel.

It is clear that the Evangelist could only have received knowledge of the events which happened " at the beginning," directly or indirectly from Mary herself. To whomever she may subsequently have revealed them, it is certain that, in the very nature of things, she was the only earthly witness of their actual occurrence. Ultimately and apart from the teaching of the Catholic Church which on other grounds we know to be based on divine revelation, we receive the narrative on the word of the Mother of Christ.

There was a Virgin.

She was saluted by the Angel Gabriel sent by God to Nazareth where that Virgin dwelt.

To her he was the first on earth to say " Hail, full of grace, the Lord is with thee. Blessed art thou among women."

She was " troubled " at his " saying " and thought within herself what his salutation should mean, for she was a Virgin.

" Though all Jewish women," writes Newman, " in each successive age had been hoping to be the Mother of the Christ, so that marriage was honourable among them, childlessness a reproach, Mary alone had put aside the desire and the thought of so great a dignity ; she who was to bear the Christ gave no welcome to the great announcement that she was to bear him, and why did she act thus towards it ? Because she had been inspired, the first of womankind, to dedicate her virginity to God, and she did not welcome a privilege which seemed to involve a forfeiture of her vow. How shall this be, she asked, seeing that I am to live separate from man ? " [2]

" And the Angel said : Fear not, Mary . . . the Holy Ghost shall come upon thee, and the power of the Most High shall overshadow thee, and therefore the Holy which shall be born of thee shall be called [a Hebraism for shall be] the Son of God." [3]

Behold the great mystery of the Virginal Motherhood set forth in the noble words of the holy Gospel, convincing in their simplicity, as they proclaim with majesty the supernatural history of the origin of our religion. In the beginning they inspired triumphant faith, the faith of the Martyrs and the Saints, as also of the little ones of

[1] Luke i 1-4.
[2] *The Glories of Mary for the Sake of her Son*, p. 352.
[3] Luke i 26-35.

Christ, who all rested with amplest security on the word of God. Such faith they will continue to inspire in Christian men and women until the end of time.

There never has been, and never will be, any other Virgin Mother, but one only. It is a unique wonder. In Mary alone we believe that motherhood was joined to virginity, and that virginity was fruitful. Blessed above all the children of men was the fruit of her virginal Motherhood. Those who believe in the Incarnation of God will expect, rather than shrink from, subordinate mysteries surrounding the great mystery of all mysteries that God became Man. Moreover, to those who believe in God behind nature it will hardly seem incredible that the Creator should, when he determined to live a human life, act independently of the " laws " or processes that he made for all others. To Mary in her childbearing it could be said with truth as to Esther of old, '' This law was not made for thee." St Ambrose teaches us that in the Holy Mass the consecration of the Body of Christ is effected by no mere human benediction, but by the words of our Lord. " He spake the word and they were made : He commanded and they were created." The Lord himself declared : " This is my Body," and his words effect what they proclaim. Surely that which is true of the " making " of the Body and Blood of Christ upon the altar is true also of their first " making " within the Virgin Mother's womb. It was accomplished by the direct word of God, the Creator of all things. We rest in his power and wisdom and no other explanation is required. As Abbot Vonier writes : " In Mary's Motherhood, God's action is supremely exclusive, absolutely unconditioned by the created law of life." [1]

It has been the firm and constant belief of the Catholic Church from the beginning that our Blessed Lady remained a spotless Virgin to the end. *Virgo ante partum, in partu et post partum :* A Virgin before her childbearing, during and after that childbearing. In the special Preface provided by the Church for the Blessed Virgin's Feasts we read the words : *quae virginitatis gloria permanente lumen aeternum mundo effudit.* " The glory of her virginity still abiding with her, she shed upon the world the everlasting Light." As light passes through the crystal leaving it uninjured, so did the Light of the World, who is from eternity, shine upon his creation when he visited the earth ; nor did his Virgin Mother suffer harm or pain in her childbearing, when Emmanuel passed from the resting-place he had chosen awhile for his habitation before he bestowed his visible presence amongst his own. Mary was his way to earth from heaven, when he came to us, " skipping over the hills, leaping over the mountains."

The Fathers of the Church remind their readers that of this mysterious passage of the body of our Lord at his birth there are analogies in the Holy Scriptures. Thus St Jerome writes : " Christ

---

[1] *The Divine Motherhood,* p. 11.

is a virgin. His Mother, too, was ever-virgin. She is Mother and Virgin. In like manner Jesus came [to his Apostles after his Resurrection] when the doors were closed. So also in his sepulchre, which was new and hewn out of hardest rock, none had been placed after him, and none was placed before him." [1]

We are reminded of the prophecy of Ezechiel : "And he brought me back to the way of the gate of the outward sanctuary, which looked towards the East ; and it was shut, and the Lord said to me : This gate shall be shut ; it shall not be opened, and no man shall pass through it, because the Lord, the God of Israel, hath entered in by it, and it shall be shut." [2]

In this manner was fulfilled the other prophecy, familiar to us all : "Behold a virgin shall be with child and bring forth a son, and they shall call his name Emmanuel, which being interpreted means God with us." [3]

It is difficult for us in the present day to imagine the horror and indignation which in the fifth century of our era was evoked by the news that certain heretics, Helvidius and Jovinian by name, had set themselves against the universal tradition of Christianity, which had been handed down from the beginning, and dared to assert that our Blessed Lady had other children after the birth of her Divine Son.

They based their heresy on certain passages of the Gospel and were answered at once conclusively by St Jerome, so that no more was heard of any doubt as to our Lady's virginity until the time of the Reformation.

Helvidius and Jovinian appealed to the passage in St Matthew's Gospel "until she brought forth her first-born son." [4] This usage of the word "until" for "before" denoting what had actually happened without any reference to what would, or would not, happen afterwards, was common amongst the Hebrews. Thus we read (Gen. viii 6 and 7) that Noah sent a raven out of the ark which did not return "*until* the waters were dried up on the earth," that is, did not return at all. Again, when it is said of our Lord that he should sit at God's Right Hand "*until* his enemies be made his footstool" are we to understand that it was only until then ? Many similar examples can be given, if necessary. St Jerome asks derisively, if anyone were to say that Helvidius did no penance until he died, would it follow that he did penance after his death ? With regard to the word "first-born" it is certain that whatever may be the case in our current English, its use amongst the Jews in no way implied that other children were born afterwards. We read even of the eternal generation of the Son : "When he bringeth his first-begotten into the world, he saith, ' Let all the angels of God adore

[1] *Apologia ad Pammach. pro lib. advers. Jovinian* (*in fine*).
[2] Ezechiel xliv 1-3.
[3] Isaias vii 14 ; *cf.* Matt. i 1-23.        [4] Matt. i 1-25.

him.' " The words " first-born " and " first-Begotten," at least in the language of the Scriptures, involve no reference to any subsequent birth. They testify simply to what they affirm—that the son to whom they refer was the first-born ; whether he was the only son, or was not, can in no way be gathered from the expression itself.

A further difficulty has arisen from the words " the brethren " and " the brothers and sisters " of our Lord. But it disappears immediately so soon as we learn that these phrases are applied in scriptural usage to all near, and even to distant, relations. Really this " difficulty " is of the same nature as that of an Englishman who might insist that the French word " *parents* " can only mean *parents* in our English sense of the word, in the teeth of information given him by a Frenchman that in his language it often means kinsfolk.

Quite independently of the teaching of the faith, it can be shown that these brothers and sisters of our Lord were the sons and daughters of Alpheus, or Cleopas, and of Mary, our Lady's sister.[1] It is clear from the Gospels that there existed not only a near kinship between our Lord and his " brethren," but also that they lived in close companionship. Indeed, it seems probable that after the death of St Joseph the Blessed Virgin made her home with her sister, so that living together they constituted but one family, much as we so often see in Italy to-day several generations living under one roof-tree.

We may recall with pleasure the words of the learned Origen : " Would that it might happen to me that I should be called a fool by the unbelieving because I have believed such things as these. The event has shown that I have not given credit to foolishness, but to wisdom. For unless the birth of the Saviour had been heavenly, unless it possessed something divine and surpassing the common things of humanity, his doctrine would never have penetrated throughout the world." [2]

When we reflect upon the position bestowed by God upon our Lady in the central mystery of the Incarnation, we may cease to wonder at the solemnity of the warning of the Fathers assembled at the Council of Ephesus : " Should any man not acknowledge that Mary is Mother of God, let him know that he is cut off from the Godhead, for without a doubt by his own act he is cut off from the knowledge of God revealed in Jesus Christ, Son of Mary the Virgin " —and " this is Eternal Life, to know thee the one true God and Jesus Christ whom thou hast sent."

---

[1] See the large edition of Cruden's *Concordance* under " Brethren " and " Sisters." Also the article in the *Catholic Encyclopedia* on " Brethren of the Lord," proving that they were not, as was once thought possible, the children of St Joseph by a previous marriage. In Italy, even now, cousins are called " brothers." A friend has told me that an Italian once said to him : " I saw my brother this morning," and when he replied that he thought he had no brothers, the answer came : " Oh yes, but I mean my brother-cousin."

[2] *Homil. vii in Lucam.*

If we turn our thoughts away from the consideration of the Christian doctrine about our Lady to the effect which that doctrine has had when realised in practice by the Christian people, we shall recognise how true devotion to Christ is inseparable from true devotion to Mary.

Terrible must be the fate of all who attempt to separate those whom God has bound together—the Mother and her Son ; on the other hand all who honour Mary as best they may will make their own the witness of St Alphonsus : " The more we honour Mary, the more we shall honour God," who, when he came to free us all, did not disdain the lowliness of the Virgin's womb.

§ II : MARY, THE MOTHER OF THE SAVIOUR

THE Blessed Virgin is the Mother of God. She is the Mother of *The Second* him whom before his birth she was commanded to call JESUS,[1] *Eve* since, as it was said to Joseph her spouse, he should save his people from their sins.[2] She is the Mother of Christ the King ; she is the Mother of the Good Shepherd, the Saviour, the Redeemer ; as such she was most closely united with him (so far as creature may be) in his redemptive work.

Such has always been the belief of the Church. The mystery of the Redemption is the analogue of the mystery of the Fall. The Wisdom of God coming to our rescue has provided an appropriate remedy, as a divine corrective, for the human folly which led to our undoing. " Where sin abounded, there doth grace much more abound." At each point of contact, or rather of contrast, there is the visible imprint of the Hand of God. A man led to our loss of the sanctifying grace of God ; a Man gave us back the gift. Death reigned in the race of Adam ; through one born of Adam's race true Life was restored to men. Death was the punishment decreed for our first father's sin ; when the Redeemer died, death was found to be the one efficacious remedy for our loss. Then at last it could be said :

> O Death, where is thy sting ?
> O Grave, where is thy victory ?

The tree in the Garden was the occasion of our loss ; our healing is to be found in the Tree on Calvary. In the divine Food given through all the ages by him who once hung upon that Tree, which is the source of immortality, we may find the antidote for the poison which lurked in the forbidden fruit of old.

Catholics are familiar with the liturgical Preface of the Passion :

" Thou didst place the salvation of the human race on the Tree, that whence death first arose, thence life should spring, and that he, who in Eden had gained his victory by the wood, by the wood should be overcome."

[1] Luke i 21.          [2] Matt. i 21.

This, then, being the principle of what we may call compensation in the divine work of the Redemption of the human race, we shall not be surprised to find that, as a woman played so large a part in our fall, so, by the side of our Redeemer, there will be another Woman co-operating in our restoration. As there is a second Adam, so is there a second Eve. As both sexes yielded to the tempter, so both sexes shall have their part to play in the fulfilment of the merciful designs of God. " I will put enmities between thee and the Woman, between thy seed and her seed " is the first of recorded prophecies.

In a well-known passage [1] St Paul teaches that " Adam is a figure of him who was to come. . . . For if by one man's offence death reigned through one, much more they who receive abundance of grace, and of the gift, and of justice, shall reign in life through one, Jesus Christ."

This doctrine—that our Lord came to undo the work of Adam, and to open the gates of heaven which had been closed to his posterity as a consequence of his sin, thus becoming Adam's antitype by way of contrast—is a favourite theme with St Paul.[2] The corresponding doctrine that the Blessed Virgin is the antitype of Eve, and that therefore she is rightly called the second Eve in the same sense that her divine Son is rightly called the second Adam, is not indeed stated expressly in Holy Scripture (though it is implied by the primeval prophecy in Genesis) ; but, none the less, the teaching of earliest Christian antiquity proves that it belonged to the Apostolic Faith and was handed down by the Apostles to the Church.

On this subject Cardinal Newman [3] has set out with magisterial authority the witness of very early Fathers of the Church. We find the truth that Mary was appointed by God to counteract the work of Eve taught before the end of the second century by St Justin in the East ; by Tertullian in the West ; and by St Irenaeus, who, having been brought up in Asia Minor in the school of St John, watered the Church in Gaul with his doctrine and his blood, and therefore belongs both to East and West.

For example, Justin wrote :

" We know that the Son of God, through means of the Virgin, became Man, so that the disobedience due to the serpent might have its undoing after the same fashion that it had its beginning, for, whilst Eve, still a virgin and undefiled, through acceptance of the word that came from the serpent, brought forth disobedience and death, Mary the Virgin, possessed of faith and joy, when the Angel brought her the glad tidings, answered : ' Be it done unto me according to thy word.' " [4]

And Tertullian :

" It was whilst Eve was still a virgin that the word crept in which produced death. Unto a Virgin in corresponding manner must be introduced the Word of God who built up life, so that by the same sex whence had come

---

[1] Rom. v 14-17.   [2] Cf. 1 Cor. xv 44-49.
[3] In his answer to Dr. Pusey's *Eirenicon*.   [4] *Tryph.* 100.

our ruin might come also our recovery. Eve had believed the serpent, Mary believed Gabriel. The fault which the one committed by believing [the evil angel] the other by believing [the good angel] blotted out." [1]

And Irenaeus :

" As Eve was seduced by an angel's word to shun God after having transgressed his Word, so Mary, also by an Angel's word, had the good tidings given her so that after obeying his Word she might bear God within her. . . . And as the human race was bound to death through a virgin, so through a Virgin it is saved ; the poise of the balance is restored, and for a virgin's disobedience a remedy is found by the obedience of a Virgin, and Mary the Virgin consoles and rescues the virgin Eve." [2]

And again :

" As Eve had become the cause of death, so has Mary become the cause of salvation to herself and the whole human race." [3]

The importance of this teaching will be understood when it is remembered that St John died not more than thirty years before the conversion of St Justin and the birth of Tertullian ; whilst St Irenaeus was the disciple of St Polycarp, who was taught the faith by the Apostle himself. Nor was there at any period a moment's hesitation on this subject. From the third century onwards it was taught in every part of the Catholic world without contradiction, and by the greatest of the Doctors of the Church, that, in the economy of our Redemption, Mary was appointed by God to undo the work of Eve.

Thus, St John Chrysostom, preaching on the Feast of Easter, dwells on the antithesis between Eve and Mary, to which I have already directed the attention of my readers. " Let us all rejoice to-day at the triumph of the Lord. He has turned against Satan the arms with which he once overcame. You ask me how : I will tell you. A virgin, a tree, and death represented our defeat : these three have all become for us principles of victory. In the place of Eve we have Mary ; in place of the tree of knowledge of good and evil, the wood of the Cross ; in place of the death of Adam, the death of the Saviour." [4]

I will allow myself before leaving this subject a short reference to the testimony of St Jerome. Jerome may be said to represent the whole Christian world, excepting perhaps Africa. He was the intimate friend of Pope Damasus at Rome, the disciple of Gregory Nazianzen at Constantinople and of the celebrated Didymus at Alexandria. Born in Dalmatia, at different periods of his career he lived in Italy, Gaul, Palestine and Syria. Now, in one of his letters he writes as though enunciating a proverb, known to all : " Death by Eve, life by Mary." [5] Whilst St Jerome was writing this in Europe, the great St Augustine in Africa expressed the same truth in all but identical words : " It is a great mystery that as it was

---

[1] *De Carne Christi*, 17.  [2] *Haer.* v 19.
[3] *Ibid.* i 33.  [4] *Hom. in S. Pascha.*  [5] *Ep.* xxii 21.

through a woman that death befell us, so through a woman it was that life was born to us—perdition by Eve, salvation by Mary." [1] This truth belongs, if anything belongs, to the earliest and universal tradition. Our Lady is the second Eve in the same sense that Christ is the second Adam, joined to him in the blessing of our reparation even as the first Eve had been joined to the first Adam in the calamity of our Fall.

Here we have a principle of our religion from which, when we reflect upon it carefully, we shall see that certain conclusions of great interest and importance will occur to the mind. For example, we are prepared (apart from all other considerations) to learn that the Mother of God, through the foreseen merits of her Son and Saviour, was preserved in the first moment of her existence from original sin (which otherwise would have overtaken her as one of Adam's descendants) and that she was even then dowered with the supernatural grace of God. This revealed truth we speak of as the Immaculate Conception of the Blessed Virgin Mary.

*The Immaculate Conception*

I would refer my readers to the essay [2] in this volume which deals with the Fall of man, for a full statement of the Catholic doctrine of original sin ; it will be sufficient to say here, that it is of the essence of that doctrine that God raised our first parents to a state above nature, bestowing upon them his sanctifying grace as a free gift to which, by nature, they had no claim. Through the sin of Adam (in which Eve bore her share) this gift was lost for all Adam's children save only for her, who alone was chosen by God to undo our first mother's evil work. Grace was bestowed not only upon Eve in the very opening of her life, but also upon Mary, that she, too, might at the first instant of her existence be found on the side of God as Satan's foe. The enmity between Mary and the tempter is no new story. Already when Gabriel hailed her she was *gratia plena*, full of grace. Divine grace was hers without stint and came to her with life itself. Thus was she fittingly prepared for the virginal childbearing through which was crushed the serpent's head.[3] The Virgin Mother of God is the Immaculate Mother of the Saviour of the world.

This truth, contained implicitly [4] in the universal Tradition of the Church, and necessarily involved in the teaching of the Fathers concerning Mary the second Eve and her entire sinlessness and purity, was solemnly defined by Pope Pius IX on December 8, 1854. With joy, therefore, we hail the Mother of God " without spot or stain or any such thing " from the first moment of her existence, until she was gathered to her eternal rest in the unveiled presence of her Lord. For the Church teaches us [5] that the Mother of God

---

[1] *De Symbol. ad Catech.*
[2] Essay x.    [3] *Cf.* 1 Tim. ii 15.
[4] In Essay i (*Faith and Revealed Truth*), pp. 33 ff., it is shown that a truth may be contained implicitly in revelation, and at a later date be explicitly defined.
[5] In the Council of Trent.

was free, through the Grace of Christ, not only from original sin, but also from the slightest actual sin. " The Blessed Virgin," writes St Thomas, " was chosen by Heaven to be the Mother of God ; but she would not have been a Mother fitting for God, had she ever sinned. Therefore we must simply confess that the Blessed Virgin never committed any kind of sin whatsoever." [1] Our Lady's office as the New Eve (*mutans Evae nomen*, Eva changed to Ave) is not the only mystery of our religion which involves her sinless conception and her fulness of grace—even more is it the direct consequence of her Divine Motherhood. She is the Holy Mother of God.

Mary's peerless sanctity, her freedom not only from original sin but also from actual sin, is the inevitable condition of her nearness to the Person of our Lord, who is the source of all supernatural holiness that has ever been possessed by any creature. In his uncreated nature he alone is essential goodness—the All-Holy God, and of him in his humanity we are told that he was separate from sinners [2]—" holy, innocent, undefiled, elevated above the heavens, separate from sinners." *Freedom from actual sin*

This last phrase should cause us to think carefully. Our Lord, after becoming man, in a real and true sense was far from being separate from sinners. It was an accusation brought against him with vehemence that he was the sinners' friend—an accusation which he was careful not to repel. With public sinners he sat at meat and welcomed them to his side and to his feet. If we call to mind his relations with the Magdalen, with the Thief on the Cross, with Peter after his fall, with countless broken-hearted men and women crushed by an intolerable weight of sin, we shall see that far from separating himself from their company he drew them always closer and closer to himself. " Come unto me *all* ye that are burdened and heavy laden." Yet it still remains true that he whose footstool is the heavens, when he visited our earth in the human nature which he assumed, remained " separate " from all that was displeasing to God. It could not be otherwise. No man might accuse him of sin, for sin could not come nigh unto him who is the Lord our God. When, then, we remember that he deigned to derive his human life from the life of his Mother, we shall share at once the feeling of St Augustine, who, when writing of the universality of sinfulness in all the descendants of Adam, " with the exception of the holy Virgin Mary," refused to entertain the question of sin where she was concerned, " since she merited to conceive and bring forth him whom all allow to have no sin," for to her was granted grace, greater than that conferred upon all others, " that she might vanquish sin in every respect." [3]

[1] *S. Theol.*, III, Q. xxvii, art. 4.
[2] Heb. vii 26.          [3] *De Nat. et Grat. contra Pelag.* xii.

The Son of Mary was without sin in virtue of the hypostatic union of his humanity with the Person of the Word ; Mary was sinless, but through the grace which God bestowed upon her in abundant measure, that she might be fitted—so far as creature could be fitted—to provide the blood, drawn from her own body, with which her Son would redeem Adam's race from the guilt and punishment of sin. His Mother was too close to him for sin to touch her. Our Lord held forth his hand and by his merits preserved the chosen creature, whom by her Motherhood he had united so closely to himself, from the slightest spot of sin which could displease him, or even for a brief moment disfigure her soul in his most holy sight. And on this account Mary his Mother rejoiced beyond measure in God her Saviour. She was redeemed in the highest way—the way of prevention—from the shipwreck that involved all the other children of Adam, all our race, in dire catastrophe. As St Francis de Sales writes :

" God bestowed upon his glorious Mother the blessedness of the two states of human nature ; for she possessed the innocence which the first Adam lost, but also enjoyed after the most excellent manner the Redemption which the second Adam obtained for men." [1]

*Tota pulchra es Maria et macula non est in te.* " Thou art all beautiful, Mary, and in thee is no stain." The Mother of God is a creature like ourselves, and like all other creatures she depends absolutely upon her Creator ; but she, alone of all creatures, is without sin, for in all creation she stands alone as having, by the power of the Holy Ghost, communicated her flesh and blood to him, who when he became incarnate upon the earth still remained " separate from sinners " and elevated above all the heavens.

Let me repeat it : by physical nearness and the nearness of his human sympathy and compassion he would indeed draw near to sinners without shrinking. During the days of his public ministry, and as he hung upon his Cross, he was no more separate from the Magdalen than from the Immaculate. On Calvary, by their side, was John the beloved, and other holy women too ; the Good Thief also was close to him in the agony of his passing. He was the Lord of all—of Mary Immaculate and of John the beloved ; of the Magdalen, of the Thief, and of the rest hard by—and of all he was the Saviour. But one was near to him in a sense that no other might ever be, for in all that goodly company one only called him Son. Once more it should be said : the sinlessness of Mary was bestowed upon her for the sake, supremely, of her All-Holy Child. Her sinlessness is part of the reverence due to God.

*Her co-operation in the work of redemption* Our Blessed Lady was united with the second Adam, her Son, both as his Mother and as the second Eve, after a fashion and to a degree impossible for any other creature. She stands alone, in a position apart, in her relation to the Redeemer and to his work of Redemption.

[1] *Treatise on the Love of God*, Bk. II, 6.

It is of the first importance that we should always bear in mind that our Lady gave free consent to the part she was called upon to play in the mystery of the Incarnation. At first she hesitated, not being certain as to the will of God in her regard. Heaven waited, as Gabriel hung upon her words, for her submission. " Be it done unto me according to thy word " was the direct response to the encouragement: " Fear not, Mary, it is as God would have it be. The Holy One to be born of thee shall be the Son of God." Our Lady's *Fiat*, when it came, was operative in its direct effect. In deep humility the Queen of Heaven bowed her head, as she spoke her word, and when she spoke, the Lord of all was made flesh and dwelt amongst us. From that tremendous moment the association of the Holy Virgin with the Incarnate Saviour and with the purposes of his coming was so close that we can never hope to grasp its full significance. It still persisted when the Lord of all gave up his human soul into his Eternal Father's hands, sin and Satan were overcome, and the world redeemed. Beneath the Cross of Calvary the Mother of God was still the handmaid of the Lord ; still she surrendered herself in complete submission. She stood by the Redeemer's side uniting her will to his : one with him, even as of old our first mother had stood by the side of Adam beneath the shadow of the tree of the knowledge of good and evil in the opening chapter of the fateful story of our race.

There is only one Redeemer, one Lord and Saviour of us all. That is the very alphabet of the Christian religion. On the other hand, every Christian is called upon, as St Paul writes, to be " a fellow-worker with Christ." We are urged to co-operate with Christ not only that by good works we may make our own salvation sure,[1] but also in order that thus we may " fill up those things that are wanting of the sufferings of Christ for his body which is the Church." [2] Nothing can be " wanting " in these sufferings themselves, for each of them is of infinite worth ; and yet something is " wanting," since our Lord has left us something to do which he looks for (however infinitesimally small when compared with what he has done), in order that through his merits, which alone give supernatural merit to anything we can do, we may both work out our own salvation, and also aid all those for whom he died. In union with him and by his grace we are permitted to share in his work " for his body, which is the Church." Again, St Paul ventured to write of himself that " he became all things to all men, that he might save all."

Every Christian, therefore, may in this sense co-operate with Christ in the work of the Redemption ; but our Lady does so in a far higher, closer, deeper sense than any other of the members of his body, in virtue of that intimate union with him and with his redeeming work, of which I have already written. The co-operation

[1] 2 Peter i 10.  [2] Col. i 24.

of the Mother with the Redeemer who was her Son differs not only in degree, but also in kind, from that of any other saint. For her consent alone he waited when he sent Gabriel to her presence. She alone is his Mother ; she alone, as the second Eve, stood beneath the Cross.

The words of St Bernard are well known : " One man and one woman have wrought us exceeding harm ; nevertheless, thanks be to God, through one Man and one Woman all things are restored . . . and indeed Christ would have sufficed. Surely all our sufficiency is of him ; but it would not have been good for us that Man should be alone. Rather was it fitting that both sexes should take part in our Reparation, for neither sex had been guiltless in our Fall." [1]

" In the Christian religion," writes Cardinal Billot,[2] " Mary is absolutely inseparable from Christ both before and after the Incarnation. Before the Incarnation in the hope and expectation of mankind, after the Incarnation in the worship and love of the Church. For, indeed, in the primeval prophecy we were shown not only Christ, but also the Woman whose child he is ; so that I seem to see in the vision granted to our first parents a type of the Christian religion as it was one day to be, as we now see it, in the image of the Virgin holding her Son in her arms upon our altars throughout the world."

Eve sinned before Adam, Mary was born before Christ. Mary gave Christ to us to redeem us from our sins. A religion that separates Mary from Jesus—the Woman from her Seed—is neither the religion of the promises and prophecies as we read of it in the Old Testament, nor the religion of their fulfilment as we see it in the New. The Fathers of the Church assure us that our Lady conceived Christ in her heart by faith before she conceived him actually in her womb. The Holy Virgin was even more closely united to her Son by grace than by nature in order to fit her, so far as might be possible in a creature, for her sublime office. Her dignity as Mother of God, her intimate union with the Saviour of the world in his work of Redemption, should be regarded together. For her dignity and for her office she was prepared both spiritually and physically, in her soul and in her body. Fr. Gallwey writes : " Our Lord loves his Blessed Mother more because of her high graces than on account of the natural tie—*but both are his own creation.*" [3]

In the New Testament we are shown the picture of Mary saluted by the angel, Mary in obedience unparalleled on earth, Mary in her deep humility, Mary giving utterance to her *Fiat*—" Be it done unto me according to thy word "—Mary overshadowed by the Spirit of

[1] *Sermo de Duodecim praerogativis B.V.M.*, i, 2.
[2] *De Verbo Incarnato*, p. 401 (Rome, 1912).
[3] *Memoirs of Fr. Gallwey, S.J.*, p. 92.

God, Mary the chosen vessel of election, Mary the Mother of the Word, and then—after her years of union with her Son in the holy house of Nazareth—Mary beneath the Cross, the head of Satan crushed, man delivered. The Fathers of the Church supply the commentary when they teach us how the Mother of God undid the work of Eve.

If we will absorb this scriptural and patristic teaching we can hardly fail to realise in some small measure the wonder of our Lady's office and function as the Mother of the Saviour of mankind, and of our Lady's share in the reparation of the evil work of our first parents. One is our Saviour. He alone redeemed us, yet he deigned to associate his Mother with his work of Redemption. Mary is the cause of our salvation, even as Eve was the cause of our ruin. This is the teaching of all antiquity.[1]

Such thoughts as these should be of much service to us when *Her* we turn our minds to the consideration of the Blessed Virgin's inter- *intercession* cession with God on our behalf. We can all co-operate with our most holy Redeemer, yet Mary's co-operation stands alone ; similarly we can all pray one for another through Christ our Lord, yet Mary's mediation and the efficacy of Mary's prayer is something by itself, unlike that of any other creature. In both cases the fundamental reason is the same—of all creatures she alone is not only the servant, but also the Mother of God. All our Lady's privileges rest ultimately on this great fact. If we consider the Catholic doctrine, we shall find that it can be set out in a few simple propositions :

1. All supernatural graces, like all gifts to man in the natural order, come from God alone as their fountain-head.

2. All supernatural graces are conferred through Jesus Christ. We pray " through our Lord Jesus Christ " and through him only. He is the only Mediator of Justice between God and man ; for he alone is both God and man. Through him alone the wall of partition created by sin between the heavenly Father and his earthly children was broken down. He is the only Saviour of mankind. Yet—

3. All members of his mystical Body can mediate with the Mediator, and through the Mediator can mediate with the Father ; this is called intercessory prayer. To this mediation St Paul constantly exhorts those to whom he addressed his letters ; and to this mediation St James attaches the greatest importance, urging Christians to " pray for one another that you may be saved." [2]

4. This mediation of Christians, one for another, is not to terminate with our earthly life, but is to continue after death. We are taught to believe in the Communion of Saints in heaven as on earth.

---

[1] Thus St Ephrem (*Op. Syr.*, tom. ii, p. 327) : " Those two innocent, those two simple ones, had been equal the one to the other ; but afterwards, one became the cause of our death, the other of our life."

[2] James v 16.

The Saints of the Old Testament, Moses, David, Elias ; the Saints of the New Testament, Mary the Mother of our Lord, St. Mary Magdalen the Penitent, the disciple whom Jesus loved with a special love, the disciple to whom Jesus gave the keys, the great Apostle of the Gentiles, still intercede for us who are left struggling *in via* (in the " estate of the way "), not yet, as they, *in patria*—in our true country which is above.

5. Amongst the prayers of all the Saints our Lady's intercession has a special place apart, as the direct consequence of her special relation to the Lord of all, who is also her Son, to whom she was so closely joined in his earthly life and work, especially at Nazareth, at Bethlehem, and on the hill of Calvary.

But, further than this, it is commonly believed amongst the faithful that *all* graces obtained for us by the Death and Passion of our Most Holy Redeemer are bestowed after the prayer of Mary. This pious opinion has been taught expressly by St Bernard, by St Robert Bellarmine, St Bernardine of Siena, St Alphonsus Liguori and other Saints ; in our own days it has received approval in the Encyclicals of one Pope after another, and quite recently has been encouraged by the fact that a Mass and Office have been granted to several religious Orders and to all the dioceses of the kingdom of Belgium in honour of the Blessed Virgin as " Mediatrix of all graces."

It is, then, believed that our Lady prays not only for some or for many of the graces we receive, but for all. Apart from the weight of authority which encourages us to believe that this is the case, it would seem to follow from our Lady's co-operation in the acquisition of grace, since it is difficult to separate the distribution of graces from their acquisition. Mary certainly co-operated by her consent to the Will of God in the divine action which *acquired all* graces, for all graces have been acquired solely by the Incarnation and Passion of her Son, in which, as we have seen, she bore her special part, even as Eve had shared in Adam's sin. Can we then be surprised at the belief of so many great Saints, as well as of the faithful generally, that she also bears her special part, by her prevailing prayer, in the *distribution* of all the graces obtained by her Son ?

To this matter we can apply the most true words of Fr. Marin-Sola, O.P. :

" The faith and filial piety of the Christian people has been the best and most powerful auxiliary of speculative logic with regard to the dogma of the Immaculate Conception, as it has been and always will be in regard to all the dogmas that do not concern the intelligence exclusively, but also the heart of man." [1]

Our hearts tell us that we owe all to Mary who gave us Jesus Christ, nor do our hearts deceive us.

[1] *L'Evolution Homogène du Dogme Catholique*, p. 331.

We read in the holy Gospel that Mary brought Jesus to the house of her cousin Elizabeth :

" And she entered into the house of Zachary and saluted Elizabeth. And it came to pass that when Elizabeth heard the salutation of Mary, the infant leaped in her womb. And Elizabeth was filled with the Holy Ghost, and she cried out with a loud voice and said, ' Blessed art thou among women and blessed is the fruit of thy womb. And whence is this to me, that the mother of my Lord should come to me ? For behold, as soon as the voice of thy salutation sounded in my ears, the infant in my womb leaped for joy. And blessed art thou that hast believed.' " [2]

From the constant Catholic tradition we know that when the babe leaped for joy when Mary spoke, at that moment, through the merits of Christ his Saviour, he was cleansed from the stain of original sin and sanctified whilst yet within his mother's womb. The birthday of the Baptist alone amongst the Saints is celebrated by the Church. In his case, clearly, it was through the mediation of Mary, when she spoke her words of salutation and Elizabeth rejoiced at her coming, that God gave the grace of Christ to the child unborn. This was the first of the graces won for men by the foreseen merits of the Redeemer of which we find express record in the Gospels. We receive it on the word of one who, we are told, was " filled with the Holy Ghost," in order that in every ensuing age men might read and ponder, and marvel as they read. It was the norm and example of graces innumerable that should be bestowed upon the children of Adam, from the day when Mary entered the house of Zachary and Elizabeth, to the end of time.

Who shall dare to separate those whom God has joined together, the Mother and the Son ? We love to linger on the hallowed words : " Blessed art thou among women, and blessed is the fruit of thy womb, Jesus." He is the Saviour ; she is the Saviour's Mother. Whence is this to me that the Mother of my Lord should come to me ? Whence is this to me that the Mother of my Lord should pray for me ?—Her prayer is all-powerful with her Lord, for he will refuse her nothing, who deigned to be called and to be her Son.

## § III : MARY, THE MOTHER OF CHRISTIANS

MARY, Mother of God, Mother of the Saviour, is also the Mother *Spiritual* of men and especially the Mother of Christians ; she is the Mother *motherhood* of all those for whose sake God became man, for whose redemption our Saviour died. God has given her to be not only the Mother of Jesus, but our Mother too, the Mother of every human creature who may read this essay, the Mother of the poor sinner who writes it. Needless to say she is not God's Mother and ours in the same sense. She is the Mother of God physically, since she gave God his human life ; she is our Mother not physically, but none

[2] Luke i 40-45.

the less really, after a supernatural manner. This spiritual mother-hood of Mary it will be the object of this section to elucidate, but I should like for a moment to pause and observe that the idea of motherhood in itself involves the idea of secondary causes. Nothing can be more certain than the fact that God ordinarily governs, sustains and aids his creatures not by his own direct action, but through the action of his creatures one upon another. This is true both in the natural order and in the order of grace.

If we glance first at the order of nature we shall find that Al-mighty God gave us our being by an act of his will, and maintains us in existence by his power ; yet in a true sense it may be said that our life was bestowed upon us by our mother at our birth. Of course *all* depends upon God. This is taken for granted and does not need to be continually repeated. Throughout life we rely upon our parents and schoolmasters and friends for the food, education, and sympathy which alone make life tolerable or even possible.

Manifold and diversified are the human relationships which are necessary to us as we pass our days upon earth. We travel from God to God, but from the beginning to the end, from the day when we were brought into the world to the day when we are placed in our coffin by human hands, we depend, absolutely, upon the good offices of our fellow-men.

We need not, then, be in any way surprised to find the same principle of secondary causes at work in the supernatural scheme which has been set up by the Divine Wisdom for our redemption and for the sanctification of our souls. To God's dealings with mankind through our holy religion, there is always to be found a parallel in that everyday natural way of living with which we have all of us, by long habit and usage, grown familiar. For example, as we need bread to sustain the life of the body, so do we need the Bread that cometh down from heaven to sustain the life of the soul— both should be our daily food ; or again, from time to time our body needs medicine as a remedy for its ills, so the Church provides super-natural medicine for the healing of the souls of her children. I need not give further illustrations, though numbers occur to the mind, but will say at once that to those who are familiar with the workings of the Providence of God, as he satisfies the necessities of both soul and body, it will be no surprise to find that, as the Almighty has given men an earthly mother to care for them in the days of their weakness, so has he given his children a heavenly Mother to watch over them in their journey through life with a mother's love and a mother's tenderness. Our true Mother is Mary, our Lady, the same Mother whom he gave to his Son, who became a child for love of men and deigned to need a mother's love.

This Catholic doctrine of the twofold Motherhood of Mary— Mother of men as well as Mother of God—depends upon many principles, to some of which I will draw the attention of my readers.

To our earthly mother we owe our earthly life. So in the supernatural order our Lady is the Mother to whom we owe the life of the soul. This life—the life of grace—depends exclusively upon him who *is* Life, and from whom all life flows. " For the life was manifested," writes St John, " and we declare unto you the life eternal, which was with the Father and hath appeared to us." [1]

" The life was manifested " when our Lord Jesus Christ was born of Mary the Virgin. Full of grace, full of love for God and man, the Blessed Virgin, as his earthly Mother, bestowed upon the everlasting Word of God his earthly life, bearing bodily him whom she had conceived by the Holy Ghost ; at the same moment, as our spiritual Mother, she bestowed upon us " the life eternal, which was with the Father and hath appeared to us." When, with the same great love still burning in her heart, she stood on Calvary's Hill, once more she gave life to man in giving her consent to the Passion and Death of her Divine Son ; for the life of our souls is due directly not only to the Incarnation, but also to the Redemption, and in each our Blessed Lady had her allotted part to play.

St Augustine writes : " Mary, alone, doing the will of God is the Mother of Christ bodily ; spiritually she is both sister and mother, and that woman alone,[2] not only spiritually, but also bodily, is mother and virgin. Surely she is not spiritually the Mother of our Head. Rather of him, the Saviour, she is spiritually born, for she is among those who have believed in him, among those who are rightly called ' the children of the bridegroom.' But in very truth she *is* spiritually the Mother of the members of our Head—that is of us—because *by her charity she co-operated in bringing about the birth in the Church of the faithful who are the members of that Head ;* whilst bodily she is the Mother of the Head himself." [3]

*Mary and the Mystical Body*

In these words the greatest of the Doctors of the Church reminds us of the emphatic teaching of the New Testament that by Baptism we are incorporated with Christ, becoming one with him. He is the Head, we are the members of his Body which is the Church.

" Saul, Saul, why persecutest thou me ? " said our Lord from heaven, for Saul of Tarsus was persecuting his Church on earth. The persecutor became the Apostle of the Gentiles, and showed that he had learned his lesson well, when writing to the first Christians he taught them that their very bodies were the members of Christ.[4] No one can rightly separate Christ for one moment from those who are united to him by a mystical but most close and real union. Our Lady, then, who is the Mother of the Head of the Body, is also the Mother of each member of the Body. Not only the natural but also

---

[1] 1 John i 2.
[2] *Illa una femina.* The word *illa* (" that famous ") marks her out from all other women and strengthens greatly the word *una.*
[3] S Aug. *De sancta virginitate,* cap. vi, 6.
[4] 1 Cor. vi 15.

the mystical Body of Christ was the fruit of Mary's virginal mother-hood. Before the birth of any one of us we belonged to our Lord as belonging to his Body. The Mother of God carried us together with her Divine Son when she visited Elizabeth and dwelt in the Holy Land. In a true sense the whole Church of God was enclosed, along with its Head, in the virginal womb of his Blessed Mother.

*The words of Christ on the Cross*      Catholic theologians teach that when our Lord gave utterance to the Seven Words from the Cross, he spoke not merely for the needs of the moment, but also officially as Redeemer of the world. He intended that these last words of his should be recorded in the Gospels, thus providing for the needs of all time that was to come. When he prayed for those who were directly responsible for his death—indeed, for them he prayed in the first place—he prayed also for all men and women who should crucify him anew by wilful sin and thus put him to open shame. When he pardoned the penitent thief, he declared his readiness to pardon all those in every age who, like the Good Thief, should confess their sins, own him as their Lord and seek forgiveness from his Sacred Heart. He prayed and made excuses for *all* sinners, when he prayed for some ; he declared his readiness to forgive *all* penitents, when he forgave one ; in like manner when he said to one disciple, " Behold thy Mother," he spoke to all. " When Jesus, therefore, had seen his Mother and the disciple standing whom he loved, he saith to his Mother : ' Woman, behold thy son.' After that he saith to the disciple : ' Behold thy Mother.' And from that hour the disciple took her to his own." [1] Our Blessed Lady stands at the foot of the Cross, not merely as the Mother of her dying son, but as the Mother of the Redeemer of man-kind. He that hath ears to hear, let him hear and heed his Re-deemer's word.

*Adoptive sonship*      Perhaps the most striking proof of the reality of Mary's spiritual motherhood will occur to us after we have considered with some care the Christian doctrine of our adoptive sonship. In a certain sense it may be said that the Creator is the Father of all his creatures, irrational as well as rational, since to him they owe their being ; but we use the word " father " in a very wide sense when we say that God is the Father of the cattle or of the birds and reptiles. In a higher sense he is the Father of all his *rational* creatures, the Father of all men and women. But this does not approach to the sense in which Christians use the word when they speak of that Fatherhood of God which belongs to them as to the brothers and sisters of Christ.

[1] John xix 26-27. There are Catholic writers who see in the word Woman, as used by our Lord to his Blessed Mother, both here and previously at Cana, a reference to the fact that our Lady is *the* Woman of Prophecy, *the* Woman who is, in a higher sense than was our first mother, the Mother of all the Living. But our Lord used the same word when addressing St Mary Magdalen, as it had previously been used by the Angels of the Re-surrection (John xx 13, 15). It seems to have been the usual mode of ad-dress in Palestine at the time.

When St John wrote, " As many as received him, he gave them power to be made the sons of God : to them that believe in his name, who are born, not of blood, nor of the will of the flesh, nor of the will of man, but of God," [1] he referred to a fatherhood and a birth and a sonship, other than those which belong purely to nature. They who were already sons of God, both as the work of his hands and as having been made as men and women after his image and likeness, received a new " power " that they might be made his sons in virtue of a new sonship, after a new birth. Already born into the kingdom of this world " of the will of the flesh, of the will of man," they should be born again of water and the Holy Ghost, through the action of God's Spirit.

A birth and consequent sonship above the gifts of nature were to be granted to those who had already been born of a birth, and thereby received a sonship, that did not pass the limits of that which concerns only this passing life. The gifts of grace were to be granted as an additional endowment to those who already possessed the gifts of nature. We find this truth insisted upon with much earnestness in the New Testament. For example, we are told that " we are not only called, but really are the sons of God " ; [2] that " we have received the spirit of adoption, whereby we cry Abba, Father " ; [3] and our Lord himself teaches his disciples when they pray to say boldly : " Our Father." If we ask ourselves how dare we thus speak—we poor sinful men—there is but one answer. Our Lord was not ashamed to call us his brethren. What he calls us, that we surely are—but if his brethren, then the sons of God by adoption. So by the gift bestowed upon us when we receive new life in the mystery of Baptism (as we had received our first life in the mystery of birth from our earthly mother), we are made the brethren of the Son of God, and his Father is our Father. But as his Father becomes our Father, so also does his Mother become our mother. From the first moment when, for our sake, he became " partaker of flesh and blood," [4] he became in time the Son of Mary as truly as from all eternity he was the Son of God. If his Father is our Father, then his Mother is our mother.

God, therefore, has given us his Mother to be our mother, and to care for us with a mother's love. The statement that our Lady is our mother is not merely a poetic expression—something which is a figure of speech. It is a strict truth, belonging to the spiritual order—to that order which is far more real, because more lasting than anything can be which will pass like a dream of the night. The Motherhood of Mary has its roots in time, but its promises are for eternity. *Mary's maternal functions*

We read in the life of St Stanislaus Kostka that he would constantly repeat, with wonderful happiness, " *Mater Dei, mater mei—*

---

[1] John i 12-13.  [2] 1 John iii 1.
[3] Gal. iv 6.  [4] Heb. ii 14.

God's Mother is my mother "—and we can, each of us, say the same. Can anything be more consoling ? Mary is *God's Mother*. To his Mother God will refuse nothing. Mary is *our mother*, so she will refuse nothing to her children, when they kneel at her feet and beg her to show to them a mother's love, to extend to them a mother's care. There is something extraordinarily tender and trustful in the devotion of Catholics to their Blessed Mother ; to which it is impossible to find a parallel. Our Lord we love supremely as our God and Saviour ; his Mother we love, for his sake, because she *is* his Mother so near to him, because she loved him so dearly and watched over him so faithfully at Bethlehem, in Egypt and at Nazareth ; we love her also because she is our mother too. If our Lord had appeared on earth, as he might have done, without a human mother to be his, he could not have been quite the same to us as he is when we read of him, as he actually did come, with his Mother by his side when he drew his first human breath at Bethlehem, and by his side when he died on Calvary. And as she was faithful to him unto the end, so we know that she will be faithful to us, who are also her children—the children of her tears.

Theologians are accustomed to point out that when God calls any creature to any office, he will give to that creature all the graces which are needed for the worthy discharge of the duties pertaining to that office. Thus, St Joseph was called to be foster-father of Christ, and we know that God gave him all he needed for this sublime dignity. But Mary was called actually to be Christ's true Mother ; her immaculate heart was, therefore, in such wise fashioned by her Creator—made so gentle and unutterably sympathetic and true, in the highest sense so womanly—in order that God made Man might receive all the wealth of affection which a mother could give to her child. This was one chief purpose and end of her creation. By one creature at least our Lord was loved with a perfect human love—and Mary loved him not only with the love of a creature for her God, but also with the love of a mother for her son. Nor should we ever allow ourselves to forget that our Lady loves us with the same loving heart with which she loves the Son to whom she gave birth at Bethlehem. Leaving out of consideration the love of God for men—with which, of course, we cannot compare any human love—next to the love of the Sacred Heart of Jesus there can be nothing so pure, nothing so deep, nothing so wonderful as the love of Mary for her children. Our Lady is not only *speculum justitiae*, the mirror of God's sanctity ; she is also *speculum amoris*, the mirror —the earthly reflection—of God's love. He has endowed his Mother with a love that is above the love bestowed upon all other creatures ; and this because of her nearness to him who is the source of all pure love, who himself is Love essential.

Our Lady, then, will care for her children in the same manner that of old she cared for her Divine Son. When he needed her care she saved him from Herod who would slay him ; she will save us from Satan. She gave him the food he needed in the days of his mortality ; she will plead for us that we may receive the Food of immortality. She will help us to find him, should we unhappily lose him by our sins, as once after weary search she found him, in the Temple at Jerusalem. If we allow her, she will rule our lives, as for eighteen years he allowed her to rule his life, when to her he was " subject " in the holy house of Nazareth. As she was with him when he died, so will she watch over our deathbed and answer the supplications we have raised to her heavenly throne, never doubting her goodness, during all the days of our life ; she will pray for us not only now, but, above all, in the dread hour when we die.

But while Mary shows herself to be our mother above all in caring for us in our spiritual warfare, yet we can also turn to her with confidence in the needs that concern our life here below. Not only did she bring Jesus to the house of Elizabeth, when he would work that great work of grace, and sanctify the unborn Baptist ; but also " the beginning of miracles " was worked by her Son at Cana of Galilee, when, at her prayer, water was changed into wine by divine power at the marriage feast. It was her sweet voice to which Christ listened then, as it is to her sweet voice to which he listens now at such a holy sanctuary as Lourdes, or, indeed, the wide world over, when, at his Mother's pleading, he gives his gifts to men.

They who see God face to face, see all things in him ; for no longer do they see as in a glass darkly, but in the light of the Eternal. This is true of all the Saints ; above all is it true of our Lady, to whom all her children turn in every trial, in every emergency, whether of soul or body, knowing that never in any age has she failed those who seek her aid, for she is the mother of us all. St Anselm of Canterbury gave expression to the mind of the Church and the feeling of Catholics when he wrote : " O Mary, if thou art silent, none will pray, none will aid ; when thou dost pray, all will pray, all will aid. Oh ! Queen most good to men, a thousand times a hundred thousand mortals cry to thee, and all are saved. I, too, will cry to thee, and shall I not receive thy help ? " [1]

I have said that our Lady's Motherhood of men, especially of Christians, seems to depend chiefly upon four great principles. (1) Mary gave us the life of the soul when she gave us Jesus Christ ; (2) she is the Mother of the members of his Body as well as of the Head ; (3) she was given to us by our Lord Jesus from the Cross in the person of the disciple whom he loved with a special love ; (4) she is the Mother of him who is our Brother, and therefore is our Mother also, even as his Father is our Father too.

---

[1] Te tacente, O Maria, nullus orabit, nullus juvabit ; te orante, omnes orabunt, omnes juvabunt. Millies centena millia hominum ad te clamant, Regina piissima, et omnes salvantur ; et ego clamabo ad te et non auxiliabor ? —Migne, P.L., tom. clix, col. 943.

But once in the Sacred Scriptures our Lady is pointed out to us in her own person as the Mother of Christians. The disciple to whose care Christ had entrusted his Blessed Mother for what should yet remain of her earthly life, tells us that he beheld a mysterious vision. Mary had passed to her great reward, when he saw the long story of the Church unrolled as in a wondrous panorama. It was to be a story of bitter, enduring conflict. " And a great sign appeared in heaven : A woman clothed with the sun, and the moon under her feet, and on her head a crown of twelve stars. . . . And there was seen another sign in heaven ; and behold a great red dragon, having seven heads and ten horns ; and on his heads seven diadems. . . . And the dragon stood before the woman who was ready to be delivered . . . that he might devour her Son. And she brought forth a man-child, who was to rule all nations with an iron rod. . . . And there was a great battle in heaven : Michael and his angels fought with the dragon, and the dragon fought and his angels. . . . And the dragon was *angry* against the woman, and went to make war with *the rest of her seed, who keep the commandments of God and have the testimony of Jesus Christ.*" [1]

In this manner, throughout all the ages, the primeval prophecy was to be fulfilled : " I will put enmities between thee and the woman, between thy seed and her seed." [2]

We read that the dragon of the vision is " that old serpent, who is called the devil and Satan " ; and we know who is the Woman, clothed with the Sun of Justice—Christ our Lord—and below her the moon—this passing world—and on her head a crown of twelve

[1] Apoc. xii 1-17.
It is well known that it is often difficult in Holy Scripture to discover whether the *direct* reference (particularly in Old Testament types) is to the Mother, or to the Church, of Christ. We are taught by writers of great authority that our Lady and the Church are merged in the Sacred Writings into a mystic unity ; for example, already in the second century St Clement of Alexandria writes : " One only Mother Virgin. Dear it is to me to call her the Church." He was speaking in the first place of the Blessed Virgin (*Paed.* i 6). And St Augustine : " His Mother is the whole Church, because through the grace of God everywhere she gives birth to the faithful of Christ" (*De Sancta Virg.* vi). It is also certain that our Lady represents and personifies the Church, as for example in her obedience : " Behold the handmaid of the Lord, be it done unto me according to thy word " ; and in her prayer as at Cana : " They have no wine " ; and in her submission to Christ : " Whatsoever he shall say to you, that do ye " ; and in her faithfulness to our Lord to the end. Therefore, we shall not be surprised if we find that some of the few writers of antiquity who have written on this Vision in the Apocalypse refer it *in the first place* to our Lady, and others to the Church. In any case, even though the direct reference be to the Church there can be no doubt that it is to the Church under the figure of the Blessed Mother of God, who is represented to us as the Mother, not only of the Man-Child who was to rule the nations with a rod of iron, but also of " the rest of her seed," who are expressly pointed out as Christians " having the testimony of Jesus Christ."

[2] Gen. iii 15.

stars ; for is she not the Queen of the Apostles, who are her crown ?
We thank God that we are " the rest of her seed," her children too.
If we endeavour to keep the commandments of God and have the
testimony of Jesus Christ, she who is the Queen of Heaven will
fight on our behalf, with Michael and his angels by her side ; for
ours is the promise of God which endureth for ever. The Woman
and her seed through all the ages, and until time shall be no more,
will crush the serpent's head.

Our Blessed Lady is the heavenly Mother under whose banner
her children shall triumph over Satan and over sin.

> *Monstra te esse matrem,*
> *Sumat per te preces,*
> *Qui pro nobis natus*
> *Tulit esse tuus.*

## § IV: MARY AND HER DIVINE SON

FROM all eternity Mary of Nazareth was chosen by God to be the
Virgin Mother of the Word made Man, to co-operate in the work
of the Redemption, and to care for her children in the land of their
exile with a heavenly Mother's love ; but she too had once, like all
other children of Adam, dwelt upon the earth, and thus was made
ready for her rich reward.

It remains, then, for us to consider what we may gather as to
our Lady's earthly life, passed by her for the most part in company
with her Divine Son. Here we are treading on very holy ground
indeed—nothing can be more mysterious than the relations of the
Incarnate God with his Blessed Mother, as he led her soul step by
step to heights of sanctity far above our mortal ken, through sorrows
unimaginable—from earth to heaven that she might, when life
was past, be crowned by his hand Queen of Angels and of men.

Any Catholic who attempts to deal with this theme must feel
something of what St Bernard felt when he wrote : " There is
nothing which gives greater joy to my heart, yet there is nothing
which inspires me with more fear than to treat of the glory of the
Virgin Mother." [1]

Still, though we take off our shoes with awe, as we approach
to contemplate the Virgin Mother's life on earth, reverently to do
so should bring us nearer to her in veneration and love—so we may
attempt the task, remembering always that we are thinking of one
who, although a creature like ourselves, nevertheless always remains
the predestined Mother of God.

The Old Testament is full of types of our Blessed Lady. Eve, *Types of*
Sara, Rebecca, Rachel, Miriam, Deborah, Ruth, Abigail, Judith, *Our Lady*
Esther—all prefigure, under one aspect or another, the Mother of
the Saviour. Her virginal maternity was foreshadowed by the yet

[1] *Serm. iv de Assumptione.*

untilled soil in Eden, by the Burning Bush and Gideon's fleece, by the Ark of the Covenant and the Eastern Gate of the Temple, and, so the Fathers of the Church assure us, by many another mysterious episode in the time of God's preparation for the coming of his Son.

I have no space in which to dwell on these figures of our Lady, nor on the prophecies which linked her name with that of her Son, who was to redeem Israel from captivity. We must come to the time of the fulfilment, when types and shadows should have reached their accomplishment in the perfection of that which they prefigured.

*The Annunciation* We find Mary first in the New Testament, as " a Virgin espoused to a man whose name was Joseph, of the House of David," when the Angel saluted her at Nazareth : " Hail, Mary, full of grace, the Lord is with thee. Blessed art thou among women."

Catholic tradition tells us that for this salutation and for this coming of the Lord, and for this high blessedness, our Lady had been prepared by her Presentation as a child in the Temple, where she had passed her early life in prayer and meditation on the ancient Scriptures, and especially dwelling on the prophecies concerning the Messias whose advent was then eagerly expected by the Jews. Already the time marked out by Daniel had arrived. Israel was waiting full of expectation. . . .

And now the Holy Virgin knew that he had come and that he was hers—wonder of wonders, he was her Son. Soon she was to see his face amidst the straw at Bethlehem, to worship him with every fibre of her being, to love him with every beating of her heart, with a love far, far beyond the love of the Cherubim and the Seraphim. She loved him with the love of the creature for her Creator and of the Mother for the fruit of her womb. This twofold relation between Jesus and Mary was to persist to the end of her life and to endure for eternity. Unless we bear it steadily in mind nothing is intelligible in the sacred narrative. We are as far away from any understanding of the mystery of Mary if we forget that she is both servant and Mother of her Lord, as we should be from any understanding of the mystery of Jesus were we to forget that he is both God and Man.

*The Visitation* I have already written something of the marvel of the Visitation when our Lady bore her Child over the hills to visit Elizabeth.[1] Elizabeth was filled with the Holy Ghost, and Mary, who was even then the living shrine of the Godhead, burst into song of a beauty unimaginable. Her soul magnified her Lord who had done such things for her, and her spirit rejoiced in God her Saviour. The Queen of Prophets was not afraid to declare aloud that all generations should call her Blessed, reaching forward through the long ages in dim futurity, for God had put down the mighty from their seat and had exalted the lowly and the meek. When we listen to the *Magnificat*, we feel it is one of the most unimpeachable of all prophecies,

[1] P. 533.

the most sublime of all thanksgivings, and the most thrilling of all poems. Mary's soul was full of joy and of holy exultation when thus she magnified the Lord before her child was born; after he had come to her, she was to bear him in her arms as she listened first to the *Nunc Dimittis* of the aged Simeon, and then to the solemn warning, "And thy own soul a sword shall pierce, that out of many hearts thoughts may be revealed." [1]

Our Blessed Lady's mind was not only steeped in the ancient *The sorrows* Scriptures—she knew that the Messias was to be the Man of Sorrows *to come* —it was also specially illuminated by God. Already she knew full well that his Mother must in large measure share her Son's appointed lot; but now the seal was, as it were, impressed upon that knowledge, as Simeon's threnody fell, like a death knell, upon her ears. In very truth a sword should pierce her inmost soul, that out of the hearts of countless millions the thoughts of the broken-hearted should be revealed. In the dim future, through the long ages inspired by Christian faith, Mary's children, stricken with grief otherwise intolerable, were to kneel before the image of the desolate Virgin, and there find comfort for their bleeding hearts. But before this could come to pass, her own life had to be lived through, her own heart pierced by the sword of agony, that thus it might be duly fashioned and made ready as the home of the hopeless and the refuge of the sinner who repents.

The glad Mother of the Lord was also to be the Mother of Sorrows—she was to be the Mother of the Crucified. Deep as the sea is thy desolation, O Virgin Daughter of Sion, and who shall be compared with thee, either in thy joys that are incomparable, or in thy grief which is beyond all measure?

Nor could the delay be long before the sword pierced our Lady's *Flight into* heart. It was but a brief period after the Blessed Virgin had shown *Egypt* her Child proudly to the homely shepherds and to the wondering Wise Men from the distant East, that she [2] "heard the voice in Rama, lamenting and great mourning; Rachel bewailing her children and refusing to be comforted because they are not." For the first time in the world's history women were weeping, their children dying, because tyrants feared and hated the Name of Christ, and Mary's heart was broken. She herself had to fly into the foreign land of Egypt, far from friends and home, because her first duty was at all costs to safeguard the life of her Son, who had been entrusted to her care. When at last Herod was dead and his threats a thing of the past, the Holy Family, Jesus, Mary and Joseph, went back to Palestine.

Our Lord was but twelve years of age; "when he remained in *Jesus lost in* Jerusalem and his parents knew it not . . . and it came to pass *Jerusalem* that after three days they found him in the Temple, sitting in the midst of the doctors, hearing them, and asking them questions . . .

[1] Luke ii 35.    [2] Matt. ii 18.

and his Mother said to him : Son, why hast thou done so to us ?
Behold thy father and I have sought thee sorrowing. And he said
to them : How is it that you sought me ? Did you not know that
I must be about my Father's business ? " [1] As we read we recognise
that he is the Divine Child. No young boy, who was merely a boy
like other boys, could rightly thus act and speak.

The relations of our Divine Lord with his Blessed Mother, as
they are recorded in the gospels, would be utterly unintelligible, were
he nothing more than a great Jewish teacher, and she only the mother
of that teacher. The key to that which otherwise would be so
perplexing may be found in the fact that he is not only Man, but
also that his Mother's soul was during her earthly life being moulded
by his hand for her eternal destiny as Queen in his kingdom. It is
the realisation of this supreme reality—as to who Jesus is and who
Mary—which opens out to our gaze, as we ponder on the gospel
narrative, a vista of transcendent loveliness and awe-inspiring
majesty. In the dealings of our Blessed Lord with his Mother no
merely human measure can be applied, for here the divine and the
human meet in sublime conjunction. Two things we know : Inscrutable are his ways and unfathomable is his love for the chosen
creature of his predilection whom, in all-wise but unsuspected ways,
he drew to a degree of nearness and of union with himself that
could be reached by no other. There can be only one Lord
Jesus Christ, and only one Mother of God. They stand apart
from all the world beside. God will deal with Mary as with no
other, for she will understand as can no other.

"And his Mother kept all these words in her heart." [2]

If the story of the loss and finding of our Lord in the Temple
is deeply charged with mystery, more mysterious far are the words
that tell us what followed : " And he went down with them, and
came to Nazareth and was subject to them." [3] *He* was the Lord
God Incarnate, *they* were his Mother and his foster-father, the work
of his hands. Amongst other purposes of his coming, Christ came
to be our example—from the age of twelve to the age of thirty no
other example is given us by him excepting that of his " subjection "
in the holy house of Nazareth. During that long reach of years
Mary and Joseph were catching from his lips the secrets of the
Kingdom which he set up in their hearts, as they learned with ever
increasing simplicity and perfection to do the will of God, his
Father.

*The public
ministry*

Great sorrows—the sorrow of Simeon's prophecy, of the Flight
into Egypt, of the Loss in the Temple—came to our Lady before the
eighteen years she passed at tranquil Nazareth ; during the sojourn
there, so far as we know, all was peace, excepting that St Joseph
died who was so dear to her, and the shadow of the Cross hung over
her through the day and through the night. She knew what had

[1] Luke ii 41-49.          [2] Luke ii 51.          [3] *Ibid.*

to come. And at last the hour struck. That which had been fore-shadowed during the three days in the Temple had to be fulfilled during the last three years of our Saviour's life. They had to be spent away from the society of his Blessed Mother. Now he was to be, during the period that immediately preceded the Passion, in a special sense about his Father's business—teaching all those who would listen to his word, training his chosen disciples for their future apostolate, laying the foundation of his Church, giving hearing to the deaf and sight to the blind, making the lame to walk, raising the dead to life, and speaking words sweeter than honey and the honeycomb, that should linger in the world, haunting the hearts of men, to the end of time—above all by undying parable and actions of heavenly kindness teaching his Father's love, for he and the Father are One. And all the time Mary, his Mother, could not be by the side of her Son. She remained in isolation with his brethren, some of whom at least believed not in him—and once again her tender heart was wellnigh broken and Simeon's sword pierced her soul.

Looking back, as we do, through nearly two thousand years of Christian history and tradition, it is exceedingly difficult, if not im-possible, to form any adequate idea of the circumstances which surrounded our Lord's public ministry. We know that he was God: none of those who were drawn to him when he began to teach had the slightest idea of any such thing—to them it would have seemed sheer madness and blasphemy of the worst kind—a sin especially hateful to the Jews. The minds of his disciples had to be attuned most carefully—first to the idea that he was the Messias, and then . . . upwards to the very heights. We see the first great step : " Whom do *men* say that I am ? . . . Whom do *you* say that I am ? . . . Blessed art *thou*, Simon, son of John, for flesh and blood hath not revealed it unto thee." [1] And then in all its dread com-pleteness : " So long have I been with thee and hast thou not known me, Philip ? He that seeth me seeth the Father also." [2] And the tremendous assertion : " Before Abraham was made I am." [3]

It is very remarkable that through all this necessarily elaborate process our Lord, from time to time, speaks almost provocatively, as though to stimulate thought in the Church in the generations yet unborn, when his Godhead should have been recognised to the full. He wished also to rivet to attention the minds of his disciples, and, indeed, of all who were listening to him, by introducing the element of surprise into his speech. Such sayings of Christ which will at once occur to the mind are : " The Father is greater than I." [4] " Why dost thou call me good ? None is good but God alone." [5] " Weep not for me ".; [6] and there are many others of a like character. The Saints and mystics of the Catholic Church have mused unceasingly upon the mysterious words which fell from the lips of Christ. From

[1] Matt. xvi 17.  [2] John xiv 9.  [3] John viii 58.
[4] John xiv 28.  [5] Luke xviii 19.  [6] Luke xxiii 28.

them they have drawn consolation, wisdom, strength, as the bee draws honey from the flower.   They have furnished matter for the profoundest reflections of Doctors of the Church, and have been one of the chief means by which Christ's servants have been drawn to the heights of contemplation and union of the soul with God.   It should hardly be necessary to say that, when rightly understood, they are all fully consistent with the true doctrine of the Eternal Godhead of the Word made Man ; but historically they furnished ammunition for the Arian heresy.   This our Lord disregarded. It was merely incidental and could not be allowed to interfere with the high purposes which ever directed his earthly life.   If men should misunderstand, let them see to it.   They would be solely responsible, for they would run counter to the warnings and to the teaching of his Church.   In this manner they would only make shipwreck of the faith.   Christ spoke for all time, for the ears of the faithful in every age ; he spoke also for the sake of those who were listening to him at the moment.   He would not go beyond *their* knowledge, since to have done so at the time would have served no useful purpose.

*Apparent repudiation*   We find the same remarkable set of facts with reference to our Blessed Lady.   Her privileges are clear and conspicuous in the Gospel, standing out in bold relief, so that it is hard to miss them. The story of the Annunciation and of the first visit to Elizabeth need no comment to bring out their full significance.   But, just as the Arian has found, in the very Gospels which proclaim the Divinity of our Lord, materials on which to ground his denials, so have others found certain incidents which they use against the Church in consequence of the honour which she pays to the Blessed Mother of our Lord.   For example, when our Lord had once been speaking to the crowds, a certain woman lifting up her voice said to him : [1] " Blessed is the womb that bore thee, and the paps that gave thee suck.   But he said : Yea rather, blessed are they who hear the word of God and keep it."

On this there are several things to be observed.   We must bear in mind that in his public speech our Blessed Lord was always intent upon inculcating a practical lesson.   Of this we have here a striking instance.   As we have already pointed out, the great Saints have insisted that our Lady is even more blessed through doing the Will of God, in which all may imitate her, than in her Divine Childbearing—a grace bestowed upon her by God in which she must of necessity stand alone.

Also, it is certain that, according to the established custom of Orientals, the woman who spoke to our Lord lifted up her voice in *his* honour, not in the honour of his Mother ; for in the East, if they wish to praise a man they will praise his ancestors, if they desire to dishonour a man they will curse his forebears to many a

[1] Luke xi 27.

generation—so that if our Lord is deprecating honour paid to any, it is that shown to himself rather than that offered to his kinsfolk, however near they might be to him. Again, there can be no doubt that his Mother had been proclaimed blessed among women both by Gabriel sent from God's Throne to Nazareth, and by Elizabeth, filled with the Holy Ghost in the house of Zachary, whilst the Baptist exulted yet unborn. Any argument or inference which would tend to lessen the force of this, and of our Lady's own testimony that all generations should call her blessed obviously proves too much and falls to the ground slain by its own weight. And yet, as a matter of fact, this saying of our Lord has created a difficulty, hard to dispel, in the minds of some people who have seen in it, however unreasonably, a disparagement of the honour shown to the Blessed Virgin by Catholics.

To take a second instance. Christ was once told by the multitude that his Mother and brethren were seeking for him. At the time he was away from them all, about his Father's business, and asked, " Who is my mother and my brethren ? " He then answered his question himself, looking upon those whom he had been teaching : " Behold my mother and my brethren. For whosoever shall do the will of God, he is my brother and sister and mother." [1]

Surely a spiritual lesson of enormous value for all time. I have already reminded my readers that St Augustine, commenting on these words of Christ, says that our Lady, in doing the will of God, became not only Mother, but sister to her Son, and Christians in every age can learn from these words to be mother and brother and sister to their Lord. Yet, I think our Lady's heart ached when she heard the manner in which she, who was his Mother in the strict sense of the word, apparently was passed over. Can we not find a faint reflection here of the anguish of her Divine Son, when, in apparent abandonment, he cried aloud to his Father in bitter agony before he died ? Not only on Mount Calvary, it was hers to share, so far as creature might, in the sufferings of Christ. The Passion of our Lord found its echo in the compassion of his Holy Mother. In truth the sorrows of Mary, the sorrows of her trans-pierced heart, were necessary not only that many thoughts should be revealed of sorrowing men and women, but also for her own perfect sanctification. Her soul had to be made perfect in the furnace of trial and tribulation. As in all things else, so pre-eminently in this must she resemble our Lord, that he was the Man of Sorrows and acquainted with grief. Of all the redeemed his Mother must be nearest to his Cross, not only on Calvary, but also in every hour of her earthly pilgrimage.

But that pilgrimage, both for Jesus and for Mary, at length was over. And now that our Lord is glorified in his Kingdom, every tear that his Mother shed on earth shall be wiped away by his pierced

*Mary's Compassion*

*Mary's death*

[1] Mark iii 31-35.

hand, and changed into a jewel in the crown upon her peerless brow. Mary must die, for this is the lot of mortals. " It is appointed unto man to die, and after death the judgement " ; and as Jesus died, so will his Mother die, for in all things, so far as may be, shall her lot be like to his ; moreover, since all her children must pass one day through the gate of death, so bitter to human nature, so their Mother will go before them, treading the same path. But in her passing hence there will be for her no bitterness, death will lead her straight to God. She had waited, obedient to the will of God who would have her remain a while on earth, the Apostles' Queen. But now the chains which held her captive at length were broken and her sinless soul winged its flight to be with her Son for ever. And Mary's judgement: " Well done, good and faithful servant." Were these words for which all Christ's servants wait expectant ever spoken as when they were addressed to her, who alone was crowned in heaven as the Mother of her Lord ?

*The Assumption*     The bodies of the holy Apostles, of the Martyrs who shed their blood for Christ, of men and women famed for their sanctity, were to be carefully preserved and venerated in the Church from the first beginnings of Christianity. Of the Mother of God no relics should remain upon the earth. Mary was taken up, body and soul, to the unveiled presence of her Son. She was the mystic Ark of the Covenant which God had sanctified. The body of the Virgin Most Holy from which the Holy Spirit had formed the body of Christ should not be permitted to see corruption. Behold the Queen in her beauty by the side of her Son, as already the Psalmist saw her in prophetic vision, in a vesture of gold wrought about with divers colours. She is the eldest daughter of the Father, and the beloved Mother of the Son, and the chosen Spouse of the Everlasting Spirit.

We, too, have to die and to meet Christ in judgement. We trust to be greeted with forgiveness and love as we enter into his Kingdom. He will not reject us, whose arms were extended wide for us upon the Cross of pain. " Who is he that shall condemn ? Christ Jesus who died for us ? " [1]

But if, notwithstanding all, our hearts fail within us at the thought of our sins and miseries, we will entreat our dear Mother, who is also the Mother of our Judge, to be to us *Felix caeli porta*, the gate of a happy eternity, that when all is passing and death is near, she may turn her eyes of mercy towards us, and show unto us at length the ever-blessed Fruit of her womb, Jesus, teaching us to trust him absolutely and to the full. So may it be for us all—we beseech thee, O loving, O kind, O sweet Virgin Mary.

O. R. VASSALL-PHILLIPS, C.SS.R.

[1] Rom. viii 34.

# XVI

## SANCTIFYING GRACE

### §I: THE STATE OF GRACE

IN one of the most beautiful of the Psalms the royal singer gives *Sanctifying* expression to the wonder which filled his mind when he looked out *grace a* upon the glories of God's visible creation. " O Lord our Lord : *positive* *reality* how admirable is thy name in the whole earth ! For thy magnificence is elevated above the heavens. . . . I will behold thy heavens, the works of thy fingers : the moon and the stars which thou hast founded." And then he marvels that a God of such magnificence and power should have any care for feeble man. " What is man that thou art mindful of him ? Or the son of man that thou visitest him ? Thou hast made him a little less than the angels : thou hast crowned him with glory and honour, and hast set him over the works of thy hands. . . . O Lord our Lord : how admirable is thy name in all the earth ! " [1]

With still greater reason can we proclaim the glory and the magnificence and the condescension of the Lord our God when we consider, in the light of Catholic theology, the wonders of a soul which God has beautified by the gift of sanctifying grace. " All the glory of the king's daughter is within," [2] and it is in a soul which is in the state of grace rather than in the starry heavens or in the wonders of the human mind that we are to find the masterpiece of God's handicraft in this world of ours. The sanctifying grace with which the souls of God's servants are endowed is far grander, far more glorious than anything which we can behold in the heavens above us or on the earth at our feet. This is a truth which we have often heard—so often, perhaps, that it has become a commonplace which we accept without appreciating its significance. But the more we study it the more we shall marvel, until we can make our own the words with which the Blessed Virgin expressed her realisation of the favour which had been granted her : " he that is mighty hath done great things to me : and holy is his name." [3]

The state of grace is not merely the absence of mortal sin, as many people seem to imagine. They look upon the soul as being in itself a very beautiful thing—a spirit, glorious in its various natural qualities, and far grander than any material object ; mortal sin can defile it and make it hideous ;. but if there is no such sin it remains resplendent in all the glory of its spiritual nature and is thus (so it is thought) in the state of grace.

[1] Ps. viii.    [2] Ps. xliv 14.    [3] Luke i 49.

Such a view of the matter, however, falls far short of the truth. The state of grace is thus made to be a mere negative thing—namely, the absence of the defiling element of mortal sin. But the fact which we have to remember is that grace [1] is a positive reality superadded to the glorious natural endowments of the soul. These endowments are not left in all their natural beauty ; they receive an additional glory which surpasses what they are in themselves far more than they themselves surpass the glories of the world around us ; and it is the possession of this additional glory, rather than the mere absence of mortal sin, which constitutes the state of grace.

The Catholic doctrine on this point is in direct opposition to the strange theories of Protestantism. Faced by his failure to control his violent and sensuous character, Luther evolved a theory which is a combination of pessimism and easy optimism. Through the fall of Adam, he maintained, our nature has become essentially evil and must ever remain evil ; it is a mass of corruption, and even the redeeming blood of our Saviour does not cleanse or heal it ; and he pressed his theory so far as to draw the conclusion that all our actions are sinful, not excluding those which we look upon as virtuous. Here we have the pessimism of the system : but now comes its easy optimism. For Luther taught that if only we will have complete confidence that the merits of Christ are actually applied to us, our sins are ignored, as it were, by God ; our souls remain indeed hideous in themselves, but God covers them over with the merits of Christ so that these are looked upon by him as being ours ; our sins are not " imputed " to us, but the merits of Christ are.

This is the famous doctrine of Justification by Faith. For the Lutheran, then. justification does not mean (as it means for a Catholic) an inner change by which the soul becomes a sacred thing, but a mere external non-imputation of sins ; and faith means, not an assent to truths divinely revealed, but a personal persuasion that the merits of Christ have been applied to us. This faith, in the Lutheran system, is the only thing which counts : good works are of no avail —indeed, they are impossible, since all our actions are made evil by the evil source from which they spring. A further conclusion from Luther's principles is that there can be no such thing as Merit, a point with which we shall deal later on.

*Protestant error explained and refuted*

In what follows there will be frequent reference to the Protestant theory of justification. This is inevitable, for, although our chief concern is with the positive statement of Catholic truth, the official statement of this truth by the Council of Trent was drawn up with direct reference to the errors of the sixteenth century.

[1] In the course of this essay whenever we use the term " grace " we shall understand by it " sanctifying grace " as opposed to " actual grace." Sanctifying grace, as we shall explain, is a permanent quality in the soul ; actual grace, of course, is a passing help given by God for the performance of some act. See Essay xvii of this work.

In the first place, then, the Council lays it down that we become just before God not through a non-imputation of sin but by an interior renovation which blots out sin. This is effected by sanctifying grace, which is explained as a reality poured forth upon us and inhering in us.

Beyond any doubt, this is the teaching of Scripture and of the great leaders of Christian thought from the beginning. Within the compass of a small essay like the present it is not possible to give an adequate exposition of scriptural texts, still less to set out the teaching of Christian writers through the ages, but there readily come to the mind a number of expressions used in the Scriptures which show most clearly that the state of grace involves a real interior change in the soul. Consider such expressions as " born again," " regeneration," " renovation," " new creature." Here, surely, we have the idea of an inner change and not of a mere non-imputation of sin. Similarly when St Paul speaks of the " new man " who is " created in justice and holiness of truth," [1] he is alluding to a marvellous change which is produced in us. Very striking, too, is the parallel which he draws between the results of Adam's sin and the restoration which has been accomplished by Christ. " As by the disobedience of one man many were made sinners, so by the obedience of one many shall be made just." [2] But the disobedience of Adam certainly brought about a real change in the souls of men, as Luther must be the first to admit : therefore Christ produces an inner change when through his grace many are made just.

The early teachers of Christian truth proclaimed the same doctrine in many striking ways. Thus in explaining the effects of Baptism they frequently compared the water of the font to a mother : as the mother forms and fashions her child, so does the baptismal water form and fashion a new creature for God. Or as God in the work of creation produced living things out of the waters, so does he bring the soul to a new life in the waters of baptism. So insistent on this inner change are the early writers, and such a high ideal did they form of it, that they did not hesitate to say that we are deified ; in fact they took this to be an admitted principle amongst Christians, for they made it a basis of argument against those who denied the divinity of the Holy Ghost. The Holy Ghost, they argued, deifies us : therefore he is God, since none but God can deify the soul.

It would be easy to quote many striking and beautiful passages from the writings of the Fathers of the Church extolling the glory of the soul which Christ has washed in his blood. All this is directly contrary to the awful teaching of Protestantism which would make the soul even of the just man a sinful thing, essentially corrupt and loathsome. There can, then, be no doubt about what is the correct view of the matter : sanctifying grace is a real quality, of surpassing

[1] Eph. iv 24.      [2] Rom. v 19.

beauty, infused by God into the soul and making that soul worthy of the Creator who fashioned it and the Redeemer who won it from the thraldom of sin.[1]

*Grace wholly supernatural*

This, then, must be our first point : grace is a positive reality superadded to the soul. But what is the nature of this positive reality ? Here we are faced by the inability of the human mind to grasp the magnificence of the glorious truth. We may use metaphors and comparisons ; we may liken grace to the brightness of white-hot steel or to the brilliance of a diamond that sparkles in the light ; but all such modes of speaking fall far short of the truth. They fail in various ways, but principally in one most important point which is necessary for a right understanding of what grace is. In all such figures of speech we compare sanctifying grace with something which is natural to the object to which it belongs ; thus the brilliance of the diamond is natural to the diamond and is in the same order of being. But sanctifying grace is not natural to the soul ; it belongs to a higher order of things. It is a supernatural quality which no created cause could possible produce. It belongs to a new and an altogether higher world. This is an aspect of the matter which calls for careful consideration, and we beg the reader's attention to what follows. The explanation shall be given with as little technicality as possible.

As the very form of the word indicates, the supernatural is something which is above, or higher than, that which is natural. But what are we to understand by the term " natural " ? In ordinary usage it has various meanings, but in Catholic philosophy and theology it has a very precise meaning which must be rigorously adhered to. The natural, then, is something which belongs to the very essence or nature of a thing (as the power of reasoning belongs to man), or flows from its nature (as the skill of a workman flows from his nature), or is necessary or suitable for the existence and development of a thing (as air is necessary for man). Thus " natural " is not to be contrasted with " artificial," and if we are to keep to the strict meaning of the words we ought not to say, for example, that it is not natural for a diamond to sparkle since in its original (or, as we say, in its natural) condition it is a dull stone. In the technical sense of the term it is quite natural for a diamond to sparkle since this follows from its very nature.

Of course what is natural for one thing may be above the nature of another thing. Thus it is natural for a man to reason, but not for a dog ; natural for wood to float in water, but not for a bar of iron.

In the light of these explanations it will be seen that the supernatural is something which is above, or higher than, what belongs

---

[1] Here no criticism is made of the Lutheran theory of Faith, but the point will be dealt with later on when we consider faith in Christ as the fundamental element in preparation for justification.

" naturally " to things ; if this something is above that which belongs naturally to any creature, it is said to be " absolutely " supernatural ; if it is above that which belongs naturally to some creatures but not to all, it is " relatively " supernatural. Thus, angelic knowledge in a man would be relatively, not absolutely, supernatural ; but for a man to enjoy the Beatific Vision of God, face to face, is absolutely supernatural, since to see God by direct and immediate vision is above the natural order of all created beings, angelic as well as human.

To the reader who desires no more than to have unfolded before him something of the glories of sanctifying grace these explanations may appear wearisome : but they are necessary not only for the avoiding of positive error but also for the gaining of a clearer and grander idea of what this wonderful gift is. Another point must be explained before we pass on—a point of great importance. A distinction has to be made between that which is supernatural considered in itself (*supernaturale in se*), and that which is supernatural because of the way in which it has been brought about (*supernaturale quoad modum*). Thus the restoration of a dead man to life is clearly supernatural : is it supernatural in itself or only supernatural in the manner of its production ? The answer is that it is supernatural not in the first way but in the second : for the thing produced (namely, life) is not in itself supernatural, though it has been produced in a supernatural way. And the same is to be said of all miracles. On the other hand, whatever belongs to God himself, or involves some sharing of what is proper to God, is supernatural in itself, transcending the order not only of what creatures do but also of what they are.

The application of all this to the question of sanctifying grace will be seen more and more as we proceed, but for the present we simply assert the magnificent truth that grace is not only a positive reality in the soul, not only a reality which no created being could produce, but a reality which in itself is higher than the whole order of created things (even angelic) and is truly divine. This brings us at once to a wonderful phrase of St Peter, who says that we are made " partakers of the divine nature." [1] Catholic theology has ever clung to the belief that here we have no mere figure of speech but the declaration of a definite fact. We really are made to be partakers of the divine nature. It is not merely that our spiritual faculties of intellect and will establish a special likeness to God in our souls ; that is true enough, but over and above this natural likeness to God a wholly supernatural quality is given to us which makes us to be of the same nature as God. In this connection we may recall the principle used by early writers in arguing the divinity of the Holy Ghost : the Holy Ghost deifies us ; in other words makes

*Grace makes us share God's nature and life*

[1] 2 Pet. i 4.

us partakers of the divine nature. St Augustine puts the matter thus : " He descended that we might ascend, and whilst retaining his own divine nature he partook of our human nature, that we, whilst keeping our own nature, might become partakers of his." St Thomas Aquinas, echoing the constant teaching of the past, declares in a passage which the Church uses for the feast of Corpus Christi : " the only-begotten Son of God, wishing to make us partakers of his own divinity, took upon himself our human nature that having become man he might make men to be gods." And we know how the Church has enshrined this wonderful truth in one of the most beautiful of the prayers at Mass. " O God, who in creating human nature, didst marvellously ennoble it, and hast still more marvellously renewed it, grant that by the mystery of this water and wine *we may be made partakers of his Godhead*, who vouchsafed to become partaker of our humanity, Jesus Christ, thy Son, our Lord."

God, then, has deigned to touch us with his finger, and in touching us has transformed us into something like himself. We shall never understand in our present life in what this partaking of the Godhead consists : how could we understand it, seeing that the nature of the Godhead is itself above our understanding ? We can, indeed, speak of it as the divine Light which shines in our souls, or as the divine Beauty which is bestowed upon us ; or we may use illustrations such as that of St Thomas Aquinas, who says that we share the very nature of God as metal in the fire shares the nature of the fire. Such ways of speaking and such illustrations are all helpful, and the Christian soul, seeking to get some faint idea of the glory of sanctifying grace, will dwell upon them with joy. But a higher and truer way of viewing the matter is to think of grace as a communication to us of the divine Life itself. For God is a living being, not a lifeless thing like the shining metal or the glistening jewel, and they who share his nature must necessarily share his very life. A wonderful thought, truly, and one which leads us far in our search for a less inadequate idea of what grace is. Let us dwell upon it for a moment.

We are familiar with the grades of life in the world around us. There is the life of the plant which separates it by an immense ocean of reality from all non-living things ; there is the life of the animal with those wonderful powers of sensation and instinct which the plant does not possess ; and there is the life of a rational being whose intellect and will raise him far above the brutes. Higher, indeed, than man there are the angels, but their life does not differ in order from the rational life of man ; it is more perfect in many ways and is not bound up with the animal life which is part of man's nature ; but it is a life of intellect and will. But there is yet a higher life, the incomprehensible, unutterable life of God, who, as the Scripture says, dwells in light inaccessible. This life of God is the fountain whence all life flows and, could we understand it, is the

explanation of how and why there are three Persons in him. To
share this life is clearly the grandest thing that can be imagined.
It would seem, indeed, to be impossible ; and impossible it certainly
would be if we were limited to the natural order of things. Nothing
in the world of created things could have brought it about and no
human mind could have guessed it. Yet in this life God has made
us share—a greater work than when he called the world out of
nothingness.

In the next section something more will be said about the nature
of this partaking of the divine life, and we shall then see how it
is a preparation for the Beatific Vision, and the basis of our claim
to be in very truth the sons of God.

There are also other wonderful aspects of the state of grace
which remain to be explained, but already we can see something of
the grandeur of the Catholic doctrine, which asserts for man, even
in the days of his earthly pilgrimage, a glory which raises him up
to the Godhead and makes him most beautiful in the sight of the
angels.

And so we make our own the words of David, " What is man
that thou art mindful of him ? Or the son of man that thou visitest
him ? Thou hast made him a little less than the angels ; thou hast
crowned him with glory and honour. . . . O Lord our Lord: how
admirable is thy name in all the earth." [1]

## §II : SONS AND HEIRS

IN this second section we are to consider two special aspects of the *Divine*
life of grace which God bestows upon us ; the first is the sonship *Sonship*
which comes with sanctifying grace, and the second is the fact that,
in a fuller sense than at first sight would seem possible, we are made
heirs of God and have already within us the beginnings of eternal
glory.

St John bids us see " what manner of charity the Father hath
bestowed upon us, that we should be called and should be the sons
of God." [2] In his infinite condescension God has made us his
children. We know how sometimes a poor child is adopted, taken
into a home, made one of the family, treated as a son or daughter,
and even given a right to inherit all that belongs to those who have
thus bestowed their love. God has done this for us—and much
more. Through the fall of our first parents we were cut off from

---

[1] Sanctifying Grace is regarded by theologians as a " Habit." The term
may be misleading, for by a habit we usually understand a customary mode
of acting, and this does not seem to fit in with the idea of Sanctifying Grace.
But habits may be either " operative " (which dispose one towards a particular way of acting) or " entitative " (which give a particular disposition to
the thing itself, like beauty). Sanctifying Grace is an " entitative " Habit.
For an explanation of " Habits," see Essay xviii, *The Supernatural Virtues*,
pp. 622 *seq.*    [2] 1 John iii 1.

him and came into existence bearing the dread heritage of original sin. But God ever wanted to bring us back, and to re-establish between himself and us the sweet relationship of father and child. For that purpose the Second Person of the Blessed Trinity became man and gave us " power to be made the sons of God." [1] Both St John and St Paul exult in proclaiming this act of divine condescension. " Dearly beloved," the first writes, with all the earnestness of the disciple of love, " we are now the sons of God : and it hath not yet appeared what we shall be. We know that when he shall appear we shall be like to him : because we shall see him as he is. And everyone that hath this hope in him sanctifieth himself." [2] To cherish the belief that we are really and truly the sons of God, and to cling to the hope that as sons we shall one day be allowed to gaze on the beauty and majesty of our heavenly Father, is to sanctify ourselves. St John himself has written few more consoling words than these. And St Paul announces the same great truth in sonorous terms that ring through the ages : there is no mistaking their emphasis. At the beginning of that wonderful little epistle to the Ephesians, in which he expounds so beautifully the mystery of Jesus, he cries out : " Blessed be the God and Father of our Lord Jesus Christ, who hath blessed us with spiritual blessings in heavenly places, in Christ : as he chose us in him before the foundation of the world, that we should be holy and unspotted in his sight in charity. Who hath *predestinated us unto the adoption of children* through Jesus Christ unto himself : according to the purpose of his will : unto the praise of the glory of his grace, in which he hath graced us in his beloved Son." Nothing, surely, could be finer than this assertion of God's condescension in making us his sons through Jesus. And to the Galatians, who were being led astray by the errors of Jewish formalism which crushed all loving sense of sonship, he writes to remind them that " when the fulness of the time was come, God sent his Son . . . that he might redeem them who were under the law : that we might receive the adoption of sons. And because you are sons, God hath sent the Spirit of his Son into your hearts, crying : Abba, Father." [3] This same idea of the liberty which belongs to us as sons dwelling, as it were, in our father's house, is expressed also in the epistle to the Romans. " You have not received the spirit of bondage again in fear : but you have received the spirit of adoption of sons, whereby we cry : Abba, Father. For the Spirit himself giveth testimony to our spirit that we are the sons of God." [4]

*More than legal adoption*

In the light of such luminous teaching it is clear that it is in a very special sense that we are the children of God. St Paul, more particularly, assigns to us a sort of legal position in the house of God, in virtue of which we have both the freedom and the rights of sons : for, as he goes on to say at the end of the passage just quoted : " And

[1] John i 12.  [2] 1 John iii 2-3.
[3] Gal. iv 4-6.  [4] Rom. viii 15, 16.

if sons, heirs also ; heirs indeed of God and joint heirs with Christ." [1]
We fail to do justice to a great and fundamental truth if we think of
our sonship in terms of some vague favour which God has shown
to us in virtue of which the term son could be used metaphorically.
We must at least assign to our sonship the meaning which adoption
had under the ancient Roman law. Amongst the Romans an adopted
son lost his legal position in the family to which he belonged by blood,
and became legally a member of the family into which he had been
adopted, acquiring all the dignities and rights which would have been
his if he had been a son by blood. In such a sense at least we must
be the sons of God. But the truth carries us further than that.
Our sonship raises us much higher, for God does for us what no
Roman could do for the child whom he had adopted : He makes us,
in a very true and wonderful way, children " by blood." To appreciate this fact we have only to apply what has already been explained
about the nature of Grace.

Sanctifying grace, as we have seen, is a positive reality infused *Actual*
into the soul by which we are made to share the divine life. At *kinship*
once we see the difference between our sonship and the sonship of
those who are sons only by legal adoption. This legal adoption
may be an act of wonderful love and condescension, and it may
bring untold blessings with it ; but the adopted son remains of
foreign blood, with the physical characteristics which he inherited
from his real parents. It is their blood that flows in his veins, their
features that are copied in his face and form. But with the sons of
God all is different. By sanctifying grace the very life of God is
imparted unto them ; they are grafted on to him, as it were ; nay,
they have been " born again," as our Saviour teaches us ; they are
a " new creature " ; they have been " born of God "—" born again
not of corruptible seed but incorruptible." [2]

This is what God has done for us when he gave us the gift of
sanctifying grace, so that we may well repeat, with that deeper
gratitude which comes with greater knowledge, the words of St John
which have been already quoted : " Behold what manner of charity
the Father hath bestowed upon us, that we should be called and
*should be* the sons of God."

" And if sons, heirs also : heirs indeed of God and joint heirs *Heirs*
with Christ." The Church ends that magnificent profession of
faith which we call the Nicene Creed with the words : " And I
expect the resurrection of the body and the life of the world to come."
The Christian looks forward to heaven as his *home*, not simply as a
place of happiness which he may reach if he is fortunate. Incorporated in Christ who reigns in glory, a true son of God, made already
a sharer in the life of God, he may look upon eternal happiness as
the completion of God's loving plan for him ; and so in a calm spirit
of hope and love he awaits the day of the Lord, not as a day of wrath

---

[1] Rom. viii 17.  [2] 1 Pet. i 23.

and vengeance but as a day of home-coming. He must for a time fight the good fight and keep the faith and accept the sufferings which may be laid upon him, for he knows the truth of the words which St Paul added to his declaration of our heirship with Christ : " Yet so, if we suffer with him, that we may be also glorified with him " ; but his whole attitude is essentially one of gladness and hope " in Christ Jesus our Lord."

*Grace and Glory*

It is well that we should stress the fact—and rejoice in it—that grace makes us truly sons and heirs, and that consequently we can look upon heaven as truly our home. But there is something more than the fact that grace gives us a right to an eternal inheritance. Grace is already the beginning of glory ; the second grows out of the first, much as the blossom grows out of the seed. How this is, the following explanations will show.

The catechism teaches us that the glory and happiness of heaven is " to see, love and enjoy God for ever " ; to behold him who is all Beauty and Truth, to love him who is all Goodness, to enjoy him who is the Supreme Good ; in a word, to possess the Beatific Vision. No created intellect can form an adequate idea of the Beatific Vision until this be actually experienced, yet theologians—guided by such hints as are given in Sacred Scripture and making use of forms of reasoning which faith has enlightened—have sought to set out the fundamental elements of the joy of the Saints. They call attention to the fact that in the Scriptures the Beatific Vision is represented as " seeing " God. Our Blessed Saviour himself told us that the pure of heart " shall see God," and that the angels in heaven " always see the face of my Father who is in heaven." [1] There is the well-known saying of St Paul : " We see now through a glass in a dark manner ; but then face to face." [2] And in St John's first epistle there is the very striking passage which has been quoted already : " Dearly beloved, we are now the sons of God ; and it hath not yet appeared what we shall be. We know that when he shall appear we shall be like to him : because we shall see him as he is." Here, as will be noticed, St John makes our future likeness to God rest upon our seeing him as he is. This doctrine of a direct vision of God in heaven has been solemnly defined by the Church and is thus a matter of faith.

Filled with the glory of the direct vision of God, the soul necessarily is drawn to him in a transport of love. It sees him in all his overpowering goodness ; it recognises that only in him can happiness be found, and that in him is *all* happiness : and the will is drawn to him in an act of love that nothing can change. It is a matter of dispute amongst theologians as to whether the vision of God or the love of God is the essential element in the happiness of the blessed in heaven, but we need not go into the question : in any case, both belong to the happiness of heaven, and the love which the soul has

---

[1] Matt. xviii 10.  [2] 1 Cor. xiii 12.

for God depends upon the knowledge which it has of him.   Hence,
whatever view we hold about the essential element of happiness in
heaven we must recognise that the direct vision of God is the foundation of the rest.   Now, this vision of God is wholly supernatural.
No created intellect can know God as he is by its natural powers—
and this applies to angels as well as to men.   Consequently, if the
soul is raised so much above its natural condition as to have a face-
to-face vision of the infinite God, some change must be wrought in
it, elevating it to an order of things that is absolutely supernatural.
The change is brought about by what theologians have aptly called
the " light of glory."

This brings us to the point which we set out to explain, viz. the
way in which grace is already the beginning of glory, as the seed
is the beginning of the blossom.   For grace is the beginning of that
" light of glory " whereby the blessed in heaven see God ; it is
something which grows into the " light of glory," and for that reason
it has been called the " seed of glory "—an expression which en-
shrines a great truth, and recalls the words of St John, who says :
" Whosoever is born of God committeth not sin : for his seed
abideth in him." [1]

The intrinsic connection between grace and glory is not the least
of the marvels of sanctifying grace.   As Bishop Hedley beautifully
expresses it in his *Retreat :*  " We are given to possess on earth a
gift of light and life which is substantially the same as the light which
shall flood us in the heavens !   For ' the grace of God is life everlasting.' [2]   The apostle is saying that the result of sinfulness is
death, and liberation from sinfulness is holiness ; it is this holiness
which he calls the ' charisma,' or grace of God ; and of this ' charisma ' he says, that it *is* life everlasting.   One would have expected
him to say that its ' result ' was life everlasting.   This would evidently be quite true.   But St Paul's vivid expression is more true ;
for grace not merely deserves the vision of God, but (the veil being
rent in two by bodily dissolution) takes, or has, that vision, as the
eye takes in the morning when sleep departs." [3]

We have just seen that the Beatific Vision consists in the face-  *Sharing*
to-face vision of God as he is in himself, and that this vision of God *divine life*
is accompanied by unutterable love and joy ; we have also explained
that sanctifying grace is the beginning of this state of glory.   But
to see God as he is in himself and to love this infinite good, is the
very essence of the divine life itself.   God alone can fully comprehend all his own infinite excellence, and the first and most fundamental aspect of the inner life of God is precisely this, that he gazes
into the depths of his infinity : indeed, it would seem that the
existence of the Second Person of the Blessed Trinity is the result
(so to speak) of this act of divine understanding.   In a way quite
impossible for us to grasp, it is in knowing and comprehending

[1] 1 John iii 9.              [2] Rom. vi 23.              [3] P. 55.

himself that God the Father begets the Son. And out of this knowledge which God has of himself there arises a mutual love of Father and Son : and this mutual love is the Holy Ghost. Hence the remark which was made in the first section, that if we could understand the divine life we should understand how and why there are three Persons in God : for this trinity of Persons is the result of the inner life of God, much as the existence of ideas in our intellect and of pictures of individual things in our imagination is the result of our life of thought and sensation. From this it follows that when the blessed in heaven are raised to the Beatific Vision they are given a real participation in the divine life itself ; and it follows also that since sanctifying grace is the " seed of glory," it is likewise, in its own measure, a sharing in the very life of God. This sharing of the divine life will reach its fulness in the Beatific Vision, but even during our present life it grows and increases, as supernatural knowledge and love of God grow stronger. " I am come that they may have life, and have it more abundantly." [1] Finally, the intrinsic connection which we have shown to exist between grace and glory throws into clearer light the wholly supernatural character of grace itself. For the Beatific Vision, as we have seen, is wholly supernatural ; neither men nor angels could possess it by any powers of their own. But if the Beatific Vision is supernatural, grace which is its " seed " must be supernatural also.

## § III : TEMPLES OF GOD

*God in the soul*

IT is a cherished part of Catholic faith that God dwells in an especial way in a soul which is in a state of grace.

This is the definite teaching of Christ himself. " If any one love me, he will keep my word. And my Father will love him : and we will come to him and will make our abode with him." [2] Elsewhere in the New Testament this indwelling of God is attributed in an especial way to the Holy Ghost. As is well known, St Paul insists upon the fact that the very bodies of Christ's true followers are the temples of the Holy Spirit. " Know you not that your members are the temple of the Holy Ghost, who is in you, whom you have from God ? " [3] Hence he draws the conclusion that these bodies which enshrine the Spirit of God are sacred things and must not be defiled by sins of the flesh. As he had said already in the same epistle : " Know you not that you are the temple of God, and that the Spirit of God dwelleth in you ? But if any man violate the temple of God, him shall God destroy. For the temple of God is holy, which you are." [4] Here he is but echoing the teaching of his Master who said to his disciples on the last night of his life on earth : " I tell you the truth : it is expedient for you that I go. For

[1] John x 10.  [2] John xiv 23.
[3] 1 Cor. vi 19.  [4] 1 Cor. iii 16-17.

if I go not, the Paraclete will not come to you : but if I go, I will send him to you." [1]

It is this great truth of the dwelling of God in the souls of his friends that we must here consider, so that we may learn more about the wonders of the state of grace.

Of course it is true to say that God is everywhere, even in the *Natural* soul of the sinner : but what concerns us here is the special way in *presence* which he is present in the soul of the just man. How is God present naturally, in everything that exists ? He is present in everything, first of all as the one who holds every single being in existence. Not only has he brought all things into existence but he also keeps them in existence by the direct exercise of his infinite power, without which they would fall back into nothingness. Just as light is dependent upon some source of light and would disappear if its source disappeared, so the very " existing " of things is dependent upon him who is the source of all existence. But God is also present in things as the cause of their every movement. He is the First Mover and the source of every movement, just as he is the source of all " existing." Hence it is true to say of every single being outside God that in him it lives and moves and has its being.

This, be it noticed, is in the natural order of things. Nothing could be, nothing could move, without this presence of God : thus by an absolute necessity, if things exist at all God must be in them. And the truth of this essential nearness of God is one of profound importance.

But there is another kind of nearness of God, based upon a totally *Super-* different action which God may exercise in the human soul. Besides *natural* the acts of supporting his creatures in being and of operating in *presence* all their actions, God deals in a totally different way with the soul that is in the state of grace. He impresses upon it that special likeness to himself of which we have already spoken ; he infuses into it a new and a higher life which is a sharing of his own and the beginning of the life of the blessed ; he implants virtues within it and acts upon it in all sorts of loving ways ; and thus he penetrates it in an absolutely supernatural manner. That he should hold us in being and should co-operate with us in all our ordinary actions is part of the natural order of things ; but this is part of a supernatural order to which we have no right whatever. And this supernatural action within us clearly establishes a special kind of presence in our souls : he was present before, but now he holds us closer to himself and establishes a new, vital union with us. God's natural presence in the soul has often been likened to the way in which water fills a sponge ; let us imagine, however, that the water possessed the power of producing at will various magnificent changes in the sponge, vitalising every particle of it, and permeating it with its own reality in such a way that it received powers of sensation.

[1] John xvi 7.

We should then say that the water had entered into the sponge in a new way. So it is with God and the soul that he adorns with sanctifying grace. He revitalises it, makes it sensitive to the touch of heavenly influences and bestows upon it something of his own beauty : and thus he makes his " abode " there.

But there is another side to this question of God's presence in the soul. How does the soul respond to the God who has deigned to come so nigh ? In virtue of the powers which grace has brought to it, the soul has gained a knowledge and love of God which could not have come to it otherwise. It knows him—though darkly, in the twilight of faith—as the supreme good ; it sets him above all creatures ; it loves him with the ardour of supernatural charity ; and it rejoices in the possession of him. This is a new bond of union. When a natural object is thought about, longed for, loved, we say that it is enshrined in the heart : we have made it present to us, though in its actual reality it be far away. But in the case of a soul in grace the God who is thought about, loved, rejoiced in, is already actually present : and by its own action the soul clasps him and will not let him go. " I found him whom my soul loveth. I held him : and I will not let him go." [1] Thus there is a closeness more intimate than could be imagined if faith did not make it known to us : a closeness based upon the natural, physical presence of God within us, made immeasurably greater by God's most loving supernatural action upon us, and crowned by the final touch of sacred intimacy when the soul clings to him as its Lord and God.

Thus does the God of heaven dwell in human souls. He dwells there as in a temple : for his sovereign rights as God are there recognised, he is adored and praised, petition is made to him ; and there he dispenses his favours. He dwells there also as a guest in a home where he is ever welcome : all that the home can produce is prepared to do him honour. And he dwells there as Friend. Between God and the soul there is mutual love—not the feeble sentiment which sometimes passes for love amongst men, but a love that is strong and true. Each, we may say, seeks the good of the other—God enriching the soul with wonderful gifts and protecting it by his loving Providence, the soul devoting itself and all its powers to God. And though God remains invisible as long as this life lasts, faith enables the soul to realise his presence and to rejoice therein. There is a striking passage in *The Interior Castle* in which St Teresa expresses this realisation of God in a very vivid manner. " It is as if, when we were with other people in a well-lighted room, some one were to darken it by closing the shutters ; we should feel certain that the others were still there, though we were unable to see them." [2]

Such is the wonderful privilege of the soul that is in the state of grace. We may rightly say that it already stands in the ante-

[1] Canticle of Canticles iii 4.
[2] *Seventh Mansion*, chap. i 12.

chamber of heaven and is separated only by the thinnest of veils from the face of God. That veil is being worn thinner and thinner as the supernatural life of the soul increases, and when it altogether disappears the presence of God will take on a new and a higher form. God will then penetrate the soul more intimately still : he will be known not by images and comparisons, not in the obscurity of faith, but directly, as he is in himself, in the full brilliancy of the Light of Glory. But already the splendour of his face is breaking upon us, and the sound of that final approach is in our ears.

It may indeed be said that this presence of God in the soul is not recognised by us, or at least that it is not recognised by many of those who are in the state of grace. This is true, and one is inclined to echo the words of our Saviour : " if thou didst know the gift of God." [1] Though God is present he is not directly perceived. He is to be known by faith, and faith in such matters presupposes instruction in the truth. It is often want of knowledge which holds back the Christian soul from a sense of God's presence which would fill it with joy and lead it on, with giant strides, towards true perfection of life. Or perhaps it is that one knows theoretically the doctrine of God's indwelling but has never made it one's own through the distractions and earthly interests of a life which, though free from serious sin, is still held down by constant tepidity. Such a life is indeed to be pitied—and to be feared : is it difficult to understand the language of the Lord who dwells in a tepid soul ? " I know thy works, that thou art neither cold nor hot. I would thou wert cold or hot. But because thou art lukewarm, and neither cold nor hot, I will begin to vomit thee out of my mouth." [2]

In this short exposition of the doctrine of the indwelling of God *Indwelling* in the soul, we have thought of the presence of God as such—God *specially* who is three in one, Father, Son, and Holy Ghost. But this in- *attributed to the Holy* dwelling is commonly attributed to the Holy Ghost, as was seen in *Ghost* the texts which were quoted at the beginning of the section. The reasons for this " appropriation," as it is called, are set out both in the essay on the Blessed Trinity and in that on the Holy Ghost ; here we need say no more than that the indwelling of God in the soul is pre-eminently an act of love, and since the Holy Spirit proceeds from Father and Son as their mutual Love it is becoming that the divine indwelling and all the operations of grace should be attributed to him, just as the works of creation are attributed to the Father.

## § IV: THROUGH JESUS CHRIST

WE have seen how intimate are the relations between God and the *All grace* soul that is in the state of grace ; and now we must see how intimate *from Christ* are the relations between that soul and Jesus Christ our Lord. For it is through Christ in his sacred humanity that we receive all the

---

[1] John iv 10.      [2] Apocalypse iii 15-16.

treasures of grace, and this in a deeper and fuller sense than many of us realise. Hence the present section : " Through Jesus Christ."

As we know, Jesus himself declared that he came into this world to restore supernatural life to fallen man. " I am come that they may have life and have it more abundantly," [1] and the evangelist who records these words tells us that " as many as received him, he gave them power to be made the sons of God." [2] " He that hath the Son hath life," proclaims the same Apostle, and " he that hath not the Son hath not life." [3] St Peter likewise tells us in terms that are stamped with his intense conviction of our dependence on Christ : " There is no other name under heaven given to men, whereby we must be saved." [4]

*Christ merits and produces grace*

How, then, does Christ procure for us that life which he came to give ? In the first place, by meriting it for us. By the whole of his life on earth, and especially by his Passion and death, Christ merited that the supernatural life which we had lost in Adam should be restored to us. " And being consummated, he became to all that obey him the cause of eternal salvation." [5] More than that, he actually produces grace in the soul by his action upon us. Just as he healed bodies by the touch of his hand or by the word of his mouth so also does he heal souls and bring back to them the life of grace. But in a deeper sense than this Christ is the cause of grace within us, and unless we have grasped this deeper sense our understanding of grace—nay, of Christianity itself—is incomplete. We refer to the important truth that the supernatural life of the soul comes to us through actual union with, or incorporation in, Christ. It is not by mere external action upon us, like the action of a seal upon the wax in which it leaves the impression of itself, or like the action of steam upon the engine which it sets in motion, that Christ produces grace in us. Rather is it like the action of a living organism that draws particles of matter into union with itself and thus makes them live. This is the very way in which Jesus himself expressed what happens. We all know his wonderful figure of the Vine and its branches. " Abide in me : and I in you. As the branch cannot bear fruit of itself, unless it abide in the vine, so neither can you, unless you abide in me. I am the vine ; you the branches. He that abideth in me, and I in him, the same beareth much fruit : for without me you can do nothing." [6] Hence the extraordinary significance of Holy Communion, the external union of the Body and Blood of Christ with our own frail humanity being both a symbol and a cause of the inner union which is aimed at. " Except you eat the flesh of the Son of man and drink his blood you shall not have life in you. . . . He that eateth my flesh and drinketh my blood abideth in me and I in him." [7]

[1] John x 10.     [2] John i 12.     [3] 1 John v 12.
[4] Acts iv 12.     [5] Heb. v 9.
[6] John xv 4-5.     [7] John vi 54-57.

This union with Christ is especially dear to St Paul, who made *Incorporation* it one of his guiding thoughts. " You are in Christ Jesus, who of *in him* God is made unto us wisdom, and justice, and sanctification, and redemption." [1] According to the great Apostle of the Gentiles, all who are redeemed are incorporated in Christ and live by his life, so that he actually becomes to them " wisdom, and justice, and sanctification, and redemption." This is no mere metaphor ; in the eyes of St Paul it is a tremendous but simple truth, upon which he insists time after time, which he uses in all sorts of connections and upon which he builds much of his preaching. Thus it is not merely " through " Christ that redemption and grace come to us, but " in " him—as he says many times. " You are dead, and your life is hid with Christ in God. When Christ shall appear, who is your life, you shall appear with him in glory." [2] " God (who is rich in mercy) . . . hath quickened us together in Christ (by whose grace you are saved), and hath raised us up together and hath made us sit together in the heavenly places through Christ Jesus. [3] That he might show in the ages to come the abundant riches of his grace, in his bounty towards us in Christ Jesus." [4] Hence he bids us " put on the Lord Jesus Christ," [5] and tells us that " ' in Christ ' we are a new creature." [6] All this leads him to that triumphant exclamation : " I live, now not I ; but Christ liveth in me " [7]—an exclamation which was echoed by the great St Augustine in the words : " Let us break forth into thanksgiving, we are become not only Christians, but Christ." [8]

The question now arises, how is this incorporation in Christ *Function* and sanctification of the soul brought about ? We answer, primarily *of faith in* and fundamentally by true faith in him. He is the one source of *Christ* grace for fallen man ; we depend entirely on the grace which he won for us by his Passion and death ; but this grace comes only to those who believe in him.[9] It is to those who " receive " him and " believe in his name " that he gives the " power to be made the sons of God." Thus before Christ can sanctify us and make us

---

[1] 1 Cor. i 30.          [2] Col. iii 3-4.
[3] In the original Greek, and also in the Latin, this is " in Christ Jesus." Abbot Vonier remarks : " The phrase ' in Christ ' occurs nearly eighty times in St. Paul's epistles ; frequently it is translated into ' by,' ' through,' ' for the sake of ' Christ. Yet such alterations ought not to deprive us of the wealth of mystical meaning contained in the original phrase ' in Christ.' " *The Personality of Christ*, p. 108.
[4] Eph. ii 4-7.          [5] Rom. xiii 14.
[6] 2 Cor. v 17.          [7] Gal. ii 20.
[8] The implications of this doctrine are more fully developed in Essay xix, *The Mystical Body of Christ*.
[9] The case of Infant Baptism is an exception, for the child is incorporated into Christ without any actual faith on its own part. This is an exception which God in his goodness has deigned to make. The special consideration of this case does not belong to the present place, but it may be remarked that according to the traditional teaching the faith of the Church takes the place of the faith of the child.

sons of God, we must " receive " him and believe in his name. And St Paul tells us that the just man lives by faith,[1] and that we are " the children of God by faith in Christ Jesus." [2]  As a modern writer has well expressed it, faith is " a kind of psychic link between the soul and Christ " [3]—a bond without which there can be no " incorporation " and no transmission of supernatural life.

At first sight it might seem as if this insistence on the function of faith were akin to the Protestant theory of Justification by Faith. But Catholic doctrine is very different.  Luther held that faith alone brought Justification, to the exclusion of all good works.  " Good works," in fact, were impossible, according to his theory of the essential corruption of our nature.  And the very faith which he so extolled was not so much an intellectual assent to the divinity of Christ and to the doctrine of the Redemption, as a personal persuasion that our sins are " covered over " and no longer imputed to us.

The stress which Luther placed on the fundamental importance of recognising Christ as our redeemer must not blind us to the essentially vicious character of his theory, which leads logically and inevitably to disregard of the laws of right conduct.  We must not treat our Saviour as a cloak to cover up our own transgressions. He is indeed our hope, our life, of whose fulness we have all received. But it is not by the Lutheran " faith " that his grace comes to us. The process of Justification is much more complex, as we now proceed to show.

The first element in the great work of Justification is the grace of God—actual grace.  No man can have faith in Christ, no man can even have a genuine desire to possess it, unless the grace of God first draw him.[4]  It is for man to accept this grace or to reject it. If he accepts it and listens to the voice of God speaking to him, he is led on to make a true act of faith ; that is, he is enabled by God to believe what has been divinely revealed, and more particularly the doctrines of the Redemption and of the forgiveness of sins. With this belief in his heart he is moved to hope in God and to love him, and to turn his heart away from sin.  Thus, under the influence of actual grace, a soul is prepared for Justification.  Hence it is not a matter of faith alone, but of faith which leads to hope and love and genuine sorrow : yet faith is the foundation of the whole process, or, as the Council of Trent puts it, " the beginning, the foundation, and the root of all Justification." [5]

---

[1] Rom. i 17.      [2] Gal. iii 26.

[3] Vonier : *A Key to the Doctrine of the Eucharist*, p. 6.

[4] Our dependence in this respect on God's help is explained in the Essay *Actual Grace* in the present volume, section iv, to which the reader is referred for several important points which have a bearing upon the present question.

[5] Session vi, chap. viii.  The whole process of preparation for Justification was carefully explained by the Council : the account in the text is a brief summary of what may be read at much greater length in this famous 6th Session.

All is now ready for actual incorporation in Christ, which will *Sacraments* bring grace and life to the soul. It is part of his gracious purpose *and faith in Christ* that this should be accomplished by means of the sacrament of Baptism, which is essentially the sacrament of a new birth in Christ Jesus. It is thus that a man " puts on " Christ. " As many of you as have been baptised in Christ have put on Christ," says St Paul ; [1] or, as he expresses it elsewhere, taking his idea from the ancient ceremony of Baptism when the neophyte was plunged under the baptismal water : " Know you not that all we who are baptised in Christ Jesus are baptised in his death ? For we are buried together with him by baptism into death : that as Christ is risen from the dead by the glory of the Father, so we also may walk in newness of life." [2] But Baptism itself presupposes the living faith in Christ of which we have spoken. " He that *believeth* and is baptised, shall be saved ; but he that believeth not shall be condemned." [3] And sometimes, as we know, the soul is justified before the waters of Baptism have flowed over it ; for faith can inspire a love and a sorrow for sin so intense that Christ does not wait for the divinely appointed sacrament of initiation but draws the soul to himself and makes it one with him.

We are speaking here of the case of one who has lived in infidelity and without Baptism and in mature years first turns to God. But faith is equally necessary for him who has lost the grace which once he had and turns again to God. Just as for the first there is Baptism, for the second there is Penance : but neither is of any avail without faith. Indeed, faith is necessary for every sacrament, whether it restores a man to the friendship of God or increases the grace which he already possessed ; for as St Thomas says, " the sacraments are certain signs which profess the faith by which a man is justified." [4] Of course they are more than signs of faith ; they are signs of the inner grace which is produced in the soul, and of this grace which they signify they are at the same time the instrumental causes ; but it is well to insist that without faith they will not achieve their effect.[5]

## §V : SUPERNATURAL ACTIVITIES

IN the course of the preceding pages much emphasis has been laid *Sanctifying* upon the fact that sanctifying grace is a form of supernatural life. *grace and supernatural* But all life is essentially a power of internal action, of self-movement *action* such as the processes of growing, feeling, thinking, willing ; and every different grade of life has its own special forms of activity. It is therefore natural for us to ask the question : What special forms of activity belong to the life of grace ?

[1] Gal. iii 27.  [2] Rom. vi 3-4.
[3] Mark xvi 16.  [4] *S. Theol.*, III, Q. 61, a. 4.
[5] The reader is referred to Abbot Marmion's beautiful book, *Christ the Life of the Soul*, for the development of points which have been briefly touched upon in the present section.

It is well to keep before our minds the truth that sanctifying grace of its very nature leads to the ineffable activity of the Beatific Vision. The life of grace is at present incomplete ; it is like the life of an embryo which does not yet show the marvels which will be revealed in the fully developed organism. It is the " seed " of a more wonderful life than has yet appeared. The full activity, then, which is proper to sanctifying grace is the activity involved in that intuitive vision of God, and that overwhelming love of him, which constitute the happiness of the blessed in heaven. But the life of grace has already its own special form of activity : What can we say about it ?

The first thing to be said about it is not easy to understand unless one is used to theological and philosophical forms of thought : but it is of fundamental importance in the present connection. To put it in a sentence, as a result of sanctifying grace actions which would have remained " natural " become intrinsically " supernatural." Here, again, we have these ideas " natural " and " supernatural," and in a somewhat different connection. We have had occasion to speak of sanctifying grace as a supernatural quality, and of the Beatific Vision as something proper to God and therefore absolutely supernatural, and in these cases it is not difficult, in the light of the explanations which have been given, to understand what is meant. But perhaps it is less easy to understand what is meant when we speak of an action becoming supernatural. Let us put the matter as follows. At the present moment the light of the sun is streaming into the room where these lines are written, through panes of ordinary clear glass ; what would be the effect if richly coloured glass were to be substituted for the ordinary glass ? The light itself would be affected and would be tinged with various colours. In a similar sort of way, when actions proceed from a soul that is enriched with sanctifying grace they receive (or may receive) a new quality because of the source from which they come. Or, just as water which comes from a peaty soil carries with it the characteristics of peat, so do the actions which proceed from grace carry in themselves the characteristics of grace itself. We cannot submit a human action to any process of examination like a chemical analysis, but if we could we should discover a new element in the activities of grace just as the chemist discovers a new element in peaty water. And that new element is " supernatural " : it belongs to the order of divine things.

When we say, then, that grace gives us the power of performing supernatural actions we do not mean that we receive the power of producing supernatural effects, like changing water into wine or the substance of bread into the body of Christ ; nor do we mean that we become capable of doing such things as reading the future or seeing the thoughts of our fellow-men ; but we mean that we become capable of performing actions which are not in any sense miraculous but are intrinsically elevated so as to become in themselves of a higher order and value.

Behind this somewhat difficult line of thought there lies a very glorious reality. Not only is the soul made beautiful by the grace which is given to it ; not only does it become a temple and a home in which God deigns to dwell ; but it receives a power of performing actions which, apart from the reward which is promised them, are more wonderful in themselves than the noblest natural efforts of the greatest genius whom the world has ever known. As breezes that blow from a land of spices are laden with perfumes, so are the supernatural actions which come from a soul in grace laden with the perfume of God himself. Nor is this surprising, for they are the actions not of man as he is in himself, but of man as he is incorporated in Christ and engrafted on the Vine whose life flows through his veins.

In the natural order of things a man acts through his various *Infused* faculties ; he thinks and reasons by his intellect, chooses by his will, *virtues* sees by his sight, and so on. In the supernatural order of which we have been speaking something of the same holds good. We have said that together with sanctifying grace man receives power to perform supernatural actions. Now, according to the common explanation of theologians, this power of performing supernatural actions is exercised through certain quasi-faculties which always accompany grace. Grace itself is a new nature—a " new creature " —and just as my ordinary nature has natural faculties which flow from it and through which I perform my natural actions, so this new nature has corresponding " faculties " by which it performs its natural acts.[1] These " faculties " are known as Infused Virtues and they differ in various important respects from ordinary virtues— so much so, indeed, that there is a danger of confusion in the use of the term virtue as applied to them. In the first place they are not acquired as the result of repeated efforts and for this reason they are called " infused "—that is, produced directly in the soul by God. In the second place they do not (at least directly and immediately) give us a facility and readiness in acting : what they do is to give us a power of performing actions which are supernatural in character.[2]

---

[1] One uses the word " faculties," or " quasi-faculties," though strictly speaking they are rather special qualities superadded to the ordinary faculties in virtue of which these are " supernaturalised " and become capable of performing supernatural actions.

[2] There is a difference of opinion amongst theologians as to whether Infused Virtues give a facility in action or not. The matter is discussed in technical works on theology ; but in any case a point to insist upon is that their direct effect is to make us capable of performing acts which are intrinsically supernatural and therefore quite different in character from actions performed through a natural virtue. One important result of this is that such supernatural acts have a true value towards eternal life, as we shall see when we deal with the question of merit. But the question of the Supernatural Virtues is dealt with in a special essay (xviii) of this work : they are spoken of here only in so far as they enter into the working of sanctifying grace in the soul.

First amongst the Infused Virtues are the three Theological Virtues by which the soul raises itself to God in supernatural Faith, supernatural Hope, supernatural Charity. That these three virtues are infused into our souls, together with sanctifying grace, is the explicit teaching of the Church : but it is the common teaching of theologians that the other virtues—Moral Virtues as they are called —are also infused by God. Thus endowed, the sons of God are enabled to live a life on earth which is glorious in the sight of their Father who is in heaven. They must struggle, indeed, against many enemies both within and without them ; the practice of virtue remains difficult, and there may be many setbacks ; as it was with labour and toil and in the sweat of his face that Adam was set to labour, so too, is it with much strain and tribulation that they must work out their salvation ; but they are the sons of God, and besides the new nature which has been given to them they possess these wonderful springs of supernatural activity.

Yet it is not sufficient that God should have given to his children this new nature and these supernatural powers of action. If these are to do all that this new life involves they have need of constant assistance. Supernatural life requires not only sanctifying grace and the Infused Virtues but also the constant assistance of actual grace— of supernatural assistance given us for the performance of special actions. This actual grace is a complement of sanctifying grace. Sanctifying grace is the essential thing ; it is this which gives us supernatural life ; but we are so weak that we cannot keep that life or do all the things which it involves unless from time to time, as circumstances require it, God comes to our assistance and gives us present help.[1] Consequently when we enumerate the great things which God has done for us in order that we may become his sons and live as heirs of heaven, we may put it thus : first he draws the soul by actual grace and thus prepares it for Justification ; then he breathes into it the breath of supernatural life by means of sanctifying grace ; at the same time he places in it those powers of supernatural life which we call the Infused Virtues ; and subsequently, instead of leaving the soul to struggle on with the means already at its disposal, he assists it in all sorts of ways by further actual graces.

*Gifts of the Holy Ghost*

But this is not the whole story of the provisions which God has made, in the ordinary dispositions of his grace, for the supernatural life of the soul. Besides sanctifying grace and actual grace and the Infused Virtues there are also what are known as the Gifts of the Holy Ghost, seven in number. These seven Gifts are mentioned by the prophet Isaias who speaks of them as endowments of the future Messias. " The spirit of the Lord shall rest upon him : the spirit of wisdom and of understanding, the spirit of counsel and of forti-

---

[1] The necessity under which we labour of being thus helped by God is explained in Essay xvii, *Actual Grace*.

tude, the spirit of knowledge and of piety : and he shall be filled with the spirit of the fear of the Lord." [1] There can be no doubt that God produces in the soul of the just man supernatural realities corresponding to the seven great names here used by the prophet, and the Church teaches us to pray that the Holy Ghost may give us this seven-fold gift ; but there is some obscurity about the way in which they are to be explained, not only in regard to each considered by itself but also in regard to their general character. What is a " gift of the Holy Ghost " ? What does it do for us ? Does it differ from the Virtues ? The answer which theologians commonly give to these questions (following St Thomas Aquinas) runs thus. The gifts of the Holy Ghost are special dispositions produced by God in the soul in virtue of which we become sensitive to the touch of actual grace. Just as some people are peculiarly sensitive to various impressions in the natural order—of sight, sound, touch, etc.—so are the children of God made sensitive to the influences which their Father exercises upon them and by which he would lead them on in the way of sanctification. A little thought will show that these dispositions produced in the soul are of very great importance in the spiritual life. By means of them the soul is brought more directly under the hand of God, responds instinctively to the touch of his grace and may be led on to the heights of sanctity.

Space does not allow that we should explain in detail the special nature of each of the seven gifts, but a few words about one or two of them may help to explain their general character and their importance in the life of grace. Let us take the first of them, the gift of Wisdom. In virtue of this gift the soul is disposed to recognise in God the infinitely good, the infinitely lovable. It does this not as the result of a cold process of reasoning, but instinctively as though by actual contact with God. It has been prepared by God to see him as the sovereign good and the moment he reveals himself it recognises him for what he is, and cleaves to him. And this is done with all the ardour of a loving son. Charity, the queen of the virtues, is thus perfected, for its operations receive a keenness and a promptness which otherwise they would not possess, and the soul is led on by rapid strides if only it does not put obstacles in the way of grace. Similarly the gift of knowledge gives to the soul a readiness in the perception of the true value of earthly things. Here again it is not a matter of cold reasoning : it is rather a sort of instinct by which the soul almost intuitively recognises that creatures are of no real value save in so far as they minister to eternal interest. Who does not see the supreme importance of such gifts in the supernatural life of the soul ?

Each gift might well be studied by itself in order that its vast, practical importance may be recognised and appreciated. We can truly apply to them those words of St Paul : " Whosoever are led

[1] Isa. xi 2-3.

by the Spirit of God, they are the sons of God." [1]  Assuredly the sons of God are led on by the Spirit of God : and the more they surrender themselves to this divine influence, the more they will approach that state of perfection to which they are called and that state of union with God which is the prelude to the end of sanctifying grace, the Beatific Vision. [2]

### § VI : GROWTH IN GRACE

*Growth possible*

WE are now in a better position to realise how wonderful is the supernatural " organism " which God has fashioned in the souls of his children.  First there is sanctifying grace itself which affects the very substance of the soul, making it a new creature, giving it a new life.  Then there are the Infused Virtues which affect the faculties of the soul and give them the power of performing supernatural actions.  Further, by the Gifts of the Holy Ghost, God gives to our faculties, already elevated by the Infused Virtues, that special sensitiveness which makes them respond more readily to his touch. And on the soul thus prepared he is ever acting by Actual Grace, as a musician might play upon an instrument of unwonted charm.

To this loving action of God it is our task to respond, so that the life of grace may grow more and more within us " unto a perfect man, unto the measure of the age of the fulness of Christ." [3]  It is this growth in grace which we must now briefly study.

Grace itself is a free gift of God who gives it in the measure which seems good to him.  " To every one of us is given grace according to the measure of the giving of Christ." [4]  To one man there are given five talents, to another two, whilst another receives only one ; but all must trade with what they have and labour to increase their store.  How is this increase to be brought about ?

*Caused by God*

We may say at once that the increase of grace is the work both of God and of ourselves, but in very different ways.  First, it is the work of God.  In some cases he gives this increase in answer to prayer.  The Church teaches us to pray for such an increase, and for this purpose puts beautiful prayers upon our lips.  Take as an example the well-known Collect for the Mass of the 13th Sunday after Pentecost : " Almighty and eternal God, give unto us an in-

---

[1] Rom. viii 14.
[2] A further study of the Gifts of the Holy Ghost would show the important part they play in Divine Contemplation and the Mystical Life. Indeed the whole theology of sanctifying grace bears upon the question of true Mysticism : but the connection between the one and the other cannot be worked out here.  Much important matter can be found in three works by three modern French Dominicans : *De l'Habitation du Saint-Esprit dans les Ames Justes* (Froget), *La Contemplation Mystique* (Joret), and *Perfection Chrétienne et Contemplation* (2 vols.), by Garrigou-Lagrange.  Another very beautiful work on somewhat different lines is *La Grâce et la Gloire* (2 vols.), by Père Terrien, S.J.  See also below, pp. 657-8.
[3] Eph. iv 13.　　　　　　　　　　　　　　　　[4] Eph. iv 7.

crease of faith, hope, and charity." Here we look to God to increase the supernatural life of our souls as an act of his goodness. But perhaps we may say that the normal and most efficacious way in which God provides for an increase of the supernatural life of our souls is by the sacraments. The sacraments are not merely touching ceremonies, beautiful in their prayers, their old associations, their symbolism, but they are actually causes of grace. God uses them as his instruments for the production, or the increase, of supernatural life, and they are meant to play an important part in our spiritual history. This part is dealt with in a special essay of this work [1] and its importance cannot easily be exaggerated. We cannot deal here with the way in which the sacraments cause or increase grace in our souls, but we would remind the reader of two things. First, that the grace caused in us by the valid reception of a sacrament is due not to our own efforts in the receiving of the sacrament, but to the sacrament itself. Of course we have certain things to do before the sacrament can produce its effect, but the effect is due not to these things which we do but to the sacrament. This is expressed by theologians technically by saying that the grace of the sacraments is produced *ex opere operato* and not *ex opere operantis*.

The second thing to which we would call attention is the truth that in the use of the sacraments it is God who is the ultimate cause of grace ; the outward rite is but an instrument which he uses for the production of this effect. Hence it is quite a mistake to suppose (as Protestants do) that the sacrament comes between the soul and God, and lessens our dependence upon him. Still less is it true that we look upon the sacraments as having a sort of magical power. Of themselves they are merely signs ; they produce grace only as used by God from whom the grace flows as from its source, and they are not independent of our dispositions.

Leaving this part of our subject with these brief remarks, we pass *How* on to consider how our own actions can produce an increase of grace *caused by* in the soul. Of course this cannot be by our own unaided efforts ; *ourselves* if we can do anything in this respect it is only in response to, and with the help of, the grace which God gives us. It is a fundamental principle of Catholic theology that we can do nothing of ourselves towards our salvation ; [2] and this is true of the growth in grace which we are here considering. But we can correspond with grace ; and by corresponding with grace we can increase the supernatural life which we already possess. This is evident from the teaching of the New Testament. We have already heard St Paul speaking of the development of the life of grace within us " unto a perfect man, unto the measure of the age of the fulness of Christ," and it is clear that this development is at least in part dependent upon our own personal efforts. A few verses further on he exhorts his readers :

[1] Essay xxi, *The Sacramental System*.
[2] See Essay xvii, *Actual Grace*, § iii.

" that henceforth we be no more children, tossed to and fro and carried about with every wind of doctrine . . . but doing the truth in charity, we may in all things grow up in him who is the head, even Christ." [1]  And St Peter says : " Wherefore, laying aside all malice and all guile and dissimulations and envies and all detractions, as new-born babes, desire the rational milk without guile, that thereby you may grow unto salvation." [2]  But this is surely an exhortation to use our own efforts so that we may deepen within ourselves the supernatural life of grace.  Hence in his second epistle he writes : " Grow in grace and in the knowledge of our Lord and Saviour Jesus Christ." [3]

Here we have another difference between the Protestant theory of Justification and the true doctrine of the New Testament.  In the Protestant theory, it will be remembered, Justification is a mere external non-imputation of sin, and this does not admit of growth ; our sins are either imputed to us or they are not.  The passages which we have quoted are meaningless unless there be, as the Church teaches, a supernatural life in which we go from virtue to virtue, are renewed from day to day and thus become more and more justified.[4]

The fact being admitted that we can grow in grace as the result of our own efforts (as contrasted with the growth which comes from God in answer to prayer or through the use of the sacraments), the question arises :  How do our efforts bring about this increase ?  We answer that it is by *meriting* an increase of grace that we are able to develop our supernatural life.  Our own efforts do not actually produce the increase, but God grants it as a reward.  And together with the increase of sanctifying grace there is a corresponding increase in the Infused Virtues and the Gifts of the Holy Ghost—all as a result of merit.  Hence there are important differences between the growth of natural life and the development of supernatural life.  To a certain extent natural life may be said to grow of itself : there is a natural development and gradual unfolding of powers, given a fit environment.  Besides this, the very actions of a living thing may be said to quicken and develop its life in so far as they perfect its natural powers by producing in them promptness, ease and accuracy in their operations.  But in the supernatural life it is different.  Grace does not grow of itself ; neither do the supernatural activities of the soul produce, or increase, the grace within it ; God alone gives grace and God alone increases it ; but, as we have said, the increase can be merited, and it is in this sense that, with the help of God, our own actions can bring about the growth of the life of grace.[5]

[1] Eph. iv 14-15.      [2] 1 Pet. ii 1-2.      [3] 2 Pet. iii 18.
[4] See *Trent*, Session VI, chap. x.
[5] We have here assumed that there is such a thing as Merit in the eyes of God—a fact which was denied by the Reformers.  The general question of Merit will be discussed in the next section.  Our present purpose is to explain that increase of grace may be merited by us but is not directly produced by us.

It might be objected that supernatural virtues, and with them *Natural* the whole supernatural life, are directly increased by our very efforts, *facility in* for it is a matter of experience that a good man who possesses the *good and* infused moral virtues is able to increase them by the practice of *growth in* virtue. Take, for example, an earnest person who for the love of *grace* God sets himself the task of acquiring greater patience ; day by day he puts a guard over himself, and checks the various movements of impatience which arise within him, and gradually acquires a habit of self-control. During all this time he is exercising the supernatural virtue of patience, and consequently it would seem that by his own efforts he is developing this virtue just as a non-religious man might develop a natural habit of patience.

This objection is worth considering for it introduces an interesting point in connection with the life of grace. In the case supposed we must notice the distinction between two quite different things. These two things are, facility in practising patience and the increase of the infused, supernatural virtue of patience. By repeated acts a man increases what we may call his natural power of restraining himself ; this increase follows the ordinary psychological laws according to which habits are developed ; but the increase of the supernatural virtue (and of grace itself) is another matter altogether. As we have already tried to explain, the infused, supernatural virtues are not so much new powers of action as qualities superadded to our natural powers of action which supernaturalise these and make them capable of performing acts which are supernatural in character. The development of facility in operation (apart from some extraordinary grace of God) must be the result of effort on our part ; the growth of grace and of the infused virtues is produced not by ourselves but by God, though it can be merited by us.

Here we are touching upon points which are dealt with in the Essay on *The Supernatural Virtues*, to which the reader is referred ; it was necessary, however, to say something about the matter in this discussion of Sanctifying Grace.

The Christian soul, then, has it within his power to increase the treasure of grace which has been committed to him. He can pray for it, he can approach the sacraments with the knowledge that these are divinely appointed means of advancing in grace, he can exercise himself in good works. And thus his soul will become more and more God-like, and the glory of the Beatific Vision (to which the whole of the supernatural order is directed) will be intensified. For there is a proportion between Grace and Glory ; the greater the first, the greater the second. But that brings us to the question of Merit, which we shall discuss in the following section.[1]

---

[1] Whilst grace can be increased within us, it is never diminished (although, of course, it can be lost altogether). This statement probably runs counter to the idea which many Catholics form of the effects of venial sin ; they look upon venial sin as weakening the supernatural life of the soul and

## § VII: GRACE AND MERIT

Possibility<br>of merit

IT is a treasured belief of the Catholic Church that the soul which is in the state of grace can merit eternal reward. This was denied by the Reformers who urged two objections against the Catholic doctrine of Merit. First, they said, if we merit in the eyes of God we are making God our debtor, which cannot be ; and secondly, they urged that to claim merit for our own actions is to take away from the sovereign merits of Christ who alone has merited for us the rewards of eternal life. We have now to show that the doctrine of Merit is clearly contained in Sacred Scripture and that the objections which we have mentioned are based upon a misunderstanding and are without any force.

The justification of the assertion that man can merit eternal reward stands out very clearly in the pages of the New Testament. St Paul certainly believed that he had merited when he wrote the well-known words : " I have fought a good fight : I have finished my course : I have kept the faith. As to the rest, there is laid up for me a crown of justice which the Lord the just judge will render to me in that day : and not only to me but to them also that love his coming." [1] Notice the words " crown of justice " and " just judge " which express so forcibly the idea of a recompense which has been merited and is due in justice. And those who suffer for Christ are encouraged by him with the thought of the reward which will be theirs. " Be glad and rejoice," he says, " for your reward is very great in heaven." [2] Very striking, too, is the glimpse which our Saviour gives us of the great reckoning which will take place at the last day. Some souls are damned. Why ? Because their bad lives have deserved it. Others are admitted to glory. Why ? Because their good lives have merited it. Just as evil action deserves its punishment so does virtuous action deserve its reward : such is the only conclusion which can be drawn from our Saviour's words.

But does not this doctr ne of Merit mean that God is made our debtor ? And is not this quite impossible ? The answer to this argument of the Protestants is easy. I may have a right to recompense from another either because l have done him a service which has put him under an obligation to me, or because he had previously promised me this recompense if I did certain things. Now it is

diminishing the amount of sanctifying grace which we possess. But there is no such diminution : if there were, long continuance in a course of venial sin could extinguish grace altogether : and this is not the case. Yet venial sins certainly imperil the life of the soul. If a man becomes habituated to venial sins he loses his sense of the sanctity of God, his self-control is weakened, self-love gets the upper hand and sooner or later a big temptation will overthrow him. Besides, a man who is careless in regard to venial sins is less likely to receive great helps from God.

It is true that God *could*, if he wished, diminish the grace in a soul, just as he can increase it. But it is certain that he never does.

[1] 2 Tim. iv 7-8.        [2] Matt. v 12.

quite true that I cannot claim a return from God on the first of these grounds, since that would indeed be to make him my debtor ; but does the objection hold if my claim is based upon a promise which he has made ? Clearly it does not. In this case God has shown himself a most bountiful Lord in promising me a reward. Apart from his promise I could have no right to a return for what I have done. This would be true even if the reward were something in the natural order of things, such as health or wealth ; still more true is it when the reward is supernatural : the Beatific Vision. But, given his promise, I have a right to the reward if I do what was required of me : God owes it not so much to me as to himself.

In this connection it is worth noticing that eternal life is both a reward and a gift. It is a gift, since we owe it to the bountiful love of God who freely chose to set it as the end of our action, and freely gives us the means of attaining it ; it is at the same time a reward, because in his wisdom God has made the possession of it dependent upon our own action.

Similarly there is no force in the second objection that the doctrine of merit takes away from the sovereign merits of Christ. For we owe it entirely to the merits of Christ that we are able to merit for ourselves. He has won for us the power of meriting ; without him we could never do anything which would merit in the sight of God. This is more wonderful than if eternal life were in no way dependent upon our own actions.

In the light of what has been said it is evident that a promise *Conditions* (or something equivalent to a promise) on the part of God is an *for merit* essential condition for real merit in his sight. But there are other conditions which it is important that we should notice. First of all no man can really merit before God unless he be in the state of grace. It is only as part of the living vine that we can bear fruit, according to Christ's own saying : " As the branch cannot bear fruit of itself unless it abide in the vine, so neither can you, unless you abide in me." [1]  And St Paul tells us that " if I should have prophecy and should know all mysteries and all knowledge . . . and have not charity, I am nothing. And if I should distribute all my goods to feed the poor, and if I should deliver my body to be burned, and have not charity, it profiteth me nothing." [2]  In other words, unless I am in the friendship of Christ by divine love, which is inseparable from sanctifying grace, I cannot merit in the slightest way, even though I seem to perform acts of heroic virtue. Hence a man is indeed sowing the sands if he remains in a state of sin and yet fancies that by performing good actions he can merit before God.

It is not surprising that sanctifying grace should be a condition for all real merit before God. Without it, we are cut off from God and in a state of enmity with him, whether we have fallen from grace or have never become his children by Baptism : how then can we

[1] John xv 4.          [2] I Cor. xiii 2-3.

expect anything from him in return for our actions ? Still more, how can we merit to share his life in heaven ? But with sanctifying grace, we are his sons, sharers of his nature ; and it is not difficult to see how becoming it is, and how much in harmony with God's loving plan, that to such sons there should be given a promise of reward for the good actions which they perform.

Another condition for merit is that the act should be done for God. This is a point concerning which there has been considerable discussion amongst theologians who differ at least in the way in which they express themselves. Our statement of this condition does not mean (as the reader may be pardoned for thinking it means) that before an act can be meritorious it must be done with the express intention of doing it for God. In fact it would seem certain that all morally good acts which are performed by a soul in the state of grace are meritorious in the sight of God, even though he is not thought of in any way when they are done. Such a soul has chosen God as its supreme good to whom all other things are subordinated ; hence until that choice is retracted all its actions are governed by the principle " God first "—in other words, by the principle of Divine Charity. Consequently we can say that every morally good action which we perform comes under this great principle and is meritorious in the sight of God. It is " done for God " in so far as it is part of a mode of life in which all is directed to God.

This may seem to be too comfortable a doctrine, since it makes the sphere of supernatural merit extremely wide and very easy of access ; but it rests on sound theological principles, and is generally admitted by theologians. And in this connection we must remember another principle which is widely admitted, viz. that all actions which we freely perform are either definitely good or definitely bad ; there is no such thing in practice as a free act which is neither good nor bad. Considered in itself, and apart from its circumstances, an act may be " indifferent," as all admit ; but it would seem that in the circumstances in which it is performed an act must be either good or bad. If we follow this opinion, which has the authority of St Thomas Aquinas and many great thinkers, we must say that the possibility of merit for the children of God is indeed wide. As long as no warping element of self-love or other similar fault enters into their actions, they will merit all the day long, even though they do not consciously refer all their actions to God. Nevertheless the merit of their actions will be greater in proportion to the way in which love of God becomes more and more a directive principle in all they do, so that the more frequently and fervently they refer their actions to God the greater will be their merit.

Besides these conditions for supernatural merit there are certain others which need not detain us, as they are more or less obvious. Thus, the act must be free and it must be performed during the course of life, since there is no merit after death. The conditions

which we have explained are the important ones and others which
might be mentioned are reducible to them.

But is eternal life the only thing which we can merit from God ? *What we*
No, there are other things which we can merit.  In the preceding *can merit*
section we saw that the just man can merit an increase of grace—
a truth which is taught explicitly by the Council of Trent.  But
whilst it is reasonably certain that we merit eternally by all good
actions, it is not so certain that every good action merits an increase of
grace.  Many theologians hold that in order that we should merit
an increase of grace our actions must reach a certain degree of fervour
corresponding to the degree of grace which we already possess.
Thus, according to this view, if our present degree of grace and of the
Infused Virtues which accompany it is equivalent to 5, and the fervour
of our action is equivalent to 3, we shall indeed win a title to eternal
reward corresponding to the value of our action, but we shall not
obtain a present increase of grace and the Infused Virtues.  Whatever
may be thought about this, it is certain, and a matter of Catholic
faith, that increase of grace can be merited.

Since sanctifying grace is necessary for merit it will be realised
that there are many important things which no man can merit.
Thus the first actual grace which a man requires to lead him to faith
in God is quite outside the sphere of merit ; it is God's pure gift,
and no amount of natural virtue can establish a title to it.  Similarly
the first infusion of sanctifying grace cannot be merited.  Nor can
the man who has fallen away from God really merit his restoration
to grace, or even the actual graces which he needs in order to recover
the life which he has lost.  We may, indeed, pray whilst we are in
the state of grace that if we should ever be so unfortunate as to lose
the friendship of God there may be given to us the grace of repentance.  But God is in no way bound to hear this prayer.

Final Perseverance, too, is a thing which cannot be merited in
the strict sense of the word.  This great gift is bound up with the
problem of Predestination and is dealt with in the essay on *Actual
Grace* (pp. 599-600).

Can we merit graces and blessings for others ?  Strictly speaking, *Merit " de*
we cannot.  Only our Saviour, who was constituted the head of the *condigno "*
human race in all matters that pertain to eternal life, could truly *"de congruo"*
merit for others.  The rest of men can pray for others, and they can
even make satisfaction for the sins of others, but they cannot merit
for them.  To merit is entirely a personal affair.  But there is a title
to reward which is lower than that of merit in the strict sense, yet
is of real value.  It is what theologians call merit " de congruo "
(merit of congruity), as contrasted with that strict merit of which
we have been speaking, and to which they give the name merit " de
condigno " (merit of desert).  This merit of congruity is based not
upon a title in justice, but upon a certain fitness, or what we may
call a reasonable expectation that in view of what we have done a

return will be made. Thus if I have shown great kindness to another, and he in turn has an opportunity of doing me some service, I shall feel it to be only natural that he should do the service. There is no question of justice ; it is a matter of what we may call " decency "— of merit " de congruo." Now, as between ourselves and God there are several things which cannot be merited in the strict sense of the word, yet they come under the head of this merit " de congruo." Hence, although the man who has not yet been justified cannot strictly merit justification, nevertheless by responding to the actual graces which are given to him he can merit it " de congruo " ; and in a similar way the sinner by his response to actual grace can merit further grace " de congruo." And this applies to meriting for others. Though we cannot merit for them in the strict sense of the word, we can merit for them " de congruo " whatever we can merit for ourselves. Hence in our efforts to obtain favours for others we must go on in patience and in trust, relying upon God to do what is best for his own glory. We cast our bread upon the running waters, trusting that God will use it for those whose welfare we have at heart.[1]

## § VIII : LOSS AND REGAIN

*Loss of grace a possibility* IT was a peculiarity of the teaching of Calvin that he held it to be impossible for a man who had once been justified to fall away. Luther did not go quite so far as this, but he taught that justification can be lost only by the sin of infidelity ; in other words, by the loss of that faith which, according to his system, justifies a man.

The teaching of the Catholic Church is that sanctifying grace is lost by every mortal sin. That grace is a thing which can be lost is clear enough. Our Saviour warned us of the danger in which we stand when he said : " Watch ye and pray that ye enter not into temptation." [2] St Paul gives the warning : " He that thinketh himself to stand, let him take heed lest he fall." [3] In the same epistle the great Apostle of the Gentiles expresses the fear which he felt : " I chastise my body and bring it into subjection : lest perhaps when I have preached to others I myself should become a castaway." [4] Scripture and Tradition are unanimous on this point of the possibility of losing the grace which we have once acquired.

*Grace and mortal sin* A little thought will show the essential opposition which exists between sanctifying grace and mortal sin. They are contraries which necessarily exclude each other. On the one hand, he who is

---

[1] The conditions for merit " de congruo " are, of course, different from the conditions for merit " de condigno." They are that the act must be morally good, it must be free, and it must be supernatural. Hence (in regard to the last condition), if a man be not in a state of grace his actions, to be meritorious " de congruo," must proceed from an impulse of actual grace. This is one reason why the first grace which a man receives cannot be merited even " de congruo."

[2] Matt. xxvi 41.     [3] 1 Cor. x 12.     [4] 1 Cor. ix 27.

in the state of grace is the son of God, a sharer in his nature, an heir to heaven, incorporated in Christ ; on the other hand, he who sins mortally deliberately turns himself away from God and seeks his good in something which is opposed to him, so that God is rejected, his enemy enthroned. It is clearly impossible, therefore, that a man should be at one and the same time in the state of grace and in the state of mortal sin. It is for this very reason that such sin is called " mortal," because it deprives the soul of its supernatural life just as a mortal wound deprives the body of its natural life. There is no such opposition, however, between sanctifying grace and venial sin, for the adequate reason that in the case of venial sin a man does not set before himself some other end than God. There is indeed something inordinate in his action, but he does not directly turn away from God and prefer some other thing to him.

Had God wished, he could have ordained that grace once lost *Restoration* was lost for ever, as he did in the case of the fallen angels. But in *of grace* his compassion he has made it possible for us to recover grace after it has been lost. There is no sin, and no combination of sins, for which he refuses forgiveness. Yet it is well that we should remember that of himself the sinner is in a helpless condition. He is dead, as far as the spiritual life of the soul is concerned, and can do nothing towards his own spiritual resurrection.

The first thing which is necessary, then, is the assistance of Actual Grace,[1] which God never withholds completely from the sinner. If his sorrow is perfect, grace is restored to him even before he approaches the consoling sacrament of Penance ; if it remains mere Attrition, the absolution of Christ's minister is required, or some other sacrament which, under the special circumstances of the case, carries with it forgiveness. But these points are explained more fully in other essays in this work and do not call for special treatment here.[2] It is more to our present purpose to call attention to two points which arise more directly in connection with our discussion of sanctifying grace, namely : How much grace is restored to us ? And what happens to the store of merit which we had acquired before our fall and lost by our sin ?

To these questions theologians do not give a uniform answer. St Thomas Aquinas held that the amount of sanctifying grace which a sinner receives when he obtains forgiveness is proportionate to the dispositions in which he returns to God ; hence grace after forgiveness may be greater than it was before, it may be less, it may be equal.[3] Other theologians maintain that after repentance and forgiveness the amount of sanctifying grace is always greater than it was before, because the whole of that which was lost is restored and an increase of grace is obtained through the sacrament which has been received and the various acts of the penitent which have merited

[1] See Essay xvii, *Actual Grace*, pp. 604-605.
[2] See Essay xxvi, *Sin and Repentance.*    [3] *S. Theol.*, III, Q. lxxxix, a. 2.

grace. Whichever of these opinions be true (and one ought to be slow in setting aside the opinion of St Thomas) it is evidently a matter of extreme importance that the sinner should return to God with all the ardour of his soul ; then he may hope that in the infinite mercy of God all the grace which he had lost has been restored to him and he may begin again with renewed energy, hope, and gratitude.

The question of the recovery of merit is closely akin. That merit is restored to us when we return to God after a fall, is the teaching of the Church : but it is explained in different ways by theologians. As in the case of the restoration of sanctifying grace, some make it proportionate to the dispositions of the penitent sinner : but others hold that the full measure of lost merit is always restored, with an addition due to present repentance. The point is one concerning which a Catholic is free to hold either opinion. In any case the goodness of God is apparent. Like the father of the Prodigal Son, he is ever ready to receive his erring child and restore him to the inheritance which he had lost.

# EPILOGUE

### HOPE AND FEAR

THERE can be no doubt that the Catholic teaching on sanctifying grace does much to encourage within us the spirit of hope. He that is mighty has done great things for us. He has made us his children, he has raised us up to a share in his nature, he has set the Beatific Vision as the end towards which we must aspire, and he has given us most wonderful endowments to enable us to reach that end. Well, then, may we hope. Yet in our hope there ought ever to be an element of salutary fear. Why ?

First of all because we cannot indulge in that strange security which the Reformers declared to be the one condition for justification. It was part of their system that in order to be justified we must have the unwavering certainty of faith that we *are* justified. This was condemned by the Council of Trent, which lays it down that " just as no pious man ought to entertain a doubt about the mercy of God, the merits of Christ and the efficacy of the sacraments ; so everyone can have uncertainty and fear concerning the possession of grace, when he considers himself and his own infirmity and want of good dispositions ; since no one can know with the certainty of faith, which admits of no error, that he has obtained the grace of God."

We cannot, then, have the certainty of faith that we are in grace ; but we can have an assurance which is sufficient for all practical purposes. Concerning the precise degree of this assurance there has been considerable discussion amongst theologians, but at any rate we can say without hesitation that a man can have a degree of certainty which excludes all real and prudent doubt. And indeed we are often expected to have such a certainty, as when we receive Holy Communion ; at such times we must be able to tell ourselves that we really and truly are in God's grace. To open the door to doubt upon our state of grace when our conscience can discover no serious sin would be to enter upon a life of anguish and stress of mind which God most certainly does not intend. If we are faced by the thought of past sins we must mourn for them and renew our heartfelt sorrow, but we must at the same time put our trust in the goodness of God and in the efficacy of the sacrament of Penance. A condition of morbid fear is altogether foreign to the spirit of Christ.

There is greater ground for fear in regard to the future. I may have reasonable certainty that I am in the grace of God, but do I know that I shall die in that grace ? I do not. Far from the mind of a Catholic must be the thought of those who look upon themselves as most certainly amongst the number of the elect, for the Church teaches that apart from a special revelation it is impossible to know which souls God has predestined. When we consider the weakness of our nature and the strength of the enemies of our soul we may well fear lest we fall from grace. Hence our Saviour teaches us to pray that we be saved from temptation. " Lead us not into temptation, but deliver us from evil." " Be sober and watch," says St Peter, " because your adversary the devil, as a roaring lion, goeth about seeking whom he may devour. Whom resist ye, strong in faith." [1] Truly it is with fear and trembling that we must work out our salvation, as St Paul tells us. [2] Nothing which we can do can really merit this " great gift " of final perseverance. We must pray for it, we must hope for it, but we cannot be certain that we shall obtain it.

Yet hope must surely temper the fear which the thought of our uncertainty creates ; not the hope of one who is conscious of his own strength, but the hope of one who, knowing his own infirmity, looks up to God in childlike trust. He has been so good to us ; he has made such wonderful provision for us ; so, whilst we fear our own weakness we are confident of his strength and his love. It is in this spirit that we listen to the words of St Paul which the Church puts before us when she celebrates the mystery of Christ's coming on Christmas night. " The grace of God our Saviour hath appeared to all men, instructing us, that denying ungodliness and worldly desires, we should live soberly, and justly, and godly in this world, looking for the blessed hope and coming of the glory of the great God and our Saviour Jesus Christ, who gave himself for us, that he might redeem us from all iniquity, and might cleanse to himself a people acceptable, a pursuer of good works. These things speak and exhort." [3]

E. TOWERS.

---

[1] 1 Pet. v 8.　　　[2] Phil. ii 12.　　　[3] Tit. ii 11-15.

# XVII

## ACTUAL GRACE

### §I: INTRODUCTORY NOTIONS

*Our
dependence
on God*

It is of fundamental importance for the right ordering of our lives that we should realise our spiritual weakness. In many of the ordinary affairs of life a spirit of self-reliance is essential for success, and men often lag behind in the keen struggle of this busy world because they have not sufficient confidence in themselves. But in spiritual matters the truth is just the other way ; it is the self-confident man that fails and the man who distrusts himself that succeeds. When the Catechism told us that " we can do no good work of ourselves towards our salvation " it was expressing a profound truth with literal exactness, not uttering a pious exaggeration. And if we do not recognise this fact we are in danger of spiritual ruin. He that thinks himself to stand must take heed lest he fall.

In speaking thus of our personal insufficiency we are not thinking merely of our natural dependence, as creatures, upon the sustaining hand of God. Every creature depends upon God, not only for its continued existence, but also for every exercise of its natural powers of action. We cannot lift a finger unless God, who is the First Cause and the First Mover, acts with us. But it is not this which we are here considering. Over and above God's concurrence with our ordinary actions there is need of his special assistance in the working out of our salvation, in such wise that if he did not give us this assistance we should most certainly perish. In a word, we need actual grace, which for the moment we will define as a supernatural help given by God for the special purpose of enabling us to perform some particular act which tends towards our salvation.

Our need of actual grace is far greater than even Catholics are at first inclined to believe ; in fact, if there is any matter of faith in which it is easy to fall unconsciously into views which are in themselves heretical, that matter is our dependence upon the supernatural assistance of God. We give ourselves credit for more than we can do by our own unaided powers.

*False ideas*

It was in the early part of the fifth century that the Church was first compelled to face the whole question of the necessity of grace. The controversy arose out of the teaching of a British monk named Pelagius who appeared in Italy in the first years of that century and soon attracted a good deal of notice. St Augustine, who was to be his chief opponent, speaks of him with respect, and he seems to have been an austere and zealous man, a practical director of souls rather than a deep theologian. He had no patience with people who distrusted themselves and for ever cried to God for help in a spirit of helplessness ; he considered all this a mark of indolence and of unwillingness to make a vigorous and persevering effort for oneself. Bestir yourself, he said in effect ; harden the will ; learn self-discipline ; watch your evil tendencies ; you are " master of your fate, captain of your soul " ; if you fall it is your own fault and you have only yourself to blame.

All this sounded very well, but there were some who raised objections. Surely, they said, Pelagius is ignoring the Fall of man, and the sad consequences involved in it for all the human race ; our nature is wounded and both the Scriptures and the Fathers rightly stress the need under which we labour of the help of God. Reasoning such as this Pelagius and his followers unhesitatingly swept aside. Adam's sin, they declared, did not harm us except by the bad example which it set ; our nature is not fundamentally evil, and man can keep from sin by the unaided power of his will ; grace comes in to make things easier for us, not to deliver us from impossibilities. They were willing to concede that in order that we may do all that God requires of us we need the external help of revelation, which makes known to us many of his commands ; but, given this knowledge through revelation, we can accomplish our task, and save our souls, by ourselves.

These issues were too serious to be ignored, and for a considerable time the western world resounded with the echoes of the controversy. And, as in other vicissitudes of his Church, God had a champion at hand in the person of the great St Augustine of Hippo who has been justly called the Doctor of Grace. From the first he saw the far-reaching consequences of these theories of the British monk and forthwith he set himself to meet the danger. The struggle was long drawn out and lasted beyond the lifetime of the saint, but it was he who dealt Pelagianism its death-blow.

It will be seen that the issues raised by Pelagius were of far-reaching and very practical importance. They involved such questions as the nature of the Fall, Original Sin, and the Redemption ; our dependence upon Christ ; the efficacy of the Sacraments ; the power of the human will. Indeed, this question of the necessity of grace is one which shows in a very striking way how a number of different dogmas which at first sight might seem to have little relation one with another are in reality mutually dependent ; and how a wonderful harmony runs through all God's dealings with men as seen in the revelation which he has given to his Church. This harmony of doctrine with doctrine is in itself no insignificant argument for the divine authorship of that body of doctrine of which the Catholic Church is the custodian.

In some of the pages which follow it will be our business to *Two sources* set out in some detail the more important ways in which we need *of weakness* the divine assistance, but before proceeding to this more detailed study it will be helpful if we glance for a moment at two sources of our weakness. If we bear these two sources in mind we shall find it more easy to realise how great is our dependence on the super-natural assistance of God.

First, then, there is the fact that we possess a fallen nature. When God created our first parents he gave them what is known as the gift of integrity. In virtue of this gift the animal part of man was subjected to the spiritual. All his actions were ruled by reason, and the lower passions did not rebel ; perfect harmony prevailed. But this gift was lost by the sin of Adam, and lost not only for Adam himself, but also for us. Henceforth a constant strife was to go on in the heart of every man, the lower rising up in opposition to the higher, the carnal against the spiritual. St Paul has spoken of this strife in a passage which has become famous even amongst non-believers. " I know that there dwelleth not in me, that is to say, in my flesh, that which is good. For to will is present with me ; but to accomplish that which is good, I find not. For the good which I will, I do not ; but the evil which I will not, that I do. Now if I do that which I will not, it is no more I that do it, but sin that dwelleth in me. I find then a law, that when I have a will to do good, evil is present with me. For I am delighted with the law of God, according to the inward man : but I see another law in my members, fighting against the law of my mind and captivating me in the law of sin that is in my members. Unhappy man that I am, who shall deliver me from the body of this death ? The grace of God, by Jesus Christ our Lord." [1]

Here we have one important source of our weakness. It would be possible, indeed, to exaggerate the difficulty and to look upon human nature as essentially and hopelessly corrupt. That was what Luther did when he taught that our nature has become so corrupt, so odious in the sight of God, that all our acts are sinful, tainted in their source. But, whilst avoiding extreme views such as this, we are forced to realise that in the loss of the gift of integrity there is a source of immense difficulty, from which we can be delivered only through " the grace of God, by Jesus Christ our Lord ".

The second source of our weakness is not so obvious as this rebellion of the lower part of man against the higher, but it is of even greater importance for a true understanding of our proper condition. To put it in somewhat technical terms, which we shall at once proceed to explain, all our natural efforts are inadequate because God has

[1] Rom. vii 18-25. In the Westminster Version, edited by Fr. Lattey, S.J., the last sentence is rendered : " Thanks be to God through our Lord Jesus Christ." The Authorised as well as the Revised Version has : " I thank God through Jesus Christ our Lord." The Douai Version used in the text follows the Latin of the Vulgate, which would seem to be based on an inferior Greek text. The sense is ultimately the same, and the Douai Version has been retained both here and elsewhere.

ordained that we should aim at the possession of a supernatural object, and should live in a supernatural order of things. Since the object to be attained and the order of things in which we are to live are supernatural, it follows necessarily that our natural efforts are insufficient ; by the very nature of the case we need supernatural help. To explain.

In a verse which gloriously expresses the wonders of our Christian calling, St John says : " Dearly beloved, we are now the sons of God ; and it hath not yet appeared what we shall be. We know, that, when he shall appear, we shall be like to him : because we shall see him as he is." [1]  Here two great truths are put before us, viz. that we are destined for the Beatific Vision and that we who have been redeemed by the blood of Christ are already the sons of God. " As many as received him, he gave them power to be made the sons of God, to them that believe in his name." [2]  But the beatific vision is something to which no creature, human or angelic, can attain by its own unaided power. God lives in light inaccessible. The object, then, which is set before us is absolutely beyond our grasp, as far as our natural powers are concerned ; no effort of our own, no matter how intense or how prolonged, could bring us within the possibility of reaching it. God, however, has freely chosen so to raise our nature above itself that we shall see him as he is. And that is not all : not only has he chosen to raise us up to the Beatific Vision, but already in this mortal life he has so elevated our nature that " we are now the sons of God " ; sons of God, not in some metaphorical sense, not merely in so far as every creature may be called the son of God because it is his handiwork, but sons of God through a change which he has wrought in us whereby we are made to share his very nature. St Peter dares to say that " he hath given us most great and precious promises : that by these you may be made partakers of the divine nature." [3]

It is of the greatest importance that we should realise this higher life to which the Christian is raised and the wholly supernatural character of that Beatific Vision to which we are called. Such a realisation is wonderfully ennobling. But what is of more direct interest for us here is the light which it throws on the question of our dependence on God. Obviously a creature who is made a partaker of the divine nature and a son of God, and who is striving to attain the glory of the Beatific Vision, must be absolutely dependent upon God. We could more easily live our natural life without air than this supernatural life without God's grace.

In the light of these general principles it will be evident that we *Correspond-* need the help of God both to save us from falling into sin and also *ing graces* to enable us to ascend to the performance of the actions which belong to our new life as sons of God. Our weak nature has to be healed,

---

[1] I John iii 2.　　　　　[2] John i 12.
[3] 2 Pet. i 4. For a fuller explanation of this see above, Essay xvi, pp. 553-555.

our lowly nature uplifted. Hence what theologians call medicinal or healing grace (*gratia medicinalis*, or *sanans*) and elevating grace (*gratia elevans*), the one to save us from our sinful tendencies, the other to lift us up to a life with God. The elevation of our nature to the divine sonship is actually accomplished by that wonderful reality which we call Habitual, or Sanctifying, Grace ; that is to say, by a real quality infused into the soul and making it Godlike—a quality which is of a permanent character, to be destroyed only by sin. With sanctifying, or habitual, grace we are not here directly concerned—the object of our study being not the permanent supernatural gifts of God to the soul, but the passing helps by which he comes to our assistance in the performance of various actions. It is to these passing helps that we give the name Actual Grace.

A reference has just been made to the grace which heals and the grace which elevates, and this distinction helps to explain the work of grace in the soul ; but it may be well to point out that these are not necessarily two distinct things. A grace which heals may at the same time elevate our faculties to the supernatural order of action. In all probability this is generally the case, and thus " healing " and " elevating " are but two effects of one and the same grace. The distinction has been mentioned here because it helps to bring out the general ideas which we are explaining on the necessity of grace.

In technical works of theology various divisions of actual grace are given which lie outside the very limited scope of the present little essay ; but there is one division the explanation of which will help towards a fuller understanding of our subject. Theologians distinguish between external and internal graces. External graces are gifts of God which are outside ourselves, such as the message of the Gospel, the example of Christ and the saints, the external circumstances of our lives ; internal graces are influences exercised by God within us, such as impulses towards good and lights on eternal truths. Of course, these two kinds of grace are often connected, the external grace being the medium, or the occasion, for the giving of the internal ; but they are obviously different in kind, and the distinction is important. In what follows we shall retain the name Actual Grace for interior grace, so that when we assert the necessity of actual grace, we mean to deny the sufficiency of merely external grace.

*Definition of Actual Grace* After these various explanations we can amplify the definition of actual grace which was given earlier on. We said that actual grace is a supernatural help given by God for the special purpose of enabling us to perform some particular action which tends towards our salvation ; we may now say, more fully, that it is a supernatural gift, internal to us and of a passing nature, whereby God helps us to avoid sin, or enables us to perform actions which tend towards eternal life.

And now we pass to the consideration of the necessity of actual grace. In this matter human reason alone is an insufficient guide ; we must rely on the revelation which God in his mercy has made to us, and on the infallible teaching of the Church. When the Catholic doctrine on the necessity of grace has been set before us we may be inclined to feel that the position is one of despair, so great is our weakness seen to be ; but further thought will lead us to a very different conclusion. It will make us see the grandeur of that wonderful scheme of Redemption whereby Christ our Lord came to our assistance, and of that equally wonderful scheme of a Church which, with its Sacraments and other means of grace, was to be an ark of salvation to us ; so that we can rejoice in that very weakness of ours which has called forth such an exhibition of loving kindness on the part of God. The thought of our weakness would indeed be terrifying if there were no strong hand to hold us ; but when we know that the arm of God is about us, fear gives place to confidence and love. " He that dwelleth in the aid of the Most High, shall abide under the protection of the God of heaven. He shall say to the Lord : Thou art my protector, and my refuge : my God, in him will I trust." [1]

## § II : THE NECESSITY OF GRACE FOR THE AVOIDING OF SIN

CAN a man keep from sin without the special help of God ? As we have seen, the Pelagians declared that he can ; it is simply a matter of the right use of our free will, they maintained, and to deny that we can keep from sin without grace is nothing less than a denial that we are free. Yet the Church teaches just the opposite and warns us that if we are to keep from sin, we must rely on the grace of God, without whose aid we shall most certainly fall. It is this teaching which we are to explain in the present section. *Inability to observe the Natural Law*

First of all, we will consider the following question : If a man lives apart from God, and receives no grace from him, can he keep the whole of the natural law ? Notice that we are limiting our question to the *natural law*—in other words, to that moral law which every normal man recognises by the light of his reason and the dictates of his conscience ; we leave out of account altogether that positive law which God has given to us through revelation. Further, our question has reference to the *whole* of the natural law. We are not suggesting that any of the dictates of the natural law, taken singly, are beyond the power of unaided nature ; that would clearly be untrue, for we have plenty of evidence of men without faith in God who avoid such offences against the natural law as drunkenness and dishonesty. No, we are referring to the whole of the natural law. Moreover, we are not going to maintain that the natural law cannot be observed for at any rate a short time ; we are thinking now of

[1] Ps. xc 1-2.

the possibility of a long-continued period in which the whole of t**
moral law is observed, and we deny the possibility of such a thin**
A man may, indeed, go on for some time—how long we do n**
pretend to say—without serious fault, but he cannot succeed i**
definitely; sooner or later there will be a serious fall in regard
one or other of the obligations which the natural law lays upon **
all, of which we are all conscious.

If we were to examine this question simply from what our ow**
reason and experience tell us of life, we might not be justified
making the bold statement that there is absolutely no one who c**
keep the whole of the moral law without the help of God. Th**
sight of so much evil, even amongst men who believe in God ar**
profess some form of religion, might make us pause, and an analys**
of the tendencies of the human heart might make us feel that soon
or later, in one way or another, by sin of the spirit if not by sin **
the flesh, men will fail to observe perfectly the dictates of the mor**
law; but would this justify us in saying universally that witho**
divine grace no man can avoid evil? Probably not; and therefo**
it is not on appeal to reason, but on the authority of God's reveal**
word, that Catholic theology bases its assertion of man's mor**
incapacity. And the passage on which we chiefly rely has alrea**
been quoted. It occurs in the seventh chapter of St Paul's Epist**
to the Romans, and requires very careful reading.

In the first chapter of this epistle St Paul paints in vivid colou**
the moral degradation into which the pagan world had fallen, ar**
in the seventh chapter he speaks of the wretched condition ev**
of the man who has the advantage of the Jewish Law. That la**
he asserts, was an occasion of sin; for by forbidding things, it creat**
a desire for them: "sin taking occasion by the commandme**
wrought in me all manner of concupiscence";[1] but it did n**
give any internal help to compensate. Hence the Jew living und**
the law finds it impossible to keep altogether from sin. "The go**
which I will, I do not; but the evil which I will not, that I do."**
There is only one means of escape; and that is, the grace of God**

Such is the thought of St Paul; and the only conclusion whi**
we can draw from it is that without the help of God which com**
to us through Christ it is impossible to keep from sin. "The la**
of the spirit of life, in Christ Jesus, hath delivered me from the la**
of sin and of death."[4]

---

[1] Rom. vii 8.  [2] Rom. vii 19.  [3] Rom. vii 25.

[4] Rom. viii 2. For a fuller exposition of the teaching of St Paul in th**
important and very difficult passage, the reader is referred to a Catho**
commentary on the Epistle to the Romans (*e.g.* Cornely in Latin, Lagran**
in French, Callan in English), or to the careful discussion of the matter
Prat, *The Theology of St Paul*, vol. i, p. 224 *seq.* It is generally admitt**
that where St Paul speaks in the first person he is not directly alluding
himself; it would seem that he is speaking in the character of a Jew livi**
under the Jewish law. Towards the end of his life St Augustine preferr**

On the strength of this teaching of St Paul, and supported by the authority of earlier Christian writers who in various ways insisted upon man's natural weakness, the champions of Catholic orthodoxy against the teaching of Pelagius strenuously maintained the necessity of help from God if a man is to keep from sin, and, although the Church has never defined the matter in so many words, there can be no doubt that this is the only true doctrine, and that it would be a grievous error for anyone to deny it. Yet it is open to some serious objections which the Pelagians were quick to seize upon. If we cannot keep the moral law without the help of God, how (it may be asked) can we logically maintain that man is free? Surely, if man *must* sin, he has no freedom in the matter. And if he is not free, but impelled by necessity to evil action, how can he be said to commit sin—since sin implies freedom to abstain from wrong? Pelagius himself put the difficulty in the form of a neat dilemma. " Is sin a thing which can be avoided, or a thing which cannot be avoided? If it cannot be avoided, it is no sin ; and if it can be avoided, man can be without it."

To meet this objection theologians introduce an important dis- *Moral, not* tinction between a *physical* impossibility and a *moral* impossibility. *physical, impossibility* There is a physical impossibility when the means which are physic- ally necessary for the doing of a thing are absent : thus, it is physic- ally impossible for a blind man to see, and for a fish to walk. Now, it will be at once evident that when a man labours under a physical impossibility, he is not free to act or not to act. A blind man is not free to see or not just as he wishes ; he is under a physical neces- sity not to see. Consequently, if we were to say that it is physically impossible for a man to keep from sin without the help of God, we should at the same time be denying his liberty, and there would be no escape from the dilemma of Pelagius. But the matter is very different if the impossibility of which there is question is a moral, not a physical, impossibility ; for in the case of a moral impossibility the means which are physically necessary for doing a thing are in- deed present, but the difficulty in the way of using those means is so great that failure is ultimately inevitable. Take the case of a man who is firing at a target. If he has not a rifle with sufficient range to reach the target it is clearly a physical impossibility for him to hit his mark. But suppose that the target is within his range : can he go on indefinitely hitting the centre every time he fires, in all con- ditions of wind and weather? We should have no hesitation in saying that this is so difficult as to be morally impossible. Each

to think that, at least in the later verses, St Paul was speaking in the person of a Christian regenerated by Baptism, but still under the influence of con- cupiscence. If this interpretation be followed we get a still clearer proof of the necessity of grace. Lagrange, followed by Callan, understands St Paul to be speaking of man in the state of innocence. In any case, we get the same conclusion—namely, that without the grace of God man is so much under the dominion of concupiscence that he inevitably falls into sin.

time he takes up the rifle it is possible for him to succeed, but we are sure that sooner or later he will fail.

Apply this to the question of the perfect fulfilment of the moral law. In every single vicissitude of life it may be physically possible for a man to observe that right order of conduct which the moral law requires, so that in each case as it arises he is free in his action ; and yet (we assert) he is sure ultimately to make a mistake. In other words, it is a moral impossibility for him to observe the whole of the natural law. He may do many things which are morally good ; he may show great moral courage in resisting various attacks of evil ; but sooner or later he will fall, not through want of freedom, not through anything which makes it impossible to continue any longer in the course of right action, but through instability.

It is to be noted that the moral impossibility of which we speak has reference, not to any one particular act considered by itself, but to a continuance of action. Thus we are not saying that a time comes when a man is faced by a difficulty which he cannot overcome ; we are simply saying that as a matter of fact a time will certainly come when a mistake will be made. When that time comes the man will have the power of succeeding—otherwise he would not be free—but he will fail to use that power.

In what has preceded we have been thinking of man as he is apart from the grace of God, and our conclusion is altogether opposed to the possibility of what we may call natural goodness. Non-religious ethical training must, in consequence, be pronounced a sad delusion ; it may, indeed, serve to teach some forms of self-restraint, and it may also contribute to develop some of the nobler qualities which lie deep in the human heart ; but it cannot arm a man against all his enemies and give him the strength he needs in every conflict. And here we have one of the dangers of purely secular systems of education. Not by such means will humanity be made sound : we have need of Christ and his grace.

*Position of the sinner* — It is worthy of special notice that St Paul clearly requires more than actual grace in order that a man may be preserved from sin ; he requires incorporation in Christ—in other words, sanctifying grace. It is " the law of the spirit of life, in Christ Jesus ", which " hath delivered me from the law of sin and of death." [1] Actual grace, indeed, is required in order that we may be upheld and strengthened in the hour of conflict, but we are given to understand that this help will not be given unceasingly except to those who " put on " Christ ; they who reject him cannot expect that the graces which belong to the sons of God will be extended to them. And this leads us to stress the important point that the man who has fallen from grace and lives in sin will most certainly fall into further sin. There is no such thing as committing one grave sin and then standing still : a man must either come back to God or come still more under the

---

[1] Rom. viii 2.

dominion of evil. If it is only by incorporation in Christ that I escape from that " law in my members fighting against the law of my mind and captivating me in the law of sin that is in my members," [1] then when I reject Christ by mortal sin I pass once more under " the law of sin." A little thought will show how this must be so. When a man sins he sets up for himself other gods. He makes his own will the end which he chooses, in contempt of God. In this state of glorified self-will—although it is not true, as Luther would have it, that all his acts are sinful—he is unable to resist the many evil influences which assail him. His efforts are doomed to failure because his will is wrong ; the compass by which he directs his life is at fault, and other sins will follow. The only way in which he can recover his power of successful resistance to the forces of evil is by turning once more to God ; he must set his will right and become again a living member of that Body of Christ outside of which there is no true life.

But—and here we see once more how terrible is the position of the sinner and how great is our dependence on God—he cannot return to God without divine grace. True, there is something in man which gives him a natural disgust with grosser forms of sin, and even the most abandoned may not be altogether free from occasional desires to escape from some of the more degrading vices ; but this is far removed from such a sorrow for sin as will win back the friendship of God. Perfect charity, which blots out sin even before reception of the sacrament of Penance, is clearly beyond the unaided powers of the sinner, as will be seen more clearly in the next section ; and even attrition, which would be sufficient to obtain forgiveness in the tribunal of Penance, is impossible without grace. The second Council of Orange, held in 529, made all this clear when it condemned those who maintained that God awaits the movement of repentance in the heart of the sinner, and that the desire to be free from sin is our own work, and not the work of the Holy Spirit. Any movement of disgust with sin and of desire for a better life which a man may experience without the grace of God is a vain, superficial thing, of no true spiritual value ; and true attrition, as the Council of Trent teaches,[2] is a gift of God, an impulse of the Holy Spirit. As the Fathers of the Council of Orange remind us in this very connection : " It is God who worketh in you, both to will and to accomplish according to his good will." [3]

There remains another question to be discussed in regard to the *Avoidance* necessity of grace for the avoiding of sin—namely, the question of *of venial sin* avoiding not merely mortal sin, but also venial sin. Of course, it is obvious that since the man who is an enemy of God cannot avoid even mortal sin he is still less capable of avoiding venial sin ; and therefore it is only in regard to the sons of God that the present

---

[1] Rom. vii 23.　　　　[2] Session XIV, chap. iv.
[3] Phil. ii 13.

question can arise. What, then, shall we say of the power of the sons of God to live a life so perfect that venial sin never enters in ?

The answer of Catholic theology is clear ; freedom from venial sin requires something quite extraordinary, which we have not the right to expect. There are several texts of Scripture which tell us that in point of fact—and from this we can argue in regard to the question of possibility—practically no man escapes altogether from venial sin. St John tells us that " if we say that we have no sin we deceive ourselves and the truth is not in us " ; [1] and in the epistle of St James we read that " in many things we all offend." [2] Everybody knows the text which says that " the just man falls seven times a day," but it would seem certain that this refers not to moral falls, but to various difficulties and tribulations. But even apart from this particular passage Scripture gives us to understand that the just man certainly does fall into various faults, and consequently our Saviour himself teaches us to pray that God will " forgive us our trespasses as we forgive them that trespass against us." Even the saints are expected to make this petition.

The Pelagians tried to explain away the force of the argument from the Lord's Prayer by saying that in using the expression " Forgive us our trespasses " God's servants were simply speaking in terms of humility, or in the name of the general mass of the people ; but this interpretation was formally rejected and refuted at the Council of Milevis, held in 416, when a number of other passages [3] were quoted as indicating the presence of sin in all men.

All this, it is true, has reference to the mere fact that even good men do actually fail to escape venial sin ; it does not refer directly to the impossibility of escaping. But the Church has not hesitated to condemn those who asserted the existence of the power of avoiding venial sins without a very special assistance from God. In a famous decree of the Council of Trent [4] they are condemned who hold that the man who has once been justified can avoid all sins, even venial sins, throughout his whole life, without a special privilege of God, such as the Church believes to have been granted to the Blessed Virgin.

It must be noticed, however, that what we have said about the impossibility of avoiding all venial sin refers to semi-deliberate sin : as for fully deliberate sin, it is possible to avoid it with the ordinary graces of God. There is clearly a great difference between the two classes—between the venial sin which we commit with our eyes open and the sin which we commit through sudden impulse or incomplete advertence. It is difficult, indeed, to avoid the former altogether, but not impossible ; but to avoid the second is quite another matter. We believe, as the Council of Trent says, that the Blessed Virgin

[1] 1 John i 8.  [2] James iii 2.
[3] Ps. cxlii 2 ; Eccles. vii 21 ; and Dan. ix 5, 15, 20.
[4] Session VI, canon xxiii.

was free even from these semi-deliberate venial sins, and the reason
for this wonderful sinlessness is to be found in her prerogative of
Immaculate Conception which included freedom from the stings
of concupiscence. Whether any other saint has been similarly free
from venial sin, we do not know ; there may be reason for thinking
that such freedom was granted to St John the Baptist, who was
miraculously sanctified before his birth, and to St Joseph, at least
from the time of his espousals to the Blessed Virgin ; but the spirit
of the Church is opposed to what one may call a tendency towards
pious exaggeration. As the Council of Milevis explained, even the
saints say in all truth " Forgive us our trespasses."

In the face of the truths laid down in this section we may well
pray that God may ever stretch out his hand to help us ; and in the
words which the Church puts upon the lips of her ministers in the
office of Prime at the beginning of each day we may cry aloud :
" Lord God Almighty, who hast brought us to the beginning of this
day, defend us throughout its course by thy power, that we may not
this day fall into any sin, but that our words and thoughts and deeds
may be directed to the fulfilment of what is right in thy sight."
Thus only shall we escape " the arrow that flieth in the day." [1]

§ III : THE NECESSITY OF GRACE FOR GAINING
ETERNAL LIFE

In the preceding section we have shown how wrong it is to suppose *Salutary*
that man is capable of avoiding sin without the help of God. As we *action*
have seen, our fallen nature is so weak that we have need of a *gratia
sanans*—that is, a grace which will heal our moral infirmities. It is
one thing, however, to avoid grievous sin, and another to obtain
eternal life ; and in the present section we are to consider how far
man is capable, by his own powers, of reaching the glorious end which
God has set him.

We have just said that there is a difference between avoiding
grievous sin and winning eternal life. Of course these two are connected in the actual order of things, but there is not an essential
and intrinsic connection between the first and the second. If God
had not raised man to the supernatural order and set the Beatific
Vision as the end to which he was to aspire, man might have lived
a life which was free from moral fault without thereby gaining
" eternal life." Now, this question of our power of gaining eternal
life presents some special features which it is necessary for us to
touch upon.

Once more we are concerned with a question which was raised
by the Pelagians. They maintained that heaven can be won by our
own efforts ; our salvation, in the full sense of the word as including
the glory of the blessed, is in our own hands. This raised the whole

[1] Ps. xc 6.

question of what theologians call "salutary acts." The term is of such importance in the theology of grace that the reader must allow us to use it, technical though it be ; but of course the use of such a technical expression makes it necessary that we should carefully explain its meaning. A salutary act, then, is one which positively serves towards the attaining of eternal life. Notice the word " positively." There are actions which serve " negatively " towards the attaining of eternal life in so far as they remove distant obstacles to salvation. Thus if a man who has no religious belief makes natural efforts to live a decent moral life, he is removing certain obstacles of vice which might stand in the way of his coming to a recognition of the truth : such efforts on his part would serve only in a negative way towards his eternal salvation. But a salutary act is one which *positively* leads to eternal life ; there is an intrinsic connection between the two. This being understood, we can state the problem raised by the Pelagians thus : Can a man perform salutary actions without the grace of God ? The Catechism gives us the answer : " We can do no good work of ourselves towards our salvation ; we need the help of God's grace." It is this answer which we must now explain and justify.

*Grace necessary*

Although the Scriptures do not use the term " salutary acts," few things are more clear from the pages of Holy Writ than that we can do nothing of ourselves towards our salvation. Listen to the words of Christ himself. " As the branch cannot bear fruit of itself, unless it abide in the vine, so neither can you, unless you abide in me. I am the vine ; you the branches : he that abideth in me, and I in him, the same beareth much fruit : for without me you can do nothing." [1]

This wonderful utterance is a perfect example of that combination of childlike simplicity and depth of meaning which is so striking a feature of the teaching of Christ. The simple peasant as he looked out over the growing plants and trees could catch the lesson which the Saviour would have him learn ; yet neither mystic nor theologian will ever be able in this life to exhaust the riches of this great truth of our dependence upon Christ. Obviously Christ is not speaking here of the way in which every man depends upon God for his existence and his natural movement. Even though a man rejects the claims of the Saviour and cuts himself off from spiritual union with him, he will still live and move in the natural order. Christ is speaking of supernatural life ; of life which is of value in the eyes of God ; of life on earth which will lead to life in heaven : and of such life he says that it cannot exist without union with him. " Without me you can do nothing." As St Augustine says in a passage which has become famous : " He does not say ' for without me you can do little ' ; but ' you can do nothing.' Whether, then, it be little or

[1] John xv 4-5.

much, without him it cannot be done, without whom nothing can be done."

And this same fundamental truth is taught over and over again by St Paul. To him there had been given " this grace, to preach amongst the Gentiles the unsearchable riches of Christ, and to enlighten all men, that they may see what is the dispensation of the mystery which hath been hidden from eternity in God." [1] These unsearchable riches he explains in many ways, returning time after time to that bold figure of Christ as the head of a mystical body made up of all who believe in him. We cannot form a really holy and salutary thought by our own power. " Not that we are sufficient to think anything of ourselves, as of ourselves ; but our sufficiency is from God." [2] We cannot will aright, we cannot act aright, without God. " With fear and trembling work out your salvation. For it is God who worketh in you, both to will and to accomplish, according to his good will." [3] And the reason for this inability of ours to act, or speak, or think in a way which will be pleasing to God, the Apostle explains in more than one place. In the fifth chapter of the Epistle to the Romans he explains how we are all spiritually dead through the sin of Adam and are brought back to life by Christ. " For if by the offence of one, many died ; much more the grace of God, and the gift, by the grace of one man, Jesus Christ, hath abounded unto many." [4] Elsewhere he speaks of all men as " children of wrath," [5] and says that we were all " concluded under sin." [6]

Thus the teaching of Christ and of his great Apostle is perfectly clear. Apart from Christ, we are spiritually dead, and no natural action of ours can have any real value unto eternal life. It is only the grace of God, which comes to us through our Saviour, which gives value to our actions and " hath quickened us together in Christ (by whose grace you are saved), and hath raised us up together and hath made us sit together in the heavenly places, through Christ Jesus. . . . For by grace you are saved through faith, and that not of yourselves, for it is the gift of God ; not of works, that no man may glory. For we are his workmanship, created in Christ Jesus in good works, which God hath prepared that we should walk in them." [7]

Our conclusion, then, is obvious : without the grace of God salutary acts are impossible. Is this impossibility a physical or a moral impossibility ? [8] Catholic theologians, bringing to the analysis of dogma an understanding that is enlightened by faith, reply that it is a physical impossibility ; there is no question of a mere difficulty in performing a salutary act, we are physically incapable of such a thing. The reason is both profound and interesting. A salutary act,

[1] Eph. iii 8-9.  [2] 2 Cor. iii 5.  [3] Phil. ii 12-13.
[4] Rom. v 15.  [5] Eph. ii 3.
[6] Gal. iii 22.  [7] Eph. ii 5-10.
[8] For this distinction see above, p. 591.

as we have explained, is one that positively tends towards the attaining of eternal life. But eternal life consists in the Beatific Vision, and this is altogether beyond the natural capacity of any creature, requiring a special elevation and illumination of the mind. Consequently, if there is to be an intrinsic connection between the Beatific Vision and the acts which positively tend to it, these acts must themselves be elevated above their natural condition. It is a contradiction to suppose an intrinsic connection and proportion between a merely natural act and a supernatural object to which that act intrinsically tends. Hence the conclusion is drawn that our salutary acts must proceed not from our unaided natural faculty, but from the faculty as elevated above its natural condition by a supernatural gift bestowed upon it by God. Without this elevation of the faculty the act could not be performed in such a way as to tend positively towards eternal life. This is not to say that we are physically incapable of performing an act which to all outward appearances will appear just the same as a salutary act ; thus a man who has no grace at all may give an alms to a beggar, just as one who is aided by grace may do ; but the former could not perform the act in such a way that it would be " salutary."

*Sanctifying grace not always sufficient*

But apart from the theological reasoning which has just been set out, it is clear from the doctrine of Scripture (which the Church has authoritatively expounded on more than one occasion) that we can do no good work of ourselves towards our eternal salvation ; we need the help of God's grace. The thoughtful reader may here raise the question : Do we need actual grace as well as sanctifying grace that our actions may be salutary ? Is not union with Christ by sanctifying grace sufficient ? Before we can give a satisfactory answer to these questions we must distinguish between the acts which a man performs in direct preparation for Justification—that is, for the passing from a state of mortal sin to a state of grace—and the acts which he performs when already in a state of grace. The acts which precede Justification, and directly prepare for it, present a special problem which will be examined in the next section, when it will be shown that actual grace is required for them. Here we will only remind the reader that of ourselves we can do *nothing* towards our eternal salvation ; therefore we cannot of ourselves prepare ourselves for Justification, which would most certainly be to do something. These preparatory acts, then, clearly require actual grace, since by hypothesis the man who performs them does not possess sanctifying grace. But what about the salutary acts which follow Justification ? Do we require actual grace for every one of them ? May we not look on man as now possessing a new nature—sanctifying grace—which has the effect of making his actions supernatural and salutary without there being need of anything further in the way of actual grace ? Perhaps we may put the matter less technically thus. Here is a man who has become a partaker of the divine nature by sanctifying grace ; can he, without any further present help from God, perform actions which are " salutary " ?

Theologians are not unanimous in the answer which they give, but the great majority reply that even the just man requires actual grace for every single salutary act which he performs. If this common opinion be accepted—and it rests on weighty arguments— we may well stand astonished at the thought of our utter helplessness in regard to the performing of actions which are of supernatural value. Not one single salutary act unless God moves me to it by a special intervention of his power and love ! And even if we do not accept this common opinion we are obliged to admit that actual grace is at least a frequent, ever-recurring necessity. In the spiritual life we cannot stand still. If we would hold what we have we must stretch out our efforts towards higher virtue, and it is certain that for this work of advancement we need a special grace of God ; the possession of sanctifying grace and the infused virtues which accompany it will not suffice. Moreover, the law which God has laid upon his children requires of them much more than the natural law requires, and sometimes the burden of its enactments is indeed heavy ; and unless God gave us present strength to do what he bids us do, we should certainly fail. Thus it is evident that if actual grace be not necessary for the performing of every single salutary act, it is something which we constantly need.

But there is still more to be said about the necessity of actual *Special* grace in our supernatural life, and what now follows leads us to the *question of* important question of Final Perseverance. In the preceding section *perseverance* it was explained that although sanctifying grace makes us sons of God it does not take away the weakness of our nature. We are still subject to concupiscence. True, as sons of God we can be sure that our heavenly Father will stretch out his hand to help us in our needs, but if he did not do so we should certainly fall into sin, sooner or later. At the second Council of Orange it was laid down that even in the case of God's holy ones his assistance is to be implored in order that they may persevere in their good works ; and the Council of Trent condemned those who held that a man who has been justified can remain in that state of holiness without the special help of God. And this uncertainty of the position of the just man is taught us repeatedly in sacred Scripture. Our Saviour taught all men, saints as well as sinners, to pray that they may be saved from temptation : " Lead us not into temptation, but deliver us from evil." " Be sober and watch," says St Peter,[1] " because your adversary the devil, as a roaring lion, goeth about seeking whom he may devour. Whom resist ye, strong in faith." Similarly St Paul bids the Philippians work out their salvation with fear and trembling,[2] and to the Ephesians he writes in words of solemn warning. " Brethren, be strengthened in the Lord, and in the might of his power.

---

[1] 1 Pet. v 8.      [2] Phil. ii 12.

Put you on the armour of God, that you may be able to stand against the deceits of the devil. For our wrestling is not against flesh and blood ; but against principalities and powers, against the rulers of the world of this darkness, against the spirits of wickedness in the high places." [1]

Be it noted that these warnings were uttered for the instruction of the faithful Christians of apostolic times, who, we may be sure, were living, for the most part, holy and fervent lives. Yet even men such as these were to understand that for continuance in good they required the assistance of God, and they were to live in holy fear lest the enemies of their souls should overcome them. But there is something else to be noticed. It is one thing to have the power of performing an action, and quite another thing to do it. Now, in order that we should continue to live a good life it is necessary not only that we should receive from God a grace sufficient to enable us to resist evil, but also that we should use that power. Consequently for continuance in good we must obtain from God not merely graces which are in themselves sufficient, but also graces which we will use. And it is obviously a special favour of God that he should give us just the ones which we will use. Well, then, may the Council of Trent say that we cannot persevere *sine speciali auxilio Dei*, without the *special* help of God—a help which is something more than the mere power to persevere. [2]

Now Final Perseverance involves all this and something more. Apart from the exceptional cases of those who have been baptised, but never reach the use of reason, and of those who are reconciled to God just before death, Final Perseverance involves two elements : firstly, a continuance in grace, and secondly, death whilst in the state of grace. The first of these, as we have seen, is dependent upon the special help of God ; the second is a special favour of divine Providence. Neither of these elements is in our power : not the first, as is evident from all that has been said ; not the second, for we cannot arrange that the hour of death shall come at a time when we are in the grace of God. Hence the Council of Trent rightly calls Final Perseverance a " great gift "—*magnum donum*. It is a gift, because it depends upon his goodwill and in no way upon our own action ; and it is indeed a great gift because it secures for us the possession of the highest good—God himself, in the Beatific Vision.

Lastly, Final Perseverance is so much the gift of God that the Council of Trent further teaches us that, apart from some special revelation, we can never be sure of it " with absolute and infallible certainty." We must ever go on " in fear and trembling," putting

---

[1] Eph. vi 10-12.

[2] Here we have the well-known distinction between *gratia sufficiens* (sufficient grace) and *gratia efficax* (efficacious grace). The first is a grace which gives the power to do a thing, but is not made use of ; the second is one which will infallibly be made use of. Something will be said later on about the explanation of *gratia efficax*.

our trust in God and committing ourselves to his hands. " Into
thy hands, O Lord, I commend my spirit." Thus the Church
teaches us to pray, that God may give us his graces in life and may
bring us to a holy death, " being confident of this very thing, that
he who hath begun a good work in you will perfect it unto the day
of Christ Jesus." [1]

## § IV: ACTUAL GRACE A FREE GIFT OF GOD

IN the present section we have to show that Grace is a free gift of *The*
God ; we have no natural right to it, we cannot merit it by our natural *statement*
powers, and we cannot even of ourselves utter a prayer for it which *explained*
will be of any real value towards obtaining it. We are absolutely dependent on God's goodwill. These are important points in the
Catholic doctrine of Grace, and they are so much opposed to our
natural ideas that they require careful attention.

The assertion that we are dependent upon God's free choice for
the obtaining of grace is really contained in the general assertion that
we can do no good work of ourselves towards our salvation. If we
could command grace, as it were, by our own efforts, we should
certainly be doing something towards our salvation. We might say,
therefore, that there is now no need to prove that grace is entirely
a free gift ; yet because of the importance of the point we must make
it a matter for special consideration. But first we must guard against
a possible misunderstanding. We are not denying that grace can ever
be merited. We are only saying that it can never be merited by any
natural action of our own. If God gives us grace, by using that
grace we can merit further grace ; but in this case the act by which
we merit is not simply our own act : it is one which is performed
through the grace of God : it is supernatural, not natural. But since
the first grace by which we begin to merit further graces is a gratuitous gift of God, the whole series which follows from it is itself
gratuitous : ultimately it depends upon God's free gift of the first
grace.

We said not only that we cannot of ourselves merit grace, but also
that no merely natural petition can be of value towards obtaining
grace. By this we mean that in the petitions which we may make
to God by our own power—making humble profession of our misery
and asking God to help us—there is nothing which he considers of
any force ; nothing which, to use human language, would persuade
or move him to grant what is asked. This is certainly true in the
present order of Providence, for we can show that God has declared
his unwillingness to accept such prayers ; whether or not it would
be true in every possible order of Divine Providence is not so clear.
Into the theoretical question of the absolute impossibility of natural
petitions having value with God, we need not enter. Let us content
ourselves with the facts of the present order.

[1] Phil. i 6.

*The teaching of the Church*    It is not difficult to show that the gratuitous character of grace is a general truth which the Church explicitly teaches. In an important passage which deals with the way in which a man prepares himself for Justification, the Council of Trent touches upon the point as follows : " The beginning of Justification in adults is to be derived from the antecedent grace of God through Christ Jesus, that is from his calling of them, by which they are called without any merits of their own." [1]    This directly excludes the idea of any merit by which the first grace leading a man to Justification is won. The second Council of Orange, which was concerned in quite an especial way with these questions of grace, is, if possible, still more explicit. It is not, the Council says, because of any merits which precede grace that a reward is given to good works which we may perform ; but the very performing of these good works is the result of a grace to which we have no right. [2]    Further, the Council declares that if a man says that the grace of God can be given in answer to human prayer, and not that it is grace itself which makes us invoke him, he contradicts the prophet Isaias or the Apostle saying the same thing, " I was found by them that did not seek me ; I appeared openly to them that asked not after me." [3]    And, again, the same Council tells us that God does not give his grace to those who without grace ask for it, but he gives grace that they may make their petitions. From all this we see that the Church definitely lays down the points with which we began this section.

*The teaching of Scripture*    But let us turn to the Scriptural authority for this teaching. It is remarkably clear, and expressed in terms of great vigour. St Paul's Epistle to the Romans is full of this theme. Neither the Jewish converts by the fulfilment of their law, nor the Pagan converts by fidelity to the natural law, have merited to be called to the true faith. The third chapter of this epistle deals in an especial way with this thought, and repeatedly both here and in subsequent passages the Apostle insists on the fact that grace is God's free gift. " If by grace," he says, " it is not now by works : otherwise grace is no more grace." [4]    (Here we are reminded that the very word which we use—grace, *gratia*, χάρις—signifies something which is freely given.) " It is not of him that willeth, nor of him that runneth, but of God that showeth mercy." [5]    " He hath mercy on whom he will ; and whom he will, he hardeneth." [6]    Very definitely in the Epistle to the Ephesians, he says : " By grace you are saved through faith, and that not of yourselves, for it is the gift of God ; not of works, that no man may glory." [7]    Other passages in the same sense we have already seen—we cannot think anything of ourselves, as of ourselves ; [8] we have nothing which we have not received, and we

---

[1] Session VI, chap. v.
[3] Rom. x 20 ; Isa. lxv 1.
[5] Rom. ix 16.
[7] Eph. ii 8-9 ; *cf.* 2 Tim. i 9.

[2] Canon xviii.
[4] Rom. xi 6.
[6] Rom. ix 18.
[8] 2 Cor. iii 5.

must not glory as if we had not received it [1]—in a word, " it is God who worketh in you, both to will and to accomplish, according to his good will." [2] And in all this St Paul is but teaching the doctrine of Christ who said : " No man can come to me, except the Father, who hath sent me, draw him." [3]

Are we, then, incapable of doing a single thing which will help in any positive way towards winning the favour of God and his grace ? Is man thrown on the ocean of life bereft of every means of salvation, and even of every means of struggling towards help ? Yes ; he is utterly helpless, completely in the hands of God, to whose mercy he owes whatever strength may come to him. We may, indeed, distinguish with theologians between negative preparation and positive preparation, allowing the possibility of the first, but not of the second ; but the distinction, though helpful in some ways, may serve only to obscure the truth in the minds of the ordinary reader. [4] The plain fact is, we are helpless ; dead, as it were ; we cannot move towards grace.

In the course of the dispute with Pelagius it was found that there *Difficulties* were many good men [5] who readily rejected the main ideas of the *from* system, but considered that statements such as those which have just *Scripture* been set down went too far. After all, they said, whilst it is true that man cannot perform a salutary act by his own power, and cannot offer indefinite resistance to the forces of evil, he surely can desire God's help ; he can knock at the door of God's mercy as a humble suppliant ; he can hope and pray for that help, without which he knows that he cannot be saved. Does not God himself bid us turn to him and he will turn to us ? " Turn ye to me, saith the Lord of Hosts, and I will turn to you." [6] And are there not the examples of the Centurion, of Zachaeus, of the Good Thief, who by their humble prayers and their holy desires merited to be accepted by the Saviour ? Do we not read in the book of Proverbs [7] that " it is the part of man to prepare the soul ? " And does not Christ himself say : " Ask, and it shall be given you : seek, and you shall find : knock, and it shall be opened to you. For every one that asketh, receiveth : and he that seeketh, findeth : and to him that knocketh, it shall be opened ? " [8]

There can be no doubt that at first sight this way of putting the matter is not without force, and we know that for a time even such a stout champion of the necessity of grace as St Augustine was misled.

---

[1] i Cor. iv 7.       [2] Phil. ii 13.       [3] John vi 44.
[4] Positive preparation for the production of an effect in a thing is the production in that thing of a definite disposition towards, or aptitude for receiving, the effect in question ; negative preparation is the mere removal of obstacles which may stand in the way of the production of the effect— or, even more remotely, the refraining from creating obstacles. In this last sense, some writers speak of negative preparation for grace in so far as a man may for a time refrain from sin, and thus not oppose grace.
[5] Called Semipelagians.     [6] Zach. i 3.     [7] Prov. xvi 1.     [8] Matt. vii 7, 8.

But a fuller examination of the language of Scripture shows the inadequacy of the argument. St. Augustine soon came to realise that the texts and examples just quoted must be understood in the light of those other texts in which our absolute helplessness is so strongly and so repeatedly emphasised. When we look at the matter in this light we see that these very prayers, desires, etc., are themselves the result of God's grace working in us, as the second Council of Orange, quoted earlier in this section, explained. The Centurion, Zachaeus, and the Good Thief did indeed seek God and were accepted ; but they sought him because he first gave them the grace to do so. Christ does in truth counsel us to ask, to seek, to knock : but first the grace to do these things must be given to us : Christ's exhortation is that we should use this grace. " It is God who worketh in you, both to will and to accomplish." [1]

The fact is that there are two classes of sayings in the Scriptures bearing upon this point. In one class we are told explicitly that we have nothing which we have not received, and that without God we can do nothing. In the other class, the necessity of grace being supposed, we are urged to make use of the graces given to us, and are told that if we do so we shall receive further graces. The two sets of texts are quite in harmony. The contrast between them is thus expressed by the Council of Trent. " When it is said *Turn ye to me and I will turn to you* we are reminded that we are free ; when we reply *Convert us, O Lord, to thee and we shall be converted,*[2] we confess that we are prevented by the grace of God "—*i.e.,* we confess that the grace of God goes before our action and enables us to produce it.

*Grace and Conversion*

There is an obvious and important connection between what we have here explained and the problem of conversion. Whether it be a case of trying to bring a non-believer to the recognition of the truth of the Catholic Church, or of moving a sinner to repentance, nothing can be accomplished without the interior grace of God. We may put before the unbeliever, in the most cogent way possible, the various arguments by which the truth is established, but this by itself will be of no avail. How far such a man is able by the unaided light of reason to grasp the force of all the arguments which establish the motives of credibility, we need not here discuss—though we would remind the reader that it is a defined truth of the Church that man can prove many of the fundamental truths, such as the existence of God and the freedom of the will, by the natural light of reason ; but it is certain that his heart will never be moved, and he will never give the assent of faith to the truths which are set before him, if the grace of God does not touch him. " No man can come to me, except the Father, who hath sent me, draw him." [3] Of course, the careful exposition of Catholic truth is an external grace of which God often makes use as a channel through which, as it were, the

[1] Phil. ii 13.          [2] Lam. v 21.          [3] John vi 44.

interior grace is poured into the soul of the unbeliever, and one man may be a better channel than another ; moreover, one man may be more zealous in winning interior graces from God for the souls of those to whom he appeals ; but in the end it is God, and God alone, who gives the increase. "Neither he that planteth is anything, nor he that watereth ; but God that giveth the increase." [1] And the same is true of the sinner who has fallen from grace. A new start has to be made. He has cut himself off from God, is living in enmity with him, and cannot do anything which is meritorious in his sight ; and so a new order of grace has to be established. A free gift of God must be the beginning of this new order. Even the greatest saint pleading with a sinner can do nothing unless God first touch the heart.

These points of Catholic doctrine may at first sight seem to be hard sayings. Can it be true that we are so helpless as this ? And is not the effect of such doctrines likely to be an attitude of despair, or of hopeless fatalism ? Doubtless there are some people who will ask such questions in a spirit of pessimism. But he who has caught the spirit of Christianity will look upon all this in a very different light. The thought of his own helplessness will throw him back more and more on the realisation of the love of God, and he will derive not merely calmness and strength, but also true joy and confidence from this his firm belief, which nothing can shake, that the God upon whom he depends is one in whom he can trust. What do we need in order that we may have absolute trust ? We must have assurance on three points : that he on whom we depend is wise enough to know what is best for us ; that he is good enough to wish what is really for our interests ; and that he is powerful enough to obtain everything which he desires. But all these things the Christian knows of his God. Hence he is not alarmed at the thought of his helplessness. Rather does he glory in it, in the spirit of the great St Paul when he cried out, "Gladly will I glory in my infirmities that the power of Christ may dwell in me." [2]

But here arises a question which is of vital importance. Can we be certain that we all receive from God sufficient grace for our salvation ? This is the question which we will discuss in the following section.

## §V: SUFFICIENT ACTUAL GRACE FOR ALL

THE question which we raised at the end of the last section is cer- *Sufficiency* tainly a momentous one. We have seen how great is our dependence *of grace* upon God's grace, and how necessarily that grace is itself dependent *for the* upon his good pleasure ; what security have we, then, that the power *faithful* of working out our salvation has been placed within our hands ?

---

[1] I Cor. iii 7.        [2] 2 Cor. xii 9.

Is it, perchance, the case that God has not willed to give us sufficient grace to enable us to save our souls ?

A Catholic, at any rate, ought to take courage. He knows that by God's infinite mercy his soul has been washed in the waters of Baptism and that, through membership of the Church which is the Mystical Body of Christ, abundant graces are bestowed upon him. And if he reads the Scriptures he finds a number of passages which are full of encouragement and hope. He remembers, for example, the words of Christ : " This is the will of the Father who sent me : that of all that he hath given me, I should lose nothing ; but should raise it up again in the last day." [1] Or he dwells on the beautiful chapter which opens St Paul's Epistle to the Ephesians, in which the Apostle speaks so gloriously of the Christian vocation : " Blessed be the God and Father of our Lord Jesus Christ, who hath blessed us with spiritual blessings in heavenly places, in Christ : as he chose us in him before the foundation of the world that we should be holy and unspotted in his sight in charity. Who hath predestinated us unto the adoption of children through Jesus Christ unto himself : according to the purpose of his will : unto the praise of the glory of his grace, in which he hath graced us in his beloved Son. In whom we have redemption through his blood, the remission of sins, according to the riches of his grace." [2] Elsewhere the same Apostle speaks almost as though salvation were already secure for those who have been called to the Church : " We know that to them that love God, all things work together unto good, to such as, according to his purpose, are called to be saints.[3] For whom he foreknew, he also predestinated to be made conformable to the image of his Son ; that he might be the firstborn amongst many brethren. And whom he predestinated, them he also called. And whom he called, them he also justified. And whom he justified, them he also glorified." [4] There is no doubt in the mind of St Paul concerning the riches of grace given to all the faithful.

Hope, then, is a duty which rests upon us all. " We hope in the living God, who is the Saviour of all men, especially of the faithful." [5] True, we do not know for certain that we shall persevere until the end ; but we *do* know that God loves his own, and we are " confident of this very thing, that he who hath begun a good work in us, will perfect it unto the day of Christ Jesus." [6] St Peter adds his reassurance to that of St Paul : " The God of all grace, who hath called us unto his eternal glory in Christ Jesus, after you have suffered a little, will himself perfect you, and confirm you, and establish you." [7] And if the thought of future difficulty and temptation suggests a fear that perhaps we shall not have sufficient grace given to us

---

[1] John vi 39.     [2] Eph. i 3-7.
[3] More exactly, " to such as are called according to his purpose."
[4] Rom. viii 28-30.     [5] I Tim. iv 10.
[6] Phil. i 6.     [7] I Pet. v 10.

in the hour of conflict, we can console ourselves with the assurance of St Paul : " God is faithful, who will not suffer you to be tempted above that which you are able : but will make also with temptation issue that you may be able to bear it." [1]

But if it be true that all those who are living members of Christ's Mystical Body are abundantly endowed with grace, doubts may arise especially in regard to two classes of men ; firstly, in regard to those who have fallen from grace by sin and been cast forth from the wedding feast, and secondly, in regard to those vast multitudes who live in unbelief, far away, it may be, from the reach of any Christian preacher. The questions naturally arise : Is the sinner ever without sufficient grace to repent ? Has the infidel sufficient grace to save his soul ?

In regard to the sinner, although a few theologians have held that *Sinners* God sometimes gives no further graces because the mind is so blinded and the heart so hardened by sin that further grace would only add to the sinner's guilt, it is certain that sufficient grace for repentance is never withheld. " If your sins be as scarlet, they shall be made white as snow : and if they be red as crimson, they shall be white as wool." [2] " I desire not the death of the wicked, but that the wicked turn from his way and live." [3] And even to those who continue to reject his claims upon them the Almighty declares that he still pleads with them : " I have spread forth my hands all the day to an unbelieving people, who walk in a way that is not good after their own thoughts." [4] Christ tells us explicitly that he came " not to call the just, but sinners to penance," [5] and the story of his life is the history of a good Shepherd whose principal care is for the lost sheep ; of a merciful, forgiving Father whose arms are open to welcome back the prodigal. It is just because the man who continues in sin is ever resisting the Holy Spirit, that his position is so terrible ; hence the vigour of St Paul's language against the obstinate sinner. " Despisest thou the riches of his goodness, and patience, and long-suffering ? Knowest thou not, that the benignity of God leadeth thee to penance ? But according to thy hardness and impenitent heart, thou treasurest up to thyself wrath, against the day of wrath." [6]

Even to the worst of sinners, then, God gives sufficient grace to enable them to repent. If not at every moment, at least from time to time and when circumstances most require it, he offers them his help. Perhaps the help is given for the resisting of some temptation, and if it is used God gives another grace ; thus, by one grace after another, the sinner will be led back to God if only he corresponds. In truth the Lord " dealeth patiently . . . not willing that any should perish but that all should return to penance." [7]

[1] I Cor. x 13.  [2] Isa. i 18.  [3] Ezech. xxxiii 11.
[4] Isa. lxv 2.  [5] Luke v 32.
[6] Rom. ii 4-5.  [7] 2 Pet. iii 9.

Against what has just been said it may be objected that sometimes the Scriptures represent God as hardening the heart of the sinner and thus making it impossible for him to do penance ; and also that some sins are spoken of as being beyond the possibility of forgiveness ; thus, " he hath blinded their eyes, and hardened their heart, that they should not see with their eyes, nor understand with their heart, and be converted, and I should heal them " ; [1] and, " It is impossible for those who were once illuminated, have tasted also the heavenly gift, and were made partakers of the Holy Ghost, have moreover tasted the good word of God, and the powers of the world to come, and are fallen away : to be renewed again to penance." [2]

*No sin unpardonable*

Space does not allow a detailed explanation of these and other texts of a like nature, but some general principles may be indicated in a few words. In the first place, God never positively hardens a heart ; such a way of acting would be contrary to what we know of his attitude towards the sinner ; but sometimes he withdraws from a sinner the more striking and more abundant graces which he gives to those who are his faithful children. Or we may say that he allows the sinner to harden his own heart. Thus in Exodus [3] we read that God hardened the heart of Pharao, but it had already been stated that Pharao had " hardened his own heart." [4] In the second place, there is no such thing as an unforgivable sin ; this is clear from the positive teaching of Scripture in regard to God's willingness to forgive, though our sins be as scarlet. Each text which appears to assert the contrary can be explained. Thus, the Fathers have explained the passage from Heb. vi 4-6 in various ways. Many have understood it to refer to the impossibility of renewing the special cleansing of Baptism ; others, with perhaps greater probability, have understood it to mean that if a man has received special graces from God and then has rejected the faith which he has received, it is morally impossible for him to repent ; not because the necessary grace is denied him, but because he has wilfully sinned against the light in such a way that his whole spiritual outlook is perverted. Under such circumstances it would require a sort of spiritual miracle to save him. But whatever we may say about any particular interpretation, it is quite certain that the Church rejects the idea that any sin is unpardonable.

*Non-believers*

We must now turn to the special problem of the infidel who has never had the truths of Christianity explained to him : who has never heard of Christ and his Church ; who knows nothing of the channels of grace : how can such a man be said to receive sufficient grace to save his soul ? The problem behind this question is all the greater when we remember that no merely natural virtue will win eternal life ; nothing short of divine faith, and the supernatural action which proceeds from it, will suffice. The problem, it must be ack-

[1] John xii 40, quoting from Isa. vi 9-10.     [2] Heb. vi 4-6.
[3] Exod. ix 12.     [4] Exod. viii 15.

nowledged, is certainly a serious one; what is the answer which Catholic theology gives?

That sufficient grace really is given even to the man who never comes within the reach of the influence of Christianity, there can be no doubt. There are various texts of Scripture in which we are clearly taught that God sincerely wills the salvation of all men; and how could he will their salvation if he did not give them sufficient grace to enable them to save their souls? Of these texts we will consider just one, which is quite decisive. Writing to his disciple, St Timothy, St Paul says: " I desire first of all that supplications, prayers, intercessions, and thanksgivings be made for all men : for kings, and for all that are in high stations : that we may lead a quiet and a peaceable life in all piety and chastity. For this is good and acceptable in the sight of God our Saviour, *who will have all men to be saved*, and to come to the knowledge *of the truth*. For there is one God, and one mediator of God and men, the man Christ Jesus : *who gave himself a redemption for all*." [1] St Paul is here speaking of men who belonged to the pagan world—kings and all that are in high stations—and with direct reference to them he tells us that God will have all men to be saved, and that Christ gave himself a redemption for all. Thus we are forced to conclude that God gives grace to all men, even to pagans. To explain just how God's grace reaches those who live in the pagan world may be a difficult matter, but we can rest assured that in one way or another it does reach them; an explanation, however, may be suggested as follows.

Even amongst the pagans there is at least a vague sense both of the existence of a supreme being and of the moral law of right and wrong. Now there are various ways in which God can help a pagan to live according to the dictates of his conscience, and if the help thus given is used in the way intended by God, further helps will be given. Thus a pagan will grow in a desire to keep the moral law and in a spirit of reverence for the supreme being whose existence he recognises both by the light of reason and through the traditions around him. When a man has been led thus far by God, may we not suppose that his mind will be further illumined so that he becomes capable of making a real act of faith in God as the supreme being on whom he depends, before whom he is answerable for his actions, and from whom he may look for reward or punishment? The difficulty is that there is need of an act of real faith, by which what is believed is accepted on the authority of God; and it is not easy to see how our pagan can know that God has revealed certain things to him. But we must remember that all peoples seem to have kept some sort of tradition of a revelation made to man in the early history of our race, and surely it is possible for God to lead a pagan to a belief that certain elementary truths must have thus come from above; with the help of a further grace he can then make a real act of faith,

[1] I Tim. ii 1-6.

and finally pass on (still aided by grace) to an act of love of God. Thus he can reach the state of grace and be saved. But however we explain the process we must accept the fact that salvation is really possible for all. As St Thomas Aquinas says : " It belongs to Divine Providence to provide each man with what is necessary for salvation, as long as the man himself does not raise obstacles. For if a man who had been brought up amongst the beasts of the forest were to follow the lead of natural reason in seeking good and avoiding evil, we ought to consider it certain that God would either make known to him by interior inspiration the truths which must necessarily be believed,[1] or send someone to preach the faith to him as he sent Peter to Cornelius." [2]

In what has just been said we have taken the extreme case of a man who hears nothing of the Christian message ; other cases can be explained in the light of the principles laid down. All men outside the Church, whether they be Protestants, or Jews, or Mohammedans, or Pagans, receive sufficient means of salvation, and will not be condemned except through their own fault. But obviously men do not all receive the same amount of grace ; to all is given sufficient, but some receive more, others less ; and this inequality in the distribution of graces is one of the great mysteries which confront us. Ultimately it raises the whole question of Predestination—a question about which it may be well to say a few words in the present connection. The reader, however, is warned that the treatment must necessarily be brief. Some further explanations will be added in an appendix.

*The problem of Pre-destination*    Predestination is a fact : but what exactly are we to understand by the word ? Let us first see what it does not mean. In the sixteenth century Calvin put forward a false view of Predestination which has become famous. He taught that from all eternity God definitely and explicitly chose some men for eternal life, and just as definitely and explicitly other men for eternal damnation, his own glory being the end he sought in either case. Nothing that man is going to do affects in any way that terrible decree by which heaven is chosen for some, hell for others. As a necessary consequence we must say that God does not will the salvation of all men ; he wills the salvation only of the elect, and the rest he positively wills to force into hell. Such, stated in a few words, is the Calvinist theory of Predestination. It is easy to see its fundamental error—namely, its denial that God really wills the salvation of any but the elect. As we have already clearly shown, God wills the salvation of all and gives to all sufficient grace to enable them to save their souls ; and if some men are lost this is due to their own rejection of grace

---

[1] It is probable that a man such as we are considering would not be required to believe explicitly more than that God " is, and is a rewarder of them that seek him " (Heb. xi 6).

[2] *De Veritate*, Q. xiv, a. 11 ad 1.

and not to God's choice of their damnation. This is a fundamental truth which must be safeguarded in every theory of Predestination which a Catholic may hold. In other words, we may not say that there is a positive Reprobation of any man antecedent to his sin ; it is only because of his sin that God wills his condemnation ; he has had sufficient grace, he has rejected it, and therefore God condemns him.

Having thus guarded ourselves against a false theory of Predestination, let us try to get at a true one. St Thomas Aquinas says that Predestination is a plan existing in the mind of God according to which some men are to be saved ; and that Reprobation is the allowing of some to be lost. Contrasting the two he remarks that Predestination includes the will to grant grace and eternal glory, whilst Reprobation includes the will to permit a man to fall into fault and to punish him for that fault.[1] Hence neither Predestination nor Reprobation is merely a matter of God's foreknowledge of what is going to happen ; each involves an element of will ; in the case of the predestined God's will being to grant them first certain graces which will lead them to eternal life, and then eternal life itself as a reward ; in the case of those who are not predestined his will being to permit them to fall into sin and then to punish them for it. The chief problem, of course, is with regard to those who are to be lost. If he had wished to do so, God could have arranged the circumstances of their lives in such a way that they would have been saved ; but he has chosen to put them in the present circumstances of life in which he knows that they will be damned. Yet their damnation is their own fault, for they all receive sufficient grace to enable them to save their souls and they wilfully reject that grace.

Predestination, then, may be defined as an arrangement of things chosen by God in which he knows that some men will most certainly be saved and others most certainly damned, the salvation of the elect being directly desired, the damnation of the lost not directly desired but permitted. This is indeed a great mystery ; but whilst we tremble at the thought of the dread issues which lie within it we must ever cling fast to the fundamental truths that God truly desires the salvation of us all, that he gives each of us the means of salvation, and that damnation can come to us only through our own fault. The simple soul that clings to these beliefs is assuredly nearer to the mind of God than the man who vexes his soul with subtle problems of Predestination. For the rest, the whole spirit of Christianity as we find it set forth in the New Testament is one of quiet hope in God "through Jesus Christ our Lord." The restless mind may raise the questions : "Am I amongst the predestined ? And if I am not, what is the use of any effort on my part ? " Better would it be to meditate on words such as these of St John, who knew so well the Heart of Christ. "Dearly beloved, we are now the sons of God ;

[1] S. Theol., I, Q. 23, a. 1, 2, 3.

and it hath not yet appeared what we shall be. We know that when he shall appear we shall be like to him : because we shall see him as he is. *And every one that hath this hope in him, sanctifieth himself.*" [1]

## §VI: THE NATURE AND SOURCE OF ACTUAL GRACE

*Movements of the mind and will*

AT the end of the preceding discussions the reader may well be pardoned if he asks for a little more information about the precise nature of this Actual Grace of which we have been speaking. We defined it at the beginning as " a supernatural gift, internal to us and of a passing nature, whereby God helps us to avoid sin or enables us to perform actions which tend towards eternal life " ; but we may be asked : What sort of help is it ? or, What exactly does God do to us when he gives us this help ?

The answer to this last question is that when God gives us actual graces he acts upon our intellect or upon our will (or upon both) in such a way that we receive new light on things, and new desires of good ; or, as theologians express it, he produces in us Illuminations of the Intellect and Inspirations of the Will. To use the language of St Paul, he enlightens the eyes of our heart, that we may know what the hope is of his calling, and what are the riches of the glory of his inheritance in the saints ; [2] " for God, who commanded the light to shine out of darkness, hath shined in our hearts, to give the light of the knowledge of the glory of God." [3] Hence our Saviour can say : " Everyone that hath heard of the Father, and hath learned, cometh to me." [4] In these texts we are told that he enlightens the mind ; in others we read how he moves the heart : " I have run the way of thy commandments when thou didst enlarge my heart." [5] " No man," says our Saviour, " can come to me, except the Father, who hath sent me, draw him " ; [6] and how does he draw him except by moving his heart ?

*Immediate and mediate impulses*

These illuminations of the mind and inspirations of the will are often produced by God directly, without the medium of any creature. In all kinds of circumstances—in hours of solitude, in the midst of anxious cares, even in moments of dissipation or of wrongdoing— he touches us with his loving hand, and the great eternal truths shine out in our minds, or our hearts suddenly feel the attraction of the things of God. Thus it is that sometimes hearts are changed without apparent cause : the reason is, as Longfellow puts it in a poem in which he likens God's action to the rains which have fallen far away in the mountains and have filled the half-dried torrents, because " God at their fountains far off has been raining." It is of this immediate action of God upon the understanding and the will that the author of the *Imitation* speaks when he says : " Let not Moses, nor any of the prophets speak to me ; but speak thou rather,

---

[1] 1 John iii 2-3.    [2] Eph. i 18.    [3] 2 Cor. iv 6.
[4] John vi 45.    [5] Ps. cxviii 32.    [6] John vi 44.

O Lord God, who art the inspirer and enlightener of all the prophets : for thou alone without them canst perfectly instruct me ; but they without thee will avail me nothing." At other times God makes use of various external circumstances to produce the like effects ; through the voice of another, or through the thousand and one vicissitudes of life—pain, sorrow, separation, loss, death—he speaks to the human heart and mind. But though Paul may plant and Apollo may water, it is God who gives the increase.[1] And sometimes he does not disdain to make use of our emotional and sensitive faculties in order that he may reach the inner sanctuary of thought and will. He who made the human heart knows best how to touch it, reaching from end to end mightily, and disposing all things sweetly.

Here, indeed, an interesting field of thought opens itself out before us—the consideration of the various ways in which God may illumine our minds and stir our desires ; but we cannot now explore it further. Suffice it to have indicated in this general way the manner in which God comes to our assistance to keep us from evil and to lead us to good. Yet there is another point, closely connected with what we have been saying, to which attention may well be called, however briefly. It is this : the soul of the man who is in a state of grace is made specially sensitive to these impulses of God of which we have been speaking. Effects are produced in such a man which would not be produced in another—just as effects are produced by light on photographic paper which would not be produced on ordinary paper. This is a fact for which we cannot be sufficiently grateful. It brings God nearer to us, as it were, making his beneficent influences over us more potent, more effective ; and in virtue of it we can hope that, if we are faithful to him, we shall be led on from virtue to virtue. It is the function of the Gifts of the Holy Ghost thus to prepare our souls for the touch of the Most High, and the study of these gifts would be a most useful complement to what we are here indicating so briefly about the nature of God's action upon the soul through Actual Grace. But whether we study Actual Grace itself or those Gifts of the Holy Ghost which make us more responsive to its action within us, we shall ever find how truly we may say with the Psalmist : " The Lord ruleth me : and I shall want nothing. He hath set me in a place of pasture. He hath brought me up on the water of refreshment : he hath converted my soul." [2]

The illuminations of the mind and the inspirations of the will of

---

[1] 1 Cor. iii 6.

[2] Ps. xxii 1-3. In the foregoing account of the nature of Actual Grace, the writer has prescinded altogether from a point discussed amongst theologians : viz., is Actual Grace the illumination of the mind, and the inspiration of the will, or is it rather an impression produced upon the soul from which follow the illumination of the mind and the inspiration of the will ? To the ordinary reader the point may seem a mere subtlety ; it has its importance, but the discussion of it is outside our limited scope.

which we have spoken are not deliberate acts ; they are produced in us apart altogether from any control which we can exercise over them. But it is a point of Catholic doctrine that the salutary act which results from actual grace is itself perfectly free. The Reformers represented man as a mere automaton, and some who claimed to expound Catholic doctrine spoke of our being under the influence of an invincible impulse which took away all real freedom ; but such ideas are altogether foreign to the Catholic doctrine of grace and free will. God influences us ; he creates desires in us ; he moves us to action : , but he lays no necessity upon us in the performing of the acts by which we work out our salvation.

*All actual grace from Christ*

There can be no need to insist upon the fact that all actual grace is the work of God ; no one but the Almighty—no saint, not even the Blessed Virgin—can produce it in our souls. But perhaps there really is need to insist upon this other fact that all grace—actual and habitual—comes to us from Jesus Christ our Lord, of whose fulness we have all received.[1] In the vision of the Apocalypse we read how the four-and-twenty ancients sang a new canticle in praise of the Lamb, " because thou wast slain and hast redeemed us to God, in thy blood, out of every tribe, and tongue, and people, and nation, and hast made us to our God a kingdom and priests." The Lamb is Christ, and not only has he redeemed us, but he gives us every grace which we ever receive. It was this Lamb of God who said : " Without me you can do nothing " ; [2] and it was of him that St Paul declared : " In all things you are made rich in him . . . so that nothing is wanting to you in any grace." [3] This is a fundamental truth of Christianity, and it is of immense importance that we should realise it. In very truth Christ in his sacred Humanity is not merely an intercessor for us before the throne of God, " always living to make intercession for us " ; [4] he has not merely merited for us all the grace which we receive ; but he actually produces that grace in us. In the days of his life on earth he performed marvels with a touch of his hand or with a word of his mouth ; thus did he give sight to the blind, cleanse the lepers, heal the deaf and dumb, and free Mary Magdalen from her sins ; and now in a similar way he produces grace in our souls.

*Union with Christ*

This great truth is part of the wonderful lesson which Christ gave us when he proclaimed himself to be the Vine from whom we receive our life. " As the branch cannot bear fruit of itself, unless it abide in the vine, so neither can you unless you abide in me. I am the Vine ; you the branches : he that abideth in me, and I in him, the same beareth much fruit : for without me you can do nothing." [5] Consider the nature of the dependence here set before us. First of all, it is only by our union with Christ that we have any spiritual life : apart from him we are dead. But the Vine does more than give life ;

[1] John i 16.  [2] John xv 5.  [3] 1 Cor. i 5, 7.
[4] Heb. vii 25.  [5] John xv 4-5.

it fosters and sustains the life of its branches by a constant influence which it exercises upon them. And this most assuredly is what Christ does for all the branches which are spiritually united with him. The spiritual sap of life is constantly flowing from him to them. Or, to use the figure of speech by which St Paul expresses the same truth, Christ is the head of a body of which we are the members, and just as the head exercises a constant control of the members by elaborate systems of nerves which carry its messages to every part of the body, so does Christ constantly act upon us. These two figures—the one used by our Saviour himself, the other a favourite of the Apostle who so gloriously expounded the mystery of Christ— are no mere figures of speech ; they express a profound truth in graphic terms. The Council of Trent puts the matter in these more sober terms. " Christ Jesus constantly pours forth his grace (*virtutem*) upon those who have been justified as the head exercises its influence on the members and the vine upon the branches ; and this grace ever precedes, and accompanies, and follows their good actions." [1]

Thus, through Christ Jesus our Lord, are all things restored. It is a wonderful scheme of things—so wonderful that in the very marvels of it we may well recognise that its fashioner is God, and not mere human ingenuity. Let us consider it for a few moments. By the sin of Adam man fell from the supernatural condition of divine sonship in which our first parent had been created ; all the wonderful endowments of grace which God had intended for him were lost, and he became an outcast on the face of the earth. But God loved him with an everlasting love, and prepared for him an opportunity of being restored to grace and to glory. The central figure in the scheme of restoration was the Word Incarnate, Jesus Christ our Lord. It was through Jesus that all grace was to come ; there was to be " no other name under heaven given to men, whereby we must be saved " ; [2] " in whom we have redemption through his blood, the remission of sins, according to the riches of his grace, which hath superabounded in us in all wisdom and prudence. That he might make known unto us the mystery of his will, according to his good pleasure, which he hath purposed in him, in the dispensation of the fulness of time, to re-establish all things in Christ." [3] And this restoration which he effects in the souls of men is indeed a glorious one. In the might of his power he draws men to himself by his immediate action upon them. He fills their souls with sanctifying grace—that wonderful supernatural quality which makes them par- takers of his Deity. Together with sanctifying grace he gives them the infused virtues—Faith, Hope, and Charity, and those other virtues by which new powers of action are bestowed upon them. By the Gifts of the Holy Ghost he prepares them to respond to

[1] Session VI, chap. xvi.
[2] Acts iv 12.    [3] Eph. i 7-10.

the impulses which he intends to give them ; and then he acts upon them by his actual grace, moving their minds and wills to the knowledge and the love of sacred things, and to the fulfilment of all justice. Thus, born again to the supernatural life which they had lost, and enriched with most precious endowments, they are carried along by the impulse of his grace towards that eternal destiny which he has prepared for them. They are in his hands—his own handiwork ; nay, they are part of that Mystical Body of which he is the head— of that Vine of which he is the life. He has kept his word : " I am come that they may have life, and may have it more abundantly." [1] Having become like men by taking their nature, he makes them like himself by grace.

It is well that we should think of actual grace as part of this greater fact of life in Christ. To the man who is separated from Christ, actual grace is given in order that he may be brought into union with him ; to the man who is already united with Christ it is given in order that the union may be more complete, and that " rooted and founded in charity you may be able to comprehend, with all the saints, what is the breadth, and length, and height, and depth : to know also the charity of Christ, which surpasseth all knowledge, that you may be filled unto the fulness of God." [2]

*Union with the Church*    And for the perfecting of this great scheme Christ has given us the Holy Catholic Church, " which is his body, and the fulness of him who is filled all in all." [3] By means of her sacraments, her various rites, her prayers, the kingdom of God—which is the kingdom of grace—is extended within us. It is through her that we receive the primary gift of sanctifying grace, but we receive actual grace as well, for we may rightly say that it is as members of the Church that Christ gives us his help. True, actual grace is given also to men who do not belong to the Church ; but it is given in order that they may be drawn to the Church, and be animated by its soul even if they never visibly belong to its body. In this respect we may see once more how well Christ's own figure of the Vine corresponds with the facts of the supernatural life of souls ; for the vine draws into itself various extraneous substances which it builds up as parts of itself, and Christ by his grace draws men into union with himself that they may become part of his Mystical Body. Here, then, we who are members of the Church have every reason for humble thankfulness. Well may we thank him for the richness of that life which he has bestowed upon us ; well may we have confidence in the closeness of the influence exercised over us by him of whose fulness we have all received ; and well may we pray that we ourselves may be built up " unto a perfect man, unto the measure of the age of the fulness of Christ," [4] and that those who know him not may be brought to him who is the way, the truth and the life.

[1] John x 10.　　　　　　　　[2] Eph. iii 17-19.
[3] Eph. i 23.　　　　　　　　[4] Eph. iv 13.

## APPENDIX: SOME MATTERS OF CONTROVERSY AMONGST CATHOLICS

IT is well known that the problems of Actual Grace have raised some acute controversies amongst Catholic theologians. In the course of this little essay practically nothing has been said about these controversies, because it has seemed best to content oneself with a simple statement and explanation of the main points of Catholic doctrine on which all theologians are agreed. Nevertheless it would be unsatisfactory not to give to those readers who desire it some account of the principal points of debate ; and therefore this Appendix is added.

### I

### EFFICACIOUS GRACE

The chief controversy bears upon the question of Efficacious Grace. By Efficacious Grace we understand a grace which is infallibly followed by the effect to which it tends ; whilst Sufficient Grace—*Merely* Sufficient Grace, as it is sometimes called—is grace which is not followed by the effect to which it tends, although it carries with it the power of producing this effect. All are agreed that God gives graces which are infallibly connected with their effect, and the question arises : How are we to explain the infallibility of this connection ?

One answer is that the infallibility of the connection is to be explained simply by the fact that God foresees that if this grace is given the recipient will most certainly use it. Looked at in themselves there is no intrinsic difference between an efficacious grace and a grace which is merely sufficient ; the whole difference is in this, that one grace will be used and the other will be rejected, and God knows all this beforehand. God, it is explained, altogether apart from any act of his will by which he decrees what shall come to pass, sees from all eternity what free creatures would do in every possible set of circumstances ; thus he sees that if the grace A is given to me I will use it, and that if the grace B is given to me I will not use it ; then he chooses an order of things in which the grace A is given, and by that very fact he knows that I will actually make use of the grace.

This is known as the Molinist explanation, deriving its name from a great Spanish Jesuit of the sixteenth century, and it is the theory held by Jesuit theologians. It was put forward in opposition to another theory known as the Thomist theory which is the official teaching of theologians belonging to the Order of Preachers—*i.e.*, the Dominicans, who bear the name Thomist because they base their teaching on that of St Thomas.[1] Theologians who do not belong

---

[1] In the controversies between the rival schools there is often keen discussion about the real teaching of St Thomas, each side claiming the authority of that great Doctor.

to either of these great orders are divided on the point, some supporting one theory, some the other.

According to the Thomist school the infallibility of the connection between efficacious grace and its effect is due to something in the grace itself which infallibly brings about the result in question. Hence there is an intrinsic difference between Efficacious and Sufficient Grace. The explanation runs much as follows. Before any creature can pass from inaction to action it must be acted upon by the First Cause. Thus there must be what is called a physical premotion. But this physical pre-motion must fix, as it were, the particular action which follows ; otherwise we should have a secondary cause, which is dependent upon the First Cause for its action, arranging for a particular action independently of the First Cause. Therefore this physical pre-motion is called a physical predetermination ; it is a movement produced in the secondary cause, and its influence cannot be affected by the being which receives it. When this physical predetermination is applied to supernatural action we call it Actual Grace—Efficacious Grace.

The great difficulty urged against this theory is that it seems to destroy all freedom ; for if I am so acted upon by God that I cannot alter the movement which he produces in me and one particular act must follow, how (ask the Molinists) can I remain free ? The Thomists admit that there really is a difficulty, but reply by saying that God is capable not only of producing an act in me, but also of producing a free act ; or, more technically, he can produce not only the act, but also the " mode " of the act. This, no doubt, is hard to understand, but they claim that it is necessitated by the very nature of things ; they assert moreover that by thus attributing the determination of the free act to God we have a true explanation of that saying of the Apostle : " It is God who worketh in you, both to will and to accomplish, according to his good will." [1]

In their own turn the Thomists have serious objections to make against the Molinists, the principal being as follows. To leave to man the actual decision to correspond or not to correspond with a grace which is offered—to consent or not to consent—is equivalent to an admission that man can do something of himself towards his eternal salvation—which is Pelagianism. Moreover, the Molinist theory involves an impossible explanation of the divine knowledge ; for the Molinist supposes that independently of his will God knows from all eternity what free agents would do in any possible circumstance. This is the so-called *Scientia Media*. But this knowledge, independent of the decrees of the divine will, the Thomist declares to be impossible—and the Molinist himself admits that it is a mystery. We can easily understand how God from the consideration of his own Being can see all things possible : but how can he see what would be done by free agents in all conceivable circumstances ?

[1] Phil. ii 13.

In place of the physical predetermination of the Thomists some theologians have suggested what is known as moral determination. The suggestion is that God acts upon the will of man not physically, but morally—that is, by way of moral inducement or encouragement —this action being of such intrinsic force that consent infallibly follows. A special application of this theory was made by St Alphonsus, who postulated moral predetermination only in the case of very difficult actions.

## II: PREDESTINATION

The problem of Predestination gives rise to another controversy. All theologians must agree on two points—that God has a real will for the salvation of mankind (in opposition to Calvin), and that our salvation is the result of God's grace (in opposition to Pelagianism). This being supposed, the Thomists, supported in this matter by a certain number of eminent Jesuit theologians such as Saint Robert Bellarmine and Suarez, explain Predestination as follows. Although God has a real will for the salvation of all men, he definitely chooses some for eternal life, and leaves the others out of his choice. Having chosen these particular souls for the glory of heaven, he prepares efficacious graces for them so that they will infallibly correspond with his impulses ; for the others he prepares merely sufficient grace. Finally, reward or punishment is given according to the actions which have been performed. Of course the preparation of efficacious grace for the elect is explained differently by the Thomists and by those Jesuits who accept this general scheme of things. The former explain it by saying that God wills physically to predetermine the elect ; the latter say that by means of the *Scientia Media* he knows which graces will be successful, and then decides to give just these. Some of the Jesuit writers speak of a certain internal suitability in the grace which is efficacious, but in reality what makes it to be efficacious is the foreseen consent which the recipient will give to it. Thus there are important differences between the Thomists and the Jesuit theologians to whom we refer, but they are at one in saying that God's choice of the elect is an act of pure benevolence on his part which has nothing whatever to do with their merits or demerits. For this reason their explanation is known as the theory of Predestination *ante praevisa merita* (Predestination antecedent to the prevision of merit), because it asserts that it is not on account of their foreseen merits that the predestined are chosen. Their choice is God's free act. The chief argument for the theory is found in Scripture where those who are predestined to the glory of heaven are often represented as " elect "—*e.g.*, " They shall show signs and wonders, to seduce (if it were possible) even the elect." [1] " They shall gather together his elect from the four winds," etc. [2]

[1] Mark xiii 22.      [2] Matt. xxiv 31.

Against this theory of Predestination antecedent to the prevision of merit an obvious but very serious objection is raised by the opposing school of theologians, who hold that Predestination is *post praevisa merita*—consequent on the prevision of merit. The objection is that Predestination antecedent to the prevision of merit necessarily involves a Reprobation antecedent to the prevision of fault ; and this would seem to be directly opposed to the doctrine defined by the Church, that God's will for the salvation of men is not limited to the predestined. In other words, the Thomist theory logically leads to Calvinism. To meet this difficulty the Thomist theologians and those who agree with them on the point at issue reply that in regard to the reprobation of the wicked there is not a positive antecedent desire for their damnation, but merely a permission or a negative reprobation in the sense that God does not choose them for eternal glory. The opposite school, however, is not satisfied, and retorts that the effect is the same whether the reprobation be called negative or positive ; and they want to know how God can be said to reprobate only negatively when he deliberately provides the elect with efficacious graces, and the non-elect with non-efficacious graces.

In dealing with the objection which we have just explained some of the supporters of Predestination antecedent to the prevision of merit seem to admit the impossibility of giving a solution that is altogether satisfactory, but they insist on their claim that Predestination antecedent to the prevision of merit is clearly taught in Scripture and must therefore be accepted, even if no direct solution of difficulties is forthcoming. But the other side reply that the texts which are quoted are not satisfactory, for they either refer only to God's free gift of grace (which all allow to be antecedent to the prevision of merit), or they do not imply a choice which is independent of merit—as in the case where some fish are chosen to be kept and the bad are cast away. " They chose out the good into vessels, but the bad they cast forth." [1] Moreover, these same theologians urge, there are other texts in which eternal glory is spoken of as a prize, a reward ; and it would not really be prize or award if it had been chosen for men antecedent to the prevision of their merits. This would seem to be the more common opinion amongst Jesuit writers, and it has the support of St Francis de Sales.

### III : THE ATTITUDE OF THE CHURCH

In these discussions every Catholic is at liberty to take whichever side he prefers, provided that he is always ready to submit to any decision which the Church may make. At the end of the sixteenth century and the beginning of the seventeenth the principal points at issue in regard to efficacious grace were formally considered by the

---

[1] Matt. xiii 48.

Holy/See. Champions on each side were summoned to Rome for public debate, and the discussions went on through more than one pontificate. Ultimately it was decided to leave the two schools free to teach their own theories until such time as the Holy See might issue a definite ruling in favour of the one or the other : but each side was to refrain from denouncing the other as heretical. Consequently, although the Thomist may think that the Molinist theory logically involves a form of Pelagianism, he must not denounce Molinism as heretical ; and the Molinist must exercise a similar restraint in regard to Thomism, although he may not be able to see how it does not involve one of the chief errors of Calvin. Certainly neither side draws the conclusion which the other side says is logically involved in its premisses ; the Thomist does *not* deny freewill, nor does the Molinist deny our dependence upon God for all our salutary actions.

The history of the discussions on this question shows very clearly that Catholics are allowed great liberty of speculation when God himself has not settled a point for us by his revelation, and when the general welfare of the body of the faithful does not require that definite action should be taken. In the present case the freedom which has been allowed has certainly done no harm to the faith and practice of the faithful, and it has given occasion for some really marvellous displays of genius. But if ever circumstances should arise which make it imperative for the custody of Catholic truth that these issues should be decided by the authority of the Church, we can be sure that the Church will speak ; and if ever that day comes the world will see the wonderful spectacle of a great school of theology, with long and glorious traditions behind it, and the *esprit de corps* of a vast religious order to animate it, submitting in humble obedience to the word of Christ's Vicar on earth. Far from being a proof that Catholics do not possess that unity of belief which they claim as one of their glories, the whole attitude of the rival parties shows in reality how strong is the principle of unity amongst us ; for all are ready to submit if the Church calls upon them to do so.

E. TOWERS.

# XVIII

## THE SUPERNATURAL VIRTUES

### §I: ON HABITS

*The meaning* THIS essay is going to be all about habits. " Habit " is such a familiar
*of Habit* term that one might have hoped to leave it at that ; but unfortunately
it is a term that in current language has lost its primary significance.
If we are to understand our subject at all, we must set out at once the
older philosophical meaning of the word. William James, in the
delightful third chapter of his *Psychology*, a chapter full of good
things and sage advice, has given us what he calls " the last word
of our wisdom in the matter " of the genesis of habit. But all that
his " last word " represents is a suggested picture of the underlying
material development which corresponds to the growth of habit.
The very error that has crept into the use of the word is this genetic
idea, as though habit were essentially a growth by repetition. This
confounds the common process of the evolution of the habit with the
habit itself. I can say that a circle is a figure traced by the ex-
tremity B of a line AB which is revolving about the point A. But
the circle need not have been made that way. I can say that a
chicken is the result of an ordered evolution of a fecundated egg.
But the chicken would have been just as completely a chicken if it
had been immediately created by God. And a habit is completely
a habit if it is a modification of human nature disposing that nature
well or ill for its proper operations—whether the habit has been
gradually developed by a series of acts or has appeared at once.
Again, habit is sometimes confused with the notion of custom, as
when we say : He has a habit of reading at meals. Now, though
habits do commonly arise from repetition, and issue in repetition,
they do not essentially involve either such a cause or such a result.
There is no objection to the use of the word " habit " in the examples
we have given ; our quarrel is with the contraction of the word's
meaning to such usage. The original notion is simpler and more
comprehensive. If it were not, the supernatural virtues could not
be called habits. But we cannot avoid so calling them without
separating ourselves from the traditional theological description.
Anyhow, it is much simpler to spend a little time in determining
the true meaning, once for all, than to indulge in circumlocutions
throughout our treatment.

A habit, then, is a modification, a permanent quality added to
our nature, something that we can have or be without. It means
a *setting* of our nature, a disposition of our nature which has an effect

on the operations of our nature. When we speak of our *nature* we are looking at ourselves, our being, as a source of activity. Every being has a natural tendency to work towards the end for which it was created. In human beings we call these tendencies " appetites." We have an appetite for food, for self-preservation, for reproduction, for knowledge, company, speech, and, most generally, for happiness. Foolishly or wisely, blindly or prudently, we are ever seeking the good. Every act we perform is the result of one of our appetites, our tendencies, and is an expression of our nature. We frequently have to pull ourselves together, to brace ourselves, to direct our scattered energies, before we undertake an act. This results in a momentary " set " of our nature, as a bar of soft iron is set by the stroke of a magnet. Now, if this " set " becomes permanent, stable, it is a habit. It saves us the initial trouble of self-direction or bracing. Our nature spontaneously tends to activity ; the habit makes it tend, as if constrained, to some special activity, as the needle which, before, was indifferent, after magnetisation turns to the north. We say *as if* constrained ; for it is still possible for free-will to assert itself and to prevail over the habit. A man learns to speak French. This gives him a new perfection, a new facility, a disposition bearing on one of the faculties of his nature, that of speech. It is a thing that can come or go without changing his nature essentially ; it is an accident. He had the faculty of speech before ; this accidental perfection promotes its activity in a particular way. It does not matter in the least how the man has become possessed of the habit : he may be a Frenchman, who has learned French as his mother-tongue ; he may be an Englishman who (by a rare good fortune) has learned it at school ; or he may have received the gift of tongues. The fact is that he can speak French, and *that* is the habit.

Now I have said—and it is very important—that habit is directed to the activity of a nature, but it need not be immediately directed thereto. The immediate disposition may be, not of the faculty, but of the essence underlying the faculty. I have a habit [1] of skating. That is a disposition of the faculty by which I can use my limbs and maintain my balance. But if I am to skate or to walk or to ride, I need a more fundamental habit ; my body must be healthy. Health is a disposition of my very being ; it disposes that being considered as a source of activities. Thus it fulfils the definition of habit. For a habit is a modification of the subject, of his nature or faculties, which has a bearing on the pursuit of his end. If, like this habit of health, its direct effect is on the nature itself, it is called an *entitative* habit ; but if it immediately affects the faculties, it is called an *operative* habit. Sanctifying grace, as we shall remark later, is an entitative habit, whereas the virtues are operative habits.

[1] In absolute strictness habits can reside only in the soul, but it is common to use the word more largely for bodily dispositions.

Not every habit sets us in the right direction for the accomplishment of the true ends of our nature. Unfortunately we are much more prone to the formation of bad habits. We are constantly being warned to take care of our health, as if it were more natural for us to have bad health. Slovenly habits of speech, of dress, of deportment, are dispositions of our various faculties hampering them in the conduct of their activities for the ends of our nature, and, therefore, are bad habits.

A habit must be stable, a disposition so deeply ingrained that it is not easily movable. It is often said to be a second nature. " Habit second nature ! " said the Duke of Wellington. " Habit is ten times nature." This emphasises the fact that it facilitates the works of the nature which it perfects, so that there is a pleasure in performing them, and a promptitude which results from the absence of lengthy deliberation. Our human faculties are capable of being used either for or against the true good of our nature. We have to make up our mind how they are to be used in a given instance ; that means that we deliberate, we weigh the *pros* and *cons*. The faculty itself is ready for either line of action. The habit does something to relieve this state of indetermination, and if it is a good habit, it sets the faculty permanently towards the good.

*Good habits*  The good operative habit of which we have just spoken is called a virtue. But if we think for a moment we shall see that in using the word virtue we never get away from the idea that it has something to do with the will ; it must appear in actual exercise. Ability to play a musical instrument or to paint is a good operative habit ; but we should only grudgingly call it a virtue, unless it went further. A virtue of that kind is not in default even though it is not applied in execution. A good violinist would not cease to be a good violinist if he should choose to make the night hideous by playing badly ; he is still a violinist as completely as before. But a temperate man falls from his virtue (he does not necessarily *lose* it) if he gets drunk. A boy who can do his sums has a virtue of reckoning. This does not ensure that he always will do them. He probably also possesses a virtue of carefulness. If he fails to do his sums correctly, we say he still can do them ; he still has the first habit intact, but he has failed in the second, for carefulness is incompatible with a lack of care ; and his master takes such means as he thinks fit to consolidate the habit. Here, then, we have the true virtue, and it is in the will. That is why you can justly punish a boy for carelessness, but not for mere ignorance.

Now if we remember that a virtue is a habit which is going to help us to attain the end of our nature, and if we further realise that human nature is meant to aim at God (who alone is the all-sufficient good), we see at once that we limit very considerably the number of habits that can properly be called virtues. If we misapprehend our good, follow a false trail, the " virtue " that aids us is as false as the " good " we are pursuing. The dexterity of the pickpocket could never be called a virtue without qualification ; it is certainly much less of a virtue than the dexterity of the surgeon. But even this is not a perfect virtue unless the surgeon is in union with God by charity ; for, if he is not, his work will not take him any nearer to the one Good. He is pursuing some lower end, such as the alleviation of pain. This is not, of course, a bad end ; it is good. But its goodness lacks " the one thing necessary." And in consequence the virtue remains imperfect. We shall have occasion to remark later that any virtue in order to be perfect must come under the influence of the one supreme virtue of love of God. " If I should distribute all my goods to feed the poor, and if I should deliver my body to be burned, and have not charity, it profiteth me nothing." [1] The prudence of the miser, the boldness of the burglar, the generosity of the seducer, are all bad ; they are false virtues ; not because the men are in sin, but because the virtues are misdirected. The benevolence, marital fidelity, paternal discipline of a sinner are imperfect virtues, because though they are directed to a real good there is an abyss between them and the ultimate good.

It was necessary at the outset to show that the term " habit " does not necessarily connote repetition of acts, for the habits of infused virtue have no dependence on such repetition. But before we begin the discussion of the supernatural virtues proper, we must see how common natural habits do grow out of repetition, for the recognition of this fact has an important bearing on the spiritual life.

Consider the habit of decision. This is acquired by repeated acts of decision. The will acts sharply once. That act leaves on it an impression, in virtue of which it acts decisively the next time with a greater facility. The second act emphasises the impression. And thus a series of acts modifies the will, giving it a stable disposition to act decisively ; and this is a habit. Now, the will, perfected by the habit, decides each case promptly as it arises, and takes a positive pleasure in the sense of decisiveness. Before, it was liable *either* to clench a matter sharply *or* to shilly-shally over it. Now, it behaves as if it were its nature to be prompt and decisive in its acts. " Habit is second nature." The will is not constrained to behave in this manner. That would mean the destruction of free-will. But it is most apt to do so. You can *bet* on it. In the same way a long series of acts of kindness will produce a kindly disposition, or acts of justice a just disposition. You can guess beforehand how a just man will deal with a case which calls for his judgement ; not that you know precisely what he will do, for that depends on how he reads the circumstances of the case ; but you do know that he will not do anything unjust. All these are good habits, and so they are virtues. But we are now considering them under the aspect of merely natural virtues.

[1] I Cor. xiii 3.

Once the habit is established, it grows stronger with every act which is of an equal or greater intensity. If a man is accustomed to rise " at six sharp " every morning, the habit will persevere, and the act will grow ever easier in execution. But if for a period he allows himself to hesitate, to execute the act with less decision, then by so much will his good habit be weakened. If he fail to get up at six, and that repeatedly, the habit will go. An occasional long sleep may be very good for health, but it is not at all good for habit. Or again, consider the habit of controlling one's thoughts. Suppose that one has learned by experience that a certain train of thought, innocent in its beginning, is apt to run on into sensuality. Prudence dictates that such beginnings should be checked. It may be that for a time the checking is easy. This is one of the devil's wiles.[1] Over and over again, we " resist the beginnings." But we are not really advancing in the good habit, for the acts are of less intensity than the habit itself. We are like schoolboys whose exercises are too easy. We are lulled into a state of security, in which we think that we can easily arrest the development of the initial thought. Then a really strong temptation may sweep down upon us. If we resist now, the habit will be established much more firmly. Here, of course, a new element would be introduced, that of grace ; but we are abstracting from this at the moment.

Habits, then, increase by regular acts of an intensity equal to, or greater than, that of the habit itself. They diminish and die through contrary acts or by the cessation of the original acts. But the mere cessation of the acts does not destroy the habit directly. The direct cause of the destruction is found in those contrary debilitating influences which can be withstood only by the performance of the act. The influence of the acts is like the repair of the body by food. In the body there is a constant wear and tear which must be met by regular meals. Poisonous food will ravage and destroy the tissues ; but the absence of food will also prove fatal because the constant catabolism is not made good.

## §II: SUPERNATURAL ACTIVITY

*The equip-*
*ment of the*
*supernatural*
*man*

THE foregoing discussion of natural habits and virtues was necessary in order that we might be able to appreciate the traditional technical language in which supernatural virtue is described. There is a parallel between nature and supernature of which we must take account, if we are to attain to any comprehension, however inadequate, of the supernatural virtues. Our comprehension will always be imperfect, for the terms we shall employ, whose proper significance we have been at some pains to determine, can be applied only analogously to the problems that are now before us. This means that while the terms fit the facts to some extent, they do not completely

[1] *Cf.* Scupoli's *Spiritual Combat*, chap. xiii.

cover the facts. They are true descriptions, but inadequate descriptions. After all, these are terms used by philosophers in their description and classification of natural experience, and grace and supernatural virtue are outside the field of that experience. It is like the true but inadequate description I might give of a picture in terms of colour tones, or of a piece of music in terms of light and shade.

Our present purpose is to describe the equipment of the supernatural man. When we attempt to analyse human activity, we see that it involves the recognition of these elements : human nature, consisting of body and soul in one composite individual ; the faculties of the soul, intellect and will ; the acquired dispositions of those faculties, the habits good and bad ; and the operations which arise from these sources. Similarly, we shall now find a complex of endowments which raise a man above his own nature and bestow on this " new creature " new powers. The supernatural man has a new nature and new faculties. I have remarked already that " nature " is the name applied to an essence when the essence is regarded as the source of its activities. My human nature is the remote source of every merely human action that I perform. But each such action springs immediately from its appropriate faculty. My will and my understanding are the faculties of my soul ; they are the immediate sources of every act of willing or of intelligence. Now, all the activities of my nature, if they are normal, tend to the perfection of my nature, to that end for which my nature is designed. But God, out of his infinite goodness and condescension, has proposed to me an end, a perfection, utterly beyond any capacity of my human nature to know, to pursue, or to attain. God could render such a design feasible only by uplifting my nature, recreating it as it were, and endowing it with powers which are in no sort of continuity with its original equipment.

It will make for clearness if we give at once a scheme of our supernatural endowment and show how it runs parallel with our natural equipment. The fundamental gift is sanctifying grace, which we receive at baptism. This is our " new nature," corresponding in the scheme to our human nature. As a nature, it demands new faculties, the immediate sources of supernatural activities, by which it is able to move towards its end ; these are the theological virtues of faith, hope, and charity. Finally, to the acquired natural virtues correspond the supernatural moral virtues of prudence, justice, fortitude and temperance. Now grace and virtues are habits ; and that statement calls for some explanation.

Grace is dealt with in another essay [1] but we must for a moment dwell upon it here, in order to show how the virtues flow from it. There is a mysterious and startling phrase of St Peter, which is the best introduction to this analysis : " By these [promises] you may

[1] Essay xvi : *Sanctifying Grace.*

be made partakers of the divine nature." [1]   Here we must insist on
the word " nature."   If St Peter merely meant to say that we were
participators of the divine essence, he would only be saying what is
true of every one of God's creatures.   For every creature gets its
being from God, and, in so far as it does, it participates his being ;
though here, again, we lose ourselves in the contemplation of God's
infinite being, and say so by declaring that the word " being " is
applied to creatures only analogously.   We can decide, then, that
St Peter meant more than that.   We participate in the divine *nature*
inasmuch as God makes it possible for us to share in the divine
activity.   God's activity is to contemplate, and rejoice in, his own
divine essence.   And it is precisely that contemplation and consequent joy which he has proposed to share with us.   That is our
heaven.   But that activity itself, and every act which in this life
tends towards it, is wholly beyond the scope of our nature and
powers.   So God puts into the soul sanctifying grace in order to
dispose the soul for that vision and enjoyment which God possesses
of his own nature.   Too often grace is described as if it were merely
an operative habit ; a virtue by which a man could *work* towards his
great end, or by which his desires could be turned in its direction.
That is inadequate.   The perfecting of man's powers is the work,
not of sanctifying grace, but of the virtues which accompany it ;
grace itself perfects the very essence of the soul, and so it is called
an entitative habit,[2] just as the health which perfects our body is an
entitative habit.   It is a habit because it is an accident by which the
soul is perfected, well disposed ; it makes the soul like to God, giving
it a share in that activity which is most characteristic of God.   " By
justifying men he makes them sons of God," says St Augustine ;
" if we are made the sons of God, we are made Gods."

But, as I have said, the word " habit " is used analogously here.
Regarded as the source of our God-like activity, grace is more like
a nature than a habit.   Moreover, it is unlike a habit, in that the
perfection which it bestows breaks away from human nature, soaring
above it.   Yet it is a habit ; for it is an endowment of the soul,
disposing it for that supreme end of human nature, God himself.
So, while we remember that it is a habit, we range it in our scheme
as the supernatural correlative of nature ; and, as a nature, it demands new immediate principles of activity, just as our human
nature, the ultimate source of human activity, demands immediate
principles, like intellect and will, for each of its activities.

*The
immediate
principles of
supernatural
activity*

These new principles are the supernatural virtues.   The very
name suggests habits ; but, again, " habit " is applied only analogously.   The virtues are not like ordinary habits.   In some ways
they are more like faculties, intellect and will.   The immediate
source of an act of understanding or of reasoning is the intellect ;
so the immediate source of an act of supernatural belief is the virtue

[1] 2 Pet. i 4.        [2] *Cf.* p. 623.

of faith. That looks as if faith should be rather a supernatural faculty, and as a matter of fact, we correlate it with faculty in our scheme. But the act of belief is not completely accounted for by the virtue of faith. It springs from a more complex root. It has a human element as well as a divine. The act of believing is an act of our human intellect, supernaturalised by the virtue of faith. It is of the last importance that we should be clear about this. Grace does not do away with nature ; it perfects nature. The virtue of faith is a necessary complement of the intellect, if the intellect is to assent on the authority of God to a truth revealed by God. Again, when, by the virtue of charity I make an act of love of God, it is my own will that loves him, though that will is enabled to love him by the virtue of charity. Thus in each instance, the virtue is the perfection of a power, and from the beginning we have called the perfection of a power or faculty, a virtue, or good *habit*. A faculty cannot grow ; it can only be perfected by good habits. Now a virtue, as we shall show, can grow, as can the supernatural grace whose " faculties " the virtues are.

But there is one striking difference between the supernatural virtues and ordinary good habits, or natural virtues. It is a very significant difference, and one that secretly and in the background has been determining the course of our discussion. The supernatural virtues do not confer the same ease in operation as the natural virtues. Consider the case of a well-instructed Catholic, who knows what natural virtues are, and who knows further that the result of the sacrament of Penance is to restore sanctifying grace if it has been lost by mortal sin, and that with this grace there inevitably comes the whole series of supernatural virtues. Suppose that he has been given up to some vice such as drunkenness or impurity. That means that he has lost the virtue of temperance, and, indeed, most of the other virtues. Now he goes to confession, and he is determined to reform. He knows that he has once more the virtue of temperance in his soul. But a virtue is a good habit, and a good habit makes the good act easy and pleasant. So, full of good desires, he cheerfully faces the future, fully equipped, as he thinks, to meet the old temptations, and to win an easy victory over them. Alas ! the first real temptation that comes his way undeceives him. He finds that the shackles of his old sins are still upon him, though he knows that their guilt is forgiven. The vice is in his very flesh. In spite of his virtues, the path of holiness is steep and rugged ; the struggle is a fierce one, and he is very apt to fall. The truth is that these supernatural virtues do not give facility of action in the same way as do the natural good habits, and the reason is because they have not been developed in the same way. The virtue of temperance which is designed to enable him to be sober or pure does not seem to make the attainment of those ideals any easier.

And yet it does something to secure that attainment, in addition to making the supernatural act possible. There are two ways in which a faculty may be helped to carry out its proper act : one is by making the faculty more eager for the act itself, the other by increasing the attractiveness of the object. You can see the difference in two boys faced with the task of learning a book of Euclid. One of them has the type of mind for which the study of geometry is a pleasure ; the other has no bent for the subject, but has a keen realisation of the necessity of getting it up for the sake of an examination. Or again, a young man at the university who has a natural gift for athletics is too lackadaisical to effect anything, while another who is slow, clumsy, and flabby, will spend long afternoons at the nets, or painful hours " tubbing " on the river, because his imagination is fired by the prospect of winning his colours or of rowing in his college boat.

Now supernatural virtue acts in the second way. It bestows a special inclination to the good which is the object of the virtue. It does not in the least make the practice of the virtue any easier in itself. We should not have expected God to give such ease as a grace, for man can acquire this for himself. Each act of the virtue is possible, and a frequent repetition of the acts will produce that facility which corresponds to the natural habit. The supernatural virtue does not even negatively promote the facility by the removal of old bad habits or by the control of the passions.

A supernatural virtue, then, is like a natural virtue in this, that it perfects a natural power. The two are unlike in the kind of perfection they bestow. The supernatural virtue uplifts the faculty, and so makes it possible for that hitherto incompetent faculty to produce an act of the supernatural order ; it also gives a special inclination towards the good object, which inclination is a real help in the pursuit of the good, although it does not immediately make the pursuit easier. The natural virtue presupposes the ability to produce an act of the human order, but makes the act easier.

To complete our sketch of man's supernatural equipment, we should observe here that the Gifts of the Holy Ghost are conferred with sanctifying grace. These, too, are habits. They bestow no new power or facility, but they dispose our faculties to be responsive to God's suggestions and invitations.

## §III: VIRTUES NATURAL AND SUPERNATURAL

*Origin of the supernatural virtues* THE supernatural virtues are commonly called the "infused virtues," and this name indicates their divine origin. It would be quite proper to attribute the name " infused virtue " to any virtue immediately given by God, even though it were possible to develop such a virtue by natural means. Thus we might call the virtue of health " infused " if it had been miraculously restored ; or the Apostles' gift of tongues might be so called, though men can learn foreign languages by their own efforts. But the name is restricted to those virtues which could not be developed by any natural means, the virtues by which a man is disposed for an end surpassing the reach of human nature, for his last and perfect happiness. No repetition of acts will account for the origin of these habits. Always bearing in mind the halting nature of every comparison, and realising that any comparison of natural and supernatural must be peculiarly lame, we will try to emphasise this difference between natural and supernatural virtues by a commonplace similitude. A pearl-diver of the South Seas, by much practice, has become very expert and enduring. He can remain under water for a considerable time, and work there. But he could never undertake the work of a professional diver who has to investigate a wreck. For that a habit of quite a different kind is necessary. The diver must be clothed in a diving suit [1] and helmet properly connected with an air-pump. No efforts of diving will ever produce such a suit, though the diver can put it on when he has got it. The act of a supernatural virtue is, as we have shown, an act performed by a natural faculty after that faculty has been upraised. The faculty is only capable of the act after such elevation, and this elevation depends upon the supernatural virtue. It is therefore obvious that the supernatural act cannot generate the virtue. Even though it is possible to make a series of supernatural acts under the influence of a series of actual graces before the bestowal of the habits of grace and of the virtues, still such acts cannot beget the virtues.

Since, then, the infused virtues have no cause in the subject who enjoys them, since they are not made by him or out of anything that was in him, they, like the grace from which they flow, are spoken of in Scripture as the work of a *creation*, as a new creature : " If then any be in Christ a new creature, the old things are passed away " ; [2] " for in Christ Jesus neither circumcision availeth any thing, nor uncircumcision : but a new creature " ; [3] " and put on the new man, who according to God is created in justice and holiness of truth." [4]

Like the natural virtues they can increase : " As newborn babes, *Growth of* desire the rational milk without guile, that thereby you may grow *supernatural* unto salvation." [5] But this increase also is the direct work of God. *virtues* This is all summed up in the expression that virtue is that which God effects in us without our help (*in nobis, sine nobis*).

But all this is not to say that the sinner can do absolutely nothing towards the production of virtue. He can dispose himself for the reception of the good habit. This he can do, under the influence of actual grace, either by withdrawing his will from that which is contrary to the virtue, or by an act of the love of God which almost demands the infusion of the virtues by God. But such a disposition

---

[1] We are not here confusing the two meanings of *habitus*.
[2] 2 Cor. v 17.    [3] Gal. vi 15.    [4] Eph. iv 24.    [5] 1 Pet. ii 2.

is only a " material " disposition. It is like the preparation of the material by rough workmen for the skilled artist, the removal of knots from the wood or the hewing of the marble block on which the sculptor is going to work. And once we have the virtues, we can do more for their increase. We can never effect it ourselves, but we can merit it by acts of virtue.

*Loss of the supernatural virtues*

With regard to the loss of the virtues, here again there is complete dissimilarity between natural and supernatural. Natural virtues are lost by a succession of contrary acts or by a cessation from the practice of the virtue ; and that, because they are developed from acts. But the supernatural virtue is lost by one act opposed to the virtue, by one mortal sin. On the other hand, cessation from practice does not destroy it. To return to our former example : the diver's suit is completely effective as long as it is not torn, no matter how much it may be worn ; but one tear will make it ineffective and useless. Acquired virtues are lost by a gradual process ; the infused are lost at one step. They cannot in themselves diminish ; any injury is a mortal injury. There is no process of weakening ; it is life or death.

This looks like a paradox. What about the universally received doctrine that venial sin leads to mortal sin, and that in the spiritual life there is no standing still ? Venial sin does lead to a loss of charity, and therefore of the other supernatural virtues (exception being made with regard to Faith and Hope, as we shall explain later) ; but it is not by a process of diminution. The ease with which virtuous acts are accomplished is the result of the frequent performance of the acts. Venial sin weakens the natural habit ; and makes it harder to resist temptation ; and thus it paves the way for mortal sin, which in a flash destroys the supernatural habit. The same is true of the effectiveness of the cessation from the practice of virtue. Scupoli tells [1] us that it is a common wile of the devil to leave us in peace for a time, when he sees that we are established in virtue. If he constantly tempted us, and if, as constantly, we vanquished him, then every such act of ours would have a twofold effect : meritoriously it would strengthen the supernatural virtue (which, however, has nothing to do with the facility of the act), and efficiently it would strengthen the natural virtue, and so increase the ease with which we perform the good act. But if he leaves us alone, there is the chance that we shall grow careless in the exercise of virtue. Thus, although the supernatural virtue will not diminish, the acquired virtue will. Then he will swoop down on us when we are off our guard, and although we have the supernatural virtue which enables us to resist the temptation, human nature is weakened, and we may fall. Fervour means the subservience of all the strength of the soul and the bodily members to charity ; and by venial sin this fervour is chilled.

*Grace and nature*

As I have said, facility in the exercise of virtue depends upon an

[1] *Spiritual Combat*, chap. xiii.

acquired, natural virtue which in its genesis, growth and decay, obeys all the laws which have been laid down for such virtues. It is commonly observed that in the saints the practice of virtue grows easy by their frequent repetition of virtuous acts. Even very ordinary Christians who are trying to serve God know that the control of the tongue, patience, the restraint of appetites, ejaculatory prayers, the constant sense of the presence of God, which in the beginning meant a struggle and a deliberate self-conquest, in course of time become almost natural. Furthermore, it is a particular virtue whose exercise becomes easy, and various saints are conspicuous exponents of various special virtues : a St Francis de Sales of meekness, a St Teresa of prayer, a St Aloysius of purity, a St Francis of Assisi of poverty. Now this particular facility might conceivably arise from one of two sources : it might be attributable to a growth of the supernatural virtue by way of merit, or to the development of the corresponding natural virtue, acquired efficiently by repetition of acts. But it cannot be the first, for as we have so often insisted, supernatural virtue does not give facility ; and, moreover, as we shall presently see, all supernatural virtues grow together proportionately, so that any facility, or special intensity arising from their growth, would affect them all simultaneously ; and that is contrary to experience. The facility, therefore, must be caused by the acquired virtue.

We have remarked that the absence of facility in the practice of virtue for one who is lately converted from habits of sin is a source of disappointment and of dismay. Here, in the teaching concerning the loss of virtue, we have a corresponding source of consolation. The one act that destroys the habit of virtue does not destroy the acquired facility. The sinner can still make acts of the natural virtue, and with an actual grace he can even make the supernatural act. Thus, if he had acquired facility in making acts of perfect charity or of perfect contrition, it would be easy to imagine his speedy restoration to the state of grace, under the impulse of actual grace, even before he had time or opportunity to go to confession. It is a very practical consequence of this teaching to insist on the value of frequent acts of contrition. When we are in the state of grace we should accustom ourselves to sorrow over our past sins as offences against an infinitely good God, as treasonable acts which put us out of friendship with our eternal Lover. Then, if under a sudden temptation we have the misfortune to fall, we shall be ready with God's grace to turn to him again immediately, and not have the horror of lying in our sin until such time as we can get sacramental absolution.

This is an illustration of the way in which grace builds on nature. As the natural faculty, of itself impotent to perform a supernatural act, can act supernaturally when perfected by an infused habit ; so, too, natural habit plays its part in facilitating good acts when it is associated with the corresponding infused virtue. And this will account for the part played by natural character in the lives of the saints. It is true that God chooses the weak to confound the strong ; but if there is a strong natural character to begin with, grace has something on which to build. The saints have been men and women of great natural courage, strong will, temperate habits, remarkable for even-handed justice, great self-discipline, love of their fellow-men. It is not that God could not, or does not, give supernatural virtues in the absence of their natural counterpart. It is not that we do not sometimes find holy men and women lacking in natural prudence or fortitude. It is not that there is never a bad streak of nature to be eliminated. But, as a rule, the saint's natural character is an index of the supernatural heroism that is going to distinguish his life. St Teresa had great native courage and common sense ; St Peter had enthusiasm and zeal ; St John was by nature loving. This natural character is itself a gift of God. " Some are disposed by their bodily disposition to be chaste, or gentle, or suchlike," says St Thomas. These have a start, as it were, in the way of virtue, by the hidden, but certainly not unjust, disposition of God. Of course they have to fight nature, but it is probably in other particulars. St Francis de Sales was naturally noble and *fine*, but he had to fight against his temper. St Thomas Aquinas was subtle-minded and intelligent ; also he was chaste ; but he was allowed to be very violently tempted against chastity.

Saudreau, in *The Degrees of the Spiritual Life*, seems to make too little of this gift of God. While it may be granted that very often the character of the saints, their evident prudence, wisdom, charity, are the results of infused virtues (and Gifts of the Holy Ghost) ; that often persons of no education are wonderfully enlightened by infused knowledge ; this does not seem to be contrary to the principles we have laid down. And if, as Saudreau goes on to say, " natural defects may have a negative influence, producing an adverse effect and hindering any progress in holiness," this seems to amount to the same thing as we have declared. But this teaching is not averse to Saudreau's essential doctrine that there can be no " positive influence of the natural virtues in the way of sanctification," if by that he means that natural virtues can do nothing efficiently or meritoriously to produce an increase of supernatural virtue. As we have been at pains to state, they merely facilitate the activity. Every natural good habit that we possess can be used for advance in virtue, if only we are supernaturalised. It is safe to speak thus positively, but it would not be safe to establish comparisons between nature and grace in different individuals who were both supernaturalised. The comfort which St Bonaventure gave to Brother Giles was perfectly well founded : " an ignorant man can love God as much as one that hath great learning, and a poor simple woman can love God as much as a doctor of theology " ; nevertheless, the doctor of theology has a gift which can, and should, help him on the way to perfection and union with God ; and if, as a matter of fact, it does not, this is his fault and not the fault of his learning. St Teresa demanded *courage* of her daughters.

A clear understanding of this relation between the natural and supernatural virtues should be a help to the person who, after confession of mortal sin, still finds an unexpected difficulty in the exercise of his newly restored virtues. Now that his heart is turned away from sin, he cannot be the victim of *formal* vice. But his former bad habits have left their mark on him materially. He has a bodily disposition to sin : he may be teased by lust or crave for drink. The vice is in his flesh and in his bones. This he can eradicate according to the rules which govern the growth or decay of any acquired habit. At first he will have to fight hard, but every victory will mark a stage in natural self-conquest. A series of acts opposing the vice, a deliberate subduing of the flesh, for example, will in course of time substitute a good natural habit for the bad one ; and then the supernatural goodness which is made possible by the infused virtues will become more pleasant ; he will find the yoke sweet and the burden light.

## §IV: NATURE AND CONNECTION OF INFUSED VIRTUES

WE have seen that God has set before mankind, as the great aim *Necessity of* of existence, the enjoyment of the direct vision of himself in eternity. *infused* Of the double activity of intellect and will implied in this eternal *virtues* reward we have not now to speak. In this life there can be no such activity, for we cannot here see God face to face. But he has made us sharers of his own activity even in life, by habitual grace which gives us the adoption of sons, and by the infused virtues which enable us to aim at him as he has revealed himself to us. He must have made provision for these virtues, otherwise the gift of his grace would be imperfect. Every lowest creature has those powers which are necessary for the pursuit of its end. Merely natural man has the faculties to pursue his natural end. It is unthinkable that God should not have endowed man with what is necessary for his supernatural end. And though man's native faculties are adequate to the knowledge and love of God as known in the works of creation —physically adequate, even if, as a matter of fact, they are in his present state morally inadequate—they are wholly inadequate to the belief, hope, and love which are directed to God as our revealed supernatural end. Given the present state of the world in which God has revealed to all men himself, his power, goodness, amiability, it is physically possible for the man who has no grace or virtue to believe in God on the authority of God revealing, to hope for God's help and eternal reward, to love God as the one infinite good ; but it is not physically possible that he should do these things in such a way as will be an effective pursuit of that last end. The difference between natural and supernatural acts lies, not in their proper object, nor in the reason by virtue of which they are performed, but in the fact that the supernatural act emanates from an uplifted principle and is thereby capable of being ordained to an end which is beyond the power of nature.[1]

We can, then, distinguish three possible stages in man's knowledge and love of God. First, the merely natural man (physically speaking) can know God as his last end, and believe in him as revealed ; and St Thomas teaches us that by nature man is bound to love God above all things, and that he would be a monster if he did not. Secondly, the supernaturalised man can believe in God and hope in him in such a way as will merit an eternal reward. Thirdly, in the Beatific Vision, by an entirely new equipment, man will be able to see God as he is, face to face, and love him. In this last case, although the object of the acts is the same God,[2] there is a shade of difference in the charity, arising from the difference in the mode of apprehension by the intellect whose function it is to enlighten the will ; then we shall see face to face, now we see " as in a glass darkly."

Now the supernatural virtues are all those which are necessary for the production of acts which lead to God. These may have as their object either, first, God himself or something intimately connected with him, or, secondly, the means of approach to him. The first class, because of their preoccupation with God himself, are called the theological virtues ; the second, because of their immediate concern with conduct, are called the moral virtues. The theological virtues are three : Faith, Hope, and Charity. Faith enables us to assent to the facts of God's revelation about himself on the authority of God revealing, or to make the preliminary assents to the motives of credibility. Hope enables us to rely upon God's power and goodness for our eternal reward in himself, or for those present aids which are necessary if we are to merit that reward. Charity enables us to love God as our sovereign good, and (as a secondary connected object) our neighbour for God's sake. These virtues are the homologues of our natural faculties, for this reason : man's will needs no habit, no added perfection to enable it to be set towards its last end in the way of nature ; God himself is its object, as he is the object of the theological virtues in their own order.

Now the virtues which are concerned with supernatural conduct are the obvious homologues of the virtues which perfect the natural man, and which are necessary for him if his faculties are to be used aright in the details of conduct. They are manifold, but they are

---

[1] This is the subject of a famous controversy, the discussion of which is outside the scope of this treatment. In the text we state the view that appears to us the best.

[2] The intimate union of the blessed with God is already inaugurated " in germ " by the indwelling of the Holy Ghost in the souls of the just.

grouped under the heads of the four cardinal virtues : Prudence, Justice, Fortitude, and Temperance.   We have said that the will of itself is directed to its last end ; if it wander from the straight path to that end, this is attributable to lack of knowledge in the intellect or to wandering desires concerned with the means to the end.   So to safeguard the will from these induced errors, prudence must first of all regulate the intellect ; then justice must keep the will upright in those operations which concern our intercourse with our fellow-men as citizens of heaven ; and, finally, fortitude and temperance must preserve the will from the interference of the passions, temperance controlling impulses towards the unreasonable, fortitude conquering the obstacles which are set in the way of good.

There is an old adage to the effect that virtue stands in the middle *The golden* line.   This applies to all the moral virtues.   Their very object is the *mean* mean between excess and defect : between giving too much and too little, between taking too much pleasure and too little, between attempting too much and too little.   It does not imply that the virtue is a mean between two vices ; it is not the virtue, but the object, that is the mean, the mean between excess and defect in its own matter.   But when excess and defect are both contrary to the virtue (which is not always the fact) then there are two vices between which the virtue lies.   So, for example, we get the sequences :—

Gluttony, Temperance, Insensibility,
Rashness, Fortitude, Timidity.

But sometimes only one of the extremes is directly against the virtue, the other simply having nothing to do with it, and then there is but one corresponding vice, though the virtue is still in the mean : for example, Justice *v.* Injustice.

All this applies only to the moral virtues.   For the theological virtues, taken in themselves, there is no mean.   " The measure of the love of God," said St Bernard, " is to love him without measure." The same applies to hope and faith.   God himself is their object. In him we can never repose too great faith, for he is infinite wisdom and truth ; nor too great hope, for he is omnipotent, supremely generous and faithful to his promises ; nor can we ever love him too much, for he is the absolute good.   As we have remarked above, the idea of the mean is not derived from a consideration of opposed vices ; so the general rule is not affected by the commonly mis-interpreted sequence, Despair—Hope—Presumption.   Presumption is not an excess of hope in God's promises, but a hope for what God has not promised.   The only qualification arises from our own weak-ness, not from the virtue itself.   In the exercise of the virtues we must observe the rule of prudence, otherwise by excess of zeal we might do more harm than good.   A man might put too great a strain on his nature by setting out to make, say, ten thousand acts of charity every day.

But while there is no possibility of excess in the theological virtues, the virtue may fail by defect. In order to retain the virtue of charity we have to attach our wills so completely to God's will that we would not forsake him for any creature. We must appreciate him more highly than ourselves or anything else that he has made. But we are not bound to love him more intensely than any creature. A boy loves a game of football with far greater intensity than he loves his studies; but, for one reason or another, he has his mind made up that he will not forsake his lessons in order to play football. That means that he has a greater " love of appreciation " for his studies. The soldier going to battle has a far more intense love of his wife and family than of the duty which calls him from their company; but he has a greater love of appreciation for his duty:

> " I could not love thee, dear, so much,
> Loved I not honour more."

The first and most obvious application of this important distinction between appreciation and intensity is to the virtue of charity; but we can extend the distinction with quite definite meaning to faith and hope. By our faith we believe in God more firmly than in any creature of God; by our hope we rest our confidence on God more stably than on any of his creatures. We would relinquish anything which should be in opposition to either of these virtues rather than give up believing or hoping in God.

So much is necessary for the lowest grades of the spiritual life, but progress is marked by an ever closer identification of our will with that of God, and also by a love of ever-growing intensity. In this life we shall never attain the highest that even we are capable of reaching:

> " For a man's reach should exceed his grasp,
> Or what's a Heaven for ? "

A saint may love God more intensely than we love any creature; we should all strive so to love him; but there are endless degrees of intensity even in this life, and the greatest intensity of an act of love attainable by any saint in this life is lower than the least intensity that is found accompanying face-to-face vision in heaven.

*Solidarity of the virtues* Speaking quite generally, and, for the moment, prescinding from one striking exception, we can say that all the virtues are infused simultaneously, and exist all together, and, if they are lost, are lost all together. This statement depends on three principles:

1. The virtues are all most intimately connected with sanctifying grace. It is grace which makes the " new creature," and the virtues are the " faculties " of that new creature. Where sanctifying grace is, all the virtues must be, and, anteriorly to the appearance of the new nature, there can be no call for the new principles of operation.

2. But it is the very definite teaching of the Council of Trent that the virtues of faith and hope can remain in the soul after the

loss of sanctifying grace : " If anyone says that when grace is lost by sin, faith is always simultaneously lost, or that the faith which remains is not true faith, though it be not living faith, . . . let him be anathema." Though this definition was primarily directed against the Protestant error of justification by faith only, it clearly teaches the present truth. It says nothing about hope, but theologians are agreed that the same teaching holds for hope, for the same theological reasoning applies to both. This is the ground of the exception we have mentioned.

3. Charity is the " form " of all the virtues. That means that no virtue has its full perfection as a supernatural virtue unless it is, by association with charity, directed to the last end. This " form " is something added to the essence of the virtue, which gives it a fuller richness of being in the way of a designation. If a child puts his pennies in a money-box, he marks them for saving. If a man is sworn in as a soldier or policeman he has an added form, extrinsic to his nature, designating him for special duties. The pennies are just as much pennies even if they are out of the money-box ; the soldier or policeman is just as completely a man if he leaves the army or the police force. Charity gives the other virtues an extrinsic form of this type. It does not change their essence, but it refers their operations to man's final end. A man with the supernatural habit of fortitude is by that habit enabled to seek the means to the last end, and to conquer such difficulties as arise in the pursuit of virtue. Here we have the proximate object which specifies the virtue. But it is the charity which accompanies the virtue that directs the act of the virtue to something beyond the proximate object, to the ultimate object which is God himself. So it is only by charity that any virtue is constituted in its perfect state, the state in which it is able to fulfil the end for which all virtues are given. Now hope and faith can be present without charity ; but then we speak of them as " dead," thus opposing them to the perfect virtues " informed " by charity, which we call " living " faith and hope.

But it is only these two virtues which can persevere after the loss of grace. Charity is so intimately united with grace on the one hand, and with the moral virtues on the other, that grace, charity, and the moral virtues not only come together, but must go together. They move as one thing. Charity implies the presence of sanctifying grace. The union of the two is so intimate that many have identified them—wrongly, as we think. But charity means friendship with God. There can be no friendship without some community of life, and this, we know, is found in that participation of the divine nature which is formally given by habitual grace.

This establishes the connection of charity and grace. Now charity is inseparably linked with all the other moral virtues by prudence. Prudence has for its object the regulation of the moral virtues. There is no virtue without prudence, and there is no proper prudence without the other virtues. But if prudence demands that a man should be properly directed to his immediate ends by justice, fortitude, and temperance, much more does it demand that he should be directed to his final supernatural end by charity. So whether it be in their first appearance, or in their remaining, or in their departure, all elements act as one.

This leaves us only to deal with the exceptional virtues of faith and hope. These make their first appearance with grace and the other virtues, for the reasons already assigned. And as long as grace and charity are present they must remain. But they do not depend on charity as do the other virtues. Obviously we can believe a person, or hope in him, without loving him. Nor do they depend on the other virtues; the others rather depend on these. And as a matter of fact, common experience teaches us that sinners, who must have lost charity and with it the moral virtues, retain their hope and their faith. These are not then perfect virtues, for they lack the " form " which is necessary for perfect virtues, but they are still the true supernatural habits of faith and hope, though they are " dead." Faith can be destroyed only by a sin against faith. By such a sin hope is also destroyed, for in its very essence hope depends on faith. Hope can also be destroyed by a sin against hope.

Suppose that any mortal sin has been committed other than a sin against these two virtues. When grace is restored, sacramentally or otherwise, all the virtues come back and at once are joined with the faith and hope that are already in the soul. So even here it is true that the whole group of virtues exists together. And, of course, faith and hope are at once vivified by charity. The supernatural structure rises in three levels from faith, in the order, (1) faith, (2) hope, (3) charity and grace, and the moral infused virtues. Destroy any level of the building, and all the superstructure falls, but not the levels below.

Thus :

| Charity, Grace, Moral virtues, Gifts |
| --- |
| Hope |
| Faith |

*Co-ordination of the virtues* From the point of view of relative dignity, the theological virtues are more excellent than the moral virtues because their object is God himself, whereas the objects of the moral virtues are creatures. And of the theological virtues charity is the noblest : " the greatest of these is charity." It alone possesses God. The person loved is in a certain way in the lover, and the lover is in union with the object of his love : " He that abideth in charity abideth in God, and God in him." [1] Among the moral virtues prudence takes the lead because of its directive influence over the rest.

But from the point of view of their degree of intensity in the individual subject the virtues are all equal. Taken as virtues in the fullest sense of the term, we have seen that they receive their perfection from charity, and their intensity depends on that one thing. As charity grows they grow with it. But the same is true, generally speaking, when they are regarded in their very essence. They all come together with grace. They are habits depending on grace and required by grace, if the new nature is to perform its operations ; and so they are commensurate with grace, growing with its growth. Such growth may be by merit, which induces God to grant an increase of grace and a corresponding infusion of virtues, or by the sacraments which bear grace to the soul.

But here again we have to take account of the same exception as before. Let us consider a person whose grace and virtues have attained a certain degree equal for all. If he falls into sin, he loses all except faith and hope. These persevere in their same degree, and when grace and the other virtues are restored sacramentally, at probably a lower level on account of lack of preparation in the penitent, faith and hope will be greater than the others. Every fall means a reduction of the main body of virtues to zero while faith and hope are left, " dead " indeed, but at the same level ; every rise and period of development means that faith and hope grow with the others. Evidently, then, they will be much greater than the others. Thus, perhaps, we can account for the amazing faith and hope which we find in the most sinful Catholics, who seem to have but the rudiments of any other supernatural virtues.

With this exception, the virtues are, according to the figure of St Thomas, like the fingers of the hand, which, though different in size (as the virtues in specific dignity), are all in proportion to each other and to the hand, and all increase in equal proportion.

Now at first sight this teaching seems to be at variance with all our experience. Not only do the saints shine in the manifestation of particular virtues, but even ordinary Christians will easily do the works of one virtue while they are in constant danger of sinning against another. A good man, absolutely chaste and sober and truthful, may be very ill-tempered or niggardly ; the generous are often unjust. The petty vices of the good are the scandal of the indevout. The solution of this paradox is fairly evident at the present stage of our inquiry. In both saints and sinners we are considering the *exercise* of the virtues, which is the only thing that is open to our view. The virtue itself we can never know directly. And the thing that we remark is the constancy, the facility, the almost naturalness of the exercise. But this we know is the evidence of the

---

[1] 1 John iv 16.

corresponding acquired virtue; it does not depend upon the intensity of the infused virtue, but arises, perhaps from natural character and habit, perhaps from a special help of God. Thus is achieved the wonderful variety in the lives and examples of the saints. Each of us can find among them a model whose most manifest virtue appeals to him or is necessary for him. From our principles we know that all the virtues are present in an equal degree whether they are apparent in exercise or not.

*The virtues after death* In the damned there can be no virtue at all. The damned are confirmed in evil; for them there is no possibility of a conversion to God. And it is the function of virtue to lead to God either immediately or eventually. We are told that "the devils believe and tremble"; but this is not even the dead faith which the sinner may have had at the point of death. God cannot infuse virtue into those who are irretrievably separated from him.

The souls in purgatory have the three theological virtues. Charity they can now never lose. As they neither see God nor possess him, faith and hope are not incompatible with their state; and as they are not in a state of sin they have these virtues. And probably they have the moral virtues too.

The blessed in heaven have charity in its full development. It is the same charity as they had in life, but with the vision of God it has evolved into a greater and nobler condition. Faith they cannot have, for faith is of things not seen; nor can they have hope, for they are in possession of the highest and all-satisfying good. They cannot even be said to hope for the resurrection of the body in glory; for, though they have not as yet this perfection, they have not to struggle for it, and have the guarantee of it. "Charity never falleth away: but when that which is perfect is come, that which is in part shall be done away." [1] It is the common opinion of theologians that the moral virtues will persevere in the Beatific Vision, though it is impossible to assign the subject-matter of their activity.

§V: THE VIRTUES IN PARTICULAR

1. *Faith*

WE are now in a position to discuss each of the virtues in particular. And we shall begin with the virtue of faith. This is the supernatural habit by which our intellect is disposed to assent to all that is revealed by God, who is infinite truth and wisdom, who, therefore, "can neither deceive nor be deceived." The act of faith is treated in a separate essay of this volume, [2] and the full implication of the above definition must be sought there. Here we shall concern ourselves with the habit alone. For any act of faith the intellect

---

[1] I Cor. xiii 8, 10.    [2] Essay i · *Faith and Revealed Truth.*

must be moved by the will ; nevertheless, the virtue perfects the intellect only. The necessary disposition of the will is provided by the virtue of charity when faith is a perfect virtue ; when it is dead faith, the necessary aid for the will comes from a transient actual grace. Ordinarily, " faith works by charity." [1] As we have already explained, supernatural faith is essentially the same faith whether it be " dead " or " living," the same after the subject has fallen into sin as when he is restored to a state of grace, for charity is only an " extrinsic form."

Faith is an act of homage to God in which he takes pleasure and *The meaning* which he demands from us. If we refuse to accept a person's testi- *of Faith* mony it must be because we question either his veracity or his competence to speak in the present case. We judge of each particular case on its merits. I can believe a man, whom I know to be a rascal and a liar, if he is giving evidence against himself, and if there is nothing for him to gain by incriminating himself. But if I know that a man is truthful, and I assent to any testimony of his, I ought to assent to every testimony, as long as he is within the sphere of his competence. But if he goes outside that sphere I can reasonably refuse to credit him though I have assented to his testimony in other matters. Thus I may reject the teaching of a biologist who tells me that man is evolved from an anthropoid stock, even though I believe him when he presents to me the facts on which he bases his opinion. I do not doubt his word or his competence in his own science, but I do doubt his philosophic judgement when he goes outside that science to integrate its results in a theory.

Now when God speaks to me, I know that he is infinitely true and that all things are clear in his sight ; and therefore I pay homage to his veracity and omniscience by giving my assent to everything that he has revealed. To refuse my assent to any particular point of his revelation would be to question one of the two attributes upon which any faith rests, and therefore would be equivalent to the rejection of all faith. Such a sin destroys the virtue of faith, but such a sin is not committed unless I know that God has spoken. As a rule, I learn this through the Church.

The Church is the infallible witness to the matter of the divine *The Church* revelation. We Catholics must believe explicitly everything that we *and Faith :* thus know to have been revealed ; and implicitly, everything which *heresy* as a matter of fact the Church does teach as of divine revelation, whether we are aware of it or not. To refuse either of these assents would be to become a formal heretic ; but, in ignorance of the fact, to refuse assent to some particular, while giving the implicit assent, would result in one's being a merely " material " heretic. This distinction is of the greatest importance in a country like ours, where so many who have received the virtue of faith in baptism have, through no fault of their own, grown up in ignorance of many of the

[1] Gal. v 6.

truths of revelation. Leaving out of account the possibility of doubts about the functions or identity of the Church, their implicit faith would be guaranteed by their prevailing desire to believe whatever God has revealed. But, as long as they refuse to believe any truth which the Church teaches as of divine revelation they are material heretics ; and, of course, if in deliberate contempt of the Church's teaching they insist on picking and choosing according to their own private judgement, they are formal heretics, whether they accept much or little. There can be degrees of ignorance, but there cannot be any more or less in the extent of faith ; there, it is " all in all, or not at all." There can be degrees, however, in the intensity of faith. Hence Christ rebukes St Peter : " O thou of little faith," [1] and the Church prays, " Almighty, everlasting God, give us an increase of faith, hope, and charity."

*Temptations and doubts*  Faith is destroyed only by the sin of refusing to believe that which is adequately proposed as an object of divine revelation. Either doubt or positive rejection constitutes heresy in the baptised subject, infidelity in the unbaptised. It is important to notice that doubt involves heresy. In doubt the assent is withheld ; there is no decision on either side, whereas revelation demands the assent of faith. Those who would fly the very suggestion of heresy will sometimes say that they " doubt." They probably mean no more than that they feel the difficulties against some article of faith, or against the whole scheme of revelation. Such people should remember that " ten thousand difficulties do not make one doubt " ; that the acute realisation of difficulties presents the occasion for an act of faith ; and that such acts strengthen the natural habit, and merit an increase of the supernatural virtue. Temptations against faith are always to be rejected at once, with the same promptitude as temptations against purity. Any dalliance with them or carelessness with regard to them is most dangerous. That is why the Church prohibits the reading of certain books. Wantonly to read such books is a sin against faith, but not a sin which destroys the virtue.

Other sins against faith which cannot be called heresy are the refusal to assent to certain truths which, though not defined, are so intimately connected with defined doctrines as to bind our belief under the sanctions of one or other of the theological notes, " rashness," " proximity to heresy," " offensiveness to pious ears," and the like. Similarly the teaching of Roman Congregations to which is attached the sanction of the Pope, binds under sin.

## 2. *Hope*

*The meaning of Hope*  Hope, in general, means the longing after something which is conceived as good. But it is not the longing of desire merely. There is in hope the element of the recognition of a difficulty to be overcome.

[1] Matt. xiv 31.

I contemplate the prospect of a struggle, and that temper in me which rather enjoys a struggle is roused. But I know, too, that I am not faced with the impossibility of attaining my object. I stand a chance of winning through. Hope therefore implies four things : the surging of the desire towards something that appears as good ; a future good ; a good that is hard of attainment ; but a good that can be attained. In hoping we are like men setting out to climb a mountain peak. We see before us the goal of our desires, but it is a long way off, and we shall have hard work to reach it and many dangers from moraine and crevasse to pass on the way, and meantime the ground is heavy and the sun hot on our backs ; but we can arrive finally at the peak, and enjoy a revelation of beauty which we can only speculate about now. In our efforts we may be depending on our own strength only, or we may be relying upon the help of others.

The supernatural virtue of hope is that disposition in our souls which enables us to aspire to God as our last end, and to all the means which will enable us to achieve that end. In so hoping we realise that we cannot achieve either the end or the means by our own efforts—to depend on them would be presumption—but we look for all from God's grace. So, although this is a theological virtue, its object is not confined to God himself, but is extended, in a second-ary manner, to all those created helps which may be ours in our endeavours to reach God who is the primary object. The primary object of our hope, then, is God himself, and, indirectly, that vision of God which will constitute our happiness in heaven. The second-ary objects are the glory of our bodies after the resurrection, all spiritual and temporal goods, and, finally, the like happiness and blessings for others.

As it is well pleasing to God that we should by the virtue of faith *Errors con-* assent to the word of his truth, so it pleases him that we should rely *cerning this* on his goodness and promises, and cling to him by the virtue of hope. *virtue* But some men take up an attitude of appalling pride in the presence of their Creator, and stand over against him as if he were a man like themselves. You will sometimes hear a sinner say, " If I have done evil, then I am prepared to stand by my sin and take the appropriate punishment, rather than beg for mercy " ; and, similarly, you will find men who say that hope is a mean virtue which is unworthy of a disinterested lover. The Quietists taught that we should aim at a state of indifference to our own salvation, that there should be no disturbance of our quiet either to do good works or to resist tempta-tions however foul. Michael de Molinos fathered these opinions, and they were condemned as heretical by Innocent XI. The holy archbishop, Fénelon of Cambrai, while he could never have sub-scribed to such outrageous statements as these, did favour Semi-quietism, which taught that the virtue of hope found no place in the higher states of perfection, wherein there was no room for any self-

interest, no room for the admission of such motives as the fear of
hell or the desire of heaven. These opinions were condemned, not,
indeed, as heretical, but as rash and erroneous and pernicious in
practice, by Innocent XII.

If the virtue of hope is a perfect virtue it can never be unbe-
coming to any creature however holy. St Paul could no⁺ afford to
discard the "helmet of the hope of salvation," [1] and he encouraged
Titus "to live soberly, justly, and godly in this world, looking for
the blessed hope and coming of the glory of the great God and our
Saviour Jesus Christ." [2] But, indeed, Holy Scripture is full of encouragement to the virtue of hope : "Know you not that they that
run in the race, all run indeed, but one receiveth the prize ? So run
that you may obtain." [3]

Hope will not lead us into slackness in the pursuit of our great
end. It does not mean that we are certain of getting to heaven some
day. For although hope relies most confidently on God's goodness
and power to help us, we know perfectly well that neither of these
will avail unless we accomplish our part of the bargain. I can depend on God with the greatest certainty, but, alas ! I cannot depend
on myself. "He that thinketh himself to stand, let him take heed
lest he fall." [4] And the warning is repeated to the Philippians :
"Work out your salvation with fear and trembling." [5] I know of
faith that God will never fail me, but I have to work and pray that
I enter not into temptation, and thus prove false to myself. Moreover if I have sinned, hope is necessary for justification. Conversion
is impossible without hope, and after turning our backs on God such
conversion is required as a condition of our reacceptance by him :
"Turn ye to me, saith the Lord of hosts, and I will turn to you,
saith the Lord of hosts." [6]

*Sins against
Hope*

There are two sins against hope : despair and presumption.
Either of these will destroy the virtue of hope ; and, as we have seen
already, the loss of faith involves the loss of hope. Despair means
a relinquishing of our hope, either because we do not reckon that
God and heaven and the means necessary to attain them are worth
the trouble ; or because, while still desiring the objects of hope, we
no longer depend on the divine goodness and mercy to save us for,
and by, them. The first kind of despair is the more common, and it is
the frequent cause of worldliness and sins of the flesh. Men think
that these temporary pleasures are more to be desired than the
glory to come. Despair, though a less heinous sin than infidelity
or hatred of God, is more dangerous than either of these, because it
means the loss of the lever of hope which could pull us back to safety
when we have turned our back on God.

The second sin, presumption, is always a sin against hope, but it

---

[1] 1 Thess. v 8.   [2] Titus ii 12-13.
[3] 1 Cor. ix 24. See also Heb. xi 24 *seq.*
[4] 1 Cor. x 12.   [5] Phil. ii 12.   [6] Zach. i. 3.

is not always so directly contrary to hope as to destroy the virtue. It is important to state carefully the nature of the different kinds of presumption. There are two ways in which the presumptuous person may sin directly against hope. The first is by expecting to attain eternal happiness by one's own unaided efforts ; the second by expecting pardon without sorrow, or eternal glory without final perseverance. These sins must be very rare, but one does sometimes hear people say lightheartedly : " Oh, God would never send me to hell." In an age when men do not hesitate to judge their Creator, when they are prepared to make a God after their own psychological image, this may be commoner than would seem possible. The man who continues to sin depending on a death-bed repentance, is guilty of presumption, but this sin does not destroy the virtue of hope. There is no presumption in the attitude of the sinner who persistently keeps at the back of his mind the hope of one day amending his life and so receiving pardon ; this disposition rather diminishes the gravity of the sin. Such a sinner, however, should remember that although God has promised that he will turn to us as soon as we turn to him, he has not promised to allow us time for preparation on our death-bed.

### 3. *Charity*

" The greatest of these is charity." [1] Charity is the queen of all *Love of God* the virtues, the form, as we have seen, with which every other virtue must be endowed if it is to realise perfection as a virtue. It is the virtue which joins us to God in bonds of friendship, enabling us to love him for his own sake as a friend, to identify the movements of our will with his, *idem velle, idem nolle*. It involves the divine indwelling : " He that abideth in charity abideth in God, and God in him." [2] " The charity of God is poured forth in our hearts, by the Holy Ghost who is given to us." [3] This union with God, to be realised completely only in heaven, is the one great aim of our lives on earth. All other spiritual activities and endeavours are only the means to this end. Faith and hope are indeed directed straight to God, but faith as to the source of our knowledge, and hope as to the source of our enjoyment of him ; whereas charity is directed to him for himself alone.

It is true that we could not love God if we did not regard him as *our* good ; but though that is the necessary condition of charity, it is not its motive. It is a necessary condition, for I cannot be in a state of friendship with anyone with whom I cannot in some sense stand on common ground. If I am to love God, he must lift me up to participate in his divine life. This he does in heaven, by permitting me to find my joy in the contemplation of his goodness as he finds his own joy therein ; and on earth, by enabling me to know him by faith as the good to be enjoyed one day, and as such to love

---

[1] 1 Cor. xiii 13.  [2] 1 John iv 16.  [3] Rom. v 5.

him even now, by charity. But this love of charity exercised whether here or hereafter is not evoked by consideration of self ; the love that is *made possible* by the fact that its object is a good for me, is a love that is *evoked* by the goodness of God, for his sake alone. In the way of mere nature man must love God as his first beginning and his last end, as the source and explanation of his being ; but that love is not charity, for charity cannot be built on anything less than that participation of the divine nature which is the work of sanctifying grace. " If we say that we have fellowship with him and walk in darkness, we lie, and do not the truth. But if we walk in the light, as he also is in the light, we have fellowship one with another." [1]

That such friendship is possible is abundantly evident from Holy Scripture. " Son, give me thy heart," is God's own pleading invitation. Again, through the voice of St John he would constrain us, urging with a divine humility that he has been beforehand with us : " Let us love God, for God hath *first* loved us." We are told that they that use wisdom " become the friends of God." [2] The whole of the Canticle of Canticles is an inspired love-song lyrically celebrating the love of friendship between God and the soul. And at the end of his life, our Lord says to his Apostles : " Now I have called you friends." [3]

*Love of our neighbour*

God is the primary object of charity, but it is obvious that the love of God will issue in the love of our fellow-man. Love primarily directed to any one person must always embrace as secondary objects of love those who are united in any way with that person. We may have no natural attraction to his friends and relatives, but we love them for his sake. And so it is that as secondary objects of the virtue of charity we must love all those whom God has exalted to his friendship or to whom he offers such friendship. All the citizens of heaven are united directly with God, and, in God, are united with one another. By charity we love, for God's sake, the blessed in heaven, the souls in Purgatory, and all men on earth, for all these are actually God's friends now, or may be some day. Only the devils and the damned are excluded from the scope of our charity ; and they must be, for they cannot participate in God's friendship, they cannot love him as their supernatural end.

Of course, a man's charity must include himself, because he himself is loved by God. That is not an unnecessary thing to say, for it asserts not the obvious inclination to love oneself for one's own sake which is a law of nature, but the obligation to love oneself supernaturally for God's sake. The natural love of self for one's own sake can be directed to God, and be made virtuous, receiving a " form " from charity ; but even then it is not charity. Indeed, it may easily come into opposition with charity. My natural love of self must be conquered in deference to my love of self as a friend of God, as when my love of ease and comfort is made to give way to

[1] I John i 6–7.    [2] Wisdom vii 14.    [3] John xv 15.

my love of God's law or to the love of the poverty, humiliation, or pain, that associates me more closely with Christ.

Not only must a man love himself, but in the matter of his eternal salvation, at least, he must love himself more than any other created person. God is to be loved above all things ; then myself ; then my neighbour for God's sake. " Thou shalt love the Lord thy God with thy whole heart and with thy whole soul and with thy whole mind. This is the greatest and the first commandment. And the second is like to this : Thou shalt love thy neighbour as thyself." [1] The love of self is the norm of the love of one's neighbour.

We are bound by charity to love all men, even our enemies, for if we were to cut these off from the scope of our charity, in spite of the fact that God loves them, we should be preferring our own inclination to God's, and so offending against the first commandment : " If any man say : I love God, and hateth his brother ; he is a liar." [2] But we are not bound to love all equally. Indeed, it would not be possible to do so. We must love most those who are allied to us by blood or friendship, by natural ties, in their proper order. All that the commandment means, as a commandment, is that we should have a desire for the good of every man, be ready to pray for all and to succour them in their need when we can. When it comes to the choice of those whom we should help, we must have a regard first to our own. " Charity begins at home." Spontaneous natural friendship is perfected by the supernatural friendship of charity, and the two motives as a rule are more powerful than the one alone, though the perfection of charity might lead us, while doing no injury to claims of kith and kin, to show special affection to those who had offended us ; and so we have the counsel, " Do good to them that hate you." If I meet two men who are equally in need and who have no special claims on me, and I have but one half-crown to spare to meet that need, charity moves me equally towards both, but necessity forces me to prefer one. I can decide between the two by tossing the half-crown. But if one of the two is in my parish, or is a fellow-countryman, or is personally more attractive, I can let that circumstance be equivalent to the luck of the toss.

When we say that the law of God coincides with natural equity in demanding that we should love ourselves and those who are allied to us more than others, it is to be understood that we are thinking of the intensity of our affection and of what we can do practically for them in this life. But we can look at the order of charity in another way. As the principle of charity is the love of God, we must be conformed to God's will. So we must wish a greater good to those who shall be more deserving, irrespective of their relation to ourselves. But in this life degrees of merit are not stable ; the saint of to-day may be the sinner of to-morrow, Magdalen's seven devils may be driven out, and she may become more closely united to God

---

[1] Matt. xxii 37-39.      [2] I John iv 20.

than is Martha. So we may always hope that our friends and intimates may grow in virtue so as to outstrip others ; but when we have arrived in glory, all these degrees of union with God will be fixed for ever, so that there will be no room for such desires. We shall accept heaven's ranks as we find them ; seeing God face to face we shall rejoice in the glory of those who are nearest to him, because that is his unchanging will. But even then we shall in one way love ourselves more than our neighbours, and there will always stand the multitude of holy ties established here on earth, though they will not disturb that first consideration of loving most those who are most closely united to God.

The very essence of charity depends on union. That union with God and my neighbour spells joy and peace. A friend rejoices in the presence of his friend, and love can transcend time and space and produce a spiritual nearness when bodily presence is denied. The love of God brings him to the soul in an intimacy of union which is full of joy. In the Beatific Vision that joy will be such " as eye hath not seen nor ear heard," [1] but even in this life there is joy for the heart that loves God.

And there is peace also. For the possession of charity means that all our desires are harnessed, all our tendencies polarised. There is none of the irritation of domestic strife in our hearts. There is none of that conscious disharmony which disturbs the calm of peace. Also, between us and God there is a unity of will which guarantees us against the fundamental discord that is the lot of rebels, and makes us superior to the ephemeral troubles that destroy the peace of those who kick against the goad. There is still room for that holy fear which makes us flee from sin and the judgement to come ; but such fear does not drive out peace. Moreover, the charity which binds us to our neighbour in God secures a harmony of co-operation in the pursuit of good.

*Sins against Charity*

Any mortal sin destroys the virtue of charity. The essence of love is union of wills, and therefore the first test of love of God is the keeping of the commandments : " If you love me, keep my commandments." To commit a mortal sin is to prefer the creature to the Creator, which is obviously incompatible with the love of God above all things.

But there are some sins which are directly against the virtue of charity. Besides such sins of commission as hatred of God and scandal of our neighbour, over which we need not delay here, there are sins of omission. These arise from the neglect of such *acts* of charity as are commanded by the precept of charity. It is clear from the condemnation of certain errors of Baius [2] that such acts are commanded often, though their necessary frequency is not precisely determined. Anyhow, they are so valuable an aid to the perfection of that union with God which is the most important concern

[1] I Cor. ii 9.   [2] Michael du Bay (1513-1589).

of our life, that we should try to make them as often as is reasonably possible. We should establish the natural habit of making them easily.

It is sometimes suggested that to make an act of perfect charity *Acts of* is difficult or impossible for the ordinary man of the world. That *Charity* surely is not true of anyone who is trying to lead a Christian life. God does not command the impossible, and God does command acts of perfect charity. There is no need to take alarm at the name, *perfect* charity. It does not mean any great refinement of love. It simply means that love of God for his own sake which prefers him to any creature that might challenge his claim to the sovereignty of our hearts. It involves no sacrifice which is not equally necessary for a sacramental absolution. It is perfect, only as opposed to the imperfect, self-regarding charity, which is adequate for forgiveness of sins in the sacrament of Penance. But it does mean that one must get beyond the love of self, that one must progress from the mere fear of God or grateful love of God, to a love of friendship in which the friend is considered for himself. It does not eliminate these imperfect forms of love. It can coexist with them. As we insisted when we were dealing with the virtue of hope, we can never be so advanced as to despise these motives of sorrow or love. Instructed by faith about the supreme amiability of God, his infinite goodness and perfections, it should not be difficult to love him above all things for his sake. " We needs must love the highest when we see it." No habit could be more valuable for the man who is day by day struggling against mortal sin. For if he chance to fall, an act of perfect charity (with, of course, the implied intention of seeking later the sacramental absolution as commanded) will at once produce that disposition of soul which induces God to restore sanctifying grace, so that his sin is forgiven.

So far, we have only described an act of charity of the lowest grade of intensity. A more intense act is within the capacity of the Christian enjoying ordinary grace. By this the will rejects the intention of doing anything which, though not directly against God's will, is still not according to that will. With such charity we shall be disposed to forgo the distraction from our main end, the loitering by the way, which is implied in deliberate venial sin.

Finally, there is the advanced stage of charity which leads the soul to identify its will as completely as possible with that of God ; which reaches out, in the yearning of love, to suffer for and with the Beloved ; which welcomes such adverse circumstances as befall, or contrives self-immolation, as satisfaction for sin or expression of love. In this state the soul will not only bear with resignation to God's will poverty, hardship, and pain, but will welcome or go out to seek them, in sympathy with him who was born in a stable, worked at a bench, and died on a Cross. And this will lead to a correspondingly great charity for one's neighbour, to a zeal and desire to work

and suffer for souls, to such zeal as inspired St Paul when he said :
" But I am straitened between two : having a desire to be dissolved
and to be with Christ, a thing by far the better. But to abide still
in the flesh is needful for you." [1]

#### 4. *The Moral Virtues*

Prudence

The general discussion of the moral virtues necessitated a certain
description of each. We have now only to fill the gaps. We saw
that the first of these virtues, first because of its significance for all
the others, is prudence. *Prudence* is the rule of action ; it is the
virtue perfecting the intellect and thus guiding the will in its application of the other three moral virtues. It is, however, a distinct virtue
with its own proper subject-matter. Its procedure is first to inquire,
then to judge, then to state the case to the will for its guidance.
It " prescribes " for the will. We have already shown the difference
between true and false prudence, and we have also seen that there
is a prudence which falls between these two in that it lacks the perfection of charity. [2] As prudence deals with the details of conduct,
it is accompanied by a certain solicitude.

The vices opposed to prudence arise from the defect of any of
the three elements which appear in the exercise of the virtue. The
lack of inquiry results in precipitancy. The lack of judgement is
the second vice. Inconstancy arises from the failure to direct the
will aright, when this is under the influence of an evil passion. If
the failure is due to sheer inertia, the vice is called negligence. But
it is to be observed that these vices are not in the will, but in the
intellect, for it is the intellect which is set to good by the virtue of
prudence. Of all the evil influences which hinder prudence the
worst is the predominance of the animal appetites. Envy, anger,
avarice, ambition, deflect reason from its straight path ; but
" luxury " tends to suffocate it.

But there are vices of excess of prudence. The first is that
prudence of the flesh which, neglecting the great end of life, concerns itself with immediate pleasures. Then there is that worldly
cunning or craft which employs tortuous methods to gain its ends,
and which is comparable to the use of sophisms in argument. And,
finally, there is an undue solicitude about the things of this world,
a lack of confidence in the providence of God. St Thomas, whom
we are following throughout, tells us that the evil spirit in these
cases is that of avarice.

Justice

*Justice* is that disposition of the soul according to which we have
a constant will to render to, and preserve for, everyone his due.
It is called by St Thomas the most beautiful of the strictly moral
virtues. It regulates our relations to God and our neighbour. It
comprehends many virtues, such as religion, piety, truth, gratitude,
liberality, affability.

[1] Phil. i 23, 24.  [2] *Cf.* pp. 639–40.

*Fortitude* is a virtue which enables us to face undismayed the *Fortitude* dangers which stand in the way of the execution of our duty, to conquer fear and restrain rashness. Its most conspicuous efficacy is in conquering the fear of death, whether in war, when we have the natural fortitude of the soldier (which, of course, can be supernaturalised) ; or in martyrdom, when we have the highest type of supernatural fortitude. It was fortitude which enabled St Lawrence and St Thomas More to be so gay in presence of death, or St Joan of Arc to endure the flames which she so frankly dreaded. It does not mean the absence of fear, but the control of fear. Fear is an instinct which every man not deficient in sense or imagination must sometimes feel. The bravest soldier is not he who is thoughtless and unmoved by danger, but rather he who, fully realising the danger, has to conquer his dread of it while clinging to his post. " Are you afraid ? " sneered an old soldier, observing a recruit's blanched cheeks. " Afraid ? " was the reply, " if you were half as afraid as I am you would have run away long since." Fortitude is manifested both in defence and in attack ; but it shows up more brightly in defence, where there is no supporting ardour of onslaught or sense of superiority. The soldiers who went down with the *Birkenhead* were, at least, as brave as " the gallant six hundred " who charged at Balaclava.

Here is a good instance of the general rule that acquired virtue is a predisposition for infused virtue, that nature builds on grace. The man who is not prepared to meet and conquer the difficulties of everyday life will find it hard to conquer temptation ; he who, from boyhood, has learned self-conquest, will the more easily persevere in the pursuit of virtue. There is no limitation to the power of grace, but natural invertebrates will find it hard to walk upright to heaven.

Virtues allied to fortitude are magnanimity, patience, and perseverance. Opposed vices are " intimidity " (lack of fear where one ought to fear), cowardice, timidity, rashness, pusillanimity, ambition, vainglory, inconstancy, obstinacy.

*Temperance* is a moderating virtue. Fortitude is the " whip for *Temperance* the horse," temperance the " snaffle for the ass." As in the pursuit of virtue we have to control fear, so we have to withstand the seductiveness of pleasure, especially those most enticing pleasures which are associated with the preservation of the individual and of the race. Aristotle teaches that the temperate man uses pleasure with a view to his health, and also with a view to his efficiency. The Christian has to consider spiritual efficiency. For that he will not only restrain himself from any grave excess of the natural appetites, but he will be drawn to some discipline of asceticism, in order to ensure his strength and readiness against the day of temptation ; he will undergo spiritual " training."

We have seen that temperance is set midway between the vices of intemperance and insensibility. Insensibility means that habit (which is sufficiently rare) of attempting to break the natural order which has associated pleasure with certain necessary natural acts, a hate-inspired rejection of natural pleasures as if they were shameful or evil. Intemperance is a particularly odious vice, because it makes men brutish : " Man when he was in honour did not understand : he hath been compared to senseless beasts, and made like to them." [1]

Specifically different virtues subordinate to temperance are abstinence, sobriety, chastity, and a sense of shame. Allied virtues are continence, clemency, modesty. Opposed to one or other of these virtues are gluttony, drunkenness, unchastity, anger, cruelty, pride.

## §VI: GIFTS OF THE HOLY GHOST, BEATITUDES, FRUITS

### 1. *The Gifts of the Holy Ghost*

*The Gifts in general*　THUS is man supernaturalised. His nature is lifted up by grace, so that he becomes a partaker of the divine nature ; his natural faculties are supernaturalised by the infused virtues, the theological enabling him to believe, hope, and love in an effective supernatural way, the moral enabling him to seek supernaturally the immediate good which leads to the true last end. But even yet he is not safe. Thus equipped he can avoid sin, at least for some time, and act meritoriously, but he is still weak and blind. The flesh is prone to evil, even after the mind has been healed ; man is subject to that concupiscence, that struggle between spirit and flesh, of which St Paul writes so feelingly, " For I am delighted with the law of God, according to the inward man : but I see another law in my members, fighting against the law of my mind and captivating me in the law of sin that is in my members." [2] Moreover, the mind is still darkened by ignorance, so that we " do not even know what we should pray for as we ought." [3]

Labouring under these difficulties, the heritage of sin, man cannot avoid sin and pursue his course of sanctification throughout life, unless he is specially aided by God. He needs special helps *occasionally*, helps *ad hoc*, to eke out the general help of sanctifying grace and virtue.[4] We are like men who are living on the margin of poverty ; times of sickness or misfortune arrive when we need a " bonus " if we are not to sink under the burden. Now that additional help must come from God. God will not do the work of virtue for us ; if he did, it would no longer be ours. We must do it, but he will help us.

There must be a disposition in our souls to receive such transient helps from God. That disposition is called a Gift of the Holy Ghost. It is a permanent modification of the soul, whereby the

---

[1] Ps. xlviii 21.　　　　[2] Rom. vii 22-23.
[3] Rom. viii 26.　　　　[4] See Essay xvii, *Actual Grace*.

soul is enabled to respond swiftly and easily to the suggestions of the Holy Ghost. It is a habit of the intellect or will, by which these faculties are set in readiness to receive the light or warmth which comes from God. The faculties thus endowed can then elicit the act of virtue for which the help is given. The gifts are not to be confused with the transient help, the actual grace, itself. They are permanently in the soul when habitual grace is there. They, too, are habits. That they are not always used is our own fault, and this accounts for much of the failure in the spiritual life. They are like an auxiliary engine, or like the sail in a motor-boat. They are not intended to substitute for the virtues, but to help them out. Sometimes we meet an adverse current, or the engine is cold and will not start ; then if the sail is hoisted it may catch a breeze, and so help the boat to get under weigh ; but if the parallel is to hold, the engine must now work with the sails.

The occasion of the assistance bestowed may be almost anything ; it may be a sermon, a spiritual book, a sunset, or a storm, a sickness, a sorrow, a success, or even a sin. In divers ways the grace may come to us, clearing our minds from the obscurity of passion, stirring us from our lethargy, warming our hearts ; however it comes, the corresponding gift of the Holy Ghost must be there, disposing us to welcome it and to act upon it. We must be " tuned in " to receive the impulse and to respond to it. This disposition, this " tuning " of our souls, is the gift.

It is very clear that the gifts are different from the virtues. Both are infused by God, and both are habits. But the virtues dispose our faculties to perform those supernatural acts to which reason directs them, whereas the gifts dispose them to accept and (always aided by the corresponding virtue) to act upon, the divine inspiration. And it is because the " mover " in the second case is divine, whereas in the first it is human, that we need a nobler disposition in the second case than in the first. A student who follows the course of an advanced lecturer must be better prepared than his fellow who is addressing himself to more elementary work.

It is sometimes suggested that the difference between virtue and gift is a difference of material object simply ; that the virtues are bestowed to cope with the ordinary difficulties or ordinary acts, whereas the gifts are for the extraordinary, the heroic. But if that were true, many Christians would be habitually in possession of gifts which throughout their lives they would never be called upon to exercise. It is true that the gifts do enable us to cope with these extraordinary circumstances, but they are not designed for that purpose only.

It must not be supposed from what we have said about the need of the gifts, that actual graces cannot be offered and accepted in the absence of the gifts. They can be, and are ; by them, sinners are brought towards justification. And, of course, those in sin have not the gifts, for the gifts come and go with habitual grace. But the gifts habitually draw from God the inspirations that are necessary, and they make the acceptance of these actual graces more ready and easy.

Although they are there from Baptism, the gifts are not always used. As a rule they do not seem to come into play immediately after the subject has come to the use of reason. And, indeed, some people seem to use them very little. Although in a state of grace, they seem to respond very little to the divine suggestions. They seem to be particularly obtuse or hard-hearted. They make no advance in prayer ; they are unmortified and worldly-minded. Of course, such persons are on the way to lose both gifts and grace.

*The Gifts in particular*     As enumerated by Isaias,[1] the gifts are seven in number : Wisdom, Understanding, Counsel, Fortitude, Knowledge, Piety, Fear of the Lord. Of these, Understanding, Wisdom, Knowledge, Counsel perfect the intellect ; the other three perfect the will. Understanding is intended to help us to a firm adhesion to the truths of faith in spite of difficulties. It results in that state of mind expressed in Newman's famous phrase, " Ten thousand difficulties do not make one doubt." It also leads to a fuller comprehension of the mysteries of faith, and is the cause of the remarkable phenomenon found among Catholics, that the unlettered poor have a grip of subtleties which may baffle the educated, an insight which, in extreme cases, goes beyond the grasp even of learned theologians. The other three intellectual gifts make for a correct appreciation of spiritual values as they affect God (Wisdom) and created things (Knowledge), and as they are applied in individual cases (Counsel). Constantly during the day the earnest Christian has to decide whether to do something or to leave it undone. No mentor, no confessor, is adequate for his guidance in these particulars. In dealing with others, in carrying out the duties of his state, the conscientious man must often pause to think and pray for guidance. The question of mortification, for example, is beset with the difficulty of deciding between prudence and fervour, of discerning the voice of cowardice from that of wisdom. In all such cases the gift of counsel comes to the aid of the virtue of prudence. It is, therefore, a valuable exercise to recite frequently the two hymns to the Holy Ghost.

Piety helps in our worship of God and in our regard for the due of other men as they pertain to God, for example, the respect due to the saints. Fortitude and fear of the Lord correspond to the virtues of fortitude and temperance. The fear of the Lord is particularly concerned with the restraint of the flesh : " Pierce my flesh with thy fear." [2]

There is a special type of prayer associated with the gifts. It is the prayer of simplicity or of faith, contemplative prayer. Whereas in ordinary meditation the soul approaches God by way of discursive

---

[1] Isa. xi 2.         [2] Ps. cxviii 120.

reasoning, deliberately trying to penetrate the truths of faith and making appropriate acts of love, desire, sorrow, etc. ; in mystic contemplation all such process is abandoned, and the soul simply rests quietly at the feet of Jesus, " like those noble courtiers whose whole duty is to be found at certain hours in the presence of their king." [1] It is very common teaching that every soul in the state of grace can aspire to such prayer as this, and that no exercise is more effective for the attainment of the intimacy of divine union. But the soul must be called to this state. The prayer is a grace for which the soul is held in readiness by the gifts of the Holy Ghost. The action of the Holy Ghost may be by way of giving increased light to the act of the understanding itself so that independently of the work of memory the elements of mental experience arise in consciousness ; or it may actually supply such human elements or co-ordinate them, without any effort of the mind. Indeed, according to some writers, the Holy Spirit may infuse a gift of intuition of divine truth which is proper, not to man in the flesh, but to angelic beings, or separated souls.[2] The psychology of the question is extremely recondite, and there is much divergence of opinion about it. But, however that may be described, the action involves the gifts, and, of course, according to the general principle already laid down, the co-operation of the virtues, especially the theological virtues.

The language of the mystics has a superficial resemblance, which may be very misleading, to that of the Quietists and the false mystics of Oriental paganism. But there is one outstanding difference : in spite of the ideas of repose, quiet, wordlessness, there is in true mysticism the insistence on an intense activity of the will.

This is a subject of supreme importance in the spiritual life, which has been too much neglected in recent times. Owing to a combination of circumstances many look askance at the very word mysticism. They have been led to think that such prayer is no concern of ordinarily pious Christians. Such an opinion is a breakaway from the classical tradition. But there has been a large output of mystic literature of very varied quality in the last few years. We cannot attempt to deal with the subject here, but readers may be confidently referred to such books as Poulain's *Graces of Prayer*, Besse's *Science of Prayer*, the mystical series of the Orchard Books, and the works of the Ven. Fr. Baker.

## 2. *The Beatitudes*

When a person in the state of grace resolves, under the influence of actual grace, to perform the acts which correspond to the gifts of the Holy Ghost, he puts himself immediately under the influence of the Holy Ghost, and from this divine inspiration the beatitudes

---

[1] *De Smedt*, quoted by Poulain, p. 54.
[2] *Cf.* Billot, *De Virtutibus Infusis*, p. 191.

result. There is no specific difference between these acts and the ordinary acts of the virtues ; the only difference is in the manner of their production and the greater dignity of those which arise from the more dignified source, the divine impulse.

The rewards which are attached to the beatitudes refer primarily to the future life, but they are realised to some extent here in the lives of the saints. They are of such a nature as to compensate for the yielding of that apparent good which worldlings seek. For example, the gift of fear enables a man to withdraw from the pursuit of riches and honours ; he becomes poor in spirit, and is rewarded by gaining the kingdom of heaven. Or they give a reward corresponding to the nature of the good work : " Blessed are the clean of heart " ; cleanness of heart is derived from the gift of understanding, and is rewarded with the contemplative vision of God.

### 3. *The Fruits of the Holy Ghost*

The fruits refer to acts done under the influence of grace by virtue or by gift. The name indicates the act as being accompanied by the pleasure of spiritual activity. It is of wider application than " beatitude," which is limited to such perfect works as call for the use of the gifts. The name " fruit " suggests the spiritual joy which accompanies the exercise of a good work, and also the fact that it is the issue of the growth of the divine seed of grace in the virtuous work of the man who receives the grace. There is much discussion among the Fathers and theologians of the Church regarding the exact significance of the words of St Paul,[1] but the best opinion seems to be that the fruits are the issue of the human spirit, divinised by grace, and that they impart to the soul the delightful savour of the performance of good works. They are *acts*, products of virtue, not virtues themselves.

Here, then, we find the temporal (as opposed to the eternal) fruit of the tree of the spiritual life. Nature and grace have contributed to its production : human nature with its faculties, and the habits of sanctifying grace and the infused virtues which perfect these. We have tried to study briefly the nature of supernatural activity, which constitutes a world more real and important than the world revealed by our senses, a world of which too many live in complete oblivion. Its ultimate evolution will be revealed to us only in the next life, when we shall enjoy its eternal fruit, the reward which " eye hath not seen, nor ear heard." [2]

T. E. FLYNN.

---

[1] Gal. v 22.     [2] i Cor. ii 9.

CPSIA information can be obtained
at www.ICGtesting.com
Printed in the USA
LVHW011154200723
752377LV00020B/351/J

9 781989 905739